Strategies for Addressing Behavior Problems in the Classroom

FOURTH EDITION

Mary Margaret Kerr
University of Pittsburgh

C. Michael Nelson
University of Kentucky

Merrill
Prentice Hall

Upper Saddle River, New Jersey
Columbus, Ohio

D1451323

Library of Congress Cataloging-in-Publication Data

Kerr, Mary Margaret.
   Strategies for addressing behavior problems in the classroom / Mary Margaret Kerr, C. Michael Nelson.— 4th ed.
      p. cm.
   Rev. ed. of: Strategies for managing behavior problems in the classroom. 3rd ed. c1998.
   Includes bibliographical references and index.
   ISBN 0-13-041541-3
   1. Classroom management. 2. Behavior disorders in children. 3. Behavior modification.
4. School discipline. I. Nelson, C. Michael (Charles Michael), 1941-II. Kerr, Mary
Margaret. Strategies for managing behavior problems in the classroom. III. Title.
LB3013 .K47 2002
371.5'3 — dc21   2001034241

Vice President and Publisher: Jeffery W. Johnston
Executive Editor: Ann Castel Davis
Editorial Assistant: Keli Gemrich
Production Editor: Linda Hillis Bayma
Production Coordination: Lea Baranowski, Carlisle Publishers Services
Design Coordinator: Diane C. Lorenzo
Photo Coordinator: Valerie Schultz
Cover Designer: Ceri Fitzgerald
Cover art: VSA arts of Maine/Bernadette
Production Manager: Laura Messerly
Director of Marketing: Kevin Flanagan
Marketing Manager: Amy June
Marketing Coordinator: Barbara Koontz

This book was set in Novarese Book by Carlisle Communications, Ltd. It was printed and bound by Maple Vail Book Manufacturing Group. The cover was printed by Phoenix Color Corp.

Photo Credits:
Scott Cunningham/Merrill, pp. 79, 201, 345, 365, 411; Kenneth Kerr, p. 313; Mary Margaret Kerr, p. 208 (top); Anthony Magnacca/Merrill, pp. 129, 171; Gail Meese/Merrill, p. 281; C. Michael Nelson p. 208 (bottom); Barbara Schwartz/Merrill, pp. 39, 239; Anne Vega/Merrill, p. 3.

Pearson Education Ltd., *London*
Pearson Education Australia Pty. Limited, *Sydney*
Pearson Education Singapore Ptd. Ltd.
Pearson Educaton North Asia Ltd., *Hong Kong*
Pearson Education Canada, Ltd., *Toronto*
Pearson Educación de Mexico, S.A. de C.V.
Pearson Education—Japan, *Tokyo*
Pearson Education Malaysia Pte. Ltd.
Pearson Education, *Upper Saddle River, New Jersey*

Previous editions of this text were titled *Strategies for Managing Behavior Problems in the Classroom.*

Merrill
Prentice Hall

10 9 8 7 6 5 4 3 2 1
ISBN 0-13-041541-3

A friend is one to whom one may pour out all the contents of one's heart, chaff and grain together, knowing that the gentlest of hands will take and sift it, keep what is worth keeping, and with a breath of kindness, blow the rest away.

—*Arabian proverb*

For Jamey Joy Covaleski

M.M.K.

For my wife, Linda

C.M.N.

ABOUT THE AUTHORS

Mary Margaret Kerr received her Bachelor's and Master's degrees from Duke University and her doctorate from The American University in Washington, DC. Trained in special education and developmental psychology, Dr. Kerr has devoted her career to working with troubled children and adolescents and to teaching those who help them. The author of six textbooks and many articles, she has taught in special education and alternative education classrooms and continues to consult with school districts across the country. A former faculty member at Vanderbilt University, Dr. Kerr joined the faculty of the School of Medicine and the School of Education at the University of Pittsburgh in 1980.

In 1989, Dr. Kerr joined the Pittsburgh City Schools as Director of Pupil Services, where she administered services such as guidance, counseling, social work, drug-free schools, alternative education, health services, school security, and discipline. In 1994, she returned to her faculty position at the University of Pittsburgh, where she is Educational Director and Associate Professor of Child Psychiatry and Education. She also directs outreach services for the University's youth suicide and violence prevention center, STAR-Center. This center provides crisis response services, training, and consultation to school districts and communities across Pennsylvania.

In 1996 Dr. Kerr was appointed by the United States Court for the Central District of California as a Consent Decree Administrator for Los Angeles Unified School District. In this capacity, Dr. Kerr works with educators and parents to improve services for 81,000 students with disabilities.

When Dr. Kerr is not at work in Pittsburgh or Los Angeles, she is at home with her husband Bruce and their two children.

C. Michael Nelson began his special education career as a teacher of adolescents with learning and behavior disorders. After earning a master's degree in school psychology, he worked as a child psychologist at the University of Kansas Medical Center. He received his Ed.D. from the University of Kansas in 1969 and took a position with the Department of Special Education and Rehabilitation Counseling at the University of Kentucky, where he currently is a full professor and coordinates the graduate Personnel Preparation Program for Teachers of Students with Emotional and Behavioral Disabilities. Dr. Nelson has authored or edited over 100 professional publications, including books, textbook chapters, articles in referred journals, and multimedia instructional packages. He has prepared teachers of children and youth with behavior disorders at the pre- and in-service levels and has served as principal investigator on a number of research and personnel preparation grants. He has served as president of the Council for Children with Behavioral Disorders. Currently, he is involved in two national centers that promote research and best practices for students with or at risk for emotional and behavioral disorders: the Center for Positive Behavioral Interventions and Support, and the Center for Education, Disability, and Juvenile Justice. He also is associated with the Kentucky Center for School Safety.

PREFACE

In our preface to the third edition of this text, we observed that public and professional concerns about students with challenging behavior had increased alarmingly. Fueled by press coverage of recent acts of school violence, this trend has accelerated. America's schools are facing a crisis with regard to finding more effective ways to deal with students who exhibit challenging behavior, including those who bring weapons to school, assault other students and teachers, exhibit defiant and disruptive behaviors, and commit acts of vandalism. The strategies traditionally used to address such problems, including punishment and school exclusion, have not been effective. Policies of "zero tolerance" for misbehavior have resulted in large numbers of students, even preschoolers, being suspended and expelled, or placed in alternative programs, often without services to address their complex behavioral and emotional needs.

At the same time, national reports continue to indicate that special education programs for the segment of the school population identified as having emotional disturbance (ED) or emotional and behavioral disabilities (EBD)[1] have not been effective. These students include children and youth with internalizing disorders (social withdrawal, psychological problems, and psychiatric disorders) in addition to those with externalizing disorders such as those mentioned above. This student population remains chronically under-identified and underserved in the public schools, and identified students are educated in the most restrictive settings and experience the lowest rates of planned inclusion.[2] Status and outcome reports document poor academic achievement, high rates of grade retention, the lowest rate of high school graduation of any group of students with disabilities, and extremely poor post-school adjustment.

These issues continue to prevail in spite of the articulation of national educational policies and goals that focus more than ever on recognizing and addressing the mental health needs of children (i.e., Education 2000). Educational reform has been a major agenda in many states. Unfortunately, with regard to student behavior, most reform efforts continue to emphasize harsh and reactive punishment, applied piecemeal and too late. Excluding students with undesired behavior from schools only transfers the problem to other child-serving agencies, such as those in the fields of mental health, child welfare, and juvenile justice. These systems likewise are being overwhelmed by the sheer number of children needing services, as well as by their own set of poor outcomes (e.g., high rates of psychiatric hospitalization, out-of-home placement, and incarceration). Moreover, the cost of treatment in these systems is enormously more expensive than public education (e.g., between $35,000 and $60,000 a year to incarcerate one juvenile), and these expenses are borne by taxpayers, not the youths' parents. Professionals in all of these disciplines are recognizing that EBD is a severe disability that often cannot be adequately addressed within a single system or in one location. Accordingly, in many parts of the country, system-of-care initiatives have been developed to provide comprehensive and coordinated services to these children and their families in their local communities. Evaluation reports indicate that it is possible to meet the diverse and complex needs of these children and their families without resorting to expen-

---

[1]These terms are considered to be synonymous: The ED category continues to be used in the federal definition of this disability group, despite preference for the term EBD voiced by professional groups and families.

[2]Because students with EBD are the most underidentified special education population, the majority are found in general education classrooms, but in many instances neither they, nor their teachers, receive any special support services.

sive programs that remove the child and attempt to treat him or her out of the context of the natural environment. However, even within these systems of care, services often are applied well after the child's and family's needs have reached crisis proportions.

Fortunately, the initiatives directed toward student behavior that we cited in the third edition have continued to evolve and have been augmented by more recent advances. A national movement to improve school safety through positive and proactive measures has been gaining momentum through the creation of state and national centers for school safety and publication of strategic documents such as *Early Warning, Timely Response: A Guide to Safe Schools* (Dwyer, Osher, & Warger, 1998) and *Safeguarding Our Children: An Action Guide* (Dwyer & Osher, 2000). The 1997 amendments to the Individuals with Disabilities Education Act (IDEA) include, for the first time, requirements that schools conduct functional behavioral assessments of students with disabilities whose challenging behavior causes staff to consider a change in placement, including alternative placement, suspension, or exclusion. These assessments provide the basis for proactive behavior intervention plans. Changes also are taking place in the way behavior intervention plans are formed and implemented. Indicative of a shift in attitude and approach to dealing with challenging student behavior is the recent practice of referring to intervention plans as behavior support plans. This approach, referred to as positive behavior support, began in research involving individuals with developmental disabilities who exhibit challenging behavior. Its focus is on teaching students new, appropriate skills that are more effective than their old, undesired behaviors in achieving such desired outcomes as gaining attention and escaping or avoiding undesired events. Recently, this research has been extended to students with little or no cognitive impairment. The result is a growing intervention technology that employs information gathered from functional behavior assessments to build interventions that teach and support adaptive behaviors rather than simply responding to maladaptive or undesired behaviors with aversive stimuli.

The philosophy and practice of positive behavior support has been extended to school-wide planning as well. School-wide discipline systems that are based on establishing clear sets of behavioral expectations, teaching these expectations to students, and rewarding them for their success, have begun to replace old systems based exclusively on punishment. Evaluations of these positive approaches to school discipline provide convincing evidence of their impact on school climate and student behavior.[3] Moreover, behavioral researchers have articulated tiered models of positive behavior support, based on the concept of primary, secondary, and tertiary prevention. These models serve as guides to practitioners in making decisions regarding when, and to whom, to apply more intensive levels of intervention. Thus, primary prevention attempts to prevent initial occurrences of a problem (e.g., challenging student behavior) through universal interventions apply to all students. School-wide discipline is an example of universal intervention. Secondary prevention addresses students who are at risk for developing chronic patterns of disruptive or dangerous behavior or emotional disorders. It is applied through targeted interventions—systematic strategies that are individualized or used with small groups. Tertiary interventions address students who exhibit chronic patterns of behavior or conditions such as EBD. These intensive interventions may involve alternative placement or multiagency planning and implementation.

By tracking students' responses to each level of intervention, educators can determine when more intensive interventions are needed for which students. Monitoring student response to each level of intervention thus serves as a convenient screening tool: Students who do not benefit from universal interventions are candidates for secondary prevention activities, and those who fail to succeed when targeted interventions are applied may be in need of tertiary prevention strategies. The theme of positive behavior

[3]At the same time, evaluations of traditional disciplinary practices (e.g., in-school suspension) with students with EBD reveal that such practices are ineffective in reducing undesired behavior (e.g., Stage, 1997).

support runs across all three levels, in that the major focus of intervention is on teaching the student appropriate skills that will meet his or her needs more effectively than do the problem behaviors.

Another set of advances involves the use of technology in providing training and support for professionals who serve students with challenging behavior. Dozens of World Wide Web sites provide information and access to resources with regard to effective academic instruction, assessments and interventions for undesired student behavior, and improving school safety. Interactive, multimedia training modules (even entire courses) are available in CD-ROM and Web-based formats. These innovations, in addition to distance education courses, are increasing professionals' access to training in effective practices for students with challenging behavior. Thanks to online linkages, professionals now have greater access to another important resource—each other. Collaborative approaches to intervention planning and implementation, including wraparound planning and collaborative teaching in general education classrooms, also have improved the support base for persons who work with the full range of student behavior, from strategies that prevent or minimize initial occurrences of problem behaviors to intensive interventions for some of the most challenging pupils. As educators have become more involved in transdisciplinary systems of care for this population, their collaboration with other providers and with families has increased, which has resulted in improved support for both the student and the classroom teacher.

Finally, attention is being directed to the critical need to deliver more effective academic instruction to students with EBD. Researchers have documented the lack of effective instructional practices with this student population, and leaders in the field are calling for a focus on improving the appropriateness of curriculum and students' rates of correct academic responding. This emphasis fits well with the inclusion of direct instruction and reinforcement of appropriate social skills to replace undesired behaviors targeted for reduction in behavior support plans.

NEW IN THIS EDITION

The fourth edition of *Strategies for Addressing Behavior Problems in the Classroom* addresses school-based interventions in the context of multiple levels of positive behavior support. Universal intervention strategies are a critical foundation for targeted and intensive interventions, because they reduce the number of students who potentially need more complex and costly targeted and intensive interventions. While it may be tempting to conclude that these latter intervention levels are reserved only for those pupils who have been identified as having EBD, they should be considered for all students with troubled or troubling behavior, regardless of their labels. The features of this new edition include:

- The organization of strategies according to universal, targeted, and intensive levels of intervention.
- More links to additional intervention resources and access to professional support.

In addition, this edition preserves two important features of the previous edition, which include an emphasis on:

- The total ecology of the student and his family, taking into account the child's needs across multiple life domains and employing expanded assessment procedures to identify and incorporate environmental influences on behavior to design more proactive, positive interventions.
- Collaboration with other disciplines, agencies, and families in designing more effective services and interventions in the educational system, as well as better coordination of treatments across settings and life domains, thereby facilitating more awareness and consistency among treatment providers.

ORGANIZATION OF THE TEXT

As in the previous editions, this text is organized in three sections. Part I provides background information from the professional literature regarding assessment and intervention methodology. Part II presents specific intervention strategies organized according to broad categories of problem behavior. Part III deals with issues involving the generalization of intervention effects and the role of professional educators in the context of a system of care. However, subsections of text have been reorganized and parts have been revised substantially, both to incorporate new information and to improve readability. Many chapters include new case studies that illustrate the concepts and interventions presented.

ACKNOWLEDGMENTS

Many persons have contributed to the development of this text. Although we cannot name all those whose ideas, suggestions, and criticisms are reflected in these pages, we hope that our friends and colleagues will recognize their influences on our work.

We thank four colleagues in particular, who have written major sections for this edition:

- Dr. Terrance M. Scott, Assistant Professor with the Department of Special Education and Rehabilitation Counseling at the University of Kentucky, who contributed a new chapter on school-wide discipline and planning based on positive behavior support;
- Dr. Kristina Johnson, Psychologist at Western Psychiatric Institute and Clinic, University of Pittsburgh, and Dr. William J. Helsel, Director of Psychology and Research, Black Mountain Center, Black Mountain, NC, who co-wrote the chapter on stereotypic behaviors;
- Ms. Deborah Lange Lambert, who with the assistance of Dr. Kristina Johnson and David E. O'Connor, M.D., Adult/Child and Adolescent Psychiatrist, wrote the chapter on psychiatric problems.

We also want to thank our colleagues who contributed case studies invaluable in illustrating some of the strategies presented in each chapter: Wendy Mager; Phillip L. Gunter and Marti L. Venn; Karen Hensley; Terrance M. Scott; Wyllie Keefer and Meshelda Jackson; Li-Lin Chen; Dawn E. Cois; Kristina Johnson, Cynthia R. Johnson, and Robert A. Sahl; Pamela Johnson and Donna T. Meers; and Kristine Jolivette. For transforming our manuscript into a first-rate book, we thank our superb project editor, Lea Baranowski. Ann Davis, our editor, once again led us through the process with great skill. We also thank her assistant, Keli Gemrich, as well as the production and marketing staff at Merrill/Prentice Hall. The reviewers, whose thoughtful comments helped us improve this edition, included Dr. Karenlee Alexander, Bemidji State University; Dr. Roger Bass, Carthage College; Dr. Lisa Bloom, Western Carolina University; Dr. Amelia E. Blyden, The College of New Jersey; and Dr. Martha J. Meyer, Butler University.

We thank our colleagues in Pittsburgh and Lexington who hunted down permissions and articles, suffered through rewrites and short deadlines, and yet managed to remain cheerful: Jamey Joy Covaleski, Mary Anne Frederick, Heather Gill, Yvonne Howitz, Kristine Jolivette, Carl Liaupsin, Linda Nelson, and Tera Rak.

Our final tribute is to our families—Bruce, Rob, and Cristina Perrone, and Linda Nelson—for their love and encouragement.

M.M.K.
C.M.N.

REFERENCES

Dwyer, K., & Osher, D. (2000). *Safeguarding our children: An action guide*. Washington, DC: U.S. Departments of Education and Justice, American Institutes of Research.

Dwyer, K., Osher, D., & Warger, C. (1998). *Early warning, timely response: A guide to safe schools*. Washington, DC: U.S. Department of Education.

Stage, S. A. (1997). A preliminary investigation of the relationship between in-school suspension and the disruptive classroom behavior of students with behavioral disorders. *Behavioral Disorders, 23*, 57–76.

DISCOVER THE COMPANION WEBSITE ACCOMPANYING THIS BOOK

THE PRENTICE HALL COMPANION WEBSITE: A VIRTUAL LEARNING ENVIRONMENT

Technology is a constantly growing and changing aspect of our field that is creating a need for content and resources. To address this emerging need, Prentice Hall has developed an online learning environment for students and professors alike—Companion Websites—to support our textbooks.

In creating a Companion Website, our goal is to build on and enhance what the textbook already offers. For this reason, the content for each user-friendly website is organized by chapter and provides the professor and student with a variety of meaningful resources.

For the Professor—

Every Companion Website integrates **Syllabus Manager**™, an online syllabus creation and management utility.

- **Syllabus Manager**™ provides you, the instructor, with an easy, step-by-step process to create and revise syllabi, with direct links into the Companion Website and other online content without having to learn HTML.

- Students may log on to your syllabus during any study session. All they need to know is the web address for the Companion Website and the password you've assigned to your syllabus.

- After you have created a syllabus using **Syllabus Manager**™, students may enter the syllabus for their course section from any point in the Companion Website.

- Clicking on a date, the student is shown the list of activities for the assignment. The activities for each assignment are linked directly to actual content, saving time for students.

- Adding assignments consists of clicking on the desired due date, then filling in the details of the assignment—name of the assignment, instructions, and whether it is a one-time or repeating assignment.

- In addition, links to other activities can be created easily. If the activity is online, a URL can be entered in the space provided, and it will be linked automatically in the final syllabus.

- Your completed syllabus is hosted on our servers, allowing convenient updates from any computer on the Internet. Changes you make to your syllabus are immediately available to your students at their next logon.

For the Student—

- **Topic Overviews** — outline key concepts in topic areas

- **Characteristics** — general information about each topic/disability covered on this website

- **Read About It** — a list of links to pertinent articles found on the Internet that cover each topic

- **Teaching Ideas** — links to articles that offer suggestions, ideas, and strategies for teaching students with disabilities

- **Web Links** — a wide range of websites that provide useful and current information related to each topic area

- **Resources** — a wide array of different resources for many of the pertinent topics and issues surrounding special education

- **Electronic Bluebook** — send homework or essays directly to your instructor's email with this paperless form

- **Message Board** — serves as a virtual bulletin board to post—or respond to—questions or comments to/from a national audience

- **Chat** — real-time chat with anyone who is using the text anywhere in the country—ideal for discussion and study groups, class projects, etc.

To take advantage of these and other resources, please visit the *Strategies for Addressing Behavior Problems in the Classroom*, Fourth Edition, Companion Website at

www.prenhall.com/kerr

CONTENTS

PART 3
BEYOND THE CLASSROOM   343

Chapter 10
PSYCHIATRIC PROBLEMS   344

Chapter 11
EXTENDING INTERVENTION EFFECTS   364

Chapter 12
THE CHALLENGES OF WORKING
WITH STUDENTS WITH EBD   410

Note: Every effort has been made to provide accurate and current Internet information in the book. However, the Internet and information posted on it are constantly changing, so it is inevitable that some of the Internet addresses listed in this textbook will change.

PART I

FOUNDATIONS OF EFFECTIVE BEHAVIOR MANAGEMENT

Chapter 1 Identifying and Serving Students with Behavioral Problems

Chapter 2 Assessment-Based Intervention Planning

Chapter 3 Keeping Track of Student Progress

Chapter 4 Selecting and Evaluating Interventions

Chapter 5 Universal School and Classroom Management Strategies

IDENTIFYING AND SERVING STUDENTS WITH BEHAVIORAL

CHAPTER **PROBLEMS**

OUTLINE

OBJECTIVES

After completing this chapter, you should be able to

- Describe the process of determining students' needs for behavioral support and educational services, including the assessment data that should be collected and the decisions that should be made.
- Describe the continuum of positive behavior support for students and indicate how decisions should be made regarding which students require what levels of intervention.
- Describe the major changes in IDEA that affect school disciplinary practices for students with disabilities.
- Indicate what a definition of behavioral disorders should accomplish and indicate weaknesses of the current federal definition.
- Discuss the role of school-based teams with regard to addressing the needs of students for positive behavior support and for reducing the need to identify, label, and serve students in special education programs.
- Give a rationale for creating systemic changes in schools as a basis for preventing and responding more effectively to challenging student behaviors.

Aggressive, disruptive, noncompliant, socially inadequate, stereotypic, or withdrawn behaviors constitute a difficult set of problems for educators. Among the many questions raised in reference to pupils exhibiting challenging behaviors are the following:

- Should these pupils be formally identified as having an emotional or behavioral disorder (EBD)[1] and served in special education programs, or should they remain in regular programs and be treated as disciplinary problems?
- Are students with EBD, or those with patterns of acting out behavior, threats to school safety?
- Can the needs of students with challenging behavior or emotional problems be addressed in general education settings, or do they require services in self-contained special classes or even more restrictive settings?
- Regardless of their educational placements, what approaches to addressing these pupils' behavior problems are most effective? What skills and resources are needed to accomplish desired behavior changes?

This text offers you classroom strategies for preventing and responding to the behavior problems of students across a variety of educational status and settings. These approaches work with the full range of students, from those with severe and profound developmental disabilities to those with no disabilities, from preschool children to adults. General and special classroom teachers, consultants, psychologists, guidance counselors, and administrators, as well as other professionals and parents, have applied these methods.

The needs of many children and youth with EBD greatly exceed the service delivery capacity of the educational system (or any human services system). The outcomes that are consistently documented for this group of students, while they are in school and afterward, support the conclusion that a single agency or system alone cannot meet their needs. These outcomes include the following:

- Higher percentages of students with EBD are placed on homebound instruction and in residential, hospital, and other restrictive settings than any other group of students with disabilities (Koyanagi & Gaines, 1993).
- Students with EBD fail more courses and are retained in grade more often than students with any other disabilities. Over 75% of secondary school students with EBD have failed one or more courses, the highest rate of failure of any category of students with disabilities (Wagner, 1995). Only 42% of this population earn a high school diploma compared with 56% of all students with disabilities and 79% of youth in the general population. Their drop-out rate is 55%, compared with 36% for students with other disabilities and 21% for the general student population (Wagner, 1995).
- Only about 18% of youth identified with EBD go to college or vocational schools as compared to 22% of all students with disabilities (McLaughlin, Leone, Warren, & Schofield, 1994).
- Students with EBD have difficulty maintaining jobs and living independently; according to the most recent National Longitudinal Transition Study (Blackorby & Wagner, 1996), 47.4% of students with EBD were employed when they were 3 to 5 years out of school, and 40.2% were living independently.
- Using even low criteria for "successful" adjustment to adulthood, fewer than 25% of both graduates and dropouts of programs for students with EBD were judged to be successful 3 years after their class exited high school (Carson, Sitlington, & Frank, 1995; Weber & Scheuermann, 1997).

[1]The 1997 amendments to the Individuals with Disability Education Act (IDEA, PL 105–17) uses the label "emotionally disturbed" for this population. However, many professionals and professional organizations (e.g., the Council for Children with Behavioral Disorders) prefer the label EBD because it places equal emphasis on students' behavioral and emotional characteristics and needs.

- About 20% of all youth identified as having EBD have been arrested while in school; 58% are arrested within 5 years of leaving school. Of students with EBD who drop out of school, 73% are arrested within 5 years of leaving school (Walker, Colvin, & Ramsey, 1995).
- African Americans and males are significantly overrepresented in special education programs for students with EBD compared to proportions in the general school-age population (Chesapeake Institute, 1994).

As schools address public concerns regarding school safety and effectiveness, and simultaneously face the challenges of dealing with an increasingly complex and diverse student population, educational leaders are calling for systemic changes in the way in which student behavior is viewed and addressed. For example, it is acknowledged that schools can no longer afford to ignore the behavioral needs of students until they reach the point that special education identification is considered, or that potential threats to school safety exist. In the past, schools have adopted a relatively passive attitude toward student behavior (i.e., expecting that students will enter school with the knowledge and skills necessary to meet expectations for behavioral decorum), relying on punishment and school exclusion when behavior exceeds these often poorly defined limits. Today this stance is being replaced with the recognition that schools must be prepared to address the full range of student behavior, including teaching expectations and routines to all pupils, and responding proactively and constructively to misbehavior through a graduated system of positive interventions (Sugai, Sprague, Horner, & Walker, 2000). This new approach, **positive behavior support,**[2] is being implemented in hundreds of schools throughout the United States. It provides a context for identifying and serving students exhibiting behavior problems in general education.

[2]Terms in boldface in the text are defined in the Glossary.

Therefore, we begin this edition with an overview of positive behavior support.

POSITIVE BEHAVIOR SUPPORT

A number of years ago, professionals working with individuals with severe cognitive disabilities and challenging behavior argued that punishment of problem behaviors does not work. These punitive methods create treatment and educational environments that are aversive, and therefore counterproductive to facilitating educational progress. They proposed a new way of looking at problem behavior: these behaviors are functional communications, in that they help persons with limited cognitive and verbal skills to get what they need from other people. If the communicative function of their behavior could be identified, they argued, this information could be used to develop more effective interventions. Specifically, these individuals could be taught to use adaptive replacement behaviors that serve the same functions as the maladaptive behaviors (LaVigna & Donnellan, 1986). Two decades of research have supported the validity of these arguments.

The cornerstones of positive behavior support are:

- **Functional behavioral assessments** (FBAs) of problem behavior; and
- Positive behavioral intervention planning.

The 1997 amendments to the Individuals with Disabilities Act (IDEA '97) mandates that **Individualized Education Plan** (IEP) teams use the FBA and positive behavior intervention planning processes for all students with disabilities whose problem behavior provokes consideration of a change in educational placement, including suspension and expulsion. Recent applied research with children and youth in public school settings with so-called "mild" disabilities (e.g., EBD, attention deficit hyperactive disorder [ADHD], learning disabilities, mild mental retardation) or even no identified disabilities, has demonstrated the effectiveness of interventions based on positive behavior support (also referred to as effective behavioral support).

IDEA '97 only requires that FBAs be conducted and behavior intervention plans be developed or reviewed when a change in placement is considered. However, the strategy of waiting for a student to demonstrate problem behavior, particularly if it poses a threat to the student or to others, obviously has some drawbacks. First, interventions can be applied only if the problem behavior is observed by someone with the authority to do something. Second, interventions are reactionary; that is, they are applied after the behavior has occurred (sometimes well after). Public concerns regarding school safety have promoted researchers and practitioners to think more preventatively, and one outcome of this thinking is that the concept of positive behavior support has been broadened to an approach that may be applied to entire schools. Professionals have begun to think about schools as "host environments" and of improving the capacity of the school setting to support the use of effective practices (Sugai & Horner, 1999). Effective host environments include policies, structures, and routines that promote the use of research-validated practices (Sugai et al., 2000). It has been demonstrated that the application of strategies that promote positive behavior support across the total school environment (e.g., school-wide discipline plans) dramatically reduce discipline referral rates.[3] Accordingly, educators have had to think in terms of providing positive behavior support across the entire range of student behavior. This has been elaborated into school-wide integrated systems of intervention (Sugai et al., 2000), which emphasizes multiple levels of prevention, a model that has been widely used in pub-

lic health, but only recently has been applied by other human service agencies, including social services, education, mental health, social work, and crime prevention. The model is described in terms of primary, secondary, and tertiary prevention (see Figure 1-1).

Primary prevention strategies (*universal interventions*) focus on enhancing protective factors in schools and communities and are intended to prevent students from falling into risk. Primary prevention is universal; that is, applied through the efforts of all school staff and across all individuals. An example of a universal intervention is inoculations to prevent such diseases as polio and measles. A school-based example of a universal intervention is a school-wide focus on positive student discipline.

Secondary prevention (*targeted intervention*) involves activities that provide support (such as mentoring, skill development, and other types of specialized assistance) to students who are identified as at risk so that they will not develop patterns of problematic coping (e.g., antisocial behavior, substance abuse), or other behavioral manifestations that contribute to even more serious problems. Secondary prevention strategies

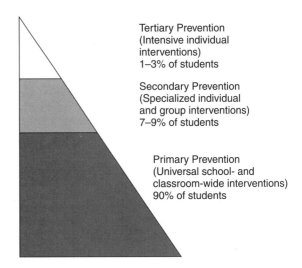

Tertiary Prevention
(Intensive individual
interventions)
1–3% of students

Secondary Prevention
(Specialized individual
and group interventions)
7–9% of students

Primary Prevention
(Universal school- and
classroom-wide interventions)
90% of students

FIGURE 1-1   Model of school-based positive behavior support.

[3]Office discipline referrals have been shown to be a useful measure of school disciplinary incidents that can be used as a basis for making decisions regarding school-wide discipline strategies (Lewis-Palmer, Sugai, & Larson, 1999; J. R. Nelson, Martella, & Galand, 1998; Skiba, Peterson, & Williams, 1998; Sugai et al., 2000).

include efforts targeted at specific problems or individuals for whom primary prevention strategies have not been effective. For example, children with thin tooth enamel may receive specialized dental care. A school-based example of secondary prevention is implementation of systematic instruction in social skills for a group of students with poor or inappropriate interactions with peers or adults.

Tertiary prevention (*intensive intervention*) targets individuals with serious problems that constitute a chronic condition and attempts to ameliorate the effects of their condition on their daily functioning. These strategies are delivered through highly specialized services that are orchestrated by a team. For example, children with chronic health conditions may receive highly specialized and ongoing treatment and their families may be shown how to manage and support their child as well as how to meet their own continuing needs. A school-based example of tertiary prevention is the implementation of a **wraparound plan** for a student who also is being served by the juvenile justice system. This plan would coordinate services across school, home, and community life domains.

Implementing Positive Behavior Support

As Sugai and Horner (1999) explain, positive behavior support consists of four interrelated systems: (a) school-wide procedures to define, teach, reward, and correct pupil social behavior; (b) specific setting procedures to address problems that arise from scheduling, monitoring, and architectural flaws; (c) classroom procedures that teachers use in their own classrooms to maintain order and motivation; and (d) individual student procedures to provide the extra resources and structure necessary to support and control the 5–7% of students who typically present 50% or more of the behavioral challenges in the school. Implementing these systems obviously requires thinking about interventions at all three levels of prevention. Moreover, applying the full continuum of positive be-havior support demands commitment and planning from the entire school building staff, as well as parents, and representatives of the school district and community. This is because effective implementation of strategies at the targeted and intensive levels depends upon that of universal interventions, which address all students and involve all school staff. Recall that the focus of universal intervention strategies is to prevent initial occurrences of problem behavior by supporting appropriate student behavior in all areas of the school building, as well as on school transportation, during field trips, athletic, and social events. Obviously, school-wide planning is an essential prerequisite to developing universal interventions, and experience has shown that at least 80% of school staff must be committed for universal systems to be effective (Sugai & Horner, 1999). Generally, the process for gaining this level of consensus involves a meeting of the entire school staff, including office workers, administrators, custodians, cafeteria workers, and bus drivers, as well as teaching faculty. In this meeting, staff receive an orientation to the model. If at least 80% of the staff consent to implement the approach, a team (e.g., School Implementation Team, School Climate Team) is formed, consisting of representatives of all the staff constituencies. This team is responsible for assessing the school environment (Todd, Horner, Sugai, & Sprague, 1999). The assessment includes examination of: (a) the physical environment to identify where behavior problems occur; (b) routines and schedules that comprise specific contexts in which problems are more likely to happen; (c) how students are monitored throughout the school; and (d) existing disciplinary responses and their effects. This assessment process is facilitated by examining school disciplinary data, which often are available in the form of office discipline referrals, discipline referrals, or behavior reports. An advantage of labeling this form a "behavior report" is that it may be used to document positive behaviors as well as disciplinary infractions, thereby focusing staff attention on the need to acknowledge and support desired student behavior.

Typically, a behavior report is a brief form containing the student's name, the behavior occasioning acknowledgment or disciplinary action (which may be a simple checklist), the location and time of the event, and the name of the staff person making the referral. Figure 1-2 is a sample behavior report developed for an alternative education program. Each item on this checklist is coded to facilitate entry into the computerized spreadsheet used to summarize and report school-wide behavior report data (Dorsey & Haywood, 2000). When behavior report data are collected systematically and entered on a spreadsheet, summary reports are easily generated, which provide useful answers to such questions as: "Where and when do most behavior incidents occur?" "Which students account for the majority of behavior reports?" "Which staff make the most referrals?" (Lewis-Palmer, Sugai, & Larson, 1999).

The team presents the results of their assessment to the staff at a school-wide meeting, and lead the staff through the process of developing a plan based on the assessment data. Specific components of **school-wide interventions** (often referred to as school-wide discipline plans) of course vary from school to school, but typical elements include: (a) establishing a set of clear behavioral expectations (rules) for students in all school areas and activities; (b) identifying strategies for teaching these expectations to students and rewarding them for complying; (c) planning alterations in physical settings and routines (e.g., removal of physical barriers to supervision, changing problematic traffic patterns); (d) establishing provisions to ensure that students are monitored at all times; and (e) making decisions about how rule violations are to be dealt with. Staff consensus must be reached on all expectations and responses to student behavior; otherwise, inconsistency of implementation will undermine the effectiveness of the plan (Lewis & Garrison-Harrell, 1999; Scott & Nelson, 1999a). A number of staff development curricula are available for implementing school-wide discipline plans, many of which are based on the principles of positive behavior support (e.g., Scott & Nelson, 1999a; Sprick, Sprick, & Garrison, 1992). Staff training workshops also are available through the National Center for Positive Behavioral Interventions and Support (www.pbis.org).

Schools that have met these implementation criteria have experienced substantial reductions in discipline referral rates (e.g., Nelson, Martella, & Galand, 1998; Taylor-Green, Horner, Sugai, & Hall, 1996). When appropriately implemented, approximately 90% of students respond positively to primary prevention. Significant reductions in discipline referrals free staff to concentrate on other duties. However, the important task that remains is to address the needs of the 10% of students with whom interventions at the universal level are *not* effective. Students in this pool may be thought of as constituting an at-risk group, in that, without additional structures and supports, they are at risk for academic failure and developing enduring patterns of disruptive, noncompliant, or antisocial behavior, as well as EBD. As Farmer, Farmer, & Gut (1999) point out, students who are likely to develop disruptive behavior disorders often have distinct risk profiles, which typically include four or more of such characteristics as academic problems, low academic motivation, problems in peer relations, associations with deviant peers, aggression, attention problems, hyperactivity, and family difficulties. Attempting to change any single risk factor without simultaneously addressing others is very difficult and not likely to succeed. Therefore, systemic changes, which occur at multiple levels and address the interconnectedness of students' behaviors, are needed. School- and classroom-wide universal intervention strategies based on positive behavior support are presented in Chapter 5.

Targeted interventions may be designed for individual students, or for a small group having similar needs.[4] Important elements of targeted

---

[4]However, we caution against assembling groups of students who share a common deficit (e.g., poor social skills) for treatment, as appropriate peer role models are important factors in social skill instruction. Furthermore, social skills are best taught in natural social contexts (Scott & Nelson, 1998).

Student Name: _____   **Date:** _____

Teacher: _____   **Grade:** _____

Time of Day: _____

Location:

- ☐ Classroom (L1)
- ☐ Parking Lot (L5)
- ☐ Rest Room (L9)
- ☐ Not on school grounds (L13)

- ☐ Gym (L2)
- ☐ Library (L6)
- ☐ Ball Field (L10)

- ☐ Playground (L3)
- ☐ Computer Lab (L7)
- ☐ Bus (L11)

- ☐ Hallway (L4)
- ☐ Office (L8)
- ☐ Auditorium (L12)

Positives:

- ☐ Perfect Attendance (P1)
- ☐ Positive Attitude (P4)
- ☐ Good Citizenship (P7)
- ☐ Appropriate Appearance (P10)

- ☐ Learns New Skill (P2)
- ☐ Compliance (P5)
- ☐ Volunteer Service (P8)

- ☐ Completes Work (P3)
- ☐ Honesty (P6)
- ☐ Improvement (P9)

Positive Actions:

- ☐ Meet with Parents (PA1)
- ☐ Public Recognition (PA4)

- ☐ Call Home (PA2)
- ☐ Tangible Reward (PA5)

- ☐ Call Home School (PA3)

Infractions:

- ☐ Tardy (I1)
- ☐ Skip Class (I5)
- ☐ Substances (I9)
- ☐ Lying (I13)
- ☐ Noncompliance (I16)

- ☐ Language (I2)
- ☐ Fighting (I6)
- ☐ Weapons (I10)
- ☐ Verbal abuse (I14)
- ☐ Disruptive behavior (I17)

- ☐ Repeated Minor (I3)
- ☐ Vandalism (I7)
- ☐ Disrespect (I11)
- ☐ Insubordination (I15)
- ☐ Verbal/Physical Intimidation (I18)

- ☐ Defiance (I4)
- ☐ Theft (I8)
- ☐ Cheating (I12)

Consequences:

- ☐ Meet w/Parents (C1)
- ☐ Changed Seating (C4)
- ☐ In-School Suspension (C7)
- ☐ Agency Referral (C10)

- ☐ Consulted Home School (C2)
- ☐ Telephoned Parent (C5)
- ☐ Suspension (C8)

- ☐ Consult Support Service (C3)
- ☐ Schedule Change (C6)
- ☐ Expulsion (C9)

How does the consequence relate to the learning process?

FIGURE 1-2   Behavior report.

Note: *Adapted from a model developed by Candice Hayward. Trainer/Assessment Specialist, Regional Office of Education #2. Jonesboro, IL. Copyright 2000. Reproduced with permission.*

interventions are functional assessments of problem behavior; identification, instruction, and reinforcement of a desired replacement behavior, effective (direct) instruction of both academic and social skills, the use of errorless learning strategies, and systematic plans for responding to problem behavior. For individual students, a **behavior intervention plan** (BIP) is developed from a functional assessment of problem behaviors and their environmental contexts. Appropriate skills are identified that can serve as functional replacement behaviors, and the use of these is taught, prompted, and reinforced. At the same time, strategies are created to facilitate success in settings where problem behaviors are likely to occur, and to respond to targeted problem behaviors, if and when they occur. Finally, a plan for collecting data to monitor occurrences of targeted and replacement behaviors is developed and decision rules are created for determining when parts of the plan need to be revised or replaced (Scott & Nelson, 1999b). Four important criteria must be met if a BIP is to be effective:

1. The plan must be written, so all aspects will be clear to everyone involved in its implementation.
2. The plan must be implemented as written.
3. The plan must be evaluated regularly and systematically against data decision rules.
4. The plan must be revised as often as needed.

Again, interventions at this level are best planned, implemented, and monitored by a team. This team, which we refer to as the Behavior Support Team, may be a subset of the team that provides support to staff in addressing school-wide, specific setting, or classroom behavioral issues (Todd et al., 1999). The team supports all persons who are working with the student (as well as the student himself) through regular meetings and consultation. Todd et al., (1999) recommend that the Behavior Support Team include at least one member who is competent in designing and providing positive be-

havior support, the staff member who requested assistance, a family member, a representative of the school-wide team, other school staff who have a good relationship with the student, and, when appropriate, the student. The team conducts the functional behavioral assessment, designs the BIP (which may be referred to as a behavior support or positive behavior support plan) and strategies for its implementation, and provides direct and consultative assistance with regard to ongoing implementation and evaluation.

Experience with secondary prevention strategies indicates that they are effective for approximately 7% to 9% of the student population. Thus, schools should anticipate that tertiary prevention will be needed for the remaining 1% to 3% of students. Tertiary prevention is accomplished through intensive interventions, which are individualized and based on multiple assessments of student, provider, and family needs, as well as their strengths. A fundamental distinction of intensive interventions is that they frequently involve providers from other human service agencies (i.e., juvenile court, child welfare, mental health) and the intervention plan extends beyond the school day. However, these intervention plans should incorporate features of other formal plans, such as IEPs and 504 Accommodation Plans (see p. 14). If educational programs and interventions for this most needy group of students are to succeed, they must occur in the context of an integrated system of services offered by numerous agencies that support the child and his family. Children and youth experiencing significant emotional and behavioral problems require many services that flexibly "wrap around" their needs at home, in the community, and the workplace, as well as in school (Clark, Schaefer, Burchard, & Welkowitz, 1992). Such integrated **systems of care** (Stroul & Friedman, 1986) are being established in many communities and several states (Epstein, Quinn, Nelson, Polsgrove, & Cumblad, 1993; Illback, Nelson, & Sanders, 1998). Integration of service delivery is characteristic of wraparound planning, which is described in Chapters 11 and 12. Thus, wraparound plans consider such life domains as employment, food, clothing, transportation, and recreation. Naturally, such plans also are developed, implemented, and evaluated by a team, consisting of providers, the family, and others who know and care about the child. The wraparound planning format and strategy developed out of systems of care initiatives that attempt to deliver intensive levels of service in natural home, school, and community settings. Figure 1-3 summaries the major characteristics and actions needed to implement all three levels of positive behavior support.

We now turn to assessment procedures used to identify and classify those students whose behavior interferes with their educational progress, as well as the early intervention strategies designed to avoid the necessity of special education labels and classification. Here, we address the issue of which students should be considered, for educational purposes, as having EBD. We also give you an overview of special education for students with EBD—who they are, how they are identified, and what services are available to them in school.

IDEA 1997 DISCIPLINARY REGULATIONS

The Education of the Handicapped Act of 1975 (PL 94–142) is a major accomplishment in terms of guaranteeing appropriate educational experiences for children and youth with disabilities. However, as the poor outcomes for students with EBD suggest, pupils whose educational performance is impaired by their emotional or behavior problems have not benefited greatly from this legislation; compared with a very conservative prevalence estimate of 2% of the school-age population, less than 1% are receiving special education across the nation (U.S. Department of Education, 1999). Koyanagi and Gaines (1993) estimate that fewer than one in three children with EBD receive the services they need. Moreover, little evidence exists that schools are dealing effectively with the emotional

and behavior problems of students *not* identified as having EBD.

Subsequent amendments to the Education of the Handicapped Act (i.e., PL 99–457, PL 101–436, and PL 105–17) substantially expand the scope of the 1975 legislation. Current provisions include a greater emphasis on programs that improve the transition of students with disabilities to adult life, a call for early intervention services to infants and toddlers (birth to age 2) with disabilities and their families, and guidelines for disciplining students with disabilities.

The most recent amendments (known as IDEA '97) have had a dramatic impact on schools' disciplinary practices regarding students with disabilities. Specifically, these amendments require that an FBA be conducted for those students with disabilities who exhibit behaviors that constitute a pattern of misbehavior or resulting in a change in educational placement (PL 105–17, §615 (K)1.B.i). The IDEA requires that:

1. Either before or not later than 10 business days after either first removing the child for more than 10 school days in a school year or commencing a removal that constitutes a change of placement under §300.519, including [removals for weapon or drug violations]—

   If the local education agency (LEA) did not conduct an FBA and implement a behavioral intervention plan for the child before the behavior that resulted in the removal—the agency shall convene an IEP meeting to develop an assessment plan.

   If the child already has a BIP, the IEP team shall meet to review the plan and its implementation, and modify the plan and its implementation as necessary to address the behavior.

2. As soon as practicable after developing the [assessment plan] and completing the assessments required by the plan, the LEA shall convene an IEP team meeting to

The goal of *Positive Behavior Support* is to create an environment that facilitates and predicts positive student behavior while maintaining plans for effective and efficient interventions for misbehavior.

THREE LEVELS OF POSITIVE BEHAVIOR SUPPORT

1. UNIVERSAL INTERVENTIONS (School- and classroom-wide)

-preventative in nature
-implemented across all staff and students

-collect and monitor school-wide data
-predict when and where problems occur

Analysis of Physical School Arrangements
Simple logistical and architectural factors should be assessed and arranged to minimize the potential for disruptive or dangerous behaviors.

√ setting physical boundaries to keep students in monitored areas
√ arranging schedules to avoid potential conflicts
√ directing student traffic to minimize student numbers in limited areas

Establish Clear and Enforceable School Rules
A set of clear rules should be developed by each teacher for his or her classroom and for the entire school. These rules must be enforceable and agreeable to all staff members.

√ staff generates a list of rules to facilitate safe learning environments
√ rules are brief, positive, aimed at problem areas, and publicly posted
√ all school staff teach rules to students through modeling, practice, & correction
√ all staff reinforce students for following rules

Plan for Supervision of All Students
Staff must be organized to supervise all areas in which students may congregate and must take responsibility to see their students transition in and out of their rooms. Even those areas which are designated out of bounds will require some degree of monitoring.

√ procedures are designated to facilitate quick assistance when requested
√ all staff take responsibility for monitoring students
√ supervision is active, teachers are moving about and interacting with students

Plan for Disciplinary Responses
A plan for how misbehaviors will be consequated must be determined in advance and in accordance with district and state policies and guidelines. As a general rule, discipline should be used to prevent further misbehavior rather than to exclude students from school.

√ consequences (positive & negative) are applied immediately
√ consequences are applied consistently across all staff and students
√ records on student discipline are kept to track repeat offenses/offenders

2. TARGETED INTERVENTIONS (Specialized individual and group)

-written individualized plans
-carried out in the school and home
-based on functional assessment

-used on students for whom universal interventions
 have not been successful
-involve effective instruction

FIGURE 1-3   Elements of positive behavior support.
Copyright 1999 by T. M. Scott & C. M. Nelson.

Key Activities and Skills

√ effective instruction (academic and social)
√ functional behavioral assessment
√ teaching and supporting functional replacement behaviors
√ knowledge of effective systems of behavior management

Behavior Intervention Plan Steps

1. Identify function of the behavior for the student
2. Identify appropriate replacement behavior(s)
3. Plan for systematic teaching of replacement behavior(s)
4. Arrange environment to facilitate success (prompting/reinforcing)
5. Design behavior management component
6. Write behavioral objectives
7. Collect data and evaluate

3. INTENSIVE INTERVENTIONS (Individual, comprehensive, interagency)

-written individualized plans
-carried out across a range of settings
-based on needs beyond just the school

-used on students for whom targeted interventions
 have not been successful
-multiagency cooperation and planning

Key Activities and Skills

√ planning for involvement of community resources as necessary
√ in-depth and continuous assessment from a variety of sources and perspectives
√ write activities into formal plans where necessary (e.g. IEPs)
√ knowledge of and ability to access full range of school support services
√ school acts as liaison for planning of wraparound services
√ planning and implementation of individualized academic and behavior plans

Wraparound

• used with individual students
• based on unique child and family needs
• built upon child, family, and provider strengths
• uses traditional and nontraditional interventions
• encompasses multiple life domains (school, home, etc.)
• resources are blended
• services are planned, implemented, and evaluated by a team
• team supports child, family, and providers
• unconditional—if the plan doesn't work, change the plan

FIGURE 1-3 Elements of positive behavior support—*Continued.*

develop appropriate behavioral interventions to address that behavior and shall implement those interventions.

Local education agencies do have the authority to move a student to another placement of the LEA's choosing (including temporary suspension) for up to 10 consecutive school days for any violation of the school's code of conduct, or to an appropriate interim alternative educational setting for up to 45 days if the student carries or possesses a weapon or illegal drugs on school premises. A change in placement of up to 45 days also is allowed if a hearing officer determines that maintaining the student in his or her current placement would be likely to result in injury to the student or others. However, a change in placement may not be made if the behavior in question is a manifestation of the student's disability. In cases where a change in placement is considered, the IEP team must perform a **manifestation determination** assessment, which means that, before a change in placement can be made, it must be established that the behavior is not a manifestation (i.e., an expression) of the student's disability (U.S. Department of Education, 2000). During any proceedings that address either discipline or alternative educational placement, the student is to remain in his current educational placement, unless the SEA or the LEA and the parents agree otherwise (§615 (j)). If the student is placed in an interim alternative educational setting, the setting must enable him to continue to participate in the general curriculum and to continue to receive services that will enable him to meet the goals specified in his IEP (§615 (k)(3)). The law also requires that, "in the case of a child whose behavior impedes his or her learning or that of others," a student's IEP team, in the process of developing an IEP (whether an initial IEP or a revision) must "consider, when appropriate, strategies, including positive behavioral interventions, strategies, and supports to address that behavior" (20 U.S.C. §1414 (d) (3) (B) (i), 1999).

These "discipline regulations" have a potentially enormous impact on how schools address students with problem behavior. First, as noted above, if a student has been (or could be) identified as having a disability, he or she may not be disciplined through long-term suspension or expulsion, unless it can be proven that the behavior which occasioned the disciplinary action was not a manifestation of the disability. Second, the emphasis placed on developing a BIP that is based on an FBA means that, in effect, problem behavior is officially viewed as an opportunity to provide positive behavioral intervention (Katsiyannis & Maag, 1998). These mandated practices are a dramatic contrast to policies that include zero tolerance for

even minor student misbehavior and "get tough" disciplinary measures that include harsh punishment and school exclusion (Nelson, 2000).

Another, less well-known feature of IDEA with respect to students with EBD is that the law supports research to *prevent* this disability. The emphasis on prevention is unique to the EBD category, and indicates a federal philosophy that is proactive with regard to initiatives that address prevention of problem behavior.

Other federal laws provide protection to individuals with disabilities, including conditions not covered under IDEA. For example, Section 504 of the Vocational Rehabilitation Act of 1973 requires that all individuals with a disability that substantially limits one or more life activities receive an education comparable to that of their typical peers through an Accommodation Plan. Students with ADHD, as well as other students with disabilities who are not considered eligible under IDEA, should be provided with services under this regulation. The Americans with Disabilities Act of 1990 (ADA; PL 101–336) addresses all types of discrimination against persons with physical or mental disabilities, primarily with regard to employment. While these laws do not afford protection from school suspension or expulsion for students with disabilities to the same extent as does IDEA, court decisions and Office of Civil Rights rulings indicate that IDEA and 504 safeguards may be applicable to students who were excluded from school before their disabilities had been verified (Katsiyannis & Maag, 1998).

BEHAVIOR DISORDERS OR PROBLEM BEHAVIORS?

As we suggested earlier, the public education system has not embraced the challenge of working with students with difficult behavior. Historically, schools have excluded these pupils or have placed them in segregated schools and classrooms (e.g., alternative education programs, self-contained special education classes) for most or all of the school day. Now that students with disabilities are spending more time in general education settings, *all* educators can expect to work with students with emotional and behavioral problems (whether they are labeled as having this disability or not).

Pupils with problem behaviors may be classified by a variety of terms, from emotionally disturbed or behaviorally disordered to autistic or psychotic; from juvenile delinquent or socially maladjusted to conduct disordered or just a discipline problem. Labels tend to have little relationship to the behaviors that children exhibit. Instead, the characteristics of the setting and teachers' standards and expectations are more predictive of students' behavior than their labels. Nevertheless, IDEA requires that pupils who are provided special education services because of their behavior deviations be defined so that the programs serving them can receive state and federal funds. This law defines students with emotional disorders (ED) as those who exhibit one or more of the following characteristics that adversely affect educational performance over a long period of time and to a marked degree:

1. An inability to learn that cannot be explained by intellectual, sensory, or health factors
2. An inability to build or maintain satisfactory interpersonal relationships with peers and teachers
3. Inappropriate types of behavior or feelings under normal circumstances
4. A general pervasive mood of unhappiness or depression
5. A tendency to develop physical symptoms or fears associated with personal or school problems

(Students with "social maladjustment" are specifically excluded from eligibility under this definition.)

Although this definition has been modified slightly over the years, essentially it is the same as when PL 94–142 was first passed. The definition has been widely criticized by the professional community (Forness & Kavale, 2000). Issues of contention include the vagueness and ambiguity of such criteria as "inability to learn," which results in confusion regarding the distinction between the ED and the learning disorders definition. The criterion of "inability to build or maintain satisfactory interpersonal relationships" would seem to define social maladjustment, yet students with this condition are specifically excluded from eligibility. Similar problems exist with regard to the remaining three criteria. An alternate definition has been drafted and was circulated for public reaction and comment in the *Federal Register* (1993). Two thirds of more than 1,200 respondents were in favor of the new definition, which is as follows:

(1) The term "emotional or behavioral disorder" means a disability that is characterized by behavioral or emotional responses in school programs so different from appropriate age, cultural, or ethnic norms that the responses adversely affect educational performance, including academic, social, vocational, or personal skills; more than a temporary, expected response to stressful events in the environment; consistently exhibited in two different settings, at least one of which is school-related; and unresponsive to direct intervention applied in general education, or the condition of a child is such that general education interventions would be insufficient.

The term includes such a disability that co-exists with other disabilities.

The term includes a schizophrenic disorder, affective disorder, anxiety disorder, or other sustained disorder of conduct or adjustment, affecting a child if the disorder affects educational performance as described in paragraph (1) (*Federal Register*, February 10, 1993, p. 7938).

The report analyzing responses to this definition (McIntyre & Forness, 1997) was never submitted to Congress for action. However, the definition contains statements that highlight "best practices" with respect to identifying and serving students whose EBD dictate a need for special education and related services. First, it emphasizes that EBD is more than a temporary response to stress and is not responsive to prereferral interventions. Second, it requires that the determination of eligibility be based on multiple sources of data that are gathered in more than one school setting. Third, it indicates that EBD may co-exist with other conditions. Fourth, it lists some of the mental health diagnoses that could make a student eligible for services if educational performanceis is also impaired, which allows for coordination of services with other agencies that provide services (Forness & Kavale, 2000).

Definitional issues notwithstanding, pupils with EBD are no more homogeneous than are children classified any other way. Furthermore, classifying a student as having a "learning disability," "mental retardation," or even being labeled "gifted" does not guarantee that emotional and behavior problems also may not exist. Therefore, we focus on strategies for preventing initial problem behavior, minimizing problems with students who are "at risk" of developing chronic patterns of maladaptive emotions or behavior, and reducing the impact of EBD on the educational outcomes of students so identified. We believe that such a focus will better serve your pupils' interests and will make you a better practitioner.

Obviously, this work is not easy! Attrition rates of educators, especially special educators, are high, and working with students who exhibit challenging emotional and behavioral problems can be highly stressful. Skill in using the strategies presented in this book may be your best protection against this stress. Other considerations and tactics for dealing with stress are presented in Chapter 12.

IDENTIFYING STUDENTS WITH BEHAVIORAL DISORDERS

Serving students through all levels of positive behavior support will lead to the identification of some whose emotional, behavioral, and academic needs dictate that special education and related services be provided so that they can benefit from their school experience. Thus, responsiveness to intervention (or lack thereof) may serve as a screening tool to identify students eligible for special education.[5] If schools adopt systemic changes based on positive behavior support, this approach hopefully will replace the practice of waiting until a student's problems become sufficiently intense to warrant a referral for special education eligibility assessment. However, current federal law establishes a process for determining eligibility based on referral and assessment. A **multidisciplinary team** (MDT) of individuals performs these comprehensive assessments and decides whether to classify the student as having EBD, determines the nature and extent of the services to be provided, and implements the service plan. Procedures commonly used to identify students with EBD include finding those students at risk for EBD through screening; implementing prereferral intervention strategies within the general education program (with appropriate documentation of the effects of these modifications on student performance); and conducting more intensive assessments to determine whether the student should be certified as eligible for special education services because of EBD (Algozzine, Ruhl, & Ramsey, 1991).

Screening

Whereas systematic school-wide screening procedures routinely are applied to detect other disabilities (e.g., sensory, psychomotor, physical, learning, and cognitive disabilities), screening for EBD typically amounts to a referral to a special education program administrator from the general education classroom teacher. Once referred, teacher-nominated students are very likely to be certified by a MDT as having EBD, especially if they exhibit **externalizing** (overt, acting-out) behavior patterns. On the other hand, students manifesting **internalizing** (withdrawn, depressed) behavior

---

[5]Gresham (1991) has conceptualized EBD in terms of resistance to intervention. He argues that certification as EBD should be applied only to students for whom universal and targeted interventions, provided in the context of a general education program, have not been successful.

patterns tend not to be referred and therefore are not identified because they are less bothersome to classroom teachers (Walker & Fabre, 1987). More systematic screening tools have been developed. For example, systematic screening techniques to identify children who are at risk have been developed for use in the elementary schools (McConaughy & Achenbach, 1989; Walker & Severson, 1990). Screening procedures also have been developed to identify children of preschool age at risk of school failure because of emotional and behavioral problems (Feil & Becker, 1993; Feil, Severson, & Walker, 1994; Sinclair, Del'Homme, & Gonzalez, 1993).

Students' school records are a rich source of screening information. Walker and his colleagues (Walker, Block-Pedego, Todis, & Severson, 1991) developed the *School Archival Records Search*, a systematic protocol for compiling and analyzing such school records data as attendance and grade promotion patterns, office referrals, health history, and anecdotal comments. These systematic screening tools are useful and effective; however, staff should receive training and support in administering such instruments as checklists, rating scales, and direct observation protocols. It also is important to be aware of legal and ethical issues involved in singling out individual students for intensive levels of screening. Before implementing school-wide screening procedures, you should consult with your school district's due process experts.

Although such procedures make identifying students with EBD more objective and accountable, they do not remove the bias that exists when identification is based on teacher referral. As Gerber and Semmel (1984) observe, referral-driven identification procedures place the general education teacher in the role of a gatekeeper who determines which students will be considered for special education services. We already have noted that the referral process is biased toward students with externalizing behavior problems. Also, some pupils are referred because their teachers simply are less tolerant of disruptive behavior. Systematic

screening, coupled with early intervention that impacts the child and his home, presents a significant opportunity to prevent the development of intractable EBD.

Prereferral Interventions

The purpose of prereferral interventions is to address the student's (and the teacher's) issues in the context of the general education environment, thereby preventing a referral for determination of special education eligibility. If your school has implemented positive behavior support, a prereferral intervention corresponds to secondary prevention, which may involve developing a BIP. However, interventions at this level do not need to be extremely complex: They may consist of program modifications that are relatively easy to implement by the general education teacher. Some of the most effective interventions are also the most straightforward. Clearly explaining expectations, modifying instruction, providing peer assistance, changing seating arrangements, removing obstacles to desired behavior, having students monitor their own behavior, and providing feedback or praise for desired performances are strategies familiar to most general educators. Figure 1-4 is a form used to document prereferral intervention strategies and their effects. Note that this form suggests only some of the potential interventions that may be attempted singly or in combination.

The difference between an informal tactic and a targeted intervention strategy, such as a BIP, is that the latter should be applied and evaluated systematically. To ensure this, it is desirable to create a building-based Behavior Support Team[6] as a resource for teachers experiencing difficulty with specific pupils (Todd et al., 1999). Although these teams may develop a plan for any student, prereferral interventions are required under IDEA prior to the MDT's meeting to determine eligibility for special education, *except* when a parent or advocate has

[6]Teams that provide assistance with prereferral interventions may be called **teacher assistance teams.**

TEACHER ASSISTANCE TEAM
Request for Assistance

Date _1/06/01_   Teacher/Team _Liz S._

IEP: Yes (No) (Circle)

Student Name _Kyle_   Grade _4_

Situations	Problem Behaviors	Most Common Result
written assignments group activities whole class instructions	won't do independent work very unorganized, no materials teases & distracts others	attempt work ask for help cooperate with other in group

1. What have you tried/used? How has it worked?
   give more individual attention
   quick payoffs (prizes)
   more parental involvement

What have you tried to date to change the situations in which the problem behaviors occur?

✓ Modified assignments to match the students skills	✓ Changed seating assignments	___ Changed schedule of activities	Other?
✓ Arranged tutoring to improve the student's academic skills	___ Changed curriculum assistance	✓ Provided extra care	

What have you tried to date to teach expected behaviors?

✓ Reminders about expected behavior when problem behavior is likely	✓ Clarified rules and expected behavior for the whole class	___ Practiced the expected behaviors in class	Other?
✓ Reward program for expected behavior	✓ Oral agreement with the student	✓ Self-management program	→ Classroom self-evaluation program at end of school day
___ Systematic feedback about behavior	✓ Individual written contract with the student	___ Contract with student and parents	

What consequences have you tried to date for the problem behavior?

✓ Loss of privileges recess	✓ (Note) or phone call to the student's parents	✓ Office referral	Other?
✓ Time-out	___ Detention	✓ Reprimand	
___ Referral to school counselor	___ Meeting with the student's parents	✓ Individual meeting with the student	

FIGURE 1-4 Teacher Assistance Team Request for Assistance.

Note: *From "Individualizing School-Wide Discipline for Students with Chronic Problem Behaviors: A Team Approach" by A. W. Todd, R. H. Horner, G. Sugai, and J. Sprague Effective School Practices, 17(4) p. 77. Copyright 1999 by A. W. Todd. Reproduced with permission.*

TEACHER ASSISTANCE TEAM

Request For Assistance

Page 2

WHEN ADDRESSING THE PROBLEM, PLEASE CONSIDER THE FOLLOWING QUESTIONS:

1. When is the problem behavior(s) most and least likely to occur?
   • On particular days of the week (e.g., Monday) or times of day (e.g., right after recess)?
   • During or after interactions with certain people (e.g., during small, cooperative group projects)?
   • During certain types of activity or tasks, (e.g., during apparently difficult or boring work)?
   • In connection with particular features of the physical environment, (e.g., noisy, crowded)?
   • Features of routine (e.g., when there are unexpected changes or when a preferred activity is canceled)?
   • During medical or physical factors (e.g., apparent hunger of lack of sleep)?
   • Other influences?

2. What do you think the student(s) may gain from the problem behaviors?
   • Attention? What kind of attention? From whom?
   • Avoid an apparently difficult or boring activity?
   • Avoid teacher interaction?
   • Get control of a situation?
   • Avoid embarrassment in front of peers?

Summary of Behavior

Setting Events & Predictors	Behaviors of Concern	Maintaining Consequences

3. Are there appropriate behaviors that the student could use that would make the problem behavior unnecessary?

4. Teacher Support Team Decision
   ☐ Some suggestions regarding interventions to try.
   ☐ Referral to a different team for assessment (speech, hearing, academic): _____
   ☐ Formation of an Action Team to conduct a Functional Assessment and develop a plan of support.

5. Date for Follow Up _____

FIGURE 1-4   Teacher Assistance Team Request for Assistance—*Continued.*

requested that an eligibility assessment be conducted. Refer again to Figure 1-4. Note that the teacher is requested to provide information concerning specification of the problem and prior efforts to solve it. Also note that the last part of the form guides the teacher to think of antecedents and outcomes that may support the problem behavior, and that the form provides space for the team to indicate follow-up activities.

There are no hard-and-fast rules concerning the duration of prereferral interventions, but 20 to 40 school days (i.e., 1 to 2 months) constitutes an adequate period for determining whether the problem can be managed without more formal procedures. To avoid the tendency to turn prereferral interventions over to special services personnel, ownership of both the problem and intervention plans should be vested in the general education program. Therefore, staff identified with the general education program are fundamental members of Behavior Support Teams. Specialized staff (e.g., special education teachers, school psychologists) may serve as ancillary team members on specific cases.

Prereferral interventions are important for two reasons: first, they emphasize making attempts to solve students' behavior problems using resources available in the general education program before considering special education referrals.[7] Second, the results of such interventions provide assessment information useful for those making decisions about pupils' eligibility for services and determining what services are needed. Again, the processes of screening and providing prereferral interventions can be managed more effectively in a system of school-wide positive behavior support. Screening is accomplished by noting which students fail to benefit from primary prevention strategies (universal interventions). Secondary prevention for these students consists of the implementation of BIPs or more informal

strategies. The need for special education and related services may be considered for students who do not benefit from these targeted interventions.

Certification

This stage initiates formal consideration of the student's eligibility for special education services. The question of whether a student is manifesting a condition that constitutes a disability is a serious matter. Therefore, IDEA requires that the student's parents be notified of the school's intent to assess the child and give their approval. Parents also should be active participants throughout the assessment and decision-making processes, including making decisions regarding the child's educational placement and development and implementation of the IEP. These due process safeguards protect students' and parents' rights, including the right to have an independent assessment of their child and to request a hearing in the event that they disagree with the decision of the MDT.

In addition to medical and sociological screening or evaluations, traditional assessment for identifying students with EBD usually consists of a battery of psychoeducational instruments, including an individual intelligence scale, norm- and criterion-referenced measures of achievement, instruments that assess perceptual-motor skills, and, less frequently, measures of personality characteristics, although their poor reliability and validity render them suspect for diagnosing EBD (Waksman & Jones, 1985). Data from these instruments may be supplemented with teacher or parent interviews, direct observation of the pupil, and anecdotal information from school records. Responsibility for this stage of the classification process often falls on school psychologists. However, as Gresham (1985) observes, school psychologists are more comfortable and competent in assessing mental retardation and learning disabilities than EBD.

Walker and Fabre (1987) offer support for this observation, noting that research suggests the be-

---

[7]Recall that the MDT must proceed with the assessment to determine eligibility if one has been requested.

havioral characteristics and performance deficits of referred and nonreferred pupils are quite similar and that assessment data typically have little impact on certification decisions. Recent improvements in screening and identification procedures have made this process more objective and systematic. For example, the state of Iowa has adopted a comprehensive assessment model for students exhibiting behavior problems (Wood, Smith, & Grimes, 1985). Other states are also developing systematic procedures for screening and identifying such pupils and providing services for them. Figure 1-5 presents a checklist from a technical assistance paper developed by Waksman and Jones (1985) to facilitate identifying students with EBD in Oregon and providing services to them. This checklist provides operational guidelines for applying Oregon's definition (which closely resembles the definition the federal law uses) to determine whether a student should be considered to have EBD for special education purposes. The items pertaining to the pupil's behavior document that the problems are severe (i.e., occur to a "marked degree"). A "long period of time" is defined as 6 months (note the exception in the case of dangerous behavior), and "adverse effects on educational performance" are documented either through academic performance markedly below capacity or through deficiencies in social skills. Finally, note the requirement that attempts to solve the problem in the general education program be documented. Wood et al. (1985) and the Council for Children with Behavioral Disorders (1987) also recommend using multiple sources of data for identifying and documenting efforts to modify the student's behavior in general education settings. The Council for Children with Behavioral Disorders, Iowa, and Oregon all urge that MDTs be used to make special education eligibility decisions.

MENTAL HEALTH ASSESSMENT. Many school districts rely on other agencies or professionals (e.g., mental health clinics, psychologists or psychiatrists in private practice) to conduct these evaluations. Mental health professionals typically use an assessment model that is considerably different from models used for educational purposes. One of the chief differences is that the mental health assessment model is based on identifying emotional or cognitive pathology that is presumed to underlie the student's behavior problems. Until recently, this medical model dominated other approaches to the assessment of emotional and behavioral problems. It is still widely used by mental health practitioners and school districts in some states.

The classification decisions resulting from mental health assessment often result in diagnostic labels that come from the **Diagnostic and Statistical Manual, Fourth Edition** (DSM-IV), published by the American Psychiatric Association (1994). The DSM-IV classifies psychological disorders along five axes or dimensions. Axis I consists of the major pattern of symptoms, or clinical disorders, that the student exhibits; Axis II describes personality disorders; Axis III addresses general medical conditions; Axis IV describes psychosocial factors that impose stress on the individual; and Axis V considers the pupil's level of adaptive functioning over the past year. A diagnosis may or may not be made on every axis, depending on the student and how much information the evaluator has about the case. However, a principal diagnosis, using the categories and accompanying diagnostic codes for Axis I and/or II, is always made. The Axis I or II categories for disorders usually first diagnosed in infancy, childhood, and adolescence are grouped into 10 classes, as shown in Table 1-1.

More specific diagnoses are made within these categories and subcategories for individual cases. For example, Table 1-2 lists the diagnostic criteria for autistic disorder.

Children may also be assigned an Axis I or II diagnosis from one of the other categories included in the system (e.g., school phobia, classified as one of the anxiety disorders; anorexia nervosa, which is one of the eating disorders). As the preceding example suggests, the DSM-IV approach to

1. At least two of the following five apply:
   a. The student is rated at or above the ninety-eighth percentile on two different acceptable problem rating scales (or similarly named subscales by two or more current teachers).
   b. The student is rated at or above the ninety-eighth percentile on two different acceptable problem-behavior rating scales (or similarly named subscales) by her current teacher and by at least one previous year's teacher.
   c. The student is rated at or above the ninety-eighth percentile on two different acceptable problem-behavior rating scales (or similarly named subscales) by one or more parents or guardians.
   d. The student is currently displaying behavior that is endangering her life or seriously endangering the safety of others.
   e. The student's observable school or classroom problem behavior is documented to be more severe than approximately 98% of her peers.

All of these apply:

2. Behavior management consultation has been provided to the classroom teacher(s) over a period of at least four weeks by a behavioral specialist, and documentation indicates that specifically prescribed and consistently employed classroom management interventions have not reduced the inappropriate behavior within acceptable limits suggested by these eligibility criteria.
3. The problem behaviors have been exhibited for over six months. This may be waived if the child is endangering her life or seriously endangering the safety of others.
   Waived: _____ Yes _____ No
4. No recent acute stressor or isolated traumatic event in the child's environment (e.g., divorce or death in the family, loss of property) can adequately explain the problem behavior.
5. No medical problem or health impairment can adequately explain the problem behavior pattern.
6. An inappropriate educational program cannot adequately explain the problem behavior pattern.
7. Culturally different norms or expectations cannot adequately explain the problem behavior pattern.
8. The child is either
   a. performing markedly below her academic potential on acceptable academic tests or school report cards (_____ Yes _____ No), or
   b. severely deficient in social skills or social competence (_____ Yes _____ No).
9. Direct observation by a school psychologist or behavior specialist has documented that either
   a. the student is displaying problem behaviors at a high frequency (_____ Yes _____ No), or
   b. the student is displaying low-frequency behaviors that grossly deviate from acceptable social norms (_____ Yes _____ No).

FIGURE I-5　Suggested EBD evaluation checklist.

Source: Waksman, S., & Jones, V. (1985, August). *A suggested procedure for the identification and provision of services to seriously emotionally disturbed students. Technical assistance papers: A series on PL 94–142 and related Oregon laws.* Portland, OR: Department of Education.

assessment is descriptive in that the diagnosis is based on a pattern, or **syndrome,** of behavior. It also is clinical because portions of the diagnosis are based on judgments and inferences made from the presenting symptoms (e.g., "failure to develop peer relationships appropriate to developmental level"). DSM-IV notes that the categories are not mutually exclusive, that children often have problems not subsumed within a single diagnostic category, and that many behavior problems do not warrant diagnostic classification. To these cautions we must reiterate our previous observation that students who have other disabilities also may exhibit EBD. Moreover, traditional diagnostic pro-

TABLE 1-1   DSM-IV Diagnostic Classifications

Mental Retardation	Predominantly Inattentive Type
Mild Mental Retardation	Predominantly Hyperactive-Impulsive Type
Moderate Mental Retardation	Attention Deficit/Hyperactivity Disorder NOS
Severe Mental Retardation	Conduct Disorder
Profound Mental Retardation	Oppositional Defiant Disorder
Mental Retardation: Severity Unspecified	Disruptive Behavior Disorder NOS
Learning Disorders	**Feeding and Eating Disorders of Infancy or**
Reading Disorder	**Early Childhood**
Mathematics Disorder	Pica
Disorder of Written Expression	Rumination Disorder
Learning Disorder Not Otherwise Specified (NOS)	Feeding Disorder of Infancy or Early Childhood
Motor Skill Disorder	**Tic Disorders**
Developmental Coordination Disorder	Tourette's Disorder
	Chronic Motor or Vocal Tic Disorder
Communication Disorders	Transient Tic Disorder
Expressive Language Disorder	Tic Disorder NOS
Mixed Receptive-Expressive Language Disorder	
Phonological Disorder	**Elimination Disorders**
Stuttering	Encopresis
Communication Disorder NOS	With Constipation and Overflow Incontinence
	Without Constipation and Overflow Incontinence
Pervasive Developmental Disorders	Enuresis (Not Due to a General Medical Condition)
Autistic Disorder	
Rett's Disorder	**Other Disorders of Infancy; Childhood; or**
Childhood Disintegrative Disorder	**Adolescence**
Asperger's Disorder	Separation Anxiety Disorder
Pervasive Developmental Disorder NOS	Selective Mutism
	Reactive Attachment Disorder of Infancy or Early
Attention Deficit and Disruptive Behavior Disorders	Stereotypic Movement Disorder
Attention Deficit/Hyperactivity Disorder	Disorder of Infancy, Childhood, or Adolescence NOS
Combined Type	

Source: *American Psychiatric Association, 1994, pp. 13–14.*

cedures usually occur in the clinician's office where the verbal reports of the child and others (e.g., parents) must be used instead of direct behavioral observation. This affects the reliability of the diagnosis (i.e., two clinicians may not arrive at the same diagnostic assessment because each receives a different report or interprets the same information differently).

The limitations of the mental health diagnostic and classification system have been widely discussed (Algozzine et al., 1991; Kauffman, 2001). Perhaps the major weakness of this approach stems from its reliance on a disease analogy, that is, on the assumption that psychological disorders are analogous to disease processes that exist within the individual. The addition of Axis IV (psychosocial stressors) classification notwithstanding, DSM-IV diagnoses tend to attribute the causes of behavior disorders to conditions within the individual.

The assessment procedures followed depend on the discipline of the evaluator (e.g., psychiatrist, psychologist, social worker), the evaluator's skills, and the diagnostic tools available. Many diagnosticians conduct structured or unstructured interviews with the student, the student's parents,

TABLE 1-2 DSM-IV Diagnostic Criteria for Autistic Disorder

A. A total of six (or more) items from (1), (2), and (3), with at least two from (1), and one from each (2) and (3).

    (1). Qualitative impairment in social interaction, as manifested by at least two of the following:

        (a). Marked impairment in the use of multiple nonverbal behaviors such as eye-to-eye gaze, facial expression, body postures, and gestures to regulate social interaction

        (b). Failure to develop peer relationships appropriate to developmental level

        (c). Lack of spontaneous seeking to share enjoyment, interests, or achievements with other people (e.g., by a lack of showing, bringing, or pointing out objects of interest)

        (d). Lack of social or emotional reciprocity

    (2). Qualitative impairments in communication as manifested by at least one of the following:

        (a). Delay in, or total lack of, the development of spoken language (not accompanied by an attempt to compensate through alternative modes of communication such as gesture or mime)

        (b). In individuals with adequate speech, marked impairment in the ability to initiate or sustain a conversation with others

        (c). Lack of varied, spontaneous make-believe play or social imitative play appropriate to developmental level

    (3). Restricted repetitive and stereotyped patterns of behavior, interests, and activities, as manifested by at least one of the following:

        (a). Encompassing preoccupation with one or more stereotyped and restricted patterns of interest that is abnormal either in intensity or focus

        (b). Apparently inflexible adherence to specific, nonfunctional routines or rituals

        (c). Stereotyped and repetitive motor mannerisms (e.g., hand- or finger-flapping or twisting, or complex whole-body movements)

        (d). Persistent preoccupation with parts of objects

B. Delays or abnormal functioning in at least one of the following areas, with onset prior to age 3 years: (1) social interaction, (2) language as used in social communication, or (3) symbolic or imaginative play.

C. The disturbance is not better accounted for by Rett's Disorder or Childhood Disintegrative Disorder

---

Source: *American Psychiatric Association. (1994)*. Diagnostic and statistical manual of mental disorders *(4th ed.), 70–71. Copyright American Psychiatric Association, Washington, DC. Used with permission.*

or others (e.g., classroom teachers). In some cases, standardized assessment procedures or instruments also may be used. These may include individually administered intelligence tests, personality tests, tests of interest or preference, language assessment instruments, behavior rating scales, or self-concept inventories. It is important to recognize that many of the instruments used, especially **projective techniques** (in which the client "projects" his personality through responses to ambiguous stimuli, such as ink blots or pictures), offer poor reliability and validity as well as inadequate norms (Salvia & Ysseldyke, 2001). The inadequacy and educational irrelevance of personality tests, as well as the threat of legal sanction arising from decisions based on their results, have led to increasing reliance on more objective procedures (Salvia & Ysseldyke, 2001).

Despite their weaknesses, clinical assessment procedures still are widely used in assessments of children and youth. A good diagnostic evaluation can be helpful, especially if the outcomes include multidisciplinary planning and follow-up activities. We have chosen to organize this text in terms of educationally relevant behavioral categories rather than those found in DSM-IV; therefore, you may need to translate psychiatric diagnoses into more useful terms. The term ED or EBD is sufficient to identify pupils for special education. Once more, we stress that is not necessary to formally classify students in order to work with them.

SCHOOL-BASED ASSESSMENT. The process used in schools for determining whether students should be considered as exhibiting EBD consists of building on the information gathered from systematic screening and prereferral or targeted intervention procedures through comprehensive assessments directed by school personnel. This process begins with a referral for formal evaluation and involves compiling information from attempts to manage the problem at the secondary prevention level, as well as systematic assessments by school staff and other professionals. Table 1-3, which is based on Kentucky's assessment procedures (EBD Task Force, 1992), summarizes the process. The compilation of prereferral screening and intervention data should demonstrate that (1) problem behaviors are perceived as extreme by more than one observer across more than one setting; (2) prereferral interventions have been attempted and have failed; (3) the problem has existed over a reasonably long period of time (except in the case of behavior that poses a hazard to life or safety); (4) the problem cannot be explained by factors such as temporary stress, medical problems, inappropriate educational programming, or cultural differences; (5) the pupil has deficits in academic performance or social skills; and (6) the problem behaviors occur at a high rate or deviate markedly from acceptable norms.

Intelligence tests have very limited utility for assessing emotional or behavior problems. However, an intellectual assessment can document that the problem is not due to cognitive impairment. (If the student has some degree of cognitive disability, it should be documented that specific programming related to this condition has not solved the student's behavior problems.) It is important to realize that students may exhibit both cognitive disabilities and behavior problems or EBD. Therefore, schools should be able to bring the needed services to the pupil in the current school placement rather than moving the student to another program unless it is decided that the latter is more appropriate. Changes in school placement require invoking due process, which includes reassessment and decision making by the MDT established to supervise the pupil's educational program, and thus cannot be made quickly or easily. Taking services to the student is more expedient and less disruptive and so is the preferred strategy.

The academic assessment may be accomplished through a variety of procedures, including individually administered norm-referenced achievement tests, curriculum-based assessments, analysis of classroom work samples and data regarding academic progress, and direct observation of time on task. Several sources of academic data should be provided to rule out the possibility that conclusions are based on inadequate samples of student performance.

Academic assessment is important for two reasons. First, in most states, EBD eligibility can be determined only if educational performance is adversely affected. Second, behavior problems and academic difficulties often are functionally related. Students who are frustrated by academic tasks and expectations that are beyond their current skill levels may act out or withdraw to avoid such tasks or to express their feelings. Conversely, problem behaviors may interfere with academic learning because they are incompatible with academic performance or because they result in disciplinary actions that cause pupils to be removed from the instructional setting.

The social competence assessment is likely to reveal social skills deficits in students considered for EBD classification because failure to establish satisfactory social relationships is a defining characteristic. Therefore, it is important that skills related to social interactions with peers and adults be assessed. Recall that in some states (e.g., Kentucky, Oregon), social skill deficits carry as much weight as academic deficiencies when identifying pupils with EBD. Social competence is a general domain referring to summative evaluative judgments regarding the adequacy of a student's performance on social tasks by an informed social agent (Walker & McConnell, 1988). Gresham and Reschly (1987) indicated that social competence is composed of two subdomains: adaptive behavior and specific social skills. Measures of adaptive behavior typically assess general independent functioning, including physical development, self-direction, personal responsibility, economic or vocational skills, and functional academic skills

TABLE 1-3 Pupil Identification Assessment Process

I. Compilation of Screening and Prereferral Data
Documentation that student's problem behaviors occur more frequently or more intensely than nonreferred peers, that such behaviors have occurred for a long period of time, and that they have not been solved through systematic management in the general education setting

Acceptable procedures
- Standardized behavior ratings completed by two or more teachers, or by teachers and parents
- Direct observation data (including data on nondeviant peer)
- Evidence that problems have occurred for a prolonged period
- Evidence that problems are not due to temporary stress or to curriculum or cultural factors
- Evidence that interventions in regular program have been systematically implemented and have not been effective
- Verification by school personnel that behavior is dangerous to student or to others

II. Intellectual Assessment
Documentation that behavior is not due to impaired cognitive functioning, or if cognitive deficits are present, that appropriate programming has not solved behavior problems

Acceptable procedures
- Acceptable individual measure of intelligence or aptitude, administered by qualified examiner

III. Academic Assessment
Documentation that academic performance or progress has not been satisfactory for a period of time

Acceptable procedures
- Individually administered norm-referenced measures of academic achievement
- Group-administered achievement tests *and* written analysis of classroom products and documentation of classroom academic progress
- Curriculum-based or criterion-referenced assessments documenting progress across curriculum
- Direct observation of academic time on task
- Samples of classroom work across time and tasks

IV. Social and Language Competence Assessment
Documentation that student is deficient in social skills or that social status is seriously affected

Acceptable procedures
- Administration of approved standardized social skills inventories or checklists
- Administration of acceptable assessments of expressive and receptive language functioning
- Administration of adaptive behavior scales
- Administration of sociometric scales or procedures
- Direct observation in unstructured social setting (include peer comparison data)

V. Social, Developmental, and School History
Documentation that problem is not due to any previously undiscovered factors or cultural differences

Acceptable procedures
- Culturally sensitive assessments and interviews with parents or guardians, referring teacher, other teachers, student
- Review of student's cumulative school records

VI. Medical evaluation
Documentation that problem is not due to health factors

Acceptable procedures
- Medical screening by physician, school nurse, or physician's assistant
- Comprehensive medical evaluation if student fails to pass screening

(Walker & McConnell, 1988). The American Association of Mental Deficiency (AAMD) *Adaptive Behavior Scale, School Edition* (Lambert, Windmiller, Tharinger, & Cole, 1981) or the *Vineland Adaptive Behavior Scale* (Sparrow, Balla, & Cicchetti, 1985) are appropriate measures of adaptive behavior. The format of these scales consists of ratings completed through interviews with persons familiar with the pupil's functioning or development in relevant settings. Social skills are the specific strategies one uses to respond to social living tasks (Walker & McConnell, 1988). Standardized measures of social skills typically consist of rating scale items completed by persons who are familiar with the student's functioning. A recommended alternate procedure for assessing social competence consists of conducting direct observations of the pupil's behavior in unstructured social situations.

The direct observation of social behavior is an important assessment tool for pupils being considered for special education services. It provides an opportunity to analyze the student's behavior in the immediate social context, enabling the assessor to identify excess and deficit problem behaviors and adaptive behavior patterns, as well as the antecedents and consequences of specific behaviors. Potential biases associated with personal judgment are reduced when using direct observation procedures. Behavioral observation strategies are described in Chapter 3.

Additional data may be collected about social, developmental, and school history through interviews with the student's caregivers, the referring teacher, other teachers, and the student. A thorough search of the pupil's cumulative school records should be conducted to assess such variables as attendance, health history, discipline reports, and previous screenings or referrals for special education evaluation. As mentioned earlier, tools such as the *School Archival Records Search* (Walker et al., 1991) are available to systematize this process. Concurrently, a medical evaluation should be performed to rule out possible health factors. Students who do not pass this screening should be referred for a comprehensive medical examination.

It is also important to assess the extent to which language development may contribute to behavior problems in school. Research consistently shows that the language proficiency of students with EBD, as a group, falls significantly below that of typical peers (Griffith, Rodgers-Adkinson, & Cusick, 1997; Kaiser & Hester, 1997; Mack & Warr-Leeper, 1992; Ruhl, Hughes, & Camarata, 1992). Pragmatic language skills, or the functional use of language to express social intentions in ways that are culturally acceptable, seem to be particularly affected (Kaiser & Hester, 1997). Therefore, assessment should address pragmatics as well as language skills more typically assessed, such as syntax, semantics, and phonology. Both receptive and expressive language areas should be addressed, of course.

Finally, assessment must take into account the potential contribution of cultural factors. Although membership in a racially or ethnically different cultural group are not reasons to overlook a student's maladaptive behavior, school personnel must be sensitive to the effects that cultural attitudes and customs may have on behavior. Students from families with low income and those who belong to a racial minority, especially African American males, are overrepresented in special education programs for pupils with EBD (Chin & Hughes, 1987; McIntyre, 1992; Peterson & Ishii-Jordan, 1993). Culturally different students may exhibit patterns of language and social behavior that conflict with the normative standards and expectations of the school. Moreover, pupils' awareness of their deviation from school norms regarding dress, extracurricular activities, and financial status may cause them to withdraw from or rebel against persons exemplifying these norms. Cultural stereotypes also may affect the expectations and reactions of other pupils and school staff, which can intensify difficulties involving cultural issues. Therefore, in assessing students with cultural differences, evaluators should attempt to determine the function that "deviant" behaviors may serve for the student (e.g., "playing the dozens," avoiding direct eye contact) with reference to her cultural group before concluding that such behavior patterns are maladaptive. When culturally appropriate behaviors conflict with staff or peer expectations, assessors should be open to the conclusions that the expectations are in error and that intervention should address adult standards for behavior in addition to (or instead of) the student's behavior.

McIntyre (1995) developed an instrument to assist in evaluating the influence of culture on behavior and learning. Intended for use in the prereferral and referral processes, the *McIntyre Assessment of Culture* (MAC) contains a student information form, a parent/home information form, and a behavior checklist. The information derived from these sources is analyzed to determine whether the behaviors of concern to educators have a cultural bias.

In summary, an adequate assessment of students referred for possible classification as EBD is comprehensive and takes considerable time. The seriousness of the decision being considered justifies this detailed evaluation process. Also, this process is multidisciplinary; no single professional is qualified to perform all of these assessments. It is appropriate and desirable to involve professionals in other roles within the school as well as outside the schools in gathering and analyzing assessment data. However, it is important that a staff member or a team of staff from the pupil's school compile and analyze the assessment data and present it to the persons who will make the certification decision.

Classification

The decision to classify a pupil as having EBD is too important to be made on the basis of limited information or by persons not familiar with all facets of the student's personality and environment. That is why IDEA requires that eligibility decisions be made by an MDT, which must include the parents or guardians (if they are not available, a parent surrogate may be appointed), the refer-

ring general education teacher, a school administrator, the special education teacher, and a person able to interpret the results of the diagnostic procedures used. Other individuals should be included as necessary. The team determines whether the assessment information supports the need for special education certification, makes decisions regarding the most appropriate educational program and placement, and evaluates the student's progress and the effectiveness of the educational services provided.

The validity of the classification decisions made by child study teams has been questioned, however. Potter, Ysseldyke, and Regan (1983) gave a large group of school professionals assessment information on a hypothetical student that reflected performance in the average range for the student's age and grade placement. They indicated that the student had been referred for special education and asked the professionals whether they believed the pupil was eligible for it. Of these professionals, 51% declared the student eligible for special education services. This study verifies that assessment data often are not used in making certification decisions (Walker & Fabre, 1987). The procedures we described in the previous sections should help to remedy this problem; however, decisions involving the judgments of persons inescapably are subjective. Careful analysis and review are needed to make this decision.

Certification that a student has EBD actually consists of a set of decisions. If the MDT decides that the pupil is eligible for services, it must determine which services are needed and in what settings they should be provided. In the past these decisions were guided by the limited range of services available in schools. Often the only alternatives were special academic instruction and behavior management in a self-contained special classroom or resource room. The availability of an increased range of special education and support services reduces the team's dependency on placing students in restrictive educational settings to provide them with needed services. Thus, the team may determine that a pupil needs systematic behavior management, highly structured academic instruction, and social skills training. However, because the school has adopted a policy of inclusion supported by such staff resources as Behavior Support Teams or consulting teacher services as well as a social skills curriculum, these services can be provided without changing the student's current educational placement. Even in schools without a wide range of services, decisions regarding what services pupils need should precede and be separate from decisions about where students will access them (i.e., where they will be placed).

When students are found to be eligible for special education, the MDT also should consider the criteria by which their continued eligibility will be determined. Too often, students with troubling behavior are given a "life sentence" in segregated special education settings. The MDT should be diligent in monitoring students' progress and should hold as many IEP team meetings during a given year as are necessary to ensure that students are making progress toward their goals and objectives. (The decision to retain the pupil in special education also should be justified through a comprehensive reevaluation and should be made by the MDT.) It is important to realize that there always will be some students whose needs require the orchestration of services from multiple agencies over extended periods of time, perhaps throughout their lives. These students and their families should receive this support through team-based systems of care, which are characterized by bringing the resources they need to home, school, and community settings, rather than relegating the child to institutional treatment.

Table 1-4 summarizes the eligibility decision-making process from screening through decertifying and returning pupils to the general education program. For a complete, step-by-step guide to the assessment of behavioral disorders, see Kentucky's Emotional-Behavioral Disability Technical Assistance Manual (Kentucky EBD Task Force, 1992).

In summary, the issue is not whether a pupil should be identified as having EBD and served through special education but whether an intervention plan needs to be designed. Unfortunately, in many cases, students not identified as having EBD receive no services or inadequate ones because schools tend to lack effective strategies for helping pupils without disabilities who exhibit behavior problems. The effectiveness of such traditional disciplinary practices as corporal punishment, suspension, and expulsion has not been proven for the majority of students with which they are used. Therefore, the dilemma is whether to identify the student as having EBD, which has potentially negative social and educational consequences (i.e., stigmatization, separation from behaviorally typical peers and from the general academic program), or not to identify in the hope that the student's problem behaviors can be remediated by using resources available in the general education program.

THE CONTINUUM OF BEHAVIORAL PROBLEMS AND EDUCATIONAL SERVICES

The range of problem behaviors encountered in schools can be described in many ways. For practical reasons, this range generally is matched to a continuum of special education interventions: the more severe the problem behavior, the more intensive the level of intervention. In the past, special education interventions have been "place oriented" (Reynolds & Birch, 1977), that is, confined to special places such as self-contained classrooms or resource rooms. This orientation has created an expectation that pupils who are referred for special education will be removed from the general education program and treated in some "special" place with a "special" set of methods. Nowhere is this expectation more prevalent than in the area of EBD. Students who are unruly, aggressive, disrespectful, threatening, or just "weird" are aversive to general education teachers; many

TABLE 1-4 Eligibility Decisions

Question	Action
I. Screening	
A. Is student "at risk"?	A. Administer screening procedure, activate teacher assistance team
B. Can student be helped through regular program?	B. Modify or adapt regular program
II. Identification	
A. Has student benefited from adaptations made in regular program?	A. Evaluate effects of regular education interventions
B. Is additional support or service needed?	B. Implement consultative intervention
C. Should student be identified as EBD?	C. Conduct assessment; hold staffing
III. Certification	
A. Should student be referred for EBD services?	
B. What services are needed?	A. Conduct child study team meeting
C. Where should services be provided?	B. Develop IEP
D. What expectations must the pupil meet to return to the regular classroom?	C. Identify least restrictive settings for pupil
	D. Specify criteria for decertification
IV. Program Evaluation	
A. Is the program working?	
	A. Implement formative and summative evaluation procedures
V. Decertification	
A. Is special education no longer needed?	A. Evaluate progress against exit criteria, conduct exit MDT meeting

such teachers report that they are unable to manage such students effectively (Lloyd & Kauffman, 1995). Others use punishment and coercive tactics in attempting to cope with undesired student behavior (Shores, Gunter, & Jack, 1993). For years, special education has served these students in segregated pull-out programs, thereby reinforcing the expectations that pupils with behavior problems cannot be taught in the mainstream and that general educators are not responsible for their management.

Unfortunately, this refer-and-remove pattern reinforces the assumption that it is the referred pupil who "owns" the problem. Seldom is it acknowledged that inappropriate expectations, curriculum, or teaching methods may contribute to the behavioral disorder. Thus, the referring teacher emerges from this process without any new skills

and with a reinforced attitude that "only a specialist can handle these students." The referred child, on the other hand, may come out of this process with a stigmatizing label and segregated in a "special" environment, perhaps never to be returned to the educational mainstream.

The integration of students with EBD into educational settings with their peers who are not disabled is a laudable goal with numerous advocates in the special education profession. The IDEA specifically requires that students with disabilities be educated, to the maximum extent possible, with peers who are not disabled. The MDT must carefully justify educational placements in more restrictive settings. Recall that students with EBD, more often than students in any other disability category, tend to be educated in the most restrictive settings (Koyanagi &

Gaines, 1993). The larger number of students in general education classrooms, teachers' lack of sophisticated training in behavior management procedures, and the unavailability of adequate technical assistance to classroom teachers make the full inclusion of many pupils with behavioral disabilities implausible. Meadows, Neel, Scott, and Parker (1994) compared the educational programming for students with EBD who were placed in mainstream versus segregated programs. They found that "placement in general education settings represented a major reduction, if not complete cessation, of [individually differentiated] programming" (p. 170).

To compound these problems, children with serious behavioral disorders do not interact well with their peers, who do not accept them (Nelson, 1988). Moreover, the general education curriculum often falls short of meeting the needs of pupils who are behind their age mates both academically and socially. Many students with mild disabilities (those who are closest to typical peers in terms of functional levels), especially those with EBD, drop out or are "elbowed out" of school by the time they reach adolescence (Edgar, 1987).

The basic dilemma is whether to redouble efforts to integrate these pupils into general academic programs (which may not meet their needs) or to educate them in segregated environments, in which they miss many of the curricular and extracurricular opportunities available in the mainstream and in which they are likely to remain throughout their public school years. Unfortunately, the dilemma has no ready solution. The most promising approach may be to continue improving and expanding the range of educational and related services across the entire continuum of educational settings in which children and youth with behavior problems are found (Kauffman & Hallahan, 1995; Kauffman, Lloyd, Astuto, & Hallahan, 1995). In schools that have adopted systemic changes based on positive behavior support, resources (e.g., Behavior Support Teams) are available to support and assist staff who serve students with challenging academic and behav-

ioral problems. This model of *supported inclusion* may improve the educational status and outcomes of both students who are at risk and those with EBD.

While the placement of students with challenging behavior in self-contained settings may not be in their best interests, there is scant evidence that current policies of full inclusion, in which students with disabilities are educated in general education classrooms with their typical peers, is acceptable or effective as the *only* placement option. Students with chronic behavior problems, including those with EBD, are the first to be excluded from general education classrooms, and the last to be returned. General education teachers are not able to meet the needs of these students in the context of a full class of other students (MacMillan, Gresham, & Forness, 1996).

There is no foreseeable resolution to the polemic debate regarding educational placement in segregated versus inclusive settings for these students. Some school districts are attempting to redesign the concept of **least restrictive environment** from a focus on placements to a focus on a continuum of services that are brought to pupils and their teachers. For example, Colorado has adopted an approach to educational programming for students with behavioral disorders based on these students' needs (Cessna, 1993). An outgrowth of the emerging policy of moving services to the student instead of moving the student to the services is an effort to design services that address the pupil's needs in the least restrictive settings, and also providing adequate support to the staff who serve the student in these settings. For students with challenging behavior, we advocate a philosophy of supported inclusion instead of full inclusion. While we described wraparound planning with regard to the most intensive level of intervention, the goal of intervention at any level of prevention should be to provide supports and services that effectively meet students' and caregivers' needs. Teacher and student support teams plan and implement interventions that are brought to the student rather than moving the student to settings where these services presumably are provided. Consistent with the philosophy we have just advocated, intervention planning should be based on the identification and assessment of strengths in both the student and settings, rather than on the mere elimination of identified deficits. Thus, administrators should view behavior problems as indicating a need for services, not a need to change a student's educational placement. The latter requires considerably more elaborate and time-consuming activities, which are likely to disrupt the student's program, with no guarantee that the new placement will benefit the pupil more than did the old one.

Again, the least restrictive placement depends on the individual student, and we urge that special education be conceptualized as a continuum of services, with consideration given to more restrictive educational placements only after interventions have been tried unsuccessfully in less restrictive settings. We also recommend that the behavioral requirements of educational settings be assessed and that those competencies be targeted for instruction in more restrictive placements so that the curriculum is functional and promotes student progress to less restrictive educational settings. Procedures for assessing the behavioral expectations of less restrictive environments have been developed (see Walker & Rankin, 1983) and are described in Chapter 11.

Finally, to change problem behavior—to teach pupils and their caregivers to use new and better skills in their total environment—you must systematically implement strategies to ensure that these skills are generalized and maintained in other settings (Rutherford & Nelson, 1988). What has been accomplished when you have taught a student to accept your correction of his or her behavior if the student blows up when corrected in algebra class? Working with pupils exhibiting behavioral disorders requires that you spend a good deal of time outside your classroom. In Chapter 11 we offer techniques and suggestions for working effectively with persons in other settings.

The concepts and strategies presented in this chapter are not yet in widespread use in many school programs. In addition, their implementation may depend on school policies developed by boards of education and administrators. You may feel powerless to use these models in your school. However, in an effort to make public education more responsive to local needs and issues, schools are moving toward management by school councils, consisting of staff, parents, and community members. These councils afford frontline staff an opportunity to participate actively in school-based decision making. Far from being futuristic ideals, the concepts and strategies we have presented are part of a currently developing technology for serving pupils who have behavior problems. In the following chapters you will learn some of this technology, as well as guidelines for judging when and where to apply it. We hope that the skills you acquire will help you to function more effectively in your professional role and to advocate on behalf of more effective services for students whose behavior reduces their chances of succeeding in the educational system.

SUMMARY

Schools today are being challenged to meet increasingly higher standards of student achievement, to create safe and effective learning environments, and to meet the needs of an increasingly diverse student population. In addressing this challenge, school staff are joining other professionals, parents, and representatives of local communities in developing innovative strategies for supporting students across the full range of potential behavior. The "discipline regulations" of IDEA '97 are compelling educators to view students with behavioral problems differently and to make fundamental changes in the way interventions are planned and delivered. These events provide a dramatic new context for thinking differently about identifying and serving students with EBD.

DISCUSSION QUESTIONS

1. How can the poor educational status of, and outcomes for, students with EBD be remedied?
2. Would you advocate identifying and certifying students with EBD to provide them with educational services, or would you favor serving them through systematic interventions in regular programs? Support your position.
3. What are the implications of positive behavior support in terms of a school's responsibility for students' social as well as academic behavior?
4. Children and youth with EBD continue to be served in residential treatment programs outside of local school districts. How does this affect the likelihood that students can successfully reintegrate into the educational mainstream?

REFERENCES

Algozzine, B., Ruhl, K., & Ramsey, R. (1991). *Behaviorally disordered? Assessment for identification and instruction*. Reston, VA: Council for Exceptional Children.

American Psychiatric Association. (1994). *Diagnostic and statistical manual to mental disorders* (4th ed.). Washington, DC: Author.

Blackorby, J., & Wagner, M. (1996). Longitudinal postschool outcomes of youth with disabilities: Findings from the National Longitudinal Transition Study. *Exceptional Children, 62*, 399–413.

Bullis, M., & Gaylord-Ross, R. (1991). Moving on: Transitions for youth with behavioral disorders. In L. Bullock & R. B. Rutherford, Jr. (Eds.), CEC *mini-library: Working with behavioral disorders*. Reston, VA: Council for Exceptional Children.

Carson, R. R., Sitlington, P. C., & Frank, A. R. (1995). Young adulthood for individuals with behavior disorders: What does it hold? *Behavioral Disorders, 20*, 127–135.

Cessna, K. K. (Ed.). (1993). *Instructionally differentiated programming: A needs-based approach for students with behavior disorders*. Denver: Colorado Department of Education.

Chesapeake Institute. (1994, September). *National agenda for achieving better results for children and youth with serious emotional disturbance*. Washington, DC: Department of Education, Office of Special Education and Rehabilitative Services, Office of Special Education Programs.

Chin, P., & Hughes, S. (1987). Representation of minority students in special education classes. *Remedial and Special Education, 8*(4), 41–46.

Clark, R. T., Schaefer, M., Burchard, J. D., & Welkowitz, J. W. (1992). Wrapping community-based mental health services. *Journal of Child and Family Studies, 1*, 241–261.

Council for Children with Behavioral Disorders. (1987). Position paper on definition and identification of students with behavioral disorders. *Behavioral Disorders, 13*, 9–19.

Dorsey, G., & Haywood, C. (October, 2000). Positive behavior intervention and support data management using Excel. Unpublished manual. Jonesboro, IL: Southern Region, PBIS Regional Office of Education #02.

Edgar, E. B. (1987). Secondary programs in special education: Are many of them justifiable? *Exceptional Children, 35*, 5–22.

Epstein, M. H., Quinn, K., Nelson, C. M., Polsgrove, L., & Cumblad, C. (1993). *Serving students with emotional and behavioral disorders through a comprehensive community-based approach*. OSERS News in Print, 5(3), 19–23.

Farmer, T. W., Farmer, E. M. Z., & Gut, D. (1999). Implications of social development research for school-based interventions for aggressive youth with emotional and behavioral disorders. *Journal of Emotional and Behavioral Disorders, 7*, 130–136.

Feil, E. G., & Becker, W. C. (1993). Investigation of a multiple-gated screening system for preschool behavior problems. *Behavioral Disorders, 19*, 44–53.

Feil, E. G., Severson, H. H., & Walker, H. M. (1994). *Early screening project (ESP): Identifying preschool children with adjustment problems*. The Oregon Conference Monograph, 6, 177–183.

Forness, S. R., & Kavale, K. A. (2000). Emotional or behavioral disorders: Background and current status of the E/BD terminology and definition. *Behavioral Disorders, 25*, 264–269.

Gerber, M., & Semmel, M. (1984). Teacher as imperfect test: Reconceptualizing the referral process. *Educational Psychologist, 19*, 137–148.

Gresham, F. M. (1985). Behavior disorders assessment: Conceptual, definitional, and practical considerations. *School Psychology Review, 14*, 495–509.

Gresham, F. M. (1991). Conceptualizing behavior disorders in terms of resistance to intervention. *School Psychology Review, 20,* 23–36.

Gresham, F. M., & Reschly, D. (1987). Issues in the conceptualization, classification, and assessment of social skills in the mildly handicapped. In T. Kratchowill (Ed.), *Advances in school psychology* (Vol. 6, pp. 203–264). Hillsdale, NJ: Lawrence Erlbaum Associates.

Griffith, P. L., Rodgers-Adkinson, D. I., & Cusick, G. M. (1997). Comparing language disorders in two groups of students with severe behavioral disorders. *Behavioral Disorders, 22,* 160–166.

Illback, R. J., Nelson, C. M., & Sanders, D. (1998). Community-based services in Kentucky: Description and 5-year evaluation of Kentucky IMPACT. In M. H. Epstein, K. Kutash, & A. Duchnowski (Eds.), *Outcomes for children and youth with emotional and behavioral disorders and their families: Programs and evaluation best practices* (pp. 141–172). Austin, TX: Pro-Ed.

Kaiser, A. P., & Hester, P. P. (1997). Prevention of conduct disorder through early intervention: A social-communicative perspective. *Behavioral Disorders, 22,* 117–130.

Katsiyannis, A., & Maag, J. W. (1998). Disciplining students with disabilities: Issues and considerations for implementing IDEA '97. *Behavioral Disorders, 23,* 276–289.

Kauffman, J. M. (2001). *Characteristics of emotional and behavioral disorders of children and youth* (7th ed.). Upper Saddle River, NJ: Merrill/Prentice Hall.

Kauffman, J. M., & Hallahan, D. P. (Eds.). (1995). *The illusion of full inclusion: A comprehensive critique of a current special education bandwagon.* Austin, TX: Pro-Ed.

Kauffman, J. M., Lloyd, J. W., Astuto, T. A., & Hallahan, D. P. (1995). *Issues in the educational placement of students with emotional or behavioral disorders.* Hillsdale, NJ: Lawrence Erlbaum Associates.

Kentucky EBD Task Force. (1992). *Emotional-behavioral disability technical assistance manual.* Frankfort, KY: Kentucky Department of Education.

Koyanagi, C., & Gaines, S. (1993). *All systems failure: An examination of the results of neglecting the needs of children with serious emotional disturbance.* Alexandria, VA: National Mental Health Association.

Lambert, N., Windmiller, M., Tharinger, D., & Cole, L. (1981). AAMD *adaptive behavior scale* (school edition). Monterey, CA: Publishers Test Service.

LaVigna, G. W., & Donnellan, A. M. (1986). *Alternatives to punishment: Solving behavior problems through non-aversive strategies.* New York: Irvington.

Lawson, H. A., & Sailor, W. (in press). Integrating services, collaborating, and developing connections with schools. *Focus on Exceptional Children.*

Lewis, T. J., & Garrison-Harrell, L. (1999). Effective behavior support: Designing setting-specific interventions. *Effective School Practices, 17*(4), 38–46.

Lewis-Palmer, T., Sugai, G., & Larson, S. (1999). Using data to guide decisions about program implementation and effectiveness: An overview and applied example. *Effective School Practices, 17*(4), 47–53.

Lloyd, J. W., & Kauffman, J. M. (1995). What less restrictive placements require of teachers. In J. M. Kauffman, J. W. Lloyd, D. P. Hallahan, & T. A. Astuto (Eds.), *Issues in educational placement: Students with emotional and behavioral disorders* (pp. 317–334). Hillsdale, NJ: Lawrence Erlbaum Associates.

Mack, A. E., & Warr-Leeper, G. A. (1992). Language abilities in boys with chronic behavior disorders. *Language, Speech, and Hearing Services in Schools, 23,* 214–223.

MacMillan, D. L., Gresham. F. M., & Forness, S. R. (1996). Full inclusion: An empirical perspective. *Behavioral Disorders, 21,* 145–159.

McConaughy, S. M., & Achenbach, T. M. (1989). Empirically based assessment of severe emotional disturbance. *Journal of School Psychology, 27,* 91–117.

McIntyre, T. (1992). A primer on cultural diversity for educators. *Multicultural Forum, 1*(2), 13–16.

McIntyre, T. (1995). *The McIntyre assessment of culture.* Columbia, MO: Hawthorne Educational Services.

McIntyre, T., & Forness, S. R. (1997). Is there a new definition yet, or are our kids still seriously emotionally disturbed? *Beyond Behavior, 7*(3), 4–10.

McLaughlin, M. J., Leone, P. E., Warren, S. H., & Schofield, P. F. (1994). *Doing things differently: Issues and options for creating comprehensive school linked services for children and youth with emotional or behavioral disorders.* College Park, MD: University of Maryland and Westat, Inc.

Meadows, N. B., Neel, R. S., Scott, C. M., & Parker, G. (1994). Academic performance, social competence, and mainstream accommodations: A look at mainstreamed and non-mainstreamed students with serious behavioral disorders. *Behavioral Disorders, 19,* 170–180.

National Association of School Psychologists (1986). *Intervention assistance teams: A model for building level instructional problem solving.* Washington, DC: Author.

Nelson, C. M. (1988). Social skills training for handicapped students. *Teaching Exceptional Children, 20*(4), 19–23.

Nelson, C. M. (2000) Educating students with emotional and behavioral disorders in the 21st century: Looking through windows, opening doors. *Education and Treatment of Children, 23,* 204–222.

Nelson, J. R., Martella, R., & Galand, B. (1998). The effects of teaching school expectations and establishing a consistent consequence on formal office disciplinary actions. *Journal of Emotional and Behavioral Disorders, 6,* 153–161.

Peterson, R. L., & Ishii-Jordan, S. (Eds.). (1993). *Multicultural issues in the education of behaviorally disordered youth.* Cambridge, MA: Brookline Books.

Potter, M. L., Ysseldyke, J. E., & Regan, R. R. (1983). Eligibility and classification decisions in educational settings: Issuing "passports" in a state of confusion. *Contemporary Educational Psychology, 8,* 146–157.

Reynolds, M. C., & Birch, J. W. (1977). *Teaching exceptional children in all America's schools.* Reston, VA: Council for Exceptional Children.

Ruhl, K. L., Hughes, C. A., & Camarata, S. M. (1992). Analysis of the expressive and receptive characteristics of emotionally handicapped students served in public school settings. *Journal of Childhood Communication Disorders, 14,* 165–176.

Rutherford, R. B., Jr., & Nelson, C. M. (1988). Generalization and maintenance of treatment effects. In J. C. Witt, E. N. Elliott, & F. M. Gresham (Eds.), *Handbook of behavior therapy in education* (pp. 227–324). New York: Plenum.

Salvia, J., & Ysseldyke, J. E. (2001). *Assessment in special and remedial education* (8th ed.). Boston: Houghton Mifflin.

Scott, T. M., & Nelson, C. M. (1998). Confusion and failure in facilitating generalized social responding in the school setting: Sometimes 2 + 2 = 5. *Behavioral Disorders, 23,* 264–275.

Scott, T. M., & Nelson, C. M. (1999a). Universal school discipline strategies: Facilitating positive learning environments. *Effective School Practices, 17(4),* 54–63.

Scott, T. M., & Nelson, C. M. (1999b). Using functional behavioral assessment to develop effective behavioral intervention plans: Practical classroom applications. *Journal of Positive Behavioral Interventions, 1,* 242–251.

Shores, R. E., Gunter, P. L., & Jack, S. L. (1993). Classroom management strategies: Are they setting events for coercion? *Behavioral Disorders, 18,* 92–102.

Sinclair, E., Del'Homme, M., & Gonzalez, M. (1993). Systematic screening for preschool behavioral disorders. *Behavioral Disorders, 18,* 177–188.

Skiba, R. J., Peterson, R. L., & Williams, T. (1998). Office referrals and suspension: Disciplinary intervention in middle schools. *Education and Treatment of Children, 20(3),* 1–21.

Sparrow, S. S., Balla, D. A., & Cicchetti, D. V. (1985). *Vineland Adaptive Behavior Scale.* Circle Pines, MN: American Guidance Service.

Sprick, R., Sprick, M., & Garrison, M. (1992). *Foundations: Developing positive school-wide discipline policies.* Longmont, CO: Sopris West.

Stroul, B. A., & Friedman, R. A. (1986). *A system of care for severely emotionally disturbed children and youth.* Washington, DC: CASSP Technical Assistance Center, Georgetown University Child Development Center.

Sugai, G., & Horner, R. H. (1999b). Discipline and behavioral support: Practices, pitfalls, and promises. *Effective School Practices, 17(4),* 10–22.

Sugai, G., Horner, R. H., Dunlap, G., Hieneman, M., Lewis, T. J., Nelson, C. M., Scott, T., Liaupsin, C., Sailor, W., Turnbull, A. P., Turnbull, H. R. III, Wickham, D., Wilcox, B., & Ruef, M. (2000). Applying positive behavior support and functional behavioral assessment in schools. *Journal of Positive Behavior Interventions, 2,* 131–143.

Sugai, G., Sprague, J. R., Horner, R. H., & Walker, H. M. (2000). Preventing school violence: The use of office discipline referrals to assess and monitor school-wide discipline interventions. *Journal of Emotional and Behavioral Disorders, 8,* 94–101.

Taylor-Green, S., Horner, R. H., Sugai, G., & Hall, S. (1996). School-wide behavioral support: Starting the year off right. Unpublished manuscript, College of Education, University of Oregon, Eugene.

Todd, A. W., Horner, R. H., Sugai, G., & Colvin, G. (1999). Individualizing school-wide discipline for students with chronic problem behaviors: A team approach. *Effective School Practices, 17(4),* 72–82.

Todd, A. W., Horner, R. H., Sugai, G., & Sprague, J. R. (1999). Effective behavior support: Strengthening school-wide systems through a team-based approach. *Effective School Practices, 17(4),* 23–37.

U. S. Department of Education. (1999). *20th annual report to Congress on the implementation of the Individuals with Disability Education Act.* Washington, DC: U.S. Department of Education, Office of Special Education and Rehabilitative Services.

U. S. Department of Education. (2000). *21st annual report to Congress on the implementation of the Individuals with Disability Education Act.* Washington, DC: U.S. Department of Education, Office of Special Education and Rehabilitative Services.

Wagner, M. M. (1995). Outcomes for youths with serious emotional disturbance in secondary school and early adulthood. *Critical Issues for Children and Youths, 5,* 90–112.

Waksman, S., & Jones, V. (1985, August). A suggested procedure for the identification of and provision of services to seriously emotionally disturbed students. *Technical assistance papers: A series on PL 94–142 and related Oregon laws.* Portland: Oregon Department of Education.

Walker, H. M., Block-Pedego, A., Todis, B., & Severson, H. (1991). *The school archival records search.* Longmount, CO: Sopris West.

Walker, H. M., Colvin, G., & Ramsey, E. (1995). *Antisocial behavior in school: Strategies and best practices.* Pacific Grove, CA: Brooks/Cole.

Walker, H. M., & Fabre, T. R. (1987). Assessment of behavior disorders in the school setting: Issues, problems and strategies revisited. In N. Haring (Ed.), *Measuring and managing behavior disorders* (pp. 198–243). Seattle: University of Washington Press.

Walker, H. M., & McConnell, S. R. (1988). *The Walker-McConnell scale of social competence and school adjustment: A social skills rating scale for teachers.* Austin, TX: Pro-Ed.

Walker, H. M., & Rankin, R. (1983). Assessing the behavioral expectations and demands of less restrictive settings. *School Psychology Digest, 12,* 274–284.

Walker, H. M., & Severson, H. (1990). *Systematic screening for behavioral disorders.* Longmont, CO: Sopris West.

Weber, J., & Scheuermann, B. (1997). A challenging future: Current barriers and recommended action for our field. *Behavioral Disorders, 22,* 167–178.

Wood, F. H., Smith, C. R., & Grimes, J. (Eds.). (1985). *The Iowa assessment model in behavioral disorders: A training manual.* Des Moines, IA: Department of Public Instruction.

CHAPTER 2

ASSESSMENT-BASED INTERVENTION PLANNING

OUTLINE

OBJECTIVES

After completing this chapter, you should be able to

- Describe the process and procedures for conducting behavioral assessments.
- Describe the issues that should be considered when identifying behaviors for intervention.
- Explain the steps for conducting a functional behavioral assessment.
- Given descriptions of recurring sequences of behavior in specific contexts, develop hypotheses describing functional relationships.
- Given the function of behavior and other assessment data, identify components of a behavior intervention plan.
- Given descriptions of target behaviors, write terminal intervention objectives and analyze these objectives by breaking them down into three to five task steps.

In Chapter 1 we described two sets of assessment decisions: those regarding students' eligibility for special education services and those involving their educational treatment (Algozzine, Ruhl, & Ramsey, 1991). This chapter deals with the process of conducting functional assessments of behavior and using this information to design interventions directed at pupils' academic performance and social behaviors. The assessment and intervention decisions discussed here are those you make as an intervention agent, whether you are a classroom teacher, a school counselor or psychologist, or some other support person in the school setting. Intervention planning requires data from various levels of assessment in order to tailor strategies to the characteristics of the students with whom they will be applied, the persons applying them, and the settings in which they are used. The purposes of these assessments are (a) to verify that a problem exists and that it warrants intervention; (b) to analyze the problem in terms of which behaviors are occurring, where they occur, and the characteristics of the settings in which the problem is seen (persons, expectations, degrees of structure, etc.); and (c) to develop hypotheses about the factors that may cause or contribute to the problem, as well as about the potential intervention strategies that address the relevant characteristics. These hypotheses are then tested by systematically implementing interventions and monitoring their effects (Wehby, 1994).

We begin by describing the process of conducting *functional behavioral assessments* (FBAs). Next, we explain how to develop a *behavior intervention plan* (BIP) based on your FBA. We conclude with a discussion of the outcomes of treatment planning assessment—namely, intervention goals and objectives—as well as how to task-analyze terminal objectives for intervention. The case study at the end of the chapter illustrates the development of a BIP.

THE ASSESSMENT PROCESS

Behavioral assessment involves the evaluation of observable student behaviors across the range of environmental settings in which they occur. As indicated in the previous chapter, traditional mental health assessment focuses on internal processes that are assumed to underlie overt behavior patterns. In contrast, behavioral assessment focuses upon the objective analysis of the overt behavior itself, which minimizes inferences about underlying conditions. Tests that measure personality constructs, attitudes, and feelings typically are not used in behavioral assessment. Because behaviors occur in a variety of settings (e.g., home, school, community), and because the behaviors that take place in one setting may not happen in others, it is important to assess student behaviors across various settings. A single environmental setting actually is comprised of many subsettings. For example, the school setting consists of classrooms, offices, a lunchroom, a gymnasium, hallways, a bus waiting area, a playground, and so forth. Settings are also referred to as **behavioral contexts,** because they include an abundance of events that occur before and after a given behavior. Even students placed in self-contained classrooms function in many contexts (e.g., reading group, science class, recess, lunch period, dismissal time). These contexts often differ in terms of other persons, behavioral expectations, the degree of structure, and the interactions likely to occur. Thus, behavioral assessments should be conducted in all settings that are relevant to planning and implementing effective interventions. Polsgrove (1987) articulated the goals of behavioral assessment as identifying specific interpersonal and environmental variables within each setting that influence behavior, analyzing the behavioral expectations of various settings, and comparing expectations and the pupil's behavior across settings. These analyses provide a comprehensive picture of the student's behavior in a range of places and among a variety of persons. They also reveal differences in expectations, structure, and social interaction patterns that characterize these settings. Table 2-1 presents guidelines for assessing behavior across the settings in which the student functions.

Thus, behavioral assessment procedures address the range of behaviors and settings that characterize each student's total environment. Such broad assessments are particularly useful in identifying potential **target behaviors,** where they occur, both immediate and remote environmental factors that influence their occurrence, and other variables that potentially may contribute to intervention planning. Within and across these environmental settings, increasingly specific and precise assessments are conducted to identify, analyze, and monitor the behaviors targeted for intervention. The decisions made by intervention agents guide this process as these persons evaluate the student's behavior relative to the characteristics of the behavioral contexts in which the student functions.

In the following paragraphs, we describe the general behavioral assessment process. This includes procedures used to determine whether a given behavior constitutes a problem that warrants an intervention. Next we describe the procedures used in developing an assessment-based intervention plan. As pointed out in Chapter 1, this is a specific process that must be followed when a student with a disability engages in behavior that causes the IEP team to consider a change in edu-

cational placement. We recommend it as the best practice for intervention planning at any point in time, regardless of the situation or whether the student has a disability.

Behavioral assessment often begins with the assumption that there is a problem. That is, the student is doing too much of something that he is not supposed to be doing, or too little of something that he is supposed to be doing. However, the decision that too much or too little behavior is occurring requires that we evaluate the behavior in question relative to the expectations for social behavior in specific settings. Therefore, it is prudent to ask whether a problem really exists, or whether our perceptions are out of line. As Howell, Fox, and Morehead (1993) point out, a problem exists if there is a discrepancy between student behavior and a standard. In other words, someone must use his or her own judgment and decide that there is a discrepancy and that it is serious enough to justify intervention. In the case of academic behaviors, making judgments about discrepancies between standards and behaviors is relatively straightforward and objective (e.g., the student is getting less than 50% correct on his assignments in language arts). However, standards for social behavior are based on the expectations of other persons, and

TABLE 2-1 Guidelines for Behavioral Assessment

Information to Be Obtained	Potential Sources of Information
1. What are the pupil's major environmental settings and reference groups?	1. Pupil, parents, other teachers, peers.
2. Who are the significant persons in these settings?	2. Pupil, parents, other teachers, peers, direct observation.
3. What behaviors occur in these settings? (List both desired and undesired behaviors.)	3. Parents, other teachers, peers, direct observation.
4. (For settings in which problem behavior occurs) Who sees the behavior as a problem?	4. Significant others in the setting.
5. What behaviors are expected in the setting	5. Significant others in the setting.
6. How does the pupil's behavior differ from these expectations?	6. Significant others in the setting.

such expectations are both personal and subjective. For example, Mr. Smith believes that pupils should not talk to each other while working; therefore, he expects students to speak only when called upon. But Ms. Peterson believes that pupils should talk to each other while working; therefore, she expects some level of noise in her classroom.

RULING OUT MEDICAL EXPLANATIONS FOR PROBLEM BEHAVIOR. A student who lacks functional communicative skills may be unable to tell you that he is striking his head because he has an earache. Or a pupil whose listlessness, lethargy, and inattention to tasks interfere with his educational performance may be unaware that he has diabetes. Mild or potentially serious medical problems may underlie student behavior problems and educators should not assume that managing the environment is the only effective way to influence behavior. Particularly if an undesired behavior pattern has a sudden onset, and if behavioral assessment procedures reveal no apparent environmental factors that affect its occurrence, you should ask the parents if they have observed any recent changes in their child's behavior, and whether the child has had a recent physical examination. In any case, it may be wise to ask the school nurse or health practitioner to conduct a brief medical screening (with parental permission). If the screening reveals any indicators of potential health problems, ask the parents to obtain a medical examination and indicate the suspected medical cause of the problem. If the parents approve, you may contact the examining physician to explain the behaviors of concern.

If there is an underlying health problem, the next step is appropriate medical intervention. While the pupil is receiving treatment, continue to observe the behaviors of concern and note any changes. Be aware that in cases of long-standing medical problems, successful medical treatment may not solve the problem immediately. For example, if the student has missed out on instruction in important skills, or if the undesired behavior originally caused by his health problem

has been reinforced (e.g., he has been able to avoid undesired tasks), solving his physical problem may not alleviate the corresponding behavior pattern.

SOCIAL VALIDATION OF PROBLEM BEHAVIORS. **Social validation** (Wolf, 1978) is a strategy for evaluating whether significant persons agree that a problem is serious enough to require intervention.[1] Several procedures can be used to validate the existence and severity of a behavior problem. The most obvious is simply to ask other persons who have daily contact with the student whether the identified target behaviors are serious problems. In the case of a serious behavior problem (e.g., aggression, stereotypic behavior), discrepancies between standards and behavior are more obvious. Students with severe disabilities or those who display bizarre or extremely deviant behaviors clearly depart from expectations for "normal" behavior. However, judgments about the seriousness of less extreme behavior problems are more difficult due to the absence of instruments and procedures for accurately measuring behavioral standards and student performance relative to these standards. One way to establish that a problem exists is to directly observe the identified student in settings where problem behaviors are occurring. Direct observation data will tell you little about the need for intervention, however, unless the problem behavior is dangerous or intolerable at any level, or unless you have some indication of what level of the behavior persons in the setting will tolerate. For example, even a single instance of physical aggression during a classroom work period is likely to be intolerable, but what about off-task, out-of-seat, or noncompliant behavior? Almost all students display some undesirable social behaviors, as well as some deficits in appro-

[1]Social validation also encompasses the acceptability of intervention procedures and goals to professionals and caregivers, as well as their satisfaction with the results of interventions (Wolf, 1978).

priate social skills. Pupils who are identified as having EBD usually are distinguished from those who are not by *excesses or deficits* in the frequency or rate at which they exhibit such behaviors rather than by differences in the *kinds* of behaviors they exhibit. It is possible that the teacher simply notices the designated student's disruptive behavior more than he or she notices the same behavior in others. One way to assess the discrepancy between the identified student's behavior and the standard for that behavior in the classroom is to simultaneously observe the target pupil and a peer whom the teacher designates as typical with respect to how much of the problem behavior he or she displays (Walker & Fabre, 1987). Comparing the frequencies of the behavior exhibited by the two students will help you assess the relative severity of the target behavior. Figure 2-1 displays a sheet of interval data collected on a target student and a selected peer (see Chapter 3 to learn how to use this direct observation tool). Note that on some behaviors the target student was much like his behaviorally acceptable peer.

Assessing differences between the student's behavior and that of behaviorally typical peers also will help you decide whether intervention is warranted. For example, one teacher may regard students who are noisy and boisterous or who violate his standards for order and routine as having serious problems that require intervention, but other staff members may view the same behavior in other settings as typical. We are not suggesting that students who act out in only one classroom should not be considered candidates for intervention; we mean only that persons' standards and tolerance for pupil behavior are subjective and vary from setting to setting or from one occasion to another. Also, because students with behavioral problems seldom display only one undesired behavior or lack only one appropriate social skill, it is necessary to decide which behaviors to act upon first. Social validation and direct observation procedures will help you evaluate the discrepancy between pupil behavior and standards. With this in-

formation, you can determine whether intervention is justified and which behaviors should receive priority for intervention. Checklists and rating scales also may be administered across persons and settings to socially validate the perception of a problem.

Another facet of social validation is consideration of whether the student's behavior is deviant with respect to the standards of his cultural reference group. The overrepresentation of culturally different learners in classes for children with disabilities, including programs for students with EBD, may be partially explained by the teachers' lack of sensitivity to culturally based behavior (McIntyre, 1996). Therefore, it should be determined that the problem behavior is not typical for the student's cultural group. Assessment procedures that may provide this information include interviews with the target student or his caregivers, in combination with rating scales, checklists, and direct observation of behavior across settings.

Methods of Assessment

A large variety of tools and procedures are available for conducting behavioral assessments. These may be used at any stage in the assessment process, from determining whether a problem exists, to conducting an FBA and monitoring student behaviors that are targeted for intervention. For example, a review of school archival records (described in Chapter 1) can help identify patterns of behavior over time, as well as events in students' lives that may influence their behavior. Interviews and direct observation procedures can be used to determine whether a problem behavior warrants intervention and to gather information across persons and settings as part of an FBA or to evaluate the effects of a BIP. We begin by describing procedures for conducting general behavioral screening as a first step in problem identification, then illustrate a range of behavioral assessment tools. In Chapter 3 we expand the topic of assessment to include strategies for ongoing monitoring of student

Behavior Observation Record

Recorder _B. Hogg_ Child _Frank_
Date _2/16/01_ Circumstance _Study Period_
+= Behavior observed at least once Length of time observed _15 min._
during interval.
−= Behavior not observed during interval.

Target Child

																TOTAL
Noise	−	+	+	−	−	−	+	+	−	+	−	+	−	+	+	8
Out of place	−	−	+	+	−	−	+	+	−	+	−	−	−	−	−	5
Off-task	−	+	+	+	+	−	+	+	+	−	+	+	+	+	+	12
Physical contact	−	−	+	−	−	−	−	−	−	+	−	−	−	−	−	2
Other _Calling out for teacher_	−	−	−	+	−	−	+	−	−	−	+	−	−	−	+	4

Peer

																TOTAL
Noise	+	−	+	−	−	+	+	−	+	−	+	+	−	+	+	9
Out of place	−	−	−	−	−	−	−	−	−	−	−	−	−	−	−	0
Off-task	−	−	+	−	−	+	−	−	+	−	−	−	−	+	+	5
Physical contact	−	−	−	−	−	−	−	−	−	−	−	−	−	−	−	0
Other	−	−	−	−	−	−	−	−	−	−	−	−	−	−	−	0

Note: Each square represents one minute of observation.

FIGURE 2-1 Target student and peer comparison observational data.

Source: *Deno, S., & Mirkin, P. (1978). Data-based program modification. Reston, VA: Council for Exceptional Children. Used with permission.*

progress and making intervention decisions from this information.

SCREENING. The screening procedures we described in Chapter 1 for identifying students with behavioral problems also should clarify whether a significant discrepancy exists between behavior and expectations, irrespective of whether the student is being considered for special education. The specific procedures used should be relatively brief and efficient so that persons in each relevant setting will be inclined to cooperate. Alternately, screening assessments may be conducted by persons who are familiar with the student's performance across most or all of the relevant behavioral contexts. Systematic school-wide screening procedures serve the purpose of establishing whether a problem exists, but, as we pointed out, these are not widely used. The traditional method of screening students for behavioral problems is through teacher referral. You will recall that referral-driven identification procedures are unreliable and tend not to identify students who are socially withdrawn. Screening for intervention planning addresses the following questions: Is *intervention needed*? If so, *in which settings should it be applied*? The assessment procedures used to answer these questions are likely to involve more time and more sophisticated procedures across more settings than those required for general screening to identify pupils at risk. However, this level of screening focuses on a limited number of students, and the importance of the decisions to be made justifies the greater expenditure of time and resources needed for these assessments. Also, you will recall from Chapter 1 that this type of screening may be accomplished through systematic analysis of behavioral referrals.

INDIRECT BEHAVIORAL ASSESSMENT. As we emphasize repeatedly throughout this text, direct observation of students' behavior is the most precise strategy for assessing behavior. However, more indirect procedures are less time consuming and simpler to use. Furthermore, many instruments are available. In this section we describe procedures checklists and rating scales, teacher rankings, self-report measures, and sociometric procedures. In addition, we describe procedures designed to measure teacher expectations and pupil social skills. The great weakness of indirect assessment tools and procedures is that they really are assessing the evaluator's opinion regarding the student's behavior rather than the behavior itself. Thus, assessment information may be distorted by the biases and expectations of the person conducting the assessment.

Checklists and rating scales generally use information supplied by a significant other (e.g., teacher, parent, sibling, or peer) to produce a picture of a target child's behavior. A checklist merely asks the responder to indicate whether he has observed specific behaviors at any time. These behaviors are selected from a list of behaviors. A rating scale gives the rater a set of items and asks him to evaluate these items with respect to a particular student in terms of how frequently behaviors occur. Less commonly, the rater responds to each item in terms of how much it characterizes the student's behavior (e.g., is very characteristic of the student; is not at all characteristic). Typically, ratings are presented in a Likert or similar numeric scale format.

Sometimes the rater may be instructed to rate how often a student engages in a particular behavior (never, rarely, occasionally, often, very frequently). If you are asked to complete a rating scale as part of a formal screening program, be sure that you have had enough experience with the child to provide valid responses. Remember, behavior ratings are only standardized ways of representing opinions regarding the presence or strength of students' behaviors. Thus, they should not be the only assessment tool used, nor are they appropriate as a basis for making intervention decisions (see Chapter 3).

Behavior rating scales may be *standardized*, meaning that tests were administered to a number of persons and, on the basis of their responses, norms and criteria for discriminating between groups were established (e.g., a conduct problem/not a conduct problem). Figure 2-2 presents a sample of items from the *Walker Problem Behavior Identification Checklist* (Walker, 1983). Rating scales also may be informal and nonstandardized, such as the instrument shown in Figure 2-3. The format shown here has the advantage of rating a group of students on the same sheet, thereby permitting comparisons. Rating scales may contain items that assess undesired or maladaptive behaviors, desired or adaptive behaviors, or both. Many rating scales are available commercially, and we suggest that you study their items, reliability, validity, norms, and recommended uses in order to identify those that are likely to be most appropriate and useful for your purposes (see McMahon, 1984).

To make the assessment of **teacher expectations** less subjective, Walker and Rankin (1980) developed a standardized rating scale format, the SBS *Inventory of Teacher Social Behavior Standards and Expectations*. It asks teachers to rate the importance

	Scale				
	1	2	3	4	5
20. Has nervous tics: muscle-twitching, eye-blinking, nail-biting, hand-wringing					.3
21. Habitually rejects the school experience through actions or comments	.1				
22. Has enuresis (wets bed)					.1
23. Utters nonsense syllables and/or babbles to himself				.4	
24. Continually seeks attention			.1		
25. Comments that nobody likes him				.2	
26. Repeats one idea, thought, or activity over and over				.4	
27. Has temper tantrums	.2				
28. Refers to himself as dumb, stupid, or incapable				.3	
29. Does not engage in group activities		.2			
30. When teased or irritated by other children, takes out his frustration(s) on another, inappropriate person or thing	.2				

Directions: The rater identifies those statements that describe the student and circles the number in the column corresponding to these statements. The circled values in each column are then added to yield a score for each of the five scales. The scales are Acting out (column 1), Withdrawal (column 2), Distractability (column 3), Disturbed Peer Relations (column 4), and Immaturity (column 5).

FIGURE 2-2   Sample items from the *Walker Problem Behavior Identification Checklist* (1983).

Source: Walker, H. M. (1983). Walker problem behavior identification checklist. Los Angeles: Western Psychological Services. Copyright ©1970, 1976, 1983 by Western Psychological Services. Reprinted by permission of the publisher: Western Psychological Services, 12031 Wilshire Boulevard, Los Angeles, CA 90025, U.S.A.

of adaptive behaviors (e.g., child takes turns, uses free time appropriately) and their own tolerance for maladaptive pupil behaviors (e.g., child whines, has tantrums, uses obscene language) in terms of how these affect their willingness to work with the students in their classrooms. This instrument is also a component of the *Assessment for Integration into Mainstream Settings* system (AIMS) (Walker, 1986), which is used to identify the minimal skill requirements of mainstream settings, to prepare the student to meet these requirements, and to assess the pupil's adjustment following mainstream placement. We describe the AIMS system in greater detail in Chapter 11.

Teacher rankings on the basis of social criteria (e.g., frequency of peer verbal interactions) have been shown to be a reliable and valid method of identifying pupils who are not socially responsive (Walker, Severson, & Haring, 1986). Figure 2-4 illustrates one such ranking procedure. The teacher initially ranks all students in the class, divides them into two groups according to the behavior pattern being considered (e.g., most and least talkative), and finally ranks all pupils according to the criterion (Hops & Greenwood, 1981). The systematic school-wide screening procedure (Walker & Severson, 1990) mentioned in Chapter 1 includes this ranking procedure. Teacher rankings offer a quick way to establish the relative standing of pupils in the group with respect to a criterion.

Another format is a **self-report.** As the name implies, this type of instrument requires that students describe their own behavior in response to a

Students	Child has close friends.	Child is frequently chosen by classmates to play on a team, study together, etc.	Child spends most of recess time playing with others.	Child volunteers for classroom "jobs."	Child answers appropriately when the teacher asks questions of the group.	Child follows most teacher instructions independently or with minimal assistance.	Child brings materials and ideas to school for inclusion or class discussions and projects.	Child initiates conversations with the teacher.	Child completes most assignments within allotted time.	Child's academic performance is about right or better than expected for his grade level.	Child regularly follows classroom rules of conduct.	Child checks over most work papers before submitting them.	Child's statements about school are usually positive.	Child attends school regularly.	Child has no known major health problems.
1.															
2.															
3.															
4.															
5.															
6.															
7.															
8.															
9.															
10.															
11.															
12.															

Teacher _____ Interviewer _____ School _____
Grade _____ Date _____ Time _____

FIGURE 2-3   Teaching rating form.

number of questions or statements. For young students or nonreaders the questions may be read orally with subsequent directions for students to color in a response area, to circle a happy or sad face, or to sort pictures into groups (Finch &

Rodgers, 1984). Self-report instruments have been designed to assess a variety of general (e.g., locus of control) and specific (e.g., anger, depression) constructs. Self-reports provide useful information, but they should be supplemented with data

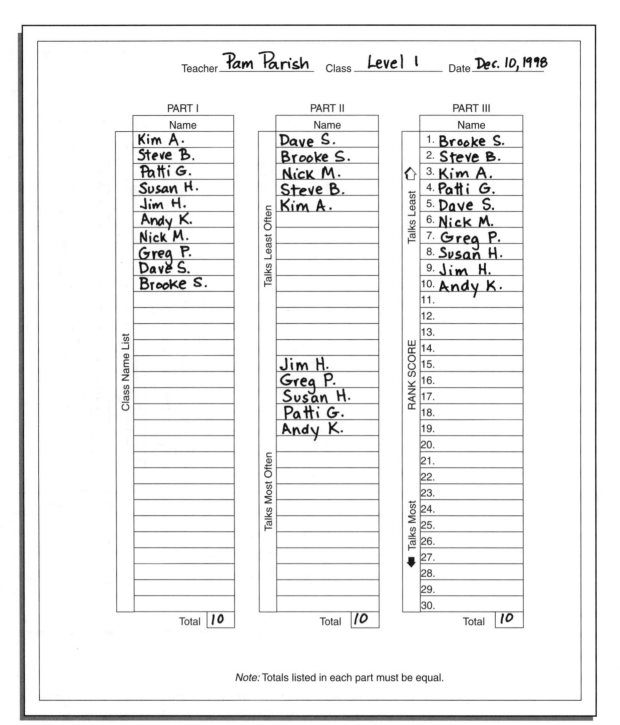

Teacher **Pam Parish** Class **Level 1** Date **Dec. 10, 1998**

PART I	PART II	PART III
Name	**Name**	**Name**

PART I — Class Name List

- Kim A.
- Steve B.
- Patti G.
- Susan H.
- Jim H.
- Andy K.
- Nick M.
- Greg P.
- Dave S.
- Brooke S.

Total **10**

PART II

Talks Least Often:
- Dave S.
- Brooke S.
- Nick M.
- Steve B.
- Kim A.

Talks Most Often:
- Jim H.
- Greg P.
- Susan H.
- Patti G.
- Andy K.

Total **10**

PART III — RANK SCORE

Talks Least ⇧
1. Brooke S.
2. Steve B.
3. Kim A.
4. Patti G.
5. Dave S.
6. Nick M.
7. Greg P.
8. Susan H.
9. Jim H.
10. Andy K.
11.
12.
13.
14.
15.
16.
17.
18.
19.
20.
21.
22.
23.
24.
25.
26.
27.
28.
29.
30.
Talks Most ⬇

Total **10**

Note: Totals listed in each part must be equal.

FIGURE 2-4   Student ranking form.

Source: *Hops, H., & Greenwood, C. R. (1981). Social skills deficits. In E. J. Msh and L. G. Terdal (Eds.),* Behavioral assessment of childhood disorders. *New York: Guilford Press, 359. Used with permission.*

from other sources, such as behavioral ratings and observations (Finch & Rodgers, 1984).

Although sociometric procedures may not be considered traditional behavioral assessment devices, they nevertheless can play a role in identifying students at risk for social behavior problems (Hops & Lewin, 1984). Before using a sociometric procedure in your classroom, check to see what, if any, parental permissions are required in order for students to participate in this process. In general, a sociometric procedure requires that students describe one another according to a predesignated set of criteria. For example, students might be asked to name their best friends or to list classmates they do not like. In this type of peer nomination, a student makes an acceptance or rejection choice about a selected number of peers. Because peer acceptance and rejection appear to be independent dimensions, both positive (e.g., "With whom would you most like to go to a movie?") and negative (e.g., "With whom would you least like to go to a movie?"), social preferences should be obtained from peers (Hops & Lewin, 1984). Asking students to make negative nominations raises ethical questions that should be weighed before using this procedure. Students' sociometric ratings of peers should be kept confidential.

Instruments that measure student **social skills** are relatively new additions to behavioral assessment technology. A number of social skills checklists and rating scales are available commercially. Remember, these instruments ask for the evaluator's opinion regarding the student's social skills; they are not direct measures of social behavior. Evaluations are more likely to be valid if they come from a variety of sources (e.g., teachers, parents, peers, and students themselves) and if they address multiple social domains (i.e., interactions across environmental settings).

The instruments and procedures just described may be used to conduct general assessments of students' social behaviors. Remember, it is important to assess student behavior across several settings and to obtain data from multiple sources in order to get a valid and comprehensive picture of pupils' behavioral assets and liabilities. While some may be useful in gathering data for an FBA, they (with the exception of direct observation and measurement) are indirect measures of behavior and should not be used by themselves, either as assessments of student behavior, evaluations of intervention effectiveness, or as FBAs. Direct observation and interviews also frequently are used to assess student behavior. We describe these in the following section, which describes developing a BIP from assessment data.

ASSESSMENT-BASED INTERVENTION PLANNING

As discussed in Chapter 1, IDEA '97 stipulates that, for the first time, schools must conduct FBAs of students with disabilities whose behavior prompts consideration of a change in educational placement, including suspension and expulsion. An intervention plan addressing the student's problem behavior then must be developed, based on the information obtained from the FBA. Because this process requires the collection of fairly large amounts of assessment data from multiple sources and over extended periods of time, we recommend that FBAs be coordinated by Behavior Support Teams. Many professionals agree that this intervention planning process represents best practice, regardless of whether the problem behavior causes school personnel to consider a change of placement (Sugai et al., 2000).[2] We describe the process of developing a BIP in terms of five steps, adapted from Scott & Nelson (1999). These steps are interrelated and include a number

[2]Assessment-based intervention planning has a relatively lengthy history with individuals with severe cognitive impairments and challenging behavior. However, research with individuals who do not exhibit cognitive impairment (i.e., those with or at risk for mild disabilities) has only begun recently, and has not yet demonstrated conclusively that assessment-based interventions produce better results than interventions that are not based on FBAs (Heckaman, Conroy, Fox, & Chait, 2000).

of subordinate components. For example, assessing the student's behavior includes identifying and describing the target behavior, determining the contexts in which it occurs and those in which it does not occur, identifying potential predictable relationships between the behavior and these contexts, and testing these relationships to establish their validity.

Step 1: Assess the Student's Behavior

The three primary outcomes of an FBA include (a) a concrete definition of the problem behavior(s); (b) identifying environmental variables reliably associated with the behavior and formulating hypotheses regarding which factors appear to predict its occurrence; and (c) identifying the function that the behavior appears to serve in meeting the needs of the individual (O'Neill, Horner, Albin, Storey, & Sprague, 1997). Initial assessments of behavior for the purpose of developing intervention plans are likely to involve informal conversations, questionnaires, checklists, and structured interviews with individuals, such as classroom teachers and parents, who have frequent contact with the student and who may be able to offer insights regarding what factors seem to predict problem behaviors (Scott & Nelson, 1999).

WHAT DOES THE PROBLEM BEHAVIOR LOOK LIKE? The task here is to develop a definition of the behavior or behaviors that will be the primary target(s) of intervention. Target behaviors should be defined or described in terms that are observable, measurable, and definable so that two or more persons can agree on their occurrence or nonoccurrence. These characteristics constitute an **operational definition** of target behaviors (i.e., what the behavior looks like). Sometimes you will be working from the verbal descriptions of behavior provided by others or from statements contained in behavior checklists. Also, you will be writing behavioral objectives based on definitions of behaviors. For these reasons, it is important

that your definitions be observable and precise. Table 2-2 provides examples of target behavior definitions derived from general statements. Study these operational definitions and practice writing some of your own in order to gain competency in this skill. While target behaviors may include those to be decreased (e.g., refusal to complete assignments, tantrums, self-injurious behavior) or increased (e.g., completion of assignments, making appropriate requests of peers, keeping hands to self), the focus of most behavior intervention plans is on behaviors to be decreased.[3]

UNDER WHAT GENERAL CONDITIONS DO PROBLEM BEHAVIORS TEND TO OCCUR? UNDER WHAT GENERAL CONDITIONS DO DESIRED BEHAVIORS TEND TO OCCUR? Several assessment instruments can help to answer these questions. For example, the *Motivation Assessment Scale* (Durand & Crimmins, 1992) and the *Problem Behavior Questionnaire* (Lewis, Scott, & Sugai, 1994) are simple paper-and-pencil tools for assessing the likelihood of problem behavior under a variety of circumstances. Touchette, MacDonald, and Langer (1985) devised a format that enables practitioners to estimate rates of targeted behaviors across time and settings. This procedure, called a **scatter plot,** is a system for rating behavior in time intervals. One scatter plot format is presented in Figure 2-5. Each day is represented by a vertical column divided into 30-minute blocks of time. The observer notes the activity taking place during each time interval and marks the interval for a given day according to whether or not the target behavior occurred. Alternately, different symbols can be used to indicate whether the behavior occurred at a high rate (e.g., a completely filled cell) or at a low rate (e.g., a slash). A blank grid indicates that the behavior did not occur. Although a scatter plot does not indicate the actual frequency

---

[3]However, behavior intervention plans also include identification of an appropriate replacement behavior.

TABLE 2-2 Examples of Target Behavior Definitions

General Statement	Target Behavior
1. Kim does not comply with teacher requests.	1. When given a direction by the teacher, Kim fails to initiate the behavior requested within 5 seconds.
2. Andy is hyperactive.	2. Andy is out of his seat more than one time in 10 minutes.
3. Fred cannot ride the school bus appropriately.	3. Fred is out of his assigned seat on the bus.
4. Betsy is aggressive.	4. Betsy hits, kicks, pushes, and calls other children names during recess.
5. Billy is withdrawn.	5. Billy initiates less than one interaction with a peer in any given 10 minute free play period.

Student: _____ John _____

Observer: _____ Ms. Lewis (teacher) _____

Dates: _____ 3/2 _____ through _____ 3/13 _____

Target Behavior:

Leaving seat without permission

Using a scatter plot involves recording the times of the day (and/or activities) in which the behavior does occur and does not occur to identify patterns that occur over days or weeks.

Time	Activity	Dates 3/2	3/3	3/4	3/5	3/6	3/9	3/10	3/11	3/12	3/13
7:30	Arrival		■								
8:00	Writing	■	■				■	■	■		
8:30	Social Skills		■				■				
9:00	Reading		■	■		■				■	
9:30	P.E.	NA	NA	NA	NA	NA	NA	NA	NA	NA	NA
10:00	Science			■				NA			
10:30	Crafts					■		NA			
11:00	Mathematics	■			■			NA	■		
11:30	Lunch							NA			
12:00	Recess	NA	NA	NA	NA	NA	NA	NA	NA	NA	NA
12:30	Projects						■				
1:00	Music		■				■				
1:30	Reading	■	■			■	■	■		■	
2:00	Mathematics		■		■		■			■	
2:30	Dismissal	NA	NA	NA	NA	NA	NA	NA	NA	NA	NA

☐ Behavior did not occur
■ Behavior occurred
NA Did not observe

FIGURE 2-5 Scatter plot.

Note: From "Facilitiator's Guide: Positive Behavioral Support" by the Positive Behavioral Support Project, p. 30. Copyright 1999 by the Department of State, State of Florida. Reproduced with permission.

with which a target behavior occurs, it does reveal patterns over time and settings. Therefore, this procedure may be used to identify relationships between problem behaviors and time of day, the presence or absence of certain persons, a physical or social setting, a particular activity, and so forth (Touchette et al., 1985).

Behavioral interviews are another useful strategy for obtaining assessment data from both children and adults. The interview should be structured to elicit specific information about the behaviors that occur, the settings in which they take place, and the antecedent and consequent conditions associated with these behaviors, including the social behavior of other persons (Conroy & Fox, 1994). An interview may be used to gather information about concerns and goals, identify factors that maintain or occasion problem behaviors, obtain historical information, and identify reinforcers (Gross, 1984). Information from two or more sources can be compared to evaluate the reliability of informants or to obtain individual perceptions of behaviors and environmental events across ecological settings. For example, Kern, Childs, Dunlap, Clarke, and Falk (1994) developed a student-assisted functional assessment interview that provides information from the student's perspective regarding expectations, curricula, and other variables in the school setting, as well as his or her perceptions about the target behaviors. The Problem Behavior Questionnaire (Lewis et al., 1994) is a teacher-based interview format that provides information from the teacher's perspective regarding the student's problem behaviors and the circumstances under which they occur as well as those under which they do not occur.

Figure 2-6 is a general interview format for identifying and analyzing target behaviors. Note that the questions are open ended (they do not limit answers by requiring only one-word responses) but structured to focus on observable events. The format also includes probes for following up on previous answers. Consult Gross (1984) or Polsgrove (1987) for more information on conducting behavioral interviews. Additional interview for-

mats are presented in subsequent chapters. Interviews and scatter plot ratings furnish information that may be used to identify times and locations where more direct assessments can be performed (Scott & Nelson, 1999). In addition, they may help identify stimuli or events that affect pupil behavior but which take place outside of the settings where the problem behavior occurs, or they may be concurrent events, such as a change in seating arrangement. These influential antecedents are known as **setting events,** and may include such variables as the student's experiences over a weekend, the time of day, a particular classroom environment, or transition periods. Setting events can set the occasion for some behaviors; that is, when they have taken place, or when they are present, the target behavior is more likely to occur.

School records often contain information that may be useful in identifying patterns of behavior or variables that may have some bearing on the student's target behavior(s). Systematic tools, such as the School Archival Records Search (Walker, Block-Pedego, Todis, & Severson, 1991) are quick and reliable methods for summarizing the sometimes large amount of data found in students' cumulative records. Pay particular attention to previous disciplinary records, anecdotal notes from meeting with caregivers, IEP team minutes, and health records.

Although it may be possible to form a hypothesis regarding the variables that predict problem behavior from the assessments described above, more information generally is required. At this point, it is useful to observe directly in settings where the target behavior occurs. Human behavior occurs in environmental contexts that contain a variety of stimuli. Some of these stimuli influence behavior either directly or indirectly. It is helpful to know precisely which stimuli affect behavior and which do not. Direct observation may enable you to identify the variables that affect student behavior. An **antecedent-behavior-consequence (A-B-C) analysis** is a direct observation format that organizes events into those that are present or take place immediately before a behavioral event and

Teacher _____

Consultant _____

Date _____

Student(s) _____

1. Can you describe for me in your own words what the problem behavior seems to be?

2. Could you be a little more specific? For example, when you say that the student disrupts the class, what exactly does she do?

3. Now I'm getting the picture. Tell me, does this behavior take place every day (period)?

4. (If no) Would you say it happens every week? Every other week?

5. Can you identify anything that seems to happen before this behavior?

6. Is there a pattern regarding when the behavior occurs (e.g., more often on Mondays, after lunch, during writing period)?

7. Let's try to figure out what the student gains from this behavior. Can you recall what happens to the student (that is, what do you do) after this behavior occurs?

8. Have you been able to notice what other students in the room do when this behavior takes place?

9. Is there anything else you can tell me about this behavior or this student?

FIGURE 2-6   Anecdotal interview recording form.

those that occur immediately afterward. We just pointed out that setting events can influence behavior, even when they take place some time before the target behavior occurs. However, more immediate antecedent events such as the task the student is expected to perform, the other persons present, or the instructions provided to the student may be important "triggers" for problem behavior. In addition, stimuli that occur subsequent to the pupil's behavior often exert a powerful influence on that behavior. For example, does the student receive social attention, praise, or criticism following specific behaviors? Does his behavior result in avoiding or escaping task demands?

An A-B-C analysis involves carefully observing and recording events that occur immediately before the target pupil's behavior, the behavior itself, and the events that take place immediately afterward. Figure 2-7 illustrates an A-B-C assessment. Note that the observer logs the time and describes the immediate antecedents, the student's behavior, and the consequences in the sequence in which they occur. An analysis of recurring antecedent and consequent events provides some clues as to which of these stimuli potentially influence behavior. Can you identify some of these events in the example? An A-B-C assessment is only useful for observing students individually; it would become too unwieldy to use with several pupils at the same time. Also, it typically is not something you can do while teaching; therefore, you may need to enlist the aid of another person (e.g., a paraprofessional) to provide instruction while you do the assessment, or vice-versa. It is important to conduct A-B-C observations for sufficient lengths of time to capture a range of behavioral sequences (both those that include instances of the target behavior and those that do not). Also conduct observations across several days to ensure that typical ranges of student performance are observed (you can ask persons in the setting to verify that such is the case). We have found it useful to perform A-B-C assessments in settings and at times of the day when the target behavior does not occur, as this information can uncover events

that predict when more desirable behavior is likely to take place (which is important for developing the BIP). By doing these assessments over a period of time and analyzing the results in conjunction with data from other sources (e.g., interviews, school records searches) it may be possible to identify setting events that influence the behavior. For example, if the problem behavior occurs more often during the first period of the day, there may be something that happens in the morning (e.g., the student doesn't eat breakfast, or is teased or bullied on the school bus).

Although the procedure is not complex, it is neither quick nor simple. We recommend 30- to 40-minute observation periods over several days to get representative samples of student behavior (remember to validate your findings against the judgments of adults in the setting, such as the classroom teacher). The A-B-C assessment routine can be confusing to persons who are not experienced. Therefore, such assessments should be performed by persons with specific training in this procedure. The purpose of an FBA is to generate hypotheses regarding which variables may influence the student's behavior. As Wehby (1994) pointed out, up to 10 hours of assessment time may be needed to evaluate functioning in all the areas required for an FBA of a given student's behavior. However, the process can be conducted much more efficiently when A-B-C assessments focus on settings and events that historically have predicted desired and undesired behavior.

While direct observation of behavior is by far the preferred strategy, alternate procedures may be used in situations where trained personnel are not available. For example, persons who are present when problem behaviors occur can be given behavior incident logs to complete as soon as possible following a behavioral incident. Data from several such logs can be summarized in a three-column format (antecedents to the behavior, a description of the behavior occurring in each incident, and events that took place immediately following the behavior). Figure 2-8 is an example of a behavior incident report format. A completed

	Student _Raymond_		Date _Oct. 29, 2001_
	Observer _Dionne McInerney_		Time _2:15 - 2:25_
	Behavior _Talking out during class discussion, off task_ Activity _Social Studies_		

Antecedent	Behavior	Consequence
Teacher says, "Everyone please get out your Social Studies notebook and pencil."	Raymond asks student next to him, "What did she say?"	Teacher says, "No talking."
Teacher asks Tommy to name the capital of Alabama.	Raymond shouts out, "Montgomery."	Tommy yells, "Shut up, Raymond."
Teacher says, "Please, Raymond, sit quietly until it is your turn."	Raymond yells, "What did I do?"	Teacher says, "Raymond, be quiet."
Teacher asks, "Which state has the largest population? Raymond, can you answer?"	Raymond says, "Uh? I didn't do anything!"	Class laughs.
Teacher asks, "Alice, which state is nicknamed the Keystone State?"	Raymond calls out, "I know. It's Pennsylvania."	Teacher says, "Raymond, I've had enough. Put your head down on your desk."

FIGURE 2-7   Sample A-B-C record.

Source: McInerney, D. (1986). Personal communication.

report may be found in Chapter 8. The disadvantage of recording only events surrounding occurrences of problem behavior is that no insight is gained about events that predict occurrences of desired behavior.

Figure 2-9 displays a format for documenting the methods used in the FBA process. This information should be updated by the Behavior Sup-

port Team as they collect information from their respective assessments.

Step 2: Propose a Hypothesis

Analysis of the data gathered through the assessment process described above leads to the identification of recurrent patterns involving setting

Directions: Fill in the boxes for each incident of the student's target behavior.

Completed by: _____ Date: _____

Student: _____ Target Behavior: _____

Describe the behavior.	
When did this behavior occur most recently?	
Where did the behavior take place?	
Who else was there?	
Was the behavior directed toward a person or property? Describe.	
What was going on immediately before the behavior?	
What happened immediately after the behavior?	
Did you observe the behavior directly?	
Comments: Describe anything that would be helpful to consider about the setting, schedule, student, etc.	

FIGURE 2-8   Behavior incident report.

Records: What records were reviewed? Conducted by:	_____ academic records (cumulative) _____ discipline records _____ previous interventions _____ other:	_____ child study notes _____ anecdotals/home notes _____ evaluations (e.g., social work, psychological)	What relevant information was obtained? _____ See attached summary/notes
Interviews: What interviews were conducted? Tools used: Conducted by:	_____ student _____ ESE teacher _____ general education teacher _____ other _____ See attached interviews	_____ parent(s) _____ Administrator _____ related services	What relevant information was obtained? _____ See attached interviews
Observations: What direct observations occurred? Tools used: Conducted by:	Location	Date/Time	What relevant information was obtained? _____ See attached observations
Other Assessments: What, if any, other assessments were conducted (e.g., ecological or classroom management inventories, reinforcer surveys, academic assessments)?			

FIGURE 2-9 Functional assessment methods.

Note: *From "Facilitiator's Guide: Positive Behavioral Support" by the Positive Behavioral Support Project, p. 30. Copyright 1999 by the Department of State, State of Florida. Reproduced with permission.*

events, antecedents, or consequences (or both) associated with occurrences of the target behavior, as well as events that are not associated with it. This analysis should enable the Behavior Support Team to answer questions about the antecedent contexts in which the behavior occurs, such as the following (Positive Behavioral Support Project, 1999):

- In what settings does the behavior occur?
- During what times of the day does the behavior occur?
- Does the behavior occur in the presence of certain persons?
- During what activities is the behavior more likely to occur?
- During what activities is the behavior less likely to occur?

Answers to questions regarding events following the target behavior suggest what functions it may serve for the student:

- What happens to the student following the behavior?
- Does the surrounding environment change in any way following the behavior?
- What does the student gain or lose?
- How do others respond to the behavior?

While the contexts in which problem behaviors occur often are the primary focus of assessment procedures, it also is important to know the variables that seem to predict instances of *desired* behavior. Therefore, remember to look at settings in which the student's behavior is appropriate, and identify setting events, antecedents, and consequences that are associated with these behavior patterns. From answers to these questions we can form hypotheses about antecedent or consequent events that predict both desired and undesired behavior. For example, the hypothesis, "When Raymond is disruptive, his teacher attends to him" predicts a relationship between Raymond's behavior and a specific consequent event: attention from the teacher. On the other hand, the hypothesis "Toya engages in self-stimulatory behavior

when approached by peers" suggests a predictable relationship between antecedents and behavior. However, keep in mind that antecedent or consequent events are not likely to be identical every time. The key is to identify events that have some common elements (Scott & Nelson, 1999). Thus, sometimes Raymond's teacher responds to his outbursts with a verbal reprimand and sometimes she takes him aside to calm him down. The common element, however, is that she consistently gives him her attention when he behaves this way. By looking at sequences in which he is not disruptive, we may be able to strengthen our hypothesis. For example, if we observe that Raymond is not disruptive when he is engaged in one-to-one interactions with the teacher, we have a better basis for hypothesizing that teacher attention is the variable that supports Raymond's disruptive behavior (i.e., he only exhibits the target behavior when he is not receiving the teacher's personal attention).

Although, as we have emphasized, human behavior is complex and influenced by many variables, all behavior can be classified into one of two broad functions: to gain access to something (e.g., peer or teacher attention, a desired item) or to escape or avoid something (e.g., an unpleasant task, a specific person or situation) (Scott & Nelson, 1999). Thus, Raymond's disruptive behavior gains attention from his teacher and peers; Toya's self-stimulatory behavior results in other persons leaving her alone (i.e., escape/avoidance). Figure 2-10 presents a format to help you analyze patterns of behavior and propose a function served by the behavior. This information will guide your hypothesis statement.

We have pointed out that the FBA process was developed in working with individuals who display challenging behavior but lack cognitive and expressive language skills. As recent research demonstrates (Shores, Wehby, & Jack, 1999), the undesired behavior of students with more extensive behavioral repertoires than those with severe disabilities also serve functions. For example, the observation that a student predictably displays disruptive behavior during certain classroom

What tends to occur before the behavior? (time of day, type of lesson, presence of certain persons, task requests, other triggers)	What tends to occur after the behavior? (student gains attention, object, control of others; avoids/escapes situation or task)	What are some testable explanations for the behavior? (behavior occurs when. . .)

FIGURE 2-10   Analysis of predictable behavior patterns.

activities resulting in his being removed from the classroom may suggest that disruptive behavior serves the function of helping him escape or avoid these task demands. In this case, providing remedial instruction or adjusting the level of task difficulty is a more appropriate response than punishing his undesired behavior (or reinforcing it by removing him from the classroom). Thus, knowledge about recurring setting event-antecedent-response-consequence relationships is important for intervention planning. However, the extensive social behavior repertoires of many students who exhibit behavioral disorders, as well as the complexity of their social interactions with peers and adults, renders the task of establishing functional relationships between their behavior and environmental variables extremely difficult, as the same target behavior may serve different functions in different settings (Shores et al., 1999).

Step 3: Assess the Validity of the Hypothesis

Our hypothesis about the relationship between Raymond's disruptive behavior and his teacher attending to it basically is an informed guess: When Raymond engages in disruptive behavior, we predict that his teacher is likely to attend. To the extent that such attention consistently follows his behavior, we can say that the function of Raymond's disruptive behavior is to gain teacher attention. However, at this point we have not *proven* that these events are functionally related. To demonstrate such proof (i.e., establish a causal relationship), it is necessary to change some of the variables involved and observe the effect on Raymond's behavior. We have observed that Raymond does not display disruptive behavior when he has the teacher's undivided attention. Therefore, one way to demonstrate a causal relationship is to assess Raymond's disruptions in situations where the teacher already is attending to him and when she is not. Another way is for the teacher not to respond to Raymond's disruptions and observe what happens to their frequency of occurrence. However, if Raymond's behavior functions to gain access to teacher attention, under the latter circumstance we would expect to see an immediate increase in disruptive behavior (see the discussion of extinction in Chapter 4). While this would validate our hypothesis, it also may create a situation that would be undesirable to the teacher. Fortunately, it isn't necessary to go through prolonged periods in which these conditions are in effect to validate a hypothesis. But

keep in mind that behavior is strongly influenced by contextual variables and other setting events (Conroy & Fox, 1994; Chandler, Fowler, & Lubeck, 1992; Shores et al., 1993). Thus, Raymond may be quite a bit more disruptive in a loosely structured language arts class than during a science lesson. Also, the same behavior may serve different functions in different settings, and very different behaviors (e.g., making barking noises, hand raising) may be equally effective in gaining attention. Therefore, it is often important to use a variety of methods to assess behavior and conduct assessments across multiple settings and sources to form a reasonable hypothesis.

Researchers refer to the process of changing conditions while observing their effects on the target behavior a **functional analysis,** because repeated demonstrations that the systematic alteration of certain events reliably increase or decrease a specific behavior indicate a predictable, functional relationship. For example, Lewis and Sugai (1996) hypothesized that peer and teacher attention was more likely following a 7-year-old boy's inappropriate behavior. To test this hypothesis, they conducted three 10-minute testing sessions that were repeated twice in a 1-hour reading period, with tasks and number of peers remaining constant in all sessions. In one session, the boy (Fred) was grouped with three peers who were observed to attend to him when he was off task. In this session, Fred's teacher was instructed to give him attention briefly and only once every 3 minutes. She also praised him for being on-task and redirected him when he was off-task. This was a high peer attention plus low teacher attention condition. In the second session, Fred was grouped with three peers who were not likely to attend to him, and the teacher delivered attention, praise, and redirects as before (low peer attention plus low teacher attention condition). In the third session, Fred was grouped with the three students who were likely to attend to his inappropriate behavior, and the teacher was prompted every 30 seconds to praise him for being on-task or to redirect him if he was off-task (high peer attention plus high teacher attention condition). Results showed that Fred engaged in the highest levels of off-task and the lowest levels of on-task behavior under the high peer attention plus low teacher attention condition. This analysis confirmed the researchers' hypothesis that Fred behaved less appropriately when he received more attention for disruptive behavior.

From a research perspective, a functional relationship cannot be scientifically proven without this level of functional analysis. However, Steege and Northup (1998) identified a range of functional assessment procedures, and evaluated the extent to which each strategy was useful in forming or confirming hypotheses regarding functional relationships. *Indirect assessment* procedures mainly rely upon interviews with persons who observe the behavior (archival records searches also would be classified as indirect). *Descriptive assessment* involves naturalistic observations of behavior, including A-B-C observations. *Brief functional analysis* entails observing target behavior in briefly alternating conditions (e.g., the procedure used by Lewis and Sugai, 1996). *Extended functional analysis* involves more prolonged exposure to each condition, usually across several sessions or days. Naturally, briefer and more indirect strategies are much simpler to implement, but at the expense of greater confidence in the validity of the hypotheses that are formed. Sugai (personal communication, 1999) offered practical advice for evaluating the validity of hypotheses. If, after using indirect and descriptive procedures to generate a hypothesis, the team has a high level of confidence in the hypothesis, a BIP based on the hypothesis (see Step 4) can be implemented. The team should gather direct observation data systematically for a sufficient period of time to evaluate the intervention. If behavior changes that are consistent with the hypothesis are observed, it is reasonable to assume that the hypothesis is valid and the intervention can be continued. If, however, the team does not feel confident in the hypothesis, or, if after the BIP has been implemented for several days the behavior does not change in the direction that would be

predicted based on the hypothesis, the FBA process should be continued. In any case, the target behavior should be directly monitored to evaluate the effects of the BIP. Data decision rules should be used as a basis for determining whether the plan, or the hypothesis, need to be revised.

If you have followed the steps to this point, you will have completed an FBA. Training in the FBA process is available in a variety of formats, including printed manuals (e.g., Gable, Quinn, Rutherford, Howell, & Hoffman, 1998; Nelson, Roberts, & Smith, 1999; O'Neill et al., 1997; Witt, Daly, & Noell, 2000) and CD-ROM (e.g., Liaupsin, Scott, & Nelson, 1999).

Step 4: Design an Intervention

If your FBA has been successful, you will have identified the function(s) served by the target behavior; that is, how the behavior "works" for the student. You also will have gathered additional information that is critical to the development of a BIP, including: (a) any setting events that increase the likelihood of the behavior; (b) specific antecedents that reliably predict the behavior; and (c) the outcome(s) or consequences that usually follow the target behavior. For example, social studies class appears to be a setting event for Raymond's disruptive behavior. The recurring antecedent event appears to be the teacher posing a question to the entire class, and the consequence is teacher attention. This information constitutes a **problem behavior pathway,** and it is useful to write down this sequence for analysis by the Behavior Support Team (see Figure 2-11).

At the same time, the team may identify the *desired* or expected behavior that should occur instead, as well as its typical outcome or consequence. These events can be identified by looking at what the other students do. The desired behavior for Raymond is to raise his hand and wait to be called upon before speaking. The consequence for this behavior is being called upon occasionally, and sometimes being praised for having the correct answer. In this case, hand raising and waiting

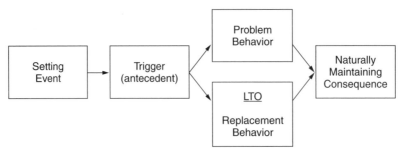

FIGURE 2-11   Functional behavior intervention pathways.

Note: Adapted from R. E. O'Neill, R. H. Horner, R. W. Albin, J. R. Sprague, and J. S. Newton. Functional Assessment and Program Development for Problem Behavior (2nd ed). Copyright 1997. Reprinted with permission of Wadsworth, an imprint of the Wadsworth Group, a division of Thomson Learning. Fax 800 730-2215.

to be called upon before speaking is a **replacement behavior**—a socially valid, effective, and efficient behavior that Raymond may use instead of blurting out. Identifying, teaching, and supporting replacement behaviors are critical features of BIPs. Replacement behaviors should be functional for the student—-that is, they should result in consequences that will maintain them. Table 2-3 illustrates functional replacement behaviors and their benefits.

The BIP must address two parallel intervention strategies: one to teach and support the replacement behavior, and one to correct or reduce the target behavior. The plan should insure that the target (undesired) behavior is no longer effective, efficient, or relevant to producing the outcomes it once did. On the other hand, the replacement behavior should be consistently effective, efficient, and relevant in terms of serving this function. To accomplish these goals, the BIP must address two issues: (a) where the student is with respect to the criterion (terminal skill level), and (b) what changes must be made in the environment to increase the student's fluency of performance and the likelihood that the replacement behavior will be used repeatedly and the target behavior will not.

INCREASING THE REPLACEMENT BEHAVIOR.
It is important to know whether the target behav-

ior reflects a deficit in the skills needed to perform as expected or a lack of incentive to perform as desired (Howell et al., 1993). For example, if a student lacks the skills necessary to gain peer attention appropriately, he may use undesired behavior to produce this effect. On the other hand, he may have the skills to perform as desired, but the problem behavior is more successful in producing outcomes that are rewarding to him. If the desired behavior is one the pupil *cannot* do (i.e., perhaps he lacks the necessary information or component skills), the appropriate intervention is instruction in the skill. Attempting to change the student's motivation to perform the skill through arranging positive or aversive consequences will be ineffective unless accompanied by relevant skill instruction. It is important to be sensitive to the possibility that pupils may be deficient in social skills. Often, teachers assume that undesired student behavior reflects the pupil's decision to misbehave. However, the student who lacks appropriate social behavior does not have a choice because alternative social behaviors are missing from his repertoire. As Howell et al. (1993) emphasize, students should be taught the social skills they lack rather than just receiving behavior management interventions to control their maladaptive behavior.

On the other hand, if the skill is something the student *can* perform (i.e., he has done it before or

TABLE 2-3 Functional Replacement Behaviors and Their Benefit

Predictor	Undesirable Behavior	Replacement Behavior and Contingency	Function of Both Behaviors	Benefit of Replacement Behavior
Addition problems with regrouping	Scream until thrown out of class	Raise hand to get assistance	Escape frustration	More math completed & less screaming
Line-up	Pushes peers and ends up at front of line	Don't touch anyone and is allowed to be the first one in line	Access first spot in line	No physical aggression in line
Reading groups	Refuses directions to read and ends up sitting alone at desk	Is allowed to sit and lay at desk after reading a predetermined number of pages	Escape from reading/access playing at desk	Student now gets some reading instruction
Robert	When Robert is near, student will engage in off-task behavior to get Robert's attention	Complete all assigned tasks and earn time to play alone with Robert	Access to Robert's attention	Student remains on-task and completes assigned tasks

From: T. M. Scott and C. M. Nelson. (1999), "Using Functional Behavioral Assessment to Develop Effective Intervention Plans: Practical Classroom Applications" Journal of Positive Behavioral Interventions, 1, pp. 242–251, copyright 1999 by PRO-ED, Inc. Reprinted with permission.

performs it in other settings), the problem behavior may be maintained by its consequences (i.e., accessing something desirable or avoiding something undesirable). In this case, the appropriate intervention consists of providing opportunities for the replacement behavior to occur, or removing obstacles to desired performance, and reinforcing the desired behavior when it occurs. At the same time, strategies are developed to reduce undesired behaviors by withholding or removing reinforcing consequences or by applying consequences designed to weaken the behavior.

Behavioral interventions would be simple if the only requirement were to tell the student what he should do and then reinforce him for doing it. But often, students either lack the skill to perform the replacement behavior or they have long histories of being reinforced for using the target behavior. Therefore, you must begin where the student is

now and work up to where you want him to be. Using the replacement behavior at rates typical of other students and with consequences that are naturally available to support it is a **long-term objective:** We want Raymond to raise his hand and wait to be called upon before speaking, which will be followed by intermittent teacher attention and praise. To get from the student's current level of performance to the long-term objective, we must think in terms of some intermediate steps or **short-term objectives.** This entails identifying some approximations to this objective, as well as strategies for addressing the consequences of both target and replacement behaviors. Regarding where to begin, a good rule of thumb is to start with the behavior the student gives you. For example, if Raymond has never raised his hand in social studies class (and that is an expectation the other students understand and meet), practice it with him in a direct instruction format (i.e., model the behavior, lead the student through its performance, test for acquisition, reward correct performance or correct errors). If Raymond can comply with the rule, but doesn't do it reliably, we look at his typical performance and set our first approximation (expectation) there. Thus, if he typically raises his hand and waits 5 seconds before speaking, we make sure to catch him as soon as he raises his hand, and provide attention (praise for hand raising). When we see an increase in compliance, we can increase the criterion to the next level (expecting him to wait a few more seconds).

As Scott and Nelson (1999) observe, it may be necessary to modify immediate goals so that the replacement behavior will serve the same function as the target behavior. For example, if the function of the target behavior is to escape or avoid an undesired academic task, it may be necessary to teach the student to use a replacement behavior that temporarily will serve the same function (e.g., asking to take a break, as opposed to creating a disruption). While this behavior is being taught, tasks can be simplified and reinforcement provided for **successive approximations** to the long-term objective.

Even though the student may have the skill to perform the desired replacement behavior, he isn't likely to do so without being directly taught. This is because the student has a history of using the target behavior successfully to produce a desired outcome. Introduction of the replacement behavior should be accompanied by a general rule and a rationale (Scott & Nelson, 1999). The rule explains when the behavior is appropriate, and the rationale describes what the consequences will be for using it. Thus, we teach Raymond the rule ("Raise your hand when you want to speak and wait for my permission before you do"), and explain the rationale for following it ("Each time you follow the rule, I will come and talk to you"). Following this introduction, the replacement behavior should be taught or practiced, using strategies that minimize failure and maximize success.

Again, replacement behaviors should serve the same function as target behaviors, but do so

more effectively and efficiently. Therefore, identify a signal that will indicate to the student when he should use the behavior. This may be a naturally occurring stimulus or time (e.g., be in your seat when the tardy bell rings) or a specific prompt (e.g., "Remember to ask for my help if you get stuck"). When the replacement behavior occurs in the presence of the stimulus, be sure to reinforce it immediately. Be prepared to prompt and guide the student to perform the replacement behavior. Remember, ensuring the student's success is the key.

It also is necessary to consider conditions in the environment that may either facilitate or inhibit the student's acquisition and use of the replacement behavior. If FBA data suggest times of the day, settings, or specific antecedent events that increase the likelihood that the replacement behavior will be used, incorporate this information into the BIP. For example, if one student is a particularly good role model for following the hand raising rule, we could seat this student by Raymond. We may even teach this student to prompt Raymond at intervals throughout the class period ("Remember the rule about hand raising"). Conversely, if there are circumstances that increase the likelihood of failure, the BIP should include strategies for avoiding these. For instance, we could move peers who are likely to respond to Raymond's blurting out further away, and place him next to students who are better at ignoring his inappropriate behavior (also, peers can be taught to ignore, and be reinforced for doing so).

REDUCING THE TARGET BEHAVIOR. The BIP also must address the issue of managing the target behavior. It is unrealistic to expect students to discard behaviors that have been successful in meeting their needs for some time. However, the focus of the plan is on teaching and reinforcement of the desired replacement behavior. Sugai (1995) suggests that instances of the target behavior be regarded as errors rather than intentional misbehaviors. The appropriate response to a mistake is to provide an error correction procedure ("No, remember the rule about hand raising"), not punishment. However, reductive procedures may be required if the target behavior poses a risk to the safety of the student himself or to others, or if it interferes with learning.[4] A review of alternative strategies for reducing undesired behavior is provided in Chapter 4, and Chapters 6 through 9 provide examples of methods for reducing problem behavior. At this point, we reiterate that the plan should insure that the target behavior is no longer effective, efficient, or relevant to serving the functions that it once did, whereas the replacement behavior is highly effective, efficient, and relevant (Sugai, 1995). The *difference* between what happens when the target and the replacement behaviors occur is more important than the magnitude of punishment that can be delivered.

Just as you should assess the environment for conditions that make the student's success (use of the replacement behavior) more or less likely and adjust these to increase the likelihood of success and reduce failure, you should also look for conditions that support or discourage use of the target behavior and modify these. By anticipating and correcting these circumstances before the target behavior has a chance to occur, we again minimize the need for punishment.

Nevertheless, if the target behavior poses a danger to the student or to others, the BIP must include strategies for crisis management. The Positive Behavioral Support Project (1999, p. 60) defines a crisis as an "unforeseen combination of circumstances posing continuous risk that calls for immediate action." Procedures for dealing with such situations should include strategies that will insure safety and rapid de-escalation of the crisis. Emergency procedures are not part of regular programmatic intervention, but are rather, reactive

strategies to prevent students who are engaging in self-injurious, aggressive, or destructive behavior from harming themselves or others. *Use of emergency procedures should be regarded as evidence that the BIP is in need of revision.* Crisis intervention plans should be monitored carefully, and if it cannot be documented that their use is decreasing over time, or if implementation of emergency procedures provokes emotional reactions from the student, the plan should be revised immediately. If emergency procedures are to be considered in conjunction with a BIP, consult your school district or agency's policies and obtain the necessary permissions from your agency and the student's caregivers (see Chapter 4). You also may need to obtain training or consultation from persons who are skilled in safe physical management procedures (Positive Behavioral Support Project, 1999).

Finally, the Behavior Support Team should obtain input from the student's educational management team (e.g., IEP team) and BIPs should be integrated into his overall program and daily routines. For example, plan goals should be written into IEPs or Accommodation Plans. At a minimum, BIPs should include descriptions of the target and replacement behaviors; intervention goals; strategies to prevent, replace, and manage target behavior(s); and mechanisms for insuring implementation and progress. Particularly if the BIP was developed in response to an incident that invoked consideration of or placement in an alternative educational setting, the team should carefully document the procedures used throughout the process (Positive Behavioral Support Project, 1999).

Step 5: Collect Data on Intervention Effectiveness and Adjust the Plan as Needed

Figure 2-12 presents a flow chart to assist you in evaluating the BIP in terms of increasing replacement behavior and decreasing the problem behavior. Careful and continuous monitoring of the effects of the BIP on the target and replacement

---

[4]Bear in mind that the target behavior will have a history of being effective and efficient in terms of the function it has performed. Therefore, just using a correction procedure when it occurs may not be sufficient (particularly when paired with a powerful reinforcer such as teacher attention). Under these circumstances, the BIP should include planned reductive consequences.

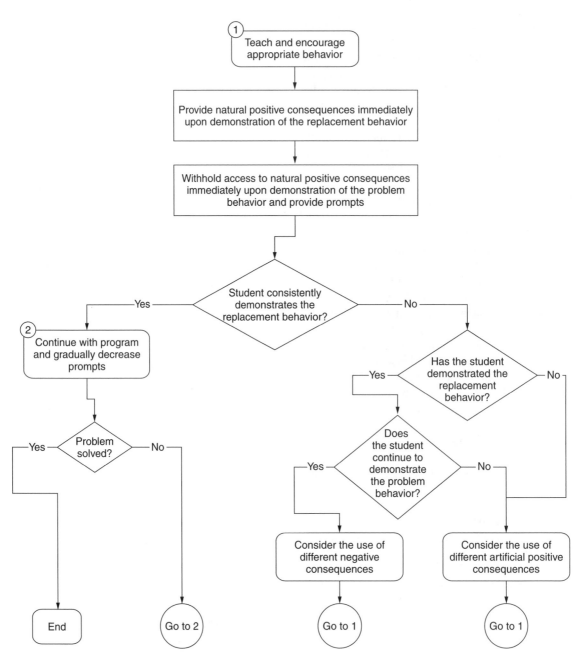

FIGURE 2-12 Consequence planning decision model.
Note: *Copyright 2000 by T. M. Scott. Used with permission.*

behaviors is critical to ensuring that the plan is working. Moreover, the team needs to be accountable to the school district or agency, and to the student's caregivers. At a minimum, data should be collected on rates of occurrence of the target behavior. We strongly recommend that occurrences of the replacement behavior be documented with equal rigor, given the BIPs focus on promoting the latter. Informal, subjective evaluations of progress are not a sufficient basis for making the kinds of sensitive intervention decisions required for adjusting BIPs. The data collected provide the basis for making decisions regarding the need for adjustments in the plan. Therefore, the team should not only gather direct observation data on the behaviors of concern, but also should use these data in making intervention decisions. Strategies for observing and recording behavioral data, as well as for making data decision rules, are presented in Chapter 3.

The long-term and intermediate objectives established for BIPs provide a framework for data collection and evaluation of the plan. Thus, the objective "During social studies class, Raymond will raise his hand and wait to be called upon before speaking on 100% of opportunities for 5 consecutive days" suggests that we should monitor hand raising and blurting out. The intermediate or short-term objective, "Given a prompt at the beginning of social studies class to remember to raise his hand, Raymond will raise his hand on 80% of the opportunities" indicates a progress marker after the intervention has been in place for a while. If short-term objectives are not met, the Behavior Support Team should reassess the intervention by looking at the data patterns, reanalyzing FBA data, or conducting additional assessments. Based on these analyses, several adjustments to the BIP may be made. The plan may be continued, but with an abbreviated timeline for evaluating outcomes. Alternately, it may be changed in some way (e.g., adding or deleting prompts, changing criteria for performance, changing consequences, redefining the behavior, or teaching a prerequisite skill that has not been mastered. Finally, the plan may be re-

placed entirely (Scott & Nelson, 1999).[5] Again, *if the plan isn't working, change the plan*; don't eject the student from the program.

The case study at the end of this chapter illustrates a BIP. Notice that the format and sequence of steps do not conform to the steps just described. However, it does include all of the essential components. Additional training in developing, implementing, and evaluating BIPs is available, again in several different formats (e.g., Gable, Quinn, Rutherford, Howell, & Hoffman, 2000; Liaupsin, Scott, & Nelson, 2001; Positive Behavioral Support Project, 1999). This chapter concludes with suggestions for writing long-term goals and objectives and breaking them down into intermediate steps. Chapters 3 and 4 provide guidelines and strategies for monitoring progress and adjusting interventions.

INTERVENTION OBJECTIVES AND TASK ANALYSIS

The beginning point of intervention, whether it consists of skill instruction or behavior management, is to write behavioral objectives that describe the behavior to be achieved following intervention. A well-written behavioral objective specifies in observable and measurable terms the terminal behavior the student is to demonstrate, the conditions under which the behavior should occur, and the criteria for acceptable performance (Mager, 1962). Table 2-4 contains examples of acceptable and unacceptable terminal instructional objectives.

Maheady, Harper, Mallette, and Sacca (1989) analyzed the IEP objectives of students who exhibit social behavior problems. They determined that the objectives for these students, who were certified as having EBD, reflected a preponderance of academic targets and few social behavioral objectives. The written social objectives tended to target behaviors related to the completion of academic tasks, such as staying on-task, completing work, and turning in assignments on time. It has been our experience that

[5]See Chapter 3 for guidelines regarding data collection and decision making.

TABLE 2-4 Acceptable and Unacceptable Instructional Objectives

Instructional Objectives	Acceptable?	Reason (If Unacceptable)
1. Arnold will behave in gym class.	No	Behavior and criteria not specified
2. Given a 45-minute study hall, Sally will remain on-task 90 percent of the time.	No	On-task behavior not specified; impossible to assess "90 percent of the time"
3. Yen-Su will interact with her peers with no hitting, kicking, biting, pushing, or verbal taunting for 30-minute lunch periods for 5 consecutive days.	Yes	
4. Washington will be punctual in arriving at school for 15 consecutive days.	No	"Punctual" not defined
5. When given a task request. Tanya will begin the task within 10 seconds without stating "I can't".	Yes	
6. Karen will refrain from biting or scratching herself for any given one-hour period.	No	Conditions not specified (i.e., instruction, prompts, or supervision to be provided during the hour)
7. Yolonda will not take any drugs during school for 20 consecutive days.	No	Impossible to monitor during intake accurately
8. When approached by a peer, Philip will emit an appropriate greeting response (make eye contact, smile, and say "hello") on 10 of 10 trials.	Yes	

many written objectives for social behaviors are inappropriate, not because the teacher failed to specify the behavior in observable and measurable terms, but for the following reasons. First, the conditions or criteria for the objective sometimes are meaningless (e.g., "90% of the time" suggests that the teacher will be observing the student constantly). Second, objectives often are not matched to the behavior that is desired (e.g., "Tony will demonstrate that he understands the classroom rules by coming to class on time"). Finally, objectives may not be matched to the intervention strategy used (e.g., "Given immediate positive consequences for completing her math assignments, Renee will remain on task for 80% of five consecutive math periods"). Less frequently, objectives are beyond the student's ability to reach or expect performance well above that of typical peers (e.g., "Linda will be on task 100% of the period"). With practice and feedback, you will become proficient at writing good instructional objectives for social skills.

Long-term behavioral objectives indicate relatively long-range desired outcomes of intervention strategies. The student may have none or some of the skills he needs to perform the desired behavior. Once you have written the objective, it is important to know whether he can perform all necessary components of the terminal behavior, because this information will affect the strategies you will use to get him there. The best way to assess the skills pupils need in order to perform a particular task (or to engage in a desired social behavior) is to observe their attempts to perform it. This establishes a starting point. Next you should conduct a **task analysis.** Essentially, task analysis is a fine-grained assessment of a task; that is, the task is broken down into sequential component steps. The number of components depends on the

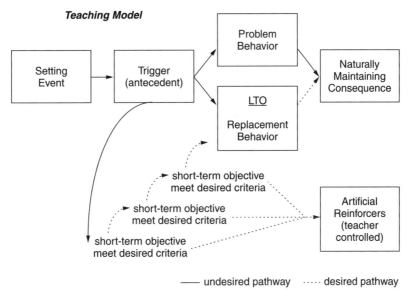

FIGURE 2-13 Teaching through successive approximations.
Copyright 1997 by T. M. Scott. Used with permission.

complexity of the task and the entry skills of the pupil (the skills the student brings to the task). A task analysis can be done by performing the task oneself, by observing someone who is proficient do it, or by outlining a logical sequence of steps (Wolery, Ault, & Doyle, 1992).

Analyzing academic or motor tasks is relatively simple. For example, most teachers are familiar with the component steps involved in solving two-place addition problems. Social skills are more difficult to analyze by task, however. One reason is that many social behaviors are performed without obvious, discrete steps. Another reason is that most persons are not accustomed to analyzing social skills systematically. Organize task steps according to one, or a combination, of the following:

1. A change in response criterion (e.g., a systematic increase in length of time engaged in desired play behavior across days or trials)
2. A progression through a sequence of discrete skills (e.g., learning social greeting responses)

3. A change in response **topography** (e.g., controlling one's temper by substituting verbal for physical reactions, such as counting to ten silently)

Once you have constructed a task sequence, assess the pupil with respect to the component steps. The evaluation will help you determine where to begin instruction and how to revise your sequence if needed. The steps included in your program can be written as instructional objectives and matched to teaching methods and materials. This then constitutes your intervention plan for a target behavior. Describe it in general terms on the student's IEP and develop it more specifically in your weekly and daily lesson plans. Your plan is not inflexible; it should be adjusted and revised as indicated by your continued assessment of the student's progress. Chapter 3 describes this phase of monitoring progress.

Figure 2-13 illustrates the process of sequencing short-term objectives to approximate a replacement behavior specified in a long-term objective.

Note that each occurrence of short-term approximations to the replacement behavior should be followed by reinforcing consequences. Because it often is not possible to arrange for these approximations to result in the outcome (function) produced by the target behavior (e.g., avoidance of difficult or undesired tasks), it may be necessary to use artificial reinforcers that are controlled by the teacher (e.g., points that can be exchanged for free time). Once the replacement behavior (e.g., asking for assistance with difficult tasks) has become established, the natural consequence (avoidance of difficult work) will be effective (e.g., the student uses the replacement behavior successfully to get assistance, thereby reducing task difficulty). For example, an early short-term objective for Raymond may be: "Given a reminder at the beginning of social studies class to raise his hand before he speaks, Raymond will raise his hand and wait to be called upon before speaking on 50% of opportunities for 2 consecutive days." Each time he remembers to use this rule, he earns a point. When he raises his hand at least half of the opportunities, he can cash in his points for time with the teacher at the end of class. Each time he meets a criterion, the standard is increased slightly. His teacher also praises his hand raising, and tries to respond to this behavior immediately and frequently. Ultimately, the function served by the target behavior (getting the teacher's attention) is better served by the replacement behavior, and the artificial consequence can be faded out.

SUMMARY

Conducting behavioral assessments involves gathering data from multiple sources of information and assessment strategies. Functional behavioral assessment is a specific example of behavioral assessment. The outcome of an FBA is a hypothesis regarding the function, or purpose, of the target behavior; that is, how it works for the student. All behavior, whether desired or undesired by others, serves one of two functions: To gain access to something desired, or to escape or avoid something aversive. Data gathered from the FBA process guide the development, implementation, and evaluation of a BIP, which includes strategies for teaching and supporting desired replacement behaviors as well as for preventing and responding to instances of targeted undesired behavior. The focus of assessment-based intervention planning is on the student's success. The BIP emphasizes strategies that strengthen replacement behaviors while seeking to prevent the occurrence of target behaviors, thereby minimizing the use of punishment. This is an important process that should be directed by a Behavior Support Team that includes persons with expertise in designing and evaluating behavioral interventions. Long-term and intermediate behavioral objectives are used to evaluate the student's progress.

DISCUSSION QUESTIONS

1. A student with a disability has demonstrated a pattern of aggressive behavior. What steps should the IEP team take before considering placement in an alternative educational setting?
2. For the situation described in Question 1, indicate several alternate instruments and procedures you could use to conduct an FBA. What questions would you attempt to answer through this process?
3. What are the components of a BIP? How should it be developed, implemented, and evaluated?
4. Assuming that the function of a student's physical aggression is to obtain items from peers, what are some replacement behaviors that the student can use to achieve this goal more appropriately?
5. What is a behavioral objective for reducing physical aggression? Write one and analyze it into three to five sequential steps.

A Behavior Intervention Plan for Tony

Wendy Mager

Tony Simpson is a 6-year-old first grader at a public elementary school. His teachers were very concerned about a range of behavior problems. The primary problem is Tony's disruptive and noncompliant behavior. During class time, Tony is highly impulsive. He gets out of his seat without permission, talks out of turn, and gets very frustrated if he has to wait for the teacher's attention. He also fails to respond to directions, especially those involving requests to engage in academic tasks.

Another problem is that Tony responds inappropriately to teacher discipline. He often does not comply with teacher attempts to redirect his behavior. When consequences are delivered, Tony becomes very hostile and disrespectful. He often yells at the teachers, making statements such as, "I didn't do anything wrong," and "That's not fair."

The third concern is Tony's inattentive behaviors during class lessons. During group work or when the teacher is providing instruction, he tends to be off-task, often sitting at the back of the area, away from others, focusing on things other than the lesson. He often looks at and fidgets with things around him (objects unrelated to the lesson). After a lesson is completed and students are working independently on an assignment, Tony has difficulty concentrating on his work. He typically hurries through the assignment, then moves on to enjoyable activities (i.e., computer) or asks the teacher, "What's next?"

Tony's behavior problems occur mostly during academic instruction times at school. They are far less severe during recess/lunchtime, and during the after-school program that Tony attends at his school. The problems seem especially noticeable during two class periods: "Special Class" (which occurs at mid-day, with subject matter rotating among computer, art, and physical education), and math class (which is the last period of the day). He also has great difficulty maintaining appropriate behavior during transitions between activities and when there is any change to the regular daily schedule (e.g., special assembly, vision screening, guest speaker in class, etc.).

The Behavior Support Team agreed that these problems merited intervention because they significantly interfere with Tony being successful at school. He currently is having difficulty being successful in both the academic and social domains, and there is reason to believe the behavior problems are associated with his academic deficits. Tony shows average or above-average learning ability, but he is functioning in the below-average range of academic achievement. Socially, Tony is fairly isolated. The other children in the class tend to ignore him; they seem to neither actively reject nor especially like him. Recently, he has made one friend—a boy in his class who has very similar behavior problems. They seem to "feed off" of one another, getting into more trouble together than either one does alone. Furthermore, Tony's behavior problems warrant intervention because they interfere with the other students' rights to a calm, orderly learning environment.

Two A-B-C assessments were completed from observations of Tony conducted in the classroom. An analysis of this information was used to develop a hypothesis about the function(s) of Tony's behavior. Tony frequently failed to comply with teacher directions by not engaging in tasks when asked, talking out without permission, and being out-of-seat. These problems seemed especially likely during transitions between activities, in math class, and in "special" classes (like art and physical education).

Several antecedent events appeared to be more immediately predictive of problem behavior. First, the presence of another boy with similar behavior problems seemed to precipitate Tony's disruptive behavior. The two boys have been described as "magnetically drawn to one another." Except for this boy, Tony tends to react negatively to directions or requests from peers. In addition, teacher warnings of impending consequences, prompts to correct his behavior or to begin work, and delivery of negative consequences for misbehavior tended to precede larger behavior problems.

Tony's teachers ignored his nondisruptive problem behavior (e.g., inattention) but when he continued to leave his seat, ignoring verbal warnings (or "marks"), he was sent to time-out for 10 minutes in a chair in an isolated section of a neighboring classroom—he pleaded with the teacher not to make him go. He was allowed to return to his classroom after the 10 minutes had elapsed and after he had completed a "reentry" sheet, which involved drawing pictures—one depicting his rule violation and another showing how he could avoid it in the future. His reentry sheet was completed by the end of the 10-minute period. Upon returning, he was directed to complete all academic work missed during the time-out, refused, and again ended up in time-out. Although teachers reported praising Tony for appropriate behavior, several brief instances of appropriate behavior received no teacher acknowledgment.

Tony himself was not interviewed about the reasons for his behavior; but his teachers were asked their impressions of Tony's reasoning. They stated that Tony almost always claims that he gets in trouble because others treat him badly—that other children provoke him and that teachers pick on him.

It was hypothesized that Tony's noncompliant and disruptive behavior functions to help him avoid tasks that are difficult for him. His rule-breaking and hasty work habits are seen as attempts to minimize the amount of time he has to spend engaged in academic tasks, particularly math. He also finds it difficult to tolerate teacher reprimands and discipline and thus avoids such by resorting to angry outbursts, which typically result in removal from the situation.

To test these hypotheses, Tony's teachers gave him a set of simple math problems. Under this condition, Tony engaged in very little off-task and inattentive behavior. In addition, the teachers did not reprimand or lecture Tony about instances of noncompliance. Tony's outbursts decreased in frequency under this condition, indicating a relationship between reprimands and outbursts. While these testing procedures resulted in a decrease in problem behavior, neither was seen as an intervention as neither was instructional to Tony. The hypothesis was validated and it appears that the function of Tony's behavior is to avoid or escape work and negative teacher attention.

To measure Tony's compliance with academic task requests, it was decided that the teacher would count the number of task requests that she makes of Tony (either individually or to the whole class) during math period each day. She also will note the number of requests with which Tony complies. Specifically, Ms. Magee will make a tally mark on her clipboard each time she gave a task direction that involved Tony (i.e., opportunity) and will circle the tally if Tony followed the direction within 10 seconds. Data will be summarized each day as the percentage of opportunities in which Tony complied with directions.

Figure A shows the BIP that the team developed for Tony.

Student: _Tony_   Teacher: _Ms. Quincy, Ms. Magee_

School: _Lee Elementary_   Date: _10/2_

Step	Action	Outcomes
1	Identify the function of the behavior. • Describe the behavior in measurable terms? • How does the behavior meet the student's needs?	*Disruptive, non-compliant behavior.* *Tony is non-compliant or disruptive to escape or avoid difficult tasks and negative teacher attention.*
2	Select a replacement behavior. • What should the student do instead? • What do successful students do? • Will the behavior help the student meet their needs?	*Tony will ask for help with difficult problems and ask to take a break when he gets frustrated.*
3	Design a teaching plan. The expected behavior includes: • Conditions • Behavior Teaching examples should: • Describe when to use the behavior • Be realistic Non-examples should: • Describe when *not* to use the behavior • Be realistic	**Expected behavior** *Tony will comply with teacher requests.* **Teaching examples** *Teach and review school rule, "follow all staff directions" with all students.* *Conduct individual sessions with Tony preceding transitions or non-preferred activities.* **Non-examples** *If Billy tells you to do something you know is wrong.* **Models and/or demonstrations** *Role play following directions with whole class.* *Teach Tony to raise his hand for help and ask for a break when he needs one.*
4	Arrange the environment to facilitate success. Consider changes to • Physical environment • Classroom procedures • Task requirements • Teacher-student interactions	**Problem situations** *(1) Tony and Billy together; (2) Work above Tony's level; (3) Lecturing; (4) Failure to reinforce requests.* **Promote success** *(1) Separate Tony and Billy; (2) Ensure work at Tony's level; (3) Don't lecture (4) Plan opportunities to reinforce requests.*

(Continued)

FIGURE A   Behavior Intervention Plan.

Step	Action	Outcomes
5	Develop consequences for desired and undesired behavior.	**Natural positive consequences** *Immediate praise for requesting help and compliance with directions.* **Withholding access to natural positive consequences** *Do not remove task demand when Tony is disruptive.* **Prompts** *Corrective prompts: "What is the rule about following directions?" "What should you do if a problem is too difficult?"* **Artificial positive consequences** *One point for each hand raise or direction followed; exchanged at end of each period for free time.* **Negative consequences** *Loss of point for each instance of non-compliance.*
	• If the replacement is not exhibited despite natural positive consequences and prompts.	
	• If the problem behavior continues despite natural consequences and prompts.	
6	Develop a plan for monitoring the behavior.	**Measurement procedures** *Count number of directions given (opportunities) in one period and number complied with; divide the latter by the number of opportunities and multiply by 100 to get % compliance.*
7	Write behavioral objectives. • Conditions • Learner • Behavior • Criteria	*Given a task direction by the teacher, Tony will comply within 10 seconds during at least 80% of opportunities for 4 consecutive days by the end of the semester.*

FIGURE A Behavior Intervention Plan—*Continued.*

REFERENCES

Algozzine, B., Ruhl, K., & Ramsey, R. (1991). *Behaviorally disordered? Assessment for identification and instruction*. Reston, VA: Council for Exceptional Children.

Chandler, L. K., Fowler, S. A., & Lubeck, R. C. (1992). An analysis of the effects of multiple setting events on the social behavior of preschool children with special needs. *Journal of Applied Behavior Analysis, 25,* 249–263.

Conroy, M. A., & Fox, J. J. (1994). Setting events and challenging behaviors in the classroom: Incorporating contextual factors into effective intervention plans. *Preventing School Failure, 38*(3), 29–34.

Durand, V. M., & Crimmins, D. B. (1992). *The motivation assessment scale*. Topeka, KS: Monaco.

Finch, A. J., Jr., & Rodgers, T. R. (1984). Self-report instruments. In T. H. Ollendick & M. Hersen (Eds.), *Child behavior assessment: Principles and procedures* (pp. 106–123). New York: Pergamon

Gable, R. A., Quin, M. M., Rutherford, R. B., Howell, K. W., & Hoffman, C. C. (1998, May). *Addressing student problem behavior—Part II: Conducting a functional behavioral assessment*. Washington, DC: Center for Effective Collaboration and Practice.

Gable, R. A., Quinn, M. M., Rutherford, R. B., Howell, K. W., & Hoffman, C. C. (2000, June). *Addressing student problem behavior—Part III: Creating positive behavioral intervention plans and supports*. Washington, DC: Center for Effective Collaboration and Practice.

Gross, A. M. (1984). Behavioral interviewing. In T. H. Ollendick & M. Hersen (Eds.), *Child behavioral assessment: Principles and procedures* (pp. 61–79). New York: Pergamon Press.

Heckaman, K., Conroy, M., Fox, J., & Chait, A. (2000). Functional assessment-based intervention research on students with or at risk for emotional and behavioral disorders in school settings. *Behavioral Disorders, 25,* 196–210.

Hops, H., & Greenwood, C. R. (1981). Social skills deficits. In E. J. Mash & L. G. Terdal (Eds.), *Behavioral assessment of childhood disorders* (pp. 347–396). New York: Guilford Press.

Hops, H., & Lewin, L. (1984). Peer sociometric forms. In T. H. Ollendick & M. Hersen (Eds.), *Child behavioral assessment: Principles and procedures* (pp. 124–147). New York: Pergamon Press.

Howell, K. W., Fox, S. L., & Morehead, M. K. (1993). *Curriculum-based evaluation: Teaching and decision making* (2nd ed.). Pacific Grove, CA: Brooks/Cole.

Kern, L., Childs, K. E., Dunlap, G., Clarke, S., & Falk, G. D. (1994). Using assessment-based curricular intervention to improve the classroom behavior of a student with emotional and behavioral challanges. *Journal of Applied Behavior Analysis, 27,* 7–19.

Lewis, T., Scott, T., & Sugai, G. (1994). The problem behavior questionnaire: A teacher based instrument to develop functional hypotheses of problem behavior in general education classrooms. *Diagnostique, 19*(2–3), 59–78.

Lewis, T. J., & Sugai, G. (1996). Functional assessment of problem behavior: A pilot investigation of the comparative and interactive effects of teacher and peer social attention on students in general education settings. *School Psychology Quarterly, 11,* 1–19.

Liaupsin, C. J., Scott, T. M., & Nelson, C. M. (2001). *Functional behavioral assessment: An interactive training module* [CD-ROM]. Longmont, CO: Sopris West.

Mager, R. F. (1962). *Preparing instructional objectives*. Palo Alto, CA: Fearon Press.

Maheady, L., Harper, G. F., Mallette, B., & Sacca, M. K. (1989, September). Opportunity to learn prosocial behavior: Its potential role in the assessment and instruction of behavior disordered students. Paper presented at the CEC/CCBD Topical Conference on Behaviorally Disordered Youth, Charlotte, North Carolina.

McIntyre, T. (1996). Guidelines for providing appropriate services to culturally diverse students with emotional and behavioral disorders. *Behavioral Disorders, 21,* 137–144.

McMahon, R. J. (1984). Behavioral checklists and rating scales. In T. H. Ollendick & M. Hersen (Eds.), *Child behavioral assessment: Principles and procedures.* (pp. 80–105). New York: Pergamon Press.

Nelson, J. R., Roberts, M., & Smith, D. (1999). *Conducting functional behavioral assessments: A practical guide*. Longmont, CO: Sopris West.

O'Neill, R. E., Horner, R. H., Albin, R. W., Storey, K., & Sprague, J. R. (1997). *Functional assessment and program development for problem behavior: A practical assessment handbook* (2nd ed.). Pacific Grove, CA: Brooks/Cole.

Polsgrove, L. (1987). Assessment of children's social and behavioral problems. In W. H. Berdine & S. A. Meyer (Eds.), *Assessment in special education* (pp. 141–180). Boston: Little, Brown.

Positive Behavioral Support Project. (November, 1999). *Facilitator's guide: Positive behavioral support*. Tallahassee, FL: Florida Department of Education.

Scott, T. M., Liaupsin, C. J., & Nelson, C. M. (2001). *Behavior interventions planning: A CD training module.* Longmont, CO: Sopris West.

Scott, T. M., & Nelson, C. M. (1999). Using functional behavioral assessment to develop effective intervention plans: Practical classroom applications. *Journal of Positive Behavioral Interventions, 1,* 242–251.

Shores, R. E., Jack, S. L., Gunter, P. L., Ellis, D. N., DeBriere, T. J., & Wehby, J. H. (1993). Classroom interactions of children with behavior disorders. *Journal of Emotional and Behavioral Disorders, 1,* 27–39.

Shores, R. E., Wehby, J. H., & Jack, S. L. (1999). Analyzing behavior in classrooms. In A. C. Repp & R. H. Horner (Eds.), *Functional analysis of problem behavior: From effective assessment to effective support,* pp. 219–237. Baltimore, MD: Paul H. Brookes.

Steege, M. W., & Northup, J. (1998). Functional analysis of problem behavior: A practical approach for school psychologists. *Proven Practice, 1*(1), 4–11.

Sugai, G. (1995, June). *Proactive classroom management.* Workshop presented at the Springfield School Improvement Conference, Springfield, OR.

Sugai, G., Horner, R. H., Dunlap, G., Hieneman, M., Lewis, T. J., Nelson, C. M., Scott, T., Liaupsin, C., Sailor, W., Turnbull, A. P., Turnbull, H. R. III, Wickham, D., Wilcox, B., & Ruef, M. (2000). Applying positive behavior support and functional behavioral assessment in schools. *Journal of Positive Behavior Interventions, 2,* 131–143.

Touchette, P. E., MacDonald, R. F., & Langer, S. N. (1985). A scatter plot for identifying stimulus control of problem behavior. *Journal of Applied Behavior Analysis, 18,* 343–351.

Walker, H. M. (1983). *Walker problem behavior identification checklist.* Los Angeles: Western Psychological Services.

Walker, H. M. (1986). The AIMS (Assessments for Integration into Mainstream Settings) assessment system: Rationale, instruments, procedures, and outcomes. *Journal of Clinical Child Psychology, 15* (1), 55–63.

Walker, H. M., Block-Pedego, A., Todis, B., & Severson, H. (1991). *The school archival records search.* Longmount, CO: Sopris West.

Walker, H. M., & Fabre, T. R. (1987). Assessment of behavior disorders in the school setting: Issues, problems and strategies revisited. In N. G. Haring (Ed.), *Assessing and managing behavior disabilities* (pp. 198–243). Seattle: University of Washington Press.

Walker, H. M., & Rankin, R. (1980). *The SBS inventory of teacher social behavior standards and expectations.* Eugene, OR: SBS Project, University of Oregon.

Walker, H. M., & Severson, H. (1990). *Systematic screening for behavioral disorders.* Longmont, CO: Sopris West.

Walker, H. M., Severson, H., & Haring, N. (1986). *Standardized screening and identification of behavior disordered pupils in the elementary age range: Rationale, procedures and guidelines.* Eugene, OR: University of Oregon.

Wehby, J. H. (1994). Issues in the assessment of aggressive behavior. *Preventing School Failure, 38*(3), 24–28.

Witt, J. C., Daly, E. J., & Noell, G. H. (2000). *Functional assessments: A step-by-step guide to solving academic and behavior problems.* Longmont, CO: Sopris West.

Wolery, M., Ault, M. J., & Doyle, P. M. (1992). *Teaching students with moderate and severe disabilities: Use of response prompting strategies.* White Plains, NY: Longman.

Wolf, M. M. (1978). Social validity: The case for subjective measurement or how applied behavior analysis is finding its heart. *Journal of Applied Behavior Analysis, 11,* 203–214.

3
CHAPTER
KEEPING TRACK OF STUDENT PROGRESS

OUTLINE

OBJECTIVES

After completing this chapter, you should be able to

- Select alternate ways to measure targeted behaviors that take into consideration the characteristics of the behavior, the setting, constraints on data collection, and the person collecting the data.
- Explain and illustrate the following measurement strategies so that a parent or paraprofessional could use them: permanent product recording, event recording, trials to criterion recording, duration and response latency recording, interval recording, and time sampling.
- Design an appropriate recording strategy for two or more target behaviors, or for monitoring multiple students who are exhibiting similar target behaviors.
- Given event or interval data collected simultaneously by two observers, select the appropriate formula for calculating interobserver agreement and calculate interobserver agreement correctly.
- Summarize and graph or chart data using techniques appropriate for the data.
- Visually analyze graphed data and write data decision rules.

In the previous chapters, we discussed assessment strategies and procedures that guide screening, identification, and assessment planning. If you follow the assessment sequence that we have been describing, you should be able to determine which students are in need of interventions that address their academic and social behavior and which behaviors you are going to target for specific interventions. You also should know how to develop an assessment-based behavior intervention plan. In this chapter, you will learn strategies and techniques for monitoring and summarizing the progress of students for whom you have developed intervention plans that address either academic or social behaviors. This chapter serves as an important bridge to Chapter 4, which presents strategies for selecting and evaluating interventions on the basis of your measures of student performance, as well as guidelines for selecting the most appropriate intervention procedures. Thus, the precise and systematic monitoring of student progress provides data upon which to base decisions regarding instructional and behavior management interventions.

Evaluating intervention programs involves many complex decisions: Should you continue with an intervention, discard it, or modify it? Is the pupil ready to move on to more complex skills or to less restrictive settings, or does he need more training at his current skill level and in the present setting? To make good decisions, you must have useful information. In behavior change programs involving powerful methods that can be misapplied, student progress must not be evaluated subjectively or casually. As White (1986) explained, "to be responsive to the pupil's needs the teacher must be a student of the pupil's behavior, carefully analyzing how that behavior changes from day to day and adjusting the instructional plan as necessary to facilitate continued learning" (p. 522). Careful monitoring is a critical element of your role as an intervention agent.

To be an effective teacher—that is, to ensure that your students are progressing as rapidly as their capacities and present educational technol-

ogy allow—you need a system for monitoring their progress on a frequent and regular basis. Because your daily planning depends upon the information you obtain from such monitoring, you are, in effect, conducting ongoing assessments of your students throughout the school year. The data you obtain serve as a basis for evaluating pupil growth, for locating flaws or deficiencies in your instructional programs or behavior intervention plans, and for evaluating the effects of program modifications. You can also improve your use of pupil performance data by implementing **data decision rules,** which are teacher-determined guidelines for responding to patterns in student performance. Data decision rules are developed by the teacher to facilitate the efficient and effective evaluation of instructional and behavior management programs. You will find guidelines for developing data decision rules at the end of this chapter.

Some educators may be able to function adequately without using systematic procedures such as those described in this text. Continuous monitoring and evaluation of student progress is one of the most time consuming of these procedures. Because most public school and educational agencies do not require teachers to monitor student progress continuously, it is the first set of skills lost from a beginning teacher's repertoire. Nevertheless, effective teachers constantly monitor, evaluate, and revise their instructional programs and intervention plans. Consequently, they are more sensitive to the instructional needs of their pupils, and they are accountable to students, supervisors, and parents for the methods they use. If you want to be an effective teacher, you must expect to spend much time and effort collecting student performance data and planning and implementing systematic interventions. The result will be greater pride in your own skill as a teacher, the recognition of fellow professionals, and more rapid progress by your students. Fuchs and Fuchs (1986) found that students whose programs are systematically monitored and adjusted through ongoing data-based evaluation procedures make greater gains than students whose programs are not monitored systematically or formatively evaluated.

We begin this chapter with an overview of measurement procedures, including common objections to student performance measurement, frequently asked questions about monitoring student performance, and the use of measurement in IEPs. Next, we present measurement considerations, followed by step-by-step procedures for data collection, assessing the accuracy of behavioral measurement, and summarizing and visually displaying data. A number of alternate strategies are described and illustrated.

OVERVIEW OF CLASSROOM MEASUREMENT

Teacher Objections to Systematic Measurement of Student Progress

Educators and supervisors lament the tendency of classroom teachers to avoid data collection, despite the emphasis placed on this function in preservice training. The most common objections are presented below, and strategies for addressing these concerns are mentioned. These strategies are described in greater detail later in this chapter.

1. **"I don't have enough time to monitor their behavior—I have to teach."** Walton (1985) surveyed general and special education teachers regarding their data collection practices. Approximately 76% reported not having enough time during the day to carry out data collection. This objection suggests a basic misunderstanding of the role of data collection. Frequently, it is seen as impractical or as a useless activity required by an administrator or bureaucrat. We understand why many teachers hold this attitude. School districts and state and federal agencies require teachers to gather and report such data as daily attendance, which students will be eating the school's hot lunch, and who will be taking the early (or late) bus home, in addition to periodic surveys, question-

naires, and lists. Because these data have little application to what the teacher does, it is no wonder that practitioners develop a repugnance for data collection in general.[1]

Still, teachers are notorious data collectors. Their grade books are full of checkmarks showing assignments turned in, scores on daily or weekly tests, counts of disciplinary actions, and so forth. Unfortunately, these data are used infrequently as a basis for evaluating pupils or programs. One solution to the problem of time constraints on data collection is to make sure the data you keep are data you will use. This does not include IQ scores, test profiles, and the like. It does include daily reading or math performance rates, spelling test scores, rates of social behaviors targeted for intervention, number of disciplinary actions, and student progress toward individual behavioral objectives. As a rule of thumb, you should carefully decide what to measure; then measure it as precisely as you can.

Another solution is to simplify your data collection. Later we describe several alternate strategies for doing this. These include using data probes, time samples, and scatter plots instead of continuous measurement, as well as auto-graphing. You also may train someone else to observe and record data, such as an aide, a fellow teacher or other staff person, another pupil, or the student whose behavior is being measured. (See page 90-91 for guidelines for training observers.)

2. **"Measuring behavior doesn't help me teach."** Nearly 45% of teachers surveyed by Walton (1985) reported that data collection procedures were of little help or only somewhat helpful to their teaching responsibilities. This objection also suggests that the teacher is not gathering useful data, that is, data that can be used to make educational decisions and upon which to base program adjustments. In response to this objection, we offer this

---

[1]Special educators have additional reporting tasks, including monitoring and revising IEPs, summarizing meetings, documenting parental contacts, and updating student portfolios.

guideline: If you do not use the data frequently, do not collect it. (Note: This guideline does not apply to data you are required to collect by your agency.) On the other hand, failure to gather data you should use is inexcusable. As Kauffman (2001) emphasizes:

> The teaching profession is dedicated to the task of changing behavior—changing behavior demonstrably for the better. What can one say, then, of educational practice that does not include reliable measurement of the behavior change induced by the teacher's methodology? It *is indefensible.* (p. 532)

If your data are not useful to you, perhaps you need to select measures that are more sensitive to what you are trying to accomplish. A common mistake is to measure the results of behavior instead of the behavior itself. For example, if you are trying to increase a pupil's use of specific social skills, do not record the number of points he earns for appropriate social behaviors each day. Instead, directly record the frequency with which these skills are exhibited.

Systematic data collection can help you accomplish many things, including: (a) making instructional decisions; (b) providing feedback for the student, yourself, and others regarding the effectiveness of instructional and behavioral management programs; (c) ensuring accountability; (d) giving you a common basis for discussion among parents, teachers, other professionals, and students; (e) giving support and reinforcement to parents, teachers, and students; and (f) increasing student performance (Cooke, Heward, Test, Spooner, & Courson, 1991; Fuchs & Fuchs, 1986; Lund, Schnaps, & Bijou, 1983). We hope you will appreciate the value of data collection by the time you complete this text.

3. **"I don't get any support or reinforcement for monitoring student progress."** Obviously, if teachers don't gather data, they shouldn't expect to be reinforced for completing this task! However, many teachers enter their profession with an earnest desire to use systematic teaching and measurement procedures, and a year later their teaching is guided by guesses and hunches. Frankly, there are no explicit reinforcement contingencies for data-based instruction in most schools. Neither your salary nor your effectiveness, as measured by most parents or administrators, depends on the objective documentation of student progress. Therefore, to maintain such a complex and sometimes difficult task, you will need to "recruit" reinforcement (Stokes & Baer, 1977). One way is to share your data with those to whom you report student progress. Parents should be more receptive to graphs or charts detailing their child's progress in, for example, learning a functional speaking vocabulary than they would be to a letter grade in language arts. Administrators too can learn to view your performance in the school by progress made toward individual student objectives. So, share your student data with everyone with whom you communicate. Show them what you are trying to do and how you are trying to measure and evaluate progress. Solicit their assistance in solving your measurement problems. In addition to getting valuable feedback and support, you are more likely to gain other teachers' cooperation with data-collection activities such as beginning to record student performances in their own classrooms.

Frequently Asked Questions about Monitoring Student Behavior

In addition to recruiting reinforcement for data-based interventions from others, you also must minimize the cost to yourself in terms of time and effort. Here are some responses to teacher's questions that may help make data collection more relevant and less aversive.

1. **"Do I need to monitor everything?"** As Scott and Goetz (1980) point out, some teachers collect data seemingly for its own sake. Gast and Gast (1981) suggest that the question "To what practical end can the data be used?" be employed as a guideline for describing how much data are

needed and how often it should be collected. And, as we said earlier, there is little purpose in gathering data to which you do not respond. So if you intend to do something about a behavior, even if your intention is only to monitor it, record it. If you have no such design, ignore it. Some behaviors will have to be ignored simply because they are not a top priority for immediate intervention. For example, if the student's IEP committee has ranked his physical aggression and the replacement behavior of hands to self as priority targets, and his occasional out-of-seat behavior as a much lower priority, you will probably want to devote more effort to monitoring the first two behaviors and let the third go until later. You may wish to conduct periodic measurement probes (see page 92) of lower priority targets in order to verify that there are no abrupt changes in their rates.

If you follow the rule of collecting only those data you can use in decision making, you also may find that you can consolidate some data. For example, if you are concerned with general classroom disruptions and don't need to respond differently to specific behaviors in this category, such as out-of-seat or talking out, count the number of disruptions rather than the number of times out-of-seat and the number of talk-outs.

2. **"What is most important for me to measure?"** Sometimes teachers waste a lot of time and energy collecting data on nonessential behaviors. The points we mentioned above will also help you avoid this pitfall. If you rank objectives and target behaviors, if you consolidate measures of behaviors, if you gather only those data to which you will respond, you should be able to cut down on this problem significantly. It does not hurt to ask, "Do I use this?" every time you review data sheets and summaries. Our emphasis on using data to make frequent program adjustments applies to your monitoring procedures as well. Remember, your monitoring strategy is also part of your program.

3. **"Isn't it simpler to measure the results of students' behavior?"** With regard to behaviors that result in an academic product, the answer to this question is definitely "yes." However, while academic performances result in a permanent product that is a reasonably sensitive measure of the behaviors that produced it, social behaviors leave no such record. For example, many persons monitor their eating by measuring their weight. They are dismayed if decreases in eating are not accompanied by immediate reductions in their weight. This may occur because weight is also affected by other factors, such as fluid retention or muscle mass. Likewise, behavioral indexes such as teacher rating or point earnings are affected by variables other than the pupil's behavior (e.g., the teacher's mood) and therefore are inaccurate measures of actual behavior. These data are convenient, and they may provide a rough estimate of student progress, but they do not provide a sufficient basis for making specific educational decisions. Further, the time and effort used in obtaining and summarizing these data can be spent more productively in more precise recording.

Therefore, instead of counting the number of points earned, it is preferable to count the behaviors that earn points (e.g., assignments completed, directions followed). Finally, if your students are interested in such information as their daily point earnings, teach *them* to record and chart these data. Indirect measures such as rating scale scores and point earnings may help an IEP or behavior support team gain a more complete perspective on a student's current status and rate of progress. When these are the *only* measures of performance, however, they are not sufficient. Therefore, if you do use indirect measures of social behaviors, get data from several sources and perspectives. Always remember to verify the accuracy of the impressions you are getting by comparing this information with data obtained from direct observation and measurement.

Teachers are not always present to observe and record student behavior when it occurs. Further, some behaviors (e.g., stealing, verbal threats) are less frequent when an authority figure is around.

However, sometimes these behaviors do have measurable effects on the environment. For example, the number of items stolen, papers torn, marks made on furniture, or objects damaged represent **permanent products** that can be counted with reasonable accuracy. These results of behavior are not based on teachers' subjective evaluations of pupils' responses, and so they are more reliable indicators of the behaviors that produced them.

The increased use of alternative assessment procedures, particularly student **portfolios,** has led many practitioners to incorporate data from such procedures as rating scales, informal criterion-referenced assessments, and curriculum-based measurement of progress in social skills curricula. We will describe some of the uses of portfolios in monitoring student progress in a later section.

4. **"How do I use student performance data once I gather it?"** If you follow our suggestions thus far, there is little danger that you will wind up gathering information that you will not use. Still, it is wise to review periodically all student programs with your supervisor or colleagues to ensure that you are gathering important data, that your data-collection procedures are appropriate, and that you are making the best use of these data. A number of teachers may be interested in informal biweekly meetings to talk about programs and review data.

A major reason teachers fail to use the data they collect is that the data are not summarized graphically. This process takes time and frequently is put off until it is too dated to be useful (Fabry & Cone, 1980). Teachers' grade books or plan books often are full of data regarding academic performances and social behaviors. However, these data are not arranged so as to show change over time. Graphing or charting organizes these data to show such changes and is critical to making program adjustments based on student performance (Fabry & Cone, 1980). More efficient techniques have been devised, some of which combine the functions of data recording and graphing or charting (e.g., Fabry & Cone, 1980; Nelson, Gast, & Trout, 1979). We illustrate these procedures later in this chapter.

Finally, because monitoring of targeted social behaviors occurs repeatedly over time and covers a relatively narrow range of behaviors, you should select your monitoring points carefully. Just as a physician knows where to find a pulse that tells important things about a patient, so too should you measure a few behaviors that describe the student adequately and that are sensitive to the changes you are attempting to achieve. You should neither measure too much or too little, nor should you monitor behaviors that are not directly related to the changes you want. That's like searching for a pulse in the wrong place—the data will tell you nothing.

The Role of Program Monitoring and Evaluation in IEPs

The IDEA mandates that the total service plan for a pupil's education be reviewed at least annually. However, as White and Haring (1980) point out, an annual review of goals and objectives is far too infrequent for any child, especially one who has a great deal of catching up to do. Annual, semiannual, or quarterly reassessments relative to the goals and objectives stated in a pupil's IEP are **static measures;** that is, they provide a report of progress at a single point in time. They also represent an evaluation process that is **summative,** meaning that measurement occurs after teaching and learning have taken place. In addition to the potential inaccuracy or unreliability of static measures, they are not made often enough to allow the teacher to make timely program decisions or precise program adjustments. Figures 3–1 and 3–2 illustrate the difference between infrequent and frequent measures of student progress. The first set of panels depict measures of six students' performances, relative to the criterion, or desired level of performance, taken at 6-week intervals. What decisions would you, as these students'

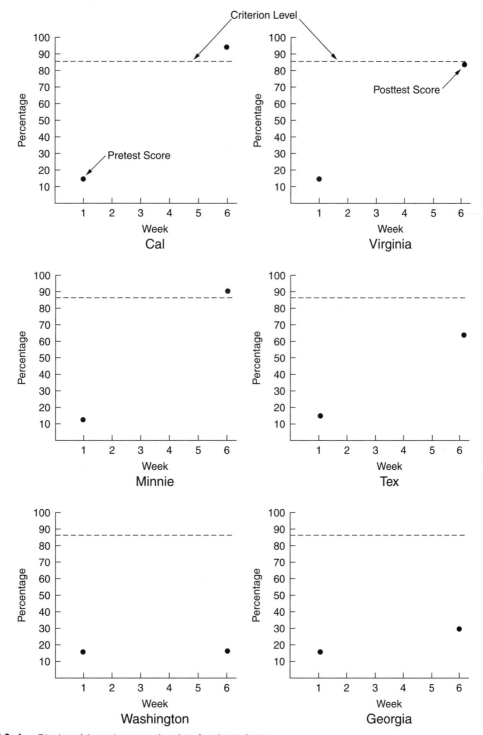

FIGURE 3–1 Display of 6-week summative data for six students

Source: *From G. M. Sugai and G. A. Tindal, "Effective School Consultation: An Interactive Approach" p. 59. Copyright 1993. Reprinted with permission of Wadsworth, an imprint of the Wadsworth Group, a division of Thomson Learning.*

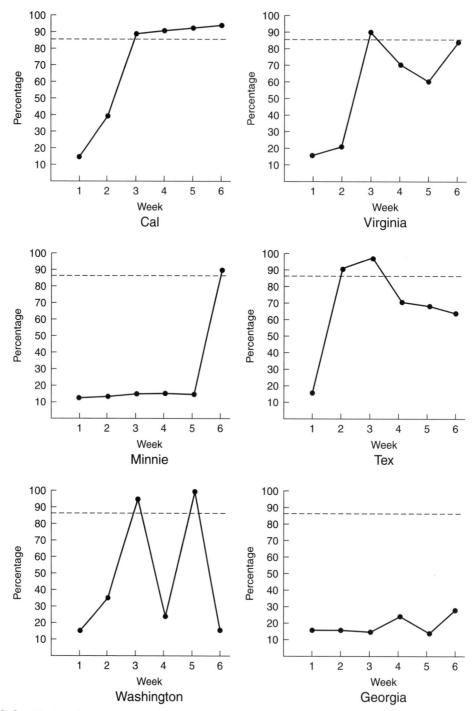

FIGURE 3–2 Display of 6-week formative data for six students

Source: *From G. M. Sugai and G. A. Tindal, "Effective School Consultation: An Interactive Approach" p. 60. Copyright 1993. Reprinted with permission of Wadsworth, an imprint of the Wadsworth Group, a division of Thomson Learning.*

teacher, be able to make about adjustments they need in their instructional programs? Now look at the second set of panels in Figure 3–2, in which the progress of these same students is reported in 1-week intervals.

This approach to measurement represents **formative evaluation;** that is, it occurs while skills are being developed. Notice how much more information is available for making instructional decisions. For example, we can see that Cal reached the criterion after only 3 weeks of instruction; he was ready to move on to another skill well before the other students. In contrast, Minnie and Georgia did not profit from the instruction offered for some time; their time (and the teacher's) was wasted on instruction that was not beneficial. Finally, Virginia, Tex, and Washington performed inconsistently, and would have benefited from some adjustments in their daily instruction. Gast and Gast (1981) point out that

> The pretest/posttest methods of determining pupil performance are only the peripheral ends of a continuum of evaluating and monitoring individual education plans. Systematic procedures that result in formative data, from which decisions of program maintenance and modification can be made, are imperative if the IEP is to be a truly functional tool for assuring appropriate education for exceptional children. (p. 3)

The following sections present a number of measurement principles and techniques. As you read, you may find yourself thinking, "I can't do all this!" You will be quite right. The measurement strategies presented here describe an ideal situation, one that can be achieved only when sufficient resources are available. Our goal is for you to understand these principles and procedures well enough to make intelligent compromises about fitting these methods to your teaching situation. For example, if you are a beginning teacher, we suggest that you attempt *some* systematic monitoring of your students' performance (e.g., on your highest ranked academic or social behavior targets). As you gain skill and confidence, you can increase the amount and sophistication of your

measurement of behavior. Furthermore, it is not necessary to do everything we suggest in order to be an effective teacher. Experienced educators develop their own decision-making strategies. (You will notice that the chapter case studies do not follow all of our guidelines regarding data collection.) As you gain more experience, you will develop your own strategies, many of them perhaps less formal than those we describe. Nevertheless, we hope you will strive for the principles presented here and will find our suggestions to be useful in your efforts to be a systematic and effective teacher.

MEASURING STUDENT PROGRESS

Progress monitoring involves four basic steps, several of which we already have highlighted: selecting a monitoring format and procedures; recording data; assessing the accuracy of data; and summarizing the data for analysis. In this section, we describe and illustrate procedures for accomplishing each of these steps.

Selecting a Monitoring Format and Procedures

This step includes several components: determining what aspects of student behavior to measure, selecting an appropriate recording procedure, and deciding what data to collect. We mention these separately, but in practice, you probably will evaluate these components simultaneously.

Deciding what to measure requires that you must first know what properties or aspects of behavior can be measured. Obviously, human behavior does not have the dimensions of a physical object; therefore, it cannot be measured in terms of height, weight, volume, or mass. However, behavior does have features that can be observed and accurately measured. The first of these is *frequency* or *rate*, which refers to how often a behavior occurs in a period of time. For example, you can measure the number of times a child hits, asks a question, or raises her hand in an hour. Second, behavior may be described or measured in terms of its *duration*: the length of a verbal interchange, the duration of temper tantrums, and so forth. Third, the *latency*, or lag time between the presentation of a prompt, or verbal instruction, and the initiation of a response (compliance), may be observed. Behavior also may be measured in terms of *intensity*, which includes its frequency and its duration: for example, recording the number and the length of a pupil's temper tantrums. Finally, behavior sometimes is measured in terms of its *magnitude*, or force, although this is difficult to do objectively without laboratory apparatus. The decision of which of these properties to measure depends upon which is best suited to the pupil, the situation, and the changes you want. For instance, if your target involves a student's compliance with adult requests, you may consider whether compliance is best characterized in terms of frequency or latency, and then, whether your goal is to increase rate, decrease latency, or both.

The selection of a monitoring format, therefore, is partly based on the characteristics of the behavior being observed and how you want it to change. If you want to increase the fluency of student responding, measure rate. If your goal is to reduce the amount of time it takes a student to do something, measure duration. However, another important consideration is convenience. Although you may want to increase the duration of on-task behavior, for instance, keeping track of it with a stopwatch is highly inconvenient, unless you have nothing else to do. We suggest alternative strategies for such problems later.

Thus, you have several decisions to make regarding the choice of the behaviors you will measure and attempt to change. The range of these **dependent measures,** or variables to be monitored, is described in Table 3–1. Study it carefully to determine which option best suits your purposes and situation.

If you are not accustomed to observing behavior systematically, it is easy to make mistakes that may adversely affect the data you collect. Because unreliable data increase the probability of bad decisions, it is imperative that your procedures be as sensitive and precise as possible. To help you accomplish this goal, we offer the following guidelines.

1. **Select a direct and sensitive monitoring format.** Consider several factors before deciding upon a format: What constraints do the observation setting place on observation and recording? What is it about the behavior observed that you want to change? How do you want the behavior to change? Remember to measure behavior directly (i.e., measure the behavior itself, not the results of the behavior; see our previous discussion of indirect measures).

Direct measures of behavior are more sensitive to the effects of your instructional programs and behavior intervention plans. Therefore, the data are more useful to you in analyzing and "fine tuning" your program. The more experience you acquire with observation and recording techniques, the easier it will become to tailor monitoring formats to the behaviors you want to measure. The major exception to monitoring behavior directly is permanent products. Written responses on worksheets, number of objects stolen, and so forth are indirect measures of the behaviors contributing to an outcome, but they are also more convenient to measure, and unless it is possible for students to cheat on every written assignment or items reported as stolen were simply misplaced, there generally is only one way to produce the outcome that is measured.

2. **Observe and collect data daily for as long as possible.** A busy teacher decided to monitor a pupil's fighting during the first 30 minutes of school. She was frustrated that her baseline data showed zero fights, even though the student had been in several that month. Fighting occurred rather infrequently, and her observation sample was too brief to capture it. Therefore, the behavior "escaped." Unless the behaviors you want to monitor occur fairly often across all settings and times,

TABLE 3–1   Summary of Dependent Measures

Dependent Measure	Definition	Considerations
1. Number	Simple count of the number of times a behavior or event occurs	1.1 Requires constant time across observational periods when response opportunities are not controlled 1.2 Requires constant number of trials across sessions/days with teacher-paced instruction
2. Percent	Number of occurrences divided by the total number of opportunities for the behavior to occur multiplied by 100	2.1 Equalizes unequal number of opportunities to respond across sessions/days 2.2 Easily understood 2.3 Frequently used measure for accuracy 2.4 Efficient means for summarizing large numbers of responses 2.5 No reference to the time over which behavior was observed 2.6 Generally should be used only when there are 20 or more opportunities to respond
3. Rate	Number of occurrences divided by the number of time units (minutes or hours)	3.1 Converts behavior counts to a constant scale when opportunities to respond or observation time varies across sessions/days 3.2 Reveals response proficiency as well as accuracy 3.3 Reported as responses per minute or responses per hour 3.4 Appropriate for behaviors measured under conditions in which opportunities to respond are not controlled 3.5 Cumbersome to use with behaviors measured under teacher-paced conditions
4. Duration (total)	Amount of time behavior occurs during an observation period	4.1 Expressed as the percentage of time engaged in behavior 4.2 Does not yield information about frequency or mean duration per occurrence
5. Duration per occurrence	Amount of time engaged in each episode of the behavior	5.1 Yields behavior frequency: mean duration per occurrence and total duration information
6. Latency	Elapsed time from the presentation of the discriminative stimulus (S^D) and the initiation of the behavior	6.1 Appropriate measure with compliance problem behaviors (long response latency) 6.2 May yield information regarding high error rate when there is a short response latency
7. Magnitude	Response strength or force	7.1 Direct measure requires automated-quantitative instrumentation 7.2 Indirect measure of magnitude possible by measuring effect response has on environment
8. Trials to criterion	Number of trials counted to reach criterion for each behavior	8.1 Yields information on concept formation (learning-to-learn phenomenon) 8.2 Post hoc summary measure

Source: Tawney, J. W., & Gast; D. L. (1984). Single subject research in special education. Upper Saddle River, NJ: Merrill/Prentice Hall. Used with permission.

you should plan to observe or have others record the events long enough to obtain an adequate sample. This is important particularly with regard to social behaviors that occur only in certain settings (such as the playground) or in the presence of very specific stimuli (such as a particular person). You can use a scatter plot (see Chapter 2) to estimate the rates of behaviors across various times of the day and activities. This assessment will help you identify when and where a target behavior occurs, so you can design your monitoring format accordingly.

Longer observation and recording periods yield more accurate records of behavior and provide a better check of your behavior intervention plan. In addition, you will be able to check for generalization of behavior changes across settings or time. If the behavior is **discrete** (has a definite beginning and ending, does not take place constantly, and is apparent when it occurs, e.g., hand raising and physical aggression), you should be able to observe and record it several times during the day. On the other hand, if the behavior is more subtle or **continuous** (there is no definite starting or stopping point between episodes, such as stereotypic or on-task behavior), you may be able to use one of the internal or time-sampling techniques described below that permit you to sample behaviors across the day.

There are no hard and fast guidelines for determining the optimal length for observation periods. Generally, you should adjust the interval to the "typical" rate at which the behavior occurs; that is, you should ensure that the data are representative of natural rates of occurrence. Infrequent target behavior requires longer observation periods. On the other hand, briefer time samples are possible for more frequent behaviors, provided they represent the rate of occurrence accurately. Ask yourself, "Do these data reflect the behavior as I evaluate it?" If the answer is "No," adjust your recording period (or reevaluate your subjective assessment of the behavior).

Although daily measurement provides the best basis for making intervention decisions, research

supports the conclusion that twice-weekly monitoring of student academic performance is as adequate as daily monitoring in terms of promoting academic achievement (Fuchs, 1986). However, priority social behaviors should be monitored daily during the initial phases of intervention (i.e., when programs are being tested and revised). Less frequent measurement probes may be taken when students have advanced to maintenance or generalization phases.

3. **Observe and record behavior where it occurs.** The teacher we mentioned who monitored her student's fighting for 30 minutes daily also ignored this guideline. Obviously, your measures of behavior are not going to be valid if your observation periods do not coincide with the times or activities during which the behavior occurs. Thus, if fighting occurs only during lunch or recess, observe in the lunchroom or playground instead of the study hall. And, as we stated earlier, if the behavior does not occur in your presence, find someone who is present when it happens and train him to monitor it. Consider asking other school staff to monitor behavior: custodians, cafeteria workers, aides, and so forth. Given proper training and supervision, peers can be reliable observers of behavior (Fowler, 1986). However, be cautious when using this tactic; peers may have a vested interest in the target student's behavioral performance. The following guidelines are suggested for training others to observe behavior systematically and reliably. It is very important that you train observers well, if you are going to base decisions on the data they collect.

- Develop a specific, observable definition of the behavior(s) to be observed. Include all instances (what is counted as an occurrence) and noninstances (what is not counted as an occurrence). Review this with the observer.
- Explain recording sheets and apparatus to the observer. Teach the observer to use the recording equipment (e.g., wrist counter, stopwatch) as well as the recording procedures (e.g., response codes, interval data sheets). Go over these procedures several times.

- Ask the observer to practice data collection. At first, you may role-play the behavior while the observer records, or use a videotape to simulate an actual situation. Later, you can sit beside the observer in the setting and label the behavior when it occurs (e.g., "That's an instance of disruption.") and have the observer record it according to your procedure. Be sure to stop immediately to answer questions or correct mistakes.
- Ask the observer to collect data in the actual situation with you (or another qualified observer) present to provide assistance.
- Ask the observer to collect data while a more experienced observer simultaneously observes and records. Assess the accuracy of the novice's data, answer questions, correct errors, and so forth. Continue checking the agreement between observers (see pages 103-104) until agreement is 80 to 90%. Do not use any of the data for making intervention decisions until this has been achieved!
- The observer is now ready to begin formal monitoring. Continue frequent checks of observer agreement (e.g., once a week, depending on the frequency of monitoring). If agreement falls below 80%, stop formal data collection and retrain this observer.

Unless there are no predictable differences in the level of the behavior across settings or activities, you should observe and record in the same setting, activity, or time period each day. Not only will this result in more comparable performance data, it also will be easier for you to remember to monitor specific performances.

4. **Keep observation time relatively constant.** If you are maintaining a frequency count of behavior, your data will be affected by the length of time you observe. For instance, there is twice as much opportunity to make appropriate verbal comments in 60 minutes as in 30 minutes If your observation period is not controlled, your data may reflect variations in the opportunity to respond rather than in the response itself. If you are unable to observe for the same amount of time each session or day, use a rate or a percent of time recording procedure (discussed later) to control for these variations. Rate data are particularly useful because they permit comparison of measures taken across different settings or for varying lengths of time.

5. **Once a behavior is defined, observe and record only responses meeting that definition.** One of us supervised a teacher who was working on a preschool child's self-injurious behavior. The teacher was counting the number of times the child slapped herself in the head or bit her fingers. The teacher reported that intervention was successful, and our observations in the classroom confirmed this. However, we could see very little change in the data. Our questioning revealed that the teacher's definition of self-injurious behavior had gradually shifted from slaps and bites to touches and mouthing. The solution to this problem is to establish a clear, written definition of the target behavior that includes both instances and noninstances. Thus, self-injurious behavior could be defined as slaps to the face or head and bites to the fingers or hands that result in an audible sound and perhaps skin reddening. Noninstances would include covering the face with hands, twisting hair with fingers, and so forth. The latter would not be counted as instances of self-injurious behavior. The best way to discriminate instances from noninstances when developing behavioral definitions is to observe the child continuously for a period of time, writing down every response as well as antecedents and consequences. This initial A-B-C assessment will not only help you establish all the forms of the behavior you will be observing, it will also help identify environmental factors that may predict occurrences (see Chapter 2). It is also desirable to conduct periodic assessments of interobserver agreement. These are especially useful if after each session the observers discuss their agreements and disagreements.

6. **Monitor only as many behaviors in as many settings as you can manage.** There is little purpose in observing and recording so many

behaviors that you have no time left for instruction or you confuse yourself and your students. Likewise, the purpose of monitoring behavior is lost if you have more data than you can act upon. Cooper (1981) suggested that the more severe the pupil's educational problem, the more behaviors should be monitored. Teachers of students with mild disabilities should monitor all responses to direct (planned academic) instruction, whereas teachers of students with severe and profound disabilities should monitor all student responses to planned academic instruction and those during social activities.

Cooper (1981) also provides several suggestions for practitioners who are just beginning to monitor student behavior:

- Begin observing one or two behaviors of one student. Gradually expand observations of the same behavior to include another student, a third, and so on. Experiment with different measurement strategies (duration, time sample, interval) to find those that are most useful, sensitive, and direct for a particular setting.
- Monitor behavior for the shortest time possible to get an adequate sample (i.e., without occurrences of behavior "escaping" measurement).
- Use other persons (classroom aides, other students) to observe, to record, and to collect observer agreement information.

- Ask persons who are skilled in recording and graphing behavior to help you analyze your measurement strategies.

You will find it possible to monitor a larger number of behaviors if you adjust your data-collection procedures to the behavior you are recording. All behavior does not need to be monitored constantly, such as when you are evaluating the maintenance or generalization of a previously taught skill. In such cases, you might employ periodic (weekly or biweekly) **measurement probes.** For example, you may observe a student once a week to see whether he continues to play appropriately with others during recess. Data probes are also useful for general monitoring (e.g., spot-checking pupils' on-task behavior) and for monitoring programs in which student progress is slow. Table 3–2 summarizes guidelines for adjusting the frequency of measurement to student and program characteristics.

7. **If you are observing in a setting other than your own classroom or school building, follow established procedures.** Each institution, residential treatment program, or school district has its own policies regarding visitors. Although we cannot prepare you for every situation, we have summarized general guidelines. These procedures are important if you are to obtain accurate data without offending anyone.

Do obtain permission to observe the student. Consult the building or program adminis-

TABLE 3–2   Guidelines for Adjusting Frequency of Monitoring

Student or Program Characteristics	Monitoring Strategy
Rapid student progress or progress through small-step sequence	Session-by-session recording (one or more per day)
Daily progress or fluctuation in student behavior, daily program adjustments	Daily recording
Slow rate of student progress	Data probes (biweekly, weekly)
General monitoring of behavior less frequent program adjustments	Data probes (biweekly, weekly)
Evaluating maintenance or generalizing previously mastered programs or steps	Data probes (biweekly, weekly, monthly)

trator and the teacher. Some agencies require parental consent. Check with the teacher or supervisor to find out if this is the case.

Do sign in and out when entering and leaving the building.

Do talk with the teacher beforehand about the purpose of your observations, what to tell the class about your visits, and the extent of your class participation.

Do enter and leave the classroom area unobtrusively, ideally during a normal break in the routine.

Do avoid being conspicuous. Sit where you can see the pupil and monitor the behavior you want to observe but out of the student's direct line of vision.

Don't interact or make eye contact with any of the students or the teacher during your observations. If a student insists on getting your attention, indicate that you are not allowed to talk and redirect her attention.

Don't participate in classroom activities.

Don't begin systematic observations until the pupils have become accustomed to your presence.

Do thank the teacher for allowing you to observe and share your data with the teacher if you can do so without disrupting the classroom.

Recording Strategies

Advances in the technology of behavior measurement have resulted in a variety of alternatives for recording. The alternatives you select depend on a number of factors, some of which are presented in Table 3–3. Your answers to the questions posed in this table will help determine which recording procedure you should use. For example, if you must observe while you are involved in direct instruction with pupils other than or in addition to the target student, you would likely choose a sampling technique or train someone other than yourself to observe and record. Following is a discussion of alternative approaches for recording behavior.

COUNTING PERMANENT PRODUCTS If your measurement strategy is based on permanent products, your choices of recording techniques are fairly straightforward. You may obtain numerical counts, rate or percent, or record the number of instructional trials required for the student to reach the criterion (see page 94). Your choice will be based upon some of the considerations listed in Table 3–3. For example, does the student not attempt any of the work assigned, or is his work inaccurate? Will you be recording student responses in a one-to-one instructional situation, in which you are presenting discrete learning trials? Do you want to increase the pupil's response speed, accuracy,

TABLE 3–3 Considerations in Selecting a Measurement Strategy

1. Definition of the behavior target	Movement/function or both?
2. Characteristics of target behavior	Frequency/duration/latency/intensity? Individual/group? High rate/low rate?
3. Goal of intervention	Change rate/duration/latency/intensity?
4. Observation situation	Your class/another class? Group/one-to-one? Teacher giving lesson/individual seatwork/recess or free time/lunch/other?
5. Person doing observation	Trained observer/untrained observer? Adult/child?
6. Time available for observation	All day/one period/portion of several periods/portion of one period?
7. Equipment available for measurement	Automatic recorder/cumulative recorder/multiple event recorder/wrist counter/timing device/pad and pencil?
8. Accuracy	High/medium/low? Interobserver agreement critical/not critical? Reliability observers trained/untrained?
9. Audience for whom data are intended	Professionals/parents/students?

or both? Will you be giving daily or weekly probes over the objective you are attempting to reach? Will the student monitor and record the target behavior himself? Will you use a peer observer? Permanent product recording is useful primarily for monitoring academic behaviors that result in written student responses, although, as we suggested earlier, some social behaviors may have results that can be measured as permanent products. Also, you can use audio or video recordings as permanent products of social behaviors. Permanent products are useful documents to include in student portfolios.

To measure behaviors that do not result in a permanent product (e.g., most human social behavior), you must rely upon observational recording techniques. A variety of these are available or you may adapt or design a recording procedure suited to your own situation. We briefly describe and illustrate several approaches, and other examples appear in subsequent chapters.

FREQUENCY OR TALLY METHOD   If you have defined target behaviors specifically and objectively, recording their frequency is relatively easy. Frequency recording is the method of choice for most behaviors that are brief and discrete (i.e., have a definite beginning and end and are best characterized in terms of their frequency rather than their duration). In some cases, a simple numerical count will be sufficient, but it generally is better to record the time period in which the behavior occurred or keep observation time constant to permit comparison across observation sessions. If observation sessions vary in length, you may convert event data to rate by dividing the numerical count by the time observed (e.g., Katy initiated a verbal interaction with a peer seven times in 30 min. Rate = 7/30 or 0.23 times per minute). This will permit comparison of your data across unequal observation periods. The case study at the end of this chapter illustrates a procedure for collecting data on students' rate of correct academic responding.

Frequency recording may be accomplished with a paper and pencil or you may use other devices.

For example, you can attach a piece of masking tape to a clipboard, watchband, or pencil, and mark on it whenever a target behavior occurs. Transfer coins or paper clips from one pocket to another or to a container whenever a target behavior occurs. Golf counters, knitting counters, button counters, and even digital stopwatches or wristwatches can be purchased at variety stores for under $10.

COUNTING NUMBER OF TRIALS TO CRITERION When you are providing skill instruction through **discrete learning trials** (i.e., presenting a fixed number of trials that consist of a specific instruction or model, the pupil's response, and a subsequent teacher response), or when you are otherwise controlling the student's opportunities to respond (e.g., through teacher-paced instructions), it is useful to monitor performance on each trial. Figure 3–3 shows a discrete trial recording format (also referred to as controlled presentation recording) for teaching a pupil to ask for teacher assistance appropriately. Note that the teacher records whether the desired response occurred following each verbal instruction, and whether a verbal prompt was needed to occasion the correct performance. Note also that the teacher has set 10 trials per training session and that the criterion for moving to the next level of delay between when the student first requests attention and the teacher responds is specified on the recording sheet. Trials to criterion data sheets may be attached to a separate clipboard for each student. Trials may spread out (**distributed trials**) over the course of a class period or a day rather than being massed together (**massed trials**). Counting the number of trials needed for the student to reach the criterion is an appropriate measurement strategy for monitoring progress through a task-analysis sequence, as in Figure 3–3.

RECORDING DURATION   If the length or the latency of a response is its major characteristic or the one you most want to change, **duration recording** may be the best method. For example,

Objective: When instructed to " show me how you ask for my help," Robert will raise his hand and sit quietly for 15 seconds. Criterion: 8 of 10 consecutive correct trials for two consecutive sessions.

Duration	Session	Trials 1	2	3	4	5	6	7	8	9	10
5 seconds	1	0	XP	XP	0	XP	XP	X	X	X	X
	2	XP	0	XP	XP	X	X	X	X	X	X
	3	XP	XP	X	X	X	X	X	X	X	X
	4	X	X	X	X	X	X	X	X	X	X
10 seconds	1	0	0	OP	OP	XP	XP	OP	OP	XP	XP
	2	XP	XP	OP	OP	X	X	0	0	XP	XP
	3	X	X	X	0	XP	XP	X	X	X	X
	4	0	XP	X	X	X	X	X	X	X	X
	5	X	X	X	X	X	X	X	X	X	X
15 seconds	1	XP	XP	0	XP	X	X	X	X	X	X
	2	0	0	XP	X	X	X	X	X	X	X
	3	X	X	X	X	X	X	X	X	X	X
	4	X	X	X	X	X	X	X	X	X	X

Scoring Key: X = correct
O = incorrect
XP = correct prompted (verbal)
OP = incorrect prompted (verbal)

FIGURE 3–3 Trials to Criterion Data Sheet

a student may have a low frequency of in-seat behavior but each episode may last several minutes, or a student may be extremely slow in following directions or in joining group activities.

Response duration or latency may be monitored by any watch or clock with a second hand or second counter, but a stopwatch is best. By starting and stopping a stopwatch without resetting it, you may record the cumulative time out-of-seat or on-task across several instances. Although a *total duration* recording procedure is more convenient, it is less descriptive than *duration per occurrence* because the latter keeps track of each event and its duration. Both of these procedures are easier to use if the observer is not occupied with direct instruction or classroom management.

Response latency recording is accomplished by starting the timer when a cue (verbal instruction, visual signal, etc.) is presented and by stopping the timer when the pupil complies with the request (e.g., "Take your seat"). Although teachers generally want to decrease latency, as when a student does not comply with teacher requests or instructions, sometimes it is desirable to increase latencies, as when students respond impulsively and thereby increase errors (Tawney & Gast, 1984).

USING INTERVAL RECORDING   Interval recording is a versatile technique for recording both discrete and continuous behaviors. It requires your full attention for observing and recording, but you can observe several behaviors or pupils simultaneously. Interval recording also may be the most practical strategy if a response occurs too frequently for each instance to be counted (e.g., hand flapping or other stereotypic behaviors). When using this technique, break the observation period down into small intervals of equal length (10, 15, or 30 sec) and observe whether the behavior occurs or does not occur in any given interval. The size of the interval should be at least as long as the average duration of a single response, but short enough so that two complete responses normally cannot occur in the same interval. You may count a behavior as occurring according to a proportion of the interval during which it took place (e.g., 50% or more of the interval) or if the behavior occurred at all during the interval. The latter procedure is easier and lends itself to higher levels of interobserver agreement. When monitoring several behaviors simultaneously, it may be easier to observe for one interval and use the next to record your observations (10 sec to observe, 10 sec to record, etc.). It is also possible to arrange your recording sheet to allow more time for observing than for recording (e.g., 15 sec to observe followed by 5 sec to record, or three observation and recording intervals per minute). Figure 3–4 shows interval data collected in 15-sec blocks. Another option for coding more than one behavior is to preprint recording sheets with the behavior codes written in each interval, as in Figure 3–5. The observer indicates a behavior's occurrence by drawing a slash through the appropriate code. Subsequent chapters contain other examples of interval recording.

In addition to being versatile, interval recording does not require sophisticated equipment. A clipboard and a stopwatch or watch with a second hand are all you need.[2] Because interval recording does not provide a measure of absolute frequency, it is not appropriate to report the total number of target behaviors that occurred in a given observation period. Instead, report the percentage of the intervals in which you observed the behavior. Calculate this by the formula:

$$\frac{\text{Number of intervals in which behavior occurred}}{\text{Total number of intervals}} \times 100 = \frac{\text{Percent of}}{\text{occurrence}}$$

With a little practice, you will become proficient in collecting interval data.

The scatter plot (Touchette, MacDonald, & Langer, 1985) described in Chapter 2 is a compromise between rating and interval-scale measurement. Once each interval (e.g., 30 min) or instructional period, the practitioner enters a code indicating her estimation of the frequency of the target behavior for that interval. However, convenience comes at the price of accuracy, because the scatter plot yields a summary estimate of the behavior rather than an indication of whether it occurred in a much briefer time period.

TIME SAMPLING   If you do not have a block of time to devote to observing and recording, if you want to sample behaviors across an extended time

[2]However, to increase the accuracy of interval recording, use a device to signal the beginning and end of an observation interval. For example, beeps or verbal signals ("50 sec . . . 1 min . . . 10 sec") may be recorded on an audiotape and replayed via an earphone for the observer to use while recording. Calculators that signal time intervals also may be used for this purpose. The audible signal they produce may distract students, however, and therefore these devices should be used when the observer is separated from the group (e.g., in an observation room), or with an earpiece so the sound can be detected only by the observer.

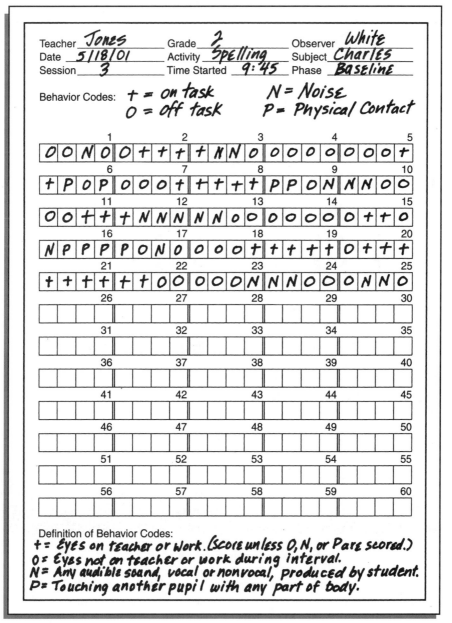

FIGURE 3–4 Sample Interval Recording Form

period or across settings, or if you are monitoring a number of pupils or behaviors, a time sampling technique may suit your needs. Time sampling is similar to interval recording, but the intervals are much longer (e.g., 1 to 20 min), less frequent, and may be variable. There are many variations to this approach. For example, you may take a 5-min sample out of every hour, or take one momentary

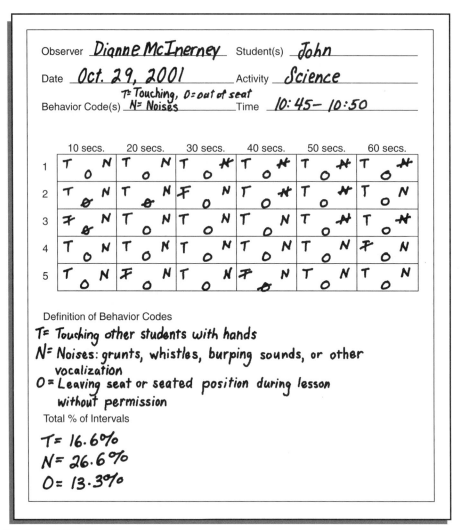

Observer _Dianne McInerney_ Student(s) _John_

Date _Oct. 29, 2001_ Activity _Science_

Behavior Code(s) _T= Touching, O= out of seat N= Noises_ Time _10:45– 10:50_

	10 secs.		20 secs.		30 secs.		40 secs.		50 secs.		60 secs.	
1	T	N	T	N	T	N	T	N	T	N	T	N
	O		O		O		O		O		O	
2	T	N	T	N	T	N	T	N	T	N	T	N
	O		O		O		O		O		O	
3	T	N	T	N	T	N	T	N	T	N	T	N
	O		O		O		O		O		O	
4	T	N	T	N	T	N	T	N	T	N	T	N
	O		O		O		O		O		O	
5	T	N	T	N	T	N	T	N	T	N	T	N
	O		O		O		O		O		O	

Definition of Behavior Codes

T= Touching other students with hands

N= Noises: grunts, whistles, burping sounds, or other
  vocalization

O = Leaving seat or seated position during lesson
  without permission

Total % of Intervals

T= 16.6%

N= 26.6%

O= 13.3%

FIGURE 3–5 Interval Recording Form

sample every 5 min, or sample behavior on a variable interval schedule. If you employ a **momentary time sampling procedure,** rate the occurrence or nonoccurrence of the target behavior immediately following a specified interval of time (Cooper, 1981). In this case, it is advisable to use a wristwatch timer to signal when to observe. Set the timer for the desired interval and when it sounds, record whether the behavior is occurring. Kubany and Slogett (1973) developed a recording form to

use in conjunction with a timer set for variable schedules averaging 4, 8, or 16 min (see Figure 3–6). The numerals in the columns indicate the number of minutes to set the timer according to each variable interval schedule. The advantage of a variable observation schedule is the unpredictability of each interval, particularly if the timer announcement is audible to students (e.g., if a kitchen timer is used). Students may be aware of the behavior being observed, but cannot predict

Target Behavior _On task (✓)_   Date ___5/18/01___

Schedule _VI 4 min._   Student ___Rob___

Teacher ___Jones___

Starting time ___8:40___

Activity ___Language Arts___

VI Schedule (in minutes)

Comments		Four		Eight		Sixteen
	2	✓	12		12	
	5	—	2		8	
	7	✓	10		28	
	1	✓	4		2	
	3	✓	6		24	
	6	—	14		6	
	4	✓	8		24	
	6	—	2		6	
	4	—	10		30	
	1	✓	14		12	
	2	✓	8		16	
	5	✓	10		4	
Came in from fire drill	3	—	6		8	
	7	—	4		30	
	2	—	12		28	
	1	✓	4		6	
	7	—	12		24	
	3	✓	14		16	
	4	—	2		12	
	5	✓	6		2	

Scoring Key: ✓ = on-task

— = off-task

FIGURE 3–6 Variable Interval Recording Form

Source: Kubany, E. S., & Slogett, B. B. (1973). Coding procedure for teachers. Journal of Applied Behavior Analysis, 6 330–334. Used with permission.

each interval and change their behavior when the timer is due to ring. This strategy is particularly useful for measuring the behavior of a group of pupils relative to classroom rules, for example. When the timer sounds, you can check which pupils are on task, in-seat, and so forth. A similar procedure is PLACHECK (Hall, 1973), which involves recording which students are engaged in a particular activity at the end of specified intervals. Pupils also may be trained to take momentary time sample data.

Observing and Recording Multiple Behaviors of Students

As some of the examples we have presented indicate, event, interval, and time sampling formats can be adapted to monitor several behaviors simultaneously. Sometimes researchers measure a number of behaviors at the same time, but we do not recommend that you attempt such complex recording systems without appropriate training. Teachers usually can observe and record up to four behaviors accurately by using appropriately constructed interval recording formats. There are occasions when you may want to monitor two students who are exhibiting the same behaviors, or when you may want to collect simultaneous data on the target pupil's behavior and that of selected peers, either as a basis for validating that the behavior warrants intervention or for setting a criterion level for a behavioral objective (see Chapter 2). One way to accomplish this using an interval format is to observe and record one student's behavior for 10 sec. Then observe and record the second pupil's, and so on, until you have sampled the behavior of all pupils you wish to observe. Observe pupils in the same sequence (Jim, then Vernon, then Carol, then Yvonne, etc.) during any single observation session but vary the sequence from session to session to avoid unintentional bias. Kubany and Slogett's (1973) variable-interval procedure or Hall's (1973) PLACHECK strategy may be used if you are observing the same behavior for each student. Figure 3–7 shows an interval recording form developed for this

purpose. When recording more than one behavior or the behavior of more than one student, be careful not to make your data-collection task too great. The advantages of having more data may be erased by the problem of low accuracy. When attempting new or complex recording procedures, practice collecting data with an experienced observer until you reach 80 to 90% agreement. Remember to recheck observer agreement frequently.

Student Portfolios

Educational reform efforts that call for increasing literacy and academic achievement among school-age children have posed a dilemma for professionals working with students with disabilities. Should these pupils be required to take standardized tests along with their typical peers, and should their scores be averaged in with those of their school or district? One response that does not place students or schools at a disadvantage is to develop alternative assessment and reporting strategies. Student portfolios are a viable alternative. A student portfolio contains information systematically compiled from relevant curricular domains that documents his change and growth over time (Swicegood, 1994). Therefore, portfolios offer a means of monitoring student progress across curricula and settings. Table 3–4 suggests the types of information you may enter into student portfolios. Portfolios are developed through a team process, involving all who participate in delivering services listed on the student's IEP.

A portfolio is a collection of a student's work over time. Together a student and his teacher systematically choose, collect, evaluate, and display papers, projects, tapes, artwork, compositions, and other items that accurately reflect the student's progress in one or more courses. In this way, portfolios use students' strengths and diverse learning styles. The student should assume increasing responsibility for managing his portfolio, and it should be reviewed and updated frequently by the student, his parents, and relevant profes-

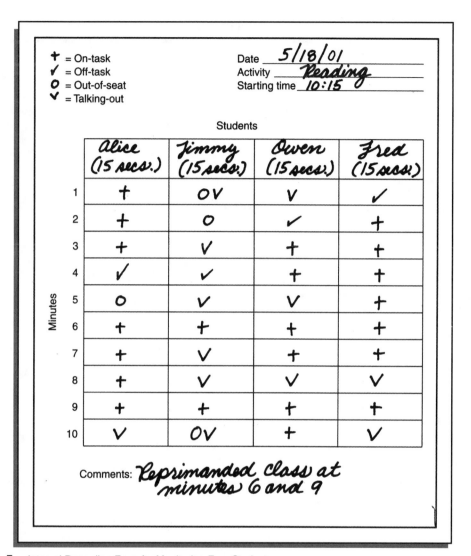

+ = On-task
✓ = Off-task
O = Out-of-seat
ⱱ = Talking-out

Date __5/18/01__
Activity __Reading__
Starting time __10:15__

Students

Minutes	Alice (15 secs.)	Jimmy (15 secs.)	Owen (15 secs.)	Fred (15 secs.)
1	+	OV	V	✓
2	+	O	✓	+
3	+	V	+	+
4	✓	✓	+	+
5	O	V	V	+
6	+	+	+	+
7	+	V	+	+
8	+	V	V	V
9	+	+	+	+
10	V	OV	+	V

Comments: *Reprimanded class at minutes 6 and 9*

FIGURE 3-7   Interval Recording Form for Monitoring Four Students

sionals. Make the shift to portfolio assessment carefully and allow sufficient time for students, parents, and staff to learn to use them properly (Swicegood, 1994). Often portfolios link classroom experiences to district or state standards. Portfolio development follows these basic steps:

1. Collect the permanent products that accurately reflect the student's performance.

2. Select permanent products, or artifacts, that illustrate specific skills or knowledge (standards).

3. Evaluate each product, using written reflections, or rubrics. Students and teachers complete this task together.

4. Compare the work products against standards, IEP objectives, or other measures.

TABLE 3–4   Possible Information to Include in Student Portfolios

---

Measures of Behavior and Adaptive Functioning
Anecdotal records or critical incident logs
Observations of behavior across settings and conditions
Behavior checklists
Interviews about interests, motivation, and attributions
Videotapes of student behaviors
Social skills ratings and checklists
Peer ratings and sociometric measures

Measures of Academic and Literacy Growth
Criterion-referenced tests
Curriculum-based assessments
Teacher-made tests in selected literacy or content-area domains
Analysis of oral reading such as informal reading inventories
Writing samples collected over time
Photographs of student projects
Running records in reading, writing, or math, such as "stories read and completed"
Classroom tests in spelling, math, etc.

Measures of Strategic Learning and Self-Regulation
Ratings and checklists of skills or strategies a student is using
Student self-evaluations of task performance
Miscue analysis procedure in oral reading
Interviews and questions about how a student performs in literacy and classroom tasks
Student thinks aloud: Verbal descriptions of strategies and operations used in different academic situations
Excerpts from teacher-student dialogue journals
Observations and ratings of study skills

Measures of Language and Cultural Aspects
Cultural interviews with students and parents
Primary language sample
Observations of student responses to changing social and classroom situations
Simulations and role-plays

Source: Swicegood, P. (1994). Portfolio-based assessment practices: The uses of portfolio assessment for students with behavioral disorders or learning disabilities. Intervention in School and Clinic, 30, (1), 9. Copyright 1994 PRO-ED. Used with permission.

5. Present the portfolio to others, through a parent-student-teacher conference, or in-class activities. Student-led conferences are a great forum for sharing portfolios with parents.

Many teachers take advantage of technology to create electronic or digitized portfolios (Barrett, 2000). Computer software assists in storing, displaying, comparing, and retrieving student work. To see examples of electronic portfolios, go to: http://transition. alaska.edu/www/portfolios/bookmarks.html.   (For

other practical tips on portfolio assessment, see Rolheiser, Bower, & Stevahn, 2000).

Using Technology to Observe and Record Behaviors

Technology has affected nearly every aspect of education, and observing and recording student behavior is no exception. A variety of computer software and hardware is available for observing behavior and for recording and plotting data from direct observations. Laptop computers are capable of recording and storing data on a number of coded behaviors, or the data can be fed simultaneously into a monitor that displays a graphic record of the data as they are recorded. Denny and Fox (1989) developed a portable microcomputer and software system for observational data collection in school settings.

A disadvantage of many computer-based observational systems is that the observer must enter data at the computer keyboard. Even laptop computers can be cumbersome and obtrusive at times. Johnson et al. (1995) designed a system that allows for unobtrusive data collection in natural settings through a remote recording device that allows the observer to enter event, interval, duration, or latency data, using a remote transmitter to send the data to where the computer is located. Some researchers (e.g., Hausafus & Torrie, 1995; Tapp & Wehby, 2000) have used bar code scanners (like those used to inventory stock in commercial establishments) and handheld computers to record occurrences of behaviors.

Sophisticated computer technology is not out of the reach of classroom observers. Many schools now have microcomputers in some or all classrooms. Programs are available that will turn a classroom computer into a data-collection and plotting instrument (e.g., Zuckerman, 1987). Handheld computers can be programmed to record data (e.g., Taylor, Fried, & Kenardy, 1990). New tools and programs are appearing almost daily. Investigate these labor-saving data-collection and analysis systems with your school's technology specialist.

Assessing Observer Agreement

If all human behavior could be observed and recorded automatically by machines (as the disk pecks or lever presses of laboratory animals are recorded), the accuracy of measurement would be a minor concern. However, we must rely upon our own powers of observation, and this raises the question of the accuracy of the observer's esti-

mates. In the classroom, if the target behaviors result in a permanent product (math worksheet, spelling test, carburetor assembled), measurement accuracy is relatively certain. But most social behaviors are ephemeral; they leave no trace. Unless you are able to obtain an audio or video recording of the student's performance, your accuracy in observing and recording behavioral occurrences is a major concern. Human observers are biased rather easily, and their measures may be influenced by many subjective factors. Also, changes in observed behaviors may be due to errors of measurement rather than to actual changes in behavior resulting from intervention procedures. Therefore, some procedures for improving and evaluating the accuracy of observational measures of behavior are necessary.

One way to improve the accuracy of observational measures is to specifically and objectively define the behaviors to be observed (Cooper, 1981), meaning observations must be confined to what the student actually does rather than reflecting a generalization or impression. Consider the difficulty you might have in measuring "hostile" remarks or "pesky" noises. Human behaviors are objectively defined if two or more persons agree on whether they occurred. It is unlikely that high interobserver agreement could be obtained for either of the behaviors we just mentioned. What is "hostile" or "pesky" to one person may not be to another. To make these behavioral definitions specific and objective, we would ask: What does the pupil do that makes you interpret his remarks as hostile or his noises as pesky? To answer this question we might prepare a list of specific behaviors, the occurrence or nonoccurrence of which two independent persons could agree upon: for example, he says to others, "Go to hell," "I don't like you," "Your momma," and so forth; he taps his pencil against his desk; he squeaks his chair; he belches.

It is not sufficient to develop definitions of target behavior about which two observers *could* agree, however. The primary criterion for evaluating the adequacy of a behavioral definition is the extent to which independent observers actually *do* agree that they have observed the same levels of behavior during the same observation period (Hall, 1973). Only then can we feel relatively confident that the data reflect what the pupil is actually doing and not measurement error. Several methods are used to assess agreement between observers. The simplest method is to calculate the percent of interobserver agreement by dividing the smaller observed frequency by the larger and multiplying by 100. This method is appropriate for event, frequency, or rate data. (Koorland & Westling, 1981). For example, if two observers counted seven and eight episodes of self-stimulation in a 30-min period, their reliability would be $7/8 \times 100 = 88\%$. Another procedure must be used when discrete units of observation, such as time intervals, problems solved, or trials, are being compared (Koorland & Westling, 1981). For each time interval or opportunity to observe the behavior, two observers may agree or disagree as to its occurrence (i.e., they both may "see" the behavior as defined, or they both may not see it, or one may see it although the other does not). Thus reliability is calculated by:

$$\frac{\text{Number of agreements}}{\text{Number of agreements} + \text{disagreements}} \times 100 = \frac{\text{Percent of}}{\text{agreement}}$$

If, for instance, on-task behavior is being observed in 10-sec blocks for 30 min, there would be six observations per minute, or 180 observations for the 30-min period. If two observers agreed (that on-task behavior occurred or did not occur) on 150 of these observations and disagreed on 30, their reliability would be

$$\frac{150}{150 + 30} \times 100 = 83\%$$

This approach is more useful when several behaviors are being observed and recorded simultaneously, when interval data are recorded, or when pupil responses to discrete learning trials are being measured. If you are unsure of the approach to use, consult someone more experienced in behavioral measurement.

There are no hard-and-fast rules for determining how much agreement is enough. When observing low levels of behavior, a single disagreement may make a difference of several percentage points when the total reliability method is used. Generally, 80% agreement is considered satisfactory but 90% or better is preferred (Koorland & Westling 1981; Tawney & Gast, 1984). Use periodic assessments of interobserver agreement to rule out gradual changes in the observers' interpretation regarding the occurrence or nonoccurrence of a behavior. Conduct these assessments at least once during each program phase, and otherwise once a week, unless you are measuring permanent products. If interobserver agreement is below 80%, check with the other observer regarding how he or she is scoring instances and noninstances of the behaviors observed before resuming formal data collection. If agreement is below 90%, follow the same procedure without interrupting formal data collection. However, in both cases you should conduct additional assessments to ensure that disagreements have been resolved.

SUMMARIZING DATA

Obviously, if your observations are recorded with a wrist counter, on scraps of paper, or on an interval data sheet, you will want to transfer the data to a central form, both for convenience and safekeeping. Such forms need not be elaborate, but they should contain all relevant information: dates, sessions, observation time, data taken, and program phase. Software spreadsheet programs can be used to quickly generate data summary forms. Figure 3–8 is a data summary sheet for rate data measured in terms of responses per minute. Such forms centralize your data for easy reference and for transfer to a chart or graph.

Data summaries can be organized to eliminate the necessity of graphing or charting. For example, Nelson et al. (1979) developed an IEP performance

Teacher **Swenson Margaret**
(last)   (first)

Student **Issacs Jean**
(last)   (first)

Target **Offers to share with peers**

Phase	Session	Number of responses	Time (minutes)	Rate (number of responses per minute)	Consequence
baseline	1	0	30	0	
	2	0	30	0	
	3	10	30	.33	
	4	0	30	0	
	5	0	30	0	
Intervention 1	6	9	30	.30	1 min. free time if .33 per min.
	7	11	30	.35	
	8	5	30	.18	
	9	9	30	.30	
	10	13	30	.42	
	11	8	30	.27	
	12	5	30	.18	
Intervention 2	13	16	30	.52	Sit by preferred peer if .42 per min.
	14	13	30	.42	
	15	18	30	.58	
	16	11	30	.35	
	17	16	30	.52	
	18	20	30	.62	
	19	17	30	.55	
	20	20	30	.64	
	21	17	30	.55	Lunch with preferred peer if .52 per min.
	22	20	30	.64	
	23	20	30	.64	
	24	18	30	.58	
	25	20	30	.64	
	26	20	30	.64	
	27	20	30	.64	
	28				
	29				
	30				

FIGURE 3–8   Rate Data Summary Sheet

chart to monitor progress on task steps or short-term objectives. Figure 3–9 shows how the system can be used to summarize performance regarding several targeted social behaviors. In this figure an X indicates that a criterion was met for a particular behavior, a / (forward slash) indicates that a criterion was not met, and the daily total indicates whether the short-term objective was met for that day.

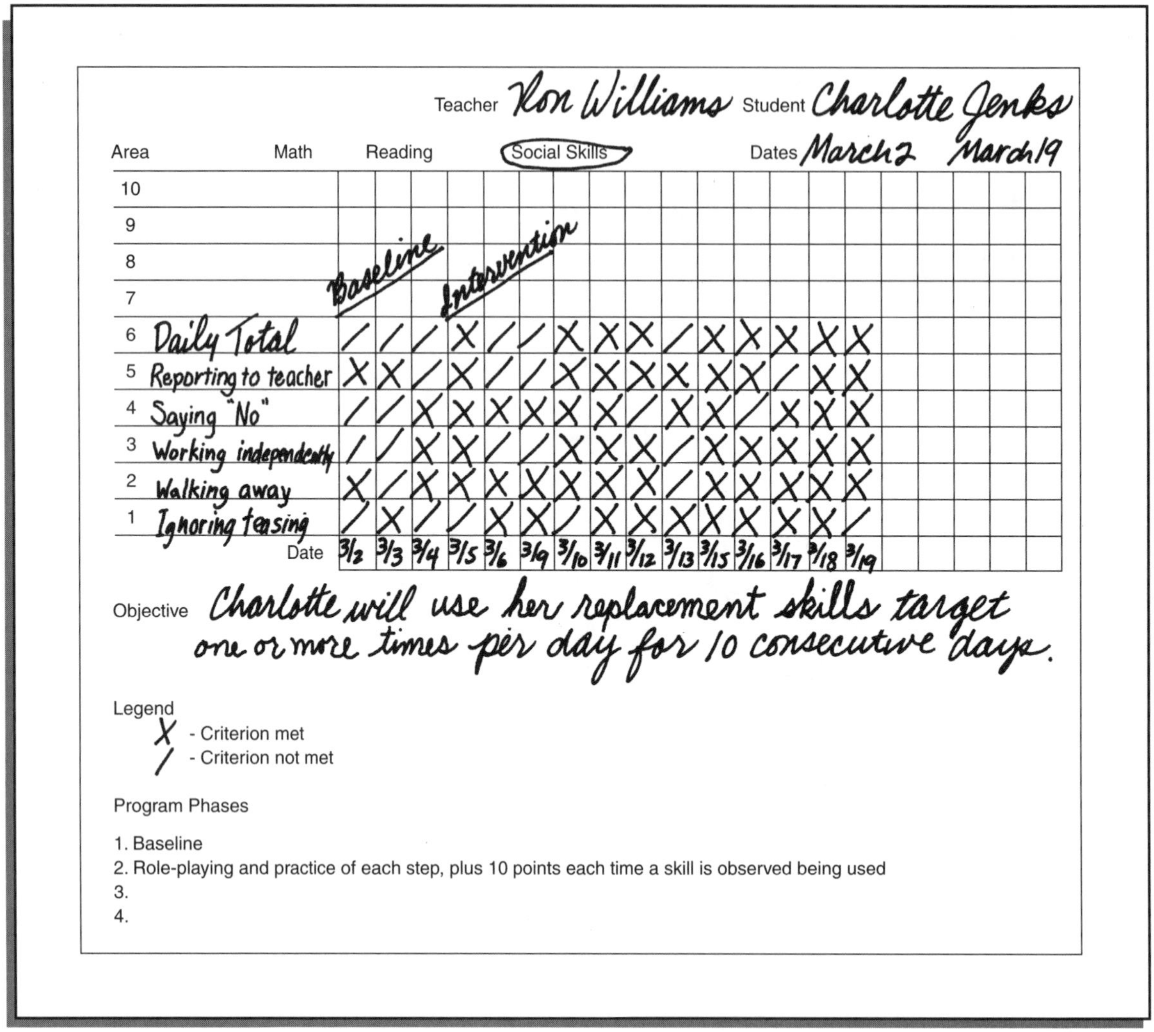

FIGURE 3–9   IEP Performance Chart

Another procedure was developed by Fabry and Cone (1980) for discrete trial recording. In this procedure, an X indicates a correct response and an O designates an error response. Figure 3–10 illustrates three uses of this procedure. The left-hand portion displays a summary of pupil responses to each trial across sessions. Here the teacher has recorded the student's performance for each instructional trial in the order that trials were presented. The middle portion shows these same data, but the teacher entered each correct student response from the bottom of the chart and each error from the top down. You can see that the student had four correct trials out of ten during session 1. An auto-graph of these data was produced by connecting the Xs representing the cumulative total of correct responses for each session. The right-hand portion summarizes the same student's performance, but this time the teacher also wrote the number of each trial ac-

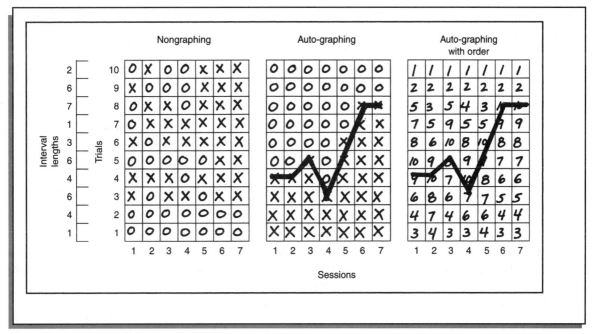

FIGURE 3–10 Auto-Graphing Data Forms

Source: Fabry, B. D., & Cone, J. D. (1980). Auto-graphing: A one-step approach to collecting and graphing data. Education and Treatment of Children, 3, 361–368. Used with permission.

cording to whether the response was correct or incorrect. Trials 3, 4, 6, and 9 in session 1 were correct; the first correct trial was 3, and the last was 9. These data also have been transformed into a graph by connecting the cells representing the last correct trial per session. The advantage of this procedure is that the teacher can collect, summarize, and graph student performance while administering instructional trials.

A final variation of Fabry and Cone's (1980) system is to substitute time intervals for trials. Interval lengths are set according to a predetermined variable interval schedule (see the left side of Figure 3–10). The teacher sets a timer for the designated interval lengths and when it sounds, enters the appropriate symbol for the pupil's behavior, as in Kubany and Slogett's (1973) procedure. These data may be arranged to create an auto-graph, just as when trial-by-trial data are recorded.

Graphing and Charting

If you employ either of the charting systems just presented, you will already have a useful visual display. However, there are other meaningful ways to present data visually. Remember that most teachers can get a variety of data pertaining to student performance. Much of it is work samples, weekly test scores, or results of standardized achievement tests. Such data are used infrequently for program decision making because these samples are not organized to be useful for this purpose: they do not show trends in student performance or compare performance to predetermined criteria. Nongraphic data summary forms such as that depicted in Figure 3–8 do organize the data, but they fail to display trends or communicate clearly to anyone who is not intimately familiar with the program or student they represent. On the other hand, graphs and charts meet these goals. A **graph** typically uses only one or two symbols to represent data (e.g., a dot or a triangle). A **chart,** however, displays from several to many symbols to represent the data. All types of graphs and charts serve three important purposes: (a) they summarize data in a manner convenient for precise, daily decision making; (b) they communicate information that is helpful in evaluating the effects of an intervention or program on a frequent basis; and (c) they provide reinforcement and feedback to those persons involved with the program.

There are as many types of charts and graphs as there are behaviors to monitor. However, these can be grouped into a few categories. The selection of any particular type depends on the considerations listed in Table 3–3, as well as on the type of data to be presented. A **bar graph** may be used to show progress toward a specific goal or objective. For example, Figure 3–11 shows a student's progress toward earning a class party through appropriate classroom behavior. This type of graph is useful for presenting data to be used by students because it is easily interpreted and may be reinforcing. Pupils also may be reinforced by filling in the graph each day. Another type of bar graph, shown in Figure 3–12, provides a better display of daily fluctuations in student performance. Bar graphs may be used to plot any kind of data and they are easily understood by pupils, parents, and other lay persons. An even simpler presentation is a star chart, shown in Figure 3–13. Charts such as these can be sent home to parents as daily or weekly reports. Charts that report the results of behavior (points earned, stars) instead of the behavior itself are reinforcing and do communicate readily, but they do not provide the kind of data useful to teachers for decision-making purposes.

The graph pictured in Figure 3–11 is a **cumulative graph;** each day's total is added to the previous day's earnings. Line graphs may also be cumulative, as shown in Figure 3–14. Although you may plot cumulative time, percentages, frequencies, or rates of either appropriate or inappropriate behavior, if the graph is to be used by the student,

plot desired behavior (e.g., time in-seat instead of time out-of-seat) so that increases in level will be associated with improvement, not regression.

A noncumulative frequency graph, or **frequency polygon,** is the most common type used in behavioral research, and is the type most useful in data-based decision making. It may be used to report frequency, rate, or percent data. Frequency polygons are illustrated in Figures 3–15 and 3–16. Numerical frequency is plotted in Figure 3–14 and rate (movements per minute) are graphed in Figure 3–15.

Figure 3–15 illustrates plotting on **equal interval graph paper** (i.e., the difference between a frequency of 15 and 16 is equal to the difference between that of 19 and 20). Figure 3–16 shows data plotted on **equal ratio** or semilogarithmic **graph paper,** on which equal changes in rate show up as identical changes in the slope of the data path regardless of their absolute rate. For example, a change in rate from 0.1 to 0.2 responses (movements) per minute or from 5 to 10 movements per minute, or an acceleration in rate of times 2, show up as identical slopes on the graph. Although equal ratio graph paper may be confusing to those who are not accustomed to it, the rules for plotting data are learned quickly. Also, this standard semilogarithmic charting paper offers several advantages: it saves time in drawing and scaling graphs; it allows behaviors occurring anywhere between 1 time in 24 hr and 1,000 times per min to be plotted on the same graph; it permits comparison across different times and activities when the amount of time or number of opportunities to respond varies; and once persons become familiar with the ratio scale, time is saved in reading and interpreting the plotted data (White, 1986). The major disadvantage of equal ratio graphing is that it is cumbersome to collect data on students' responses per minute when each response is controlled by the teacher's instruction (e.g., "Do this" . . . "Now do this" . . .) because, in order to measure only the pupil's rate of response, the teacher would have to subtract the time required to give each instruction from the time period in which response rate was

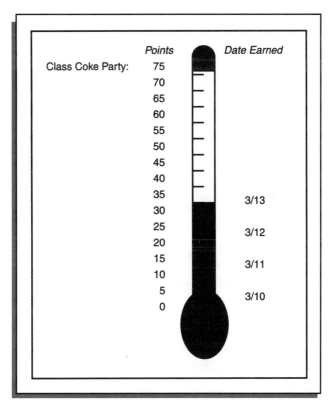

	Points		Date Earned
Class Coke Party:	75		
	70		
	65		
	60		
	55		
	50		
	45		
	40		
	35		3/13
	30		
	25		3/12
	20		
	15		3/11
	10		
	5		3/10
	0		

FIGURE 3–11   Susan's Progress Toward a Class Party

measured (Tawney & Gast, 1984). (Standard semi-logarithmic graph paper, called the Standard 'Celeration Chart, may be purchased from Behavior Research Company, Box 251, Kansas City, KS 66103.)

Graphs and charts may be designed to display either student progress or performance. A **progress graph** or **chart** shows the time it takes a student to master a set of objectives (Deno & Mirkin, 1978). For example, Figure 3–17 is a chart of a student's progress toward mastery of a set of sight words. A **performance chart** or **graph,** on the other hand, reports a change on a single task or behavior (Deno & Mirkin, 1978). The same type of data may be charted either way. For example, Figure 3–18 shows student daily performance on the same set of sight words. Whether you select

progress or performance graphs depends on the kind of data you will be using to make decisions: daily performance or sequential progress (Deno & Mirkin, 1978). Your choice will also be influenced by your instructional strategy. If you have task-analyzed your terminal objective, for instance, progress charting will be more suitable. Performance graphs or charts are better suited for monitoring most social behaviors, unless you are using direct teaching procedures to shape a particular skill or behavior.

The communication function of charts and graphs is not fulfilled if they are cluttered or inconsistent or if the reader cannot follow what is being reported. Tawney and Gast (1984) indicate that graphic presentations of data should communicate to the reader the sequence of baseline

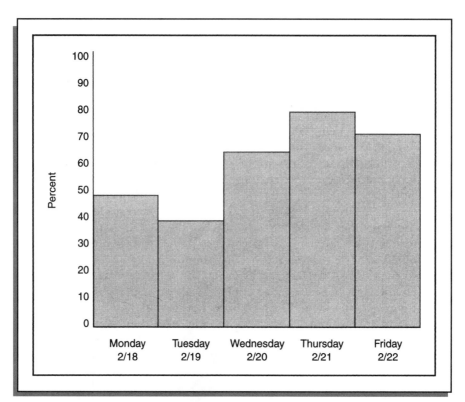

FIGURE 3–12   Arnold's Percent of Assignments Completed

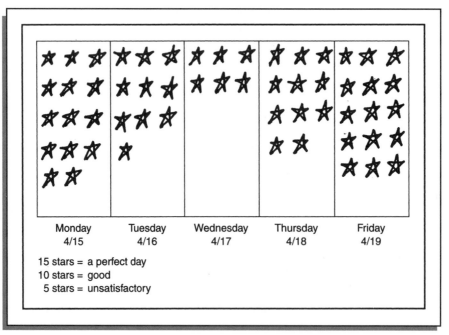

15 stars = a perfect day
10 stars = good
 5 stars = unsatisfactory

FIGURE 3–13   Mary's Good Behavior Chart

Foundations of Effective Behavior Management

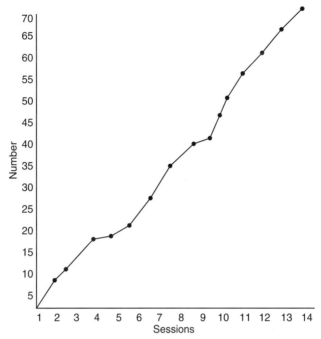

FIGURE 3–14 David: Math Facts Learned

and intervention conditions, the time spent in each condition, the independent and dependent variables, the experimental design used, and the relationships among variables. Figure 3–19 identifies the major components of a frequency polygon or simple line graph. Because charts use a variety of symbols to represent the data, they require more elaborate legends, but the basic parts are the same. Condition lines are used to designate where changes in conditions are made. Generally, behavior graphs begin with a baseline condition, followed by intervention conditions that may include phase changes (adjustments in the intervention; e.g., a change in the schedule of reinforcement). Intervention conditions and phases should be labeled descriptively, but briefly, so the reader knows what conditions are in effect at any given time. The examples we have

provided in this chapter illustrate the range of options possible without grossly violating these guidelines. With practice you will be able to construct useful graphs quickly and efficiently. Your pupils can learn to construct graphs and plot data too (self-graphing may be a reinforcer for students interested in their own progress). A number of software programs are available for creating charts and graphs.

As we mentioned at the beginning of this section, one of the principal uses of charts and graphs is to facilitate decision making by educators and intervention planners. While displaying data in these formats helps us understand how target behaviors are being affected by intervention procedures, decisions can be made more precisely and expediently if the data are visually analyzed and objective rules are developed. This process is described next.

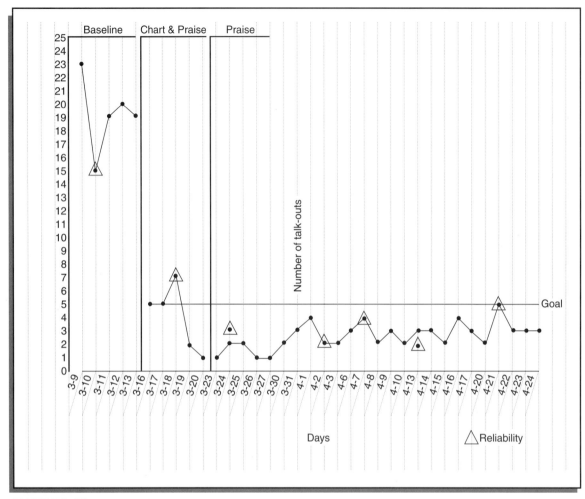

FIGURE 3–15   Kay: Talk-Outs

USING DATA TO MAKE DECISIONS

The professional who is directly responsible for managing the target student in settings where targeted behaviors occur must be able to evaluate interventions continuously and make or recommend adjustments to intervention procedures on the basis of these evaluations. **Data-based decision making** is a technology designed to assist practitioners in conducting ongoing formative evaluations of student performance as part of the teach-

ing or intervention process. It uses data collected systematically to measure targeted academic and social behaviors.

One of the first skills required for data-based decision making is determining what the collected data are telling you. In other words, you must know how to analyze data. There are two approaches to behavioral data analysis: statistical and visual. The debate between proponents of both approaches has been long standing and lively. We advocate the visual method because visual analysis is more conservative (Parsonson &

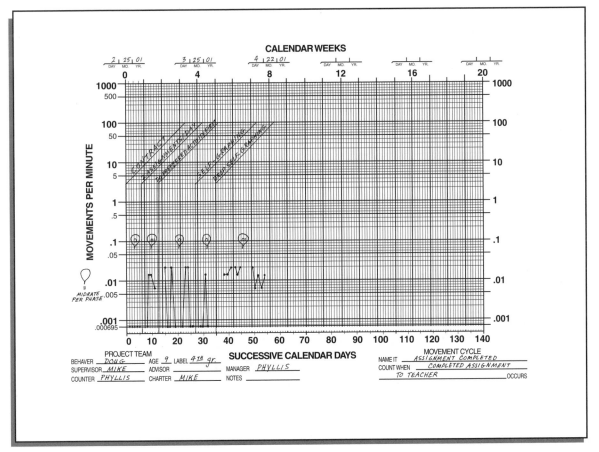

CALENDAR WEEKS

FIGURE 3-16   Doug: Rate of Assignment Completion

Baer, 1978). In addition, visual inspection is more realistic for practitioners.

Formative evaluation, then, is based upon ongoing data collection. These data are used to decide when to change an instructional or behavior management program as well as which components of a student's program to alter, remove, or replace. Obviously, this task cannot be accomplished without data that are sensitive to variations in students' daily performances and that are reliable measures of those performances. If your data are sensitive and reliable, you can make good program evaluation decisions from visual analysis.

Formative evaluation based on visual data analysis (data-based decision making) amounts to identifying **functional relationships** between environmental variables and the target behavior being measured. This is accomplished by systematically manipulating certain environmental variables (curriculum, reinforcement, instructions, etc.) one at a time while keeping other variables as constant as possible.[3]

Before implementing an academic or social intervention, assess the student's current performance. Instead of a static pretest approach, which may not represent the pupil's typical performance, measure target behavior across several sessions or days. Your intervention data then can

[3]Recall that this is the same process used to verify hypotheses generated through functional behavioral assessments.

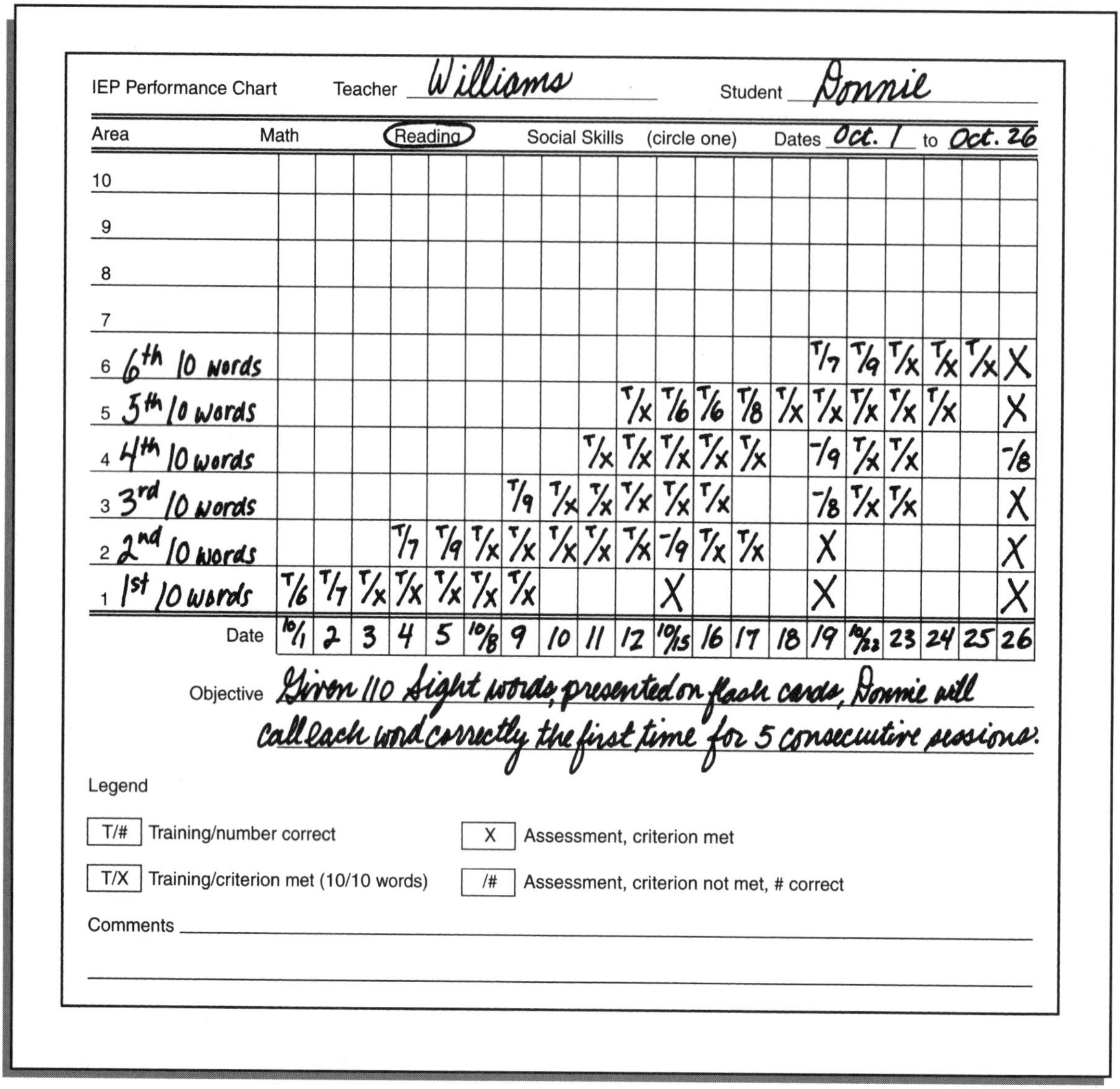

IEP Performance Chart Teacher _Williams_ Student _Donnie_

Area Math (Reading) Social Skills (circle one) Dates _Oct. 1_ to _Oct. 26_

	10/1	2	3	4	5	10/8	9	10	11	12	10/15	16	17	18	19	10/22	23	24	25	26
10																				
9																				
8																				
7																				
6 6th 10 words															T/7	T/9	T/x	T/x	T/x	X
5 5th 10 words											T/x	T/6	T/6	T/8	T/x	T/x	T/x	T/x	T/x	X
4 4th 10 words									T/x	T/x	T/x	T/x	T/x		T/9	T/x	T/x			/8
3 3rd 10 words							T/9	T/x	T/x	T/x	T/x	T/x			/8	T/x	T/x			X
2 2nd 10 words						T/7	T/9	T/x	T/x	T/x	T/x	T/x	T/9	T/x	T/x	X				X
1 1st 10 words	T/6	T/7	T/x	T/x	T/x	T/x	T/x			X					X					X
Date	10/1	2	3	4	5	10/8	9	10	11	12	10/15	16	17	18	19	10/22	23	24	25	26

Objective _Given 110 sight words, presented on flash cards, Donnie will call each word correctly the first time for 5 consecutive sessions._

Legend

T/#	Training/number correct		X	Assessment, criterion met
T/X	Training/criterion met (10/10 words)		/#	Assessment, criterion not met, # correct

Comments _____

FIGURE 3–17 Progress Chart: Sight Words

be compared to this pre-intervention or **baseline data** to determine whether your program is effective. Thus, the purpose of collecting baseline data is to determine current levels and trends in behavior, as well as to see whether any environmental variables present during the baseline period are affecting it.

There are no hard and fast rules for determining the length of a baseline condition. Length depends on the level of the behavior, its variability, and whether it shows a trend in the direction of the criterion level, as well as such factors as the effects of the target student's behavior on others and the amount of time left in the school term. If baseline

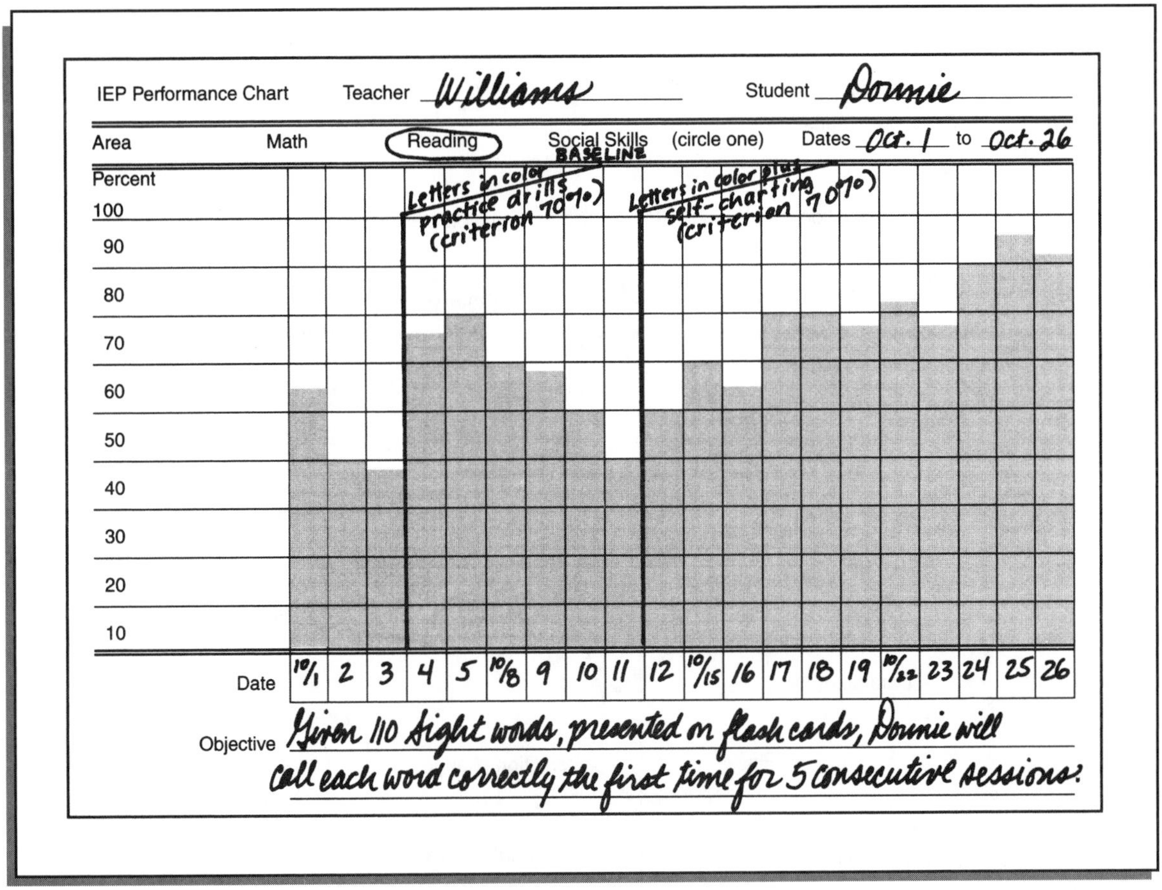

FIGURE 3–18 Performance Graph: Sight Words

data are highly variable or show a trend in the direction of the desired criterion level, consider extending the baseline phase while looking for sources of variation or factors contributing to trends. A minimum of three baseline data points generally are recommended for academic target behaviors (e.g., White & Haring, 1980), although White (1971) demonstrated that a *minimum* of seven data points is needed to project a reliable performance trend. You should collect five to seven baseline data points on social behavior targets, unless circumstances prohibit it.

Baseline data provide a relative standard against which subsequent program changes may

be evaluated, so it is essential to analyze these data as carefully as those gathered during intervention conditions. The visual display of data via graphs and charts provides a convenient summary across various baseline and intervention conditions. Within these conditions, the data may be characterized in terms of level, trend, and stability. Straightforward and useful procedures for analyzing data about these characteristics on simple line graphs have been developed.

ANALYZING LEVEL The magnitude of the data in terms of the scale value on the ordinate, or Y-axis, of the graph is its level. Tawney and Gast

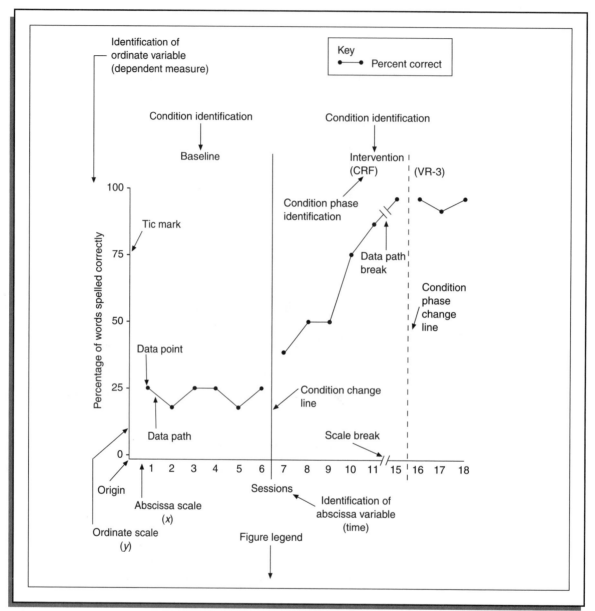

FIGURE 3–19   Basic Components of a Simple Line Graph

Source: *Tawney, J. W., & Gast, D. L. (1984). Single subject research in special education. Upper Saddle River, NJ: Merrill/Prentice Hall. Used with permission.*

Note: Draw condition lines between sessions; do not connect data points in adjacent conditions: set 0 on the ordinate scale above the abscissa.

(1984) describe two characteristics of level that are important in data analysis. Within a given condition, level may be analyzed with regard to stability and change. *Level stability* refers to the variability of the data points around their median. Data that vary no more than 15% from the median value would be considered stable. Level stability reflects the degree to which behavior is affected by planned or unplanned variables. For example, unstable data following the introduction of an intervention suggest that the other variables may be influencing the behavior as much as the intervention procedures (Tawney & Gast, 1984).

Level change refers to the amount of relative change in the data within or between conditions. To determine the amount of level change within a condition, find the ordinate values of the first and last data points in the condition, subtract the smallest from the largest, and note whether the change is occurring in a therapeutic (improving) or contratherapeutic direction, based on the intervention objective. Knowledge of the amount of level change within a condition is useful for deciding whether it is appropriate to change conditions. For example, if a level change is occurring in a therapeutic direction during baseline conditions, it may be unnecessary to begin an intervention. To find the amount of *level change between adjacent conditions* (e.g., baseline and intervention), identify the ordinate values of the last data point of the first condition and the value of the first data point of the second condition. Then subtract the smaller from the larger, and note whether the change is in an improving or decaying direction. The amount of level change between baseline and intervention conditions is an indication of the immediate impact of the intervention on the target behavior (Tawney & Gast, 1984).

Another important characteristic to consider when evaluating changes in data between conditions is the amount of *overlapping data points*. This is determined by noting the proportion of data points in adjacent conditions that fall within the same range. For example, if more than 50% of the data points during an interven-tion condition fall within the range of baseline data points, it may be concluded that the intervention has only weak effects (Parsonson & Baer, 1978). However, the trend of the intervention data must also be considered.

ANALYZING DATA TRENDS Data paths seldom follow straight lines, nor do they increase or decrease in even increments. This can create difficulty in making reliable judgments about whether rates of behavior are accelerating, decelerating, or remaining relatively stable. A relatively simple way to analyze data trends is to draw **trend lines** (also called lines of progress) that depict the general path of the data within a condition. This can be done by the freehand method, which involves drawing a line of "best fit" that bisects the data points (Parsonson & Baer, 1978). This method takes very little time but the trend lines produced are likely to be inaccurate (Tawney & Gast, 1984). A more reliable procedure is to draw a *split-middle line of progress* (White & Haring, 1980), as explained in Figure 3–20. This method may be used to analyze trends in data plotted either on equal interval or equal ratio (semilogarithmic) graph paper, and with a little practice you can do it quickly.

Data trends often reveal important and useful information. For example, an increasing (accelerating) trend indicates that the target behavior is probably being reinforced. A level trend suggests that reinforcement is serving to maintain the behavior at its current rate. A decreasing (decelerating) trend indicates that extinction or punishment contingencies are in effect. Such trends may show that contingencies unknown to or unplanned by intervention agents are operating. For example, if a baseline trend is in the direction of your intervention criterion, and you implement an intervention, it would be difficult to attribute a continued change in a therapeutic direction (were this to occur) to the intervention because the behavior was changing anyway. On the other hand, if the baseline trend is stable or in a direction opposite to the intervention criterion, you could justifiably hypothesize that therapeutic changes following the

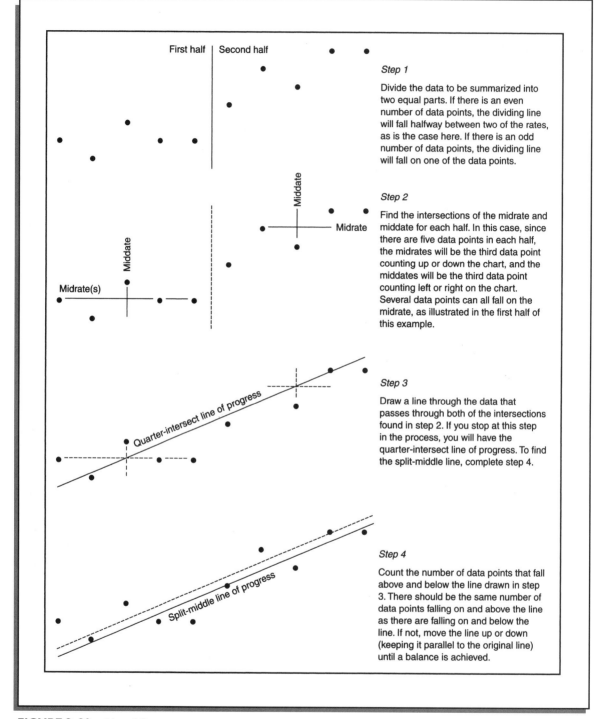

First half | Second half

Step 1

Divide the data to be summarized into two equal parts. If there is an even number of data points, the dividing line will fall halfway between two of the rates, as is the case here. If there is an odd number of data points, the dividing line will fall on one of the data points.

Middate

Midrate

Step 2

Find the intersections of the midrate and middate for each half. In this case, since there are five data points in each half, the midrates will be the third data point counting up or down the chart, and the middates will be the third data point counting left or right on the chart. Several data points can all fall on the midrate, as illustrated in the first half of this example.

Middate

Midrate(s)

Quarter-intersect line of progress

Step 3

Draw a line through the data that passes through both of the intersections found in step 2. If you stop at this step in the process, you will have the quarter-intersect line of progress. To find the split-middle line, complete step 4.

Split-middle line of progress

Step 4

Count the number of data points that fall above and below the line drawn in step 3. There should be the same number of data points falling on and above the line as there are falling on and below the line. If not, move the line up or down (keeping it parallel to the original line) until a balance is achieved.

FIGURE 3–20   Line of Progress

Source: *White, O. R., & Haring, N. G. (1980). Exceptional teaching (2nd ed.). Upper Saddle River, NJ: Merrill/Prentice Hall. Used with permission.*

initiation of an intervention condition were the result of your procedure.

ANALYZING DATA STABILITY   The stability of data is the variability of individual data points around the trend line. Gable, Hendrickson, Evans, and Evans (1988) suggest drawing a window of variance around the trend line to indicate the amount of desired stability around the trend. This is done by drawing parallel dotted lines representing a 15% range above and below the trend line. (This range can be computed by determining the medians for both halves of the data within a condition and calculating values within 15% of these, but it is simpler to estimate this variance visually.) Howell, Fox, and Morehead (1993) recommended that the window of variance should encompass at least 80% of the data points. Any extreme variation or sudden change in your data that is not associated with a planned condition indicates that something unanticipated is affecting the target behavior, and you should attempt to find out what it is through conducting further functional assessments. This information may help you adjust the intervention or control extraneous variables affecting the student's performance.

Determining data trends during intervention may also help you assess functional relationships and troubleshoot your program. Parsonson and Baer (1978) provided several guidelines. For example, stable intervention data following a variable baseline indicates that recurring baseline variables may be the treatment variables (e.g., differential teacher attention that was not controlled systematically during baseline). Weak program effects are suggested by variable intervention data or by considerable overlap between data points in baseline and intervention conditions. This problem is less critical if the overlap diminishes later during the intervention phase. A delayed therapeutic trend in the intervention data (i.e., no positive change followed by a change in the desired direction) may indicate the presence of initial training steps that are redundant or a waste of time. Figure 3–21 presents stylized graphs illus-

trating several intervention trends, and their interpretation. As you become more proficient in analyzing data visually, you will also be able to interpret trends more accurately.

Data trend analysis tells you whether an instructional program or intervention is working and can prompt you to remove or revise an ineffective strategy, but waiting for a trend to emerge may take too long. Practitioners who must make day-to-day program decisions need rules to expedite their decision making. Fortunately, empirical data decision rules have been developed for academic targets (Deno, 2000; White & Haring, 1980). To implement these rules, follow these steps:

1. Obtain and plot baseline assessment data for at least 3 days (or sessions if more than one instructional session takes place each day).
2. Determine a desired terminal criterion level. This may be established arbitrarily by the curriculum, by assessing peers, from data obtained in previous programs with the student, from normative data on the target behavior, if available, or by comparing the performance of peers who are fluent in the skill being measured. Plot this on the graph at a location corresponding to when you expect the criterion to be reached (see step 3).
3. Set a date when you want to meet the criterion. Also plot this on the graph.
4. Draw a line of desired progress from the median (middle value) of the last three baseline data points to the criterion level and date.
5. Change the program if the student's progress fails to meet or exceed the line of desired progress for three consecutive days or sessions (White & Haring, 1980).

Figure 3–22 illustrates a data decision graph for an academic target.

Data decision rules for social behaviors are not as clear-cut, because student performance,

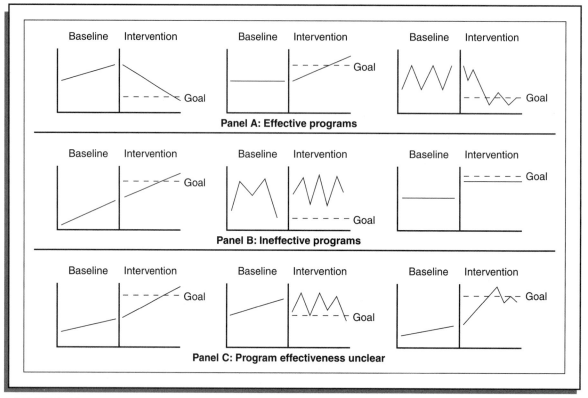

FIGURE 3-21 Interpretation of Data Trends

rather than sequential progress, is generally measured. Therefore, it is more difficult to establish a line of desired progress. You may, however, set your criterion in terms of a *daily level of desired performance* and base your decisions on the following steps:

1. Obtain 5 to 7 days (or sessions) of baseline data (more if the data are extremely variable or a therapeutic trend is apparent).
2. Set and graph terminal criterion level and date, just as for academic targets.
3. Write a data decision rule for the program (e.g., change the program if performance does not meet the criterion in a particular phase for three consecutive sessions or days).
4. Collect intervention data and adjust the program according to your rule.

These are guidelines rather than rules; they should be applied flexibly. Different behaviors and circumstances will require different data decision guidelines.

When setting criterion levels for targeted social behaviors, keep in mind an **ecological ceiling** (Howell et al., 1993). This means simply to acknowledge that it is unrealistic (and unfair) to expect students to demonstrate rates of targeted behaviors at levels that are not typical of peers in the same settings. Thus, a zero rate of talk-outs is an unreasonable criterion if the usual rate of peer talk-outs is five per hour. By assessing peers who are exhibiting acceptable rates of the target behavior, you can establish reasonable criterion levels. Lines of desired progress or performance should reflect an appropriate ecological ceiling rather than at an arbitrarily chosen rate.

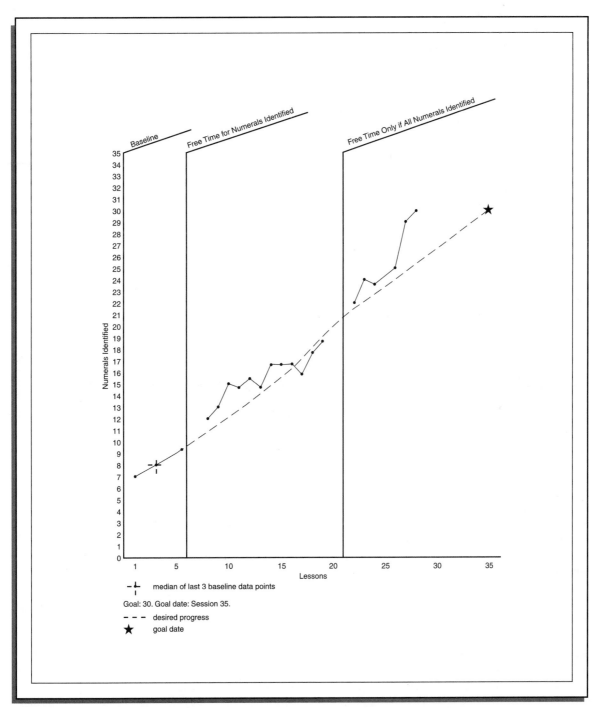

FIGURE 3–22   Data Decision Graph: Academic Program

A Procedure for Monitoring the Rate of Student's Correct Academic Responding

Phillip L. Gunter and Marti L. Venn
Valdosta State University

Ms. Smith was teaching math to a group of students in a third-grade classroom. The group was primarily comprised of students without disabilities; however, some students with behavioral disorders were in the group. Ms. Smith wanted to be sure that she was instructing her students effectively since her training program had not prepared her to teach students with behavior disorders. However, because she was also a first-year teacher she seemed to have little time for self-reflection of her instruction and she knew that her principal would only observe her teaching twice that year.

She was reading a copy of *Beyond Behavior* (Vol. 9, No. 4) in the faculty lounge. This is a professional magazine with information for those teaching students with behavior disorders. She found an article by Gunter, Hummel, and Venn (1998) that provided a protocol for determining whether classroom instruction was effective based on the number of correct responses students in the classroom gave (see Figure 3–23). One of the primary aspects of the use of this protocol was its simplicity. Therefore, she decided that she would attempt to use the protocol to determine if her classroom instruction was effective.

To do this, Ms. Smith placed a video camera at the back of her room during instruction of the math class and videotaped her instruction. She waited until the end of the school day to review the recorded lesson. She rewound the tape to the first part of the class period in which new information was presented. She used the self-evaluation protocol from the Gunter, Hummel, and Venn article and her digital watch. When she began reviewing the tape, she entered the time in hours, minutes, and seconds (10:00:00)

on the protocol sheet for starting time, and when she came to the end of instruction of new information, she entered the time again in hours, minutes, and seconds (10:19:30) in the space for ending time. While watching the lesson for the total time of 19 min and 30 sec, Ms. Smith recorded the number of correct responses that were given by each student she called on or the correct response of the group if she had asked for all the students to respond simultaneously. She used her best teacher intuition for group responses to determine if at least 80% of the students responded correctly.

To record the correct responses, Ms. Smith simply made a tally mark in the box on the form for frequency of correct responses. Examples of correct responses included Jimmy's response of "6" when asked, "What is 2 × 3?" Additionally, a correct response was marked when 80% of the class responded "In the one's column" when asked, "Where do we put the 2 from the number 12 when we multiply 2 × 6?" She did not mark a correct response when Frank answered "sum" when asked, "What is the term used to define the answer of multiplying two numbers?" since "product" would have been the correct answer. During the 19 min and 30 sec she recorded 73 correct responses made by students in the classroom during math instruction.

To make the calculations on the protocol, Ms. Smith first subtracted the starting time from the ending time of the observation and entered 19 min and 30 sec in the spaces for length of observation. The 19 min were multiplied by 60 and that product (1140) was added to the remaining seconds (30) of the observation. The total seconds (1170) were then divided by 60 to result in a whole number and a decimal (19.5 min). She then counted the number of tally marks she made (73) and divided that number by the time (19.5). The result is the rate of correct responses per minute (3.74).

Next, Ms. Smith compared the rate of correct responses she observed to that rate recommended in the effective instruction literature as presented on the bottom of the protocol. She noted that the rate of correct responses observed (3.74) was greater than the minimum number recommended (3) for instruction of new material to be effective (Gunter & Denny, 1998).

The entire process took less than an hour for Ms. Smith to complete, and she had a description of her academic instruction that had at least some foundation in empirically validated procedures. Had Ms. Smith found that the level of correct responses from students was lower than that recommended, she could use a different protocol like the one developed by Gunter and Reed (1997) to possibly help determine the cause for student failure to reach the number of correct responses required for instruction to be effective. This more elaborate self-evaluation procedure requires the observation of several teacher and student behaviors but allows the development of a functional behavioral hypothesis for both academic and social behaviors of students.

For drill and practice independent work the process might be modified to determine the effectiveness of the instructional session. The same protocol can be used to evaluate only correct academic responding but instead of observing videotaped instruction, the teacher can simply count the number of problems or tasks completed correctly on permanent product samples and divide the number correct by the amount of time needed to complete the work. In this aspect of academic instruction, the rate of correct responses expected would be at least 8 per minute (Gunter & Denny, 1998).

Teacher _____ Ms. Smith _____ Observer _____ Ms. Smith _____

Date ___ 10/30/00 _____ Starting time ___ 10:00:00 _____ Ending time _ 10:19:30 _____

Length of observation in minutes ___ 19 _____ and seconds ___ 30 _____

X60

____ 1140 _ plus ____ 30 _____ = ___ 1170 _____ seconds

/60

= __ 19.5 _____ time

Frequency of Correct Responses

卌 卌 卌 卌 卌 卌 卌 卌 卌 卌 卌 卌 卌 卌 ///	Frequency of correct responses __ 73 ____ Divided by Time __ 19.5 ____ = Rate of correct responding __ 3.74 ____

For instruction of new material, the rate of correct responses should be at least 3 per minute.
For drill and practice instruction, the rate of correct responses should be at least 8 per minute.

FIGURE 3–23   Calculating the Rate of Correct Responding

SUMMARY

This chapter has addressed the important area of monitoring student performance. The range of procedures for measuring human behavior is expanding rapidly. We have attempted to present important considerations regarding the collection and use of behavioral data in educational settings and to provide sample strategies that you may use in designing your own procedures for monitoring students' educational progress. Although there are no tangible incentives to encourage data-based instruction or intervention, research indicates that pupils whose teachers monitor their performance make greater progress than those who do not (Fuchs, 1986). Practice in data collection and graphing will increase your fluency and confidence.

DISCUSSION QUESTIONS

1. What are some of the factors that contribute to teachers' unwillingness to collect behavioral data? Suggest strategies for overcoming these resistances.
2. Suggest alternate recording strategies for the following behaviors and situations: a low-rate behavior that occurs on the playground; a high-rate behavior that occurs across a number of settings; a behavior that is characterized by its duration; a behavior that is continuous; several behaviors exhibited by more than one pupil.
3. Talk with a teacher who has used portfolios to document students' progress over time. What are some of the advantages and limitations of portfolio assessments compared with more traditional approaches?
4. If your school or program has access to a computer-based observational system, obtain a copy and experiment with different types of data collection. How does it compare with "hard copy" observational data-collection procedures?
5. Why is interobserver agreement an important consideration in measuring social behavior? How can it be influenced by such factors as low or high rates of targeted behaviors?
6. Describe the features of well-constructed graphs and charts and how these contribute to clear communication.
7. Differentiate between equal interval and equal ratio graphs and between performance or progress charts. What circumstances influence decisions about which to use?
8. How do data levels, trends, and stability affect decisions about changing intervention conditions?
9. What is a functional relationship? How is a functional relationship demonstrated between an intervention and a target behavior?

REFERENCES

Barrett, H. C. (2000). Electronic portfolios = Multimedia development+portfolio development. Paper prepared for presentation at the SITE 2000 and NECC 2000 Conferences. Available at: http://transition.alaska.edu/www/portfolios/twoframeworks.html

Cooke, N. L., Heward, W. L., Test, D. W., Spooner, F., & Courson, F. H. (1991). Student performance data in the classroom: Measurement and evaluation of student progress. *Teacher Education and Special Education*, 14, 155–161.

Cooper, J. O. (1981). *Measuring behavior* (2nd ed.). Columbus, OH: Merrill.

Denny, D., & Fox, J. (1989). Collecting and analyzing continuous behavioral data with the TRS model 100/102 portable laptop computer. *Journal of Special Education Technology*, 9, 181–189.

Deno, S. L. (2000). Academic progress as incompatible behavior: Curriculum-based measurement (CBM) as intervention. *Beyond Behavior*, 9(3), 12–16.

Deno, S. L., & Mirkin, P. K. (1978). *Data-based program modification: A manual.* Reston, VA: Council for Exceptional Children.

Fabry, B. D., & Cone, J. D. (1980). Auto-graphing: A one-step approach to collecting and graphing data. *Education and Treatment of Children, 3,* 361–368.

Fowler, S. A. (1986). Peer-monitoring and self-monitoring: Alternatives to traditional teacher management. *Exceptional Children, 52,* 573–581.

Fuchs, L. S. (1986). Monitoring progress among mildly handicapped pupils: Review of current practice and research. *Remedial and Special Education, 7* (5), 5–12.

Fuchs, L. S., & Fuchs, D. (1986). Effects of systematic formative evaluation: A meta-analysis. *Exceptional Children, 53,* 199–208.

Gable, R. A., Hendrickson, J. M., Evans, S. S., & Evans, W. H. (1988). Data decisions for instructing behaviorally disordered students. In R. B. Rutherford, Jr., C. M. Nelson, & S. R. Forness (Eds.)., *Bases of severe behavior disorders in children and youth* (pp. 75–89). San Diego, CA: College-Hill Press.

Gast, D. L., & Gast, K. B. (1981). Educational program evaluation: An overview of data-based instruction for classroom teachers. In *Toward a research base for the least restrictive environment: A collection of papers* (pp. 1–30). Lexington, KY: College of Education Dean's Grant Project.

Gunter, P. L., & Denny, R. K. (1998). Trends, issues, and research needs regarding academic instruction of students with emotional and behavioral disorders. *Behavioral Disorders, 24,* 44–60.

Gunter, P. L., Hummell, J. H., & Venn, M. L. (1998). Are effective academic instructional practices used to teach students with behavioral disorders? *Beyond Behavior, 9*(3), 5–11.

Gunter, P. L., & Reed, T. M. (1997). Academic instruction of children with emotional and behavioral disorders using scripted lessons. *Preventing School Failure, 42,* 33–37.

Hausafus, C. O., & Torrie, M. (1995). Scanning to the beep: A teacher-tested computer-based observational assessment tool for the distance education classroom. *Tech Trends, 40*(5), 26–27.

Hall, R. V. (1973). *Managing behavior—behavior modification: The measurement of behavior* (Part 1). Lawrence, KS: H & H Enterprises.

Howell, K. W., Fox, S. L., & Morehead, M. K. (1993). *Curriculum-based evaluation: Teaching and decision making* (2nd ed.). Pacific Grove, CA: Brooks/Cole.

Johnson, H., Blackhurst, A. E., Maley, K., Bomba, C., Cox-Cruey, T., & Dell, A. (1995). Development of a computer-based system for the unobtrusive collection of direct observational data. *Journal of Special Education Technology, 12*(4), 291–300.

Kauffman, J. M. (2001). *Characteristics of emotional and behavioral disorders of children and youth* (7th ed.). Upper Saddle River, NJ: Merrill/Prentice Hall.

Koorland, M. A., & Westling, D. L. (1981). An applied behavior analysis research primer for behavioral change personnel. *Behavioral Disorders, 6,* 164–174.

Kubany, E. S., & Slogett, B. B. (1973). Coding procedure for teachers. *Journal of Applied Behavior Analysis, 6,* 339–344.

Lund, K., Schnaps, L., & Bijou, S. (1983). Let's take another look at record keeping. *Teaching Exceptional Children, 15,* 155–159.

Nelson, C. M., Gast, D. L., & Trout, D. D. (1979). A charting system for monitoring student progress in instructional programs. *Journal of Special Education Technology, 3,* 43–49.

Parsonson, B. S., & Baer, D. M. (1978). The analysis and presentation of graphic data. In T. R. Kratochwill (Ed.), *Single subject research: Strategies for evaluating change* (pp. 101–165). New York: Academic Press.

Rolheiser, C., Bower, B., & Stevahn, L. (2000). *The portfolio organizer: Succeeding with portfolios in your classroom.* Alexandria, VA: The Association for Supervision and Curriculum Development.

Scott, L. C., & Goetz, E. M. (1980). Issues in the collection of in-class data by teachers. *Education and Treatment of Children, 3,* 65–71.

Stokes, T. F., & Baer, D. M. (1977). An implicit technology of generalization. *Journal of Applied Behavior Analysis, 10,* 349–367.

Swicegood, P. (1994). Portfolio-based assessment practices: The uses of portfolio assessment for students with behavioral disorders or learning disabilities. *Intervention in School and Clinic, 30*(1), 6–15.

Tapp, J. T., & Wehby, J. H. (2000). Observational software for laptop computers and optical bar code time wands. In T. Thompson, D. Felece, & F. Symonds (Eds.), *Behavioral observation: Computer assisted innovations and applications in developmental disabilities,* (pp. 71–81.) Baltimore: Paul H. Brookes.

Tawney, J. W., & Gast, D. L. (1984). *Single subject research in special education.* Columbus, OH: Merrill.

Taylor, C. B., Fried, L., & Kenardy, J. (1990). The use of a real-time computer diary for data acquisition and processing. *Behaviour Research and Therapy, 28,* 93–97.

Touchette, P. E., MacDonald, R. F., & Langer, S. N. (1985). A scatter plot for identifying stimulus control of problem behavior. *Journal of Applied Behavior Analysis, 18,* 343–351.

Walton, T. W. (1985). Educators' responses to methods of collecting, storing, and analyzing behavioral data. *Journal of Special Education Technology, 7* (2), 50–55.

White, O. R. (1971). A pragmatic approach to the description of progress in the single case. Unpublished doctoral dissertation, University of Oregon, Eugene.

White, O. R. (1986). *Precision teaching–precision learning.* *Exceptional Children, 52,* 522–534.

White, O. R., & Haring, N. G. (1980). *Exceptional teaching* (2nd ed.). Columbus, OH: Merrill.

Zuckerman, R. A. (1987). Data [Computer program]. Kent, OH: Kent State University, Department of Special Education.

SELECTING AND EVALUATING INTERVENTIONS

CHAPTER 4

OUTLINE

OBJECTIVES

After completing this chapter, you should be able to

- Describe six principles of applied behavior analysis and give examples from school situations.
- Describe professional, legal, and ethical guidelines affecting the use of behavioral interventions.
- Locate and use information systems and Internet services that provide intervention planning resources.
- Identify appropriate and inappropriate intervention alternatives for given behaviors and circumstances, and provide a rationale for each decision.
- Identify the major types of single-subject research designs and give the uses and limitations of each.

In the preceding chapters, we described procedures for screening and identifying students who require intervention for their behavior problems, for assessing these students for the purpose of intervention planning, for developing a behavior intervention plan, and for monitoring students' progress during intervention. Using these strategies, you decide with which students you will intervene and what behaviors will be the focus of your interventions. Further, you assess these behaviors and form some tentative hypotheses regarding why they are occurring. Using this information, you design a behavior intervention plan that includes strategies for teaching and supporting desired replacement behaviors as well as for addressing the targeted problem behaviors if they occur. Finally, you plan ways to monitor behaviors in the settings in which they occur or where they are expected to occur. This chapter describes strategies for selecting and evaluating interventions based upon these decisions and actions.

Behavioral interventions are based on a set of principles that explain the relationship of human behavior to immediate environmental events that occur before (antecedent stimuli) or after (consequent stimuli) the behavior being studied. As you have seen, learning about the relationships between these antecedent and consequent stimuli enables us to identify events that predict where and when behavior will occur. Mastering the principles of applied behavior analysis will help you understand the way behavior functions, the environmental factors that influence it, and how this knowledge may be used in designing interventions. We begin with a brief explanation of these principles, followed by a description of systematic procedures used by behavior analysts to influence behavior. Next, we present guidelines that affect the choice of procedure, followed by a discussion of intervention planning. We conclude with a description of specific procedures for evaluating interventions formatively; that is, for the purposes of determining their effectiveness.

PRINCIPLES OF APPLIED BEHAVIOR ANALYSIS

Applied behavior analysis implies that the practitioner is interested in more than the simple behavior management. It implies an interest in understanding behavior and its functional relationship to environmental events (Baer, Wolf, & Risley, 1968). The behavior analyst therefore studies behavior in the context of the immediate situation. As you will recall from Chapter 2, this involves examining stimuli that precede and follow the behavior. Diagrammatically, the model may be represented as A-B-C: (A) antecedent stimuli, which precede behavior (B), and those stimuli that occur predictably as consequences (C) of the behavior.

The following principles describe how this model operates. A word of caution before proceeding: *Under no circumstances should specific behavior analysis techniques be used by practitioners who do not thoroughly understand the principles upon which they are based.* These techniques are a powerful set of tools but they are easily misapplied. Therefore, you should master them through reviewing basic texts on applied behavior analysis and behavior management, such as Alberto and Troutman (1999), Cooper, Heron, and Heward (1987), Kazdin (2001), Malott, Malott, & Trojan (2000), Wolery, Bailey, and Sugai (1988), or Zirpoli & Melloy, (2001), as well as through competent supervised practice in the implementation and evaluation of behavior management procedures.

Principle I

Behavior is controlled by its **consequences.** This principle is the heart of behavior analysis, yet it is also the least understood. Most persons assume that behavior is controlled by preceding, or antecedent, stimuli. Consider the teacher who wants a pupil to sit down. She might say, "Sit down." This clearly is an antecedent (A) to the student sitting (B). If the child sits, it is obvious that the antecedent controlled her behavior. But what if the pupil does not sit down after receiving the instruction? The normal tendency is to repeat the command until it is followed, varying voice intensity and adding gestures or threats. Antecedent stimuli effectively control behavior when they enable the student to discriminate that certain consequent stimuli will follow that behavior. Thus, the pupil is more likely to sit if she knows there is a predictable relationship between sitting (or remaining standing) and consequent events. Repeated association with consequences enables the student to learn that sitting when asked will likely be followed with positive consequences, or that being out of seat is likely to result in different consequences. She has thus acquired a discrimination. If she consistently sits upon request, this behavior is under antecedent **stimulus control.** This means that pupils respond appropriately to antecedent stimuli (A) without always having to experience direct consequences (C) for their behavior. For example, stimulus control over behavior has occurred when students respond to the request "Take out your science books" by getting out the appropriate text and not by leaving their seats, shouting, or daydreaming. The teacher who has stimulus control over pupil behavior experiences a minimum of crisis situations and both teacher and pupils work in an orderly and productive atmosphere. Unfortunately, some teachers fail to provide predictable consequences for students who do not follow their instructions, with the result that pupils learn to rely on other discriminative stimuli: how often the command has been repeated, how loudly it is given, or how red is the teacher's face.

The behavior of most children is at least partially under stimulus control by the time they begin school. However, a significant number (both those with disabilities and typical students) do not respond appropriately to antecedent stimuli. Getting antecedents such as teacher directions and instructional materials to function as discriminative stimuli for desired behavior is accomplished by systematically applying positive consequences to appropriate responses made in the presence of those stimuli. For instance, if you want pupils' desks to be the stimulus that controls in-seat behavior, apply positive consequences (attention, praise, points) for students who sit at their desks, and apply different consequences (ignoring, verbal reprimands, loss of points or privileges) for students who are not at their desks.

Developing stimulus control with students with challenging behavior may require many systematic applications of consequences. Begin by reinforcing approximations of the desired behavior (e.g., praising a student for only a few seconds of in-seat behavior). This process is known as **shaping.** As Sugai (1995) emphasizes, teachers' behavioral expectations often are considerably above students' abilities to perform. Therefore, he advises that after you have identified the behavior you *expect*, decide what behavior you can *settle for* and build up to your behavioral expectation through shaping. It is important to begin with the behavior the student gives you rather than the behavior you demand. If you expect too much initially, the student will fail. The process of reinforcing closer and closer approximations to desired behavior must be carried out slowly and systematically, and the hierarchy of steps must be adjusted according to the behavior of individual students. This again emphasizes the importance of behavior analysis and underscores the need for a thorough understanding of behavior principles and their application.

Consequences can affect behavior in three ways. Some consequences *strengthen* or increase the frequency of the behavior they follow; others *weaken* or decrease behavior; whereas other consequences *maintain* preceding behavior at its current level. On the other hand, neutral consequences have no effect on the behavior they follow. Only consequences that strengthen, weaken, or maintain behavior have a functional relationship to that behavior. Moreover, consequences are always defined by their effects: strengthening consequences increase behavior, weakening consequences decrease it, and maintaining consequences keep behavior at the current level.

Principle II

Behavior is strengthened or maintained by **reinforcement.** Reinforcement functions in two ways. **Positive reinforcement** occurs when the presentation of a consequence maintains or strengthens behavior over time. Remember that procedures, as well as consequences, are defined by their effects. For example, Madsen, Becker, Thomas, Koser, and Plager (1968) found that when first-grade teachers told their pupils to sit down, higher rates of out-of-seat behavior occurred. Thus, the direction to sit down (or, more precisely, the teacher attention that accompanied it), given when students were out-of-seat, actually served as positive reinforcement for out-of-seat. In other words, out-of-seat behavior functioned to access teacher attention. It is important to keep in mind that what is a reinforcer for one student may not be for another. The way to determine whether a given stimulus may be an effective reinforcer is to observe whether it results in an increase in behavior when the opportunity to obtain it depends on the display of that behavior (see Chapter 2).

Behavior also may be strengthened or maintained if it functions to avoid or escape an aversive stimulus. This is called **negative reinforcement.** Aversive stimuli are those that people choose not to encounter. Just as reinforcers vary from student to student, what is aversive to one person may not be to another. However, most of us avoid stimuli that involve the threat of physical pain or discomfort, the loss of something that is reinforcing (e.g., money), or personal embarrassment. Think about how the aversive stimuli in the following examples strengthen or support the behavior: slowing down upon seeing a radar trap, closing the window to stop a draft, adjusting the water temperature before stepping into the shower, or sitting when requested because by doing so the student will avoid a reprimand from the teacher. These are examples of behaviors that are influenced by negative reinforcement. Because negative reinforcement emphasizes aversive stimuli, it may promote escape and avoidance behaviors other than those

the teacher intends to strengthen. For instance, a child may learn to avoid reprimands by not coming to school. Therefore, the most effective strategies for increasing desired behavior are based on positive reinforcement.

Principle III

Behavior is weakened by withholding the consequences (usually social) that have maintained it. This process is called **extinction.** For example, if your attention has consistently followed a pupil's out-of-seat behavior, and you withhold attention each time the student is out-of-seat, over time you can expect this behavior to occur less frequently. However, for extinction to work you must know which consequences have been supporting the behavior, and these consequences must be under your control. Therefore, extinction is likely to be ineffective in reducing behaviors for which you cannot identify or control the reinforcer (e.g., social interactions between pupils, bullying, or **self-stimulatory behavior** [SSB]) or in reducing a behavior that has been maintained by intermittent positive reinforcement. Out-of-seat behavior, for instance, may be maintained by reinforcement from the student's peer group instead of (or in addition to) teacher attention. If so, the teacher's ignoring out-of-seat behavior will have little effect. Once again, such examples emphasize the analysis component of applied behavior analysis, for only by studying antecedents, behaviors, and consequences can you understand their interrelationships and apply appropriate procedures. Extinction has been used with success in reducing mild behavior problems (e.g., disruptive classroom behavior, off-task, and tantrums) and, in combination with differential reinforcement of appropriate behavior, in reducing more serious problems such as aggression (Alberto & Troutman, 1999).

Attempting to weaken behavior through extinction takes time. At first, you will likely see an immediate, but temporary, increase in the undesired behavior. Hold your ground when this occurs and give the procedure time to work. For example, if your attention has maintained the target behavior and you initiate an extinction procedure, be prepared for a temporary increase in rate and intensity. Thus, the student who repeatedly calls out to get your attention may increase his calling out and perhaps add standing up, yelling, or coming to you for several days after you first apply extinction. Alberto and Troutman (1999) suggest some strategies to help you control your attention under such circumstances: become involved with another student, read or write something, recite something to yourself, or leave the room (if possible). If you cannot tolerate a temporary increase in the behavior, extinction is not a good choice. If using extinction does not achieve the desired effect after a fair trial (depending on the student's past history of reinforcement for the behavior), conduct a functional behavioral assessment. Also consider alternative strategies if you cannot control other sources of reinforcement (e.g., peer reactions) for the target behavior, if the target behavior is likely to be imitated by other pupils, if you are not able to withhold your attention consistently, or if alternative behaviors that you can teach and reinforce have not been identified (Alberto & Troutman, 1999; Zirpoli & Melloy, 2001).

Principle IV

Behavior is also weakened by **punishment.** There are two classes of punishment. The first involves presenting an aversive consequence immediately after a response has occurred (e.g., a verbal reprimand for inappropriate use of hands). The second involves removing a positive consequence following a response (e.g., taking away a minute of recess time or a point for making noises). This type of punishment differs from extinction because the consequence being removed is arbitrarily chosen rather than the consequence that maintains the undesired behavior. Also, something is actually taken away, rather than being withheld. Just as with reinforcement or extinction, punishment is defined by its effects (i.e., the behavior must decrease in fre-

quency when the consequence is applied). Therefore, you must analyze the procedure over a period of time. For example, if your verbal reprimands result in an increase in the undesired behavior, punishment has not been implemented. Thus, reinforcing or aversive consequences are not defined by the practitioner's judgment of their value to the student. For example, if standing in the corner for talking-out results in an increase in this behavior, the consequence functions as a reinforcer.

Whenever the use of punishment is considered, always target a desired **replacement** behavior (ideally, one that will serve the same function as the undesired behavior) to teach and reinforce. This is known as the **fair pair rule** (White & Haring, 1980). Overreliance on punishment creates educational environments that are unpleasant and sets the occasion for coercive exchanges between you and the student. Therefore, we urge you to administer positive reinforcers (e.g., attention, praise, points) four times more than reductive procedures. When students are used to receiving positive reinforcement and know which behaviors are likely to earn reductive consequences, withholding of reinforcement is more effective in reducing undesired behavior, thereby lowering the necessity for more intrusive and aversive procedures (Ferster & Culbertson, 1982).

Principle V

To effectively influence behavior, consequences must consistently and immediately follow the behaviors they are meant to control. A planned, systematic relationship between a behavior and a consequence is referred to as a **contingency.** Although some contingencies in the environment are naturally systematic and predictable (failing to adjust cold water to warm before stepping into the shower results in goose pimples), many are not. A teacher sometimes may allow pupils to leave their seats without permission and at other times reprimand them. To the extent that such practices diminish the predictability of a contingency, so too is the teacher's stimulus control over behavior weakened. Much teacher praise is not systematically contingent on desirable behavior. Consistency is one of the most taxing requirements of effective behavior management, but in the long run, effort here will save a great deal of frustration and suffering.

Principle VI

Behavior is also strengthened, weakened, or maintained by **modeling** (Bandura, 1969). Modeling involves the alteration of one's behavior through imitating the performance of that behavior by a model. Models may be live or vicarious, adults or children, and the behavior imitated may be appropriate or inappropriate. Children more readily imitate the behavior of models who are similar to them in some way, who have high status, and who have been reinforced. If a model's behavior is punished, the same behavior is more likely to be suppressed by the imitator (Bandura, 1969). It is important to apply planned consequences consistently to all students who serve as models for others.

Although these principles have been described separately, they seldom operate in isolation. For example, teachers often apply positive reinforcement to desired behavior (e.g., in-seat) and extinction to incompatible undesired behavior (e.g., out-of-seat). In this and the following chapters we will present a number of strategies based on these principles. First, however, remember that the complexity of behavior analysis and of behavioral interventions requires that practitioners be well versed in these principles, as well as in data-collection and evaluation procedures. An alternative is to have access to a consultant with demonstrated competence in the principles and techniques of behavior analysis.

SYSTEMATIC PROCEDURES FOR INFLUENCING BEHAVIOR

The above principles explain the effects of environmental events on behavior and how these ef-

fects may be enhanced or weakened. Using their knowledge of these principles, behavior analysts have designed procedures to strengthen or weaken behavior.[1] These are summarized in Table 4–1. Note that we have arranged them in two groups according to their influence on behavior: those that maintain or increase behavior (enhancement procedures) and those that decrease behavior (reductive procedures). You also may have heard these sets of procedures referred to as those that *accelerate* or *decelerate* behavior. Within each category, we have listed procedures from those that are least intrusive or restrictive to those that are most intrusive or restrictive. **Intrusiveness** refers to the extent to which interventions impinge or encroach on students' bodies or personal rights (Wolery et al., 1988) as well as the degree to which they interrupt regular educational activities. Thus,

TABLE 4–1 Enhancement and Reductive Procedures

Enhancement Procedures	Reductive Procedures
Self-regulation	Differential reinforcement
Social reinforcement	Extension
Modeling	Verbal aversives
Contracting	Response cost
Activity reinforcement	Time-out
Token reinforcement	Overcorrection
Tangible reinforcement	Physical aversives
Edible reinforcement	
Tactile and sensory reinforcement	

[1]The focus of the strategies described here is on the consequences of behavior. Recall from previous chapters that antecedent variables also may have functional relationships to behavior, and therefore also can be used in behavior enhancement or reduction strategies. Strategies involving the use of both antecedent and consequent stimuli are described in Chapters 6 through 9.

more intrusive interventions potentially involve the risk of interfering with students' rights (e.g., to freedom of movement, bodily integrity), of exposing them to physical risks (e.g., through restraint or aversive stimuli), or of interrupting their normal educational programs. (Those interventions that pull the teacher away from normal instructional routines are also intrusive because such an interruption affects the educational program for other students.) **Restrictiveness** involves the extent to which an intervention inhibits students' freedom to be treated like all other pupils (Barton, Brulle, & Repp, 1983).

We describe each of the major enhancement and reductive procedures briefly here. More detailed descriptions appear in Chapters 6 through 9, along with examples of how these are applied singly and in combination with other methods. In reviewing these, it is important to keep in mind that this hierarchy is based on our own beliefs regarding which interventions are more or less intrusive or restrictive. Other authorities may place the same interventions in a different hierarchy, although there is growing consensus about the relative intrusiveness/restrictiveness of alternate reductive procedures in particular (Nelson & Rutherford, 1988; Wolery et. al., 1988; Zirpoli & Melloy, 2001). Also note that although we describe these procedures separately, in practice they usually are combined as intervention packages that are applied together to increase their effects on behavior.

As you read about specific intervention strategies in the following sections, keep in mind that the best approach to addressing behavior problems is to prevent them. The most effective prevention strategy is to actively engage students in academic instruction that is appropriately matched to their abilities. Students who are interested, involved, and successful in their academic work are far less likely to engage in undesired behavior. Until recently, neither researchers nor practitioners have devoted much attention to the need for effective instruction with students who exhibit problem behavior (Gunter & Denny, 1998; Gunter,

Hummel, & Venn, 2000). On the other hand, Shores, Gunter, & Jack (1993) observed high rates of negative exchanges between students with EBD and their teachers, and other studies have found that teachers give easier tasks to students with problem behavior (Carr, Taylor, & Robinson, 1991), or have significantly fewer instructional interactions with them than with less disruptive students (Gunter, Jack, DePaepe, Reed, & Harrison, 1994; Wehby, 1997). (See Chapters 5 and 6 for more information on these issues.) Fortunately, the need for greater attention to the academic needs of students with behavior problems is being recognized. Consult Kameenui and Darch (1995) for strategies that specifically address the prevention of classroom behavior problems through effective instruction. Another approach to preventing behavior problems is to teach and reinforce desired nonacademic behaviors in students (Scott & Nelson, 1999). This includes teaching students both school- and classroom-wide rules and routines, reinforcing their compliance, as well as teaching appropriate social skills and strategies for resolving conflicts. These strategies are emphasized throughout this text.

Behavioral Enhancement Procedures

SELF-REGULATION   Self-regulation actually includes three procedures: **self-monitoring, self-evaluation,** and **self-reinforcement.** We consider these the least intrusive and least restrictive of the enhancement procedures because after students have been taught to use these strategies they may do so across a wide range of situations without interrupting ongoing activities. Most students learn to monitor their own performance ("Am I doing this right?"), evaluate it ("Yes, that's right"), and administer reinforcement or corrective feedback ("So far, so good") without systematic training. However, pupils with behavior problems often appear deficient in these skills (Polsgrove, 1979). Although self-regulation procedures have shown much promise in terms of changing behavior (Nelson & Polsgrove, 1984), because they are usually private events, it is difficult to objectively establish the degree to which students use them. However, changes in overt behaviors that result from self-regulation procedures (e.g., self-recording, verbal reports, target behaviors) may be monitored to evaluate the extent to which these strategies are used. One factor in its success appears to be training in self-regulation prior to allowing students to control reinforcing events (i.e., to decide when they have earned reinforcement) (Polsgrove, 1979; Zirpoli & Melloy, 2001). A number of self-regulation strategies are described in the self-mediated interventions sections of Chapters 6 through 9.

SOCIAL REINFORCEMENT   Like self-regulation, social reinforcement consists of several operations: feedback, attention, and approval. However, social consequences are mediated by another person. Social reinforcement may be delivered easily and nonintrusively. Used by itself, contingent social feedback has been shown to have only weak effects, but attention and approval have been found to be powerful reinforcers for both typical learners and students with disabilities, particularly those who are developmentally younger (Nelson, 1981). Teacher attention, even when paired with frowns, warnings, and reprimands, may be a potent reinforcer, especially with students who tend to be ignored except when they misbehave (Walker, 1995). Furthermore, it has been shown that such students receive proportionately more teacher attention than pupils who are not deviant (Walker, 1995; Walker, Hops, & Fiegenbaum, 1976), which may strengthen their undesired behaviors. However, when teacher attention and approval (e.g., praise) is made contingent upon desired student behavior, it is very effective in strengthening or maintaining these behaviors.

Unfortunately, teachers do not appear to use praise frequently, even in classrooms for students with EBD. Descriptive studies report praise rates of from 1.2 to 4.5 times per hour per student (Gable, Hendrickson, Young, Shores, & Stowitschek, 1983; Shores, Jack, Gunter, Ellis, DeBriere,

& Wehby, 1993; Van Acker, Grant, & Henry, 1996; Wehby, Symons, & Shores, 1995). Cantrell, Stenner, & Katzenmeyer (1977) observed that the ratio of praise to reprimands is more critical than rates of praise, per se. Authorities suggest that this ratio should be 3:1 to 4:1, in favor of praise (Shores et al., 1993; Walker, Colvin, & Ramsey, 1995). But the research cited above indicated that teachers use reprimands two to four times as much as praise (Gable et al., 1983; Shores et al., 1993; Van Acker et al., 1996; Wehby et al., 1995)! As these data suggest, a major problem with attention and approval is getting teachers to use the technique. Breyer and Allen (1975) were unsuccessful in their attempts to train a teacher with 23 years of teaching experience to praise appropriate behavior and ignore inappropriate behavior. However, they did persuade the teacher to implement a token system, which resulted in positive changes in rates of teacher approval and disapproval. We hope you will make liberal use of praise in your daily interactions with students.

Aside from being used more frequently than reprimands, in order for attention and praise to control student behavior successfully, they must have been established as **conditioned reinforcers** through repeated pairings with previously established reinforcers. Their effectiveness also depends upon whether strong competing reinforcers exist for undesired behavior, and whether the teacher uses them contingently and delivers them immediately following desired behavior (Nelson, 1981; Shores, Gunter, Denny, & Jack, 1993). Praise is more effective when it is genuine, describes the desired behavior exhibited, and is applied consistently. However, it should not disrupt the behavior being emitted and should not involve the same phrase (e.g., "Good") time after time (Wolery et al., 1988). Table 4-2 illustrates the variety of ways to praise desired student behavior. With older pupils or those with more severe disabilities, social consequences tend to work better in combination with other behavior enhancement procedures.

TABLE 4–2 Sample Praise Statements

1. You're doing a good job!	41. Keep working on it, you're getting better.
2. You did a lot of work today!	42. You're doing beautifully.
3. Now you've figured it out.	43. You're really working hard today.
4. That's RIGHT!!!	44. That's the way to do it!
5. Now you've got the hang of it.	45. Keep on trying!
6. That's the way!	46. THATS it!
7. You're really going to town.	47. You've got it made.
8. You're doing fine!	48. You're very good at that.
9. Now you have it!	49. You're learning fast.
10. Nice going.	50. I'm very proud of you.
11. That's great!	51. You certainly did well today.
12. You did it that time!	52. That's good.
13. GREAT!	53. I'm happy to see you working like that.
14. FANTASTIC!	54. I'm proud of the way you worked today.
15. TERRIFIC!	55. That's the right way to do it.
16. Good for you!	56. You're really learning a lot.
17. GOOD WORK!	57. That's better than ever.
18. That's better.	58. That's quite an improvement.
19. EXCELLENT!	59. That kind of work makes me very happy.
20. Good job, (name of student).	60. Now you've figured it out.
21. You outdid yourself today!	61. PERFECT!
22. That's the best you've ever done.	62. FINE!
23. Good going!	63. That's IT!
24. Keep it up!	64. You figured that out fast.
25. That's really nice.	65. You remembered!
26. WOW!	66. You're really improving.
27. Keep up the good work.	67. I think you've got it now.
28. Much better!	68. Well, look at you go!
29. Good for you!	69. TREMENDOUS!
30. That's very much better.	70. OUTSTANDING!
31. Good thinking!	71. Now that's what I call a fine job.
32. Exactly right!	72. You did that very well.
33. SUPER!	73. That was first-class work.
34. Nice going.	74. Right on!
35. You make it look easy.	75. SENSATIONAL!
36. Way to go!	76. That's the best ever.
37. Superb!	77. Good remembering!
38. You're getting better every day.	78. You haven't missed a thing.
39. WONDERFUL!	79. You really make my job fun.
40. I knew you could do it.	80. You must have been practicing!

Source: *Walker, H. M., Golden, N., Holmes, D., McConnell, J. Y., Cohen, G., Anderson, J., Connery, A., & Gannon P. (1981).* The SBS social skills curriculum: Teaching interactive competence and classroom survival skills to handicapped children. *Eugene, OR: University of Oregon. Reprinted with permission.*

MODELING Having another person demonstrate desired behavior has been used successfully to accelerate these behaviors in students of all ages and levels of disability (Kazdin, 2001). Also, vicarious modeling through films or printed materials has been effective with students who do not have severe cognitive impairments. Modeling is especially useful for teaching complex behaviors such as social skills (Gelfand & Hartmann, 1984). Modeling is most effective if the model is highly regarded by the student (e.g., a school athlete), the model is like the student in some way (e.g., age or sex), the student observes the model receive reinforcement for the desired behavior, the modeled behavior is in the target student's repertoire, and the target student is reinforced on other occasions when he displays the desired behavior (Bandura, 1969, 1977). Undesired behaviors also may be reduced if students observe a model who receives aversive consequences as a result of the target behavior. As with social reinforcement, modeling is likely to be used in conjunction with other procedures and is a component of behavioral rehearsal and role-playing, both of which are used in several social skills training packages. Broden, Bruce, Mitchell, Carter, and Hall (1970) and Strain, Shores, and Kerr (1976) observed positive behavior changes in some nontarget children when positive consequences were applied to a target pupil's behavior. Kazdin (2001) suggests that reinforcement becomes a discriminative stimulus for nonreinforced peers because it signals the probability that similar behavior on their part will be reinforced. If students have a history of positive reinforcement for appropriate behavior, a statement such as "I like the way Tommy is waiting his turn" increases the probability that other pupils will imitate this behavior. However, to be effective with more disruptive children, modeling should be accompanied by the consistent application of consequences.

CONTRACTING   A behavioral or **contingency contract** is a formal, written agreement negotiated between the student and other persons. A contract usually specifies the behavior(s) to be increased (or decreased), the consequences to be delivered contingent upon satisfaction of the contract's terms, and the criterion for determining whether the terms of the contract have been fulfilled (Rutherford & Polsgrove, 1981). Contracts are written so that the student's access to a **high-probability behavior** (one that has a high probability of occurrence) is made contingent upon a **low-probability behavior.** Although contracts are

more intrusive in terms of the time required to negotiate, write, monitor, and fulfill, they do not restrict the student's freedom to participate in normal educational activities. Contingency contracts have been used effectively to increase desired replacement behaviors as well as to reduce undesired behaviors (Walker et al., 1995; Zirpoli & Melloy, 2001). However, they must be carefully monitored and adjusted according to students' progress. Behavioral contracts may be used as a group contingency. The teacher negotiates individual contracts with students, but access to high-probability behaviors may be arranged on a group basis by setting aside a special area for such activities. Pupils also may select a variety of reinforcing events from a **reinforcing event menu** (RE menu) (Homme, 1970). Contracting is low cost and effective (Zirpoli & Melloy, 2001), but the process takes time. Procedures for developing contingency contracts are explained in Chapter 8.

ACTIVITY REINFORCEMENT   Providing the opportunity to engage in preferred or high-probability behaviors contingent upon completion of less preferred or low-probability behaviors (Premack, 1959) is an effective reinforcement procedure with both typical students and those with disabilities. It is a relatively intrusive procedure because the reinforcing activity must be identified and access to it made contingent upon the occurrence of desired target behaviors. However, high-probability behaviors do not necessarily have to be such major events as a class party or an extra recess; the opportunity to engage in a preferred academic task (e.g., reading, tutoring a peer) can be used as a reinforcer for a less-desired academic activity (e.g., working on a composition). Activities are often used as back-up reinforcers in token systems or behavioral contracts. As indicated above, access to activity reinforcement may be scheduled for a group of students at specific times of the day. Students may select their preferred activity from a menu or reinforcers, or they simply may earn "free time" in an area that contains a variety of interesting things to do. Students may even bring items from home (games, CDs, models to build). When free time is used as a reinforcer, the teacher typically awards tickets representing a certain amount of free time (e.g., 1 min, 5 min). When free time is scheduled, all students with tickets are allowed to "cash in" one ticket to enter the free time area. Then a timer is set, and when it goes off students must cash in another ticket to remain in the area. To insure compliance with this arrangement, be sure to teach students the routine for returning from the free time area and provide occasional "surprise" reinforcement for prompt return (e.g., another ticket that can be spent to return immediately to the free time area). Also make sure that students do not have access to free time activities outside of the specified area or other than during specified free time.

TOKEN REINFORCEMENT   A **token economy** is a behavior management system involving nonsocial conditioned reinforcers (e.g., points, chips, paper clips, etc.) earned for exhibiting desired academic or social behaviors that may be exchanged for back-up reinforcers of predetermined token value. Token systems have been used in regular and special classrooms, with children exhibiting mild to severe disabilities, with preschoolers and adults, and with social and academic behaviors (Kazdin, 1983). Token economies may be used with students individually, but they are more often applied with groups. They also may be adapted to fit any situation, or they may be combined with a variety of other management strategies (see Walker, 1995). The essential ingredients of a token system include tokens, back-up reinforcers (tangibles or activities) for which tokens may be exchanged, contingencies specifying the conditions under which tokens may be obtained or lost, and the exchange rate of tokens for back-up reinforcers.

A variety of back-up reinforcers is possible: classroom or school privileges, activities, trinkets, clothes, costume jewelry, toys, or even such large items as bicycles. Some community agencies (e.g., the Chamber of Commerce, Volunteers of America, church groups, labor unions) may be willing to conduct drives or donate items. Cast-off items from your basement or attic may prove valuable in a token system. However, remember that preferred activities are also effective reinforcers, and they are much less expensive and present no storage problems. Therefore, consider using such activities as listening to music, talking with a peer, using a computer, or playing a game as back-up reinforcers.

Because tokens are conditioned reinforcers, their value derives from association with previously established consequences. Teach students to value tokens by pairing their presentation with an existing social or tangible reinforcer or by **reinforcer sampling;** that is, giving pupils a number of tokens and letting them purchase back-ups immediately (Ayllon & Azrin, 1968). Over a period of days, fade out the paired reinforcer or delay token exchange and make receipt of tokens contingent upon desired behaviors. As your system evolves, increase the length of intervals between token exchanges. This teaches pupils to delay gratification and encourages saving for larger items, which, incidentally, are desirable skills in our economic system.

Token systems offer a number of advantages. Because each student can select from a variety of back-up reinforcers, pupil satiation and loss of reinforcer power are not likely problems. Also, tokens can be delivered more easily than individualized tangibles, and simply by announcing that a student has earned a token, your praise and approval develops as a conditioned reinforcer. If tokens are awarded contingent upon academic performance, incompatible social behaviors are reduced in most cases (Ayllon & Roberts, 1974; Hundert & Bucher, 1976; Marholin & Steinman, 1977; Robinson, Newby, & Ganzell, 1981). Also, with such contingencies, little time is lost from teaching as a result of behavior management. In addition, the requirement that tokens be awarded influences the teacher to interact frequently with pupils. With activities as back-ups, the cost of the system is minimal. Specific guidelines for setting up a classroom token system are presented in

Chapter 6. Although tokens may be delivered quickly and easily, the time required to develop a token system makes this a more intrusive intervention. A major problem with token systems is teachers' failure to phase out tokens in preparation for moving pupils to less restrictive environments where token systems are not in effect.

TANGIBLE REINFORCEMENT Nonedible items (e.g., stickers) that are reinforcing for particular students are **tangible reinforcers.** Often they are used as back-up reinforcers in token economies, but they may also be used as immediate reinforcers for desired student behavior. Many types of tangible reinforcers are inexpensive, but because the same item may not be reinforcing to every student, delivering the correct reinforcer to each student immediately contingent upon desired behavior makes this an intrusive procedure. One effective use of tangible reinforcers is to award them only on occasion (e.g., placing a sticker on a particularly good student paper) or as a surprise. This application provides some variety in routine, so that the effectiveness of usual reinforcers (e.g., praise, points) doesn't diminish.

EDIBLE REINFORCEMENT Suffering the same drawbacks as tangibles, **edible reinforcers** also involve several other disadvantages. First, the student must be in a state of relative deprivation for the edible item. Thus, pretzels, popcorn, or even M&Ms® may be ineffective immediately after breakfast or lunch. Second, students have varying food preferences, which again makes delivering the right reinforcer to every student immediately contingent upon desired behavior rather difficult. Third, because these are consumable items, health factors such as food allergies and parental preferences must be taken into account. Finally, many public schools have policies restricting the use of edible items in classrooms. Edibles have been widely effective, especially with developmentally younger pupils. Fortunately, behavior analysis technology has advanced to the point where teachers seldom have to rely exclusively on edible reinforcement.

TACTILE AND SENSORY REINFORCEMENT The application of tactile or sensory consequences that are reinforcing has been used almost exclusively with students exhibiting severe disabilities, especially in attempts to control self-stimulatory behavior (Stainback, Stainback, & Dedrick, 1979). The teacher must first identify sensory consequences that appear to be reinforcing (e.g., vibration, movement, touch) and then arrange for these consequences to follow desired behavior. For example, if the student self-stimulates by rubbing her palm, the teacher can rub the pupil's palm immediately contingent upon a desired behavior. Alternately, the teacher can allow the student to rub her own palm when the desired behavior occurs. Among the risks of such a procedure is that of strengthening SSB even further. Before considering tactile or sensory reinforcement, evaluate such possibilities and consider parental wishes and whether the SSB interferes with the acquisition of more adaptive behaviors, or select toys or other devices for the student to use that provide sensory stimulation or feedback like that received through SSB (Wolery et al., 1988).

Behavioral Reduction Procedures

Although behavior enhancement procedures should dominate intervention strategies at all levels, many students are adept at manipulating situations so that their inappropriate behavior results in positive reinforcement. Also remember that teacher attention, even when accompanied by reprimands or other negative reactions, may be positively reinforcing to some pupils. Students who are constantly punished may develop a tolerance for aversive consequences and the accompanying attention may be a powerful reinforcer, especially if the pupils' appropriate behaviors are largely ignored.[2] Used by itself, positive reinforcement of

[2]Straus and Field (2000) found that the use of harsh physical (e.g., spanking) and psychological (e.g., shouting, threatening) punishment by parents of children with high rates of antisocial behavior is so prevalent that they referred to it as "an implicit cultural norm," independent of social or ethnic factors.

appropriate behavior is generally thought to be effective in encouraging low rates of undesired behavior of pupils with relatively mild behavior problems, but even with these students it should not be assumed that positive reinforcement alone will be effective. For example, Pfiffner and O'Leary (1987) found that increasing the density of positive reinforcement alone was ineffective in maintaining acceptable levels of on-task behavior and academic accuracy in first- through third-grade students with academic or behavioral problems, unless they had previously experienced negative consequences. Research with individuals exhibiting more severe behavior disorders consistently indicates that a combination of positive reinforcement and punishment procedures is superior to either reinforcement or punishment alone (Shores, Gunter, & Jack, 1993).

This discussion of reductive procedures will help you establish a repertoire of interventions that should be used before behavior gets out of control. For example, what should you do if a pupil breaks a rule, ignores a direct request, or persistently engages in off-task or disruptive behavior? Having command of a range of reductive interventions can help you quickly resolve such problems before they become crisis situations. Later in this chapter, you will find guidelines and policies regarding the use of aversive consequences. Subsequent chapters present intervention procedures for dealing with inappropriate behavior and problem or crisis situations.

Remember that the range of reductive procedures is limited by the need for strategies that are less intrusive and restrictive. Nevertheless, several procedures can be applied with minimal interruption of instructional interactions: extinction, verbal reprimands, response cost, and timeout. In the following discussion, keep in mind that such techniques should be used only in the context of systematic positive reinforcement of desired behaviors through strategies involving differential reinforcement.

Procedures for reducing undesired student behavior have received an enormous amount of atten-

tion from professionals who deal with children and adults exhibiting challenging behavior. Consequently, the research literature on the topic of reductive strategies and techniques is extensive. It is matched by the tradition in our schools of attempting to control unwanted pupil behavior through reactive management strategies involving the administration of aversive consequences. Fortunately, this thinking is giving way to more proactive procedures, such as a recognition of the influence of a sound and relevant curriculum, interesting instructional activities, appropriate stimulus control, and positive classroom structure on increasing desired student behaviors (Darch, Miller, & Shippen, 1999; Rutherford & Nelson, 1995). These antecedent events are clearly prerequisite to the effective management of maladaptive behavior and are discussed at greater length in Chapter 5.

In addition, as pointed out in Chapter 2, research on functional behavioral assessment (FBA) is leading to the identification of antecedents and consequences that are functionally related to undesired pupil behavior (Shores, Wehby, & Jack, 1999) and to strategies for encouraging the use of desired replacement behaviors (Carr & Durand, 1985). However, keep in mind that behavioral enhancement procedures alone are not sufficient to decelerate undesired behavior in pupils who exhibit moderate to severe behavioral disorders (Axelrod, 1987; Gast & Wolery, 1987; Walker, 1995). The following continuum of reductive procedures is arranged from least to most intrusive and restrictive. It is likely that the more intrusive and restrictive procedures we describe will be aversive to both students and teachers. Note that federal law requires that behavior intervention plans (BIPs) be based on FBAs. Recall that BIPs should include direct instruction of replacement behaviors and the systematic use of behavior enhancement strategies, and that changing antecedent events that predict problem behavior may be an effective intervention.

DIFFERENTIAL REINFORCEMENT The strategy of **differential reinforcement** was described in our discussion of stimulus control. The procedure involves increasing reinforcement for replacement behaviors, while attempting to reduce or eliminate reinforcement for undesired target behaviors. Accordingly, differential reinforcement is a fundamental component of behavior intervention plans. Four strategies are involved in differential reinforcement. **Differential reinforcement of low rates of behavior** (DRL) is applied by providing reinforcement when the targeted behavior occurs no more than a specified amount in a given period of time (e.g., if fewer than three talk-outs are observed in a 1-hr period, the student earns five bonus points). **Differential reinforcement of other behaviors** (DRO, which Dietz and Repp, (1983), appropriately renamed differential reinforcement of the *omission* of behavior) requires that the target behavior be suppressed either for an entire interval (whole interval DRO), or only at the end of an interval (momentary DRO). **Differential reinforcement of incompatible behaviors** (DRI) and **differential reinforcement of alternate behaviors** (DRA) involve reinforcing behaviors that are functionally incompatible with (i.e., cannot occur at the same time) or that are simply alternatives to the target behavior (Dietz & Repp, 1983; Kazdin, 2001; Zirpoli & Melloy, 2001). DRL is appropriate for relatively minor behavior problems that can be tolerated at low rates, whereas DRO, DRI, and DRA may be used with severe behavioral disorders. However, because direct consequences (i.e., loss of reinforcement) are not provided for target behaviors under DRI and DRA, they may take longer to work than DRL or DRO, and they may be ineffective if the target behavior has a long history of reinforcement or has been maintained by other sources of reinforcement (Polsgrove & Reith, 1983).

EXTINCTION   As we explained earlier in this chapter, withholding social reinforcers (e.g., attention) will reduce undesired behavior if the reinforcer being withheld is the one that maintained the target behavior and is consistently and contingently withheld. However, this is a relatively weak procedure for controlling severe maladaptive behavior (Stainback et al., 1979) and is inappropriate for behaviors reinforced by consequences that are not controlled by the teacher (e.g., talking-out, aggression, SSB) or that cannot be tolerated during the time required for extinction to work, such as **self-injurious behavior** (SIB). Nevertheless, many pupil behaviors are maintained because they result in peer or teacher attention, and therefore extinction can be effective, particularly when combined with differential reinforcement. **Sensory extinction** (Rincover, 1981) is an intrusive procedure in which the sensory consequences of SSB or SIB are masked so that reinforcement is effectively withheld (e.g., covering a table top with felt to eliminate the auditory feedback produced by spinning objects). The need to monitor student behavior carefully and to use special equipment limits the usefulness of sensory extinction beyond very specific circumstances (see Chapter 9).

VERBAL AVERSIVES   Of the range of verbal aversives used by adults to influence children's behavior (i.e., warnings, threats, sarcasm, ridicule, etc.), reprimands are the most effective and ethical. Other types are usually not applied immediately or consistently following undesired behavior; they imply consequences that are not likely to be carried out (e.g., "If you do that one more time, I'll kick you out of class for a week!"); or they involve evaluations that are personally demeaning to students (e.g., "You're the worst student I've ever had"). Appropriate reprimands provide immediate feedback to students that their behavior is unacceptable and they serve as discriminative stimuli that punishment contingencies are in effect. Verbal reprimands have been used effectively with many mild and moderate behavior problems (Rutherford, 1983), but by themselves are less successful with severe behavior disorders. However, they should be used with caution because one provides attention when delivering a reprimand and this can be a potent reinforcer. Therefore, reprimands should be brief and to the point (e.g., "No hitting") rather than accompanied by lectures or explanations. Obviously, the student should know in advance which behaviors are not allowed so that a reprimand is not an occasion for a discussion (e.g., the pupil says "What did I do?"). O'Leary, Kaufman, Kass, and Drabman (1970) found that soft, private reprimands were more effective than those given loudly and in public. Van Houten, Nau, MacKenzie-Keating, Sameoto, and Colavecchia (1982) demonstrated that reprimands are more effective when accompanied by eye contact and when delivered in close proximity to the target pupil. In addition, they found that reprimanding one student for behavior that another student was also exhibiting reduced the problem behavior of both students. If the student fails to correct her behavior, provide a more intrusive back-up consequence (e.g., response cost) instead of another reprimand or a threat. Note: Never ask a pupil whether he "wants" to go to timeout, the principal's office, and so forth. Such verbalizations merely invite the student to challenge your statement (e.g., "No, and you can't make me!"). When reprimands are associated with other aversive back-up consequences (e.g., response cost, timeout), they acquire conditioned aversive properties and subsequently are more effective when used alone (Gelfand & Hartmann, 1984).

RESPONSE COST   This involves the loss of a reinforcer, contingent upon an undesired behavior (Kazdin, 2001; Polsgrove, 1991). It differs from extinction in that the reinforcer is taken away rather than withheld and is not the reinforcer that has maintained the target behavior. The consequence lost may be an activity, such as a privilege or a portion of recess time, or a token. Variables that influence the success of response cost include the type of behavior on which it is used, the ratio of fines to reinforcers, and the amount of cost imposed (Polsgrove & Reith, 1983). Response cost has been used successfully with various children in different settings without the undesirable side effects (escape, avoidance, aggression) sometimes observed with other forms of punishment (Kazdin, 2001). It is easily used in conjunction with a token system (Walker, 1983, 1995), and compares favorably with

positive reinforcement in controlling behavior (Hundert, 1976; Iwata & Bailey, 1974). On the other hand, McLaughlin and Malaby (1972) found positive reinforcement to be more effective, presumably because the teacher had to attend to disruptive students when taking away points.

Response cost contingencies can be arranged so as to limit this kind of attention. For example, you can post the number of points or minutes of an activity that can be lost for given rule violations and simply give the pupil a nonverbal signal (raising a finger, pointing) indicating what has been lost. (Examples of cost penalties are given in Chapter 6.) It is important to maintain a balance between cost penalties and reinforcers earned, so that a pupil does not get "in the hole" with no chance of obtaining any positive reinforcers. Once all opportunity to earn reinforcers has been lost, you hold no contingencies over undesired behavior; that is, there's no reason for the student to behave appropriately (Zirpoli & Melloy, 2001). As with any aversive system, you should negotiate systematic response cost penalties with your pupils before they are used. Strategies involving response cost are described in Chapters 6 through 9.

TIMEOUT   Like differential reinforcement, **timeout** from positive reinforcement involves several possible strategies, ranging from planned ignoring to putting the student in a secluded place for a period of time (Nelson & Rutherford, 1983). Three levels of timeout may be used in the instructional setting. **Planned ignoring** involves the systematic withdrawal of social attention for the length of the timeout period. Like extinction, it will be effective if teacher attention during time-in is associated with positive reinforcement, and other sources of reinforcement can be controlled during timeout. The effectiveness of planned ignoring may be increased by the addition of a discriminative stimulus to aid staff in identifying which students are eligible for reinforcement and which are not. For example, Foxx and Shapiro (1978) gave disruptive students a "timeout ribbon" to wear while they were exhibiting appropriate behavior. The ribbons were discriminative stimuli for staff to deliver high levels of reinforcement. When a student misbehaved, her ribbon was removed and reinforcement was withheld for 3 min. Salend and Gordon (1987) used a group contingency timeout ribbon procedure to reduce inappropriate verbalizations in students with mild disabilities. **Contingent observation** requires the student to remain in a position to observe the group without participating or receiving reinforcement for a specified period. Having the pupil take timeout without leaving the setting offers the advantage of being able to observe his behavior during the timeout condition.

Exclusionary levels of timeout (i.e., when the pupil is removed from the immediate instructional setting) are intrusive and restrictive. Therefore, these should only be used as back-up consequences when less intrusive interventions have not been effective, and only with school district approval and written parental consent. **Exclusionary timeout** involves the student being physically removed from an ongoing activity. In **seclusionary timeout,** the student is removed from the instructional setting, generally to a specified area, such as a timeout room. As discussed later in this chapter, there are a number of legal and ethical concerns when using these levels of timeout.

The levels of timeout and procedures to follow should be carefully planned when using this intervention. Also, timeout periods should be brief (1 to 5 min) and students should be taught how to take timeout appropriately before it is used. Timeout has been effective in reducing severe maladaptive behaviors when combined with procedures to enhance desired behavior (Kazdin, 2001; Nelson & Rutherford, 1988; Zirpoli & Melloy, 2001). However, effectiveness has been shown to vary depending upon the level used and its duration, whether a warning signal precedes placement in timeout, how it is applied, the schedule under which it is administered, and procedures for removing pupils from timeout (Gast & Nelson, 1977; Polsgrove & Reith, 1983; Rutherford & Nelson, 1982; Twyman, Johnson, Buie, & Nelson, 1993). Perhaps the most

important variable affecting the success of timeout is whether the time-in setting is more reinforcing. When students may escape or avoid unpleasant demands or persons, or when they may engage in more reinforcing behavior (e.g., SSB) while in timeout, this clearly is *not* a good intervention to choose. It is also an inappropriate option when the student is likely to harm himself while in timeout. One state (Maine) has passed legislation requiring that timeout rooms be unlocked, well ventilated, sufficiently lighted, and that safe supervision be provided to students in timeout (Lohrmann-O'Rourke & Zirkel, 1998). Figure 4–1 presents a statement from Kentucky's Commissioner of Education regarding the use of seclusionary timeout. Kentucky's specific guidelines for using timeout may be found at www.state.ky.us/agencies/behave/homepage.html.

OVERCORRECTION   There are two types of overcorrection procedures. **Positive practice overcorrection** involves having the student repeat an arbitrarily selected behavior (e.g., arm movements) contingent upon the occurrence of an undesired target behavior (e.g., stereotypic hand wringing). **Restitutional overcorrection** requires the student to overcorrect the effects of her behavior on the environment (e.g., returning stolen items and giving one of her possessions to the victim). Overcorrection has primarily been used with students with stereotypic behaviors, including SSB and SIB. In general, both types of overcorrection have been effective, but the procedures are time consuming and often aversive to both students and staff. Also, while overcorrection has been touted as teaching the student appropriate replacement behaviors (primarily through positive practice), research has not supported such claims (Luiselli, 1981). Specific guidelines for using overcorrection are provided in Chapter 9.

PHYSICAL AVERSIVES   Substances having aversive tastes and odors, sprays of cold water, electric shock, slaps, pinches, and spankings illustrate the

October 13, 2000

Dear Superintendent:

Many of you have asked us for guidance in relation to the use of timeout for students. Additionally, the department has been made aware of concerns about the improper use of timeout for students. These concerns cover issues such as leaving a student in a seclusionary timeout setting for excessive amounts of time, placing the student in a seclusionary timeout setting without proper supervision, using spaces for seclusionary timeout that are not safe, and continuing to implement timeout even after repeated use has failed to reduce the student's inappropriate behavior.

In an effort to provide assistance and address these concerns in a comprehensive manner, the Kentucky Department of Education is sending this information to school superintendents, directors of special education, principals, and parent resource centers to help promote effective policies for implementing appropriate uses of seclusionary timeout for all students. I encourage you to distribute this information to all staff that work with these students and to the parents of these students so that everyone involved can work cooperatively to ensure the student's educational success.

There are no federal or state regulations that address the use of seclusionary timeout; however, suggested below are guidelines and ideas to consider in planning for the use of seclusionary timeout with students. The information provided is based on recent research and practice in the field, guidance from the Office of Special Education Programs, United States Department of Education, and court cases on the subject.

Timeout is a procedure that involves denying a student access to all sources of reinforcement (e.g., teacher and peer attention, participation in ongoing activities) as a consequence of undesired behavior. The purpose is to reduce future occurrences of such behavior. Timeout may be implemented on three levels: (a) contingent observation; (b) exclusionary; and (c) seclusionary. Contingent observation requires the student to remain in a position to observe the group without participating or receiving reinforcement for a specified period. Exclusionary timeout denies access to reinforcement by removing a student from an ongoing activity, while seclusionary timeout removes the student from the instructional setting as a means of denying access to reinforcement. The use of all levels of timeout, especially exclusionary or seclusionary, must be premised on assurances that the student's behavior is not a reaction to ineffective instruction.

First and foremost, the use of seclusionary timeouts should only be considered as part of a continuum of interventions and strategies (e.g., teaching and rewarding positive behavior alternatives, not responding to undesired student behavior that is performed for the purpose of obtaining attention, taking away points or privileges as punishment) used with students who display inappropriate behaviors. The use of seclusionary timeout is a drastic measure that should be used as a last defense measure as part of an overall program to instruct the student in appropriate behaviors. How and when seclusionary timeout may be used with a student with disabilities should be thoroughly discussed and explained at the Admissions and Release Committee (ARC) meeting so that everyone involved with the student has a clear understanding of the topic. Use of any timeout must be documented by the ARC in the Individual Education Program (IEP) along with addressing the use of positive behavior supports. Prior to being placed in such a setting, the student, whether he or she attended the ARC, should fully understand circumstances under which he or she may be put into timeout and what to expect from the experience (e.g., length of time and expectations for release).

Prior to the use of seclusionary timeout, the school staff should have knowledge of the student's social and developmental history and any other relevant information about the student's disabilities and background. Additionally, the use of seclusionary timeout should only be used with students when data supports the reduction of the student's inappropriate behavior. The following are guidelines for implementation of effective seclusionary timeout:

FIGURE 4–1   Letter Concerning Use of Timeout

Source: *Copyright 2000 by the Kentucky Department of Education. Reproduced with permission.*   (*Continued*)

GUIDELINES FOR EFFECTIVE USE OF TIMEOUT
(For more detailed information on the use of timeout, visit the Behavior Web Page
at http://www.state.ky.us/agencies/behave/homepage.html)

1. **Obtain Parent/Guardian Permission to Use TimeOut.** Schools may want to consider obtaining written consent from parents or caregivers before using seclusionary timeout as an intervention. If the child has a disability, the use of any form of timeout should be a part of the IEP or 504 plan. The discussion of the timeout should include the specific procedures that will be used, including the circumstances leading to the use of timeout and its effect on the student's behavior. Communication should be made with the parents or caregivers whenever seculsionary timeout has been used as a form of intervention.

2. **Only Use Timeout as One Component of an Extensive Array of Behavior Interventions.** Timeout, and especially seclusionary timeout, should never be used in isolation as the only behavior intervention being applied. Timeout is only one component of an effective behavior change strategy, and seclusionary timeout is near the end of the spectrum of more restrictive approaches to reducing undesired or challenging student behavior. Timeout must always be used in conjunction with an array of positive reinforcement, and timeout may be implemented on several levels, with the most restrictive version being seclusionary timeout. Procedures should be designed to teach students how to appropriately take a timeout, through role playing and modeling, with a clear understanding of what behaviors can lead to timeout and how the student can avoid this procedure. Seclusionary timeout should only be used when other less restrictive interventions have been attempted and documentation verifies they have been ineffective. Most often when other less extreme procedures are used appropriately, it is not necessary to use seclusionary timeout.

3. **Do Not Engage in Power Struggles with Students.** Forcing a student through physical means to take a seclusionary timeout should be avoided. When you engage in physical power struggles with a student, it becomes a no-win situation. It has been documented that this typically leads to an escalation of the situation and can also lead to injury of students and staff. If a student is posing physical danger to self or others, a plan of action should be in place and staff should be properly trained on its implementation.

4. **Avoid Excessive Use of Timeout.** Children should not be secluded in a timeout setting for more than 5–10 minutes at a time, depending on the age of the child, and never more than 15 total minutes. Repeated applications of timeout that exceed 15-minutes maximum would not meet these guidelines. The appropriateness of timeout for children and youth at each end of the age spectrum (3-21) is questionable and should be avoided. The continued use of seclusionary timeout must be based on data supporting its effectiveness in reducing a student's inappropriate behavior, and if this data does not exist, the use of this procedure should not be implemented. If a student is using seclusionary timeout as a way to escape or avoid instruction as determined by a functional behavior assessment (FBA), timeout will not be effective.

5. **Never Lock a Student in a Closed Setting and Maintain a View of the Student at All Times.** Students should never be placed in a timeout setting secured with locks or latches or in a fully enclosed area that prevents staff observation and access to the student. For more details on physical design of a seclusionary timeout setting, consult the Behavior Web page.

6. **Maintain Thorough Written Records.** Detailed written records should be kept of use of seclusionary timeout, including the student's name, date, time and incident; prior interventions used, length of timeout and results.

7. **Assess When Timeout is Not Working.** Functional behavior assessments (FBA) should be performed whenever data indicated that timeout is not effective.

I hope this information will provide assistance to staff on this topic. If additional information is needed, please contact Laura McCullough or Toyah Robey in the Division of Exceptional Children Services at (502) 564-4970.

Sincerely,

Gene Wilhoit, Commissioner

FIGURE 4–1   Letter Concerning Use of Timeout—*Continued.*

range of physically aversive stimuli that have been used. Such procedures have been shown to be an efficient and effective means of reducing severe maladaptive behaviors (Rutherford, 1983; Stainback et al., 1979). However, the frequency with which the use of such aversives are abused; the occurrence of undesired side effects; and the objections by parents, educators, and community groups have limited the application of these most intrusive and restrictive procedures. The Council for Exceptional Children (1993) adopted a policy statement regulating the use of physical interventions (see Table 4–3). Behavior management procedures that are not consistent with this policy are indefensible.

Even less defensibly, many school districts sanction the use of corporal punishment with students in spite of the absence of empirical studies demonstrating its effectiveness (Rose, 1983; Zirpoli & Melloy, 2001), and policy statements of professional organizations that specifically prohibit its use. The general trend has been away from using aversives and toward greater use of procedures to decrease undesired behaviors by increasing functional and desired replacement behaviors through behavior enhancement strategies.

OTHER PROCEDURES   Other reductive procedures, such as in-school suspension and temporary exclusion from school, are also available. These procedures are quite disruptive to students' educational programs, and their use with pupils who have been certified as having disabilities is carefully regulated by federal and state laws. The development of strategies based on positive behavior support fortunately has opened up numerous options to educators concerned with reducing maladaptive student behaviors. It is important that you learn to use such strategies effectively in your daily work with students. The "front line" of school discipline is the immediate context (classroom, hallway, cafeteria, etc.), *not* the principal's office.

No matter how mild, use procedures that involve aversive stimuli systematically in conjunction with positive reinforcement, and monitor their effects carefully. Master a hierarchy of such consequences and plan specific techniques for each level in the hierarchy so you will have alternate intervention strategies for any given behavior or situation. Then when you apply a selected consequence, use it at maximum intensity (e.g., a firm "No" instead of a plaintive "It hurts my feelings when you do that"). Give students choices when applying consequences (e.g., "You may go back to work or you may take a timeout"). This indicates to pupils that they have control over the consequences they receive. If the student returns to work, give positive reinforcement (e.g., praise, a point). If undesired behavior persists, apply the stated consequence. Reinforce student decisions to take point or timeout penalties by praise and attention after the penalty has been paid (e.g., "I appreciate the way you took your timeout"). Note, however, that reinforcement for accepting consequences appropriately should not be equal to or greater than the reinforcement the student would receive for exhibiting appropriate behavior in the first place. If pupils can obtain strong reinforcers by engaging in undesired behaviors then taking a mild penalty, they will learn to use such behaviors to initiate the chain of events leading to reinforcement. Reserve more restrictive procedures (e.g., overcorrection or suspension) for situations in which it is documented that the above procedures have been ineffective, and pay careful attention to due process and to other procedural considerations discussed later in this chapter. Avoid using strategies that reduce students' academic engaged time or that remove them from the instructional setting. The large number of existing intervention alternatives has placed greater demands on practitioners to make appropriate choices. This decision-making process has been made easier through the emergence of professional guidelines and decision models, which are discussed next.

TABLE 4–3 CEC Policy on Physical Intervention

The Council recognizes the right to the most effective educational strategies to be the basic educational right of each special education child. Furthermore, the Council believes that the least restrictive positive educational strategies should be used, as it relates to physical intervention, to respect the children's dignity and personal privacy. Additionally, the Council believes that such interventions shall assure the child's physical freedom, social interaction, and individual choice. The intervention must not include procedures which cause pain or trauma. Lastly, behavior intervention plans must be specifically described in the child's written educational plan with agreement from the education staff, the parents, and, when appropriate, the child.

The Council recommends that physical intervention be used only if all the following requirements are met:
- The child's behavior is dangerous to herself/himself or others, or the behavior is extremely detrimental to or interferes with the education or development of the child.
- Various positive reinforcement techniques have been implemented appropriately and the child has repeatedly failed to respond as documented in the child's records.
- It is evident that withholding physical intervention would significantly impede the child's educational progress as explicitly defined in his/her written educational plan.
- The physical intervention plan specifically will describe the intervention to be implemented, the staff to be responsible for the implementation, the process for documentation, the required training of staff, and supervision of staff as it relates to the intervention and when the intervention will be replaced.
- The physical intervention plan will become part of the written educational plan.
- The physical intervention plan shall encompass the following provisions:
  - A comprehensive analysis of the child's environment including variables contributing to the inappropriate behavior;
  - The plan to be developed by a team including professional and parents/guardians, as designated by state/provincial and federal law;
  - The personnel implementing the plan shall receive specific training congruent with the contents of the plan and receive ongoing supervision from individuals who are trained and skilled in the techniques identified in the plan;
  - The techniques identified in the physical intervention plan are approved by a physician to not be medically contraindicated for the child (a statement from the physician is necessary); and
  - The impact of the plan on the child's behavior must be consistently evaluated, the results documented, and the plan modified when indicated.

The Council supports the following prohibitions:
- Any intervention that is designed to, or likely to, cause physical pain;
- Releasing noxious, toxic or otherwise unpleasant sprays, mists, or substances in proximity to the child's face;
- Any intervention which denies adequate sleep, food, water, shelter, bedding, physical comfort, or access to bathroom facilities;
- Any intervention which is designed to subject, used to subject, or is likely to subject the individual to verbal abuse, ridicule, or humiliation, or which can be expected to cause excessive emotional trauma;
- Restrictive interventions which employ a device or material or objects that simultaneously immobilize all four extremities, including the procedure known as prone containment, except that prone containment may be used by trained personnel as a limited emergency intervention;
- Locked seclusion, unless under constant survelliance and observation;
- Any intervention that precludes adequate supervision of the child; and
- Any intervention which deprives the individual of one or more of his or her senses.

The Council recognizes that emergency physical intervention may be implemented if the child's behavior poses an imminent and significant threat to his/her physical well-being or to the safety of others. The intervention must be documented and parents/guardians must be notified of the incident.
- However, emergency physical intervention shall not be used as a substitute for systematic behavioral intervention plans that are designed to change, replace, modify, or eliminate a targeted behavior.
- Furthermore, the council expects the school districts and other educational agencies to establish policies and comply with state/provincial and federal law, and regulations to ensure the protection of the rights to the child, the parent/guardian, the education staff, and the school and local educational agency when physical intervention is applied.

Source: *Council for Exceptional Children, (1993).* CEC Policy on Physical Intervention. *Adopted by the Delegate Assembly, San Antonio, TX. Used with permission.*

148 Foundations of Effective Behavior Management

GUIDELINES FOR SELECTING AND DEVELOPING INTERVENTIONS

Legal and Ethical Guidelines

As we have pointed out, the tradition of relying upon the application of aversive consequences to reduce undesired behaviors in schools continues. However, interventions based on positive behavior support are beginning to provide viable alternatives to this practice. Best practices for children and youth who exhibit chronic and severe acting-out behavior typically include procedures for teaching and reinforcing appropriate replacement behaviors as well as planned reductive strategies (Walker et al., 1995). Verbal reprimands, response cost, timeout, overcorrection, and any physical aversive are all considered punishment procedures if they result in the deceleration of behaviors upon which they are contingent. (Based upon observations of its side effects, extinction also is perceived as an aversive event by some students.) As Nelson and Rutherford (1988) observe, "the excessive and inappropriate use of aversive procedures constitutes one of the more sensitive areas of special education practice" (p. 143). Concerns regarding the potential and real abuse of aversives have led some professional organizations to adopt policies severely limiting the use of reductive procedures that involve aversive stimuli. For example, the Association for Retarded Citizens' resolution "calls for a halt to those aversive practices that deprive food, inflict pain, and use chemical restraint in lieu of programming. . . ." (The Association for the Severely Handicapped Newsletter, 1986). The Association for the Severely Handicapped (1981) resolution

> supports a cessation of the use of any treatment option that exhibits some or all of the following characteristics: (a) obvious signs of physical pain experienced by the individual; (b) potential or actual physical side effects, including tissue damage, physical illness, severe stress, and/or death, that would properly require the involvement of medical personnel; (c) dehu-

manization of the individual because the procedures are normally unacceptable for persons who are not disabled in community environments; (d) extreme ambivalence and discomfort by family, staff, and/or caregivers regarding the necessity of such extreme strategies or their own involvement in such intervention; and (e) obvious repulsion and/or stress felt by peers who are not disabled and by (community) members who cannot reconcile extreme procedures with acceptable standard practice. . . .

Other professional groups (e.g., the Council for Children with Behavioral Disorders, 1990) have prepared detailed position statements addressing the use of punishment procedures. In addition, the Council for Exceptional Children, the National Education Association, and the National Association of School Psychologists have adopted positions against the use of corporal punishment with all students. The Council for Exceptional Children (www.cec.sped.org) has drafted specific professional policies for the use of school exemption, exclusion, suspension, or expulsion, as well as physical intervention for students with disabilities.

The position statements cited above were adopted for the purpose of guiding professional practice. However, they clearly do not prohibit all use of aversive procedures, nor are practitioners, especially those not belonging to the respective professional organizations, legally bound to follow these policies. Educators are legally required to follow federal and state laws that regulate the use of disciplinary procedures. As Yell and Peterson (1995) pointed out, a dual standard exists for disciplining nondisabled students and those with disabilities. The latter group includes those protected under IDEA and Section 504 of the Rehabilitation Act of 1973. In addition, the U. S. Supreme Court's *Honig v. Doe* (1988) decision established that normal disciplinary procedures customarily used for dealing with school children (e.g., restriction of privileges, detention, and removal of students to study carrels) may be used with students exhibiting disabilities. However, disciplinary procedures that constitute a unilateral decision to change the placement of students with disabilities are severely limited, except in cases where the student brings a weapon to school, commits a drug offense, or a hearing officer determines that the district has demonstrated that maintaining the student's current placement is substantially likely to result in injury to the child or others. In such cases, the student may be placed in an interim alternative educational setting (AES) for up to 45 days. However, students placed in an AES must have access to the general education curriculum, continuation of IEP-specific activities, a FBA, and implementation of positive strategies to address behavior. The law also requires that, beginning in 1998–99, states provide annual reports to the Secretary of Education on the number of students with disabilities who are placed in these alternative settings, the acts that precipitated their removal, and the number of these students who are subject to long-term suspension or expulsion (U.S. Department of Education, 2000). Reports concerning the proportion of students with disabilities who are subject to long-term suspension or expulsion are in conflict. These federal reporting requirements hopefully will establish whether students with disabilities are disproportionately represented, either in terms of their commission of weapons or drug violations, their placement in interim AES, or both. Whatever the outcome, it is certain that school disciplinary practices, especially for students with or suspected of having disabilities under IDEA, Section 504, or ADA, will be carefully scrutinized in the foreseeable future.

Yell and Peterson (1995) have grouped school disciplinary policies into three categories. *Permitted procedures* include those that are part of a school district's disciplinary plan and are used with all students (e.g., verbal reprimands, warnings, contingent observation timeout, response cost, and the temporary delay or withdrawal of goods, services, or activities). Physical restraint or immediate suspension are permissible in emergency situations; however, recall that IEP teams are held strictly accountable to state and federal regulations on the use of suspension for students with disabilities. No legal restrictions exist regarding the involvement of the police if a law has been violated (Maloney, 1994). *Controlled procedures* include interventions the courts have held to be permissible if they are used appropriately, are not abused, and are not used in a discriminatory manner. These include exclusion timeout, seclusion/isolation timeout, in-school suspension, and out-of-school suspension. Suspensions up to 10 days are permitted.[3] *Prohibited procedures* are those that involve unilateral decisions (i.e., decisions not made by the student's IEP committee or educational team) affecting educational placement and include expulsions and indefinite suspensions. This applies even if the student's behavior is dangerous to himself or to others. The only exception allowed is when it can be proven that the behavior resulting in suspension or expulsion is not a manifestation of the student's disability, and courts have tended not to agree with IEP committees who have ruled that such is the case, especially with regard to students with EBD (Yell & Peterson, 1995).

Educators are also obligated to follow local school district policies regulating the use of aversives, but many districts do not have such policies, so your best source of guidance is case law. Lohrmann-O'Rourke and Zirkel (1998) reviewed judicial rulings since 1990 concerning the use of aversive techniques. They found that few court cases have involved the use of electric shock or noxious substances, but case law does support these procedures under narrowly defined circumstances and with careful attention to statutory due process procedures. On the other hand, courts have provided wide constitutional boundaries on corporal punishment, but have stressed that appropriate administrative process be followed when parents file grievances against schools and educators. Conversely, parents must present sufficient evidence of disparate treatment based on disabilities when corporal punishment is used with their children.

[3]Twenty years of case law has defined suspensions or expulsions of more than 10 days in a school year as a change of educational placement subject to the stay-put provision of IDEA (U.S. Department of Education, 2000).

The courts have also offered qualified support for the use of restraints and timeout.

The absence of clear legal guidelines for many reductive procedures and the observation that corporal punishment is used in many schools despite rulings against it may cause you to wonder whether to be concerned with these issues. The precaution offered by Barton et al. (1983) should clear up this ambiguity: "Any person who provides aversive behavioral therapies for persons [with disabilities] without knowledge of the current legislative and litigative mandates governing such provision and concern for the rights of the individual invites both professional and personal disaster" (p. 5). In fact, the U. S. Supreme Court has ruled that if punishment is found to be excessive, the teacher or school officials who are responsible may be held liable for damages to the student (Singer & Irvin, 1987). Thus, you may avoid using punishment procedures altogether or use them carefully and with proper attention to student and parental rights (Wood & Braaten, 1983). Reductive procedures may be necessary with highly disruptive and aggressive pupils, but they should be used in combination with procedures for teaching desired replacement behaviors. Further, as Wood and Braaten (1983) stated, corporal punishment "has no place in special education programs" (p. 71).

The possibility of legal sanctions is a compelling reason for school districts to adopt policies regulating the use of reductive procedures. Singer and Irvin (1987) suggested that students' and teachers' rights concerning intrusive or restrictive procedures should be safeguarded through establishing school district procedures. These are still valid today and include the following:

- Obtaining informed consent, including a detailed description of the problem behavior, previously attempted interventions, proposed intervention risks and expected outcomes, data-collection procedures, and alternative interventions; and a statement of consent from the parents, including the right to withdraw consent at any time.

- Review by a school district human rights committee. (Such review procedures are not found in most school districts, but they should be developed.)
- Due process procedures to regulate school district actions when intrusive behavior management techniques are used. (Again, few school districts have developed such procedures. However, "formal IEP processes must be used if disciplinary methods for any [student] are a regular part of a child's (with disabilities) educational program" [p. 50]. Intrusive interventions require a level of review beyond regular IEP procedures [e.g., human rights committee review].)
- Use the least restrictive alternative. Restrictive interventions must be aimed at educational objectives and those proposing an intervention must prove that less intrusive methods are not the best approach and that the proposed intervention is the least restrictive alternative.

Wood and Braaten (1983) suggested that school district policies regarding the use of punishment procedures include definitions and descriptions of procedures that are permitted and those that are not allowed; references to relevant laws, regulations, court decisions, and professional standards; and procedural guidelines that contain the following elements:

- Information concerning the use and abuse of punishment procedures.
- Staff training requirements for the proper use of approved procedures.
- Approved punishment procedures.
- Procedures for maintaining records of the use of punishment procedures.
- Complaint and appeal procedures.
- Punishment issues and cautions.
- Procedures for periodic review of procedures used with individual students.

Resources that can be used in drafting such policies include guidelines in the professional literature for specific interventions (consult the references cited in the earlier sections of this chapter). As noted earlier, parent and professional organizations, such as the Association for Retarded Citizens, the NEA, and CCBD have developed policies and guidelines regarding intervention procedures. The CCBD guidelines are particularly useful for practitioners.

This discussion has considered the impact on, and acceptability by, persons directly affected by behavioral interventions. The IEP committee format provides a means of socially validating the goals, the appropriateness, and the acceptability of intervention procedures; that is, the extent to which caregivers and significant others agree with the objectives and methods of intervention programs (Wolf, 1978). In planning interventions for typical students, take care to assure that intervention objectives and procedures are seen as appropriate and necessary by those persons who are involved and concerned with pupils' well-being and educational progress. School policies regulating the use of behavior reduction procedures should apply to all students, not just to those with disabilities.

The acceptability of interventions to practitioners is also a relevant issue, especially because some procedures will be recommended to general educators working with pupils having disabilities in mainstream settings. Research on this issue has revealed that, in general, more restrictive interventions (e.g., timeout and psychoactive medications) are viewed as less acceptable than such interventions as positive reinforcement of desired behavior, although more restrictive procedures are seen as more acceptable with students exhibiting highly deviant behavior (Kazdin, 1981; Witt, Elliott, & Martens, 1984). Student and teacher ethnicity also have been suggested as factors affecting treatment acceptability (Pearson & Argulewicz, 1987). Witt and Martens (1983) recommended that professionals ask five questions regarding the acceptability of an intervention (even one whose effectiveness has been documented in the literature) before implementing it:

1. Is it suitable for general education classrooms?
2. Does it present unnecessary risks to pupils?
3. Does it require too much teacher time?
4. Does it have negative side effects on other pupils?
5. Does the teacher have the skill to implement it?

CONSIDERATIONS IN SELECTING REDUCTIVE PROCEDURES Legal and ethical factors also place limits on what reductive procedures can be used with pupils. However, these do not provide specific guidelines concerning which procedures represent the appropriate alternative for specific problem behaviors. Although decisions regarding these choices should be made by students' IEP teams, it is important that this group have guidance from persons who are technically knowledgeable about intervention procedures and their effects, side effects, advantages, and drawbacks. Furthermore, teams should feel comfortable that the recommendation to intervene with a reductive procedure occurs in the context of an educational environment that is positive, structured, and productive. In this section we provide guidelines from the professional literature for making intervention suggestions.

Braaten (1987) suggested three principles that govern the appropriate use of reductive procedures:

1. The priority given the target behavior justifies the level of intervention.
2. Interventions based on positive reinforcement of incompatible or alternative behaviors have been demonstrated to be ineffective.
3. Less restrictive or intrusive procedures are attempted first.

We elaborate on each of these principles in the following discussion.

PRIORITY OF THE TARGET BEHAVIOR Earlier, we introduced the *Fair Pair rule* (White & Haring,

1980), which applies to the identification of desired replacement behaviors for each undesired behavior targeted for reduction. Further, we indicated that desired replacement behaviors could be selected by assessing the skills pupils need in their current or potential future environments. But what criteria should be used in deciding which of the student's undesired behaviors to target first? Braaten (1987) suggested a hierarchy of such behaviors. *Low-priority* target behaviors are those that are annoying but not harmful to others (e.g., teasing, off-task). *Mild-priority* targets include behaviors that frequently interfere with the achievement of classroom or individual student goals (e.g., defiance, pushing, minor property damage). *Moderate-priority* targets are behaviors that repeatedly or significantly interfere with goal achievement or with other class members (e.g., fighting, avoiding school, abuse of staff). Behaviors that are *high-priority* targets involve persistent, generalized alienation or agitation that is excessively disruptive to self and others (e.g., physical assault, stereotypic behaviors, total noncompliance). Finally, *urgent-priority* targets involve extreme risk and require expert intervention (e.g., behaviors that are life-threatening or that risk serious injury to self or others). By reviewing the student's problem behaviors with regard to this hierarchy, you can determine which behaviors may be ignored or monitored to ensure that they are not increasing to obtrusive levels and target these for intervention after higher priority undesired behaviors have been reduced.

DOCUMENTATION THAT ENHANCEMENT INTERVENTIONS HAVE NOT BEEN EFFECTIVE Braaten, Simpson, Rosell, and Reilly (1988) recommended that schools should use disciplinary procedures in accordance with the *principle of hierarchical application*, which requires that more intrusive procedures be used only after less intrusive procedures have failed. We hope that you have seen ample need to attempt interventions that strengthen desired behaviors before considering reductive procedures. By differentially reinforcing behaviors

that are incompatible with or alternative to undesired targets, you may be able to avoid using punishment procedures entirely. In targeting replacement behaviors, remember to consider possible functions of the pupil's maladaptive behavior. If you can identify a replacement behavior that serves the same function and you can systematically reinforce it, the chances are doubly good that you will not have to use aversive consequences to reduce the undesired target behavior. However, for strategies based on enhancement procedures to be most effective, remember that you should identify reinforcers for both desired and undesired behaviors and be able to control the pupil's access to sources of positive reinforcement. Furthermore, in documenting that reinforcing interventions have been ineffective, we assume that you have implemented the intervention systematically, collected data on its effects over an adequate period of time, and evaluated its effects on the target behavior with respect to level, trend, and stability (see Chapter 3 for guidelines on data-based evaluation of interventions).

USE LESS RESTRICTIVE OR INTRUSIVE PROCEDURES This principle suggests that once the decision to use reductive procedures has been made you should consider those that intrude the least upon the student's body, rights, or curriculum. Consider a wide range of alternatives that address both the antecedents to and consequences of the undesired target behavior. Wolery et al. (1988) describe four categories of setting events in the immediate environment that may influence behavior. The *instructional dimensions of the environment* include the types of materials, activities, and instruction that are provided as well as the sequence of activities. For example, if the target behavior occurs mainly when certain activities are scheduled, perhaps these activities are too difficult or are boring to the student. The *physical dimensions of the environment* that may influence behavior include lighting, noise, heat, the physical arrangement of the environment, and the time of day. Variables related to the *social dimensions of the* *environment* include the number of other students, the number of adults, the behavior of others toward the student, and the pupil's physical proximity to others. Finally, *changes in the environment* that potentially affect student behavior include changes in schedule, the physical arrangement of the setting, and the home environment. By being a careful student of the pupil's behavior and staying informed of changes in her other life settings, you should be able to identify antecedent conditions setting events that affect her. If a functional relationship between the target behavior and any of these variables is discovered, attempt interventions that address these factors before considering reductive consequences.

If you have tried reductive procedures not based on the application of aversives (i.e., differential reinforcement, extinction) and found them ineffective, you are now faced with choices from among the punishment options listed in Table 4-1. Two principles will help you make a selection. The **principle of the least intrusive alternative** (Gast & Wolery, 1987) directs you to use the simplest effective intervention based on data available in the research literature. This principle implies that intervention agents must keep up with current research literature on behavioral interventions, which is reported in a variety of professional journals. We encourage you to subscribe to some of these journals independently or through your professional organization (e.g., Council for Children with Behavior Disorders [CCBD], Council for Exceptional Children), and to allow some time each week for professional reading.

Although behavioral interventions have been proven effective across numerous settings, intervention agents, and target individuals, outcomes vary with the unique characteristics of persons and settings so effectiveness is always relative. Thus, the question of what works must address with whom and under what circumstances (Nelson, 1987). Another principle, the **criterion of the least dangerous assumption,** is useful when conclusive data are not available regarding the effectiveness of a particular intervention and the circumstances

surrounding it. As stated by Donnellan (1984), "in the absence of conclusive data, educational decisions should be based on assumptions that, if incorrect, will have the least dangerous effect on the student" (p. 142). For example, an intervention package involving DRI and response cost could be assumed to have less dangerous effects than one that includes overcorrection. One cautionary note: be sure to continuously evaluate the effectiveness of behavior reduction procedures. A less restrictive or intrusive intervention that is ineffective not only is a waste of your time, but it also may contribute to the student's increasing adaptation to more aversive consequences (Azrin & Holz, 1966).

While this discussion has focused on reductive procedures, be aware that strategies based on positive reinforcement can also be misapplied and abused (Kazdin, 2001). For example, inappropriate contingencies of reinforcement may directly support undesired behavior, as when teachers attend to maladaptive student performances while ignoring adaptive behavior when it occurs. One reason that interventions involving aversive procedures are evaluated more critically is that their misuse usually involves greater risks to the student (although there are several exceptions, such as the teacher who attends to SIB).

Decision Models for Reducing Undesired Behaviors

In Chapter 1 we described a model for restructuring schools that is based on integrated systems of intervention that address the full range of students' social behavior. There we suggested that office discipline referrals (ODRs) or behavior reports, when systematically collected and analyzed, yield a basis for making decisions regarding which interventions to use, in what settings and with which students. Lewis-Palmer, Sugai, and Larson (1999) have provided some guidelines for making such decisions. For example, if 40% of students have at least one ODR, or the average number of ODRs per student is greater than 2.5, a school-wide system of positive behavior support is needed. If 60% of all

ODRs come from classrooms, or if less than 10% of classrooms account for more than 50% of ODRs, attention should be directed toward establishing classroom-wide systems of positive behavior support. Systems of positive behavior support in non-classroom settings are indicated if more than 35% of ODRs are made from, or more than 15% of students are referred from, these settings. Students who receive more than five ODRs in a month should be considered for targeted (i.e., behavior intervention) plans. Finally, the need for intensive intervention planning should be considered for students who receive more than 10 ODRs in a given month, especially if they have been receiving secondary prevention support. Intensive interventions, including crisis plans, should also be considered if a small number of students are destabilizing the school environment.

The above are general guidelines that can be used to decide upon the location, level, and to whom interventions should be applied. However, a more detailed analysis is necessary to match precisely the intervention strategy to the characteristics of the pupil, the setting, and the target behavior.[4] Several decision models have been devised for this purpose (e.g., Evans & Meyer, 1985; Gaylord-Ross, 1980; Wolery et al., 1988). The common elements of these models are the formation of hypotheses regarding why problem behavior is occurring and systematic assessment of these hypotheses through manipulation of potential maintaining variables. For example, the model developed by Gaylord-Ross (1980) includes reinforcement, ecology, curriculum, and punishment components. In terms of *reinforcement*, if you hypothesize that a student's behavior is maintained by positive reinforcement and that you are able to control access to the reinforcer, extinction would be a viable intervention. On the other hand, if the behavior is maintained by negative reinforcement (e.g., the student escapes or avoids tasks or settings by en-

gaging in the target behavior), the task itself can be modified to make it less aversive or you can provide additional help (e.g., prompts, instructional assistance). Or, if the behavior occurs due to an insufficient amount of positive reinforcement, increasing the density (i.e., amount and availability) of reinforcement through differential reinforcement might be the best choice.

Interventions based on hypotheses regarding the *ecological setting* stress determining whether problem behaviors occur because of crowding, the lack of engaging objects, or the presence of environmental pollutants (heat, noise, light). Changes in these variables constitute the appropriate intervention in such cases. However, recall that more remote setting events, such as those occurring in the home, may need to be considered (Conroy & Fox, 1994). Hypotheses based on curriculum variables derive from the observation that problem behaviors vary according to particular tasks. Interventions addressing this component involve making appropriate adjustments in the curriculum (e.g., modifying overly difficult tasks, changing non-preferred tasks).

Punishment is the last component in the Gaylord-Ross (1980) model, which indicates that the other hypotheses should be entertained first. We cannot overemphasize the importance of trying to "read" the pupil's behavior correctly; interventions chosen without regard for maintaining variables may be doomed to failure. For example, if a student's disruptive behavior is maintained by escape from undesired tasks, using timeout actually may increase this problem. The systematic, continuous assessment of identified target behaviors in the settings in which they occur is crucial to identifying their relationships to variables that may influence them, to selecting appropriate intervention strategies, and to evaluating and adjusting these interventions.

Resources for Intervention Planning

Fortunately for the practitioner, tremendous growth has occurred in the amount of resource materials for developing interventions for addressing

[4]The best way to match an intervention to these behavioral and contextual variables is to perform a functional behavioral assessment.

academic difficulties or social behavior problems. In addition to the materials and sources mentioned above, there are social skills curricula (see Chapter 7), which represent proactive strategies for teaching appropriate social skills and replacement behaviors. Other resources present strategies for the management of specific problem behaviors. For example, Algozzine (1993) developed a practical guide for dealing with a variety of instructional and behavior management problems. The practitioner can look up a particular behavior problem in this loose-leaf notebook (e.g., physical aggression toward peers, off-task behavior) and locate alternate strategies for dealing with it. The guide includes reference citations and additional readings for each strategy. Howard and Sprick (1998) offer the *Teacher's Encyclopedia of Behavior Management: 100 Problems/500 Plans*. Sprick and his colleagues have developed an extensive variety of materials on behavioral interventions (see the Sopris West web page, www.sopriswest.com).

A number of quick reference guides have been published by Sopris West. These include *The Tough Kid Book* (Rhode, Jenson, & Reavis, 1993) and the *Tough Kid Tool Box* (Jenson, Rhode, & Reavis, 1994), which present suggestions and materials for assisting in the development of proactive behavior management strategies and ideas for dealing with students who are noncompliant, disruptive, and aggressive. *Project RIDE* (Responding to Individual Differences in Education) (Beck & Gabriel, 1990) and *Project RIDE for Preschoolers* (Utah State Office of Education, 1993) are building- and classroom-based support systems for teachers, including computer tactics banks and video libraries that present and illustrate a number of proven, cost-effective strategies. Sopris West also provides training to school districts that adopt these materials. A 16-volume series, *How to Manage Behavior*, is available from Pro-Ed (http://www.proedinc.com). This series provides detailed instructions regarding the use of such strategies as extinction, contracting, token system, timeout, and attention and approval. The Council for Exceptional Children (www.cec.sped.org) also publishes materials ad-dressing students with EBD, as well as behavioral interventions. These include several minilibraries on issues affecting students with EBD, and those who work with them. These short booklets contain useful information for practitioners about issues and strategies concerning working with students who exhibit problematic behaviors.

In using such resources, it is important to recognize the need for adequate training or access to skilled consultation to avoid the tendency to apply the tactics presented in "cookbook" fashion, without appropriate accommodation to individual circumstances. The rapid development of computer-based information services has also produced numerous on-line resources for practitioners with access to computers with modems and Internet accounts. The Internet offers practitioners access to a variety of websites. Table 4–4 lists some of the sites that offer resources for working with children with academic and behavioral problems.

Developing an Intervention Plan

Individual education plans for pupils certified as having EBD should contain objectives and strategies for targeted social behaviors. (We often are surprised to read IEPs for such pupils that contain no plans for intervening with their social behavior problems.) However, these strategies lack the specificity needed to guide intervention efforts on a day-to-day basis. Moreover, students who are not certified as having disabilities will not have IEPs.[5] Wolery et al. (1988) indicated that a specific intervention plan should be developed for each social behavior that is targeted for reduction. The components of a BIP were described in Chapter 2 and should address the following: a behavioral objective, what will be done, who will do it, how it will be done, when it will be done, when it will be reviewed, who will review it, and what will happen

---

[5]Students with disabilities who are not identified by IDEA are protected under Section 504 of the Rehabilitation Act of 1973 and should have a written accommodation plan that includes disciplinary plans (Yell & Peterson, 1995).

TABLE 4–4 On-line Resources

Teacher Resources

http://www.cas.psu.edu/docs/pde/bec.html
Basic Education Circulars

http://www.classroom.net
Classroom Connect (K-12)

http://www.asri.edu/CFSP/brochure/abtcons.htm
Consortium on Inclusive Schooling Practices

http://www.eduweb.com/adventure.html
Educational Web Adventures

http://ericeece.org
Elementary and Early Childhood Education

http://www.ericsp.org/
ERIC Clearinghouse on Teaching and Teacher Education

http://www.ed.gov/free
Federal Resources for Educational Excellence

http://www.ideapractices.org/ideadepot/
schoolswork.htm
Ideas for Lesson Plans

http://www.irsc.org
Internet Resources for Special Children (IRSC)

http://curry.edschool.virginia.edu/go/cise/ose/informat
ion/interventions.html
Intervention Techniques for Individuals with Disabilities

http://www.ericsp.org/lesson.html
Lesson Plans

http://www.ericsp.org/internet.html
Other Educational Internet Sites

http://www.nbpts.org
The National Board for Professional Teaching Standards

http://www.nichey.org/pubs/genresc/gr2.htm
National Information Center for Children with Disabilities

http://www.irsc.org/disability.htm
Resources for Specific Disabilities

http://www.capecod.net/schrockguide
Schrock's Guide for Educators

Agencies and Organizations

http://www.ky.state.us/agencies/behave/
homepage.html
Behavior Web Page

http://www.air-dc.org/cecp/
Center for Effective Collaboration and Practice

http://www.cjcj.org
Center on Juvenile and Criminal Justice

http://www.ncsu.edu/cpsv/
Center for the Prevention of School Violence

http://www.colorado.edu/cspv
Center for the Study and Prevention of Violence

http://www.kysafeschools.org/
Kentucky Center for School Safety

http://www.edjj.org
National Center on Education, Disability, and Juvenile Justice

http://www.nsscl.org/
National School Safety Center

http://www.iir.com/nygc/
National Youth Gang Center

http://ojjdp.ncjrs.org/
Office of Juvenile Justice and Delinquency Prevention
(U.S. Department of Justice)

http://www.pbis.org
OSEP Technical Assistance Center for Positive Behavioral
Intervention and Supports

http://www.pavnet.org/
Partnership Against Violent Network

http://www.ed.gov/offices/OESE/SDFS/
Safe and Drug-Free Schools Program

Research in Education

http://scov.csos.jhu.edu/Crespar/CReSPaR.html
Center for Research on the Education of Students Placed
At Risk

http://ericir.syr.edu/
Educational Resources Information Center (ERIC)

http://ncrtl.msu.edu/
National Center for Research on Teacher Learning

Educational Publications

Professional Journals
http://www.edweek.org/
Education Week

http://www.ed.gov/NCES/naep/
National Assessment of Educational Progress

http://www.edweek.org/tm/tm.htm
Teacher Magazine

Educational Departments

http://goldmine.cde.ca.gov
California Department of Education

(Continued)

TABLE 4–4 On-line Resources—*Continued.*

Educational Departments	Mental Health
http://www.lacoe.edu/doc/prc/prc.html Los Angeles County Office of Education Library and Media Services **http://www.lalc.k12.ca.us/dept/web.html** Los Angeles Learning Center **http://www.lausd.k12.ca.us/welcome.html** Los Angeles Unified School District **http://www.ed.gov/** U.S. Department of Education	**http://www.dmh.cahwnet.gov/** California Department of Mental Health **http://www.psywww.com/** Psychological Disorders **http://edweb.sdsu.edu/CSP/spwww.html** School Psychology Homepage **http://www.bcpl.net/~sandyste/school_psych.html** School Psychology Resources

if the plan is ineffective or if undesired side effects occur. Given the many legal, ethical, and practical considerations that must be taken into account in using reductive procedures, such plans are best worked out by a team. Initial intervention plans can be developed by IEP teams, but for daily decision making and for those students who do not have IEPs, behavior support teams should include persons who are readily available to review data, discuss problems, and make decisions about plan revisions as required. Data-based evaluation strategies, which were described in Chapter 3, are valuable tools for intervention teams.

EVALUATING BEHAVIORAL INTERVENTIONS

Powerful intervention strategies, especially those that are restrictive or intrusive, require precise and sensitive evaluation procedures to ensure that students do not spend unnecessary amounts of time in ineffective programs. Good evaluation procedures also protect those who carry out interventions, in that they provide feedback that may be used to adjust or change procedures that are inappropriate, incorrectly applied, or simply do not work as planned. Unlike assessment, which yields information regarding the current status of a student, evaluation involves assessing the impact of a program on a pupil's current status. Recall from

Chapter 3 that evaluation may be *summative*, occurring after teaching and learning have taken place, or *formative*, which means it occurs as skills are being formed (Howell, Fox, & Morehead, 1993). Traditionally, most educational programs are evaluated summatively (e.g., once or twice a year), when it is too late to make any program changes based on the data obtained. Formative evaluation, however, is an integral part of the teaching process.

Two sets of behavioral procedures are used in conducting formative evaluations of student programs. The first is *data-based decision making* which we described in Chapter 3. Recall that this process involves comparing student performance or progress to a desired level and making adjustments based on this comparison (Deno, 2000). The second procedure is to apply a **single-subject research design** to identify and isolate specific variables that have a direct cause-effect relationship to target behavior. We discuss these procedures separately, although both have much in common and may be used simultaneously. (The case study at the end of this chapter illustrates the use of a single subject research design to evaluate a classroom intervention procedure.)

Single-Subject Research Designs

By using data decision rules and by learning to visually analyze data, you should become skilled at systematically evaluating interventions and making appropriate decisions. However, while data-based decision-making procedures are extremely useful in determining whether an intervention is working, they do not provide a convincing demonstration that the intervention is responsible for changes in target behaviors. Other uncontrolled factors may influence the behavior simultaneously with the intervention, and these offer **competing explanations** for observed changes (e.g., something else in the setting was altered, the student became more mature, or gained insight). Single-subject research designs control for the effects of such extraneous variables through systematic manipulation of intervention variables over time while the target behavior is monitored.

At this point, many teachers say they do not care whether these variables are uncontrolled as long as something works to change behavior. The problem with this attitude is that it may lead to using nonfunctional procedures or complex interventions that place extensive demands on the teacher. For instance, a teacher designed a group contingency (see Chapter 6) to reduce a disruptive behavior of a fourth-grade class. The game involved points, back-up consequences, and much of the teacher's time. It was, however, very effective and the teacher used the game with subsequent groups for several years. Unfortunately, the effects weren't always as dramatic as the first time. Had the teacher been able to determine which components of the game were responsible for its effectiveness, the game could have been adjusted to the demands of each new situation. Further, some components could have been dropped, thereby simplifying the procedure and reducing the demands on the teacher. The point is that you should use the simplest procedures that are also effective. If praise is an effective reinforcer, why develop an elaborate token economy?

Single-subject research designs are useful not only in controlling for the effects of unsystematic variables and for isolating the essential components of intervention "packages"; understanding them will also help you interpret studies reported in the research literature. While you may not be interested in conducting such rigorous research yourself, knowledge of single subject research designs will help you interpret the research reports

that you read as part of your professional growth plan. The reference lists at the end of each chapter will give you an idea of the journals reporting research in areas of interest or concern to you.

Now, we briefly describe three single-subject research designs. For more comprehensive explanations, you may wish to consult a single-subject design book (e.g., Tawney & Gast, 1984). The information in our discussion of data-based decision making regarding the length of baseline phases and the determination of stability or trends in data through visual analysis applies here as well. You may also apply data-decision rules within phases of a single-subject design.

Withdrawal and reversal designs, also referred to as A-B-A-B designs, involve collecting pre-intervention (baseline) data (A), followed by an intervention condition (B), a withdrawal or reversal of intervention procedures (A), and finally reinstatement of the intervention (B). If the target behavior, continuously measured during all conditions, changes in accordance with the condition in effect, it may be concluded that the intervention is effective. Although A-B-A-B designs are commonly referred to as **reversal designs,** a "true" reversal design involves a reversal of intervention contingencies in which the intervention is withdrawn from one behavior (e.g., in-seat) and simultaneously applied to an incompatible behavior (e.g., out-of-seat). The purpose of this manipulation is to demonstrate that the intervention procedure (e.g., teacher attention delivered contingent on the target behavior) has a functional relationship to the behaviors to which it is applied. Reversal designs are uncommon in the applied research literature because of the understandable reluctance of researchers and practitioners to directly reinforce undesired behavior once it has been reduced (Tawney & Gast, 1984). **Withdrawal designs,** on the other hand, involve simply removing the intervention during the second A condition. In other words, baseline conditions are reinstated. Figure 4–2 shows a withdrawal design used to evaluate the effects of timeout contingent on a student's temper tantrums. It may be concluded that timeout was effective in this case because the pupil's

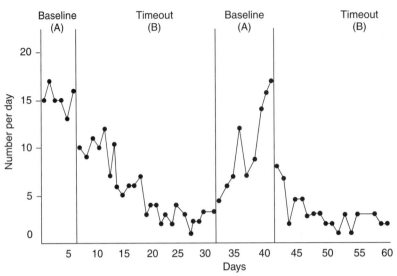

FIGURE 4–2 Tantrums

rate of tantrums decreased when the intervention was applied. (The second replication of baseline and intervention conditions establishes timeout as the variable that was probably responsible for the observed effects. Without this replication we could not be sure that timeout was responsible for changes in the target behavior, because other uncontrolled events may have been introduced at the same time as the timeout contingency.) Changes in levels and trends of the target behavior in accordance with repeated introduction and withdrawal of the intervention demonstrates that manipulation of the timeout contingency controlled the student's tantrums, regardless of any uncontrolled events that may have taken place.

Multiple baseline designs provide a means of evaluating an intervention without a return to baseline conditions. The effectiveness of a program is demonstrated by applying it sequentially across different students, across different behaviors in the same student, or across different conditions or settings with the same student and behavior. If the measured behaviors change in the desired direction only when the intervention is applied, it may be concluded that the intervention was effective. Figure 4–3 illustrates a multiple baseline design across behaviors. The teacher's

goal was to increase the pupil's oral responses to questions. Baseline data were collected on two classes of oral responses: simple yes-no answers and more elaborate verbal responses. Next, intervention was applied to yes-no responses only, while baseline data were collected on other verbal responses. After a stable trend in the former was apparent, intervention was applied to other verbal responses. The conclusion that the teacher's procedures were responsible for the changes in the pupil's oral responses is allowed because neither class of verbal behavior changed until the intervention was applied. The same sequence is followed in the other types of multiple baseline designs; that is, baseline data are collected across multiple students or settings and then the intervention is staggered across students or settings.

Multiple baseline designs are applicable to a variety of situations. However, they require two or more replications (two or more students, settings, or behaviors),[6] prolonged baselines, and target behaviors that can be separately altered without changing the rate of the behavior still in baseline (Tawney & Gast, 1984).

[6]Three replications across students, settings, or behaviors are recommended for demonstrating a functional relationship.

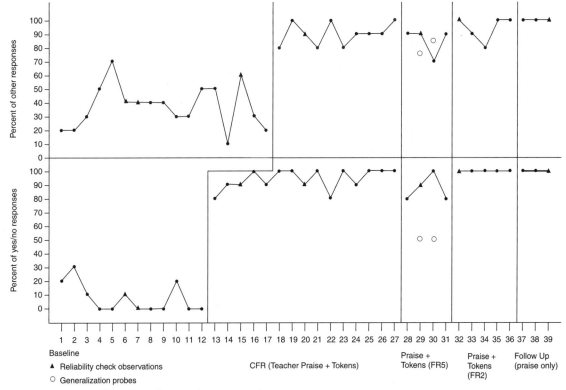

FIGURE 4–3 Percent of Verbal Responses per Opportunity

A variation on the multiple baseline is the **multiple probe design.** It differs from the former in that data probes, or periodic assessments, rather than continuous data, are recorded for the settings, behaviors, or students to which the intervention has not yet been applied. This variation is particularly useful if you are unable to monitor all target behaviors each day (Tawney & Gast, 1984).

The **changing criterion design** (Hartmann & Hall, 1976) actually is another variation of the multiple baseline design, but it may be used with only one student, one behavior, or in only one setting. Following the baseline phase, an intervention program is applied through a series of increments in criterion levels. If the rate of the target behavior changes as the criterion is altered, it may be concluded that the intervention was responsible (Hartmann & Hall, 1976). For example, Figure 4–4

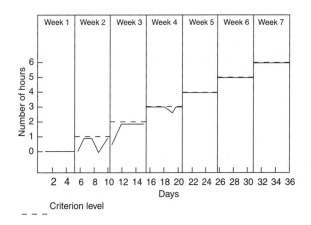

FIGURE 4-4 Chris: Time Spent in Classroom

Source: *Worell, J., & Nelson, C. M. (1974). Managing instructional problems: A case study workbook. New York: McGraw-Hill, p. 216. Used with permission.*

shows a changing criterion design used to evaluate a program to increase a student's time in his classroom. Each week, the criterion was increased in terms of time in the classroom. Chris' performance also increased in response to these criterion changes. This design is especially appropriate for evaluating programs in which a stepwise progression is desired, such as when a new skill is being acquired (Tawney & Gast, 1984).

SUMMARY

Designing intervention strategies from among the variety of behavior change procedures currently available requires complex decisions that are best made by a team of professionals and advocates for the students involved. Professional guidelines and school district or agency policies should be considered in making such decisions. Ultimately, it is the responsibility of primary behavior change agents to make informed decisions regarding intervention strategies from among the range of available behavior enhancement and reductive procedures. These choices should be based on their knowledge of the current research literature, of ethical and legal constraints, and of the characteristics of the student and the settings in which interventions are to be applied. Frequently these procedures must be combined or used in novel ways to fit the circumstances in which they are to be used. Formative evaluation procedures based on continuous and precise measurement of target behaviors therefore are needed for studying and for adjusting interventions. Formative evaluation reduces the chances that students will be subjected to ineffective or unnecessarily aversive procedures. These skills are the basic tools of applied behavior analysis practitioners.

CHAPTER 4 CASE STUDY

Using the Timer Game to Reduce Disruptive Classroom Behavior[7]

Karen Hensley

In my first year as a special education teacher, I was assigned to a primary-level (ages six through eight) self-contained class for children with EBD. Not being trained in this area, I was pretty nervous and insecure from the beginning. The first few weeks of school reinforced my apprehension.

I had established a token system, using points for completing academic assignments and for following classroom rules. Points were exchanged each day for free time to engage in such quiet play activities as puzzles, games, assembling models, and coloring. However, the system didn't prevent off-task behavior and inappropriate social interactions, which frequently disrupted the classroom routine and atmosphere. My pupils (four boys and one girl) would attempt to gain attention or distract others through talking, name-calling, arguing, and occasional open warfare.

Strategy

I had enrolled in a graduate level behavior management class during my first semester of teaching; now I elected to do my class project on disruptive classroom behaviors. I realized that if the students followed my classroom rules requiring teacher permission to talk or to leave one's seat, disruptive behavior would occur less often. Therefore, I selected talking-out and out-of-seat as target behaviors. I also identified nonverbal noises as a target, because my

[7] Used with the author's permission.

students often used this tactic to distract other pupils or to get my attention. For recording purposes, I defined these as follows:

1. Talking-out—pupil speaks or makes verbal noises without turning over his "Help" sign and waiting for teacher attention.
2. Out-of-seat—pupil's bottom is no longer touching the chair but pupil doesn't have teacher permission to be up.
3. Nonverbal noises—repeated kicking, tapping, or other motions that result in an audible sound that is noticeable to me.

My aide and I collected baseline data on these behaviors for six days; I observed three ten-minute time samples each day, scattered across several independent work periods. For recording purposes, I divided each ten-minute period into 40 fifteen-second intervals. If any of the target behaviors occurred in an interval, I entered a code in the box corresponding to that interval (T = talking-out, O = out-of-seat, N = noises). We entered only one symbol per behavior in each interval, no matter how many times it occurred or how many students were doing it. I found that I could measure these behaviors accurately while performing other teaching duties. I attached recording sheets to the clipboard I normally carry with me during independent work.

The intervention strategy consisted of a timer game. I set a kitchen timer for an average of ten minutes. When the timer rang, my aide or I gave all students who were showing appropriate behavior a point along with verbal praise. At the end of the period, these points could be exchanged for "special" free time, provided the student had earned 80 percent of the possible points. Students who failed to meet this criterion had to remain in their seats during free time.

During baseline, I observed that talking-out occurred more frequently than out-of-seat or nonverbal noises (see Figure 4–5). Since it was also the problem of greatest concern to me, I began the timer game with this behavior alone (a multiple baseline design was used in my study). After six-days, I added out-of-seat behavior to the contingency and added nonverbal noises on day 22. Reliability observations were made by my aide at regular intervals. Our independent records showed that we were consistently in agreement.

On the 33rd day I began phasing out the timer. Gradually, I lengthened the interval between timer rings from an average of 10 minutes to an average of 20 minutes. I did this so that students' good behavior would become a discriminative stimulus for awarding points rather than the sound of the timer. Also, I conducted two follow-up checks to assess generalization and maintenance. The first was conducted in the school library during independent work supervised by the librarian. The second was done during another period in my class.

Outcome

Figure 4-5 shows the percentages of disruptive behavior for all students. All three behaviors steadily decreased. This decrease was least dramatic for nonverbal noises, probably because these were most difficult to detect. By the end of my intervention, all three behaviors were occurring during less than 10 percent of the work period. These changes were maintained during my follow-up observations.

At this writing, I am still fading out the timer game. Soon I will drop the timer altogether and just catch my pupils "being good" as a basis for awarding points. I also plan to drop the special free time. My original goal, which was to reduce the occurrence of these three behaviors to less than 20 percent, has been met, and my classroom is a much quieter and more productive place in which to work.

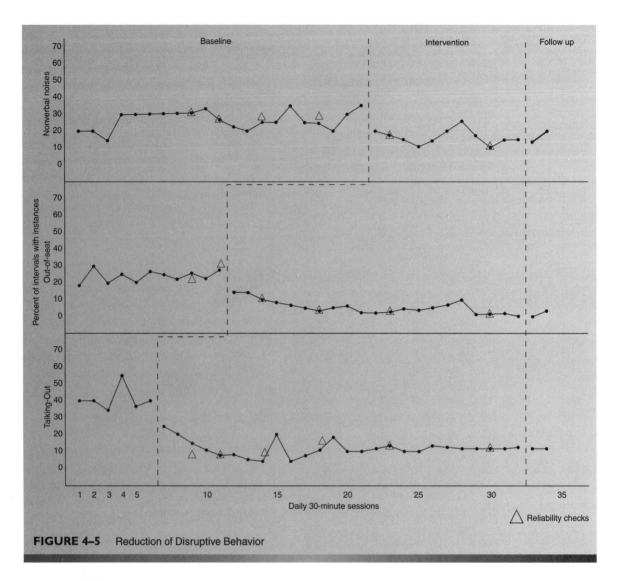

FIGURE 4–5   Reduction of Disruptive Behavior

DISCUSSION QUESTIONS

1. Give an example showing how each of the following principles affects behavior in classroom situations: positive reinforcement, negative reinforcement, extinction, punishment, modeling.
2. Why is the concept of a contingency important in determining the effectiveness of behavioral change procedures? Give

examples of both planned and unplanned contingencies.
3. What procedures and policies should be addressed in developing guidelines for behavioral interventions in schools? Develop a model set of guidelines.
4. A student engages in disruptive behavior almost every day in math class. This results in her being placed in timeout for the remainder of the math class. Comment on

the effectiveness and appropriateness of this intervention.

5. Describe alternate intervention strategies for reducing the disruptive behavior of the student described in question 4, based on your hypothesis regarding the function of her behavior.

6. For what behaviors and circumstances are the following designs appropriate: withdrawal, reversal, multiple baseline, multiple probe, changing criterion?

REFERENCES

Alberto, P. A., & Troutman, A. C. (1999). *Applied behavior analysis for teachers* (5th ed). Upper Saddle River, NJ: Merrill/Prentice Hall.

Algozzine, R. (1993). *Problem behavior management: Educator's resource service*. Gaithersburg, MD: Aspen Publishers.

The Association for the Severely Handicapped Newsletter. (1986, February). Volume 12, No. 2.

Axelrod, S. (1987). Doing it without arrows: A review of Lavigna and Donnellan's Alternatives to punishment: Solving behavior problems with non-aversive strategies. *The Behavior Analyst*, 10, 243–251.

Ayllon, T., & Azrin, N. H. (1968). *The token economy: A motivational system for therapy and rehabilitation*. New York: Appleton-Century-Crofts.

Ayllon, T., & Roberts, M. (1974). Eliminating discipline problems by strengthening academic performance. *Journal of Applied Behavior Analysis*, 7, 71–76.

Azrin, N. H., & Holz, W. C. (1966). Punishment. In W. K. Honig (Ed.), *Operant behavior: Areas of research and application* (pp. 380–447). New York: Appleton-Century-Crofts.

Baer, D. M., Wolf, M. M., & Risley, T. R. (1968). Some current dimensions of applied behavior analysis. *Journal of Applied Behavior Analysis*, 1, 91–97.

Bandura, A. (1969). *Principles of behavior modification*. New York: Holt, Rinehart, & Winston.

Bandura, A. (1977). *Social learning theory*. Upper Saddle River, NJ: Prentice Hall.

Barton, L. E., Brulle, A. R., & Repp, A. C. (1983). Aversive techniques and the doctrine of least restrictive alternative. *Exceptional Education Quarterly*, 3, 1–8.

Beck, R., & Gabriel, S. (1990). *Project RIDE: Responding to individual differences in education* (elementary and secondary version). Longmont, CO: Sopris West.

Braaten, S. (1987, November). Use of punishment with exceptional children: A dilemma for educators. Paper presented at the 11th annual Conference on Severe Behavior Disorders of Children and Youth, Tempe, AZ.

Braaten, S., Simpson, R., Rosell, J., & Reilly, T. (1988). Using punishment with exceptional children: A dilemma for educators. *Teaching Exceptional Children*, 20, 79–81.

Breyer, N. L., & Allen, G. J. (1975). Effects of implementing a token economy on teacher attending behavior. *Journal of Applied Behavior Analysis*, 8, 373–380.

Borden, M., Bruce, C., Mitchell, M. A., Carter, V., & Hall, R. V. (1970). Effects of teacher attention on attending behavior of two boys at adjacent desks. *Journal of Applied Behavior Analysis*, 3, 205–211.

Cantrell, R. P., Cantrell, M. L., Huddleston, C. M., & Wooldridge, R. L. (1969). Contingency contracting with school problems. *Journal of Applied Behavior Analysis*, 2, 215–220.

Carr, E. G., & Durand, V. M. (1985). Reducing behavior problems through functional communication training. *Journal of Applied Behavior Analysis*, 18, 111–126.

Carr, E. G., Taylor, J. C., & Robinson, S. (1991). The effects of severe behavior problems in children on the teaching behavior of adults. *Journal of Applied Behavior Analysis*, 24, 523–535.

Conroy, M. A., & Fox, J. J. (1994). Setting events and challenging behaviors in the classroom: Incorporating contextual factors into effective intervention plans. *Preventing School Failure*, 38(3), 29–34.

Cooper, J. O., Heron, T. E., & Heward, W. L. (1987). *Applied behavior analysis*. Upper Saddle River, NJ: Merrill/Prentice Hall.

Council for Children with Behavioral Disorders. (1990). Position paper on use of behavior reduction strategies with children with behavioral disorders. *Behavioral Disorders*, 15, 243–260.

Council for Exceptional Children. (1993). CEC Policy on Physical Intervention. Adopted by the CEC Delegate Assembly, San Antonio, TX.

Darch, C., Miller, A., & Shippen, P. (1999). Instructional classroom management: A proactive model for managing student behavior. *Beyond Behavior*, 9(3), 18–27.

Deno, S. L. (2000). Academic progress as incompatible behavior: Curriculum-based measurement (CBM) as intervention. *Beyond Behavior*, 9(3), 12–16.

Dietz, D. E., & Repp, A. C. (1983). Reducing behavior through reinforcement. *Exceptional Education Quarterly*, 3, 34–46.

Donnellan, A. M. (1984). The criterion of the least dangerous assumption. *Behavioral Disorders*, 9, 141–150.

Evans, l. M., & Meyer, L. H. (1985). *An educative approach to behavior problems: A practical decision model for interventions with severely handicapped learners*. Baltimore: Paul H. Brookes.

Ferster, C. B., & Culbertson, S. (1982). *Behavioral principles* (3rd ed). Englewood Cliffs, NJ: Prentice-Hall.

Foxx, R. M., & Shapiro, S. T. (1978). The timeout ribbon: A non-exclusionary timeout procedure. *Journal of Applied Behavior Analysis*, 11, 125–143.

Gable, R. A., Hendrickson, J. M., Young, C. C., Shores, R. E., & Stowitschek, J. J. (1983). A comparison of teacher approval and disapproval statements across categories of exceptionality. *Journal of Special Education Technology*, 6, 15–22.

Gast, D. L., & Nelson, C. M. (1977). Legal and ethical considerations for the use of timeout in special education settings. *Journal of Special Education*, 11, 457–467.

Gast, D. L ., & Wolery, M. (1987). Severe maladaptive behaviors. In M. E. Snell (Ed.), *Systematic instruction of the moderately and severely handicapped* (3rd ed.) (pp. 300–322). Upper Saddle River, NJ: Merrill/Prentice Hall.

Gaylord-Ross, R. (1980). A decision model for the treatment of aberrant behavior in applied settings. In W. Sailor, B. Wilcox, & L. Brown (Eds.), *Methods of instruction for severely handicapped students* (pp. 135–158). Baltimore: Paul H. Brookes.

Gelfand, D. M., & Hartmann, D. P. (1984). *Child behavior analysis and therapy* (2nd ed.). New York: Pergamon Press.

Gunter, P. L., & Denny, R. K. (1998). Trends, issues, and research needs regarding academic instruction of students with emotional and behavioral disorders. *Behavioral Disorders*, 24, 44–50.

Gunter, P. L., Hummel, J. H., & Venn, M. L. (2000). Are effective academic instructional practices used to teach students with behavior disorders? *Beyond Behavior*, 9(3), 5–11.

Gunter, P. L., Jack, S. L., DePaepe, P., Reed, T. M., & Harrison, J. (1994). Effects of challenging behavior of students with E/BD on teacher instructional behavior. *Preventing School Failure*, 38, 35–46.

Hartmann, D. P., & Hall, R. V. (1976). The changing criterion design. *Journal of Applied Behavior Analysis*, 9, 527–532.

Homme, L. E. (1970). *How to use contingency contracting in the classroom*. Champaign, IL: Research Press.

Honig v. Doe, 479 U.S. 1084. (1988).

Howard, L. S., & Sprick, R. A. (1998). *Teacher's encyclopedia of behavior management: 100 problems/500 plans*. Longmont, CO: Sopris West.

Howell, K. W., Fox, S.L & Morehead, M. K. (1993). *Curriculum based evaluation: Teaching and decision making* (2nd ed.) Pacific Grove, CA: Brooks/Cole.

Hundert, J. (1976). The effectiveness of reinforcement, response cost, and mixed programs on classroom behaviors. *Journal of Applied Behavior Analysis*, 9, 197.

Hundert, J., & Butcher, B. (1976). Increasing appropriate classroom behavior and academic performance by reinforcing correct work alone. *Psychology in the Schools*, 13, 195–200.

Iwata, B. A., & Bailey, J. S. (1974). Reward versus cost token systems: An analysis of the effects on students and teacher. *Journal of Applied Behavior Analysis*, 7, 567–576.

Jenson, W. R., Rhode, G., & Reavis, H. K. (1994). *The tough kid tool box: A collection of classroom tools*. Longmont, CO: Sopris West.

Kameenui, E. J., & Darch, C. B. (1995). *Instructional classroom management*. White Plains, NY: Longman.

Kazdin, A. E. (1981). Acceptability of child treatment techniques: The influence of treatment efficacy and adverse side effects. *Behavior Therapy*, 12, 493–506.

Kazdin, A. E. (1983). Failure of persons to respond to the token economy. In E. B. Foa & P. M. G. Emmelkamp (Eds.), *Failures in behavior therapy* (pp. 335–354). New York: Wiley.

Kazdin, A. E. (2001). *Behavior modification in applied settings* (6th ed.). Belmont, CA: Wadsworth.

Lewis-Palmer, T., Sugai, G., & Larson, S. (1999). Using data to guide decisions about program implementation and effectiveness: An overview and applied example. *Effective School Practices*, 17(4), 47–53.

Lohrmann-O'Rourke, S., & Zirkel, P. A. (1998). The case law on aversive interventions for students with disabilities. *Exceptional Children*, 65, 101–123.

Luiselli, J. K. (1981). Behavioral treatment of self-stimulation: Review and recommendations. *Education and Treatment of Children*, 4, 375–392.

Madsen, C. H., Jr., Becker, W. C., Thomas, D. R., Koser, L., & Plager, E. (1968). An analysis of the reinforcing function of "sit down" commands. In R. K. Parker (Ed.), *Readings in educational psychology* (pp. 265–278). Boston: Allyn & Bacon.

Maloney, M. (1994). How to avoid the discipline trap. *The Special Educator*, Winter Index, 1–4.

Malott, R. W., Malott, M. E., & Trojan, E. A. (2000). *Elementary principles of behavior* (4th ed.). Upper Saddle River, NJ: Prentice Hall.

Marholin, D., & Steinman, W. (1977). Stimulus control in the classroom as a function of the behavior reinforced. *Journal of Applied Behavior Analysis, 10,* 465–478.

McLaughlin, T. F., & Malaby, J. (1972). Intrinsic reinforcers in a classroom token economy. *Journal of Applied Behavior Analysis, 5,* 263–270.

Nelson, C. M. (1981). Classroom management. In J. M. Kauffman & D. P. Hallahan (Eds.), *Handbook of special education* (pp. 663–687). Englewood Cliffs, NJ: Prentice Hall.

Nelson, C. M. (1987). Behavioral interventions: What works and what doesn't. *The Pointer, 31*(3), 45–50.

Nelson, C. M., & Polsgrove, L. (1984). Behavior analysis in special education: White rabbit or white elephant? *Remedial and Special Education, 5,* 6–17.

Nelson, C. M., & Rutherford, R. B., Jr. (1983). Timeout revisited: Guidelines for its use in special education. *Exceptional Education Quarterly, 3,* 56–67.

Nelson, C. M., & Rutherford, R. B., Jr. (1988). Behavioral interventions with behaviorally disordered students. In M. C. Wang, M. C. Reynolds, & H. J. Walberg (Eds.), *The handbook of special education: Research and practice* (Vol. 2, pp. 125–153). Oxford, England: Pergamon Press.

O'Leary, K. D., Kaufman, K. F., Kass, R. E., & Drabman, R. S. (1970). The effects of loud and soft reprimands on the behavior of disruptive students. *Exceptional Children, 37,* 145–155.

Pearson, C. A., & Argulewicz, E. N. (1987). Ethnicity as a factor in teachers' acceptance of classroom interventions. *Psychology in the Schools, 24,* 385–389.

Pfiffner, L. J., & O'Leary, K. D. (1987). The efficacy of all-positive management as a function of the prior use of negative consequences. *Journal of Applied Behavior Analysis, 20,* 265–271.

Polsgrove, L. (1979). Self-control: Methods for child training. *Behavioral Disorders, 4,* 116–130.

Polsgrove, L. (Ed.). (1991) *Reducing undesirable behaviors* (CEC *mini-library: Working with behavioral disorders*). Reston, VA: Council for Exceptional Children.

Polsgrove, L., & Reith, H. J. (1983). Procedures for reducing children's inappropriate behavior in special education settings. *Exceptional Education Quarterly, 3,* 20–33.

Premack, D. (1959). Toward empirical behavior laws: I. Positive reinforcement. *Psychological Review, 66,* 219–233.

Rhode, G., Jenson, W. R., & Reavis, H. K. (1993). *The tough kid book: Practical classroom management strategies.* Longmont, CO: Sopris West.

Rincover, A. (1981). *How to use sensory extinction: A non-aversive treatment for self-stimulation and other behavior problems.* Lawrence, KS: H & H Enterprises.

Robinson, P. W., Newby, T. J., & Ganzell, S. L. (1981). A token system for a class of underachieving hyperactive children. *Journal of Applied Behavior Analysis, 14,* 307–315.

Rose, T. L. (1983). A survey of corporal punishment of mildly handicapped students. *Exceptional Education Quarterly, 3,* 9–19.

Rutherford, R. B., Jr. (1983). Theory and research on the use of aversive procedures in the education of moderately behaviorally disordered and emotionally disturbed children and youth. In F. H. Wood & K. C. Lakin (Eds.), *Punishment and aversive stimulation in special education* (pp. 41–64). Reston, VA: Council for Exceptional Children.

Rutherford, R. B., Jr., & Nelson, C. M. (1982). Analysis of the response-contingent timeout literature with behaviorally disordered students in classroom settings. In R. B. Rutherford, Jr., (Ed.), *Severe behavior disorders of children and youth* (Vol. 5, pp. 79–105). Reston, VA: Council for Children with Behavioral Disorders.

Rutherford, R. B., Jr., & Nelson, C. M. (1995). Management of aggressive and violent behavior in the schools. *Focus on Exceptional Children, 27*(6), 1–15.

Rutherford, R. B., Jr., & Polsgrove, L. (1981). Behavioral contracting with behaviorally disordered and delinquent children and youth: An analysis of the clinical and experimental literature. In R. B. Rutherford, Jr., A. G. Prieto, & J. E. McGlothlin (Eds.), *Severe behavior disorders of children and youth* (Vol. 4, pp. 49–69). Reston, VA: Council for Children with Behavioral Disorders.

Sajwaj, T. (1977). Issues and implications of establishing guidelines for the use of behavioral techniques. *Journal of Applied Behavior Analysis, 10,* 531–540.

Salend, S. J., & Gordon, B. D. (1987). A group-oriented timeout ribbon procedure. *Behavioral Disorders, 12,* 131–137.

Scott, T. M., & Nelson, C. M. (1999). Universal school discipline strategies: Facilitating positive learning environments. *Effective School Practices, 17*(4), 54–64.

Shores, R. E., Gunter, P. L., Denny, R. K., & Jack, S. L. (1993). Classroom influences on aggressive and disruptive behavior of students with emotional and behavioral disorders. *Focus on Exceptional Children, 26*(2), 1–10.

Shores, R. E., Gunter, P. L., & Jack, S. L. (1993). Classroom management strategies: Are they setting events for coercion? *Behavioral Disorders, 18,* 92–102.

Shores, R. E., Jack, S. L., Gunter, P. L., Ellis, D. N., De-Briere, T. J., & Wehby, J. H. (1993). Classroom interactions of children with behavior disorders. *Journal of Emotional and Behavioral Disorders, 1,* 27–39.

Shores, R. E., Wehby, J. H., & Jack, S. L. (1999). Analyzing behavior in classrooms. In A. C. Repp & R. H. Horner (Eds.), *Functional analysis of problem behavior: From effective assessment to effective support,* (pp. 219–237). Baltimore, MD: Paul H. Brookes.

Singer, G. S., & Irvin, L. K. (1987). Human rights review of intrusive behavioral treatments for students with severe handicaps. *Exceptional Children, 54,* 46–52.

Stainback, W., Stainback, S., & Dedrick, C. (1979). Controlling severe maladaptive behaviors. *Behavioral Disorders, 4,* 99–115.

Strain, P. S., Shores, R. E., & Kerr, M. M. (1976). An experimental analysis of "spillover" effects on the social interaction of behaviorally handicapped preschool children. *Journal of Applied Behavior Analysis, 9,* 31–40.

Straus, M. A., & Field, C. (15 August, 2000). *Psychological aggression by American parents: National data of prevalence, chronicity, and severity.* Paper presented at the meeting of the American Sociological Association, Washington, DC.

Sugai, G. (1995, June). Pro-active classroom management. Workshop presented at the Springfield School Improvement Conference, Springfield, OR.

Tawney, J. W., & Gast, D. L. (1984). *Single subject research in special education.* Upper Saddle River, NJ: Merrill/Prentice Hall.

Twyman, J. S., Johnson, H., Buie, J. D., & Nelson, C. M. (1993). The use of a warning procedure to signal a more intrusive timeout contingency. *Behavioral Disorders, 19,* 243–253.

U.S. Department of Education. (2000). *21st annual report to Congress on the implementation of the Individuals with Disability Education Act.* Washington, DC: U.S. Department of Education, Office of Special Education and Rehabilitative Services.

Utah State Office of Education. (1993). *Project RIDE for preschoolers.* Longmont, CO: Sopris West.

Van Acker, R., Grant, S. H., & Henry, D. (1996). Teacher and student behavior as a function of risk for aggression. *Education and Treatment of Children, 19,* 316–334.

Van Houten, R., Nau, P. A., MacKenzie-Keating, S. E., Sameoto, D., & Colavecchia, B. (1982). An analysis of some variables influencing the effectiveness of reprimands. *Journal of Applied Behavior Analysis, 15,* 65–83.

Walker, H. M. (1983). Applications of response cost in school settings: Outcomes, issues, and recommendations. *Exceptional Education Quarterly, 3,* 47–55.

Walker, H. M. (1995). *The acting-out child: Coping with classroom disruption* (2nd ed.). Longmont, CO: Sopris West.

Walker, H. M., Colvin, G., & Ramsey, E. (1995). *Antisocial behavior in school: Strategies and best practices.* Pacific Grove, CA: Brooks/Cole.

Walker, H. M., Hops, H., & Fiegenbaum, E. (1976). Deviant classroom behavior as a function of combinations of social and token and cost contingency. *Behavior Therapy, 7,* 76–88.

Wehby, J. H. (1997, November). Teacher interactions in SED classrooms: Implications for academic and social behavior. Paper presented at the 21st Annual Conference on Severe Behavior Disorders of Children and Youth, Tempe, AZ.

Wehby, J. H., Symons, F. J., & Shores, R. E. (1995). A descriptive analysis of aggressive behavior in classrooms for children with emotional and behavioral disorders. *Behavioral Disorders, 24,* 51–56.

White, O. R., & Haring, N. G. (1980). *Exceptional teaching* (2nd ed.). Upper Saddle River, NJ: Merrill/Prentice Hall.

Witt, J. C., Elliott, S. N., & Martens, B. K. (1984). Acceptability of behavioral interventions used in classrooms: The influence of amount of teacher time, severity of behavior problem, and type of intervention. *Behavioral Disorders, 9,* 95–104.

Witt, W. C., & Martens, B. K. (1983). Assessing the acceptability of behavioral interventions used in classrooms. *Psychology in the Schools, 20,* 510–517.

Wolery, M., Bailey, D. B., & Sugai, G. M. (1988). *Effective teaching: Principles and procedures of applied behavior analysis with exceptional students.* Boston: Allyn & Bacon.

Wolf, M. M. (1978). Social validity: The case for subjective measurement or how applied behavior analysis is finding its heart. *Journal of Applied Behavior Analysis, 11,* 203–214.

Wood, F. H., & Braaten, S. (1983). Developing guidelines for the use of punishing interventions in the schools. *Exceptional Education Quarterly, 3,* 68–75.

Worell, J., & Nelson, C. M. (1974). *Managing instructional problems: A case study workbook.* New York: McGraw-Hill.

Yell, M. L., & Peterson, R. L. (1995). Disciplining students with disabilities and those at risk for school failure: Legal issues. *Preventing School Failure, 39*(2), 39–44.

Zirpoli, T. J., & Melloy, K. J. (2001). *Behavior management: Applications for teachers and parents* (3rd ed.). Upper Saddle River, NJ: Merrill/Prentice Hall.

UNIVERSAL SCHOOL AND CLASSROOM MANAGEMENT STRATEGIES

5

OUTLINE

OBJECTIVES

After completing this chapter, you should be able to

- Explain the concept of early identification and intervention from a universal prevention perspective.
- Describe the components and procedures involved in a school-wide prevention system.
- Describe how to identify predictable problems across various school settings.
- Give examples of how rules, routines, and physical arrangements are used to prevent predictable problem behaviors.
- Describe how school-wide and classroom rules should correspond—when they should be the same and when they can vary.
- Indicate which aspects of classroom setting events are likely to influence pupil behavior and how they may be altered to increase the probability of desired behavior.
- Describe the advantages and disadvantages of level systems and their application in classroom management programs.

This chapter was written by Terrance M. Scott, Ph.D.

School problems involving weapons, violence, and student safety have garnered increasing media attention in the past few years (Lichter, Lichter, & Amundson, 1999), promoting a community perception of ever-present danger in schools (Brooks, Schiraldi, & Ziedenberg, 2000; Leone, Mayer, Malmgren, & Meisel, 2000). However, the vast majority of problems in schools do not involve violence and, in fact, children are less likely to be victims of violence when they are in school than when they are anywhere else, including their own homes (Elliott, Hamburg, & Williams, 1998; Snyder & Sickmund, 1999). Teachers' concerns about student discipline tend to be about simple, repetitive, and annoying problems such as "disrespect," "noncompliance," and "lack of responsibility for work completion" (Scott, 2001). Still, these concerns may reflect a greater focus on a perceived increase in the rate of problem behaviors rather than on their intensity. Because small problems tend to become larger when not dealt with immediately, repeated minor problems sometimes become overwhelming simply because they occur across a significant proportion of the student population. The most obvious solution is to prevent these frequent but minor behavioral infractions and to react more effectively when they do occur.

Effective prevention requires forethought about the reasons for common behavior problems, as well as insight into the factors that seem to predict these. If we can predict when, where, and why problems occur across the school and in the classroom, we can design strategies to prevent them. While these strategies likely will not prevent all problems, they will decrease their frequency. As you will see later, reducing the number of students who exhibit minor behavioral incidents will help to identify those students who need more individualized and intensive intervention.

This chapter presents examples of a variety of assessment and intervention strategies for the prevention of problem behaviors across the school and in the classroom. These strategies represent *universal interventions* as defined by Walker, Colvin, & Ramsey (1995): they are applied to all students in a group and address the "margins" in which the boundaries between acceptable and unacceptable student behavior typically are not clear. The objective of preventative behavior management is to analyze and structure social interactions in such a way as to minimize the occurrence of behaviors requiring targeted intervention. Management procedures and systems intended for specific behavior problems are emphasized in subsequent chapters. Many potentially difficult situations can be prevented through careful assessment, effective educational programming and behavioral support, and appropriate group behavior management. Thus, universal behavior management should be viewed as a set of proactive strategies that reduce the need for targeted interventions for the majority of pupils.

The typical focus of strategies for behavior management is on acting-out (externalizing) behavior problems. This focus may appear to overlook behavioral deficits, that is, the absence of socially desirable behaviors. However, many students whose behavioral excesses create management problems also are deficient in academic skills and appropriate social behaviors (Kauffman, 2001). Behavior management aimed at preventing or reducing the occurrence of behaviors that interfere with productivity and learning will be more effective if the curriculum simultaneously addresses pupils' social skill deficits. Students who consistently break rules of conduct, whose inappropriate behaviors repeatedly disrupt order in the school, or who fail to correct their undesired behavior when exposed to the school's available disciplinary measures should be assessed with respect to desired academic, social, and school survival skills, and their deficits in these areas should be addressed through appropriate school-wide and classroom curricular interventions.

It would be simple to assume that every problem behavior is "owned" by the student (i.e., that behavior problems are attributable to students' personal characteristics and histories). The assertion that students are responsible for their own behavior is inarguable, and many students do have physical and psychological disabilities that affect their behavior. To be certain, we must attempt to identify and provide support for these students' special needs. However, it is a mistake to assume that all student misbehaviors are the product of permanent physical characteristics or personality traits. In the first place, this perspective suggests that educators can do nothing to prevent problem behavior. The attitude that the cause of the student's problem behavior is centered within the child relegates intervention to a reactive mode only, in which we wait for problem behavior to occur, then attempt to alter the student's motivation to exhibit the behavior, often by using punishment. Second, assuming that misbehavior is an unavoidable trait encourages the use of more intrusive treatment options (i.e., medications, prosthetics, etc.) without first assessing the effects of less intrusive options. Providing students with effective instruction in the necessary skills to manage their own behavior surely is more empowering than simply giving them a pill. Third, although there are obviously students whose behaviors are the result of physical or personality traits, even these pupils can benefit from environmental arrangements that predict success as well as effective instruction in self-management. For example, research indicates that students with ADHD respond best to low dosages of psychostimulant medication in conjunction with effective behavioral interventions (Forness, Kavale, Sweeney, & Crenshaw, 1999). An instructional perspective on addressing problem behavior focuses on external environmental variables that can be altered much more effectively and efficiently. This approach also assumes that desired student behavior can be learned, reinforced, and maintained.

Because certain environmental conditions in the school may predict or contribute to occurrences of problem behavior, this chapter begins with a discussion of the value of prevention in behavior management. School-wide prevention strategies, including assessment of school-wide behavioral issues and implementation of universal interventions by all school staff, are described next. This focus on prevention is continued in the following section, which addresses classroom management strategies, including effective instruction and other approaches.

PREVENTION AS EFFECTIVE BEHAVIOR MANAGEMENT

Aside from being annoying, time consuming, and distracting, minor problem behaviors are predictive of more chronic and pervasive problem behaviors in the future (Kauffman, 2001; Walker et al., 1995). For this reason, systematic screening to identify students who are at risk for displaying patterns of maladaptive behavior, as well as early intervention practices, have been widely advocated as a preferred practice in the effort to prevent student failure (Kauffman, 1994; Scott & Nelson, 1999; Walker, Severson, & Feil, 1994). However, this chapter suggests another interpretation of early intervention, one that focuses on the prevention of problem behaviors throughout the school, as opposed to the more familiar method of identifying individuals at risk for failure. While traditional early identification and intervention are effective practices, evidence suggests that the number of children identified as at risk for school failure because of their patterns of undesired behavior can be reduced significantly if prevention focuses first on the larger environment (Nelson, 1996; Scott, 2001). These prevention strategies are termed *universal* because they involve assessment, analysis, and action taken by all staff and affecting all students, locations, times, and problems. The goal of this chapter is to help you create productive learning environments in which the occurrences of challenging student behavior are minimized.

In the average school, a significant portion of the student population can be expected to display problem behaviors at some time (Horner & Sugai, 2000; Sugai et al., 2000). However, not all of these students require targeted intervention strategies (including behavior intervention plans). Some pupil misbehavior occurs because the environment sets the occasion for problem behavior. Environmental variables that may contribute to such behavior include the absence of clear and consistent rules and consequences, problematic routines, or providing inadequate supervision of common areas (e.g., halls, playground, lunchroom). While 80% to 90% of students probably can function adequately even under such circumstances, some students (as many as 10%) will experience failure (manifested as recurring behavior problems) if these environmental deficits prevail. These are the students who are likely to receive multiple behavior reports or office discipline referrals (ODRs), who spend large amounts of time in the principal's office or in suspension, or who are excluded from school altogether because of their behavior. Such punishment exacerbates the academic skill deficits exhibited by many students in this group (Gunter, Hummel, & Venn, 1998; Sulzer-Azaroff & Mayer, 1991) because they spend so much time out of the learning environment. When they return to the classroom, their lack of skill makes academic work aversive, increasing the likelihood that they will engage in behavior that leads to escape and avoidance (e.g., disruption, noncompliance). If these students continue to fail, they will develop patterns of antisocial behavior or maladaptive coping mechanisms that contribute to lifelong failure. And their failure is our failure, because individuals who exhibit such patterns become lifetime consumers of the most expensive programs and services that we support as taxpayers—institutionalization, incarceration, and the like (Centers for Disease Control and Prevention, 1995). Thus, universal prevention strategies promote success among a group of students for whom small failures accumulate to become large failure. In this sense, universal systems can be conceptualized as early intervention, because not only do these strategies prevent many students from exhibiting the types of failures that annoy, distract, and burden educators, they also help more students be successful in school. Without universal strategies, the numbers of students whose behav-iors require targeted intervention too often outpace available services and supports.

The task is to determine which students are, in fact, candidates for specialized intervention systems and which are having problems because the school environment is not consistent in supporting appropriate and desired student behavior. When school staff can reliably predict the times, places, and contexts in which problem behaviors are likely to occur, they have the information necessary to effectively prevent these failures. When the environment is arranged to prevent predictable minor behavior problems for the majority of students, the 7% to 10% who truly are in need of targeted intervention will be identified as a distinct group, because they continue to exhibit problem behavior even when universal supports are in place. Universal prevention strategies reduce the number of students who might otherwise be unnecessarily exposed to these more labor-intensive targeted interventions. Thus, the implementation of universal strategies is the first step in an early intervention process. Universal assessment and intervention strategies may be applied across the entire school as well as at the classroom level.

SCHOOL-WIDE MANAGEMENT STRATEGIES

Typically, students whose behavior problems have been frequent or intense enough to come to our attention are students who repeatedly have failed in a variety of academic and social contexts (Kauffman, 2001). As explained above, every new failure strengthens a pattern of failure that, over time, greatly decreases the likelihood that the student in question will ever experience success (Walker et al., 1995). Operating under the principle that what can be predicted can be prevented, we must determine the contexts and conditions under which problem behaviors are most likely to occur.

School-Wide Prevention

Descriptions and analyses of school-wide systems of prevention are appearing more frequently in the professional literature (Horner & Sugai, 2000; Dwyer, Osher, & Warger, 1998). Chapter 1 presented a model of positive behavior support in which prevention and intervention strategies are organized into three levels that address the full range of student behavior (Sugai et al., 2000). You will recall that this model involves three levels of systemic prevention: (1) universal systems— prevention strategies applied across the school for all students, (2) targeted systems—school-wide and individualized prevention and response strategies aimed at approximately 10% of the school population for whom universal systems were not sufficient, and (3) intensive systems—individualized prevention and response strategies aimed at the approximately 1–3% of students for whom both universal and targeted systems have been insufficient. Each level can be characterized in terms of strategies that are unique and increasingly intensive, and by the specific portion of the school population upon which it is focused. The foremost concern at the three levels is prevention. However, whereas targeted and intensive interventions are much more prescriptive and individualized, the focus of universal systems is on the identification and amelioration of environmental factors that predict failure across the total student population. Research has demonstrated that systems of positive behavior support have been successful in decreasing problem behaviors across a range of elementary, middle, and high schools of varying sizes (e.g., Chapman & Hofweber, 2000; Lohrmann-O'Rourke et al., 2000; Mayer, Butterworth, Nafpaktits, & Sulzer-Azaroff, 1983; Scott, 2001). Targeted and intensive strategies are described in detail as individual interventions in Chapters 6 through 12.

Using Behavior Incident Data

The best predictor of when, where, and under what conditions problem behavior will occur in the future is the history of when, where, and under what conditions it occurred in the past (Scott & Nelson, 1999; Scott, 2001). When available, such school data as ODRs generally provide the simplest method of evaluating the predictors of past problem behaviors. As pointed out in Chapter 1, many schools summarize data on behavior problems, collecting data on ODRs or other behavioral incidents. This information can be used as a basis for making decisions about where and when prevention strategies are needed, as well as the types of strategies likely to be effective (e.g., Nakasato, 2000). Of course, this information is only useful if it provides sufficient data on the environmental conditions that were associated with each problem. For example, if behavior referral forms include information on when and where behavioral incidents or disciplinary infractions occur, these data may be summarized over time and used to answer questions about settings or times of the day where problem behaviors are most likely to occur across the school, or to identify students who are receiving multiple behavioral reports.

This level of information is critical to the development of effective prevention strategies. For example, if ODR data indicate that problems frequently occur in the hallways, a logical prevention strategy may be to improve supervision in the halls. However, continuous hallway monitoring throughout the day would require a substantial effort on the part of the staff. If the ODR or behavior report form also includes the time that the behavior incident occurs, analysis of ODR data collected over several days may suggest that supervision needs to be increased only for a specific time (e.g., during the lunch hour). Thus, the use of behavior incident data can facilitate strategic planning to create procedures that are more effective and more efficiently delivered, as staff are not being asked to exert extra effort that results in small, if any, gains in prevention. The content and complexity of a school-wide data collection form is completely dependent upon the types and amount of information desired. That is, if a school wishes to assess the predictability of problem behaviors

DATE	2-5-00		NAME	Sally Jones		STAFF	Ms. Shank

TIME:	LOCATION		BEHAVIOR		SPECIAL ED.	Yes / No
8–9 _____	classroom	_____	fighting	_____		
9–10 _____	hallway	_____	disrespect	✓		
10–11 _____	lunchroom	✓	stealing	_____	GENDER	Male / Female
11–12 _____	gym	_____	vandalism	_____		
12–1 ✓	playground	_____	noncompliance	_____		
1–2 _____	bus stop	_____	out of bounds	_____	MINORITY	Yes
2–3 _____	library	_____	safety violation	_____		No

FIGURE 5–1   Sample ODR form.

by time and location, this information must be included on the data collection form. Similarly, if a school is interested in determining whether staff respond differently to problem behaviors of special versus general education students, information regarding student characteristics and outcomes must be included on the form. Each school must develop its own data collection form to answer its own unique questions and fit its own unique needs. Typically, data forms that are small, easily carried, and formatted as a checklist (as opposed to requiring a written report) are the easiest to use and promote the greatest level of staff consistency in use. An example of an ODR form is presented in Figure 5–1.

Once behavior incident data have been collected, they must be summarized so that analyses can be performed regularly and with ease. A simple method of summarizing data is to enter it on a spreadsheet. To accomplish this, a school might design a procedure in which all ODR forms are placed into a box in the office. Each Friday, an office worker can transfer data from the forms onto the spreadsheet—generating a weekly summary of all behavior problems. Figure 5–2 presents an example of a weekly ODR summary. Note that the information summarized for Acme Elementary allows school staff to quickly see who had problems, what those problems were, where they occurred,

and who observed them. Additional characterizing information (e.g., educational placement, student gender, or minority status) also can be summarized as necessary to answer school questions. In Acme Elementary the staff might determine from their analysis of weekly data summaries that behavior problems are predictable in the cafeteria during the lunch hour. Additionally, it appears that Sally Jones is having multiple problems and that fighting seems to be a common problem. Collecting and summarizing this information is the first step in school-wide decision making. The data are a compass, directing staff to where more information should be gathered. For instance, the data from Acme Elementary may suggest that Ms. Otis and Ms. Shank should be asked about the exact nature of problems in the lunchroom and what they see as potential solutions. Furthermore, staff would likely want to look further into Sally Jones' problems. Appropriate questions to ask about Sally include what seems to predict her behavior problems and which teachers are most likely to have more in-depth information. The staff at Acme Elementary would continue to collect data and summarize it weekly throughout the year, while at the same time they would analyze the entire database for emerging trends across months.

While data collection and analysis across the school is the most effective and efficient way to

Acme Elementary—Office Referral Summary February 1–5					
Student	**Date**	**Time**	**Location**	**Problem**	**Referred By**
Smith, Jeff	2–1	12:15	lunchroom	fight	Mr. Otis
Jones, Sally	2–2	3:10	field	vandalism	Ms. Hawkins
Blake, Eddy	2–4	7:30	bus stop	fight	Mr. Hanks
Orr, Jenny	2–4	12:10	lunchroom	stealing	Ms. Shank
Jones, Sally	2–5	12:20	lunchroom	disrespect	Ms. Shank

FIGURE 5–2   Weekly ODR summary.

identify the predictors of behavioral failure, many schools do not use ODAs or do not routinely summarize data in a manner that allows access to the level of information necessary for designing effective prevention systems. In such cases, the next best strategy is to survey the school staff to identify problem behaviors they see most often in the school, as well as when and where these problems are observed (Scott & Hunter, in press; Scott, 2001). This process is time consuming but does offer the advantage of engaging all staff and encouraging their input regarding problem behaviors to which they most often respond. This staff engagement also may encourage them to be more involved in the process of developing strategies to prevent these predictable problems.

Designing School-Wide Systems

Whether by collecting behavior incident data or by surveying staff, identified predictable problems should be addressed by prevention strategies that are agreed upon by the entire school staff. A rule of thumb is that for every identified problem, staff should determine whether the problem could be prevented by (a) a simple rule that students could be taught, (b) adapting an existing routine or creating a new routine, or (c) changing the physical structure of the environment or the presence of

adults in the environment. As mentioned in Chapter 1, a specific team may be created to oversee the implementation of school-wide universal interventions. However, the same staff who fill out the behavior reports or who respond to school-wide problem surveys should participate in designing prevention strategies. Regardless of which strategy (rule, routine, physical arrangement) or combination of strategies is determined to be the best solution, it must be adopted by the entire school staff. If more than one strategy is identified as a viable solution, the staff must then decide which strategy or combination is the easiest and least expensive method of affecting the desired change. Again, once a strategy or set of strategies has been agreed upon, it must be put into place and applied consistently throughout the school. At this point, if it doesn't already exist, a data collection procedure should be developed to monitor the identified problems and evaluate the effectiveness of the adopted solutions. When data determine that selected strategies are not successful, staff must convene and adjust or design alternate strategies.

Adapting school rules is most easily accomplished when the initial set of school-wide rules are developed under a set of "big ideas" that can be used across the school, rather than a laundry list of specific rules that vary by location and context. For example, Finster Elementary School has removed their lists of "don'ts" that had served as the school-wide rules. In its place, they have taught all students three basic school expectations: respect yourself, respect others, and respect property. On the first day of school all faculty took time to teach each of the expectations. *Respect yourself* was defined as "keep yourself safe and learning," *respect others* was defined as "treat others the way you want them to treat you," and *respect property* was defined as "treat property that does not belong to you as you would like others to treat your property." Once students understood these big ideas, faculty and staff urged them to come up with examples of rules that would help them meet each expectation. On the playground, students determined that allowing the first person in line to have the final word in judging play would help to keep the game moving and thus would demonstrate respect for self and others. In the classroom, students felt that calling out was not respectful to those with their hands raised and so decided that the rule should be to raise your hand when you wish to speak.

The concept of big ideas to teach school-wide rules has several advantages. First, students are actively involved in establishing the rules across all locations and contexts in the school. Second, all rules are tied into a school-wide rationale that helps students (and staff) remember them. Third, when students do not live up to any of the expectations, correction can be accomplished simply by asking the student, "Were you being respectful of others?" Follow-up can then involve instruction and the question, "What would be a better way?" Lastly, when school-wide data reveal unanticipated problem behavior, the same expectations can be used to create new rules aimed at preventing those predictable problems. Thus, school-rules are never rewritten, only expanded.

The following sections present more concrete examples of how predictable problem information is used to develop or adapt rules, routines, and physical arrangements in the school. Look at the map of a portion of a school building presented in Figure 5–3. Assume that summaries of ODR data indicate that hallway A outside the music room is an area in which pushing and shoving, arguments, and

even some vandalism have occurred. A closer inspection of these data indicate that these problems tend to be evenly distributed through the day, except during the noon hour when no music classes are held. Knowledge of when and where problems are occurring can lead staff to develop hypotheses regarding why these problems take place. For example, suppose that many students are using this hallway at the same time (i.e., leaving and entering the music room). In addition, students are going in both directions throughout the hallway and are not under the immediate supervision of their teachers. Given this information, here are some simple rules, routines, and physical arrangements that could be introduced or adapted to prevent these problems.

RULES A pertinent question is: Could students be taught a simple rule that might prevent this problem? One explanation for the problem is that students are milling about through the hallway in a haphazard manner. Therefore, a strategy might be to teach all students the rule, "Keep to the right when in the hallway." It is reasonable to assume that, if students stay to the right, much of the pushing and shoving will be eliminated, because students no longer will be crossing paths going in opposite directions. In addition to the potential effectiveness of a strategy, staff must also consider how realistic it would be to put in place. At face value, there seems to be no reason to believe that this strategy would be difficult to implement, and thus it appears to be an effective and realistic solution. However, it is up to the staff to decide whether the strategy will be adopted.

ROUTINES Is there a simple routine that can be implemented or an existing routine that can be adapted that might prevent this problem? Again, staff must think back to the identified problem and why it is occurring. Recall that many students were in the small hallway area at one time. One change in routine that might be considered is to arrange for students in the music room to completely vacate the room prior to the next group entering. Another possible change in routine is to allow the

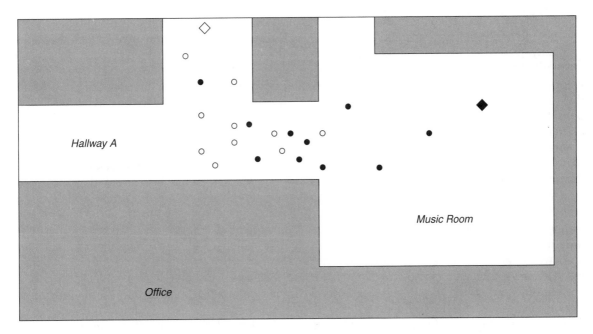

● = students leaving the music room

○ = students entering the music room

◆ = music teacher

◇ = teacher escorting entering students

FIGURE 5–3 Conditions predicting student problems.

students in the music room to exit by the other door to the room rather than through the door in the hallway. By using one door as an entrance and another door as an exit, contact between students going different directions in the hallway can be avoided. Again, whether either one of these strategies is adopted will be determined by the staff after considering all possible solutions.

PHYSICAL ARRANGEMENTS Is there a simple physical arrangement that could be introduced to prevent the problem? Recall that lack of immediate supervision was identified as a possible reason for behavior problems in that hallway. One strategy might be to ask the music teacher to stand in the music room doorway when dismissing and admitting students. In addition, the

teacher escorting the students entering the room could be asked to lead the group through the hall, making certain that the line is orderly and that students are following the rules established for this transition. As with the other alternative strategies, this one has face validity. A bigger issue with regard to changing student supervision patterns is the degree of effort required to implement those changes. The more difficult the change, the less realistic and the more likely that it will be abandoned over time. In this case, the staff changes appear to be fairly simple, although this again will be the decision of the staff. Once each of these strategies has been considered, the staff must determine which one or combination might realistically be implemented and be effective in preventing the problem.

Again, when school-wide prevention strategies are adopted by all staff, implemented consistently and fairly, monitored to evaluate their effects on student behavior, and adjusted as needed according to school-wide data collection, significant reductions have been observed in rates of ODRs and behavior incidents. Responding to these incidents ordinarily requires large amounts of time by some school staff (e.g., discipline dean, assistant principal), but more often than not, the results are less than desired in terms of serving as a deterrent to student misbehavior. School-wide prevention strategies must be owned by the entire school, meaning that the general education program must take the major role in their implementation. When properly implemented, school-wide behavior management establishes an important context for prevention efforts at the classroom level. Several resources are available to facilitate training in school-wide discipline planning. For example, see Colvin, Sugai, and Kameenui (1994); Mayer, Butterworth, and Spaulding (1989); and Sprick, Sprick, and Garrison (1992). The case study at the end of this chapter illustrates how a school-wide behavior management plan was developed.

CLASSROOM MANAGEMENT STRATEGIES

At the classroom level, a wide range of universal interventions have been developed for dealing both with students exhibiting disabilities and those who are typical. As emphasized at the beginning of this chapter, the appropriate context for a classroom behavior management program is a school-wide disciplinary plan (Colvin, Kameenui, & Sugai, 1993; Walker et al., 1995) that connects the teacher's strategy with expectations and consequences that exist throughout the school building.

Extending School-Wide Strategies

School-wide systems of positive behavior support typically extend only to the commons areas of the school, including the hallway, playground, cafeteria, restrooms, etc. School staff vote on the expectations that they'd like to see in place and agree to carry out the strategies upon which consensus has been reached. However, these strategies normally do not translate directly to the classroom. That is, even when school-wide strategies are in place, teachers maintain their autonomy regarding the management structure and style within the confines of their own classrooms. Despite this autonomy, teachers must be careful that classroom structures do not contradict school-wide expectations or set students up to fail in the larger school environment. For example, if all school staff agree that no gum is allowed, no teachers should allow gum in his or her classroom. To do so would set students up for failure if they forget to dispose of their gum before moving into the hallway or are seen carrying gum on campus. Similarly, if the school decides to use conflict managers to mediate disputes between students, every teacher should support that strategy in his or her classroom. The goal is to establish consistent expectations and procedures, thereby encouraging students to engage in behaviors that will promote their success.

Aside from considering the school-wide rules that logically should be applied to the classroom, teachers must consider their own classrooms in much the same manner as the entire staff considered circumstances that appeared to predict student failures throughout the school. Teachers can think back and identify the times, places, and conditions under which problem behaviors have most often occurred in their classrooms. Then, they can use the same procedure as followed in school-wide planning (i.e., developing classroom rules, routines, and physical arrangements). But in this case, the teacher has autonomy in deciding which strategies should be adopted. As before, strategies should be considered in terms of expected effectiveness and the effort required to implement them. In the end, classroom teachers develop their own classroom management structure which both fits within the school system and provides the most efficient and effective strategies for preventing student failure.

Recall that behavior management in the school involves facilitating student success in group settings. This focus also should be maintained in your classroom. Strategies to facilitate success in this setting involve organizing the curriculum, arranging and individualizing instruction, evaluating students' acquisition of skills and information, and adjusting instructional and behavior management procedures according to their progress. Managing student behavior is a necessary, if not sufficient, condition for accomplishing your major goal—facilitating pupils' learning. The teacher who cannot maintain behavior within reasonable limits through positive management procedures will face constant frustration and personal dissatisfaction and is likely to find those same feelings expressed by students and their parents.

In the classroom, the specific management goals expressed by teachers are likely to include increasing such desired student behaviors as attending to tasks, remaining in-seat, following teacher directions, using time productively, and giving correct academic responses (Gresham & Reschly, 1987). These behaviors correspond to a "model behavioral profile" (Hersh & Walker, 1983), but note that they have little to do with developing students' peer relationship skills (Gresham & Reschly, 1987). Teachers are also concerned about decreasing behaviors that are dangerous, disruptive, or incompatible with the completion of academic tasks. The majority of pupils also would like to achieve these goals. That is, they want to be academically and socially successful in school. Therefore, it is important to negotiate with students when setting expectations for classroom behavior. Your expectations will more likely be accepted if you consider those of your students. Again, the majority of students want to be successful in school, both with other students and adults. It is necessary to look to the problems that inhibit this success and assess to determine why students fail. The answers to these questions are the key to facilitating success for all students.

The following discussion of classroom behavior management focuses on decisions and strategies aimed at the prevention of occasions in which one or more students exhibit behaviors that disrupt the learning environment or are potentially dangerous. A classroom management system should be a flexible, operating framework, not a rigid, intolerant set of rules and consequences. As a matter of principle, use the system most natural (i.e., that involves the fewest number of contrived or "extra" factors, such as points or tangible reinforcers) and easy to operate. Artificial systems usually must be diminished for pupil behavior to generalize to classroom environments where such procedures are not in use. In accordance with this principle, classroom management procedures are presented here in an ascending order of complexity, along with factors that influence the effectiveness of the procedures used. The emphasis is on strategies that have been shown to have positive effects on the classroom environment: effective instruction and effective classroom-wide and individual behavior management strategies.

Effective Instruction as a Management Tool

The least intrusive and most natural behavior management strategies are, of course, good teaching practices. The literature on effective teaching indicates that such strategies as using brisk instructional pacing, reviewing students' work frequently, giving systematic and constructive corrective feedback, minimizing pupil errors, providing guided practice, modeling new behaviors, providing transitions between lessons or concepts, and monitoring student performance are strongly related to pupil achievement and attitudes toward learning (Bickel & Bickel, 1986; Brophy & Good, 1986; Kameenui & Darch, 1995; Rosenshine & Stevens, 1986). Detailed descriptions of these instructional behaviors are beyond the scope of this text. However, the purpose behind the use of such effective instructional strategies is to increase the likelihood of student success. The focus of the following discussion is on the important issue of facilitating success in students who have, or are at risk of developing, repetitive academic and social failure in the school. For those interested in more information and monitoring of these instructional behaviors, Sugai and Tindal (1993) have developed an "effective teaching profile" of these skills, which provides a succinct summary of the outcomes of research on instruction as well as a self-assessment checklist (see Figure 5–4).

One view of management is that it involves controlling student behavior. However, if we view management from an instructional perspective, the issue is predictability. That is, you want to be confident that students will behave in specific ways under specific conditions. For example, when you give the prompt, "What is 2 + 2?", you

want to know that the student will respond predictably with the answer "4." Similarly, when presented with an assignment, a request to pay attention, or a frustrating situation, you want to be confident that the student will respond appropriately. Therefore, control is simply the ability to predict that a student will respond appropriately to a given environmental condition or demand. The way to achieve this predictability is through effective instruction.

Effective instruction demonstrates for the student that a particular response will result in success—the most important reinforcer available to you and your students. When success is predictable, students are more likely to repeat the behaviors that lead to successful outcomes in the future. As a teacher, you must demonstrate the

---

Effective Teaching Profile

Place an X on the scale to indicate the extent to which the teacher displayed the best teaching practices. Connect each X to display a teaching profile.

Yes_____ No   1. Brisk pacing
Yes_____ No   2. Specific explanations and instructions for new concepts
Yes_____ No   3. Allocated time for guided practice
Yes_____ No   4. Cumulative review of skills being taught
Yes_____ No   5. Regularly varied assessments of learning of new concepts
Yes_____ No   6. Regular and active interactions with individual students
Yes_____ No   7. Frequent and detailed feedback
Yes_____ No   8. Varied forms of positive reinforcement
Yes_____ No   9. Positive, predictable, and orderly learning environment
Yes_____ No   10. Maintenance of student attention within and across instructional activities and materials
Yes_____ No   11. Reinforcement for task completion
Yes_____ No   12. Appropriate selection of examples and nonexamples
Yes_____ No   13. Consistent application of contingencies for rules and expectations
Yes_____ No   14. Appropriate use of model/demonstrations
Yes_____ No   15. Appropriate use of behavior rehearsal (role-plays)
Yes_____ No   16. Smooth transition within and between lessons
Yes_____ No   17. High rates of correct student responding

FIGURE 5–4   Teaching behaviors of effective teachers.

Source: *Sugai, G. M., & Tindal, G. A. (1993). Effective school consultation: An interactive approach. Pacific Grove, CA: Brooks/Cole. Used with permission.*

specific conditions under which specific behaviors are appropriate (i.e., will result in success). Thus, you teach students that "4" is the correct response to a specific class of math problems (e.g., 1 + 3, 2 × 2, etc.) but not correct in response to a much larger class of problems (i.e., all other math problems). When students respond predictably in the presence of the relevant discriminative stimuli but not in the presence of all other stimuli, the discriminative stimulus is controlling (i.e., predicting) behavior. The concept of stimulus control is the very heart of instruction. You must teach students how to behave (academically and socially) in a variety of relevant circumstances. When stimulus control has not been established, you cannot predict a student's response and the chances for failure are high.[1]

As mentioned, the goals of classroom behavior management are to develop stimulus control over pupil behavior and to prevent problem situations from occurring. These must be accomplished in group settings where you are responsible for delivering instruction. Consequently, appropriate classroom management interventions are those that are less intrusive and restrictive; they may be implemented without significant interruption of ongoing activities and without removing students or instructional staff from the teaching setting. Remember the main premise of this chapter: *prevention is the most effective early intervention strategy.* Thus, your task is to use the instructional techniques required to facilitate regular predictable student success.

PRE-CORRECTION The least intrusive prevention strategy is to teach students the rules and routines that will facilitate their success. Pre-correction originated as a strategy for making adjustments in academic instruction before a student had an opportunity to make errors (Colvin, Sugai, & Patching, 1993; Kameenui & Simmons,

1990). Academic pre-correction focuses on instructional areas in which the teacher anticipates the student will make errors. Using pre-correction involves thinking ahead to the problems, conditions, or contexts in which stimulus control is not yet firmly established. Applying this strategy to prevent student failure in social behavioral areas is a matter of teaching rules and routines for students to follow, usually during times or routines that typically are less highly structured than academic lessons, such as transitions between lessons or classes. One pre-correction strategy is to simply provide a verbal reminder of the stimulus-response relationship (e.g., "Remember that when the bell rings we need to put our work away before we can be dismissed" or "If someone calls you a name during this activity what would be a good thing to do?"). Walker et al. (1995) describe the application of pre-correction to social behavior in seven steps:

1. Identify the context and the likely problem behavior.
2. Specify the expected behaviors.
3. Systematically modify the context.
4. Conduct behavioral rehearsals.
5. Provide strong reinforcement for expected behaviors.
6. Prompt expected behaviors.
7. Monitor the plan (Walker et al., pp. 176, 178).

Figure 5–5 presents a pre-correction checklist and plan for a student who has experienced difficulty entering the classroom following recess.

PROMPTS AND CUES Pre-correction involves using a verbal prompt that is delivered prior to behavior. But prompts and cues can be verbal, tangible, and even sensory and may be used prior to behavior, along with the behavior, or as part of a corrective sequence after a behavior. The rule of thumb for prompts and cues is to use the least amount or least intrusive prompt necessary to facilitate a successful response. Because prompts are typically not naturally occurring, be careful not to allow them to become the only stimulus that sets the occasion for appropriate behavior.

---

[1]To learn about effective teaching strategies for addressing students with specific learning difficulties, consult Mercer and Mercer (2001).

Pre-Correction Checklist and Plan	Teacher _____ Sarah Enlow _____
	Student _____ Dominic Smith _____
	Date ____ 11 ____ / ____ 15 ____ / ____ 01 ____

☐ 1. Content	Students entering classroom immediately after recess.
Predictable behavior	Enter shouting, laughing, and pushing before complying with teacher direction.
☐ 2. Expected behavior	Enter the room quietly, go to desks, begin task, keep hands to self.
☐ 3. Context modification	Teacher meets students at door, has them wait and then go to desk to begin entry tasks.
☐ 4. Behavior rehearsal	Teacher reminds students just before recess of expected behaviors. Asks Dominic to tell what are expected behaviors.
☐ 5. Strong reinforcement	Students are told that if they cooperate with teacher requests, they will have additional breaks and 5 extra minutes for recess.
☐ 6. Prompts	Teacher gives signals at the door to be quiet and points to activity on chalkboard. Teacher says "hush" to noisy students and praises students who are beginning work.
☐ 7. Monitoring plan	Teacher uses a watch to measure how long it takes for all students to get on task and counts how many students begin their tasks immediately (within 10 seconds).

FIGURE 5–5   Example of a completed pre-correction checklist and plan for Dominic.

Source: *Colvin, G., Sugai, G., & Patching, B. (1993). Precorrection: An instructional approach for managing predictable problem behaviors. Intervention in School and Clinic, 28(3), 143–150.* Copyright PRO-ED. Used with permission.

Prompts should be used only to draw a student's attention to the natural discriminative stimuli that should control behavior and then be systematically faded so that the desired behavior occurs reliably in the presence of the naturally occurring discriminative stimulus. For example, the dismissal bell, rather than the teacher's verbal reminder, should be the discriminative stimulus for students to put away materials, straighten their desks, and leave the classroom in an orderly manner.

Prompts and cues may take the form of gestures, sounds, signals, notes, signs, modeling, or any other physical display that will increase the probability of success. Prompts and cues can be used in the same circumstances as pre-correction, namely, to remind students to use appropriate behaviors prior to the occurrence of a condition that predicts high failure rates. Once students begin the behavior or routine, you can provide hints, suggestions, reminders, and questions designed to facilitate success (e.g., "Remember to wait for the student who is at my desk to return to his seat before coming up"). Finally, if a student has failed to demonstrate the appropriate behavior, prompts and cues can be used to help lead him back through the situation and see the stimuli that should have signaled the appropriate behavior (e.g., "When you approached me, Johnny was at my desk so I didn't have time to help you—when I'm working with someone else when you need me what should you do?"). Even when applying a negative consequence for misbehavior under these conditions, it is advisable to use corrective prompts and cues to decrease the likelihood of repeated failure in the future. When misbehaviors are regarded as errors rather than intentions to be "bad," it is more logical to apply a correction procedure than punishment.

USING ATTENTION AND PRAISE EFFECTIVELY

The research on pupil-teacher interactions summarized in Chapter 4 suggests that the typical behavior management practices of teachers who work with students exhibiting problematic behaviors are not conducive to pupil achievement or desired social behavior. In fact, many teachers have received no formal training in effective behavior management practices. Shores (1993) interviewed 20 teachers regarding their use of behavior management strategies with students with EBD. Practically all of the teachers he interviewed reported that they learned about the classroom management strategies they were using from other teachers or from their own experience; only one teacher reported learning about the system she used from a teacher preparation program. The following paragraphs describe strategies that have been proven effective when teachers are taught to use them competently.

Chapter 4 also indicated that teacher-administered social reinforcement includes three kinds of teacher behavior: feedback, attention, and approval. Feedback typically occurs as a consequence of particular behaviors (finishing a task, breaking a rule). However, by itself, the effects of feedback are weak (Madsen, Becker, & Thomas, 1968; O'Leary, Becker, Evans, & Sudargas, 1969). On the other hand, contingent teacher attention has been shown to strongly influence behavior. Attention differs from approval in two ways: it need not involve any verbal behavior and it is not necessarily positive.

Using teacher attention involves applying differential reinforcement. When appropriate behavior occurs, provide natural reinforcement such as attending, standing near, touching, looking at, or interacting with the student. Inappropriate behavior is placed on extinction, or ignored, by looking away, moving to another part of the room, or calling attention to another child. Early applied behavior analysis researchers demonstrated that simply providing such differential attention is a powerful strategy: it has been used to eliminate regressive crawling (Harris, Johnston, Kelly, & Wolf, 1964), reduce aggression (Brown & Elliot, 1965), increase following instructions (Schutte & Hopkins, 1970), and accelerate correct academic performance (Zimmerman & Zimmerman, 1962).

As you know, attention is a potent natural reinforcer for most students. However, in cases where it is not, teacher attention must be established as a **conditioned reinforcer** (a consequence that has acquired reinforcing properties through association with previously established reinforcers). If your attention does not appear to function as a reinforcer, you should repeatedly pair it with the presentation of a consequence that already has been demonstrated to be reinforcing, such as points or tangibles.[2] Gradually and systematically fade the artificial reinforcer until attention alone produces the desired effect. This process may take time for many pupils with severe problem behaviors. Other students may reveal an extensive repertoire of inappropriate attention-getting behaviors (e.g., raising a hand and saying, "Hey teacher!," getting up to ask a question). Clearly stated rules governing how teacher attention may be solicited are helpful, but they serve little purpose if you even occasionally respond to the inappropriate activity. Using your attention as a behavior management tool requires a high degree of self-monitoring and self-control.

[2]However, before concluding that your attention is not a reinforcer, think about how the student in question responds when your attention is available versus when it is not. For example, if you observe that the student's behavior is appropriate when you are working with him individually but episodes of undesired behavior commonly occur when your attention is directed elsewhere, your attention is, in fact, a reinforcer.

Teacher approval or praise involves the same contingencies as attention and may be verbal or nonverbal. However, in using approval the teacher usually specifies the desired behavior verbally, such as "I like the way you are working" or "You really did a good job on your algebra assignment." Nonverbal approval (smiles, pats on the back) also may be effective (Kazdin & Klock, 1973). The contingent use of approval is more critical than the amount of approval, per se (Becker, Thomas, & Carnine, 1971; Kazdin & Klock, 1973), but use contingent praise four times as often as verbal aversives (Alberto & Troutman, 1999).

Used systematically and consistently, these "good teacher skills" will strengthen the behaviors that most teachers desire in their pupils: compliance with teacher requests and instructions, on-task behaviors, cooperative interactions with others, and low rates of noise and disruption. Most teachers prefer to use the least intrusive management strategies that produce these results. As stated, the most appropriate group behavior management procedures are those that are more natural and easier to implement. For example, praise and attention are more natural and easier to administer than tokens, and tokens are easier to deliver than edible reinforcers. Similarly, extinction and response cost are less intrusive behavior reduction procedures than timeout or overcorrection. Each teacher must decide what range of interventions is best for his or her classroom. In practice, the procedures that you choose will be based on your own experience and feelings of competence with them. Effective classroom teachers use a range of enhancement and reductive interventions to influence student behavior, and they develop the ability to "read" situations and behaviors on the spot and apply interventions appropriately and in a timely fashion. You should strive to develop proficiency with a range of interventions so that you can use each of them effectively.

BEHAVIORAL MOMENTUM This is based on the observation that the performance of a behavior may act as a discriminative stimulus for the continuation of that behavior (Carr, Newsome, & Binkoff, 1976). Behavioral momentum actually is a proactive, nonaversive strategy for developing behavioral compliance. The teacher issues a set of simple requests that are discriminative stimuli for compliance responses (i.e., high-probability requests) immediately prior to giving a request identified as the discriminative stimulus for problem behavior (i.e., low-probability request). The "momentum" developed by responding appropriately to high-probability requests increases the probability of compliance with the low-probability request. For example, the teacher may deliver several requests that have been discriminative of compliance ("Show me your finger," "Point to your nose," "Tell me your name") and intersperse in the chain a low-probability request ("Point to the blue triangle"). For behavioral momentum to be effective, the student must have a history of responding appropriately to other examples of compliance requests in the same response class (Davis & Brady, 1993). Successful compliance should always be followed with reinforcement. This strategy has been effective with developmentally young children.

The strategy of permitting students to make choices among tasks and curricula has shown promise with students exhibiting behavior problems. Although an extensive body of research literature is developing on allowing students with cognitive disabilities to make choices, this research is only beginning to be applied to students with behavioral problems. However, it has been demonstrated that allowing students with EBD to choose tasks and instructional materials resulted in increased academic engagement and reduced disruptive behavior (Dunlap et al., 1994; Jolivette, Wehby, Canale, & Massey, 2001).

Group Management Systems in the Classroom

Among the behavior enhancement strategies described in Chapter 4, modeling and teacher reinforcement are more or less informal and naturalistic management techniques. On the other hand, token systems and group contingencies (described in Chapter 6) are universal interventions that require proportionately more strategic planning and effort during implementation. The preferred approach is to use effective instruction, contingent praise and attention, and the reinforcement that comes from student success to facilitate appropriate student classroom behavior. However, in both general and special education classrooms, a number of pupils may be found who require some type of behavior management, which suggests that a group behavior management plan may be needed. Behavior analysis techniques could be applied to individuals but this tactic would present several problems. First, it would be necessary to identify and deliver individual consequences to each pupil. Although tokens, for example, can be delivered easily to many students, and later exchanged for individual back-up reinforcers, delivering different consequences immediately contingent upon the behavior of individual pupils can be complicated and exhausting. (One reason the number of pupils in classes for students with EBD is restricted by state laws is because so much individual programming is required.)

Delivering reinforcers immediately is virtually impossible unless you can establish a conditioned reinforcer for all students. As you have seen, praise can become a conditioned reinforcer by pairing its delivery with an existing reinforcer. Both points and praise statements may be used as conditioned reinforcers. Points offer the advantage of being concrete and additive; once a student reaches a specified total, he may exchange points for back-up reinforcers.

Group management systems are also flexible: They may be applied to an entire group of students, to individuals within the group, or to any combination. Thus, two pupils may receive the same number of tokens for performing different tasks or for reaching different criterion levels. Within such a system, individualization is accomplished by adjusting reinforcement contingencies.

The same conditioned reinforcer is given to all pupils, but for different behaviors or on different reinforcement schedules.

Specific classroom behavior management systems are described in detail in Chapter 6. The following discussion addresses behavior management considerations and strategies in special classroom settings. These self-contained classrooms, or even segregated special schools, may be the least restrictive environment for students identified as EBD. Their need for individualized behavior support, including direct instruction in academic and social skills provided by educators who are well trained in these strategies in addition to behavior management procedures, is not easily met in general education classrooms (Kauffman & Hallahan, 1995; Kauffman, Lloyd, Astuto, & Hallahan, 1995).

BEHAVIOR MANAGEMENT IN SPECIAL CLASSROOM SETTINGS Day-to-day classroom behavior management can be one of the most complex and demanding tasks faced by educators who work with groups of students who exhibit serious problem behavior. Pupils who are chronically disruptive, defiant, withdrawn, or aggressive, or who engage in nonfunctional stereotypic behaviors and who possess minimal social or functional communication skills often are difficult to manage even in one-to-one situations. Fortunately, like other students, these pupils respond to proactive and preventative behavior management strategies. Systematically teaching and rewarding desired academic and social behaviors are fundamental to effective behavior management in alternative education programs, as well as in self-contained or resource classrooms. With universal classroom management strategies in place, individual student problem behaviors will be minimized. However, *they will not be eliminated.* Therefore, it is important to have a repertoire of effective techniques for managing individual student behavior.

When you encounter students who, in spite of your best efforts at prevention, continue to exhibit challenging behavior, it may be tempting to blame their behavior problems on the underlying "pathology" supposedly inherent in students who have been certified as "behaviorally disordered" or "emotionally disturbed." As pointed out earlier, this attitude is inappropriate, and although not all classroom misbehavior is attributable to inappropriate behavior management, whether at home or in school, pupils with histories of reinforcement of their tantrums, defiance of authority, aggressive acts against others, or noncompliance will exhibit such behavior in situations when others will not. The key to effective management of these behaviors lies in the teacher's ability to analyze and adjust variables in the immediate environment; specifically, the antecedents and consequences that predict both maladaptive and desired behavior.

As the previous discussion has suggested, the behavior management procedures used by teachers may, in fact, predict problem situations. This observation has been documented in a number of studies. For example, White (1975) and Thomas, Presland, Grant, and Glynn (1978) studied rates of teacher approval and disapproval and found that most teachers gave disapprovals at higher rates than they gave approvals. Both sets of investigators suggested that teachers experience greater reinforcement for using disapprovals (i.e., the use of disapprovals is strengthened through negative reinforcement, in that disapprovals quickly, though temporarily, terminate undesired child behavior). Thomas et al. (1978) also conjectured that teachers feel appropriate behavior deserves little recognition. As noted in Chapter 4, more recent research has reported similar findings (e.g., Shores, Gunter, & Jack, 1993).

Johns and Carr (1995) have identified additional negative behavior management techniques that effective teachers seldom exhibit:

- Forcing a student to do something she doesn't want to do
- Forcing students to admit to lies
- Demanding confession from students

- Using confrontational techniques
- Asking students why they act out
- Punishing students
- Making disapproving comments
- Comparing a student's behavior with other students' behavior
- Yelling at students
- Engaging in verbal battles
- Making unrealistic threats
- Ridiculing students

Engaging in these practices greatly increases the chances that students with established patterns of challenging behavior, as well as those on the "margins" with respect to classroom behavior, will act out. They provide fertile soil for the cultivation of crisis situations. To the extent that you can avoid these practices and instead use the effective teaching skills listed in Figure 5–4, you and your students will experience a much more productive classroom climate.

USING ANTECEDENTS AND CONSEQUENCES SYSTEMATICALLY In addition to the *types* of antecedents and consequences you can use, it also is important to attend to *how* you use them. Here are some variables to consider: the specific antecedents you will use as discriminative stimuli for student behavior; the contingencies of reinforcement or punishment you will establish; how you will arrange the delivery of reinforcement or punishment; and who will administer positive and negative consequences. You should consider each of these factors in developing or altering a classroom behavior management system. For example, what rules and instructions will you provide students? How will you relate specified desired and undesired behaviors to planned consequences? Can you deliver these consequences immediately following behavior so as to maximize their effectiveness? If not, what alternatives can you use? Which schedule of reinforcement[3] is best under various circumstances? Do

---

[3]Schedules of reinforcement are described in Chapter 11.

you control the consequences of pupil behavior? If not, who does, and how can you enlist the aid of these agents to help you establish desired behavior patterns?

Thinking about how you will answer these questions before entering the classroom can help you avoid serious problems later. However, do not expect to prevent all problems at this stage, and do not walk into the classroom with a fully developed management system. Each system must be individually tailored and should be developed in cooperation with students, not imposed upon them.

As indicated earlier, antecedent stimuli include a range of setting events that may influence student behavior, some of which are beyond your control (e.g., students' sleep schedules, nutrition, events occurring at home). However, if you can identify patterns in your students' behavior that apparently are not related to school or classroom factors, you may be able to establish links with parents or other professionals who can give you information to functionally assess the relationship of these setting events to student behaviors. Perhaps you can then have input on collaborative interventions to alter their influence on behavior. Within the classroom, such setting events as the physical arrangement, schedule of events, instructional materials, and teacher proximity have been shown to affect student behavior. These variables can be managed through **structuring.**

As defined by Haring and Phillips (1962), structuring refers to clarifying the relationship between behavior and its consequences. For many children and youth who exhibit challenging behaviors, this relationship has been anything but clear, either because of an absence of rules, inconsistent application of consequences for behavior, or ability to outmanipulate the adults who control these consequences. Such pupils enter education programs with the expectation that their wishes will prevail or that the social world is a chaotic place where nothing can be predicted. Haring and Phillips designed the structured approach to make these youngsters' environment more predictable as well as to provide a basis for behavior change.

As used here, the term *structuring* differs somewhat from that described by Haring and Phillips. For the purpose of this discussion, structuring refers to a range of antecedent variables that the teacher may use to influence pupil behavior: the planning of physical space, daily schedule, rules, teacher movement patterns, and stimulus change. These strategies are analogous to school-wide behavior management systems. They are explained in detail in Chapter 6.

A **levels system** is a comprehensive behavior management strategy that establishes a hierarchy of increasing expectations for behavioral improvement with increasing student reinforcement and decreasing behavioral structure. Levels systems are used to help students progress from the academic and social skills they exhibit upon entry into the system to levels at which they may be expected to make successful transitions to less restrictive settings. Typically, students advance through a sequence of four or five levels, each associated with higher expectations for academic performance and social behavior, as well as with greater student autonomy and access to more naturalistic reinforcers. For example, at the first level, a student may be expected to follow basic classroom rules, attempt all academic assignments, and work in a 1:1 relationship with the classroom teacher or paraprofessional. At more advanced levels, expectations may include fulfilling the terms of individual contingency contracts, completing assignments with a high degree of accuracy, and working independently in group settings, which may include participation in mainstream classes. Advancement through the levels is based upon periodic assessments of student progress against specific criteria for academic and social behaviors. Considerations in the development of a levels system include the following (Reisberg, Brodigan, & Williams, 1991):

1. Clearly define the levels or steps in the system.
2. Clearly define the desired behaviors students must exhibit to progress through the system.

3. Clearly define inappropriate behaviors (and their consequences) that prohibit student advancement or will cause students to regress at each level.
4. Clearly define the reinforcers students may earn at each level.
5. Clearly define the criteria for placement and movement within the system.
6. Develop procedures for continuous evaluation and measurement of student performance.
7. Develop procedures to facilitate frequent communication between all parties.

For a complete description of levels systems as a strategy for helping students transition to less restrictive settings, see Chapter 11.

Although levels systems enjoy widespread popularity in more restrictive educational programs for students with behavioral problems, their efficacy in promoting successful transitions to less restrictive environments has not been demonstrated (Smith & Farrell, 1993; Scheuermann, Webber, Partin, & Knies, 1994). Scheuermann et al. (1994) suggested that levels systems may, in fact, violate some legal requirements associated with the due process and the least restrictive environment regulations of IDEA. Specifically, the right to an education in the least restrictive environment may be abridged, in that access to general education classrooms is treated as a privilege and is not based on whether the student can benefit from such participation. In addition, to the extent that criteria for placement in a given level and movement among levels are the same for all students, levels systems are not consistent with the individualized program requirement of the law. Even the placement of students in mainstream school settings based on their status in the levels system (e.g., lunch in the cafeteria) violates their right to have decisions regarding their participation in such settings made by their IEP teams. Scheuermann et al. (1994) proposed a model for designing individualized levels systems based on the curriculum for a given student.

SUMMARY

Planning and operating positive and productive school and classroom environments are important elements of success in teaching any group of students at any level. Without effective behavior management, teachers and pupils both are likely to be dissatisfied with the time they spend in school. This chapter has provided information about assessing environments and developing strategies to prevent student failures across the school and in the classroom. These strategies involve the use of effective instruction to develop stimulus control over student social behaviors in group settings. When the norm for the group is appropriate and desirable behavior, individual behavior problems are less likely to occur, and if they do, you can manage them without having to simultaneously worry that other students are going to be out of control. The following points summarize the procedures that are critical to success in managing classroom social behavior.

1. Prevention is the most effective form of behavior management. Think ahead to the times, places, and conditions under which failures are most likely to occur and develop consistent strategies involving rules, routines, and physical arrangements to prevent those problems.

2. Collect data on target behaviors at the school, classroom, and individual student levels. This is a critical feature of effective management, but it is also the one most often left out. Without objective, reliable measures of the behaviors targeted for change and the conditions that predict those problems, you will have no basis on which to judge the effectiveness of your management program or for making decisions regarding program adjustments. Data collection should occur on a daily basis, and if you relate it to the academic program (such as when the system is based on academic performance rates or accuracy), this process need not be a significant additional burden. Remember too that students can be taught to monitor and record their own academic and social behavior.

3. Set expectations that are specific, clear, and fair. The most effective expectations for behavior are stated behaviorally and include clear criterion statements. This enables both staff and students to clearly evaluate progress. In your own classroom, base your expectations on those for the entire school and have your students participate in translating these into specific classroom rules.

4. Set contingencies that are clear and fair. Contingencies are the "rules" of the system; they specify which consequences will follow which behaviors. The best contingencies are few in number, are positively stated, and are easily understood. The ideal contingency is one in which the response automatically produces the consequence, but in education, the natural consequences of behavior are often long term and tend to be ineffective in the short run (e.g., failure to turn in assignments results in a failing semester grade). Therefore, devise contingencies that relate behavior to immediate consequences, even if these contingencies must be arbitrary and artificial.

5. Negotiate the system with pupils. If you open yourself to pupil input, you will likely find that your students also are distressed by a chaotic and confusing environment or by being unable to meet teacher or parental expectations for academic performance. Students can participate in identifying target behaviors and setting goals for school-wide and classroom management. In addition, they can help you operate the program: monitoring behavior, giving tokens, tutoring classmates, keeping records of points saved and spent, or operating a token store. If you develop a management system with students, it will be more to their liking than if you impose it on them.

6. Base the selection and application of any school-wide or classroom behavior management system on a careful study of each individual situation. Management programs are not fixed entities applied to all groups of children. Rather, they are infinitely flexible and varied and may be designed to suit any set of circumstances. In the classroom, the variables you should take into account in setting up a program include the developmental maturity, number, and other characteristics of your group; the enthusiasm and effort you are willing to put into the program; your ability and willingness to adjust the program; and the long-range effects of the system on students and on you. This may seem like an overwhelming array of variables, but it is actually no more than you should consider when implementing any intervention, whether it be a new reading curriculum or a recess period.

CHAPTER 5 CASE STUDY

Problems at Happy Elementary School

Happy Elementary is an inner-city school of approximately 450 students, 92% of whom qualify for free or reduced lunch. With a 10-year pattern of decreasing statewide achievement scores, the district's highest rate of suspension, and an escalating number of ODRs, Happy Elementary is identified by the state as a school in crisis. Principal Ruth Jones is determined to make a difference. She brings the faculty and staff together and asks for their input and ideas regarding possible solutions. There is general agreement among all that something needs to be done—but suggestions for change are varied, fragmented among cliques, and often contradictory. Principal Jones is aware that any change efforts that are not agreed upon and adopted by the entire school are unlikely to be implemented widely or consistently enough to have an effect on the school as a whole. She determines that the school must come together and generate a school-wide plan that is acceptable to all and calculated to prevent their predictable problems.

Principal Jones again calls all faculty and staff together and proposes a school-wide solution. As a group they identify the conditions in the school that best predict problem behaviors and then brainstorm simple preventative solutions to those problems. Next, the group votes to determine consensus as to which of the strategies will be adopted on a school-wide basis. Principal Jones assures all that decisions are to be made by the group, with no one individual having any more say than any other. She then reminds all that, once they have come to consensus and agreed upon an expectation or strategy, that expectation or strategy becomes the school policy upon which all faculty and staff will be expected to abide. She makes clear, "Once you agree upon a solution, I'm going to make sure you follow through." The staff agree that decisions need to be made on a school-wide basis and determine that 80% staff approval will be the criterion for consensus regarding school-wide decisions. Further, all agree that, regardless of their individual feelings about any particular expectation or strategy, once consensus is reached, all will abide by that decision and will both teach the expectations to the students, consistently enforce the rules, and follow through with strategies for responding to student behavior.

Determining School-Wide Rules and Strategies

The first task in determining school-wide rules and strategies is to identify the areas, times, and conditions in which problem behaviors are most likely to occur. Ideally, the staff at Happy Elementary would go to their school-wide data to make these determinations. However, although ODR and suspension data exist, those data identify only the student and the behavior. Identifying predictable locations and times across the school would require a search of every student file in an attempt to recall each incident and the conditions surrounding it. Obviously, this is too large a chore to be realistic for Happy Elementary. In the absence of hard data, at a school-wide meeting, the staff identify the areas and times that they see as most predictive of problems across the school based on their experiences in the school over the past year. Principal Jones divides the entire faculty and staff into several small groups by common role in the school. For example, she asks that the instructional assistants, primary grade teachers, intermediate grade teachers, specialists, secretaries, custodians, and additional adults (including involved parents) form small groups. Each of these groups is then asked to form a list of predictable problems, times, and locations across the school. After a 20-min period, Ms. Jones calls the entire group back together to list the identified problems by area. As each area of the school is listed, small group spokespersons relate the problems and times they see. When each physical area of the school has been covered and all staff have had an opportunity to give their impressions, a comprehensive list of the schools predictable problems has been created.

Principal Jones then asks each small group to reconvene to brainstorm the strategies and rules that might be developed as a method of preventing the identified problems. This time, she asks each group to spend 10 min focusing on each specific area of the school. She reminds them to spend their time concentrating on prevention, sets the timer, and asks the groups to begin with a specific setting. When the timer goes off at the end of 10 min, Principal Jones prompts the groups to move to the next setting and continue. Once all of the settings have been covered, Principal Jones reconvenes the large group and again records the responses of the smaller groups. She reminds the large group that these responses represent only brainstorming and that there should be no critique of the proposed strategies until they are all recorded. Then, for each area of the school, Principal Jones goes through the list of possible solutions and asks the group as a whole to determine (1) whether each solution would solve the problem if it were consistently put into effect and (2) whether those that would be effective could realistically be adopted and implemented by all as part of a daily school-wide procedure. Only those solutions that are deemed to be *both* effective and realistic by at least 50% of the group move forward for a vote.

One last time, Principal Jones goes back through the locations of the school, this time asking for the group as a whole to vote on each. She reminds them that a "yes" vote signifies a willingness to adopt the rule or strategy across every staff member and all times. The criteria set for accepting a rule or strategy on a school-wide basis is 80% consensus by the staff. When 80% consensus is not achieved, additional solutions are generated or some compromise is reached through group discussion. For example, when student pushing and shoving in the stairway before school was identified as a problem, several solutions were suggested, including releasing the students individually, 10 sec apart. Although all agreed that sending the students individually would likely be effective, less than 50% agreed that this was a realistic solution because of the time required to implement and monitor it. Therefore, this strategy was removed from consideration. However, another potential solution was to teach the students to go to the right side of the stairs and always hold the railing with their right hand. This rule would encourage the students to maintain some distance from one another as they ascended and descended the stairs. In addition, by keeping their right hands on the rail, the students would have to move in single file. The majority agreed that this was both logical and reasonable. A vote was taken

and 85% of the group reached consensus that this should be a rule that is taught to the students and consistently modeled and enforced by all staff. This same process was repeated for each identified problem and area.

Developing School-Wide Data Collection Systems

The staff of Happy Elementary now has decided what steps they will take to decrease predictable problem behaviors across the school. The next step is to determine what outcomes they wish to measure and the simplest way to measure them. Because the school is considered to be in crisis in several areas, several potential goals could be adopted by the group. However, Principal Jones has persuaded the group to focus on larger outcomes for measurement, rather than developing a longer set of more specific goals. That is, the rule about keeping to the right on stairways may decrease problems here, but what effect will this have on suspensions or office referrals? Still, there must be some way of measuring whether stairway problems are decreasing so that the staff will know if their strategy is effective. The staff agree that their major goals will be to decrease student suspensions/expulsions and to decrease ODRs. They will do this not by changing the way they use those disciplinary procedures, but by preventing the problem behaviors that lead to them. Next, the staff rewrite their ODR form to include more information, including the time, location, and outcome of problem behaviors. This information is then summarized weekly in a spreadsheet, allowing the staff to monitor the effectiveness of the strategies they implemented as a school.

Monitoring and Evaluation

Each month, the staff look at the data reported from the ODR forms. Because the forms include outcomes as a category, suspensions/expulsions can be monitored using the ODR generated database. The school can assess the agreed-upon strategies across each identified time and location. This information is used to evaluate the effectiveness of rules and strategies and to determine new times and locations that may be becoming predictors of problems. In this way, the school stays on top of problems, providing new solutions for problem situations before those problems bring themselves to staff attention in a more painful manner. Principal Jones shares the data with staff monthly and the staff make new decisions depending on what the data show.

Sustaining Programs

As time goes by, staff and student changeover, new problems, and changing cultures or conditions will likely affect every school. Although it is not necessary to repeat this process every year, Principal Jones realizes the importance of formative evaluation of the school-wide agreements. In addition to the monthly data meetings, the staff meets at the beginning of each year to revisit their plans, making certain that all new staff are aware of the school-wide agreements and prompting a new round of teaching for the new students.

Principal Jones knows that the system her school has created will not prevent all problem behaviors. The behavior of some students will require much more intensive and individualized intervention. However, her staff understands that when they design the school to prevent problems across all students, the number of students who present ongoing problems will decrease, which will free up the time and resources needed to design and implement the specific interventions necessary to facilitate the success of these more challenging students.

DISCUSSION QUESTIONS

1. Finster Elementary has determined that several students are wandering to the far end of the field during recess and are playing behind a group of trees. This is a very popular location because there is a play structure in that location, but it is far from the playground where the vast majority of students play. Many problem behavior referrals seem to have emanated from this location. Because of a staff shortage and scheduling difficulties, only one teacher supervises the playground during recess. Think of some simple rules, routines, and physical arrangements. What could Finster Elementary do to prevent these predictable problems?

2. When Ms. Peters says to her students, "Please line up quietly to go to the lunch room," her first-grade pupils immediately line up in single file with no disruptive behavior. When Ms. Thomas issues the same request to her class, there is a great deal of running, shouting, and fighting among her first-grade students to be first in line. Explain the difference between the behavior of these two groups in terms of stimulus control and suggest how Ms. Peters may have established stimulus control over the behavior of lining up.

3. Ms. Thomas often uses a loud voice, threats, and spankings to attempt to control her class, but her pupils are among the most unruly in the building. Why has this happened?

4. What strategies would you recommend that Ms. Thomas use to improve her stimulus control over student behavior during these transition times?

5. If you were to set up a resource room for elementary-age pupils with EBD, how would you structure it? How would you structure a resource room differently for junior high school students?

REFERENCES

Alberto, P. A., & Troutman, A. C. (1999). *Applied behavior analysis for teachers* (5th ed.). Upper Saddle River, NJ: Merrill/Prentice Hall.

Becker, W. C., Thomas, D. R., & Carnine, D. (1971). Reducing behavior problems: An operant conditioning guide for teachers. In W. C. Becker (Ed.), *An empirical basis for change in education* (pp. 129–165). Chicago: Science Research Associates.

Bickel, W. E., & Bickel, D. D. (1986). Effective schools, classrooms, and instruction: Implications for special education. *Exceptional Children*, 52, 489–500.

Brooks, K., Schiraldi, V., & Ziedenberg, J. (2000). *Schoolhouse hype: Two years later*. Washington, DC: Justice Policy Institute.

Brophy, J., & Good, T. L. (1986). Teacher behavior and student achievement. In M. C. Wittrock (Ed.), *Handbook of research on teaching* (3rd ed.) (pp. 328–375). New York: Macmillan.

Brown, P., & Elliott, R. (1965). Control of aggression in a nursery school class. *Journal of Experimental Child Psychology*, 2, 103–107.

Carr, E. G., Newsome, C. D., & Binkoff, J. A. (1976). Stimulus control of self-destructive behavior in a psychotic child. *Journal of Abnormal Child Psychology*, 4, 139–153.

Centers for Disease Control and Prevention. (1995). Youth risk behavior surveillance—United States, 1993. *Morbidity and Mortality Weekly Report*, 44, 6–7.

Chapman, D., & Hofweber, C. (2000). Effective behavior support in British Columbia. *Journal of Positive Behavior Interventions*, 2, 235–237.

Colvin, G., Kameenui, R. J., & Sugai, G. (1993). Reconceptualizing behavior management and school-wide discipline in general education. *Education and Treatment of Children*, 16, 361–381.

Colvin, G., Sugai, G., & Kameenui, E. (1994). *Curriculum for establishing a school-wide discipline plan*. Eugene, OR: Project PREPARE, Behavioral Research and Teaching, College of Education, University of Oregon.

Colvin, G., Sugai, G., & Patching, B. (1993). Pre-correction: An instructional approach for managing predictable problem behaviors. *Intervention in School and Clinic*, 28, 143–150.

Davis, C. A., & Brady, M. P. (1993). Expanding the utility of behavioral momentum with young children: Where we've been, where we need to go. *Journal of Early Intervention*, 17, 211–223.

Dunlap, G., dePerczel, M., Clarke, S., Wilson, D., Wright, S., White, R., & Gomez, A. (1994). Choice making to promote adaptive behavior for students with emotional and behavioral challenges. *Journal of Applied Behavior Analysis*, 27, 505–518.

Dwyer, K. P., Osher, D., & Warger, W. (1998). *Early warning, timely response: A guide to safe schools*. Washington, DC: U.S. Department of Education.

Elliott, D., Hamburg, B., & Williams, K. (Eds.). (1998). *Violence in American schools*. New York: Cambridge.

Forness, S. R., Kavale, K. A., Sweeney, D. P., & Crenshaw, T. M. (1999). The future of research and practice in behavioral disorders: Psychopharmacology and its school implications. *Behavioral Disorders*, 24, 305–318.

Gresham, F. M., & Reschly, D. J. (1987). Issues in the conceptualization, classification, and assessment of social skills in the mildly handicapped. In T. R. Kratochwill (Ed.), *Advances in school psychology*. Hillsdale, NJ: Lawrence Erlbaum Associates.

Gunter, P. L., Hummel, J. H., & Venn, M. L. (1998). Are effective academic instructional practices used to teach students with behavior disorders? *Beyond Behavior*, 9, 5–11.

Haring, N. G., & Phillips, E. L. (1962). *Educating emotionally disturbed children*. New York: McGraw-Hill.

Harris, F. R., Johnston, M. K., Kelly, C. S., & Wolf, M. M. (1964). Effects of positive social reinforcement on regressed crawling of a nursery school child. *Journal of Educational Psychology*, 55, 35–41.

Hersh, R. H., & Walker, H. M. (1983). Great expectations: Making schools effective for all students. *Policy Studies Review*, 2, 147–188.

Horner, R. H., & Sugai, G. (2000). School-wide behavior support: An emerging initiative. *Journal of Positive Behavior Interventions*, 2, 231–232.

Johns, B. H., & Carr, V. G. (1995). *Techniques for managing verbally and physically aggressive students*. Denver, CO: Love.

Jolivette, K., Wehby, J. H., Canale, J., & Massey, N. G. (2001). Effects of choice making opportunities on the behavior of students with emotional and behavioral disorders. *Behavioral Disorders*, 26, 131–146.

Kameenui, E. J., & Darch, C. B. (1995). *Instructional classroom management: A proactive approach to behavior management*. Reston, VA: Council for Exceptional Children.

Kameenui, E. J., & Simmons, D. C. (1990). *Designing instructional strategies: The prevention of academic learning problems*. Columbus, OH: Merrill.

Kauffman, J. M. (1994). Taming aggression in the young: A call to action. *Education Week*, 13, 43.

Kauffman, J. M. (2001). *Characteristics of emotional and behavioral disorders of children and youth* (7th ed.). Upper Saddle River, NJ: Merrill/Prentice Hall.

Kauffman, J. M., & Hallahan, D. P. (Eds.). (1995). *The illusion of full inclusion: A comprehensive critique of a current special education bandwagon*. Austin, TX: Pro-Ed.

Kauffman, J. M., Lloyd, J. W., Astuto, T. A., & Hallahan, D. P. (1995). *Issues in the educational placement of students with emotional or behavioral disorders*. Hillsdale, NJ: Lawrence Erlbaum Associates.

Kazdin, A. E., & Klock, J. (1973). The effects of nonverbal teacher approval on student attentive data. *Journal of Applied Behavior Analysis*, 6, 643–654.

Leone, P. E., Mayer, M. J., Malmgren, K., & Meisel, S. M. (2000). School violence and disruption: Rhetoric, reality, and reasonable balance. *Focus on Exceptional Children*, 33(1), 1–20.

Lichter, S. R., Lichter, L. S., & Amundson, D. (1999). *Merchandizing mayhem: Violence in popular culture*. Washington, DC: Center for Media and Public Affairs.

Lohrmann-O'Rourke, S., Knoster, T., Sabatine, K., Smith, D., Harvath, B., & Llewellyn, G. (2000). School-wide application of PBS in the Bangor area school district. *Journal of Positive Behavior Interventions*, 2, 238–240.

Madsen, C. H., Jr., Becker, W. C., & Thomas, D. R. (1968). Rules, praise, and ignoring: Elements of elementary classroom control. *Journal of Applied Behavior Analysis*, 1, 139–150.

Mayer, G. R., Butterworth, T., Nafpaktits, M., & Sulzer-Azaroff, B. (1983). Preventing school vandalism and improving discipline: A three-year study. *Journal of Applied Behavior Analysis*, 16, 355–369.

Mayer, G. R., Butterworth, T. W., & Spaulding, H. L. (1989).*Constructive discipline: Building a climate for learning—A resource manual of programs and strategies*. Los Angeles: Los Angeles County Office of Education.

Mercer, C. D., & Mercer, A. R. (2001). *Teaching students with learning problems* (6th ed.). Upper Saddle River, NJ: Merrill/Prentice Hall.

Nakasato, J. (2000). Data-based decision making in Hawaii's behavior support effort. *Journal of Positive Behavior Interventions*, 2, 247–251.

Nelson, J. R. (1996). Designing schools to meet the needs of students who exhibit disruptive behavior. *Journal of Emotional and Behavioral Disorders*, 4, 147–161.

O'Leary, K. D., Becker, W. C., Evans, M. B., & Sudargas, R. A. (1969). A token reinforcement program in a public school: A replication and systematic analysis. *Journal of Applied Behavior Analysis*, 2, 3–13.

Reisberg, L., Brodigan, D., & Williams, G. (1991). Classroom management: Implementing a system for students with BD. *Intervention in School and Clinic*, 27, 31–38.

Rosenshine, B., & Stevens, R. (1986). Teaching functions. In M. C. Wittrock (Ed.), *Handbook of research on teaching* (3rd ed.) (pp. 376–431). New York: Macmillan.

Scheuermann, B., Webber, J., Partin, M., & Knies, W. C. (1994). Level systems and the law: Are they compatible? *Behavioral Disorders*, 19, 205–220.

Schutte, R. C., & Hopkins, B. L. (1970). The effects of teacher attention on following instructions in a kindergarten class. *Journal of Applied Behavior Analysis*, 3, 117–122.

Scott, T. M. (2001). A school-wide example of positive behavioral support. *Journal of Positive Behavioral Interventions*, 3, 88–94.

Scott, T. M., & Hunter, J. (in press). Initiating School-Wide Support Systems: An administrator's guide to the process. *Beyond Behavior*.

Scott, T. M., & Nelson, C. M. (1999). Universal school discipline strategies: Facilitating learning environments. *Effective School Practices*, 17, 54–64.

Shores, R. E. (1993, April). General classroom management strategies: Are they effective with violent and aggressive students? Paper presented at the Council for Exceptional Children Annual Convention, San Antonio, TX.

Shores, R. E., Gunter, P. L., & Jack, S. L. (1993). Classroom management strategies: Are they setting events for coercion? *Behavioral Disorders*, 18, 92–102.

Smith, S. W., & Farrell, D. T. (1993). Level system use in special education: Classroom intervention with prima facie appeal. *Behavioral Disorders*, 18, 251–264.

Snyder, H. N., & Sickmund, M. (1999). *Juvenile offenders and victims: 1999 national report*. Washington, DC: Office of Juvenile Justice and Delinquency Prevention.

Sprick, R., Sprick, M., & Garrison, M. (1992). *Foundations: Developing positive school-wide discipline policies*. Longmont, CO: Sopris West.

Sugai, G., Horner, R. H., Dunlap, G., Hieneman, Lewis, T. J., Nelson, C. M., Scott, T., Liaupsin, C. J., Sailor, W., Turnbull, A. P., Turnbull, H. R. III, Wickham, D., Ruef, M., & Wilcox, B. (2000). Applying positive behavioral support and functional assessment in schools. *Journal of Positive Behavioral Interventions*, 2, 131–143.

Sugai, G. M., & Tindal, G. A. (1993). *Effective school consultation: An interactive approach*. Pacific Grove, CA: Brooks/Cole.

Sulzer-Azaroff, B., & Mayer, G. R. (1991). *Behavior analysis for lasting change*. Fort Worth: Holt, Rinehart and Winston.

Thomas, J. D., Presland, I. E., Grant, M. D., & Glynn, T. L. (1978). Natural rates of teacher approval and disapproval in grade-7 classrooms. *Journal of Applied Behavior Analysis*, 11, 91–94.

Walker, H. M., Colvin, G., & Ramsey, E. (1995). *Antisocial behavior in school: Strategies and best practices*. Pacific Grove, CA: Brooks/Cole.

Walker, H. M., Severson, H. H., & Feil, E. G. (1994). *The Early Screening Project: A proven child-find process*. Longmont, CO: Sopris West.

White, M. A. (1975). Natural rates of teacher approval and disapproval in the classroom. *Journal of Applied Behavior Analysis*, 8, 367–372.

Zimmerman, E. H., & Zimmerman, J. (1962). The alteration of behavior in a special classroom situation. *Journal of the Experimental Analysis of Behavior*, 5, 59–60.

6 CHAPTER DISRUPTIVE BEHAVIOR

OUTLINE

OBJECTIVES

After completing this chapter, you should be able to

- Explain the four types of behavioral interventions and give examples of each.
- Select the best intervention for a student's disruptive behavior.
- List 10 reinforcers appropriate for an elementary or secondary classroom.
- Design and implement a token economy.
- Design and carry out a group contingency.
- Design and carry out a self-monitoring procedure.

My first year of teaching, I'd come home after school and sit on the couch with beverage in hand, staring blankly at the wall, dreading going back to work the next day. . . . I knew that I could not keep up with the constant struggle for control in my room for the next 25 years. (Ozvold, 1996, p. 159)

Like this teacher, you may worry about behaviors that rob you of precious instructional time and disrupt classroom routines. Your concerns are valid: Disruptiveness often leads to early school withdrawal, grade retention, and conduct problems (Vitaro, Brendgen, & Tremblay, 1999).

There is no single precise description of disruptive behavior because youngsters can misbehave in a variety of ways. Students can climb on furniture, grab classmates' materials, make obscene noises or gestures, verbally or physically defy the teacher, touch their classmates, or run through the hallways. Confronted with these behaviors, teachers may react emotionally, use ineffective approaches, and ultimately burn out. In this chapter you will discover new options for addressing disruptive behaviors.

How do you decide whether to intervene to change a disruptive behavior? First ask yourself whether the behaviors interfere with the personal freedom and learning of others. Many behaviors will annoy and irritate you. However, as a veteran middle school teacher once advised, "In this classroom, you must pick your battles carefully; you can't take on everything!" Next, consider the purpose, or **communicative function,** of the behavior. Here are some possible reasons why students disrupt classroom activities:

- To gain your attention (positive or negative)
- To get the attention or approval of classmates
- To avoid doing work
- To gather information; for example, to test the limits of your authority or to find out whether the rules will be enforced
- To make a boring class more interesting!

Because the disruptive behaviors that irritate you may not even faze your colleagues, it's important to have agreement on **target behaviors,** rules, and sanctions. To facilitate this process, stick to precise descriptions of target behaviors, as discussed in the earlier chapters. When you are really clear about the behavior you want to change, you narrow the scope of the problem. This makes it easier to interpret the behavior and find just the right intervention. As you and your teaching colleagues discuss students' behavior, try to agree on how you will help students to learn and follow the school rules. After all, research has shown that *school-wide* behavioral interventions work (Colvin, Kameenui, & Sugai, 1993; Nelson, Colvin, Petty, & Smith, 1995). Here are the guidelines offered by the University of Oregon's Project PREPARE (Colvin et al., 1993):

1. *Take a consistent approach to discipline problems*; it is important to send clear and consistent messages to students.
2. *Approach discipline as an instructional opportunity*, preparing students before expecting them to act in a certain way, offering them practice, review, and feedback. Consider the steps outlined by Colvin et al., 1993, for teaching students how to behave during transition times:
   - Identify the transition behaviors and the times when these behaviors are needed.
   - Identify times when you can explain the transition rules and behaviors.
   - Identify ways to practice and times to practice.
   - Identify reminder times and strategies.
   - List reinforcers.
   - Name correction procedures.
   Does this format remind you of a lesson plan? That is the idea. Additional detailed lesson plans for teaching appropriate behaviors during elementary school transition times are available by writing to J. Ron Nelson, Ph.D., Eastern Washington University, Department of Applied Psychology, Cheny, WA 99004.
3. *Think of discipline as a tool to improve school success*, not as an "end unto itself" (p. 369).

4. *Use preventive and proactive approaches more than reactive responses.*
5. *Ensure that administrative and teaching leaders are fully involved in the planning process.*
6. *Agree among yourselves to change and participate as you develop your school's discipline approaches.*
7. *Take time to learn new approaches.* After all, one study showed a 50% decrease in office referrals for schools that set up this approach (Colvin et al., 1993, pp. 369–370).

In summary, faculty planning based on sound policies will prevent many behavioral crises. Let's turn now to classroom-level strategies. We present four categories of interventions: environmentally mediated, teacher-mediated, peer-mediated, and self-mediated. In each section you will find examples of strategies to use in your classroom.

ENVIRONMENTALLY MEDIATED INTERVENTIONS

By **environmentally mediated strategy,** we mean that some aspect of the classroom environment is altered to prevent or to address behavioral problems. For example, you might modify your rules, curricula, schedules, seating, and the general physical layout of your room. Two important ideas may help you when considering environmental strategies. First, merely altering the environment is not a powerful intervention strategy. Environmental modifications should be combined with other strategies. Second, those other strategies depend on a sound environment that discourages disruptive behavior and that supports the other, more powerful interventions. In other words, environmental modifications are necessary if other strategies are to be successful, but not sufficient alone to change misbehavior.

The most essential prerequisites to effective classroom management are an appropriate and relevant academic curriculum and effective instructional practices (Shores, Gunter, Denny, &

Jack, 1993; Sugai & Tindal, 1993). An appropriate and relevant curriculum is one that meets each student's individual needs and that he or she perceives as important and meaningful. In the case of students with IEPs, this prerequisite is often assumed to be a given; unfortunately, research does not bear out this assumption. The correspondence between student assessment data and instructional goals is often poor (Shores et al., 1993). A curriculum that is poorly matched to students' aptitudes and interests (e.g., too difficult, too easy, or boring) is likely to be aversive, thus setting the stage for escape and avoidance behavior.

Appropriate goals and curricula are fair, functional, and meaningful to students. Undesired behavior may be one way (perhaps the only way) the student communicates that "This is too hard," "I don't like this," or "This is baby stuff." Inappropriate expectations or curricula generate frustration, dissatisfaction, and rebellion, thus setting the stage for behavior problems. If the teacher reacts punitively, he may initiate a self-perpetuating cycle of crises. By functionally analyzing problem behaviors in relationship to variables inherent in specific curricula and settings, you can identify potential causes and address them without resorting to procedures that involve aversive consequences. If your goals and curricula are fair and important to students, you can also prevent many problems from occurring in the first place.

Even experienced teachers make two other mistakes. The first is to assume that students know what is expected of them. An indication of this problem is the absence of clear rules for classroom behavior. Either rules are nonexistent or they are worded too generally (e.g., "show respect for other persons," "use good manners"). Vague rules may be explained so that pupils understand them (e.g., showing respect means keep hands and feet to yourself, do not interrupt when others are talking, take turns, etc.), but often they are not. The second mistake is to punish students for their failure to exhibit a behavior that they do not know how to perform (e.g., following directions, remaining in-seat). This problem relates to the failure to correctly discriminate the difference between a skill deficit and a performance deficit, which was discussed in Chapter 2. It is most often a response to students' noncompliance. Although noncompliance may reflect a pupil's decision not to follow a rule or direction, it may also indicate that the student does not know what behavior is expected, that there are obstacles to the student performing as desired, or that the student lacks the skills to exhibit the desired behavior. Attempt to correct the problem first through interventions based on positive reinforcement.

Take a look at Table 6–1, which gives examples not only of student rules, but also of student and teacher responsibilities.

The following questions make up an informal checklist to help you assess the potential sources of problem behaviors:

- Is what I am teaching useful or important to the students?
- Do the pupils know what I expect them to do?
- Are there any obstacles to the students performing as desired?
- Do students have the ability to perform as expected?
- What are the consequences of desired performance?
- What are the consequences of nonperformance?
- When does the problem behavior occur?
- What is different about students who are not displaying the problem behavior?
- How can I change my instruction to help pupils develop the skill I am trying to teach?

Physical Space

Imagine you have just walked into the room where you are going to spend the next nine months with students, some of whom have not yet learned to control their behavior. Perhaps the room is arranged as the previous teacher left it, or maybe you find yourself staring at nothing more than boxes and packing crates. Your first thought might be, "How can I arrange this to suit what I want to do here?" The answer to the first part of this question depends on how much thought you have given to the second part; that is, the arrangement of your classroom is determined by how you intend to use it.

Following are several considerations intended to help you plan for the full use of your classroom, not restrict it.

1. How many students will you have in the room at one time? Twenty students impose more restriction on room use than ten. However, you can plan to use different areas for more than one activity; a science area can also be used for art, provided equipment can be stored and retrieved easily.

2. How should your pupils' seats be grouped? The answer to this depends on both the behavioral patterns of your students and their activities. Extremely active or disruptive children should sit farther apart, and independent seatwork calls for less physical proximity than a group project.

3. What kinds of activities will be taking place in your classroom? You will want to provide some physical activity, particularly if you have young children or if your curriculum includes activities requiring space for free movement. Will two or more kinds of activities be going on simultaneously? One student listening to rap music as earned reinforcement can be disruptive in the middle of your civics group. It is wise to set up separate areas if space permits. If not, adjust your schedule so that quiet activities go on at one time and noisy or physical activities at another.

4. Consider also whether any students need to be isolated, and if so, whether only for certain activities or for most of the day. By isolation we mean physical (usually visual) separation from classmates, not timeout (although this too is a consideration in planning the physical layout of your classroom). Using a cubicle or separate desk space need not be punishing. If you explain it as a way to get work done on time, a student may appreciate

TABLE 6-1 List of Rules

Recommended Rules	Student Expectations	Teacher Responsibilities
Enter the classroom quietly.	Walk in and speak softly. Put away belongings. Take assigned seats.	Stand at the door. Wait to share conversations with students. Establish areas for putting away coats, turning in assignments, and so on. Create a permanent seating arrangement. Recognize appropriate behaviors.
Begin work on time.	Listen to/read instructions carefully. Begin to work immediately.	Prepare practice assignments in advance. Expect students to begin work promptly. Monitor student behavior. Recognize appropriate behaviors.
Stay on task.	Ignore distractions from others. Continue to work without interruptions.	Assign developmentally appropriate tasks. Check for student understanding. Provide positive and corrective feedback. Monitor student behavior and assignment completion progress. Prevent/end distracting behaviors. Recognize appropriate behaviors.
Complete work on time.	Check assignment completion requirements. Ask questions for understanding. Set goals for assignment completion.	State complete assignment information, including a grading criteria. Provide appropriate models and demonstrations. Teach goal setting. Allow sufficient class time to work. Recognize appropriate behaviors.
Follow directions at all times.	Listen carefully. Ask questions for understanding. Do as all teachers request.	Gain student attention. Give clear directions for particular situations. Check for student understanding. Provide examples and/or demonstrations. Monitor student behavior. Recognize appropriate behaviors.
Listen while others speak.	Maintain a positive body posture. Look at the person. Note important information. Signal for more information.	Teach listening skills. Model good listening skills. Encourage verbal elaboration. Encourage "risk free" active participation.
Use appropriate language.	Avoid angry and foul words. Use kind words to tell how you feel.	Teach appropriate statements for avoiding conflicts. Teach techniques for self-control. Model respect toward students and peers. Recognize appropriate behaviors.
Keep hands, feet, objects to self.	Avoid hitting, kicking, or throwing things.	Teach safety habits and procedures. Teach techniques for self-control. Recognize appropriate behaviors.

Source: *From Rademacher, J.A., Callahan, K., & Pederson-Seelye, V.A. (1998). How do your classroom rules measure up?* Intervention in School and Clinic, 33, 284–289. Reprinted with permission.

the opportunity. When cubicles are called *offices* and students understand they are used to facilitate studying, competition frequently develops over access to them. One word of caution, however: Under no circumstances should a study carrel be used as a means of chronically separating a disruptive student, or as a timeout area. All children deserve as much educational and personal assistance as you can provide. "Out of sight, out of mind" is not an acceptable strategy.

5. Finally, you should consider how movement in the classroom is to be regulated. When pupils need help, will they come to you or will you go to them? Will student movement be restricted ("Raise your hand to get permission") or free? Will you require them to line up before leaving the room or not? How will you regulate movement to and from learning centers or the free-time area? How will students be monitored in these areas? Regardless of whether you want an open, free classroom or a highly structured one, you will need to make decisions such as these and design your classroom accordingly.

Obviously, there are other factors to consider when planning your classroom. Much of what you do will be dictated by elements you will not discover until you see your room—the amount of storage space or the location of windows, lights, blackboards, sink, and counters. Look at your potential classroom when you interview for a job. Otherwise, you might end up in a storage closet or a converted locker room! For good information on planning classroom space, see Wong & Wong, 1998; Crosser, 1992.

Daily Schedule

This part of structure has to do with your general daily routine—how you sequence your classes and activities. A dependable classroom schedule is good for both you and your pupils. Students generally like the security of a routine, and if you nearly suffer a breakdown trying to get through the math period, there is some comfort in knowing

that in 30 min you can get to that biology project both you and the pupils like!

The job of setting up a daily schedule is often half done for you. Recesses, lunch, and planning periods are usually determined by school administrators, and like it or not, you will have to organize your day around these set activities. Such scheduled events can be used to good advantage simply by applying Grandma's Law[1]: First eat your vegetables, then you may have your dessert. Applying the law to a schedule means teaching handwriting just before recess and requiring work to be done before recess.

You might also consider Grandma's Law when trying to decide what should come first in the school day. Begin the day with a warm-up activity, usually a simple direction-following task, to get the children settled and ready for work. Then you might schedule the most challenging tasks for morning. Thus, you get pupils over a big hurdle early in the day. Another strategy is to alternate lessons that are easy and more difficult, more active and less active. Consider several other variables when setting up a daily schedule. Obviously, routine should be balanced by a reasonable variety of activity, lest school become boring or aversive. But variety does not mean keeping your pupils guessing what is going to happen from one day to the next. You can plan both variety and routine if you vary specific tasks frequently but depart from the routine schedule less often.

Another consideration is the physical activity of your pupils during the day. Children need to have some times in the day set aside for physical games and activities. Even though you can work for long periods in one place, do not assume that 9-year-olds can do the same. Plan for some physical activity at least every hour, even if it is only to stand and stretch or to get a drink of water.

Make sure your pupils understand the schedule. Telling them is not enough. Use direct instruction to teach the schedule and take students

[1]Grandma's Law actually is an euphemism for the **Premack Principle** (Premack, 1959).

through it several times before assuming they know the routine. However, do not be afraid to change the schedule if it is not working satisfactorily. This is good advice for secondary school teachers. Middle and high school schedules can be complicated, and pupils without the skills to get around properly may get into trouble.

Rules

Rules are verbal statements regulating behavior. Not only do they tell pupils which behaviors will be tolerated and which will not, they also serve as cues to the teacher as to which behaviors should be followed with which consequences. Consider these guidelines for establishing rules:

1. *Select the fewest possible number of rules.* Too many rules are difficult to remember, and frequently are so specific that pupils easily can find exceptions to them. For example, one teacher, who was concerned about fighting in the classroom, developed a long list of rules: No hitting, No shoving, No biting, No name-calling, and so forth. She later substituted just one rule—Remain in your seat during our quiet seatwork—because in-seat behavior was incompatible with behaviors leading to, and involved in, fighting.

2. *Use different rules for different situations.* Obviously, rules for classroom activities should be different from playground, lunch line, or bus-waiting-area rules. Some pupils need to be taught that different situations call for different behavior. Clearly stated rules can help them make this discrimination.

3. *Rules should be stated behaviorally and they should be enforceable.* Thus, the rule "Show respect toward others" invites differing interpretations of what constitutes respect or disrespect and is not easily enforceable. The rule "No talking when my back is turned" is behaviorally stated but would be difficult to enforce. Rules that are not enforceable invite tattling as well as limit-testing, both of which can lead to disruptions.

4. *Rules should be stated positively; that is, they should describe appropriate and desired student behaviors rather than those to avoid.* This focuses attention on positive replacement behaviors rather than on inappropriate pupil activity. For example, the rule "Wait to be called upon before speaking" is preferable to "No talking."

5. *Rules should be reasonable.* The most common response to an unreasonable rule is to challenge it, which may lead to a serious power struggle. Another option is to give up rather than try to meet the expectation. Thus, the rule "All homework must be in before first period" is reasonable only if all students are capable of meeting it; that is, no student has a night job and the homework is within all pupils' ability to complete. The best way to ensure that rules are reasonable is to develop them with students.

6. *There must be consistent consequences for rule fulfillment or infraction.* This does not mean the use of threats or lectures. Rule consequences should be posted with the rules themselves or taught until all pupils know them thoroughly. Posted rules and consequences, incidentally, are a tremendous help to substitute teachers or new classroom paraprofessionals. Without consequences, rules have little effect on behavior. Therefore, consistent teacher follow-through is critical, including praise or points for following rules and systematic withdrawal of attention or other reinforcers (or presentation of aversive consequences) for their infraction. Avoid bending the rules for specific pupils or situations unless you have planned it with students in advance.

Teacher Movement Patterns

Teachers who spend more time among their students exert greater stimulus control over their behavior than teachers who remain at their desks. Gunter et al. (1995) observed that increasing the amount of time teachers spent away from their desks during independent activities increases student academic engagement. Fifer (1986) found that increased teacher movement decreased undesired student behavior and increased positive interactions between pupils and teacher. Teacher movement also increases proximity to students, and closer proximity is associated with the increased power of both social reinforcement and punishment (Shores et al., 1993).

As you travel around your classroom, you may notice that some pupils are overly dependent on your attention, flagging you down or chronically approaching your desk. Help students to design and use a signaling device (see Figure 6–1) to show whether teacher assistance is needed. This procedure reduces the need for students to be out-of-seat to get teacher attention and may help them stop to think before calling on you.

FIGURE 6–1 Signaling device for a child's desk.

TEACHER-MEDIATED INTERVENTIONS

Once you have adopted good environmentally mediated interventions, you can select from among many **teacher-mediated strategies** proven to improve students' behavior. This section tells how to increase your effectiveness as you help your students learn new behaviors.

Monitoring Teacher Verbal and Nonverbal Behavior

What you say or do not say may be your most powerful strategy for remedying disruptive behavior. In contrast to what you might expect, your negative comments will actually *increase* misbehavior (Walker, 1995). Teacher attention to undesired behavior, though negative, seems to function as positive reinforcement. Buehler, Patterson, and Furniss (1966) and Solomon and Wahler (1973) have documented this. Furthermore, both of these studies demonstrated that peer attention to inappropriate responses exerted more powerful control over child behavior than did the adult reactions.

Shores et al. (1993) conducted numerous studies of the interactions between general and special education teachers and students with emotional and behavior disorders. Teachers responded less than half the time to students raising hands and requesting assistance with tasks. Such teacher neutrality creates an unpleasant classroom environment, which encourages pupil escape and avoidance behaviors.

As Walker (1995) found, the cumulative effect of disproportionate teacher attention (in addition to peer support and attention) to acting-out children's misbehavior is to strengthen undesired behavior patterns. The unfortunate result of this combination of events is a classroom situation in which the teacher relies on progressively more aversive management practices (public reprimands, sending children to the principal's office, suspensions, etc.). These measures may have temporary suppressive effects for some students, but they have no effect or—worse still—a strengthening effect on undesired behaviors of other pupils. In summary, patterns of unintentional teacher reinforcement of problem behaviors lead to cycles characterized by high levels of student misbehavior and aversive teacher countercontrol (Shores et al., 1993).

A common side effect of aversive teacher control is power struggles between the teacher and some, or all, pupils. Like adults, children react negatively to aversive management. If they sense that the teacher is reacting from frustration or feels out of control of the situation, they may respond with even more intensive misbehavior. We all know teachers who are "naturals" at disciplining students. These individuals have distinctive speaking voices that command students' attention without screaming. You, too, can have an authoritative but courteous voice. First, ask a colleague to role-play some situations with you. Pretend that you are stopping a rambunctious student in the corridor. Ask your colleague to tell you honestly how you sound. Do you sound angry and out of control? Do you convey authority without losing your "cool"? Are you meek or apologetic? Now practice again. This activity might seem silly at first, but it makes you more aware of your verbal reactions, especially in stressful situations.

Next, concentrate on your facial expressions, gestures, and posture. Ask a colleague for feedback on how you look. Research has shown that 80 percent of the message received by a person in a stressful situation is nonverbal. **Self-monitoring** is a great (and even fun) way to gain control of your verbal and nonverbal messages. Here is a simple activity to help you monitor your verbalizations (e.g., praise, reprimands, nags, repeated requests) and body language (e.g., hands on hips, tightened fists, clenched jaw, pointing a finger, standing too close, arms folded across chest):

1. Obtain at least 50 pennies or paper clips.
2. Place the pennies or paper clips in one pocket.

3. Each time you find yourself saying something negative or using a gesture you'd like to avoid (e.g., pointing at students), move a penny or a paper clip to the other pocket.
4. At the end of the day, count the items in each pocket and record your scores.
5. Record your scores on an individual chart. Try to improve your record the next day.
6. For more fun, challenge a friend to track her statements and gestures, too.

In our case study at the end of this chapter, you'll read how a frustrated middle school teacher surveyed her middle school students about her management approaches, including praise requests, and reprimands.

Reprimands

Admonishing students who misbehave is a teaching tradition. Your **reprimand** is more effective when you use the following guidelines:

- Make your reprimand privately, not publicly. Humiliating or embarrassing a student is likely to increase that student's resentment and may create an unsafe situation (Gun Safety Institute, 1993). Raising your voice repeatedly merely desensitizes students to your reprimands. Students may be more inclined to listen to what you are saying when you use a normal speaking voice.
- Look at the student while you are speaking (Van Houten, Nau, MacKenzie-Keating, Sameoto, & Colavecchia, 1982). Do not insist that the student give you eye contact, however, as this may violate a student's cultural traditions or humiliate him.
- Stand near the student while you are talking to her (Van Houten et al., 1982). However, a good idea with anyone is to remain at least one leg length away from the individual, to honor that individual's personal space needs (National Crisis Prevention Institute, 1987).
- Do not point your finger at the student. This habit, shared by many educators, can be very

difficult to break. Try self-monitoring your gestures, or ask students to help you.
- Do not insist on having the last word, especially with teenagers.

Physical Interactions with Students

Most of your interactions with student problems will be, and certainly should be, verbal, not physical. We advise that you do not engage in any physical interactions that you would deem inappropriate with an unfamiliar adult. Whereas a handshake may be appropriate and courteous, touching a student in any other way may lead to problems, especially with students who have a history of acting-out behaviors or who have been victims of abuse. Naturally, there will be good exceptions to this rule, but a conservative stance is usually best. Adolescents who are developing their own sexual identities are often confused about physical affection. Hypersensitive to your initiations, they may misunderstand your intentions. This likelihood increases when teenagers are under stress, angered, or embarrassed.

Physical interventions for aggressive students create their own problems. Avoid physical confrontations whenever possible, taking precautions to protect yourself and others. Maintaining the recommended three-foot distance is one way to develop the habit of honoring students' personal space needs.

The Praise-and-Ignore Approach

Sometimes we ignore problem behaviors, only to be disappointed in the results. Our failure to control behavior may be due to a misunderstanding of the basic principles that underlie this intervention. Here are five guidelines for an effective praise-and-ignore approach:

1. Remember that ignoring will not work unless the reason for the student's behavior is to gain your attention. Use an A-B-C analysis to determine this.
2. Remember that when an ignoring intervention is successful, disruptive behavior will increase before decreasing. Do not give up when students test to see if you will give in and pay attention to their antics.
3. Develop ways in which other adults can distract you from the student who is being disruptive so that you do not find yourself giving the student attention. Let others present know to ignore the student's disruptive behavior.
4. Be sure to **praise** the student for appropriate behaviors. Ignoring without praise will not work; it's merely "going cold turkey."
5. Consider the "peak" of the **extinction** curve before you begin this strategy. If you will not be able to tolerate (ignore) the behavior as it accelerates, select a different strategy. Remember that the problem behavior almost always worsens (e.g., swearing may escalate to hitting) before it gets better as the ignored child tries to get your attention.

Differential Reinforcement of Other Behaviors

Differential Reinforcement of Other Behaviors (DRO) is a strategy whereby you reinforce the nondisruptive behaviors when they occur during a specified time interval. One simple way to use the DRO approach is through a timer game (illustrated in the Chapter 5 case study). To help you get started in planning a DRO approach, Table 6–2 lists undesirable behaviors along with preferred incompatible alternatives.

Differential Reinforcement of Low Rates of Behavior

Differential Reinforcement of Low Rates of Behavior (DRL) has been applied to swearing, inappropriate questioning, and negative verbal statements. Zwald and Gresham (1982) targeted teasing and name-calling. Here are the steps they took:

1. The teacher posted and discussed class rules, telling the group the maximum number of teasing/name-calling

TABLE 6–2 Undesirable Behaviors and Preferred Incompatible Alternatives

Undesired Behavior	Positive Incompatible Alternative
Talking back	Positive response such as "Yes Sir" or "May I ask you a question about that?" or "May I tell you my side?"
Cursing	Acceptable exclamations such as "Darn."
Being off task	Any on-task behavior: looking at a book, writing, looking at the teacher, etc.
Being out of seat	Sitting in seat (bottom on chair, with body in upright position).
Noncompliance	Following directions within _____ seconds (time limit will depend upon age of student); following directions by second time direction is given.
Talking out	Raising hand and waiting to be called on.
Turning in messy papers	No marks other than answers; no more than _____ erasures; no more than three folds or creases.

Source: *From Webber, J., & Scheuermann, B. (1991) Accentuate the positive … eliminate the negative! Teaching Exceptional Children. Fall, 1991,* p. 15. Reprinted with permission.

occurrences allowed to still obtain reinforcement for that day.

2. The teacher made a mark on the blackboard for every teasing/name-calling verbalization. These verbalizations were not discussed or reprimanded.

3. Each boy selected positive reinforcement from a reinforcement menu mutually decided upon by the teacher and class members. The reinforcement menu for each day consisted of a hot drink (hot chocolate, tea, or coffee), free reading, or listening to the radio.

4. To prevent the number of teasing remarks from getting out of hand if the students went beyond the limit set for the day (thereby losing that day's reinforcement), the teacher gave a larger reward at the end of the week if the group had five or fewer "extra" recorded teasing remarks for the week. The large reinforcer was 20 min of free time on Friday.

5. A line graph was posted so that class members could graphically see their progress. The extra teasing remarks (the number of remarks that exceeded the imposed limit) were recorded on a bar graph so the students could observe whether they would obtain free time at the end of the week (p. 430).

Trice and Parker (1983) reduced obscene words in a resource room by using DRL and a response cost. Specific words were targeted, and each time a student said one of the six targeted words, he got a colored marker. At the end of the period, the markers were tallied and the students' behavior was posted on a graph. A 5-min detention (the response cost) was required for each marker. Under the DRL condition, students received praise each time the tally fell below the mean tally for the day before; students whose tallies were higher received no comment. The authors cited the response cost procedure as more immediately effective than the DRL procedure.

Public Posting

Public posting is a successful, relatively simple strategy that combines an environmental intervention with a teacher-directed approach. In public posting, students receive visual feedback about their performance (e.g., a poster telling them how well they have performed a given behavior). Two studies illustrate the versatility of this intervention. Both were conducted with secondary school students, but there is no reason why the public posting strategy would not be effective with younger students as long as they understand the contents of the poster.

Jones and Van Houten (1985) used public posting to change seventh graders' disruptive behavior (i.e., noises, pushing, teasing, "showing off," leaving seats) during science and English classes. Before trying the posting, the authors instituted pop quizzes to see whether these would remediate the misbehavior, but they were not entirely successful, so the authors turned to the public posting of each student's daily quiz score. The public posting resulted in decreased disruptive behaviors as well as in similar or improved quiz scores for the seventh graders. Caution: You may prefer to post student's grades with their student numbers to protect confidentiality.

In a second study of public posting, Staub (1987) sought to improve the rambunctious hall behavior of middle school students during change of classes. Large posters at each end of a very busy corridor gave students the following information: the percentage change in the daily occurrence of disruptive behavior (as compared with the day before) and the "best record to date" of decreasing disruptive behaviors. To enhance the public posting strategy, the dean gave verbal feedback and praise matching the posters to each classroom during the first minute of classes. This simple and inexpensive intervention proved successful in reducing the disruptive behaviors of the middle school students.

Contingency Contracting

We call a written explanation of contingencies a **contingency contract.** This is a useful procedure, even for young children (Allen, Howard, Sweeney, & McLaughlin, 1993). General guidelines for implementing a contingency contract would include the following:

- Explain to the student what a contract is. Your explanation will depend upon the conversational level of the child, but it may be helpful to use examples of contracts that the student will encounter.
- Share examples of contracts with the student.
- Ask the student to suggest tasks that might be included in a contract between student and teacher. Write these down.
- Suggest tasks that you would like to see the student accomplish, and write these down.
- Decide on mutually agreeable tasks. If a third party is to be involved in the contract, be sure that the party also agrees on the tasks that you have selected.
- Discuss with the student possible activities, items, or privileges that the student would like to earn. Write these down.
- Negotiate how the student will earn the reinforcers by accomplishing portions or all of the tasks.
- Identify the criteria for mastery of each task (time allotted, achievement level, how the task is to be evaluated).
- Determine when the student will receive the reinforcers for completing tasks.
- Determine when the contract will be reviewed to make necessary revisions or to note progress.
- Make an extra copy of the contract. Give this copy to the student and any third party involved. Home-based contracts, as they are called, have proven quite successful (Kelley & McCain, 1995; Smith, 1994). Smith (1994) offered parents of K–7 students a workshop and workbook, invited them to identify school behaviors of concern to them, and then set up weekly parent-teacher evaluation charts. Once a week students received a simple "yes" or "no" from their teacher, telling whether or not they had met the behavioral goal. Parents issued rewards and certificates when children met their weekly goals. These parent-initiated contracts improved the children's behavior and were appreciated by the parents.
- Sign the contract, get the student to sign the contract, and if there is a third party involved, ask the third party to sign the contract.

I, __Randy__ (student), agree to do the following at school:

1. __Try not to interrupt the teacher__

   on this schedule: __during social studies class__

2. __Try to work without disturbing other kids__

   on this schedule: __during math__

I, __Mr. Jameson__ (teacher), agree to provide assistance as follows:

   __Arrange for Randy to take part in the social studies discussion, by calling on him daily. Move Randy away from the gerbils.__

We, __the Bergers__ (parents), agree to provide privileges as follows:

   __provide Randy with ✓ marks on the chart posted in the kitchen. When Randy earns 50 ✓s, he can buy a gerbil. We will also try to have conversations about the news at home.__

We have read and discussed this contract in an after-school meeting on __2/16__. and we hereby sign as a way of making our commitment to this arrangement.

We will all meet on __2/28__, to reevaluate the contract.

Signed __Randy Berger__ (student)
       __JJ Jameson__ (teacher)
       __Anita Berger__ (parent)
       __George Berger__ (parent)

Date __2/16__

FIGURE 6–2 Home-based report.

Figure 6–2 provides an example of a contract for a disruptive child. Notice that it is a **home-based contract,** in which the parents have agreed to participate. Involving parents (or other persons important to the child) is an excellent way to strengthen a contingency contract. At the bottom of the home-based contract is an important fea-ture: the review date. This frequent review allows everyone involved to offer suggestions for how the procedure can be improved before major problems arise. Did you also note that the rein-forcers within the contract tend to be educational activities? By selecting special privileges that en-hance your academic program, you move away from the tendency to "bribe" students into improved performance.

We will address contracting again when we come to self-monitoring. First, let's turn to another powerful contingency management tool, the token economy.

Token Economy Programs

The **token economy** is a widely used classroom intervention system. Token systems have been used in regular and special classrooms, with children exhibiting mild to severe disabilities, with preschoolers and adults, and with social and academic behaviors. They also may be adapted to fit any situation, or they may be combined with a variety of other intervention strategies (see Walker, 1995). The essential ingredients of a token system include tokens, back-up reinforcers (tangibles or activities) for which tokens may be exchanged, contingencies specifying the conditions under which tokens may be obtained or lost, and the exchange rate of tokens for back-up reinforcers.

A variety of back-up reinforcers is possible: classroom or school privileges, activities, trinkets, clothes, costume jewelry, toys, or even such large items as bicycles. Some community agencies (e.g., the Chamber of Commerce, Volunteers of America, church groups, labor unions) may be willing to conduct drives or donate items. Cast-off items from your basement or attic may prove valuable in a token system. However, remember that preferred activities are also effective reinforcers, and they are much less expensive and present no storage problems. Therefore, consider using such activities as listening to music, talking with a peer, or playing a game as back-up reinforcers.

Because tokens are conditioned reinforcers, their value derives from association with previously established consequences. Teach students to value tokens by pairing their presentation with an existing social or tangible reinforcer or by reinforcer sampling; that is, giving pupils a number of tokens and letting them purchase back-ups immediately. Over a period of days,

fade out the paired reinforcer or delay token exchange and make receipt of tokens contingent upon desired behaviors. As your system evolves, increase the length of intervals between token exchanges. This teaches pupils to delay gratification and encourages saving for larger items, which, incidentally, are desirable behaviors in our economic system.

Token systems offer a number of advantages. Because each student can select from a variety of back-up reinforcers, pupil satiation and loss of reinforcer power are not likely problems. Also, tokens can be delivered more easily than individualized tangibles, and simply by announcing that a student has earned a token, your praise and approval develops as a conditioned reinforcer. If tokens are awarded contingent upon academic performance, incompatible social behaviors are reduced in most cases. Also, with such contingencies, little time is lost from teaching as a result of behavior intervention. In addition, the requirement that tokens be awarded influences the teacher to interact frequently with pupils. With activities as back-ups, the cost of the system is minimal.

Token economies have been successful in decreasing such disruptive behavior as jumping out-of-seat, and they have been successful in increasing attention and academic performance (see Chapter 7). Following are the resources you will need for initiating a token economy program:

- Back-up reinforcers appropriate for your classroom group
- Tokens appropriate for your group
- A kitchen timer, if you plan to reinforce behaviors by measuring their duration
- A monitoring sheet on which to record the tokens or points earned
- Token dispensers, containers, or devices to denote the gain or loss of tokens

You will need a couple of hours to get materials together and to get the monitoring sheets duplicated. Then plan to spend about 30 min a day for the first week of the program introducing the tokens and orienting students to the program. After the first week, the program should require no more than 20 min a day in addition to the time spent delivering tokens. (Note: Programs may differ in the amount of time required.)

To begin the program, select target behaviors for your class. Some of the behaviors you list should be ones you presently take for granted. Select easy behaviors to ensure all students can earn a few tokens from the beginning of the program. Select target behaviors that are compatible with your classroom rules. Include behavioral targets from your students' IEPs. Sample target behaviors developed for a primary classroom token economy could include the following:

- Say hello to teachers when you arrive at school.
- Hang up your coat when you come to school.
- Put your lunch away when you arrive at school.
- Pick up your work for the day and take your seat.
- Eat lunch within the allotted time.
- Line up for activities outside the room.

To ensure that the selected target behaviors are appropriate, ask yourself the following questions:

1. How can I describe this behavior in words the student(s) can understand?
2. How can I measure this behavior when it occurs? If the behavior is measured in terms of time (on-task for 10 min, no outburst during a 15-min period, solving a certain number of math problems within a specified amount of time), assign the tokens or points on the basis of a token-to-time ratio. If the behavior is measured in terms of frequency (percent correct on a worksheet, number of positive verbal comments to a peer, number of independent steps in a self-care task), award tokens or points on the basis of a token-to-frequency ratio.
3. How will I know when this behavior is exhibited?
4. How important is this behavior? You will not be able to initiate the program with all

of the behaviors you identify, so you may have to rank them. Start with some behaviors that you can alter successfully.
5. Is the behavior one that you wish to reduce or eliminate? You can handle this behavior in two ways. The first approach is to reward a behavior that is incompatible with the problem behavior. For example, reward in-seat behavior to reduce classroom wandering. The second approach is to fine the student. We call this a response cost. If the student wanders around the room, he loses a privilege.
6. Does this behavior occur in other settings? If so, you may want to extend the token economy program to include other classes or the home. You will need to monitor the behavior in those settings, so include space on your monitoring form or develop a different form for those settings.

As you present these target behaviors or rules to your students, remember that research has shown that a daily review of the rules strengthens the effectiveness of the token economy (Rosenberg, 1986). Use this supplemental activity by calling on students and asking them to state the rules and the tokens or points that the behaviors can earn. Rosenberg (1986) found that a mere 2-min review each day improved students' responses to the token economy intervention.

Selecting reinforcers and fines is the next step. If your students can help, let them develop a list of reinforcers. Think of items or events that will be enjoyable and that can be obtained within the school. Some ideas for involving students in identifying their own reinforcers might include the following:

- Ask students to draw, write, or select from a set of pictures those items or events that appeal to them.
- Allow students some free time, and observe what they choose to do.
- Allow students to "sample" reinforcers by placing them in an accessible place and

recording which items the students select frequently.

Selecting tokens is the next step. These may take the form of checkmarks, stamps, or other marks on a form. However, you may want to use tangible items, especially with young children. In considering the types of tokens to use, you must consider the following variables:

- The age of the students
- The skill level of the students
- The likelihood that students will destroy, eat, or cheat with respect to the tokens
- The expense of the tokens
- The durability of the tokens
- The convenience of using the tokens
- Tokens that are being used in other programs within the same setting (Do not use these!)

Once you have chosen tokens for your program, select an appropriate container or form for them. Counterfeiting may be prevented by using a special color marking pen, by awarding tokens at specified times, or by awarding bonus points for honesty and deducting points for cheating.

You may have seen token economy programs that were included in a **level system.** A levels system lists and organizes behavioral targets and their consequences in a kind of hierarchy or set of levels (Schuermann, Webber, Partin, & Knies, 1994). The example in our case study includes four levels. There are advantages (such as efficiency) to having levels for your token economy, but the levels system must carefully consider the legal rights of protected students.

Here are two legal concerns (as cited by Scheuermann et al., 1994):

1. *Ignoring the* IEP *process.* Examples include requiring all students to enter at the first level, requiring class consensus before allowing a student to move to a level, establishing target behaviors based on group instead of individual needs,

advancing or moving down based on group performance, or any other action that is not part of an individualized consideration of the student's needs.
2. *Overlooking the concept of least restrictive environment* (LRE). Examples include denying students' access to the general education setting through a requirement that students must earn the right to attain general education placement. Other examples include restricted access to peers during class or lunch. The checklist in Figure 6–3 will help you evaluate your level system.

As students learn to manage their behavior, their reinforcers should reflect their increasing ability to handle classroom freedom. Moreover, their reinforcers should provide them with a smooth transition to the less restrictive main-stream environment where frequent and tangible reinforcers are not common. After all, we cannot expect any child to leave a special education classroom willingly if that classroom resembles a toy department.

Another component of your token economy will facilitate the development of new—and unexpected—skills. Issue "bonus points" for spontaneous behaviors that you would like to recognize but did not include in your monitoring forms.

Finally, be sure that you review your token economy program with your students at least once a month. Remember that you will have students at different levels at the same time, so you will need to examine how each student is functioning. If you find that a student is not moving from one level to another, make the higher level a bit easier to reach, or reexamine your lower level to see why the student is not succeeding. This review is similar to assessing students' progress in academic curricula or materials. Through careful initial planning and regular monitoring of students' progress, your token economy will be a success. Tips for making your token economy successful follow on page 218 (Bicanich, 1986).

Answer each of the following questions regarding your level system.

I. Access to LRE

A. Are mainstreaming decisions made by each student's IEP committee, regardless of the student's status within the level system?   Yes   No

  If no, check below:

  _____ 1. Students are required to attain a predetermined level before they can attend a mainstream class.

  _____ 2. Mainstream classes are predetermined (e.g., P.E. for students on Level 2, P.E. and music for students on Level 3, etc.)

II. Placement in the level system

A. Are students initially placed in the level system at the level that is commensurate with their needs and strengths?   Yes   No

B. Is initial placement in the level system based on current, valid assessment?   Yes   No

III. Curriculum

A. Does each student have individual target behaviors designated in addition to those designated for the whole group?   Yes   No

B. Are group expectations considered by each student's IEP committee to determine whether those expectations are appropriate for each individual student?   Yes   No

C. Are criteria for mastery of target behaviors developed individually?   Yes   No

D. Is the sequence of target behaviors developed individually for each student, based on that student's needs and areas of strength?   Yes   No

E. Are target behaviors differentiated as skill deficits or performance deficits?   Yes   No

F. Are reinforcers individualized?   Yes   No

G. Do you avoid using access to less restrictive environments/activities and nondisabled peers as reinforcers?   Yes   No

IV. Procedures

A. Are advancement criteria (criteria for movement from one level to the next) individualized for each student?   Yes   No

B. Are advancement criteria based on recent, relevant assessment data as well as expectations for age peers in general education environments?   Yes   No

C. Does each student's IEP committee determine whether advancement criteria are developmentally appropriate for a particular student?   Yes   No

D. Are behavior reductive strategies used separately from the level system (i.e., downward movement is not used as a consequence for inappropriate behavior or for failure to meet minimum criteria for a given level)?   Yes   No

  If no, check below:

  _____ 1. Downward movement is used as a consequence for inappropriate behavior.

  _____ 2. Downward movement is used as a consequence for failure to earn minimum points for a certain number of days.

V. Efficacy

A. Is each student's progress through the level system monitored?   Yes   No

B. Is there a problem-solving procedure if data indicate a lack of progress through the level system?   Yes   No

C. Do students consistently "graduate" from the level system?   Yes   No

D. Do behaviors that are addressed in the level system maintain over time and generalize across environments?   Yes   No

E. Do students who complete the level system maintain successfully in less restrictive environments?   Yes   No

F. Are self-management skills incorporated into the level system?   Yes   No

Each "No" response indicates a potential problem with your level system. For information on how to remediate the problem, refer to the corresponding section in the text.

FIGURE 6–3   Levels system checklist.

Source: *Scheurmann, B., & Webber, J. (1996). Level systems: Problems and solutions. Beyond Behavior, 7, 13. Reprinted with permission.*

Do

- Include your students, whenever possible, in planning your token program.
- Deliver the reinforcement only as a consequence of the desired behavior.
- Let the student know why a reinforcer is being given.
- Give some free tokens at the beginning of your program.
- Reduce tokens gradually so that more work is done for each reinforcer.
- Review all rules frequently.
- Exchange tokens formally.
- Consider reinforcers that are controlled by the peer group.
- Change reinforcers whenever boredom sets in. (If you become bored, your students have probably been bored for some time!)
- Make the number of tokens needed consistent with the difficulty or effort required to perform the behavior.
- Keep reinforcers appropriate to your system's levels.
- Keep a record of tokens earned for everyone to see.
- Include behavior/reinforcers and response cost/fines on the same classroom poster but in separate columns.
- Combine praise with tokens so that social reinforcement can eventually be used alone.
- Withdraw material reinforcers gradually and let social reinforcement maintain the behaviors.
- Encourage students to compete with themselves to earn tokens as they improve their own behavior.

Do Not

- Use tokens that students can obtain outside your system.
- Give away the best reinforcers at the beginning; high-level reinforcers (the best ones) should cost more and be more appealing.
- Spend tokens for your students; let them choose for themselves.

- Let students stockpile tokens.
- Let students "go in the hole."

The two case studies at the end of this chapter illustrate token economy programs for young children and teenagers, respectively.

Timeout from Reinforcement

Timeout from reinforcement was introduced in Chapter 5. As you recall, this potentially powerful procedure takes away or reduces the reinforcers students might otherwise enjoy. Detention and in-school suspension are school-wide interventions that build upon the concept of timeout from reinforcement.

PEER-MEDIATED INTERVENTIONS

What? Turn over behavioral intervention to the very class giving you such a hard time? It may sound completely out of the question. Yet many studies have proven that peers can be effectively trained to change their classmates' behaviors. Here are some reasons to adopt **peer-mediated strategies:**

1. Peers make good behavioral managers. The research has proven this repeatedly. In fact, several studies have shown that peers teach skills as well as or better than adults do.
2. Nondisabled students from toddlers to high schoolers can model and teach their peers, making it a highly versatile tool.
3. Both those teaching and those taught have benefited in the many studies of peer tutoring, whether the targets were social or academic behaviors (Lloyd, Crowley, Kohler, & Strain, 1988; Sugai & Chanter, 1989).
4. Carefully implemented peer-mediated interventions provide invaluable opportunities for appropriate social interaction among children with disabilities or within an integrated setting.
5. Through teaching others, children learn to discriminate between appropriate and

inappropriate social responses (Sugai & Chanter, 1989).

Peer-mediated interventions take advantage of a student's peer group to alter problem behaviors or to teach new ones. These interventions are especially appealing to adolescents, who prefer their contemporaries. The entire class can be involved in changing an individual's disruptive behavior or the disruptive behavior of the whole class.

Group Goal Setting and Feedback

This intervention is based on a group discussion in which peers vote on a fellow student's behavior. Each student receives a behavioral goal. Either daily or twice a week, students meet in a highly structured, 20-min group discussion to vote and give feedback under adult direction. Here are some target goals for your consideration:

- Rob will help another student during recess.
- Mario will go from his class to the library without getting a detention slip.
- Cristina will not swear during her morning classes.
- Alexa will stay awake in classes after lunch.
- Bonifacio will attend his last class.

The goals are very specific. You may wonder why they are not more ambitious; after all, wouldn't we want Alexa awake all the time? Shouldn't Bonifacio attend all classes? Two rationales support these goals. First, the behavior may be specific to a particular class. Second, the goal should shape successive approximations. We will succeed in changing behavior if we break the goal into small, attainable target behaviors and reinforce students for mastering them.

Steps for directing **group goal setting and feedback** are outlined in Table 6–3.

Peer Monitoring

To give you an idea of the versatility of peer-mediated interventions—even with younger children—take a look at a **peer-monitoring** proce-

dure. Carden-Smith and Fowler (1984) taught kindergarten children to issue and withdraw points from their classmates. To introduce the strategy, they initiated a teacher-directed points program. The eight children received or lost a point for obeying or disobeying each of these rules: cleaning up after play, waiting appropriately, and going to and from the bathroom appropriately. After a few training sessions, the class was divided into two teams that changed membership each day. Each child on each team then earned (or lost) teacher-distributed points for the designated behaviors. In this system, the token exchange was simple: Children with three points each day could vote on and participate in play activities; children with two points could participate but not vote; children with one point were required to remain inside and complete clean-up chores.

The peer-mediated feature of the program built upon the introductory teacher-directed program. During the peer-mediated intervention, the teacher appointed a team captain who issued and withdrew points from classmates. (The privilege of team captain was awarded students who had earned three points the previous day.) The program showed that even young children with learning and behavior problems could manage a basic token economy. Remember to get approval through the IEP process before using this procedure.

Peer Management

Students can learn to reinforce and ignore their classmates' misbehavior through a **peer manager strategy,** peer confrontation. Peer confrontation is a combined teacher-directed and peer-mediated intervention in which elementary school students alter one another's problem behaviors (Salend, Jantzen, & Giek, 1992). The peer confrontation works this way: The teacher calls on the group with questions such as, "Who can tell Jake what problem he is having with his behavior?" or "Who can help Sarina figure out a different way to be acting right now?" The teacher then selects a volunteer, who explains the problem behavior and offers an

TABLE 6–3 Strategy for Conducting Group Goal Setting and Feedback

1. For each student in the group, develop a social behavior objective written in language the student can understand. Typical goals might be to speak up in the class discussion times, to share materials with others on the playground, to play baseball without teasing classmates, or to play with at least one other child at recess.
2. Write each student's name, goal, and the date on which the goal was announced on a separate sheet in the group notebook. Record the feedback of the student's peers each day during the group session.
3. Schedule a 15- to 20-min daily session for the group goal-setting and feedback sessions.
4. Ask everyone to sit in a circle for the group session. Instruct students that this is a time when everyone will speak and that no one is to speak out of turn. Explain further that each student has some behavior that warrants improvement and that the time will be spent talking about our behavior goals.
5. Explain to each student on the first day of the group goal-setting session what her goal is for the next week or two. It is recommended that individual goals be maintained for at least 10 school days.
6. On subsequent days of the group goal-setting session, turn to the first student sitting next to you in the group, announce that student's goal, and state either "I think you made your goal today" or "I don't think you made your goal today." Then provide limited feedback in the form of a statement to support your evaluation. A typical evaluation statement might be, "I like the way you cooperated with Charlie on the playground" or "I don't like the way you took the baseball away from Jane."
7. Request that the student sitting next to the target individual now evaluate that individual's progress toward the goal. Reinforce eye contact with the target student and other constructive feedback. Be certain that each student in the group provides both an evaluation and a feedback statement. Repeat this process until each student in the group has provided the target individual with an opinion and a feedback statement.
8. Tally the votes of making or not making the goal and announce the result. If the student has made the goal, invite others in the group to give her a handclap or other reinforcement you have chosen. If the student has not made the goal, the group makes no response.
9. Repeat this process until all members of the group have received feedback on their goals.
10. If the group has developed a consistently productive performance, you may decide to allow one of the students to be the group leader. This student then reads each student's goals and requests feedback from members of the group. These goals could still be teacher assigned, or in the case of an advanced group, the goals could be self- or peer assigned.

Source: From Kerr, M. M., & Ragland, E. U. (1979). PowWow: A group procedure for reducing classroom behavior problems. The Pointer, 24, 92–96. Reprinted with permission of the Helen Dwight Reid Educational Foundation. Published by Heldref Publications, 4000 Albemarie St., N.W., Washington, DC 20016. Copyright 1986.

alternative. Students learn this strategy through teacher-led practice and role-playing. Here are some guidelines for using peer confrontation effectively:

1. To minimize embarrassment, consider calling upon the entire group for a quick assessment of the class members' behavior: "How are we doing? Does anyone notice a problem we need to correct?"
2. Watch for signs that students are avoiding the activity or the approach or are trying to "gang up on one another." These effects of punishment were observed only initially in two studies (Salend et al., 1992), but you may find that your group responds differently.
3. Emphasize positive responses when you teach the system to your students. Role-play correct responses.
4. Don't use this approach unless you have a good relationship with your students, as they may feel that you are singling out their behavior publicly. Encourage students to offer behavioral alternatives and to de-emphasize comments regarding the problem behaviors. One of the advantages of peer interventions such as this one is

that it gives students an opportunity to solve behavioral problems and to express alternatives in words that make sense to their peers.

5. Be sure children's participation is cleared through their IEP teams, if applicable.

Peer Extinction and Reinforcement

Recall what you read earlier in this chapter about the importance of reviewing classroom and school rules with students. Could you use peer managers to review and provide feedback on rule following and rule violations?

Group-Oriented Contingencies

Token systems are powerful behavior intervention systems, but they do not necessarily take into account the interactions among students. Also, because reinforcement is based on individual performance, the teacher must deal with record keeping. Individual differences in the amount of reinforcement may create jealousy, competition, and theft of tokens.

On the other hand, contingencies related to group characteristics take advantage of social reinforcers controlled by the peer group and are adaptable to a variety of situations. A **group contingency** also reduces the number of individual consequences the teacher must deliver, which saves time from behavior intervention duties.

The basic characteristic of **group-oriented contingencies** is group reinforcement. Whether the target is an individual student or the entire class, the group shares in the consequences of the behavior. In many cases, group-oriented contingencies are devised to deal with specific problem behaviors. Nevertheless, they can be used to establish appropriate behaviors and to prevent problems. There are three categories of group-oriented contingencies: dependent, independent, and interdependent.

In a **dependent group-oriented contingency** the peer performance of certain group members determines the consequence received by the entire group (Williamson, Williamson, Watkins, & Hughes, 1992). This arrangement works best when the behavior of the large group is better than that of the target student or students. This may not be the best plan for a group whose behavior is generally disruptive. The primary characteristic of an **independent group-oriented contingency** is that the same consequence is applied to individual group members. Contingency contracting is an independent group-oriented contingency. In an **interdependent group-oriented contingency,** each student must reach a prescribed level of behavior before the entire group receives a consequence.

Which of the three types is the most effective? Research is mixed (Brantley & Webster, 1998). To be sure that a group-oriented contingency does not create negative peer pressure, observe these guidelines:

- Use a group reinforcement rather than a response cost.
- Be sure that the behavior target and criteria are within the students' reach.
- Include "language loopholes" that make the contingency easier to master and harder to sabotage (e.g., as soon as . . . whenever . . . if . . .).
- "Easy in . . . easy out": Use the principle of successive approximations.
- Avoid language that implies an ultimatum, such as "If you don't do . . ., then I will do. . . ." "Unless you do . . ., we will not do. . . ."
- Get a colleague to help you as you write your contingencies. Consider together the worst-case scenario for your proposed group-oriented contingency and alter your contingency accordingly.

Table 6–4 illustrates the three types of group contingencies. Pay special attention to each example. Can you identify the "loophole" in each one? How was an ultimatum avoided?

One nice variation of a group contingency is the "Hero Procedure," in which one student earns reinforcers for the rest of the group. As one teacher

TABLE 6–4 Group Contingency Arrangements

Type of Group Contingency	Examples
Interdependent	If all students turn in homework on a given day, I will put two marbles in the jar. If, on Friday, there are at least eight marbles in the jar, I will add a shooter (large) marble. When the jar is full, the class will have a pizza party—teacher's treat!
	Each table of students has a can with six Popsicle sticks. I take away a Popsicle stick when a student breaks a rule. If the group still has five sticks on Friday, they get to pick out a treat from the treat bag.
	If everyone remembers to bring his math books to class for four consecutive days, they will not be assigned homework for the fifth day of class.
Independent	Each student with fewer than one tardy per grading period will receive a free homework pass.
	Each student who finishes his research project on time will receive a "dog ate my homework" pass.
Dependent	If a student who returns to the classroom from the in-school suspension room has a good day (i.e., no warnings and classwork completed), all students will get to drop their lowest daily classwork grade. (This recognizes the supportive role of classmates.)
	Three students in this class served detention last week for pushing in the hall. If these three students do not get detention for two weeks, the entire class will get to play their favorite music during indoor recess.
	As soon as a group of students completes their science project, the class wins a free homework pass.

described this intervention (Briand, personal communication, 1986), "Not only does this procedure help to improve the target student's behavior, but it also stops other class members from reinforcing that behavior that you have deemed inappropriate—they want to get the reinforcers!" Here is an example of a group-oriented procedure that incorporates a hero procedure:

This will be a three-week mathematics estimation contest. If anyone in your class guesses the correct number of cubes in the container, everyone in the class will receive a prize. If more than one person (within or across classes) guesses the correct number, more than one class will receive prizes. If no one guesses the correct answer, then the person guessing closest to the correct number during week 3 will be the winner and his/her class will receive prizes. Each week you will receive written information about whether you guessed correctly or were too high or too low in your estimation. (Williamson et al., 1992, p. 418)

Good Behavior Game

The Good Behavior Game (Barrish, Saunders, & Wolf, 1969) is yet another variation on a group contingency. This intervention involves teams of students competing on the basis of their behavior in the classroom (Saigh & Umar, 1983; Salend, Reynolds, & Coyle, 1989). Salend et al. (1989) used the Good Behavior Game in an individualized format to improve the behaviors of high school students in a special education classroom. Students joined a team according to their target behaviors (e.g., inappropriate verbalizations, cursing, drumming/tapping). Each team, therefore, had a common goal. Salend et al. (1989) reported that the teams created positive peer pressure and that students enjoyed being rewarded for their behavioral improvements. This individualized approach (basing the team target behaviors on identified needs of students) is a good way to comply with the requirements of your students' IEPs. Figure 6–4 is a consultant's description of the Good Behavior Game for a group of "rowdy" sixth graders.

SELF-MEDIATED INTERVENTIONS

One of our goals with students who are disruptive is to promote self-control of their problem behaviors. For example, students whose behavior has responded to a token economy can become gradually more independent of external control when they use self-management strategy (Scott, 1998). In recent years we have learned more about such valuable tools as self-instruction and self-evaluation (Lam et al., 1994). (For a review of self-management research with students who have behavioral disorders, see Nelson, Smith, Young, & Dodd, 1991.) In this section we focus on three procedures: self-monitoring, self-evaluation, and self-instruction.

Self-Monitoring

Self-monitoring or **self-recording** allows the student to record his own behaviors. Perhaps you have tried self-monitoring for dieting, smoking cessation, or tracking your physical fitness goals. Another way to think of self-management is the correspondence between what we say we are doing (or will do) and what we do (Miller, Strain, Boyd, Jarzynka, & McFetridge, 1993). Some authors call this a "say-do reinforcement" or "do-say reinforcement" model (Paniagua, 1990). Before you begin a self-monitoring program, consider the suggestions in Table 6–5.

One of your decisions in designing this intervention is to select a practical monitoring form. Figure 6–5 shows the monitoring form used by Keith.

Space is provided for tallies each day and period, although you might find that your student will at first need to monitor in only one or two periods a day. Printing the target behavior definition at the bottom of the form is a good idea; it helps

the child remember what she is monitoring. The form could be modified for an older or more sophisticated student.

Once you have trained a student to self-record, you can move to a behavioral intervention program. During the first few days of the program (at least 3 days), ask the student to self-record disruptive behaviors without additional intervention. The data from these sessions will provide you with a baseline assessment of the student's performance. The next step in this program is to establish contingencies under which the student receives a reinforcer for reducing the number of disruptions per session. A student might use a contract form to record the reinforcement to be earned by controlling problem behaviors. In still another approach the student might self-reinforce without using tokens or contracts. For some students, self-recording alone may reduce disruptions.

Whether you use self-monitoring alone or as part of a larger behavioral intervention system, encourage students to reduce disruptions and increase appropriate behavior relative to their own baseline performance. For example, a student whose baseline assessment indicates that he is off task 80% of the period could be encouraged to improve his performance little by little until he reaches a mutually agreed-upon goal (e.g., on task 80% of the period). By setting small but reasonable goals for students and gradually increasing expectations for their behavior, you help ensure that the self-monitoring program will be successful. This strategy is referred to as **shaping** of successive approximations (see Chapter 4).

Self-Evaluation

Self-evaluation requires a student to assess the quality of her behavior, while in self-monitoring the student simply counts her behavior. Even very young children can learn to self-evaluate their behaviors. Miller et al. (1993) taught four preschoolers with disabilities to self-evaluate their behaviors with a "thumbs up" or "thumbs down" signal

Dear Mrs. Schaeffer,

I'm aware from our conversation that you are having a difficult time with your sixth graders. You told me that they can't seem to get to class on time and that it takes them at least 10 minutes to settle down.

I talked with you briefly about the possibility of trying out a game that requires team members to work toward a goal to win a reward. Here are some specifics about setting up this game:

1. It's been called the "Good Behavior Game," but your class can choose any name for it (e.g., "Party! Party Possibilities").

2. If you have not yet established and posted conduct rules for your room, do so before you start the game.

3. To set up rules, talk with the students and allow them input. Suggest your own ideas and consider theirs. Agree upon a limited number of reasonable rules, and write them behaviorally in language the students understand. Examples:

   - Do not kick, hit, shove, or push other students.
   - Keep your hands and feet to yourself.
   - Raise your hand when you want to say something.
   - Talk when it's your turn.

   Set up contingencies (the relationship between behaviors and their consequences), and maintain consistent consequences when rules are broken.

4. Find out what might be powerful reinforcers for the students. Poll them, or offer them the possibility of free time for the last half of a Friday class each week. (I will use this as a sample reinforcer for the remainder of this program description.)

5. Divide the class into two teams.

6. Review rules and contingencies with the students.

7. State that 80% of each team's members will be required to reach or exceed this goal: to have at least one marker left out of three next to their names at the end of class each day. If 80% of a team reaches this goal, team members will be rewarded with free time on Friday. The 80% criterion (as opposed to a higher percentage) is set to prevent the same one or two disruptive students from ruining a team's chances of winning free time. Unreasonably high criterion levels might lead to low morale and lack of motivation among team members. For students who have serious behavior problems, repeated failures to achieve the goal in a game where "all must achieve to receive" could lead to their being ridiculed, ostracized, or scapegoated. Prevent this by specifying a reasonable criterion and by setting up individual problems and/or contingencies for the extremely disruptive students.

8. Explain to the students that the goal must be reached in one specified class period during the first week. During the second week, it must be achieved in two specified classes. Continue adding a period per week until you're at the point where the goal must be achieved during all periods the students are with you for instruction.

9. Hang a poster or use bulletin boards for each team, listing the members. At the beginning of each class, every student should have three markers next to his or her name. (For markers, use rock concert ticket stubs, small, laminated mock "record albums," or some other easily made or acquired items.)

10. Remove one marker from beside a student's name each time he or she breaks a rule (e.g., punches somebody, arrives late).

11. At the end of the period, determine if 80% of each team's members have at least one marker next to their names. If 80% or more of one team achieved criterion, they win the privilege of receiving 20 minutes of free time during the last half of a Friday class. At this time, they will be free to go to the cafeteria for a "party." Enlist the aid of another staff member who can supervise the students as they talk, listen to radios or tape players, and drink cans of pop that they've brought or bought. The other team will be required to

FIGURE 6–4 A consultant's description.

Source: *Prisby, personal communication, 1987.*

complete work in the classroom during the same period on Friday. If 80% of both teams achieve the goal, then all students will be awarded free "party" time.

12. Run the game for entire class periods. Even though most of this group's problems occur during the first 10 minutes, you don't want to operate it for 10 minutes and then leave 30 minutes open to possible disruptions. Set the rules and contingencies for the full 40 minutes. Self-control will probably be hardest to demonstrate during the initial 10 minutes, but it may get easier once they get over that "hump" each day. And we hope that it will increase throughout the course of the game.

13. Remember to provide lots of positive verbal reinforcement for both groups and individual team improvements.

14. Again, severely disruptive students may be good candidates for individualized behavior management programs. You may want to consider what you'll do, though, when students occasionally lose all three markers in the same class. To prevent their getting completely out of control once they've broken three rules and lost all markers, perhaps you could arrange the following: If a student breaks four rules in one class period, he or she receives one day of detention. If he or she breaks five rules, he or she is assigned to two days of detention, and so on.

Good luck with this game!

Mrs. Prisby

FIGURE 6–4   A consultant's description—*Continued.*
Source: *Prisby, personal communication, 1987.*

TABLE 6–5   Guidelines for Self-Management Strategies

1. Consult the section on token economy programs for ideas about selecting appropriate target behaviors.
2. Decide how this behavior might be measured most easily by the student.
3. Some studies have shown that students perform better when they record an academic behavior rather than merely recording whether they are on task (Lam, Cole, Shapiro, & Bambara, 1994). Students may use a self-correction aid to see if they have completed a math problem right, for example. Even though this procedure takes a bit of time, the results indicate that it is a preferable approach.
4. Be sure your students can correctly identify the target behaviors, through explanation, discussion, and practice.
5. Consider using a question format. For example, the student's form might read: "Did I get this problem right?" YES _____ NO _____
6. Reinforce students not only for improvements in their performance but also for not cheating! Unannounced teacher-monitoring of the student's target behaviors will allow you to see if the student is recording his behavior honestly.
7. If a student is oppositional to the procedure, supplement it with a positive contingency for cooperation or with another strategy (Lam et al., 1994).
8. Try to make the self-monitoring as minimally intrusive as possible (Reid & Harris, 1993).
9. Choose a behavior that is relevant to the student (Reid & Harris, 1993).
10. Work with the student to develop a procedure that is enjoyable, not a chore (Reid & Harris, 1993).

	Reading	Math	Language Arts	Science	Social Studies	Total
Monday	//		/	//	/	⑥
Tuesday	/	/	/		/	④
Wednesday	//		//		///	⑦
Thursday		/	///	/	//	⑦
Friday	/	/	///			⑤

I will put a tally mark in the box each time I get out of my seat without asking permission during class. I know I am out of my seat when my backside is not touching my chair and I have not asked permission to leave my seat.

Name **KEITH**   Date Begun **2-22**   Teacher **COVALASKI**

FIGURE 6–5   Self-monitoring form.

TABLE 6–6   Guidelines for Training Students to Use Self-Instruction

1. Analyze the task for the student, listing necessary steps. For example, the task might involve specific steps such as reading the problem, writing out the necessary information, and performing the operations. Or the task might be more generic, requiring steps such as getting out pencil and paper, opening the text to the correct page, not talking to others, or signaling when help is needed.

   Consider including specific questions about task demands, planning statements, self-guiding instructions, coping statements for errors, and self-praise statements.

2. With help from the student, rewrite the steps in the student's conversational style. For example, one primary school student developed these self-instructions:

   "Okay, to be a good student, I need to stay in my seat, not bother others, and complete my assignment. I have to take my time and do the work the way Mrs. Smith showed me. Good, I did it. Right on!"

3. Practice the self-instruction procedure with the student. Begin by saying the words together aloud. Then whisper as the student self-instructs aloud. Finally, have the student whisper alone.

4. Enable the student to use the self-instructions in the classroom. If possible, allow the student to whisper quietly; this may be more effective (and easier to monitor!) than covert, or silent, rehearsal.

Note: *The material for this table was taken from Albion, F. Development and implementation of self-monitoring/self-instruction procedures in the classroom. Paper presented at CEC's 58th Annual International Convention, Philadelphia, 1980.*

as the teacher pointed to visual depictions of appropriate behaviors on a poster. Behaviors included cleaning up the play area, following teacher instructions, and interacting with peers appropriately.

Self-Instruction

In a **self-instruction** program, the student is trained to whisper statements that will help accomplish the task. Table 6–6 provides guidelines for using a self-instruction procedure. Be sure to analyze the self-instructional task before attempting to use this procedure with a student.

SUMMARY

This chapter offers you many suggestions for managing or preventing disruptive behavior. Schoolwide strategies include detention and in-school suspension. In these, as in all approaches, we urge close communication among staff and with families. Our teacher-mediated strategies include the ever-popular token economy—an outstanding way to set up classroom-wide contingencies. To enhance your overall contingency management, plan group contingencies. Finally, the self-management strategies promote generalization of new behaviors to other settings.

CHAPTER 6 CASE STUDY

Token Economy[1]

Wyllie Keefer

My classroom is a part-time resource room with the students coming on various schedules. My 13 students are in sixth, seventh, and eighth grades, with the majority of students in eighth. The age group is between 11 and 14 years old. There is such a diversity of abilities among the students that grade-level curriculum is difficult to assess on a general basis. Some students are nonreaders, some do not know their multiplication tables, while others are on grade level but behavior problems have deterred them from academic success.

When needed, the students who are the readers or mathematicians are the classroom peer tutors. Their special abilities come in handy when other students are having difficulties in their mainstream classes or particular assignments in the resource room. Two of my students are extremely talented in art and are

always excited and interested in any lesson or project dealing with art.

Our school day begins at 7:40 A.M. and ends at 2:33 P.M. There are eight periods a day; each period is 42 min long. Most of my students spend first period in my room (directly after first period is homeroom). First period usually goes very well, with a calm environment.

I bring my students to my room from study halls, for extra monitoring time, if I sense there may be trouble brewing or a potential crisis. Many days my students are sent to my room to have tests read to them, to get help with classwork/assignments, or if their behavior is disrupting a mainstream class. I have a full-time aide so there are always two adults in our room for the kids to model. Together with our students' current IEP teams, we designed a four-level behavior chart listing "Earners" and "Losers." To be sure that our students really understood the four levels, we made four posters. Each poster showed the "Earners" and "Losers" for that level. We placed

[1]Reprinted with author's permission.

the posters next to each other on our classroom wall. We included the values assigned to these behaviors so there was no question as to how much a behavior earns or loses (see Figure 6–6).

The selection of behaviors to be targeted is a group activity. The students are asked to contribute their ideas of expected or appropriate behaviors in school, to include along with my expectations.

I divided the chalkboard into four sections and labeled them Level I to Level IV. The students then participated and decided which behaviors would be listed at which level.

- Level I—Behaviors everyone can do, easy to achieve.
- Level II—Slightly more demanding than Level I.
- Level III—Bigger effort, trying to make a change.
- Level IV—Major effort, highest level.

Bonuses

Students can earn extra points (money) when they go "beyond the call of duty" and do something out of the ordinary. For example, a student of mine recently found a wallet filled with money, credit cards, and a driver's license. Other students were arguing over how they would split the cash. My student grabbed the wallet from them and turned it into the office. As it turned out, the wallet belonged to the art teacher. She was not only relieved but impressed that one of the "special" students had fought to do the right thing. This deed of honor earned a lot of bonus bucks! Bonuses will always be positive and awarded as surprises. Other examples would be when one student compliments another, lends a pencil, or helps another student or teacher. In my particular environment, there are many opportunities to reward behavior, however small!

The design of our checkbook money system is twofold. Each student receives his own personal checkbook. With help from the art teacher, the class creates their own checkbook covers made from heavy cardboard and wallpaper samples. I have designed checks and withdrawal slips.

For *earners*, the student receives *deposits*; for *losers, withdrawals*. Behaviors are assigned a dollar amount. Each period the student self-monitors the behaviors that were exhibited, negative or positive. At the end of the period, we schedule five minutes to go over their checklist and we agree on deposits or withdrawals earned. Mainstream teachers also have checklists and are familiar with our system. They have a supply of previously made deposit slips with money amounts and behaviors on them. They check each behavior earned or lost during that particular period. Each student brings back the deposit slip to enter the earned or lost amounts into their accounts.

The second advantage of using a fictitious banking system is to teach the students, for their employable future, that if they do a good job, they will get a paycheck, or perhaps a bonus/raise. If they do a bad job, argue, or forget their responsibilities, they can be fired, lose pay, and so on. They learn how to keep and balance a checking account, along with practicing basic, consumer math.

The banking system is not only a self-monitoring system but is also an interdependent contingency. Every student is responsible for her behaviors, and the class can benefit or lose out, together. My former classroom was an "every person for himself" classroom. I changed it because I believe a group plan helps students learn that together everyone achieves more. The more "money" each student "earns," the more reinforcers the group has to choose from.

The students know how often their behavior will be monitored by referring to the timeframe listed at the bottom, at each level, of the chart

Earners

Level I		Level II		Level III		Level IV	
Behaviors	**Cost**	**Behaviors**	**Cost**	**Behaviors**	**Cost**	**Behaviors**	**Cost**
Try to follow classroom rules	$2	Respect others	$3	Ignore other student's inappropriate behavior	$4	Follow classroom rules all day	$5
Be in seat when bell rings	$2	Bring book, pen/pencil & worksheet to class	$3	Participate in class	$4	Complete all assignments and turn them in on time	$5
Stay in your seat	$2	Bring homework & worksheets to class	$3	Hand in completed assignments 80% of the time	$4	Use appropriate behavior 90% of the time	$5
Raise your hand	$2	Neat papers	$3	Work without disturbing others	$4		
Use kind & courteous language	$2	Appropriate behavior on bus, in hallways, or in cafeteria	$3	Keep checkbook current and correct	$4	Be self-monitored 90% of the time	$5
Write down assignments	$2	Remain on task 70% of the time	$3	Organize school work	$4	Have no discipline offenses all week	$5
Have all teachers fill out deposit slip	$2	Start and try to complete assignments 70% of the time	$3				
Greet adults and classmates	$2	All teachers filled out deposit slip	$3				

Losers

Level I		Level II		Level III		Level IV	
Break a classroom rule	$1	Have physical or verbal outbursts	$10	Fail to turn in assignments	$3	Receive anecdotals, DT, ISS, or OSS	$20
Use vulgarities, swearing, or inappropriate gestures	$5	Argue	$2	Disrupt class	$15	Miss assignments	$4
Be out of seat	$1	Not be prepared	$2	Cheat on checkbook	$3	Break a classroom rule	$4
Be tardy	$1	Be off-task	$2	Receive anecdotals, DT, ISS, or OSS	$3		
Receive anecdotals, DT, ISS, or OSS	$5	Receive anecdotals, DT, ISS, or OSS	$10				
Have physical or verbal outbursts	$5	Fail to keep checkbook up-to date	$2				
Fail to keep checkbook up-to-date	$1						

Monitoring

To be monitored at the end of each period (5 min.)	To be monitored at the end of each period (5 min.)	To be monitored at the end of each day	To be monitored at the end of each week on Fridays (1/2 hour)
Also on Fridays (1/2 hour)	Also on Fridays (1/2 hour)	Also on Fridays (1/2 hour)	

FIGURE 6–6 Level system poster.

posted in the classroom. They are reminded when we go over the plan together before implementation.

The reinforcers and response costs are posted in the classroom. Students know that anecdotals (office referrals), DT (detention), ISS (in-school suspension), and OSS (out-of-school suspension) are included as "losers," based on our school-wide plan.

When I initially introduced the idea of a banking system for behavior, I was delighted that my students thought it would be a lot of fun and a challenge. (They did suggest that the plan include *real* money!) They helped me make a list of reinforcers that they would like to be able to earn with their "bank accounts" (see Table 6–7).

Here are my troubleshooting guidelines:

- *If a student loses the checkbook*: Student's behavior for that period goes to zero.
- *If students cannot decide on the same reinforcer for the week*: The class must resolve this problem among themselves. They may discuss the situation, vote majority rules, secret ballot, or other ways the students come up with to solve the problem, or they may vote to have alternate choices.
- *If a student does not move up to the next level*: An individual contract will be made between the teacher and student. The student will choose a particular reinforcer he or she would like to earn.
- *If a mainstream teacher will not cooperate*: For example, a student chooses to "buy" a test or homework assignment and the teacher does not agree. The mainstream teacher must then decide to offer other reinforcers that are acceptable and achievable in their room.

Including New Students

Before a new student arrives in class, we review the program within their IEP team. We figure an average balance for her initial deposit into the checking account. Depending on which level the class is on, the new student will be observed for two weeks and an individual adjustment will have to be made as to her needs and level.

Modifications to the System

Controlled/creative tinkering is an important factor to consider when designing and making successful any behavioral management plan. Problems may arise at any point of my banking/checkbook plan. I discuss problems with the students as a group. They have helpful suggestions, ideas, and negative comments. This plan is for them and I take their concerns or the question/problem at hand and deal with it on an individual basis. Sample modifications are to "up the ante," to increase the dollar amounts for deposits, to provide earners or losers, or to re-arrange the levels or change the reinforcers.

Summary of the Steps
For the Banking System

1. Discuss behavioral management plan with students. Introduce the Bank checking account system.
2. Help each student make a checkbook out of heavy cardboard and wallpaper samples.
3. Complete each checkbook with a check register, checks, and a supply of deposit slips. (The teacher designs and copies behavior deposit slips.)
4. IEP teams, students, and teachers will decide upon behavior earners and losers (to be sorted into Levels I–IV) and the reinforcers the students want to earn.
5. Draw charts for earners, losers, and reinforcers. Post it in the classroom.
6. Each Monday, the class decides on which reinforcers the whole class will be working toward for the week.
7. Each Monday, deposit the following dollar amounts into their accounts:

Level I	$10.00
Level II	$20.00
Level III	$30.00
Level IV	$40.00

8. Each period, check off behaviors on preprinted deposit slips.

TABLE 6–7 Reinforcers to Accompany Banking System

Reinforcers			
Level I—Minimum Balance $12	**Level II—Minimum Balance $24**	**Level III—Minimum Balance $36**	**Level IV—Minimum Balance $48**
10 min of free time at the end of each period	Mrs. Keefer to buy new game for the room	Get a pet (hamster, rabbit, gerbil) for the classroom	Walk to bowling alley (bowl for two periods)
Skip a homework assignment	Make a treat in the home-ec room	Help work in the school store	Paint wall mural in classroom
Movie day	Go to the library for an extra period	Eat lunch at the high school	Use weight room at high school
Popcorn party	Have a free day	Walk to Taco Bell or Dairy Queen	Go to Heights Elem., read to a class
Can of pop	Have a pizza party	Use gym for free time	Hold a car wash for the faculty
Candy store coupon	Skip a test	Do a special tech-ed project	Walk to Heights Plaza
Computer time	Listen to music in room	Do a special art project	Take a field trip

9. Instruct each student to keep their checkbooks current.
10. Students *add* earners, *subtract* losers, and enter total deposits or withdrawals on their check register.
11. Monitor students according to the level timetables.
12. Supplementary procedures: If a student does not cooperate, consider the following consequences:

    Written assignment as to why they are having problems
    Extra assignments to earn a (+) higher balance
    Detention
13. Bonus points/additional money earned entitles a student to:

    Choose an additional *reinforcer*
    Become Bank President, monitoring some part of the system
    Offer suggestions from the students
14. If the students have saved enough money, at any time, they may write a check to "buy" the following:

Study Hall pass	$ 3.00
A homework pass	$10.00
A detention pass	$15.00
A day of In-School Suspension pass	$20.00

(I have discussed this with the administration, and they have given me their approval.)

A Combination Program Created for an Inclusive Preschool Classroom: Token Economy and Self-Monitoring[1]

MeShelda Jackson

The following program describes a token economy in combination with a self-monitoring system for a preschool classroom of typically developing children, children with behavioral disorders, a teacher, a teacher's aide, and a part-time speech-language pathologist. The children's ages range from three to five years. Some of the behaviors identified by their IEP teams include temper tantrums, kicking, pushing, and hitting. Self-management is incorporated through the children's use of a self-monitoring sheet.

Component One: Classroom Rules Posters

First, the IEP teams select appropriate behaviors for the classroom and its learning centers. Next, we classroom teachers take pictures of each child displaying the appropriate behavior in the classroom and at their centers. The general classroom rules are posted in the front of the room. Next the children and the adults discuss and show pictures of inappropriate and appropriate behaviors in the classroom and at each learning center. Then my aide and I post pictures of the children exhibiting appropriate behaviors on the rules chart, one for each center area and one general chart for the classroom. The pictures allow the children to identify themselves exhibiting appropriate behavior. Before the children go to their centers each day, we review the rules (see Figure 6–7).

Component Two: Token Economy

The tokens for the token economy system are kept in each adult's apron pocket. Circles are used as tokens for the charts. The yellow circles mean the child gets the number of circles by that specific rule. The white circles mean that the child loses the number of circles by that rule. Each child starts the day earning tokens for exhibiting any of the appropriate behaviors previously discussed. A child can earn up to four circles in one center. Each time they exhibit the positive behavior, they get a yellow circle to place on their self-monitoring sheet. If they do not exhibit the appropriate behavior, they lose one or more white circles. If they have earned all four circles when time is up at the learning center, they can select from reinforcers previously decided upon before they go to their next activity. Here is a list of sample reinforcers chosen by the adults and children:

> stickers
> hugs
> having a book read to you
> emptying the wastebasket
> holding the flag for the morning pledge
> erasing the board
> feeding the fish
> leader of the line (recess, lunch, or other field trips)
> being in charge of a game or activity
> watering the plants
> free time in the center of your choice
> choosing a friend with whom to play
> sitting with the teacher at lunch

Component Three: Peer Management

At the end of each center activity, the children decide if anyone did not exhibit the appropriate behavior. We all discuss how to improve the behavior for the next center activity.

[1]Reprinted with author's permission.

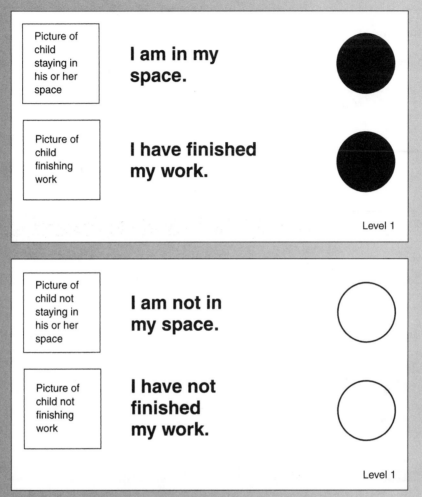

| Picture of child staying in his or her space | I am in my space. | ⬤ |
| Picture of child finishing work | I have finished my work. | ⬤ |

Level 1

| Picture of child not staying in his or her space | I am not in my space. | ◯ |
| Picture of child not finishing work | I have not finished my work. | ◯ |

Level 1

FIGURE 6–7 Examples of charts for classroom rules.

The teachers' job is to praise the specific positive behaviors whenever we see them. Any one of us in the room can distribute tokens. When the appropriate behavior is exhibited, we provide the circle as soon as possible. We keep a separate card on each child that explains his behavior/s to be decreased.

We then record on the card the frequency and the area where the behavior occurred. The teacher should record positive and disruptive behaviors that occur. A check is added every time the child exhibits the target behavior or positive behavior. For each level, the behaviors are checked all during the day after each center activity.

If the child continues to perform inappropriate behavior (hurting, throwing, hitting, or kicking, etc.) after the loss of circles, then the first step is to remind the child about the appropriate behavior and review the rule with her. The

| Student's Name _____ |
| Behavior _____ |

Center	Mon	Tue	Wed	Thu	Fri	Total
Reading						
Math						
Science						
Art						
Play						
Music						
Teacher						
Classroom						
Total						

FIGURE 6–8   Behavior checklist for teachers.

next consequence is to remove the child from the activity and ask her to sit in a chair for two minutes, away from the activity. She has to state the rule before returning to play. If the child continues to demonstrate inappropriate behavior, the positive reinforcer previously earned for that level is taken away (response cost).

DISCUSSION QUESTIONS

1. Which strategies are preferable for younger students? Older students?
2. When are peer-mediated strategies preferable to teacher-mediated approaches?
3. How can several strategies be combined to reduce disruptive behaviors?
4. What are some possible mistakes one might make in implementing a token economy?
5. For what disruptive behaviors is self-monitoring a good choice?
6. What is the importance of levels within a token economy?
7. Describe the hierarchy of timeout from reinforcement strategies.
8. How can parents be involved in interventions for disruptive behavior?
9. What can a teacher do to *prevent* disruptive behavior?
10. Give three examples of ways we measure disruptive behaviors.

REFERENCES

Alberto, P. A., & Troutman, A. C. (1999). *Applied behavior analysis for teachers: Influencing student performance* (5th ed.). Upper Saddle River, NJ: Merrill/Prentice Hall.

Allen, L. J., Howard, V. F., Sweeney, W. J., & McLaughlin, T. F. (1993). Use of contingency contracting to increase on-task behavior with primary students. *Psychological Reports*, 73, 905–906.

Barrish, H. H., Saunders, M., & Wolf, M. M. (1969). Good behavior game: Effects of individual contingencies for group consequences on disruptive behavior in a classroom are reviewed with the class. *Journal of Applied Behavior Analysis*, 2, 119–124.

Bicanich, P. (1986). *So you want to try a token economy*. Unpublished manuscript, University of Pittsburgh.

Brantly, D. C., & Webster, R. E. (1998). Use of an independent group contingency management system in a regular classroom setting. *Psychology in the Schools*, 10, 60–66.

Buehler, D., Jr., Patterson, G. R., & Furniss, J. M. (1966). The reinforcement of behavior in institutional settings. *Behavior Research and Therapy*, 4, 157–167.

Carden-Smith, L. K., & Fowler, S. A. (1984). Positive peer pressure: The effects of peer monitoring on children's disruptive behavior. *Journal of Applied Behavior Analysis*, 17(2), 213–227.

Colvin, G., Kameenui, E. J., & Sugai, G. (1993). Reconceptualizing behavior management and school-wide discipline in general education. *Education and Treatment of Children*, 16(4), 361–381.

Crosser, S. (1992). Managing the early childhood classroom. *Young Children*, 47(2), 23–29.

Fifer, F. L. (1986). Effective classroom management. *Academic Therapy*, 21, 401–410.

Gunter, P. L., et al. (1995). On the move: Using teacher student proximity to improve student's behavior. *Teaching Exceptional Children*, 28 (1), 12–14

Jones, D. B., & Van Houten, R. (1985). The use of daily quizzes and public posting to decrease the disruptive behavior of secondary school students. *Education and Treatment of Children*, 8(2), 91–106.

Kelley, M. L., & McCain, A. P. (1995). Promoting academic performance in inattentive children: The relative efficacy of school-home notes with and without response cost. *Behavior Modification*, 19(3), 357–375.

Lam, A. L., Cole, C. L., Shapiro, E. S., & Bambara, L. M. (1994). Relative effects of self-monitoring on-task behavior, academic accuracy and disruptive behavior in students with behavior disorders. *School Psychology Review*, 23(1), 44–58.

Miller, L. J., Strain, P. S., Boyd, K., Jarzynka, J., & McFetridge, M. (1993). The effects of classwide self-assessment on preschool children's engagement in transition, free play, and small group instruction. *Early Education and Development*, 4(3), 162–181.

National Crisis Prevention Institute, Inc. (1987). *Nonviolent crisis intervention: Participant workbook*. Brookfield, WI: National Crisis Prevention Institute, Inc.

Nelson, J. R., Colvin, G., Petty, D., & Smith, D. J. (1995). *The effects of a school-wide instructional discipline program on students' social behavior in common areas of the school*. Unpublished manuscript, Eastern Washington University.

Nelson, J. R., Smith, D. J., Young, R. K., & Dodd, J. M. (1991). A review of self-management outcome research conducted with students who exhibit behavioral disorders. *Behavioral Disorders*, 16(3), 169–179.

Ozvold, L. A. (1996). Does teacher demeanor affect the behavior of students? *Teaching and Change*, 3(2), 1996, 159–172.

Paniagua, F. A. (1990). A procedural analysis of correspondence training techniques. *The Behavior Analyst*, 13, 107–119.

Premack, D. (1959). Toward empirical laws: I. Positive reinforcement. *Psychological Review*, 66, 219–233.

Rademacher, J. A., Callahan, K., & Pederson-Seelye, V. A. (1998). How do your classroom rules measure up? *Intervention in School and Clinic*, 33(5), 1998. 284–289.

Reid, R., & Harris, K. (1993). Self-monitoring of attention versus self-monitoring of performance: Effects on attention and academic performance. *Exceptional Children*, 6(1), 29–40.

Rosenberg, M. S. (1986). Maximizing the effectiveness of structured classroom management programs: Implementing rule-review procedures with disruptive and distractible students. *Behavioral Disorders*, 11(4), 239–247.

Saigh, P. A., & Umar, A. M. (1983). The effects of a good behavior game on the disruptive behavior of sudanese elementary school students. *Journal of Applied Behavior Analysis*, 16 (3), 339–344.

Salend, J. S., Jantzen, N. R., & Giek, K. (1992). Using a peer confrontation system in a group setting. *Behavioral Disorders*, 17(3), 211–218.

Salend S. J., Reynolds, C. J., & Coyle, E. M. (1989). Individualizing the Good Behavior Game across type and frequency of behavior with emotionally disturbed adolescents. *Behavior Modification, 13*(1), 108–126.

Scheuermann, B., Webber, J., Partin, M., & Knies, W. C. (1994). Level systems and the law: Are they compatible? *Behavioral Disorders, 19*(3), 205–220.

Scott, T. M. (1998). Moving from token economies to teaching self-management. *Reaching Today's Youth, 2,* 28–30.

Shores, R. E., Gunter, P. L., Denny, R. K., & Jack, S. L. (1993). Classroom influences on aggressive and disruptive behavior of students with emotional and behavioral disorders. *Focus on Exceptional Children, 26*(2), 1–10.

Smith, S. E. (1994). Parent-initiated contracts: An intervention for school-related behaviors. *Elementary School Guidance & Counseling, 28,* 182–187.

Solomon, R. W., & Wahler, R. G. (1973). Peer reinforcement control of classroom problem behavior. *Journal of Applied Behavior Analysis, 6,* 49–56.

Staub, R. W. (1987). *The effects of publicly posted feedback on middle school students' disruptive hallway behavior.* Unpublished doctoral dissertation, University of Pittsburgh.

Sugai, G., & Chanter, C. (1989). The effects of training students with learning and behavior disorders to modify the behavior disorders of their peers. *Education & Treatment of Children, 12*(2), 134–151.

Sugai, G., & Tindal, G. (1993). *Effective school consultation: An interactive approach.* Pacific Grove, CA: Brooks/Cole.

Trice, A. D., & Parker, F. C. (1983). Decreasing adolescent swearing in an instructional setting. *Education and Treatment of Children, 6,* 29–35.

Van Houten, R., Nau, P. A., MacKenzie-Keating, S. E., Sameoto, D., & Colavecchia, B. (1982). An analysis of some variables influencing the effectiveness of reprimands. *Behavior Journal of Applied Analysis, 15,* 65–83.

Vitaro, F., Brendgen, M., & Tremblay, R. (1999). Prevention of school dropout through the reduction of disruptive behaviors and school failure in elementary school. *Journal of School Psychology, 27*(2), 205–226.

Walker, H. M. (1995) (2nd ed.). *The acting out child: Coping with classroom disruption.* Longmont, CO: Sopris West.

Webber, J., & Scheuermann, B. (1991) Accentuate the positive . . . eliminate the negative! *Teaching Exceptional Children,* Fall, 13–19.

Williamson, D. A., Williamson, S. H., Watkins, P. C., & Hughes, H. H. (1992). Increasing cooperation among children using dependent group-oriented reinforcement contingencies. *Behavior Modification, 16*(3), 414–425.

Wong, H. K., & Wong, R. T. (1998). *The first days of school: How to be an effective teacher.* Mountain View, CA: Harry K. Wong Publications, Inc.

Zwald, L., & Gresham, F. (1982). Behavioral consultation in a secondary class: Using DRL to decrease negative verbal interactions. *The School Psychology Review, 11*(4), 428–432.

7 IMPROVING SCHOOL SURVIVAL SKILLS AND SOCIAL SKILLS

CHAPTER

OUTLINE

OBJECTIVES

After completing this chapter, you should be able to

- Describe three assessment approaches for problems in social skills and school survival skills.
- Describe three environmental modifications to improve social skills and school survival skills.
- Plan a teacher-mediated intervention for a student with poor social skills.
- Plan a comprehensive sequence of peer-mediated interventions for a socially withdrawn child.
- Use a group contingency procedure to modify off-task behaviors.
- Develop a self-monitoring procedure to improve students' academic productivity.

SCHOOL SURVIVAL SKILLS: AN INTRODUCTION

The first part of this chapter addresses limitations in **school survival skills,** those behaviors that enable a student to get the most from instructional interactions. Research has shown that many students simply do not learn to adjust to the demands of the school setting. Consider these vignettes:

> Andy was never really a troublemaker, but he just didn't seem to "get his act together" at school. His projects were always incomplete and he often showed up late for classes, resulting in repeated detentions. Sometimes he forgot he had detention and wound up having to go to the in-school suspension room for a day or two. We never seemed to find the right intervention for Andy, and he developed a reputation as a "loser."

> Yvonne just didn't seem to fit into any classroom. She wasn't exactly a behavior problem, but she was no angel either. For example, she would never answer the questions I asked, and I found myself repeating questions to her just because she was daydreaming during our discussions. Sometimes I actually wondered if she had a neurological problem, but her pediatrician said she was fine. Let's face it: Yvonne was a "space cadet."

> How could I ever forget Corrado? I never could put my finger on his problem. He was a nice enough kid but he was totally disorganized. His assignments always looked like they had been run over, and his test papers were decorated with doodles. No amount of lecturing could ever change that kid. I wonder what ever happened to him?

> I guess you could call five-year-old Lila unmotivated or lazy. She really got under my skin because she never did what I asked the first time. Every request turned into a battle. She was fine as long as you didn't ask her to do anything.

These recollections may sound familiar to you. Regardless of the description or diagnosis you use, the behaviors will be your real concern. Figure 7–1 lists some of the behaviors we discuss in this section of the chapter.

ASSESSING SCHOOL SURVIVAL SKILLS

Many of the problems in Figure 7–1 will be obvious to you and to the other teachers. In a large secondary school, however, you may not have a chance to compare notes with a student's other teachers. Consider using a pencil-and-paper checklist for assessing a student's specific skill limitations. The School Survival Skills Scale is appropriate for middle and high school students.

As you read through the items of the School Survival Skills Scale, consider the skills and problems thought to be most important for high school students (Kerr, Zigmond, Schaeffer, & Brown, 1986).

Important Skills
1. Meets due dates.
2. Arrives at school on time.
3. Attends class every day.
4. Exhibits interest in academic work.
5. Accepts consequences of behavior.

Problem Behaviors
1. Seldom completes assignments.
2. Cannot follow written directions.
3. Gives "back talk" to teacher.
4. Falls asleep in class.
5. Is quick to give up.

Focus your intervention efforts on these skills and problems first. By the way, similar rankings have resulted from work with elementary school children (McConnell et al., 1984; Walker & Rankin, 1983). Notice the emphasis on compliance and academic productivity; as you prepare children for inclusion at any grade level, be sure to give these skills special attention.

Sue Perfetti and her colleagues (1999, personal communication) developed a self-assessment for secondary students to use in determining what adaptations and modifications they needed in the classroom. Suggestions for students who experience difficulty in taking notes follow on p. 242.

Date _____

Student's Name _____   Teacher's Name _____
                    (please print)   (please print)

Circle the appropriate response.
Student's Grade   9   10   11   12   This student is in your class for:
Student's Sex   M   F   Homeroom   Social Studies
Student's Special Ed Classification   English   Science
SED   LD   EMR   VH   HI   PH   Math   Other _____

Directions: *Please read each statement and circle the corresponding letter that best describes this student's typical behavior. Be sure that you mark every item.*

This student	Never	Sometimes	Usually	Always	Not Observed
1. . . . stays awake in class.	N	S	U	A	X
2. . . . gets to class on time.	N	S	U	A	X
3. . . . complies with requests of adults in authority.	N	S	U	A	X
4. . . . stays calm and in control of emotions.	N	S	U	A	X
5. . . . brings necessary materials to class.	N	S	U	A	X
6. . . . is persistent even when faced with a difficult task.	N	S	U	A	X
7. . . . asks for help with school when necessary.	N	S	U	A	X
8. . . . responds to others when they speak.	N	S	U	A	X
9. . . . arrives at school on time.	N	S	U	A	X
10. . . . completes assigned work.	N	S	U	A	X
11. . . . behaves appropriately in a variety of settings.	N	S	U	A	X
12. . . . manages conflict through nonaggressive means.	N	S	U	A	X
13. . . . organizes study time efficiently.	N	S	U	A	X
14. . . . can concentrate on work without being distracted by peers.	N	S	U	A	X
15. . . . works well independently.	N	S	U	A	X
16. . . . accepts the punishment if caught doing something wrong.	N	S	U	A	X
17. . . . turns in assignments when they are due.	N	S	U	A	X
18. . . . speaks appropriately to teachers.	N	S	U	A	X
19. . . . follows written directions.	N	S	U	A	X
20. . . . talks calmly to an adult when perceived to be unjustly accused.	N	S	U	A	X
21. . . . uses time productively while waiting for teacher.	N	S	U	A	X
22. . . . attends class.	N	S	U	A	X
23. . . . exhibits interest in improving academic performance.	N	S	U	A	X
24. . . . is good at taking tests.	N	S	U	A	X
25. . . . appropriately handles corrections on classwork.	N	S	U	A	X
26. . . . identifies the central theme of a lecture (demonstrates by stating or writing the main ideas and supporting facts).	N	S	U	A	X

Please Check to Make Sure All Items Are Marked

FIGURE 7–1   School survival skills scale.

Source: *From Zigmond, N., Kerr, M. M., Schaeffer, A., Brown, G., & Farra, H. (1986). The School Survival Skills Curriculum. Pittsburgh: University of Pittsburgh. Reprinted with permission.*

- Provide outline of lecture.
- Have student fill in the blanks of a structured outline.
- Have another student carbon copy notes.
- Allow students to tape record lessons.
- Photocopy teacher or student notes.
- Use graphic organizers/premade outlines.
- Provide skeletal outline.
- Provide word bank.
- Highlight key words and important ideas.
- Allow extra time for taking notes.
- Provide activities to practice getting the main idea.
- Implement note-taking learning strategies.
- One-to-one check for information with students.
- Make sure students have key points.
- Demonstrate abbreviated or speed writing techniques.
- Compare note-taking strategies with partner or teacher.

(To obtain a copy of the Secondary Instructional Support Strategies and Intervention Lists produced by Apollo-Ridge School District, contact Dr. Susan Perfetti at ARIN Intermediate Unit, 2895 Route 422 West, Indiana, PA 15701-8300.)

Homework completion, another important skill, can be assessed through the Homework Problem Checklist (Anesko, Schoiock, Ramirez, & Levine, 1987); see Figure 7–2.

As you analyze a student's classroom performance, consider the research on children's perceived control and autonomy in the classroom. Children hold *strategy beliefs* (about what it takes to perform well) and *capacity beliefs* (whether the child has "what it takes"). In the academic domain, a clear picture emerges (Skinner, Wellborn, & Connell, 1990). The children most actively engaged in the classroom are those who believe effort is an important cause of school success and failure, and they themselves can exert effort (high-effort strategy and capacity beliefs); that although ability is not necessary for success, they themselves are smart (low-ability strategy beliefs and high-ability

capacity beliefs); and that they have access to powerful others and are lucky (high powerful others and luck capacity beliefs). In contrast, children who are most disaffected from school activities believe they are incapable of exerting effort and are not smart (low effort and ability capacity beliefs); that powerful others and luck are needed to succeed, but they themselves cannot influence others and are unlucky (high strategy and low capacity for powerful others and luck); and that they don't know the causes of success and failure in school (high unknown strategy beliefs). Pairs of strategy and capacity beliefs for each of the five causes examined in the academic domain (effort, ability, powerful others, luck, and unknown) are strong predictors of children's behavior and emotion in the classroom (Patrick, Skinner, & Connell, 1993).

Students' beliefs are not the only ones that influence academic performance. Your own perceptions, beliefs, standards, and expectations play a significant role in your students' study habits. Studies of effective schools have demonstrated that teachers with higher classroom expectations take more responsibility for seeing that their students learn. Moreover, these effective teachers believe in their ability to help students (Fuchs, Fuchs, & Phillips, 1994). As you develop your own standards and expectations, ask yourself these questions:

- Is there a clear expectation for an alternative, appropriate behavior in this setting? Be sure your students have clear, appropriate expectations for performance. Are the rules posted or orally reviewed for the student?
- Is the behavioral expectation developmentally appropriate for this student? Perhaps the environment or the social situation is too demanding (or too boring) for a student at this developmental level.
- Has the student received training in alternative appropriate behaviors? If you're unsure about a student's skills, review these skills as a teaching assessment. Remember that some students require regular review and

Child performs (−1) below grade level in most subjects
(0) on grade level in most subjects
(+1) above grade level in most subjects

For each statement check one:	Never (0)	At Times (1)	Often (2)	Very Often (3)
Fails to bring home assignments and necessary materials (textbook, dittos, etc.)				
Doesn't know exactly what homework has been assigned.				
Denies having homework assignment.				
Refuses to do homework assignment.				
Whines or complains about homework.				
Must be reminded to sit down and start homework.				
Procrastinates, puts off doing homework.				
Doesn't do homework satisfactorily unless someone is in the room.				
Doesn't do homework satisfactorily unless someone does it with him/her.				
Daydreams or plays with objects during homework session.				
Easily distracted by noises or activities of others.				
Easily frustrated by homework assignment.				
Fails to complete homework.				
Takes unusually long time to do homework.				
Responds poorly when told by parent to correct homework.				
Produces messy or sloppy homework.				
Hurries through homework and makes careless mistakes.				
Shows dissatisfaction with work, even when he/she does a good job.				
Forgets to bring assignment back to class.				
Deliberately fails to bring assignment back to class.				

FIGURE 7–2 Homework problem checklist.

Source: *Reprinted with permission from Anesko, K. M., Schoiock, G., Ramirez, R., and Levine, F. M. (1987). The homework problem checklist: Assessing children's homework difficulties.* Behavioral Assessment, 9, 179.

practice in order to maintain their self-help and social skills.

- Has the student suddenly lost the skills? If so, then contact as many other persons involved with the student as possible. See if there is a health or family change that may be responsible for the sudden behavioral change. Remember, many problem behaviors may be the result of anxiety or depression and this may reflect a serious but treatable problem.

- Has the problem occurred before? Can you identify any similarities between the episodes? Consider using an A-B-C analysis to determine what causes or maintains the behavior. Perhaps the behavior is being reinforced.

- Are other students engaging in the same behavior? There's a possibility that the student is imitating others. Reevaluate the contingencies for the other students. Are they being reinforced? How can you alter the contingencies for the target student and peers?

Once you have answered these questions, you will want to ensure that your classroom environment supports your efforts to improve your students' on-task behavior. The following guidelines for curricular modifications include ways to prevent a child from experiencing the repeated failure or the unwarranted success that can be demoralizing to a child's sense of self-worth and achievement. The goal is to make the classroom environment challenging but predictable, allowing students a sense of control and accomplishment.

- Schedule ample time for a student working at a typical pace to complete the assignment, but, if you have planned a task carefully, do not give in to a student's complaints that it is too long.
- Place work materials in a designated storage area, off your desk, so that the student must take responsibility for picking up and returning work.
- Plan tasks that will challenge students but will occasionally allow them to experience some failure so that they will learn how to handle frustration. On the other hand, let students know when an assignment is difficult or encompasses new knowledge or skills.
- Let students know how they are performing. Help students develop a sense of competence by sharing your evaluations with them. Encourage self-evaluation by asking questions ("How do you think you worked in algebra today?" "Did you organize your study time well for this exam?").
- Do not assist students every time they request help. Establish guidelines for requesting help (perhaps a signaling device on the student's

desk) and follow these guidelines. Encourage students to help themselves by using the dictionary, reference books, or study guides. Promote peer assistance and peer tutoring (discussed later in this section).

With these general guidelines in mind, let's turn now to teacher-mediated strategies that you can use to improve your students' work habits.

TEACHER-MEDIATED STRATEGIES

Managing Routines

As Wong and Wong (1998) point out, "The number one problem in the classroom is not discipline; it is the lack of procedures and routines. . . . A procedure is simply a method or process for how things are to be done in a classroom" (pp. 167, 169). They recommend a three-step procedure for teaching classroom procedures:

1. State, explain, and demonstrate the routine.
2. Rehearse and practice the procedure.
3. Reteach, rehearse, practice, and reinforce the procedure until it becomes routine.

Several studies offer suggestions for helping students and teacher manage routines and transitions. For examples, *public posting* and *positive reinforcement* were combined to reduce the transition time of middle school physical education students. Students who made the transitions within the designated times had their names displayed on a poster. If their names appeared nine or more times, they earned reinforcer activities they had chosen in a survey. The teachers reported an immediate and substantial decrease in transition times. Moreover, after four weeks, the student no longer required the public posting and reinforcers (Dawson-Rodriques, Lavay, Butt, & Lacourse, 1997).

"Beat the buzzer," a strategy wherein students are asked to complete their clean-up or move to their new activity before the buzzer sounds, facilitates the transition of young and developmentally delayed children (Wurtele & Drabman, 1984). Sainato, Strain, Lefebvre, & Rapp (1987) successfully modified this teacher-directed intervention by having children move to their next activity and ring a bell themselves when they arrived. Your classroom should include a large wall clock to help students who want to remain on schedule. It may also be useful in giving students some idea about how much time has elapsed during a work period and how much time remains for them to complete work. If you work with a student who seems easily upset when the school schedule changes, arrange a time to review the schedule with the student. Suggest that she use a highlighter pen to mark special or important dates (e.g., the date a term paper is due, the date and time for auditions for the school chorus, or the deadline for ordering class rings).

Homework Strategies

Finishing homework is an essential study skill (Epstein, Polloway, Foley, & Patton, 1993; Roderique, Polloway, Cumblad, Epstein, & Bursuck, 1994). In an attempt to raise academic standards, many schools are placing special emphasis on homework completion. Consider these suggestions as you develop your own homework policy:

- Assess your students' homework difficulties, including the perceptions of their parents and other teachers. The Homework Problem Checklist (Epstein et al., 1993) is a useful interviewing tool.
- Present very clear and specific directions with all assignments.
- Teach students time-management skills (presented later in this section).
- Make it relevant! Help the student understand the connection with his classwork. Share sample assignments from general education or less restrictive settings (Epstein et al., 1993).
- Assign homework that emphasizes proficiency, maintenance of skills already learned, or generalization of those skills and knowledge to another situation or example. Be sure that the

homework is neither too novel nor too complex. A good rule of thumb is to assign homework on which an unsupervised student would achieve 70 percent to 80 percent accuracy (Epstein et al., 1993).
- To ensure that you can provide adequate and timely feedback on homework, be as efficient as you can. Consider self-correcting assignments, peer-monitored homework, or other assistance.
- Keep in mind that elementary-level students primarily learn good study habits and independent review strategies from their homework assignments (Cooper, 1989; Rosenberg, 1989). Short, successful assignments work best.
- Establish the routine early in the school year. Begin with written explanations to parents and students about the homework schedule and subjects. Collect homework after each assignment. Provide homework folders for students to take back and forth from school to home; these may help those who are likely to misplace their papers.
- Don't assume that a student will understand spoken homework assignments. Encourage the use of written assignments. (You may write them for younger students; older students may use an assignment book.)
- Involve parents. Have parents sign completed homework but do not expect parents to teach their students material that has not been learned in school. (Parent-developed ideas for helping students with disabilities organize their schoolwork and schedules are available at: www.ldonline.com; www.chadd.org; www.schwablearning.org).
- Pair students to work on homework (see Olympia, Andrews, Valum, & Jensen, 1993).

Instructional Modifications

To assist students with attentional problems, CH.A.D.D. and Dr. Sydney Zentall published the guidelines shown in Table 7–1.

TABLE 7–1 Principles for Remediation

Principles of Remediation for Excessive Anxiety

- Do not attempt to reduce activity, but channel it into acceptable avenues.
  - Encourage directed movement in classrooms that is not disruptive.
  - Allow standing during seatwork, especially during end-of-task.
- Use activity as a reward.
  - Give activity (errand, clean board, organize teacher's desk, arrange chairs) as individual reward for improvement.
- Use active responses in instruction.
  - Use teaching activities that encourage active responding (talking, moving, organizing, working at the board).
  - Encourage diary writing, painting, etc.
  - Teach child to ask questions that are on-topic.

Principles of Remediation for Inability to Wait (Impulsivity)

- Give the child substitute verbal or motor responses to make while waiting and, where possible, do encourage daydreaming or planning in the interim.
  - Instruct the child on how to continue on easier parts of tasks (or do a substitute task) while waiting for teacher's help.
  - Have the child underline or rewrite directions before beginning or give magic markers or colored pencils for child to underline directions or relevant information.
  - Encourage doodling or play with clay, paper clips, or pipe cleaners while waiting or listening to instructions.
  - Encourage note taking (even just cue words).

Note: Dr. Barkley also suggests the teacher actively focus on and reward short intervals of waiting and gradually increase the length of the period.

- Where inability to wait becomes impatience and bossiness, encourage leadership but do not assume that impulsive statements or behavior are aggressive in intent.
  - Suggest/reinforce alternate ways (e.g. line reader, paper passer).
  - For children who interrupt, teach them to recognize pauses in conversations and how to hang onto ideas.
  - Cue child about upcoming difficult times or tasks where extra control will be needed.
  - Instruct and reinforce social routines (hellos, goodbyes, please, thank-you).

Principles of Remediation for Failure to Sustain Attention to Routine Tasks and Activities

- Decrease the length of the task.
  - Break one task into smaller parts to be completed at different times.
  - Give two tasks, with a preferred task to be completed after the less preferred task.
  - Give fewer spelling words and math problems.
  - Use fewer words in explaining tasks (concise and global verbal directions).
  - Use distributed practice for rote tasks, rather than mass practice.
- Make tasks interesting.
  - Allow work with partners, in small groups, in centers.
  - Alternate high and low interest tasks.
  - Use overhead projector when lecturing.
  - Allow child to sit closer to the teacher.
- Increase novelty, especially into later time periods of longer tasks.
  - Make a game out of checking work.
  - Use games to over-learn rote material.
  - Do not teach or reinforce "dead-man's behavior"—that is, do not assume the child is not paying attention just because s/he looks out the window or at another child. Do not make on-task behavior a goal, without changing the nature of the task or learning environment.

TABLE 7–1   Principles for Remediation—*Continued.*

Principles of Remediation for Noncompliance and Failure to Complete Tasks

- Generally increase the choice and specific interest of tasks for the child.
  - Allow a limited choice of tasks, topics, and activities.
  - Determine child's preferred activities and use as incentives.
  - Bring child's interests into assignments.
- Make sure tasks fit within child's learning abilities and preferred response style.
  - Allow alternate response modes (typewriter, computer, taped assignments).
  - Alter assignment difficulty level (give advanced level assignments or lower the level of difficulty).
  - Make sure disorganization is not a reason for failure to complete tasks.

Principles of Redemption for Difficulty at the Beginning of Tasks

- Generally increase the structure and salience of the relevant parts of tasks and social settings.
  - Prompt child for verbal directions (i.e., use written directions in addition to verbal ones; encourage note taking).
  - Structure written assignments and tests (i.e., use graph paper for math; state standards of acceptable work, being as specific as possible).
  - Point out overall structure of tasks (topic sentences, headings, table of contents).
  - Allow work with partners or in small groups with quiet talking.
  - Color, circle, underline, or rewrite directions, difficult letters in spelling, or math process signs.

Principles of Media for Completing Assignments on Time

- Increase the use of lists and assignment organizers (notebooks, folders).
  - Write assignments for child in a pocket notebook.
  - Write assignments on the board. Make sure the child has copied them.
- Establish object-placement routines to retrieve routinely used objects such as books, assignments, and clothes.
  - Encourage routines of pocket folders with new work on one side and completed graded work and class notes organized chronologically on the other.
  - Encourage parents to establish places for certain things at home (books, homework).
  - Organize desk or locker with labels and places for certain items.
- Use color and physical/spatial organizers.
  - Before leaving one place for another (walking out of the door) teach routine of child self-questioning—"Do I have everything I need?"
  - Tape prompt cards in desks, on books, or on assignment folders.

Increasing Planning and Sequential Organization of Thought

- Practice planning.
  - Practice planning different activities (what is needed, how to break tasks into parts).
  - Practice estimating time needed for activities.
  - Teach outlining skills.
- Practice sorting, ordering, and reordering.
  - Teach the use of a word processor to reorder ideas.
  - Teach the child to take notes on lectures or on written materials in three columns (main points, supporting points, questions).

Principles of Remediation for Poor Handwriting

- Reduce need for handwriting.
  - Do not have child recopy material. It will get progressively worse instead of better.
  - Allow student to copy a peer's notes or the teacher's notes.

TABLE 7–1 Principles of Remediation—*Continued.*

- Accept typed or taped assignments.
- Reduce standards on some assignments and make relevant standards clearer on important assignments.
- Color, circle, or underline parts of letters that children typically fail to close in cursive writing.
- Allow reduced standards for acceptable handwriting.
- Display particularly good samples of the child's work.

Principles of Remediation for Low Self-Esteem

- Generally recognize child's strengths and efforts.
- Call attention to areas of the child's strengths by allowing for a consistent time each day or week during which child can display his/her talents.
- Recognize that excessive activity can also mean increased energy and productivity.
- Recognize that bossiness can also be leadership potential.
- Recognize that attraction to novel stimulation can also lead to creativity.
- Increase child's feelings of success by increasing child's skills.
- Recognize these children's playfulness and use it to develop skills.
- Mark student's correct performance, not the mistakes.

Source: *From Fowler, M. (1995).* Educators Manual: Children and Adults with Attention Deficit Disorders. *Plantation, FL: Children and Adults with Attention Deficit Disorder (CH.A.D.D.), pp. 15–16. Reprinted with permission.*

Many students require modifications of the curriculum. Here is an example of a Curriculum Modification Ladder:

1. Can the student do the same as peers (e.g., paragraph writing)?

If not, can . . .

2. the student do the same activity but with adapted expectations (e.g., write five sentences about a topic)?

If not, can . . .

3. the student do the same activity but with adapted expectations and materials (e.g., write five sentences about a picture)?

If not, can . . .

4. the student do a similar activity but with adapted expectations (e.g., select and rearrange words to make a sentence)?

If not, can . . .

5. the student do a similar activity but with adapted materials (e.g., arrange words on a card to make a sentence about a picture)?

If not, can . . .

6. the student do a different, parallel activity (e.g., use a computer typing program or put pictures in a computer)?

If not, can . . .

7. the student do a different activity in a different section of the room (e.g., do a computer game matching pictures to words)?

If not, can . . .

8. the student do a functional activity in a different section of the school (e.g., matching pictures to words with younger students, peer helper, or instructional aide)?[1]

TEACHING SCHOOL SURVIVAL SKILLS

One of your best approaches to improving your students' time on task is to teach them the important skills they lack. Several publishers now offer study skills curricula (e.g., Seaman, 1996). One example of a school survival skill you might teach is **time management.** Meeting deadlines is a critical skill for school success. Even young children can begin thinking about the length of assignments and how to accomplish them. Middle and sec-

[1]DeBoer, A. L., & Fister, S. (1995). *Strategies & Tools for Collaborative Teaching.* Longmont, CO: Sopris West.

ondary school teachers may put their class assignments on a website, or provide agendas for the student to record assignments and projects.

For the High School Student: Improving Reading, Taking Tests, and Planning for the Future is a free, well-written handbook for teens with learning difficulties. It is available at: www.schwablearning.org/main.asp?page=2.4.7.

Combining Contingency Management with Other Strategies

When you develop *contingency contracts, token economies, group-oriented contingencies,* or other reinforcement and *response-cost* systems, remember to include school survival skills. By emphasizing these skills you communicate the importance of good student work habits. Highly valued by teachers, these skills are essential for students who are working in general education classrooms. Recent research has demonstrated the effectiveness of token reinforcement for improving academic performance (McGinnis, Friman, & Carlyon, 1999). Figure 7–3 shows how a token economy can also incorporate school survival skills.

Group contingencies are powerful peer-mediated strategies that can be especially useful for older students whose poor academic skills are the result of having too much fun in the classroom. (Refer to Chapter 6 for guidelines.)

To illustrate how a combination of interventions might work, here are the suggestions made by a teacher who wanted to increase the productivity of eighth graders:

1. At the beginning of the class, review classroom procedures. Or, ask an individual student to state one without looking. Give a coupon to students who can recite the procedures.
2. Use a 1-inch voice; avoid yelling or publicly reprimanding students.
3. Don't disrupt students deep in concentration by stopping at their desk and talking to them.
4. Provide a reward or incentive. Put lottery tickets/coupons in the "jackpot" with the names of students who have done a thorough job with their work. When the jackpot is full, provide a classroom prize and have a drawing for individual prizes.
5. Provide choices for students. For example, "You can do 20 simple math problems worth 2 points each or 10 harder ones worth four points each." "You can do this equation sheet about figuring out your car payments, or you can do this equation sheet about how many Barbies are sold each month."
6. Make sure that you monitor students as they work. After 10 mins, say, "You should have completed at least 8 problems." Save the last 10 min for them to check each others' work. They usually like this. They like it even better if an assignment is done well by everyone and the teacher makes it worth more points.
7. Recognize students who are doing what they are supposed to do. This can be nonverbal. Write a student a note and put it on her desk or on his worksheet for the next day. Put a sticker or a stamp on his class folder, or a coupon in the jackpot. (See Figure 7–4 for sample coupons.)

(E. Liston, personal communication, 1999).

PEER-MEDIATED STRATEGIES

Peer Tutoring

Peer tutoring, a successful way of structuring academic activities to involve peers, relies upon the principles of peer modeling and peer teaching. The peer tutor must be a student who wants to do the tutoring, who may or may not have the content area skills but who can follow teacher directions and learn from a model. Use your judgment when pairing students for tutoring. Do not select a tutor who may embarrass or criticize the target student. When using a cross-age peer tutor (someone from another class), plan a schedule that is mutually convenient and decide how to evaluate the student tutor's involvement. Studies have shown that

The token economy I have set up is based on points. The reason I selected points as their "tokens" is with this age they understand what points mean. Even though points are a bit abstract, students know that they earn them for doing well. They also understand the more points they have the better reinforcers they receive. By utilizing this system, they are also using their addition and subtraction skills. If they have problems, calculators may be used. The students are also learning how to manage their points by saving them to buy something that is more valuable.

I have a monitoring sheet for each student with questions they can answer to monitor their behavior. The behaviors are listed in question form on the sheet. The questions are asked in words the students can understand. Their behaviors are measured after each class. I have allowed 10 min of class time for the students to fill out their sheets. In this time I will also be providing feedback. They will earn points for positive behavior and lose points when they display negative behavior.

The students will be introduced and given directions for their self-assessment sheets before they begin to self-monitor their own behavior. The class rules and the directions for the self-monitoring sheets will also be reviewed each morning before class begins. The students will begin with 3 free points every Monday before the class starts. The students will be responsible for answering six questions for targeted positive behavior and three questions for targeted negative behavior. The student will be given a range of 1, 3, and 5 for positive behavior and 0, 3, and 5 for negative behavior. The 1 and 0 mean the student never displays the behavior, the 3 means the student sometimes displays the behavior, and 5 means the student always displays the behavior. Depending on whether the behavior is positive or negative, these numbers will be added or subtracted from the student's total points. The student is to fill in the chart during the time allowed after the class period. I will be monitoring the students during class and fill in my list when they complete their sheets. I will have a list for each class and will keep them in a behavior folder and tally the points after school onto a master list. While the students are completing their sheets, I will also walk around the room to provide feedback on their class and behavior performance by giving verbal or physical praise. At the end of the day, the students will hand in their sheets and I will sign off on each period if I agree with the points they have awarded themselves. If I disagree strongly I will give the points they awarded themselves, but I will write them a note telling them the discrepancy. The next time I will average the points and write them a note. I will also remind the students that bonus points are awarded if our total points match.

The students will tally up their points at the end of the day and choose their reinforcers. They will hand in their sheets and I will go over their scores to see if they match mine. The reinforcer(s) will be at their desks when they arrive to school the next day. A note will be attached giving them feedback. If there is a problem, they will receive a note and will be asked to set up an appointment to talk to me about their points. A chart will also be hung in class to keep track of points and "advertise" how everyone is doing.

The students will also be awarded bonus points for spontaneous good behavior. I will have a list of example bonus items hanging up by the reinforcers. The students will also have the chance to write down on their self-monitoring sheet what they did to earn bonus points. Bonus points are worth 1 point for each positive behavior. Students can earn bonus points a variety of ways. They may earn them for improving their behavior from the day before, praising a peer, helping a peer, helping the teacher, resolving a dispute, walking away from a fight, receiving the best score from advertising sheet, etc. The students will also be given 3 free points to start with every Monday to help them earn points. Every day I will also pick one question on the sheet that will be worth double points. I will announce the question at the end of the day so the students can add this in to their total. The free points, double points, and bonus points will be awarded to keep the students from getting "in the hole."

When a student begins to earn the maximum points in good behavior and does not display the targeted inappropriate behavior it will be time to change the target behaviors. The student's target positive behavior will be more difficult, but something that will help to transition to a "regular education class." The changes will be discussed with the student, and we will decide together what he or she needs to work on. The targeted inappropriate behaviors will also change when he or she can control the behaviors listed on the self-monitoring sheet. The student may be able to control those behaviors without the sheet to remind them. They may also be displaying other inappropriate behaviors that were not targeted because of the degree of need to control the others. This will also be discussed with the student and appropriate changes will be made. The reinforcers will also be decreased because they need to be able to display appropriate behaviors naturally without receiving a physical reinforcer. They will not receive the reinforcers as often, and they will become less valuable to the student. This change will also be discussed with the student to let them know the rules are changing because they are progressing. When it is time for a change, the student's self-monitoring sheet will change by targeting new behaviors we want to increase or decrease. The class rules will stay the same, but self-monitoring sheets can always be modified due to the students' changing needs.

FIGURE 7–3   Token economy.

Source: *Zeher, C. (2000). Personal communication. Reprinted with permission.*

I was caught doing my work well! Coupon good for one gel pen.	I did an awesome job on my assignment. Free assignment pass.	I did my work 100% right! I get to tutor someone from another group.
I checked over my work and corrected my errors. Coupon good for a cool eraser.	I didn't get any wrong! Go to lunch early pass.	I was doing my thing, and it was the right thing to do! Coupon to run an errand with a friend.

FIGURE 7–4 Sample coupons.

Source: *From Liston, E.(1999). Personal communication. Reprinted with permission.*

peer tutoring for students with disabilities in general education settings is more effective if those students are tutors for at least part of the time. However, students with disabilities do not require pairing with nondisabled students for this intervention to work (Mathes & Fuchs, 1994).

Selecting the task for peer tutoring is an important step. Give first priority to the subject area in which the target student has difficulty. Choose academic tasks that are best taught through a "model or prompt plus feedback or praise" format. Good choices include spelling, vocabulary, sight words, and foreign language vocabulary; math facts; scientific formulas; and dates and names in social studies. Select academic tasks that require discrete responses and simple evaluation procedures (e.g., keeping a written tally of the number correct and errors; sorting flashcards into mastered and nonmastered piles). Plan tasks that require relatively brief 15- to 20-min sessions. Trained tutors are more successful than those who are inexperienced (Fuchs, Fuchs, Bentz, Phillips, & Hamlett, 1994). While tutor preparation should be specific to the content of the lessons, general guidelines for tutor training would include the following:

1. Pinpoint the task and analyze it before you begin.
2. Collect all needed materials.
3. Explain the goal of tutoring to the tutor.
4. Explain the task to the tutor, as much as you think is needed.
5. Instruct the tutor in the use of the materials.
6. Explain how the data are to be collected.
7. Role-play the actual tutoring procedures with the tutor.
   a. Model the teaching and the feedback/praise with the tutor and the target student.
   b. Ask the tutor to try being the student for a couple of steps.
   c. Provide feedback to the tutor.
   d. Role-play some problems the tutor may encounter.
   e. If needed, train the tutor to use particular phrases to reinforce the student.
   f. Provide the tutor with sample data and have her record them.
   g. Meet with the tutor before the first session to review the procedures.

h. Meet daily after the tutoring session to answer questions.

i. Reinforce the tutor for her efforts.

For a detailed explanation of tutor training in elementary mathematics, see Fuchs et al. (1994). Fister (1996) has written a chapter on classroom-wide peer tutoring guidelines. Preparation of preschool tutors is described in Tabacek, McLaughlin, & Howard (1994).

In the future, computers may facilitate classroom peer-tutoring programs. The Class-wide Peer Tutoring-Learning Management System developed at the University of Kansas with a grant from the U.S. Office of Special Education Programs assists teachers in planning, implementing, monitoring, and trouble-shooting their classroom tutoring programs. For information on this software programs, go to: www.lsi.ukans.edu/jg/CWPT-LMS/.

Cooperative Learning

The link between social skills and school survival skills is apparent in one of our most popular instructional strategies—**cooperative learning.** This approach holds promise for students with behavioral problems. Rutherford, Mathur, and Quinn (1998) combined social communication training with cooperative learning for incarcerated female teenagers. Their program included 12 half-hour lessons focused on social communications skills: conversational questions, positive comments to/about others, and positive self-inferences. The skills were taught using two procedures: direct instruction of target skills and cooperative learning activities. Components of direct instruction included skill rationale and identification, modeling, practice, social reinforcement, and self-instruction (Mathur & Rutherford, 1994; Rutherford, Chapman, DiGangi, & Anderson, 1992; Sugai & Lewis, 1996). A rationale was included to explain the relevance and clarify the critical aspects of each target communication skill. In skill identification, students in each cooperative learning group were asked to verbally repeat the

steps involved in the target communication skills. Teacher and **peer modeling** was included in each lesson to demonstrate the correct performance of each of the skills. After the skills were modeled, students were provided with several opportunities to practice the skills and analyze social situations that may require the use of the skills. Team members and trainers provided constructive **feedback** and **social reinforcement** for positive student performance. A self-instruction component consisted of providing a cue card the following day in the library that served as a **self-mediated strategy** for prompting the students to perform the target skills.

Cooperative group activities required students to be individually accountable for acquiring information and also responsible for their team's performance. An interdependent group contingency was incorporated where rewards were only given to cooperative learning groups whose entire membership worked together to ensure that all members in their group performed the skills. Students accomplished through practice and corrective feedback (pp. 358–359).

Sutherland, Webby, & Gunter (2000) warn against placing students with emotional and behavioral problems in cooperative learning situations without an adequate assessment of their prerequisite group skills (e.g., leadership, decision-making, conflict resolution, and communication). Also, try to incorporate all of the five components thought to make cooperative learning effective (i.e., positive interdependence, individual accountability, promotive interaction, group processing, development of small group social skills). For a discussion of the five components, see Johnson & Johnson (1991); for a description of different kinds of cooperative learning groups, see Goodwin (1998).

SELF-MEDIATED STRATEGIES

In this section we describe programs in which the student serves as the primary agent of change. These self-mediated strategies, which were introduced in Chapter 6, are strongly recommended for dependent students or students who are manipulative or oppositional when confronted with adult demands. Moreover, these interventions are "portable," in that the student can carry his self-monitoring form from class to class. Self-monitoring has the added advantage of freeing teacher time for instructional activities (Levendoski & Cartledge, 2000; Snyder & Bambara, 1997).

Figure 7–5 shows a student/teacher evaluation form used in student-led middle school conferences. This form allows the student to self-evaluate school survival skills and compare self-ratings with teacher ratings.

Hertz and McLaughlin (1990) awarded tickets to middle school students when their self-monitoring scores closely matched those of their teachers. Students then exchanged tickets for reinforcers.

Figure 7–6, a case study, describes how a nine year-old learned to proofread her math.

A critical aspect of a successful **self-management** program is the reduction or **fading** out of teacher participation in the program. Once a student has shown a consistent ability to self-monitor or self-instruct behavior, reduce your involvement in the program. Consider the steps outlined in Table 7–2 for elementary school children, but this "game" might not be appropriate for adolescents. Rather, meet with the student to discuss termination of the self-evaluation activities and to recognize achievement of the student's goal. Self-management strategies may be used in combination. For example, a student might monitor his behavior, record it, and then graph his results. DiGangi, Maag, & Rutherford (1991) combined self-monitoring with self-graphing for two older elementary school students and found that academic performance and **on-task behavior** improved even more when the students graphed the results of their self-monitoring.

RECOGNIZING AND ASSESSING SOCIAL SKILLS PROBLEMS

Success in school depends in part on students' social or interpersonal skills. Many children and adolescents with behavior disorders have very poor social skills. Their inability to respond in social situations and make friends can lead to the disruptive, aggressive, or offensive behaviors you read about in other chapters. This chapter addresses **social skill deficits** that lead to social withdrawal and other classroom adjustment problems. (Chapter 8 describes additional social skills instruction for the unique needs of students with aggression and anger-management problems.)

Social withdrawal, a very serious problem, refers to a cluster of behaviors that result in an individual escaping or avoiding social contact. This may be intentional, as in extreme cases of **elective mutism** (an uncommon syndrome involving a refusal to speak by someone who can talk), or it may reflect a broader lack of **social competence,** as is often found in children or adults with retardation, psychotic behaviors, or **autism.** Social withdrawal may result from a lack of specific social skills or it may have its origins in a history of rejection and punishment associated with social interaction. In many cases, social withdrawal may be maintained by negative reinforcement: the child continues the specific form of withdrawn behavior because she escapes or avoids social contact, which apparently constitutes an **aversive stimulus** for her. In other cases, behaviors incompatible with social interaction, such as *self-stimulatory behavior*, may be maintained by self-produced reinforcement. Thus, social withdrawal covers a broad and complex range of problem behaviors.

For a long time, social withdrawal was not considered a serious problem in the field of special education or in related disciplines. Even today, an extremely quiet child, seldom enjoying the benefits of positive relationships with others but creating no observable problems for his teachers, may drift unnoticed from one school year to the next. Yet, the consequences of untreated social withdrawal can be extremely serious. Unless a child can learn to interact with others at a reasonably competent level, access to less restrictive settings and subsequent learning opportunities may be seriously curtailed.

Student _____ Date _____

A = Almost Always
S = Sometimes
R = Rarely

		Science		Social Studies		Math		Language Arts	
		Teacher	Student	Teacher	Student	Teacher	Student	Teacher	Student
I come to class prepared.	A								
	S								
	R								
I pay attention during class.	A								
	S								
	R								
I follow directions.	A								
	S								
	R								
I participate regularly in class.	A								
	S								
	R								
I stay on task during individual and group activities.	A								
	S								
	R								
I keep an organized notebook, folder, and binder.	A								
	S								
	R								
I complete my assignments accurately, neatly, and carefully, as required by teacher.	A								
	S								
	R								
I bring and use my Agenda.	A								
	S								
	R								
I prepare for tests and quizzes.	A								
	S								
	R								
I spend time reviewing class notes regularly.	A								
	S								
	R								
Last Nine-Weeks Grade									

FIGURE 7–5 Subject evaluation form.

Source: From Harrison Middle School. (2001) Baldwin-Whitehall School District, Pittsburgh, PA. Reprinted with permission.

The Story of the Proofreading Card

By Cristina Carlson

When I was 10 years old, I brought home an "F" on a math pretest. Although it wasn't a grade, I was very, very upset. The week before, I got a "C" on the real test. My teacher said that I read too fast and made careless errors. (I think I am a lot better in reading than in math.)

Then one day after math class, Mrs. Carrick called me over to her desk and said, "I know you're not doing so well in math, and I think there's a solution. Let's talk about this. First, tell me what steps you use when you take a test."

"I put my name on the paper, read the question, do the work, and put down the answer."

"Aren't you proofreading?" she asked.

"What's that?" I replied.

"Proofreading. Proofreading is going over your work to make sure it's correct."

I thought, "Why didn't I do that before?"

Ms. Carrick and I made a proofreading card that I used every day to remind me. Here it is.

Step 1. Take a deep breath.
Step 2. Remember that you are a speedy reader, so slow down.
Step 3. Say the directions to yourself.
Step 4. Even if you feel confident, proofread:
- ☐ Check to be sure you didn't skip anything
- ☐ Proofread your work
- ☐ Proofread your answer.

I did all four steps.
Signed: _____ Date: _____

After a few days I began to catch my mistakes. On my English test, I didn't put a period. On my math homework, I skipped a step in multiplication. I left a letter out of my spelling word.
And on my next math test, I got a 96%—an A!

FIGURE 7–6 Proofreading case study.
Source: *Reprinted with permission of the author.*

As stated in earlier chapters, rating scales and checklists are useful assessment and monitoring techniques for an initial look at a student's problem behaviors. For example, you might use a problem behavior checklist or the evaluation checklists taken from a social skills curriculum to get a general picture of the social skill problems experienced by one of your students. To make this assessment especially helpful, solicit the ratings from as many significant others as possible, including the parents, teachers, and other professionals who know the child. Do not overlook the student's previous teacher, who might be a valuable source of information.

The Scale of Community-Based Social Skill Performance and the Test of Community-Based Social Skill Knowledge (Bullis & Davis, 1997) allow you to assess students' interactions with others in a community setting.

The information you gather from checklists and ratings can give you a starting place for further, more finely grained assessments, including behavioral interviews and **direct observations.** Moreover, a curriculum-based **checklist** can clue you in on

TABLE 7–2 Guidelines for Reducing Teacher Input in Self-Management Programs

1. For self-management programs that involve a group of students, divide the group into two teams. List students' names, according to teams, on the chalkboard.
2. Announce that only one group will be lucky and have its self-management records checked each day. The same group will be eligible for bonus points.
3. Flip a coin each afternoon, designating one group heads and one tails. The winning team has self-monitoring cards checked for reliability with teacher records. If each member of the team has a reliable score, team members then win bonus points or reinforcers.
4. Remember, promote the idea that being checked is a privilege.
5. Continue this procedure for at least seven school days.
6. During the next stage of the fading program, announce that a new game is beginning.
7. Place all students' names, written on paper strips, into a jar. Draw two names each day. These two lucky students receive the opportunity to earn bonus points or reinforcers.
8. After a period of at least seven school days, adjust the program so that you draw only one name. Maintain this stage of the program for at least one school week.
9. At the completion of the final phase, discontinue checking.

Source: *Material presented in this table was taken from Alford, F. (1980). Self-management for teachers. Nashville, TN: George Peabody College for Teachers.*

where to begin in the sequence of skills taught in that particular instructional program. Finally, a checklist or **rating scale** allows you to compare quickly the views of several individuals about the student's behavior.

Interviews are especially important in the assessment of social skills because others in the child's life are apt to have strong convictions about the student's social relationships and functioning. Some questions you might ask in a social assessment interview include the following:

- Who are this student's friends?
- What social situations are difficult for this student?
- What "social mistakes" does this student make?
- Does this student initiate social interactions?
- What social skills does this student have?
- What do others say about this student's social behavior?
- What skills does this student need to be more socially successful?
- Can this student maintain a social interaction?
- In what situations is this student socially successful?
- What behavior does this student exhibit in these situations?

Analogue measures refer to a **role-play** or behavioral rehearsal in which an individual demonstrates how he would respond in a given social interaction. You have probably used analogue measures and not realized it. For example, you may have asked a student to describe how he would respond to a certain social situation. Analogue procedures may help you understand a student's social perception and the skills he needs to learn in order to respond successfully to a given social situation.

Direct observations allow you to look at social skills and related problem behaviors. These skills and problems will be the focus of your planning and teaching activities. Table 7–3 offers examples taken from research studies. Use the observational strategies discussed in earlier chapters to monitor social interactions. Review the section on interval recording for specific guidelines.

REMEDIATING SOCIAL WITHDRAWAL

General Considerations

There are some strategies that you should always avoid when dealing with social withdrawal.

TABLE 7–3 Sample Definitions of Social Behaviors

Behavior Category	Definitions	Authors
Motor-gestural	This included all positive physical contacts such as brushing another person's arm while reaching for something; cooperative use of an object such as looking at a book with another person, exchanging pens, or taking turns placing puzzle pieces; touching and/or manipulating the same object or parts of the same object; all other gestural movement directed to another person such as handling an object, pointing, motioning to "Come" or "Go away," shaking head to indicate "Yes" or "No," and waving.	Dy, Strain, Fullerton, & Stowitschek (1981)
Vocal-verbal	This included all positive vocal expressions or verbalizations which by virtue of content, e.g., "Hey you," "Uh-huh" (while nodding), clearly indicated that the person was directing the utterance to another individual.	
Approach gestures	. . . consisted of any deliberate behavior of the child which involves the hand(s), arm(s), or other body parts in a motion directed to another child, e.g., an inward circular hand and arm motion, repeated bending and straightening of forefinger while arm extended towards a peer.	Gable, Hendrickson, & Strain (1978)
Play organizer	Verbalizations or responses to verbalizations wherein a child specifies an activity, suggests an idea for play, or directs a child to engage in a play behavior.	Odom, Hoyson, Jamieson, & Strain (1985)
Share	Offers or gives an object to another child or accepts an object from another child by taking the object in hand or using it in play.	
Share request	Asks a child to give an object to the speaker.	
Assistance	Helps another child complete a task or desired action which he or she could not complete or do alone.	
Complimentary statement	Verbal statement indicating affection, attraction, or praise.	
Affection	Patting, hugging, kissing, or holding hands with another child.	Odom, Hoyson, Jamieson, & Strain (1985)
Negative motor-gestural	Hitting, pushing, sticking out tongue, taking unoffered objects, or destroying others' constructions.	
Negative vocal-verbal	Crying, shouting, calling another child an ugly name, and refusal to engage in a requested behavior or corrections.	

One of these is coercion, or **punishment,** designed to "make the child come out of herself." Unfortunately, classmates often ridicule and tease their withdrawn peers, making initiating simple interactions even more difficult for the student. Try to help classmates recognize that social withdrawal is a problem for that student, and consider using one of the **peer-mediated interventions** to assist her.

Another strategy to avoid is leaving the isolate individual alone. Isolate children who are left alone for long periods may develop additional serious problems, rather than learning skills that improve their social interactions. Timeout procedures are thus inappropriate interventions for the socially withdrawn.

A third approach to socially withdrawn students—one that has not proven effective—is to accept their social isolation as a developmental phase and simply to await their decision to approach their classmates. Unfortunately, many withdrawn children have not learned the social skills required to develop social relationships with their classmates and cannot learn them without help. Maturation as a singular intervention on social withdrawal is not effective; children do not simply outgrow this problem; the more they avoid people, the less opportunity they have to develop personally reinforcing situations.

Organizing the Environment to Promote Social Interaction

You can alter the environment of the classroom, playground, or free-play room to facilitate cooperative interactions. Given the seriousness of social skills problems, early interventions have dominated the research on children's social skills. Odom &

Strain (1984) named activities that facilitated or inhibited social interactions in early childhood classrooms. These are shown in Table 7–4.

TEACHER PROMPTING AND REINFORCEMENT

One intervention procedure is prompting and reinforcement. As the name suggests, this procedure requires you to prompt and reinforce an isolated pupil's peer interactions. Even though this procedure is fairly simple, research studies conducted over a number of years have indicated that it is successful, particularly with young children. The following suggestions outline a teacher prompting and reinforcement procedure:

1. Arrange the free-play area using activities highlighted in Table 7–4. Invite the target individual and the nontarget students to play in the free-play area for a period of at least 15 min.

2. **Prompt** a nondisabled student to initiate play with the target individual by using a

TABLE 7–4 Facilitative and Nonfacilitative Activities across Settings with Mean Frequencies of Positive Social Behavior Per 5-Min Session (in Parentheses)

	Facilitative Activities	Nonfacilitative Activities
Structured play	Going to a grocery store (25.3)	Road and car (9.96)
	Having a picnic (16.1)	Building with blocks (9.4)
	Playing doctor (13.6)	Kitchen (7.54)
	Washing babies (10.27)	Garage (7.2)
	Gluing (17.0)	Stencils (5.43)
	Doing Puzzles (13.2)	Drawing (4.86)
	Parquetry (12.5)	Bristle Blocks (4.83)
	Stamping (10.0)	Playing with playdough (4.1)
Learning center	Working jobs (12.4)	Manipulatives (3.89)
	Doing puzzles (12.4)	Using rice tables (3.3)
	Pasting (8.9)	Using water table (1.2)
	Parquetry (8.7)	Showing and telling (8.3)

Source: *Reprinted with permission from Odom, S., & Strain, P. (1984). Classroom-based social skills instruction for severely handicapped preschool children. Topics in early childhood special education. (Vol. 4 No. 3 pp. 97–116).*

phrase such as, "Why don't you ask Kylea if she would like to play with the blocks?" This type of prompt is a play organizer.

3. Use a prompt such as, "Hand Tamika the truck," to share a material.

4. Use a prompt when asking the child to assist another student. You may do this by using a phrase such as, "Help Kathy roll the truck into the blocks."

5. Reinforce any interactions between the students, but try not to interrupt their play by focusing on the behaviors of one child. Make your reinforcement as brief as possible; research has shown that teacher reinforcement tends to interrupt the ongoing social interaction of two children.

6. Once the students have established a fairly steady rate of interacting with one another during free-play times, reduce the number of prompts and reinforcement instances that you provide. For example, if you have been prompting the students on an average of once every 30 sec or once every minute, reduce the number of prompts to one every 3 to 5 min.

7. Remember that a peer trainer can be used to provide prompting and reinforcement. If you feel that you have gotten the intervention off to a good start, consider using a peer to maintain it.

Social Skills Instruction

Faced with the many choices in social skills curricula, you may wonder how to make a good choice. Consider these guidelines and essential features:

Setting. Social skills instruction should take advantage of naturally occurring situations, to increase the likelihood that the new skills will generalize and be reinforced by others.

Assessment. Instead of a "one size fits all" approach, carefully consider your students' individual social skills deficits and be sure that the social skills instruction meets those needs. This is an important factor in maintaining the students' participation in the intervention (sometimes referred to as treatment adherence).

Cultural sensitivity. Be sure that your social skills instruction is responsive to your students' diverse cultural and linguistic backgrounds. *Social interactions by their nature are personal and values-laden, so we urge you to tap other resources* (e.g., Cartledge & Milburn, 1996; Franklin, 1992) before assessment and instruction begin. For example, you may teach students to maintain a firm handshake or look directly at the other person, only to discover that this is not condoned in their culture (Lee & Cartledge, 1996).

Competing behaviors. Analyze competing behaviors and what maintains them. For example, if a student avoids stressful social interactions by refusing to participate in student groups, then rearrange the contingencies so that the student finds it more rewarding to participate and less rewarding to withdraw. Remember, the "old" behaviors have served the student for a long time and may be hard habits to break. Your goal is to make the new behaviors more meaningful for the student (Gresham, 1998). Again, be sure that you are not contradicting deeply held cultural beliefs.

Modeling. The first step in most social skills teaching programs is to introduce students to examples of the social skill through live, audio, or video modeling. Usually, one skill, broken down as much as possible, is the focus of each vignette or lesson. To incorporate peers, call on various students in your class to demonstrate social skills during a lesson. Use as many naturally occurring examples as possible to strengthen the new behaviors.

Role-Playing. After an initial demonstration, the social skills program may call for a role-play of the targeted skill. To facilitate this component, encourage students first to discuss the demonstration and to think of real-life situations in which they might use the skill. Following this discussion, arrange student-designed role-playing or follow a scripted role-play from the curricular materials. [Before teaching a lesson, be sure that you would feel comfortable role-playing the social skill yourself. Also, double-check with other resources to ensure that you are not violating students' cultural beliefs and traditions. For example, many Native Americans prefer to stand 2–3 feet from their conversation partner, while many European-Americans are comfortable within 20–36 inches (Lee & Cartledge, 1996)].

Performance feedback. Letting students know how they performed the skill during the role-play is crucial. Some of the most helpful (and candid) feedback (e.g., approval, praise, constructive criticism) will come from the other group members. A good rule is to encourage positive, supportive feedback while indicating aspects of the behavior that the student could improve. Adult supervision is very important during this phase. A helpful strategy is to have the student immediately replay the scene so that the group can give feedback on the improved performance.

Generalization and maintenance. By now these terms are familiar. The chance to "overlearn" and repeatedly practice the social skills in other settings is vital to a youngster's social development. Self-monitoring can be an essential feature of this transfer-of-learning phase. Many social skills programs include "behavioral homework" and notes sent home to reinforce the skills outside of the classroom. One way to increase the generalization of social skills out of school is first to ask parents which social skills are important to them. Also, try to incorporate different "trainers." In one consultation

experience a teacher of junior high school students with moderate disabilities "primed" various faculty colleagues to enter her classroom and initiate certain social interactions, including gentle teasing for a student having trouble with this kind of interaction. She simply posted her "social skills needs list" in the teachers' lounge each Monday.

Figure 7–7 illustrates strategies to improve the effectiveness of social skills instruction in three key dimensions: programming generalization, facilitating treatment adherence, and increasing social validity (Hansen, Nagle, & Meyer, 1998). Additional information on social skills instruction is in Chapter 8.

Many teachers prefer to develop their own social skills lessons. For example, Sharpe, Brown, & Crider (1995) developed the following procedures for promoting social skills with the physical education curriculum:

1. Five minutes of talk by the teacher at the beginning of each intervention day, defining objectives of teacher-independent sport conflict resolution, lack of off-task behavior, and increased peer leadership and support behaviors in the context of active participation in a team sport.

2. Verbal definition by the teacher of the following general social characteristics in talks before and after class: (a) good winners: the absence of bragging, taunting, and so on, and the occurrence of positive and supportive feedback toward opposing team members; (b) good losers: the absence of peer accusations and negative blaming behavior and the occurrence of positive congratulatory behaviors; (c) peer respect: the absence of negative peer interactions with student referees and designated team leaders and the occurrence of referee and team leader supportive behaviors; (d) enthusiasm: the absence of negative peer comments to

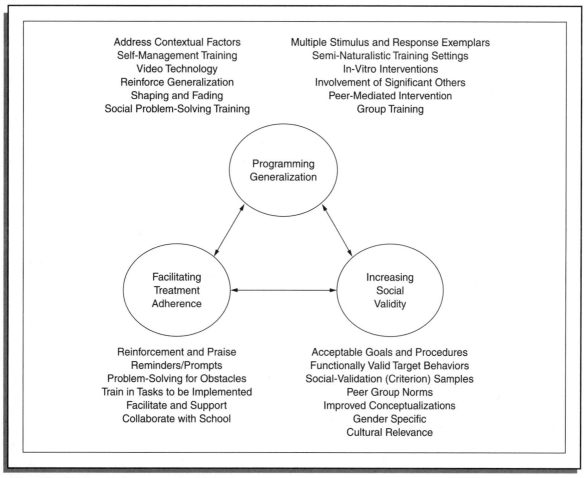

Address Contextual Factors
Self-Management Training
Video Technology
Reinforce Generalization
Shaping and Fading
Social Problem-Solving Training

Multiple Stimulus and Response Exemplars
Semi-Naturalistic Training Settings
In-Vitro Interventions
Involvement of Significant Others
Peer-Mediated Intervention
Group Training

Programming
Generalization

Facilitating
Treatment
Adherence

Increasing
Social
Validity

Reinforcement and Praise
Reminders/Prompts
Problem-Solving for Obstacles
Train in Tasks to be Implemented
Facilitate and Support
Collaborate with School

Acceptable Goals and Procedures
Functionally Valid Target Behaviors
Social-Validation (Criterion) Samples
Peer Group Norms
Improved Conceptualizations
Gender Specific
Cultural Relevance

FIGURE 7–7   Enhancing the effectiveness of social skills instruction.

Source: *From Hansen, D. J., Nagle, D. W., & Meyer, K. A. (1998). Enhancing the effectiveness of social skills interventions with adolescents.* Education and Treatment of Children, 21, *508. Reprinted with permission.*

other peers engaged in the activity and the occurrence of peer encouragement and positive feedback behaviors; (e) content effort: the absence of competent bystander behavior (i.e., student movement within an ongoing activity without demonstration of the skills involved in that activity) and the occurrence of active participation; (f) conflict resolution: resolving game activity conflicts without teacher help; and

(g) peer helping and organization: occurrence of peer instruction and support in skill content and organizational tasks.

3. On a rotating class roster, preactivity designation of (a) two students with shirts and whistles to function as referees throughout the team sport to be played, (b) two students to function as activity team captains who were charged with the supervision of all organization and

student preparation required for that activity (e.g., team division and organization, equipment organization, citing rules of play, etc.), and (c) teacher refrain from intervention in all conflicts arising from the activity played for a 2-min minimum to observe changes in students' ability to resolve conflicts independently of adult guidance.

4. Verbal feedback and written recording of a team-by-team teacher evaluation of the social characteristics listed in Item 2 were conducted at the end of each intervention day. Written records consisted of assigning a positive or negative score to each of the seven general social characteristics based on either a larger positive or negative frequency count of these behaviors for each team. Each social characteristic that received more negative than positive instances on frequency tabulation was listed once in the minus score column, and each that received more positive instances was listed in the plus column. A total score for each team was calculated as the sum of the column scores and ranged from -7 to $+7$ for that day. The 5-min postclass talk session included specific feedback regarding recommended social behavior change for the next activity class, based on the minus scores for that day (pp. 404–405).

Token Reinforcement

Chapter 6 described token reinforcement in detail. Here, we call your attention to a study of token reinforcement to improve the social interactions of preschool children. Wolfe, Boyd, and Wolfe (1983) devised a system whereby targeted socially withdrawn children wore bright yellow "happy face" charts with boxes marked to indicate the intervals during which they played cooperatively. Happy face stickers placed on (or removed from) the charts constituted the tokens. Following is a description of the intervention (Wolfe et al., 1983):

Training the target children to play in a cooperative, nonaggressive manner consisted of the following procedures. All children in the classroom were told that sharing time was about to begin, and the target children were given their happy face charts to wear. All of the children in the class were then encouraged to find a play activity and a friend with whom to share the activity. Once the target children had found an activity and friend, a bell signaled that the play program had begun. During the next minute, general praise was given to the group of children for cooperative play (e.g., "I like the way everyone is playing") and specific praise was administered to the target children contingent upon appropriate play (e.g., "I like the way Jimmy is playing with Billy"). At the end of 1 min, the bell rang and the teacher placed happy face stickers on the charts of target children who had engaged in cooperative play for the entire minute. Target children who had not earned a happy face were prompted to engage in cooperative play by the teacher and were reminded of the backup reinforcers they could earn (i.e., outside playtime). In the event a target child did not engage in play following this prompt, a gentle physical prompt was used to lead the child to a play activity. This prompt was repeated every 3 to 5 min for any target child who did not engage in cooperative play. The cycle of 1-min play periods, signaled by the bell, was repeated 15 times during each session.

At the end of the session the teacher counted the happy faces on each child's card and praised the child for his/her efforts to share with others. Initially, the backup reinforcer (10 min of outside play) was administered for earning eight or more stickers. This criterion was gradually increased over several sessions to 12 stickers. Children who did not earn enough tokens to go outside were allowed to look at books and play with toys inside the classroom while the other children went outside. Subsequently, they were reminded of this missed opportunity the following day before the training session was begun. The token reinforcement program continued in the morning for 20 sessions, and then was extended to include the afternoon sessions as well. Once a target child displayed an 80% rate of cooperative play on three consecutive sessions in either the morning or afternoon setting, a fading procedure was implemented that involved a gradual lengthening (over several sessions) of the required interval of cooperative play from 1 min to 5 min. When the child was able to play for a 5-min duration before reinforcement with an overall rate of cooperative play exceeding 80%, the happy face chart was discontinued. Intermittent verbal praise was used in the classroom, and outside play was continued as a reward at the end of each session contingent upon an 80% rate of cooperative play. (pp. 4–5).

You will notice that this intervention actually combined several of the teacher-mediated strategies we have recommended: prompting, praise, and feedback. This approach also incorporated peers as interventionists, which is discussed in the following section.

PEER-MEDIATED STRATEGIES

In a peer-mediated intervention, a member of the individual's peer group, rather than an adult, is the primary agent of change in behavior. Why should you consider peer involvement in social skills training? Consider the response offered by Hollinger (1987):

> To date, social skills training interventions consistently focus exclusively on the children who are identified as those with the behavior problems or low social status. Yet social behavior and status are defined in part by other persons in the target child's life. Consequently, it may be important to consider peers' perceptions in social skills training, thus focusing on interactive exchanges rather than discrete behaviors (Strain, Odom, & McConnell, 1984). It seems especially important to address negative social perception biases among peers in their interactions with behaviorally disordered children. (p. 22)

By including peers in the intervention, you increase the likelihood that they will alter their attitudes towards the socially unskilled child.

Few aspects of behavioral change have experienced such growth as the peer-mediated interventions for socially challenged children and adolescents. Entire volumes now offer suggestions for incorporating peers in social skills training (e.g., Strain et al., 1984). Naturally, we can highlight only the more basic, classroom-tested approaches here. We begin with peer-mediated strategies for young children or those who have more severe problems: peer imitation training, peer social initiation, and peer prompting and reinforcement.

Peer Imitation Training

Peer imitation training requires a classmate of the isolate child to model appropriate social behaviors for the student to learn. Peer imitation training is particularly well suited for students with severe behavioral disorders who do not exhibit appropriate social behaviors. This training is the most intensive peer-mediated intervention we describe, for it involves not only the peer model but an adult who prompts and reinforces the isolated student. Table 7–5 gives you ideas for selecting a good peer behavior model.

Once you have selected a peer model, begin the program. Table 7–6 provides general guidelines for conducting a peer imitation session. You may want to modify them according to the chronological and intellectual level of the peer model selected.

In Table 7–6 the peer model is cued to demonstrate target behaviors. The peer model should demonstrate social behaviors from a predesignated list, repeating them until the withdrawn student consistently imitates them. One source for generating a list of target behaviors is the IEP for the isolate student. For example, you may want the student to learn how to ask other children to play. In this case, you might have the peer model say a standard phrase such as, "I want to play with you. Here is a toy." This is a verbal target behavior. You might also want the student to learn motor skills such as how to hand a toy to another child without throwing it. You would then direct the model to offer a toy gently so that the isolate child could observe this and learn to do it. Other examples of

TABLE 7–5 Peer Imitation Training: Selection of Peer Behavior Model

1. Select a student who attends school regularly to promote continuity of the intervention.
2. Select a student who frequently exhibits appropriate social skills with other students.
3. Select a student who can follow a teacher's verbal instructions reliably and can imitate a teacher model.
4. Select a student who can concentrate on the training task for at least 10 min per target individual.

Source: *Material was taken with permission from Kerr, M. M., and Strain, P. S. (1979). The use of peer social initiation strategies to improve the social skills of withdrawn children. In A. H. Fink (Ed.),* International perspectives on future special education. *Reston, VA: Council for Exceptional Children.*

TABLE 7–6 Steps in Conducting a Peer Imitation Training Session

1. Seat the children about two feet apart and facing one another.
2. Station a trainer behind each child in a "shadowing" style.
3. The trainer behind the peer model whispers in the child's ear to cue the target behavior (e.g., "Kevin, drink from your cup").
4. The model child drinks from his cup.
5. The trainer behind the target child says, "See what Kevin's doing? You do it too!"
6. If the target imitates the modeled behavior, the trainer offers verbal praises and affectionate pats.
7. If the target does not imitate the modeled behavior, the trainer behind the target physically guides (handshapes) the desired behavior (e.g., guides the hand-held cup to the child's mouth).
8. The trainer gradually fades physical guidance and continues to reinforce successive approximations.
9. When the target can successfully imitate the peer model while seated across from each other, move the training to a less structured setting (e.g., a free-play situation).
10. When the peer model exhibits an appropriate behavior, approach the target and say, "See what Kevin's doing? You do it, too!"
11. Provide physical guidance if the target fails to imitate.
12. Fade physical guidance and reinforce successive approximations.

Source: *This table was contributed by Thomas P. Cooke.*

suitable target behaviors are smiling, pushing a toy, adding a block to a tower, throwing a ball, offering a verbal compliment, sharing, hugging, and patting. Remember that target behaviors are not always selected from play activities but might be behaviors from a self-help or prevocational activity, as illustrated in Table 7–6.

It is important that you think about where you would like the peer imitation to take place. If your peer imitation intervention relates to play behaviors, plan training in a free-play area of the classroom or during an outside recess period. If you are attempting to use peer imitation training for, say, self-help or pre-academic skills, then shift the intervention session to a setting that has the materials for these activities. You may find it helpful in the

initial sessions to conduct the training when other students are not present. This enables the student who is challenged to pay close attention to the peer model. The private peer training also allows you to give more attention to the intervention sessions.

Peer Social Initiation

In **peer social initiation,** the peer trainer is required to make social bids to a withdrawn child or children. These bids may be vocal-verbal or motor-gestural (asking the isolate child to play, giving the isolate child a toy, or helping the child to use a particular material). This procedure has been used successfully with both children who have severe behavioral disorders and those with normal to

TABLE 7–7 Peer-Mediated Social Initiation Procedure: Preparing the Peer Trainer

1. Explain to the peer trainer what is expected during the training sessions. Modify the explanation to suit the conversational level of the individual. Examples of this brief explanation are, "Try your best to get other children to play with you," "To get others to play with you, give them a toy."
2. Train the peer trainer to expect rejection. This is accomplished by the adult's taking the role of an isolated individual. In every other instance of the peer trainer making a social initiation toward the adult, ignore the initiation. Pause for 10 sec or more, then explain to the child that your ignoring the initiation is a behavior the trainer is likely to encounter with the isolate student. Explain this in a manner that encourages the trainer to continue trying. For example, you can say something like, "Children will not always want to play, but you need to keep trying very hard."
3. Repeat the role play, first training the peer to hand you a toy or to otherwise make a motor-gestural initiation. Then train the student to make vocal-verbal initiations.
4. Carry out the role play using each of the toys or play materials that are in the free-play setting. Cue the peer trainer about any toys that have a particular appeal to the isolate individual. Introduce cue cards depicting each toy at this time, if necessary.
5. Continue practicing the role plays during daily 20 min practice sessions until the peer trainer can reliably make repeated social initiations towards you. Keep in mind that peer training in the research reported has typically required at least four sessions, with additional sessions needed for a severely handicapped peer trainer.
6. Be sure to reinforce the peer trainer's participation during each training session.

Source: *Material was taken with permission from Kerr, M. M., and Strain, P. S. (1979). The use of peer social initiation strategies to improve the social skills of withdrawn children. In A. H. Fink (Ed.). International perspectives on future special education. Reston, VA: Council for Exceptional Children.*

mild disabilities (James & Egel, 1986; Ragland, Kerr, & Strain, 1978).

In addition to using the general resources listed for peer interventions, you may want to make a set of cue cards to assist the peer trainer in carrying out his role. Each cue card should display a picture of a toy or play activity that the isolate child enjoys. Peer trainers need a little reminder to move from one play material to another during the training session, which the cue cards accomplish when displayed in the play area.

Select a peer trainer for this intervention according to the criteria listed in Table 7–6. Research studies reveal the ability of even very young children (3-years-old) or children who have developmental delays (moderate retardation) to carry out this simple intervention. Table 7–7 outlines the basic steps of preparing a peer trainer for intervention sessions. If you are working with a peer trainer who has developmental delays, this training may take longer than the four 20-min sessions suggested. In addition, you may find it helpful to

provide frequent, tangible reinforcers to a trainer who has developmental delays.

When you are ready to schedule intervention sessions on a daily basis, allow enough time to enable the peer trainer to work with one isolate student at a time for a 10-min interval. Do not plan to ask the trainer to work with several students at one time because it becomes too difficult a role for the peer trainer and is not sufficiently intensive an intervention for the withdrawn pupils. Rather, "taking turns" is preferred. You may notice, however, that while the peer trainer is working with one student, others in the group play more cooperatively and frequently with each other.

The first few days of a peer social initiation intervention may leave you with the discouraging feeling that this intervention will not work at all. This is because when first approached by the peer trainer, isolate children have a natural tendency to ward off these approaches through temper tantrums and other oppositional behaviors. You

TABLE 7–8   Peer-Mediated Social Initiation Procedure: Conducting the Intervention Sessions

1. Set aside at least 6 min for each target individual during the play session.
2. Try to use the same free-play area with the play materials suggested each day.
3. Before each intervention session, review with the peer trainer the activities that are most likely to succeed.
4. Remind the peer trainer before each session that the pupils may not respond at first but to keep trying.
5. Remind the peer trainer to play with only one target individual at a time. It helps if the adult in the session reminds the peer trainer when to change toys and when to begin play with another student.
6. Reinforce the peer trainer for attempting to play with the withdrawn individuals. If the session is going slowly, you may wish to reinforce the peer trainer during the session. Otherwise, provide the peer trainer with some form of reinforcement at the end of the session.

and the peer trainer must not give up at this point. Rather, the peer trainer should continue to make initiations toward the children, and you should reinforce these efforts. You may find that in the initial session, you will also need to prompt, either physically or verbally, the isolate student's responding to the peer trainer. This initial difficult period generally lasts no more than four or five sessions, after which pupils cooperate and begin to enjoy their interactions. Table 7–8 displays the basic steps in conducting the intervention sessions.

Peer Prompting and Reinforcement

Peer prompting and reinforcement, like teacher prompting and reinforcement, refers to the use of a trainer to assist withdrawn children in playing with each other. Again, verbal and physical prompts and frequent reinforcers are used. Research on this procedure has not been extensive, but the initial work has shown that a peer trainer could successfully use the procedure to increase the cooperative play behavior of two children who have severe behavioral disorders (Strain, Kerr, & Ragland, 1979). Consider the peer prompting and reinforcement strategy as a follow-up to peer social initiations. Once an isolate student begins to respond reliably to the peer trainer, a different playmate can be introduced by using the peer prompting and reinforcement strategies described in Table 7–9. Do not train a peer to carry out both interventions (peer social initiations and prompt-

ing/reinforcement) at once; this would be too complex a task.

Peer Management Strategy

Young students who are socially withdrawn may benefit from playing "class manager," a role studied by Sainato, Maheady, and Shook (1986). In their study, the withdrawn kindergartners took turns directing pleasurable classroom activities: feeding the class pet, ringing the "clean-up bell," collecting milk money, and opening two play areas. This effort succeeded in improving social interactions and sociometric ratings.

Peer Coaching

Peer coaching, like peer imitation, involves students and adults who provide instruction. The purpose of this intervention is to teach withdrawn pupils social skills to gain them peer acceptance. Children who are socially withdrawn realize more opportunity to engage in social learning if they are trained to increase their acceptance by peers.

Peer Tutoring

Research shows that academic peer tutoring can have a positive influence on peer social interactions, although researchers cannot always document how and why (Cook, Scruggs, Mastropieri, & Casto, 1986).

TABLE 7–9 Peer-Mediated Prompting and Reinforcement Strategy

1. Select a peer as suggested in the previous intervention strategies.
2. Plan at least four 20-min training sessions to prepare the individual for her role as peer trainer.
3. Explain to the peer trainer that you want assistance in helping other children to learn to play. Explain further that the role of peer trainer is helping children play with each other and letting them know they are doing a good job.
4. Train the peer trainer by inviting two children into the play session, and practice with the trainer prompting and reinforcing them for playing together. Unlike other peer-mediated procedures, training for peer prompting and reinforcement should take place "on the job," using the isolate students from the beginning.
5. By modeling the strategies with the isolate children present, assist the peer trainer to think of ways to prompt and reinforce the isolate children.
6. Remind the peer trainer before each intervention session to try to get the two children to play with each other rather than directly with the peer trainer.
7. Set aside the time and materials and location described in previous peer training intervention for the actual training sessions.
8. Remember to reinforce the peer trainer for efforts after each session.

Peer-tutoring guidelines, as presented earlier, may help your students expand their opportunities to practice both social and academic skills. Consider peer tutoring as a supplementary social skills training activity, relying on more direct interventions to teach new social skills (see Scruggs, Mastropieri, Veit, & Osguthorpe, 1986; Scruggs, Mastropieri, & Richter, 1985).

Another goal for peer tutoring may be a shift in attitudes toward children who are behaviorally challenged. Shisler, Osguthorpe, and Eiserman (1987) found that nondisabled sixth-graders rated their tutors with behavior disorders more positively after their tutoring experience. According to Johnson and Johnson (1984), the tutoring may allow nondisabled students to view their peers with disabilities in a different, less stereotyped role (Shisler et al., 1987).

This section closes with a look at the benefits of peer-mediated interventions for *all* students. Rob, a child without disabilities, has learned helpful ways to accommodate his classmates with special needs. His ideas are listed in Figure 7–8.

SELF-MEDIATED STRATEGIES

Self-management strategies for the remediation of social withdrawal have not been explored ex-

tensively in research literature. However, newly emerging self-management strategies offer promise for an isolate student who is aware of her difficulty and wishes to have a role in remedying it. For example, this intervention might be very useful for adolescents included in a general education setting. The self-management strategies discussed here are similar to those discussed in other chapters; the primary difference is in the target behavior selected. In choosing target behaviors for self-management procedures, it is a good idea to have the student participate.

The primary resource for helping students carry out a self-managed intervention for social withdrawal is a self-recording data sheet. Students should record their own performances to visibly show their progress towards meeting the goal of increased social interactions. (Chapter 6 contained information on developing a self-recording sheet.)

The purpose of self-recording is to make the student aware of positive interactions with others and how to increase them. Thus, the intervention is twofold. First, the teacher or counselor describes to students examples of social initiations and responses. Second, students collect data on their own interactions. A third component, self-reinforcement, may supplement the intervention, or the teacher or counselor may provide the reinforcement to the

Helping a Child with Disabilities
by Rob Perrone, age eight

1. Call the child by his or her name, not "the handicapped kid."
2. Be kind to the child, and remember: this involves patience.
3. When you start out, ask the teacher, "May I help this child?"
4. Wait until the teacher says you can do it.
5. After the teacher says "Yes," then you go over to the child.
6. Ask the child what they're doing, or what they're writing, or what they're interested in.
7. Then probably ask them, [not in a mean way, but nicely], "You know, I've heard that you kind of have some trouble in doing . . ."
8. The child will say, "Yeah, but . . . I still have some friends."
9. Then you say, "I'm here to help you out with your disability and help you do things like your classmates."
10. Then, say it's time to line up for gym and the child is in a wheelchair, you would say, "I'm going to help you in gym, also. I'll come and help you along with your teacher to play the sport."

YO! THIS IS A NEW PART OF THE PRESENTATION!!

11. If the child has trouble in behavior . . . approach them not like you're a really sweet person. But more like, "Hey, yo, Dude, What 'ya doin?" so they feel comfortable. Then, if they start acting up, just say, "Calm down, [whatever their name is. Not like "Bad kid," or "Sick Kid,"]
12. Do not say this even with a kind voice--no matter what--to this child: "I know that you're not very good at behavior and you're not well-liked."
13. SURE, SURE. I KNOW YOU WANT TO KNOW WHY? WELL:

First of all, it would seem mean to them. Second of all, it would be like telling them that just because they have a simple disability that they can't be liked. Third of all, it would just probably make them do the same thing.

FIGURE 7–8 Helping a child with disabilities.

Reprinted with permission of the author.

14. For a kid who just plays a little too rough, first of all, don't say, "Do you want to play this sport that he DOES like?" [Now I know it sounds kinda mean, but the sport he likes he probably plays too rough.] Your first move when you come into the room is to definitely ask the teacher. See if the teacher will give you some information on how to work well with this child. Say, "When you have gym class, I'll probably come and help you out a little bit in case you start getting a little rough. Because the school doesn't want anyone to get hurt." Whatever you do, don't start screaming at the kid. This probably isn't my best advice for the rough-housing kid. Ask the teacher if you want really good information, because mine's probably not right. My advice might not be the best.

15. And if the child is shy, invite him to take a walk with you with his mom or something or a friend. This only works in a city. When you see a pigeon, say, "I'm gonna get that bird." And then run after it. That works because it's funny and it will get the child to laugh. Believe me, I did it to my best friend, and it worked.

16. If the child does not have trouble in behavior but--say--listening, then you would use this approach. Probably try to make the activity a little more fun or humorous. Or a little more exciting, so he or she would want to look at it. Make sure that you get the message but make sure that it is still a little humorous or fun.

Approach #2: You might just tell another student to tell them, "Can you say to this kid, 'Hey Buddy! You know how I get all my good grades?' I try to listen my best, so I hear everything the teacher is saying so I get the maximum amount you are supposed to learn."

Whatever you do, don't tell them that just because you can't listen well means that you won't get good grades Because they might get good grades in one thing but not in another thing.

FIGURE 7–8   Helping a child with disabilities—*Continued.*

student. Here are examples of target behaviors for a student to record:

- Raising my hand in classroom discussions to say something.
- Asking a question during the class meeting.
- Helping another student in my class on an assignment.
- Answering a question when another student asks me something.
- Saying "hello" to one of my classmates.
- Asking my classmate to eat lunch next to me.
- Asking someone in my class to play with me at recess.
- At recess, telling others they are doing a good job.
- Lending someone a pencil or paper during class.
- Sitting next to one of my friends during lunch.
- Bringing a toy for someone else to play with in school.
- Telling someone what I did after school yesterday.
- Signing up to tutor another person in my class.
- Asking someone else to help me with my self-recording project.

Self-monitoring is a good way to extend your social skills training program, as suggested by Kelly et al. (1983), who found that self-monitoring improved the social interactions between adolescents who had behavior disorders and their vocational supervisors. In this case, self-monitoring was combined with role-playing and didactic training. Students rated themselves and then discussed their ratings with their teacher. When students monitored their interactions, their social skills showed greater **generalization** to a setting for which they were not trained.

SUMMARY

This chapter began with remedies for students who lack school survival skills—those behaviors necessary to meet one's academic potential. School survival skills are crucial for students included in general education classrooms, and several strategies have proven effective in preparing students for this transition to general education. Try one of these interventions—after you have determined through careful assessment what skills a student lacks.

This chapter concluded with a focus on the social skill problems of your students. Beginning with checklists to gather global opinions about students' functioning, we moved to the more precise assessments, sociometric measures and direct observations. In addition to measuring a student's one-to-one interactions, consider how well a student functions within a group context. Moreover, you must adapt group activities within the classroom to the individual strengths and weaknesses of the students while challenging them to improve their ability to work with others. The capacity to function within small and large groups is crucial to successful inclusion. Many strategies were highlighted in this chapter, from environmental modifications for young children to social skills curricula for adolescents. In general, the more didactic, curriculum-based approaches are well suited to students whose limitations are mild to moderate or who have the skills but lack consistency and judgment about when and how to use them. The prompting and reinforcement strategies, conducted by the teacher or by a trained peer, meet the needs of young students or those with more severe disabilities whose social interactions may still be rudimentary.

Teaching Social Skills

Li-Lin Chen

This week the goals of my social skills program are that students will initiate a conversation, make eye contact, and smile with adults (teachers). In addition, students must get at least five marks on the group contingency according to the agreement between their self-recording charts and the teachers' recording sheet. On Monday students will practice initiating a conversation with an adult or a teacher. On Tuesday they must make eye contact as well as starting a conversation with adults (teachers). On Wednesday they will initiate a conversation with eye contact as well as smile at the adults (teachers). (Naturally, our program continues throughout the year.)

Monday
Homeroom (15 min)

00:00–00:05 (Teacher's greeting)

The teacher says, "Good morning everyone! How are you today?"

She lets students feel free and comfortable to talk.

00:06–00:15 (Introduction of today's topic)

The teacher talks about today's topic, starting a conversation with the following questions:

How do you start a conversation?
What do you do when you meet someone?
What are some other ways you can start a conversation?
Why is conversation important?

(Students can respond or ask questions if they do not understand. The teacher lists what they say on the blackboard and keeps a list on paper so that she and the students can discuss it next time.)

The teacher talks about the self-recording procedures to the entire class—including when and how to record. The teacher then asks students to start a conversation with any adult (teacher) in math, art, music, English, and social skills classes, not including the homeroom period. She hands out paper to every student and explains how to use the self-recording chart by drawing a chart on the board. Then they copy the chart onto their paper. They can place a "Y" mark on their chart if they initiate a conversation with adults (teachers) before, within, or at the end of the classes. The maximum total marks that can be earned for the week is 21. Each needs to write his name, the date, and the topic of the day on his recording chart so that he can learn to be responsible for it and also to remember what he should do for the day. The chart will be like the one in Figure 7–9.

The teacher must tell students the reason why other teachers are joining them to record their behavior by starting a conversation with teachers, in class or out of class, every day. Then they will talk about the group contingency: where it will be placed (public posting in this classroom), how the group contingency will apply in starting a conversation with adults (teachers), and how the entire class or each individual will earn rewards—the teacher lets them recommend rewards and vote for the most popular for the entire class (assuming that they like free time, reading storybooks, and computer games).

Name				
Date				
Purpose				
Math	Social Skills	Music	English	Art

FIGURE 7–9 Self-recording chart.

The Group Contingency

When each student has earned five "Y" marks in a week on their self-recording chart (this must agree with the records kept by their teachers), the whole class will have a 10-min free conversation time in the social skills class the following week. (Where there is disagreement, the teacher clarifies by talking to the student and those teachers.)

A point will be earned for each additional "Y" mark over five "Y" marks.

Each student who accumulates nine points by Friday can choose a favorite storybook to read with a friend during free time or recess time next week.

Each student who accumulates more than ten points by Friday can play a 15-min computer game with a friend during recess or free time next week.

3rd Period (60 minutes)

00:00–00:10 (Review)

The teacher asks how they initiated a conversation with their math teacher. She lets the students respond freely. She asks how they started the conversation. How did they record for themselves? What did they say?

00:11–00:25 (Introduction to starting a conversation with adults)

The teacher mentions the morning's response list and then discusses it in depth. She explains to students what it means to start a conversation and how they can start a conversation with adults (teachers). Give good examples from the math class. (Remember to make sure that each student understands how to initiate a conversation.)

00:26–00:40 (Demonstration of the skill)

The teacher will ask a student to volunteer to role-play initiating a conversation. For example, the volunteer will act as a bookstore owner and the teacher as a customer. The teacher might say, "Good morning! I am looking for a cookbook. Can you help me?" The teacher will then give each student in the room the opportunity to initiate a conversation.

00:41–00:55 (Role-play of the skill)

The teacher pairs off students and gives them some situations to let them practice with their partners, such as in a restaurant, a clothing store, a bookstore, an ice cream store, or a flower shop. After they practice one situation, the teacher asks them how they did and asks one of the pairs to come forward to demonstrate. The teacher then begins a discussion with the class about how their example can be improved. During this discussion the pair can incorporate the improvements into their situation. So as not to embarrass the pair, the discussion should accentuate the positives as well as pointing out the areas that need improvement. If time allows, each pair should be given the opportunity to demonstrate their role-play situation in front of the class.

00:56–00:60 (Reinforcement)

Ask the students what they remember. Review the procedures of self-recording. Remind students of the rewards for the whole class or each individual.

The End of the Day (15 min)

00:00–00:15 (homework)

The teacher begins by collecting all of the self-recording charts. (The teacher should also collect the other teachers' charts and make sure that they agree with the students'.) Next, the teacher passes out the homework sheet to each student and explains what they need to do at home (see Figure 7–10). The sheet should be signed by their parent and returned during homeroom period the following morning.

Tuesday
Homeroom (15 min)

00:00–00:05 (collecting parents' slips)

The teacher collects the parents' slips from all students, and asks how they did with their assignments and if there are any questions. (Remember to call student's parent if they do not turn in the slip and write down specific student's response.)

00:06–00:15 (Review of self-recording charts)

Under each student's name on the group contingency poster, the teacher writes each student's total marks. The poster should be placed on the wall where everyone can obviously see it. If there is a disagreement about the marks, the teacher arranges time to meet with the student and teachers, encouraging those students who have only a few marks, and praising those who gained many marks. Then the teacher will hand

out paper and ask the students to draw their self-recording chart. It should include each student's name, date, and the topic of the day, as defined by the teacher. The teacher announces that they can mark a "Y" when they initiate a conversation with adults (teachers) in math and social skills classes. After the social skills class, they will record a different social behavior according to today's criterion.

3rd Period (60 min)

00:00–00:15 (Recording marks in your social skills class and introducing the new social skill)

The teacher marks a "Y" on the recording chart when any student starts a conversation with her. She praises those students who initiate a conversation, especially those ten students with behavioral problems.

Next, the teacher introduces today's behavioral skill—initiating a conversation and also making eye contact with adults (teachers) by asking questions or showing examples:

What do you do when you meet someone? (For example, when you saw your friend in the mall, what did you do? Did you wave your hand or call his or her name?)

What else did you do besides talking? Did you look at your friend or did you avoid looking at him/her?

After students respond to these questions, the teacher asks them why they reacted the way they did and explains why we need eye contact when talking to people. She also discusses some exceptional situations such as when speaking to people with different cultural backgrounds.

00:16–00:30 (Demonstration of the skill)

The teacher tells them about her own story:
  I am shy; therefore, I try not to talk to people. One time, Lillian, one of my best friends,

Dear Parents,

Good evening! Thank you for taking the time to read this letter. The purpose of this letter is to ask for your help with your child's homework. The focus of this week at school is emphasis on initiating a conversation while making eye contact, and smiling with adults (teachers). This process has been divided into three steps. The first step is to initiate a conversation with adults (teachers). The second step is not only initiating a conversation but also making eye contact with adults. The third step is initiating a conversation, making eye contact and smiling while talking with adults (teachers). Today please pay attention to and encourage your child to start a conversation with you when your child wants to watch TV, to have a drink, to ask you to sign this sheet, to ask permission to play with neighbors, etc. On Tuesday, it would be helpful if you could take your child to the library or a bookstore where he or she could practice initiating a conversation while making eye contact with adults. On Wednesday, possibly you could take him or her to a friend's home where your child is able to practice initiating a conversation, making eye contact, and smiling while talking to adults. Please do not hesitate to call me if you have any questions. I will be very glad to hear from you. Have a nice evening! Please remember to detach the answer slip from this homework sheet, sign it, and remind your child to return it to me. Thank you again.

Sincerely,

Carol

08/02/00

I agree to guide my child to finish his or her homework.

Signature _____

Date _____

FIGURE 7–10 Homework sheet.

saw me and called my name, so I had to talk to her. She made direct eye contact while speaking to me, which made me very uncomfortable and I felt like going away. However, I respected her and didn't want to embarrass her, and because she was so nice, I was encouraged to look at her while talking to her. That experience helped me to make the effort to look at people when I am talking to them.

The teacher asks for a discussion about her incident with Lillian, asking what they would have done. The teacher then speaks directly to each student, making sure to make eye contact. The class should then discuss each student's reaction to this and ask the students to describe how it made each feel.

00:31–00:45 (Role-play)

The teacher should ask for four volunteers or pick four students for a role-play situation. One will be a waiter. Three of them will be friends going to have dinner at the Pizza Hut. The waiter gives them menus. They need more time to think, so they ask him to come back later. After he comes back, everyone takes a turn to order his or her own pizza. The teacher will then initiate a discussion of the role-play and ask for feedback from the class.

The teacher asks another four students to come forward, with one student acting as a children's bookstore manager and the others as customers. Each customer will request a book that they want and buy it. They need to initiate conversations and make eye contact. Once again, the teacher asks for a discussion of this role-play situation and asks for feedback from the class.

The teacher should pair off the students and have them take turns practicing being a taxi driver or passenger. The taxi driver needs to know where to go, so his passenger needs to give him the directions. Both of them should make eye contact during their conversations. The teacher should try to monitor each pair and offer help where needed. The pair that demonstrates the best activity should replay their situation for the whole class. Their peers can give them feedback and opinions.

00:46–00:60 (Review)

The teacher should ask students to sit in a circle (the teacher sits with them). Discuss what they learned in the last 45 min. How did they feel when the teacher asked them to come forward to role-play? During this time they can ask questions and express their opinions. The teacher reminds them that they mark a "Y" only when they initiate a conversation and make eye contact with the adults (teachers).

The End of the Day (15 min)

00:00–00:15 (Homework)

The teacher collects and checks students' self-recording charts to see how they are doing in math, music, English, and art classes (the teacher should also collect the teachers' recording sheet). If some students do not earn any marks today, the teacher encourages them to try again tomorrow. Explain the next homework assignment. Their mother or father should take them to a library or bookstore. Their job is to initiate a conversation with some of the people who are there, remembering to make eye contact.

Wednesday
Homeroom (15 min)

00:00–00:10 (Talking about the homework)

The teacher will begin by asking where student's parents took them and how they initiated a conversation: "Did you make eye contact? Was it very difficult? Why or why not?" The teacher writes their responses and feelings on the board to keep as a record.

00:11–00:15 (Review of self-recording charts)

The teacher records each student's total marks on the group contingency poster under their names, discussing the marks each student earned on Monday and Tuesday. She reminds the students about the class reward and the individual student rewards and the conditions on which they are based. This can encourage those students who have not reached five marks to do better. Next, the teacher hands out paper and asks them to draw their self-recording chart, including name, date, and today's topic (the teacher will announce this to the class). Once again the teacher reminds them to mark a "Y" on their self-recording charts for their math and social skills classes according to yesterday's criterion (starting a conversation and making eye contact with adults (teachers)). After the social skills class, the self-recording chart will be based on today's criterion.

3rd Period (60 min)

00:00–00:15 (Recording marks in your class and introducing the new social skill)

The teacher will mark a "Y" on her recording sheet when any student starts a conversation as well as makes eye contact. She praises those students verbally. Then, the teacher introduces today's social behavior: initiating a conversation, making eye contact, and adding a "smile." She gets them started by beginning the discussion as follows:

> Do you remember the role-play situation yesterday which included three friends and a waiter at the Pizza Hut? (If they do not remember, ask one volunteer student to describe it.) If the waiter had said "Good evening" without smiling, how would that make you feel? (Let students discuss this question.) Then, if one of the three friends ordered pizza without a smile, how would the waiter respond? Would he smile in return? Why or why not?

These discussions among the students help them to discover how important it is to smile and make eye contact when talking to someone.

00:16–00:30 (Demonstration of the skill)

The teacher walks around the classroom and chooses students randomly, asking "How are you?" and making sure to smile and make eye contact. Then the teacher asks how this made them feel and begins a discussion with the students.

00:31–00:45 (Role-play)

The teacher groups students in pairs and gives them some situations from which to choose to practice with their partners (a shoe store, a candy store, a movie theater, etc.). The teacher asks them to pay much attention to their smile when their partners start a conversation and to be sure to make eye contact with each other. If their peers do not smile while practicing, their partners should correct them right away and practice it again. (During their role-play, the teacher needs to observe their role-play and choose one of the pairs to demonstrate for the entire class.) If time permits, the teacher can invite other pairs to come forward.

00:46–00:60 (Review)

The teacher begins a discussion by asking, "Do you like it when someone talks to you with a smile on their face? Why or why not? Can anybody tell me what social skills we learned this week?" (The teacher may need to give them some hints.) Next, the teacher looks at the group contingency and encourages their efforts, reminding them of the class reward and individual rewards to provoke them to practice the social skills they have learned.

The End of the Day (15 min)

00:00–00:15 (Homework)

The teacher collects and checks students' self-recording charts to see how they are doing in other classes. If any students did not receive marks since Tuesday, she arranges a time to meet with those students privately. She discusses their previous homework assignments and encourages them to practice their skills initiating conversations, making eye contact, and smiling while making conversation.

DISCUSSION QUESTIONS

1. What are the most important school survival skills for mainstreamed students?

2. How can you assess school survival skills?

3. What are five ways you can increase the opportunities for your students' skills to generalize to other, less restrictive settings?

4. What environmental modifications can assist a student who is overly dependent on the teacher?
5. What is the most effective way of using self-instruction as an intervention for on-task behavior?
6. What are the dos and don'ts of social skills interventions? Discuss them.
7. Why is there such emphasis on peer-mediated interventions?
8. What does research suggest about environmental modifications for improving social skills?
9. Will peer tutoring lead to improved social skills? Why or why not?
10. What are the essential components of a social skills intervention? Illustrate them.

REFERENCES

Anesko, K. M., Schoiock, G., Ramirez, R., & Levine, F. M. (1987). The Homework Problem Checklist: Assessing children's homework difficulties. *Behavioral Assessment,* 9, 179–185.

Bullis, M., & Davis, C.(1997). Further examination of two measures of community-based social skills for adolescents and young adults with emotional and behavioral disorders. *Behavioral Disorders,* 23(1), 29–39.

Cartledge, G., & Milburn, J. F. (1996). *Cultural diversity and social skills instruction: Understanding ethnic and gender differences.* Champaign, IL: Research Press.

Cook, S. B., Scruggs, T. E., Mastropieri, M. A., & Casto, G. W. (1986). Handicapped students as tutors. *Journal of Special Education,* 19(4), 483–492.

Cooper, H. (1989). Synthesis of research on homework. *Educational Leadership,* 47(3), 85–91.

Dawson-Rodriques, K., Lavay, B., Butt, K., & Lacourse, M. (1997). A plan to reduce transition time in physical education. *Journal of Physical Education, Recreation, and Dance,* 68(9), 30–34.

DeBoer, A. L., & Fister, S. (1995). *Strategies and Tools for Collaborative Teaching.* Longmont, CO: Sopris West.

DiGangi, S. A., Maag, J. W., & Rutherford, R. B. (1991). Self-graphing of on-task behavior: Enhancing the reactive effects of self-monitoring on on-task behavior and academic performance. *Learning Disability Quarterly,* 14(3), 221–230.

Dy, E. B., Strain, P. S., Fullerton, A., & Stowitschek, J. J. (1981). Training institutionalized, elderly mentally retarded persons as intervention agents for socially isolate peers. *Analysis and Intervention in Developmental Disabilities,* 1, 199–215.

Epstein, M. H., Polloway, E. A., Foley, R. M., & Patton, J. R. (1993). Homework: A comparison of teachers' and parents' perceptions of the problems experienced by students identified as having behavioral disorders, learning disabilities, or no disabilities. *Remedial & Special Education,* 14(5), 40–50.

Fister, S. L. (1996). Peer tutoring. In K. R. Reavis, M. T. Sweeten, W. R. Jensen, D. P. Morgan, D. J. Andrews, & S. L. Fister (Eds.). *Best Practices: Behavioral and educational strategies for teachers,* pp. 99–108.

Fowler, M. (1995). *Educators Manual: Children and adults with attention deficit disorders.* Plantation, FL: Children and Adults with Attention Deficit Disorder (CH.A.D.D.).

Franklin, M. E. (1992). Culturally sensitive instructional practices for African-American learners with disabilities. *Exceptional Children,* 59(2), 115–122.

Fuchs, L. S., Fuchs, D., Bentz, J., Phillips, N. B., & Hamlett, C. L. (1994). The nature of student interactions during peer tutoring with and without prior training and experience. *American Educational Research Journal,* 31(1), 75–103.

Fuchs, L. S., Fuchs, D., & Phillips, N. (1994). The relation between teacher's beliefs about the importance of good student work habits, teacher planning, and student achievement. *Elementary School Journal,* 94(3), 331–345.

Fuchs, D., Fuchs, L. S., Reeder, P., Bahr, M. W., & Moore, P. (1989). *Mainstream assistance teams: A handbook on prereferral intervention.* Nashville, TN: Vanderbilt University.

Gable, R. A., Hendrickson, J. M., & Strain, P. S. (1978). Assessment modification, and generalization of social interaction among multihandicapped children. *Education and Training of the Mentally Retarded,* 13, 279–286.

Goodwin, M. W. (1998). Cooperative learning and social skills: What skills to teach and how to teach them. *Intervention in School and Clinic,* 35(1), 29–33.

Gresham, F. (1998). Social skills training: Should we raze, remodel, or rebuild? *Behavioral Disorders,* 24(1), 19–25.

Gresham, F. M., & Cavell, T. A. (1986). Assessing adolescent social skills. In R. G. Harrington (Ed.), *Testing adolescents* (pp. 93–123). Kansas City, MO: Test Corporation of America.

Hansen, D. J., Nagle, D. W., & Meyer, K. A. (1998). Enhancing the effectiveness of social skills interventions with adolescents. *Education and Treatment of Children*, 21(2), 489–513.

Hertz, V., and McLaughlin, T. F. (1990). Self-recording effects for on-task behavior of mildly handicapped adolescents. *Child & Family Behavior Therapy*, 12(3), 1–11.

Hollinger, J. D. (1987). Social skills for behaviorally disordered children as preparation for mainstreaming: Theory, practice, and new directions. *Recent Advances in Special Education*, 8(4), 17–27.

James, S. D., & Egel, A. L. (1986). A direct prompting strategy for increasing reciprocal interactions between handicapped and nonhandicapped siblings. *Journal of Applied Behavior Analysis*, 19(2), 173–186.

Johnson, D. W., & Johnson, R. T. (1984). Classroom learning structure and attitudes toward handicapped students in mainstream settings: A theoretical model and research evidence. In R. L. Jones (Ed.), *Attitudes and attitude change in special education: Theory and practice* (pp. 118–142). Reston, VA: Council for Exceptional Children.

Johnson, D. W., & Johnson, R. T. (1991). *Learning together and alone: Cooperative, competitive, and individualistic learning* (3rd ed.). Boston: Allyn & Bacon.

Kelly, W. J., Salzberg, C. L., Levy, S. M., Warrenfeltz, R. B., Adams, T. W., Crouse, T. R., & Beegle, G. P. (1983). The effects of role-playing and self-monitoring on the generalization of vocational social skills by behaviorally disordered adolescents. *Behavioral Disorders*, 9(1), 27–35.

Kerr, M. M., Zigmond, N., Schaeffer, A. L., & Brown, G. (1986). An observational followup study of successful and unsuccessful high school students. *High School Journal*, 71, 20–32.

Lee, J. W., & Cartledge, G. (1996). Native Americans. In M. Cartledge, & J. F. Milburn, *Cultural Diversity and Social Skills Instruction*. Champaign, IL: Research Press.

Levendoski, L. S., & Cartledge, G. (2000). Self-monitoring for elementary school children with serious emotional disturbances: Classroom applications for increased academic responding. *Behavioral Disorders*, 23(3), 211–224.

Mathes, P. G., & Fuchs, L. S. (1994). The efficacy of peer tutoring in reading for students with mild disabilities: A best-evidence synthesis. *School Psychology Review*, 23(1), 59–80.

Mathur, S. R., & Rutherford, R. B. (1994). Teaching conversational social skills to delinquent youth. *Behavioral Disorders*, 19(4), 294–305.

McConnell, S. R., Strain, P. S., Kerr, M. M., Stagg, V., Lenkner, D. A., & Lambert, D. L. (1984). An empirical definition of school adjustment: Selection of target behaviors for a comprehensive treatment program. *Behavior Modification*, 8, 451–473.

McGinnis, J. C., Friman, P. C., & Carlyon, W. D. (1999). The effect of token rewards on "intrinsic" motivation for doing math. *Journal of Applied Behavior Analysis*, 32(3), 375–379.

Odom, S. L., & Strain, P. S. (1984). Classroom-based social skills instruction for severely handicapped preschool children. *Topics in Early Childhood Education*, 4(3), 97–116.

Olympia, D., Andrews, D., Valum, L., & Jensen, W. (1993). *Homework Teams: Homework management strategies for the classroom*. Longmont, CO: Sopris West.

Patrick, B. C., Skinner, E. A., & Connell, J. P. (1993). What motivates children's behavior and emotion? Joint effects of perceived control and autonomy in the academic domain. *Journal of Personality and Social Psychology*, 65(4), 781–791.

Ragland, E. U., Kerr, M. M., & Strain, P. S. (1978). Effects of social initiations on the behavior of withdrawn autistic children. *Topics in Early Childhood Special Education*, 13, 565–578.

Roderique, T. W., Polloway, E. A., Cumblad, C., Epstein, M. H., & Bursuck, W. D. (1994). Homework: A survey of policies in the United States. *Journal of Learning Disabilities*, 27(8), 481–487.

Rosenberg, M. S. (1989). The effects of daily homework assignments on the acquisition of basic skills by students with learning disabilities. *Journal of Learning Disabilities*, 22, 314–323.

Rutherford, R. B., Chapman, L., DiGangi, S. A., & Anderson, K. A. (1992). *Teaching social skills: A practical instructional approach*. Ann Arbor: Exceptional Innovations.

Rutherford, R. B., Mathur, S. R., & Quinn, M. M. (1998). Promoting social communication skills through cooperative learning and direct instruction. *Education and Treatment of Children*, 21(3), 354–369.

Sainato, D. M., Maheady, L., & Shook, G. L. (1986). The effects of a classroom manager role on the social interaction patterns and social status of withdrawn kindergarten students. *Journal of Applied Behavior Analysis*, 19(2), 187–195.

Sainato, D. M., Strain, P. S., Lefebvre, D., & Rapp, N. (1987). Facilitating transition times with handicapped preschool children: A comparison between peer-mediated and antecedent prompt procedures. *Journal of Applied Behavior Analysis*, 20(3), 285–291.

Scruggs, T. E., Mastropieri, M. A., & Richter, L. (1985). Peer tutoring with behaviorally disordered students' social and academic benefits. *Behavioral Disorders*, 11(1), 283–294.

Scruggs, T. E., Mastropieri, M., Veit, D T., & Osguthorpe, R. T. (1986). Behaviorally disordered students as tutors: Effects on social behavior. *Behavioral Disorders*, 12(1), 36–44.

Seaman, J. (1996). *Teaching kids to learn: An integrated study skills curriculum for grades 5–7*. Longmont, CO: Sopris West.

Sharpe, T., Brown M., & Crider, K. (1995). The effects of a sportsmanship curriculum intervention on generalized positive social behavior of urban elementary school students. *Journal of Applied Behavior Analysis*, 28(4), 401–416.

Shisler, L., Osguthorpe, R. T., & Eiserman, W. (1987). The effects of reverse-role tutoring on the social acceptance of students with behavioral disorders. *Behavioral Disorders*, 13(1), 35–44.

Skinner, E. A., Wellborn, J. G., & Connell, J. P. (1990). What it takes to do well in school and whether I've got it: A process model of perceived control and children's engagement in school. *Journal of Educational Psychology*, 82(1), 22–32.

Snyder, M. C., & Bambara, L. M. (1997). Teaching secondary students with learning disabilities to self-manage classroom survival skills. *Journal of Learning Disabilities*, 30(5), 534–543.

Strain, P. S., Kerr, M. M., & Ragland, E. U. (1979). Effects of peer mediated social initiations and prompting/reinforcement procedures on the social behavior of autistic children. *Journal of Autism and Developmental Disabilities*, 9, 41–54.

Strain, P. S., Odom, S. L., & McConnell, S. (1984). Promoting social reciprocity of exceptional children: Identification, target behavior selection, and intervention. *Remedial and Special Education*, 5, 21–28.

Sugai, G., & Lewis, T. J. (1996). Preferred and promising practices for social skill instruction. *Focus on Exceptional Children*, 19, 1–16.

Sutherland, K. S., Webby, J. H., & Gunter, P. L. (2000). The effectiveness of cooperative learning with students with emotional and behavioral disorders: A literature review. *Behavioral Disorders*, 25(3), 225–238.

Tabacek, D. A., McLaughlin, T. F., & Howard, V. F. (1994). Teaching preschool children with disabilities tutoring skills: Effects on preacademic behaviors. *Child & Family Behavior Therapy*, 16(2), 43–63.

Walker, H. M., & Rankin, R. (1983). Assessing the behavioral expectations and demands of less restrictive settings. *School Psychology Review*, 12, 274–284.

Wolfe, V. V., Boyd, L. A., & Wolfe, D. A. (1983). Teaching cooperative play to behavior-problem preschool children. *Education and Treatment of Children*, 6(1), 1–9.

Wong, H. K., & Wong, R. T. (1998). The first days of school: How to be an effective teacher. Mountain View, CA: Harry K. Wong Publications, Inc.

Wurtele, S. K., & Drabman, R. S. (1984). "Beat the Buzzer" for classroom dawdling: A one-year trial. *Behavior Therapy*, 15, 403–409.

8 CHAPTER AGGRESSIVE BEHAVIORS

OUTLINE

OBJECTIVES

After completing this chapter, you should be able to

- Offer four reasons why students engage in antisocial behavior.
- Conduct a functional analysis of aggressive behavior.
- Identify alternatives to verbal confrontations with students.
- Implement three interventions for teaching students with aggression.

AN INTRODUCTION TO ANTISOCIAL BEHAVIOR

This chapter will offer suggestions on how you can help students who exhibit **aggression**—one form of **antisocial behavior.** Consider these facts:

- Antisocial behavior early in a child's school career is the single best predictor of delinquency in adolescence.
- Antisocial behavior that is not changed by the end of third grade should be treated as a chronic condition. . . .That is, it cannot be cured but can be managed with the appropriate supports and continuing interventions.
- Early intervention in home, school, and community is the single best hope we have of diverting children from this path (Walker, Colvin, & Ramsey, 1995, p. 6).

Because antisocial behavior is the result of many factors, the prevention and intervention approaches must also be multifaceted. No doubt, you will be called upon to participate in the classroom aspects of a program. However, to orient you to *all* of the components needed to prevent or intervene in antisocial behaviors, we offer this brief overview. (For a more comprehensive discussion, see Wasserman & Miller, 1998.)

> Community conditions contributing to violence are those in which the social organizations (family and community standards) disintegrate and youth are not bonded to conventional norms. Although these tend to be low income areas, it is the lack of social organization, and not poverty per se, that contribute to violence. Low-income neighborhoods with strong social structures do not have the same level of crime. Socially isolated families with few resources and alternative activities for children are prone to produce violent youth.

> Problem behaviors tend to cluster, and it is uncommon for a child to engage in only one type of antisocial behavior. Violence is often associated with drug use, drug dealing, gang involvement, or absenteeism. The most powerful way of dealing with risk groups is to assess the combination of risk factors. No single factor is individually an overwhelming influence on violence.

> Normal transitions (home to kindergarten or elementary school to middle school) are points when children are at greater risk of disruptive behavior and make excellent points for intervention.

> Aggressive behavior in elementary school and lack of parental supervision in early adolescence are powerful predictors of subsequent criminal behavior. Youth who are involved in violence are likely to have witnessed it early in their lives. Aggressive youths often misjudge or misinterpret others' behaviors as threatening and are prone to strike back. Feeling threatened also leads to the possession of weapons for self-protection. The use of weaponry increases the incidence of violence for youth who are not generally antisocial by nature. Exposure to violence, in their homes and neighborhoods, can lead to symptoms similar to post-traumatic stress syndrome, like those seen in children raised in war zones (Mulvey, 1993, pp. 8–9)

Aggressive behavior may be learned behavior, particularly if a student lives in a violent family, community, or culture. Studies have reported that over three-fourths of children surveyed had seen at least one act of violence (Mulvey, Arthur, & Reppucci, 1993). Much of this violence occurred at home and was witnessed by children in the primary grades. Teens involved in violence are more likely to have witnessed and experienced violence than their nonviolent peers are.

Research on violence in schools is becoming more accessible for educators who want to improve the safety of their workplace. These websites feature up-to-date information on school safety:

National School Safety Center: www.nssc1.org
Center for the Study and Prevention of Violence: www.colorado.edu/cspv/
National Association of Attorneys General/National School Boards Association: www.keepschoolssafe.org

Directions: Complete this checklist for each aggressive behavior the student has exhibited.

Person Completing Form **Mrs. Blouze**   Student **Helen A.**   Date **Nov. 6**

Describe the behavior	When did this behavior most recently occur?	Where did this behavior take place?	Who else was in the setting?	Was the aggression directed toward anyone or toward property? Whom? What?	What was going on immediately (15 min) before the aggressive behavior?	What happened immediately (15 min) after the aggressive behavior?	Did you directly observe the behavior?	Comments: (Describe anything that was unusual about the schedule, setting, or student when the event took place, or anything you think would be helpful to consider.)
Came into room, threw book on desk, refused to open it. Threw book on floor. "Sassed" me. Refused to leave. Resisted, was verbally abusive, then hit me.	Yesterday	Regular Reading Class	Other Students (entire class)	More towards teacher	Was in art and came down the hall to reading class.	I told her again to open that book. Told her to pick it up. Told her to leave room. Took her hand to lead her. Buzzed the principal's office.	Yes	She seems to come to class already mad or upset.

FIGURE 8–1   Checklist for assessing aggressive behaviors.

DOCUMENTING AGGRESSIVE BEHAVIOR

Some of the direct observational and interview strategies you learned in earlier chapters will help you document aggressive behavior. One tool you can use is **antecedent-behavior-consequence (ABC) analysis.** We begin with this assessment and continue with functional explanations for aggression, which the ABC may uncover. Because many aggressive acts take place suddenly and without warning, you can't really plan to observe and record systematically as you do with other behaviors. To circumvent this problem, look at Figure 8–1, an "after-the-fact" ABC checklist for recalling aggressive incidents. To begin, describe the aggressive or destructive behavior in the far left column, using as many specific terms as possible. Second, write the date and time period of the aggressive incident, if known. Next, identify the location and all other participants or observers. State whether the aggressive behavior was directed toward property and/or persons and identify any personal injury or property damage. Then describe as accurately as possible what happened before and after the aggressive behavior. Note whether you directly observed the behavior or received the report of it. Finally, add any comments helpful in predicting future aggression. Those involved should complete this form independently; they may have a tendency to "color" each other's account of what actually took place. Remember, you need an objective retelling of the situation. Try to capture each person's recollection soon after each incident. By comparing facts and independent impressions, you may form useful hypotheses about the antecedents (triggers) to a student's aggressive behavior. For example, you may notice that a student is aggressive only toward younger students or only during unsupervised transition activities. The form may also reveal that others inadvertently reinforce aggressive behaviors. For example, a student cursed aloud to his easily embarrassed teacher because it resulted in expulsion from History, his most difficult subject. Can you detect any clues in Figure 8–1 that might explain Helen's actions?

Use the after-the-fact ABC form to detect patterns in the aggression so that you and others can "see it coming" in the future. To predict aggression, it helps to have a good grasp of why aggression happens. In the next section, we offer interventions that focus on the physical attributes of your classroom.

ENVIRONMENTALLY MEDIATED STRATEGIES

Physical Characteristics of the Classroom

Striepling (1997) offered these for minimizing aggression:

Depending on the level of disruption in a building, the physical characteristics of a classroom may include any or all of the following. The door

is solidly constructed, not easily broken or broken through. It contains a window enabling someone looking in to view most of the classroom and some inside to look out to survey the hallway. The door is attached to its frame by hydraulic dampers, so that the harder one pushes, the slower the door closes. In addition, the door is key-lockable, permitting the teacher to keep intruders out. The teacher's desk is also of solid construction and (as is true of all the desks and tables in the room) bolted to the floor so that it cannot be used to block anyone's movement, upturned as a blockade, or picked up and thrown in the midst of a fight. Furthermore, it is placed strategically in the room to maximize the teacher's ability to see the room, move about the room, and (if necessary) escape from the room. Student desks or tables are arranged with sufficient space between them to minimize potential crowding and inadvertent bumping. Both the layout and grouping of student furniture ease movement by students as transitions take place and promote the teacher's access to students. Any call-for-assistance devices in the room are also easily accessed by the teacher. The floor plan allows the teacher to move swiftly about the room or even to leave for reasons of personal safety. . . .

There are few, if any, hidden corners or closets. There are also few, if any, objects lying around that might serve as weapons such as staplers or scissors. All such materials are marked for identification and kept in a locked closet under teacher control. The storage area is located so that the teacher is able to continue viewing the class at the same time materials are being retrieved. The room is well lit; its lights are controlled by a key (not a switch); and its windows are small and made of unbreakable materials. The entire window is covered with decorative grillwork. The interior of the room is painted (at least in part) with bright colors with a hard-surface paint. Few or no graffiti or other marks of vandalism exist in the room, because whenever such defacement takes place, it is swiftly recorded, removed, and repaired. Because of hard work on the teacher's part, most of the students feel that this is their room, and vandalism is infrequent. The class' personal touch is expressed as much as possible, with plants, a cushioned area, wall displays of student work, and similar evidence that "This is our place."

Although these accommodations will help minimize aggression, some of them plainly have a negative side. . . . For these reasons, physical alterations in the classroom must be made cautiously. Changes should reflect the nature and severity of the aggression level in a particular class, school, and community. They should be considered only as interim solutions as the school and the community work toward creating a safer space for children (pp. 43–44).

Now let us turn to targeted interventions for students with aggression.

TEACHER-MEDIATED STRATEGIES

Early Intervention

We cannot overemphasize the importance of early intervention, the single most powerful method for preventing adolescent delinquency (Walker, Severson, Feil, Stiller, & Golly, 1998.) As Loeber and Farrington (1998) advised, "It is never too early." Studies have shown that young children can develop prejudicial beliefs if they are not helped with early negative feelings about differences among people (see Hohensee & Derman-Sparks, 1992). The First Step to Success program developed by Walker, Stiller, Golly, Kavanagh, Severson, and Feil (1997) is a proven early childhood intervention for K–2 classrooms.

To select the most effective intervention we need to understand the individual student. Keller and Tapasak (1997) offer a helpful description of individual characteristics that contribute to aggression. These are shown in Table 8–1. Review this list carefully as you select your targeted interventions.

Academic Intervention

Students who struggle academically are at higher risk for antisocial behaviors, according to many studies. Too often academic frustration leads to classroom outbursts. Therefore, your careful assessment and instruction is in itself a major intervention for antisocial behaviors. Be sure that you request a comprehensive academic assessment for any student who is exhibiting serious aggression. Also, use the functional behavior assessment strategies described in earlier chapters to identify adaptations and accommodations that will help a student become more responsive to your instruction. Penno, Frank, & Wacker (2000) identified several accommodations based on *functional analyses* for their teenaged students:

- using the computer for mathematics
- working with a peer tutor
- shortening assignments
- self-monitoring

By carefully selecting these accommodations based on individual student data, the teachers were able to reduce behavior problems as well as improve academic performance. Chapter 7 describes other adaptations and modifications. Keep in mind that you may need to modify and adapt your interventions for aggression as well as your academic instruction. For example, be sure that the student can follow the scripts for role-plays or understand the terms of your token economy. Also, be sure that your interventions do not violate the student's cultural beliefs (see Burnette, 1999; Cartledge & Milburn, 1996).

Verbal De-escalation

A teacher may inadvertently provoke a student to react aggressively, especially if that student has a tendency to overreact to stressful situations. A verbal confrontation can escalate quickly into aggression. How can you avoid unnecessary verbal confrontations with your students? Here are a few ideas.

1. **Misbehavior or Mother Nature?** The misbehavior may be part of a normal developmental phase. All adolescents sometimes feel the need to prove their increasing autonomy and individuality.

TABLE 8–1 Characteristics of Students Who Exhibit Aggression

Student Characteristic	Description	Targeted Interventions
Arousal-heightening interpretation of external stimuli	An event triggers anger and self-statements that arouse anger. For example, "This teacher is frowning at me. She probably hates me anyway, so I might as well make trouble for her."	• Anger-management training, so the student can identify events that "set him off" • Self-instruction on coping statements and self-evaluation of behaviors • Teaching students to read accurately others' social cues
Heightened affective arousal	Individual overreacts to an event or stimulus.	• Relaxation training • Verbal de-escalation to model more appropriate behaviors for the student • Encouraging the student to talk about her feelings • Helping the student work out alternative behaviors for problem situations. • Helping the student "save face" by providing privacy and alternatives
Ineffective communication	Students may lack the communication skills to negotiate a resolution, express a complaint, or share feelings.	• Conflict resolution training • Social skills training • Problem-solving skills training • Behavioral contracting (to confirm verbal resolutions)
Mismanagement of contingencies	Aggressive behaviors are being reinforced; alternatives are being punished or extinguished. For example, bullies escape consequences for their behavior, so they continue their intimidation of others.	• Functional behavior assessment to determine what motivates the behavior • Contingency management strategies such as token economy, contracting, time out from reinforcement, Good Behavior Game
Prosocial values deficits	The student has the skills and self-control to manage his anger but chooses not to.	• Prosocial values training, and/or • Problem-solving interventions, combined with other interventions to promote generalization and maintenance
Cognitive and academic skill deficits	Student is struggling with school curriculum, or student is not responding to interventions because of academic or cognitive difficulties.	• Assessment of student's cognitive and academic skills • Adapting classroom instruction • Adapting the intervention

Source: Adapted from information contained in Keller, H. R., & Tapasak, R. C. (1998). Classroom management. In A. P. Goldstein, & J. C. Conoley (Eds.), School violence intervention: A practical handbook (pp. 107–120). New York: Guilford Press.

Some of these ways are not much fun for adults! For example, teenagers often engage in verbal confrontations to prove that they can "win" with an adult. Adults may be caught off guard and participate in these confrontations, making matters worse for everyone. As teenagers struggle to develop their own identities, they often reject adults' characteristics. This rejection may take the form of teasing adults. For example, we have had students say to us, "Did you really want your hair to look like that?" or "Haven't you gained an awful lot of weight since last semester?" Here is one of our favorites: "Is your mother still picking out your clothes for you, teacher?" Although you may not condone all expressions of a teenager's autonomy, you may feel better if you keep this behavior in its developmental context. One way to respond to teasing is to poke fun at yourself whenever possible. This lessens the tension and models a healthy sense of humor.

2. **Pick your battles.** An experienced middle school teacher once advised us, "You've already been a teenager. It's their turn!" Many confrontations are not worth the effort of winning; calmly turn down the invitation to do battle. When you let students win on inconsequential issues, you avoid major power struggles. This also allows the student to save face.

3. **Later!** Suggest a later, private conference to the student who tries to create a public scene. Privacy prevents public embarrassment, and the passage of time often will reduce the student's vehemence. An absent-minded teenager may forget what was bothering him in the first place!

4. **The last word can be lethal.** Avoid needing the last word. As one principal said, "Teenagers need the last word a lot more than I do!" Many teacher assaults are the result of an adult's insistence on getting the last word, rather than letting the student leave the interaction mumbling something under her breath. Statements such as, "I heard what you said! Now come back here and apologize!" can worsen an already tense situation. If a student is still really angry, you cannot have a rational conversation. Take time to talk about the issues later. In so doing, you are also showing students how to get their own emotional reactions under control.

5. **Is anybody listening to me?** Listen! Students often tell us that this is really what they want. By listening to the student's complaint (just as a well-trained customer service representative would listen to your problems with a service or product), you may reduce the student's hostility and negotiate a good conclusion. Listening usually reduces affective arousal and lowers the emotional "thermometer." Active listening also models an important communication skill for students.

6. **Sarcasm isn't funny.** Sarcasm escalates tension. Adolescents may misread the intent of your communication, perceiving your comments as hostile. In other words, your well-intended wit may backfire.

7. **Save face.** Saving face is important to all of us. Embarrassing or humiliating a student never helps and could get you hurt. In fact, research by the Gun Safety Institute has shown that youth who are prone to carry guns believe that shame can only be undone through aggression (Clough, personal communication, February 25, 1993). For example, youth who are more likely to carry guns endorsed these beliefs: "If someone insults me or my family, it really bothers me, but if I beat them up, that makes me feel better." "If someone disrespects me, I have to fight them to get my pride back." "A kid who doesn't get even with someone who makes fun of him is a sucker" (Meador, 1992, p. 31).

8. **Don't sweat the small stuff.** Ignore minor rule infractions when you think you can:

"Juan, sit down and open your book, please."
[No response.]
"Sarah, you're ready; why don't you get us started?"

9. **Set limits, but avoid ultimatums.** Offer the student a choice, or an out whenever possible. The following conversations illustrate this idea. Ultimatum: "Janice, you either get to civics class right now

TABLE 8–2 Nine Variables That Affect Compliance

1. **Format.** The use of questions instead of direct requests reduces compliance. For example, "Would you please stop teasing?" is less effective than "I need you to stop teasing."
2. **Distance.** It is better to make a request from up close (i.e., one meter, one desk distance) than from longer distances (i.e., 7 meters, across the classroom).
3. **Two Requests.** It is better to give the same request only twice than to give it several times (i.e., nag). Do not give many different requests rapidly (e.g., "Please give me your homework, behave today, and do not tease the girl in front of you").
4. **Loudness of Request.** It is better to make a request in a soft but firm voice than in a loud voice (i.e., yelling when making a request to get attention).
5. **Time.** Give the student time to comply after giving a request (3 to 5 seconds). During this short interval, do not converse with the child (arguing, excuse making), restate the request, or make a different request. Simply look the child in the eyes and wait for compliance.
6. **Start Requests.** It is more effective to make positive requests of a child to start an appropriate behavior (e.g., "Please start your arithmetic assignment") than to request him/her to stop an inappropriate behavior (e.g., "Please stop talking").
7. **Nonemotional Requests.** It is better to control negative emotions when making a request (e.g., yelling, name calling, guilt-inducing statements, and roughly handling the child). Emotional responses decrease compliance and make the situation worse.
8. **Descriptive Requests.** Requests that are positive and descriptive are better than ambiguous or global requests (i.e., "Please sit in your chair, with your feet on the floor, hands on your desk, and look at me" is better than "Pay attention").
9. **Reinforce Compliance.** It is too easy to request a behavior from a child and then ignore the positive result. If you want more compliance, genuinely reinforce it.

Source: Jensen, W. R. (1996). Reprimands and precision requests. In H. K. Reavis, M. T. Sweeten, W. R. Jensen, D. P. Morgan, D. J. Andrews, & S. Fister (Eds.), Best Practices: Behavioral and educational strategies for teachers (p. 57). Longmont, CO: Sopris West. Reprinted with permission.

or go to the office. This is no time for a personal conversation!" Setting limits, with two options: "Janice, it's time for sixth period. If you can't stop your conversation with your friend now and move on to class, you will need to spend some of the afternoon break making up your work. The choice is up to you." This approach helps students learn the critical skill of interpersonal problem solving.

10. **Take charge of yourself.** Stay in control of your own emotions. Irritable, overreactive teachers will experience repeated, unsuccessful confrontations. Students can always tell which teachers they can "set off." If you are angry, then take some time, cool off, and collect your thoughts. Not every verbal challenge requires your immediate response.

We cannot overemphasize the importance of getting to know your students, their personal beliefs, and their cultural backgrounds and traditions. You may unwittingly alienate students through your tone of voice, gestures, body language, eye contact, and choice of words. For example, an owl sticker sent home on a child's assignment may convey the wrong message: in Vietnam, the owl is a symbol of death (Yao, 1988). You can't be expected to understand another culture entirely, but you should make every effort to find out as much as you can from colleagues, readings, and training experiences. Asking students and their families about their traditions—especially when you get an unexpected reaction—can go a long way towards minimizing these unintended signals.

Table 8–2 offers 9 factors that affect a student's compliance with your requests.

Anger Management Training

The goal of **anger control training** is to help students identify the antecedents to their anger, identify their own reactions, and select good behavioral choices. Figure 8–2 describes an individual anger management intervention: the anger thermometer.

Hammond and his colleagues developed excellent interventions for helping African American youth to manage their anger. In *Dealing with Anger* (Hammond & Gipson, 1994), students learn a three-step approach: "Givin' it; Takin' it; Workin' it out." Once again, the training offers modeling (through a series of videotaped examples), role-plays, visual clues (e.g., flashcards), and homework assignments. Students also learn to recognize and analyze components of angry interactions. *Dealing with Anger* and PACT (Hammond & Yung, 1995) are available from Research Press (2612 N. Mattis Ave., Champaign, IL 61821).

Social Competence Training

As Table 8–1 indicated, aggressive classroom behavior may reflect a social skills deficit. Many students simply lack the skills to manage difficult interpersonal situations. For example, a student may not know how to express a complaint without resorting to anger and profanity. A student who has never seen adults disagree peaceably cannot be expected to resolve conflicts effectively. Students may misread the social cues of others, overlook important social signals, and have trouble solving problems in a social situation (Dodge, Bates, & Pettit, 1990; Huesmann, Guerra, Miller, & Zelli, 1992). Social competence training (SCT) helps students through a curricular approach that focuses primarily on overt aggression, as compared with covert acts such as stealing and vandalism (Wasserman & Miller, 1998).

One of the most effective approaches to teaching alternative, prosocial behaviors to aggressive students is the Prepare Curriculum, which includes seven components. One of these, Skillstreaming, can be used in the classroom. It consists of four parts: modeling, role-playing, performance feedback, and transfer of learning (Goldstein, 1999). This program can be taught to 6 to 12 participants who are assessed as having similar skill deficits. Problem situations are task-analyzed and modeled for the students by their teacher or through audiovisual aids. Table 8–3 lists some of these psychological skill areas.

After students have witnessed good ways to manage difficult situations, they role-play these skills themselves. Goldstein (1987) described the role-play as follows:

> A brief, spontaneous discussion almost invariably follows the presentation of a modeling display. Trainees comment on the steps, the actors, and often the occurrence of the situation or skill problem in their own lives. Because our primary goal in role-playing is to encourage realistic behavior rehearsal, a trainee's statements about individual difficulties using the skill can often develop into material for the first role-play. To enhance the realism of the portrayal, the main actor is asked to choose a second trainee (co-actor) to play the role of the significant other person in his or her life who is relevant to the skill problem. It is important that the main actor seeks to enact the steps just modeled. The main actor is asked to briefly describe the real problem situation and the real person(s) involved in it. The coactor is called by the name of the main actor's significant other person during the role-play. The trainer then instructs the role-players to begin. It is the trainer's main responsibility, at this point, to be sure that the main actor keeps role-playing and attempts to follow the behavioral steps in so doing. The role-playing is continued until all trainees in the group have had an opportunity to participate, even if all the same steps must be carried over to a second or third session. However, even though the framework (behavioral steps) of each role-play in the series remains the same, the actual content can and should change from role-play to role-play; the skill deficiency problem as it actually occurs in each trainee's real-life environment should be the content of each role-play. When the role-plays are completed, each trainee should be better armed to act appropriately in real situations. (p. 220)

The Anger Thermometer helps students increase their awareness of the signs and symptoms of anger (see Rotheram, 1987). Essential to its application is a problem-solving component. In order to use the Anger Thermometer effectively, students explore their past anger history. This includes examining the consequences of their behaviors as well as what prompted their responses.

USING THE ANGER THERMOMETER

To use the Anger Thermometer, an adult works with a student. The relationship involves a sharing of information about how we recognize that we are angry. The easiest starting point is the most obvious: extremes in behaviors. Using a scale of 100° to 0°, the adult can begin to establish a feeling range. First, establish with a student the maximum reaction: the level that is unacceptable to attain. Next, identify this as 100°. Let's use the example of a student who is referred to a school-based counselor for chronic fighting. Fighting would be a 100° or unacceptable level. After establishing the maximum level, help the student identify the 0° level. Nothing is bothersome at the 0° level. In our example, the 0° level might be "chillin'," or just "hangin' out with friends."

INCREASING SELF-AWARENESS BY ACCESSING MORE KNOWLEDGE ABOUT OURSELVES

It is usually more difficult to look inside ourselves than to describe how we appear to others. One way to begin this process is to ask, "How do you look to someone else when you have such an intense level of anger that you would fight? Say you're at 100°." The opposite question might be "What do you look like when you have absolutely no anger? You're just chillin'?" This step begins a collaborative effort to explore behavior changes that accompany anger at various levels of intensity. These behaviors might include shouting, making a fist, swearing, pointing a finger at someone, threatening, pushing, etc. The clinician should acknowledge these behaviors and feelings as real and understandable, yet identify for the student that these behaviors are only one option and there are other behavioral choices.

It helps to provide a real example from your own experience that demonstrates your reaction to anger and how you managed it. This expression of your own struggle and positive outcome is often a motivating demonstration for the student.

RECOGNIZING THE BODY'S CUES

There are probably as many different body cues and variations of anger as there are people. Helping youth recognize these cues can, in turn, improve their awareness of their emotional states. Once they can identify their emotional states, they can begin to manage their uncomfortable feelings.

Listing behaviors that indicate anger can help students to understand that anger presents itself in many ways. Here are some examples from our students.

- I was so angry I turned as red as a beet.
- I couldn't see—my vision was blurry.
- I couldn't hear words, only my heart pounding.
- My mouth was dry as cotton.
- There was sweat on my forehead—I was soaked from sweating.
- I trembled from my head to my toes—my eyelid twitched.
- My hand was balled up into a fist.
- I bit my lip so hard that I tasted blood in my mouth.

EMPATHY AND TOLERANCE—NOT ACCEPTANCE

The goal of the Anger Thermometer is to increase the student's options/choices for behavior. To use this model students must grasp what made them angry and why their reaction was inappropriate and got them into trouble. This exercise can precede a program for anger control or a more comprehensive program for conflict resolution.

As you work with your students, be careful not to reinforce the inappropriate behavior. Don't say "This situation made you angry," or "That person made you mad," but instead say "You became angry," or "You got mad." In this way you acknowledge their anger, imply their responsibility for their behavior, but do not necessarily accept their angry reaction.

FIGURE 8–2 The anger thermometer.

Source: *Brian W. McKain, M.S.N. Reprinted with permission of the author.*

HELPING STUDENTS EXAMINE THEIR PERSONAL ANGER HISTORY

Recognizing the signs and symptoms of anger is the first and easiest part of the exercise. Identifying what "lit the fuse" can be more difficult. Ask the student, "The last time your anger level reached 50° or 100°, do you remember what triggered your anger?" Often, recalling the event will trigger emotional memories. Once students identify what made them angry they can assign a degree of intensity or temperature to their response. To do this it helps to list: (1) the specific event; (2) the approximate date and time; (3) what occurred before and after the event; (4) the level of anger [i.e., 20°, 50°, etc.] (This helps students evaluate their emotional response in a cognitive fashion, perhaps for the first time). Finally, students discuss what they liked or didn't like about their response to the event. (It is important for the student to identify what behaviors they want to change and why. This also gives the student the opportunity to discuss alternative behaviors.) Encourage the student to give as many details as possible. This will give the adult/helper more information to understand the student's point of view. Also, it is important to make the student feel that their thoughts and feelings are important to the adult/helper.

LOOKING FOR SUBTLE CUES

The cognitive exercise of rating a response allows the student to classify and create a hierarchy of intensity. When the student has rated these various levels, they can then judge from their own value structure whether their response was an appropriate level of response. This process can be the basis for establishing with the student the purpose for using the Anger Thermometer. Without the proper motivation, this can become an academic exercise with little chance of real-life application. Remember that our goal is to help our students recognize what degrees of temperature they can reach and still engage in problem solving. Often by the time they reach 100° the climate may be too "hot" to try to resolve the issues that made them angry.

USING YOUR HEAD INSTEAD OF YOUR GUT TO SOLVE PROBLEMS

Self-questioning, "What else could I do; what other choices could I make?" can begin the process of recognizing appropriate reactions to anger. The student at this point has been able to: (1) recognize signs and symptoms of anger; (2) assess the intensity of his or her anger; (3) recognize the behavior that results from these emotions; and (4) stop, think, and make an informed choice, based on the consequences of the behaviors. After this the progression to teaching problem-solving skills is a natural and logical next step.

The problem-solving steps include: (1) identifying the problem; (2) identifying the options; (3) choosing one option and following through with it; (4) evaluating the choice and the consequences; and (5) deciding if you have to make a different choice based on the current evaluation of the situation.

Once a student is aware of the behavioral cues, they assess what their next move will be. Often a student is aware of the more obvious cues and gradually becomes aware of the more subtle behaviors. The overt behaviors such as making a fist or shouting might be the more obvious indicators of anger. Once they become more aware, they may notice that they are tensing their jaw muscles, feeling hot, their leg is shaking, or their eye is twitching.

ANGER THERMOMETER IN CONTEXT

For the Anger Thermometer to be useful, the participants must communicate clearly and trust each other. The student who is referred for issues of anger control has to be able to focus, to use cognitive abilities, and to be motivated to change their behaviors.

If the student was involved in a fight, it is important to discuss what motivated this behavior. If he has a hot temper and has been in fights before, anger management and use of the Anger Thermometer could be appropriate. On the other hand, if issues related to his ex-girlfriend's new boyfriend caused the fight, then the appropriate intervention might be mediation.

REFERENCE

Rotheram, M. J. (1986). The evaluation of imminent danger for suicide among youth. *The American Journal of Orthopsychiatry, 57,* 102–110.

FIGURE 8–2   The anger thermometer—*Continued.*

TABLE 8–3 Psychological Skill Areas for Aggressive Students

Asking for help
1. Decide what the problem is.
2. Decide whether you want help with the problem.
3. Identify the people who might help you.
4. Choose a helper.
5. Tell the helper about your problem.

Giving instructions
1. Define what needs to be done and who should do it.
2. Tell the other person what you want him to do and why.
3. Tell the other person exactly how to do what you want done.
4. Ask for the other person's reaction.
5. Consider that reaction and change your direction if appropriate.

Expressing affection
1. Decide whether you have warm, caring feelings about another person.
2. Decide whether the other person would like to know about your feelings.
3. Decide how you might best express your feelings.
4. Choose the right time and place to express your feelings.
5. Express affection in a warm and caring manner.

Expressing a complaint
1. Define what the problem is and who is responsible.
2. Decide how the problem might be solved.
3. Tell that person what the problem is and how it might be solved.
4. Ask for a response.
5. Decide whether you want to try again.
6. If it is appropriate, try again, using your revised approach.

Responding to contradictory messages
1. Pay attention to those body signals that help you know you are feeling trapped or confused.
2. Consider the other person's words and actions that may have caused you to have these feelings.
3. Decide whether that person's words and actions are contradictory.
4. Decide whether it would be useful to point out any contradiction.
5. If appropriate, ask the other person to explain any contradiction.

Responding to anger
1. Listen openly to the other person's angry statement(s).
2. Show that you understand what the other person is feeling.
3. Ask the other person to explain anything you don't understand about what was said.
4. Show that you understand why the other person feels angry.
5. If it is appropriate, express your thoughts and feelings about the situation.

Preparing for a stressful conversation
1. Imagine yourself in the stressful situation.
2. Think about how you will feel and why you will feel that way.
3. Imagine the other person(s) in that stressful situation. Think about how that person(s) will feel and why he (they) will feel that way.
4. Imagine yourself telling the other person(s) what you want to say.
5. Imagine the response that your statement will elicit.
6. Repeat the above steps, using as many approaches as you can think of.
7. Choose the best approach.

Source: Reprinted with permission from Goldstein, A. P. (1987). Teaching prosocial skills to aggressive adolescents. In C. M. Nelson, R. B. Rutherford, Jr. & B. I. Wolford (Eds.), Special education in the criminal justice system. pp. 223–226. Upper Saddle River, NJ: Merrill/Prentice Hall.

Determining responsibility
1. Decide what the problem is.
2. Consider possible causes of the problem.
3. Determine the most likely causes of the problem.
4. Take actions to test which are the actual causes of the problem.

Setting problem priorities
1. List all the problems currently pressuring you.
2. Arrange this list in order, from most to least urgent.
3. Take steps (delegate, postpone, avoid) to temporarily decrease the urgency of all but the most pressing problem.
4. Concentrate on solving the most pressing problem.

Dealing with being left out
1. Decide whether you're being left out (ignored, rejected).
2. Think about why the other people might be leaving you out of something.
3. Consider how you might deal with the problem (wait, leave, tell the other people how their behavior affects you, talk with a friend about the problem).
4. Choose the best way and do it.
5. Show that you understand the other person's feelings.
6. Come to agreement on the steps each of you will take.

Persuading others
1. Decide on your position and predict what the other person's is likely to be.
2. State your position clearly, completely, and in a way that is acceptable to the other person.
3. State what you think the other person's position is.
4. Restate your position, emphasizing why it is the better of the two.
5. Suggest that the other person consider your position for a while before making a decision.

Following instructions
1. Listen carefully while the instructions are being given.
2. Give your reactions to the instructor.
3. Repeat the instructions to yourself.
4. Imagine yourself following the instructions and then do it.

Responding to the feelings of others (empathy)
1. Observe another person's words and actions.
2. Consider what the other person might be feeling and how strong the feelings are.
3. Decide whether it would be helpful to let the other person know that you understand his feelings.
4. If appropriate, tell the other person in a warm and sincere manner how you think he is feeling.

Responding to a complaint
1. Listen openly to the complaint.
2. Ask the person to explain anything you don't understand.
3. Show that you understand the other person's thoughts and feelings.
4. Tell the other person your thoughts and feelings, accepting responsibility if appropriate.
5. Summarize the steps each of you will take.

Responding to persuasion
1. Listen openly to another person's position.
2. Consider the possible reasons for the other person's position.
3. Ask the other person to explain anything you don't understand about what was said.
4. Compare the other person's position with your own, identifying the pros and cons of each.
5. Decide what position to support, based on what will have the greatest long-term benefit.

(Continued)

TABLE 8–3 Psychological Skill Areas for Aggressive Students—*Continued.*

Responding to failure
1. Decide whether you have failed.
2. Think about both the personal reasons and the circumstances that have caused you to fail.
3. Decide how you might do things differently if you tried again.

Dealing with an accusation
1. Think about what the other person has accused you of (whether it is accurate, inaccurate, said in a mean way or in a constructive way).
2. Think about why the person might have accused you (have you infringed on the person's rights or property?).
3. Think about ways to answer the person's accusations (deny, explain your behavior, correct the other person's perceptions, assert, apologize, offer to make up for what has happened).
4. Choose the best way and do it.

Dealing with group pressure
1. Think about what the other people want you to do and why (listen to the other people, decide what their real intent is, try to understand what is being said).
2. Decide what you want to do (yield, resist, delay, negotiate).
3. Consider how to tell the other people what you want to do (give reasons, talk to one person only, delay, assert).
4. If appropriate, tell the group or other person what you have decided.

The next stage of training is performance *feedback*, in which the actors in the role-plays receive comments on how they enacted the skills. Goldstein stressed the importance of specific encouraging comments here. Finally, students experience the transfer of training, a phase in which overlearning is emphasized. Students reexperience the modeling, role-plays, and performance feedback many times in order to ensure that they have really captured the important skills they lack. For more information about this and the other six components, you might want to review Goldstein's *The Prepare Curriculum: Teaching Prosocial Competencies* published in 1999 by Research Press.

To enhance a social skills curriculum, give students "behavioral homework assignments," writing assignments for their notebooks, "cue cards," and other learning aids. Moreover, try to link the skills with real-life situations by offering relevant teaching examples, role-plays, and discussion topics. Also, social skills training is more effective when combined with other interventions specifically targeted to aggression (e.g., anger control training) and when parents are involved.

Remember, students with antisocial behaviors need contingency management as well as direct skills training. To maintain intervention gains and increase generalization or transfer of these skills across settings and persons, involve as many other persons as possible in the intervention planning and implementation. This chapter's case study demonstrates how skills training and contingency management work together to improve students' self-control.

Contingency Management Strategies

Contingency management has been discussed throughout this text in procedures such as token economies, contingency contracts, and timeout from reinforcement. This section explains how to manage the contingencies that influence aggressive behavior in your classroom. For example, students may act tough because they are reinforced by the way other people react to them. By creating a crisis, these students stop all routines, gain abundant attention from peers, and scare, embarrass, or immobilize adults in authority. Throwing work materials or swearing at the teacher may give a student a way out of a difficult lesson; avoidance of the unpleasant work is the student's reinforcer.

The first step in designing a contingency management intervention is to **pinpoint** the target behavior(s). Focus your attention on (1) identifying and modifying behaviors that immediately precede acts of aggression, destruction, or theft; and (2) identifying and modifying the not-so-immediate setting events that precede aggression, such as situations at home that "spill over" to school (Conroy & Fox, 1994). Take another look at Figure 8–1. You'll see that one column is devoted entirely to immediate antecedent events. Antecedents are good target behaviors on which to intervene (e.g., teasing remarks, initial physical contact with another student, subvocal utterances, facial flush, movement of an arm to a fighting position). For example, intervene with a student fighter not after the fight has begun but when that student first teases or picks the fight; or stop and let a student "vent" verbally when you first notice that he has had a rough morning on the bus.

Aggression may be intermittently reinforced and thereby strengthened unless all adults advocate the same position: aggressive behavior will not be tolerated. Take bullying, for example. Bullies intimidate their victims so that they will not report to authorities; knowing that they won't be punished is reinforcing to bullies. For bullying to cease, adults must find out about it so that they no longer inadvertently reinforce the bully's covert behavior. [For a bully-proofing program, see Garrity, Jens, Porter, Sager, & Short-Camilli, C. (1994).]

Token Reinforcement and Response Cost

When using a token economy to reduce aggression, apply a response cost or fine to aggressive acts as well as to behaviors that predict aggression or destruction of property. The following lists display part of a teacher's classroom token economy for aggressive students.

Points may be earned for:
- Walking away from a fight.
- Ignoring someone who teases.
- Accepting teacher feedback.
- Keeping hands off others.
- Using an acceptable word instead of a swear word when angry.

Points will be lost for:
- Fighting or hitting.
- "Mouthing off" at a school visitor.
- Teasing a classmate.
- Threatening a classmate.
- Blocking a classmate's free movement in class or in the halls.

Note that students earn points for actions that inhibit aggression. Recall our discussion of the role that stimulus control plays in maintaining or reducing aggression. By identifying behaviors that inhibit aggression as well as those that provoke hurtful behavior, this teacher controlled the stimuli preceding aggression through token reinforcement and response cost.

Here are guidelines for implementing a response cost (RC) contingency:

- The RC system should be carefully explained before applying it.
- RC should always be tied to a reinforcement system, preferably involving points.
- An appropriate delivery system should be developed.
- RC should be implemented immediately after the target behavior or response occurs.
- RC should be applied each time an instance of a target behavior occurs.
- *The student should never be allowed to accumulate negative points* (that is, go in the hole with point totals).
- The ratio of points earned to those lost should be controlled.
- The social agent using response cost should never be intimidated from using RC by the target student.
- *Subtraction of points should never be punitive or personalized.*
- The student's positive, appropriate behavior should be praised as frequently as opportunities permit (Walker et al., 1995, pp. 66–67).

A response cost (removal of smiley faces from a Good Behavior Chart) combined with rewards (for keeping a smiley face on the chart during a 40-min period) successfully reduced aggression in a preschool classroom, as reported by Reynolds & Kelley (1997).

Contracting

Contingency contracts, introduced in Chapter 4, have effectively reduced destructive actions, including fighting, property damage, fire-setting, and verbal aggression (Walker et al., 1995).

Timeout from Reinforcement

Many aggressive students, like classroom disruptors, fail to complete academic tasks because they are expelled from the instructional setting at each outburst. As a result aggressive students may develop a "double disability" requiring remediation in both academic and social skills. When using timeout with an aggressive student, remember that it is best (and easiest) to apply it before the child loses control or becomes assaultive. For this reason, behaviors pinpointed for timeout should be antecedents to aggression (teasing, threats, lifting an arm to "deck" someone). Also provide reinforcement for incompatible, acceptable actions once the student returns to the ongoing classroom activities. In the case of timeout strategies, consult with your supervisor about school policies.

Another form of timeout from reinforcement is in-school suspension. (For guidelines on how to implement an In-School Suspension program, see Rhode, 1996.) If this program is implemented properly and if the student is motivated to return to his classroom, then the separation from classmates (e.g., time spent in the In-School Suspension program) may reduce aggression and reinforce more appropriate classroom behavior. Unfortunately, studies of students referred for in-school suspension have uncovered frequent teacher disapproval and other aversive approaches (Hartman & Sage, 2000).

Keep in mind that overreliance on negative interventions can set into motion a vicious cycle: Perceiving the classroom teacher as biased and hostile, the student experiences heightened affective arousal, which leads to an angry outburst. Faced with the student's anger, the teacher escalates the situation by resorting to even more coercive practices. Before long, the student is experiencing only negative interactions, reaffirming his belief that "The teacher is out to get me" (Gunter, Denny, Jack, Shores, & Nelson, 1993). To break this cycle, start with many positive reinforcements in your classroom, then tailor your targeted interventions according to the guidelines outlined in Table 8–1.

CRISIS INTERVENTION WITH PHYSICAL AGGRESSION

In spite of your best efforts to prevent behaviors that threaten the physical safety of an aggressive student or of others in the classroom, a situation may erupt into violence before you can intervene. We hope that these instances will be rare if you employ the strategies described in this chapter. However, when violent behavior does occur, you should know what to do. If you work with potentially aggressive students, take an annual refresher class on nonviolent crisis intervention. Local police departments or mental health programs often offer these classes. Be sure that your class is offered by a certified professional who has time to provide concrete examples.

It helps to have a well-rehearsed crisis response plan. The guidelines in Table 8–4 will help you prepare for this situation and prevent harm. This "drill" also alleviates the anxiety of adults in the building. Just compare this drill with others we use to prepare ourselves for potentially serious (yet less frequent) events such as a fire or tornado.

Occasionally you may work with a student whose aggression is a result of irrational thinking, hallucinations, or another psychiatric problem, or

TABLE 8–4 Readiness Drill for Aggressive Events

1. With your principal and at least one other teacher whose room is nearby, develop a plan for getting help when the aggressive child loses control. This plan should include:
   a. transmitting a signal to the nearby adult or an alternate if that person is not available.
   b. the type of assistance you will need. For example, you might want the adult to come to your class and escort your other students out of the room so that they do not reinforce or taunt the target student.
   c. how you will notify the principal. You may want a second colleague to do this for you.
   d. how you will handle the aggressive student(s). This plan will depend in part on your school's policies. Interventions presented later in this chapter will help you.
2. Develop a "signal" that you can give to a dependable child in your classroom. This signal should be different from anything else the children may have encountered. For example, you might paint a wooden block a particular color. (If you also wish to notify the principal, you might want two such signals given to two students or their alternates.)
3. Select an alternate in the event that the designated child is absent the day you need to use your procedure.
4. Tell the students that you have an important drill for them to practice, like the fire and other drills to which they are accustomed. You do not need to declare the circumstances under which you would activate your readiness plan. If the students can read, give them a handout outlining the steps they are to take. If they are not capable readers, you might want to show an abbreviated set of steps on a poster.
5. Practice the drill, including the activities of the other adults. Begin with a weekly practice until the students and adults can complete the activities smoothly. Then have a monthly "surprise drill."
6. If at any time the drill does not proceed as you planned, revise the steps and inform everyone of the revision.

you may want to help a student trying to cope with a violent family member. Consider these guidelines offered by an advocacy organization for families affected by mental illness:

Don't Threaten. This may be interpreted as a power play and increase fear or prompt assaultive behavior by the individual.

Don't shout. If the person with a mental illness seems not to be listening, it is not because he or she is hard of hearing. Other "voices" are probably interfering.

Don't criticize. It will only make matters worse. It cannot possibly make things better.

Don't squabble with other family members over "best strategies" or allocations of blame. This is no time to prove a point.

Don't bait the individual into acting out wild threats. The consequences could be tragic.

Don't stand over the individual if he or she is seated. Instead, seat yourself.

Avoid direct, continuous eye contact or touching the individual.

Comply with requests that are neither endangering nor beyond reason. This provides the individual patient with an opportunity to feel somewhat "in control."

Don't block the doorway. However, do keep yourself between the individual and an exit. (Adapted from the Alliance for the Mentally Ill of Southwestern PA, 1996)

PEER-MEDIATED STRATEGIES

A student's peer group can play a major role in intervention programs to reduce aggressive and destructive behaviors. For example, the peers may take part in a group contingency or learn to ignore or respond in a new way to teasing or threats by the target student. Some of these peer-mediated procedures have been described in detail in previous chapters, so we will only mention them here.

TABLE 8–5 Guidelines for Implementation

The peer confrontation strategy is composed of five major parts. During each stage, the teacher should praise the target student(s) and peers for engaging in appropriate responses.

1. Identify the problem.
   - Identify the specific behavior(s).
   - Operationally define the target behavior(s) (e.g., verbal or gestural threats such as shaking a fist at another student; raising the middle finger; stating "I'll shoot you").
   - Teach all students to identify positive and neutral behaviors of peers.
   - Teach all students to identify negative behaviors of peers (e.g., hitting, name calling).
   - Teach all students to discriminate between acceptable and negative behaviors.
   - Teach all students to identify target behavior(s) as they are exhibited naturally.
2. Determine the effects of the problem behavior on others.
   - Teach students to recognize various types of effects. Categories might include tangible effects (e.g., "all our equipment will be broken"), intangible effects (e.g., "We'll be late for class" or "He'll lose face"), short-term effects (e.g., "we'll get detentions"), or long-term effects (e.g., "We may not get to go on the field trip at the end of the project").
   - Teach students to predict possible effects resulting from a specific behavior.
3. Conduct problem solving.
   - Teach students to precisely describe the problem behavior (e.g., "Mike's hand is in the air; he's getting ready to hit").
   - Discuss the consequences of the behavior.
   - Brainstorm alternative target student responses. Prompt students to offer a number of positive behavioral options to the target student.
4. Deliver mild punishment—as appropriate.
   - This might take the form of a verbal reprimand, presented in close proximity to the target student.
5. Provide "booster training" (e.g., periodic retraining) to ensure appropriate performance.
6. Monitor the long-term effect of behavior changes on the target student(s).

Source: *Reprinted with permission from Arllen, N. L. Gable, R. A., & Hendrickson, J. M. (1996). Using peer confrontation to reduce inappropriate student behavior.* Beyond Behavior, 7(1), 22–23.

Good Behavior Game

Kellan, Rebok, Ialongo, & Mayer (1994) described long-term effectiveness of the Good Behavior Game (see Chapter 6) in reducing aggression of first graders. Its effectiveness earned the Good Behavior Game a citation as one of 450 national "Blueprints for Violence Prevention" model programs.

Peer Confrontation

In this strategy, peers confront the inappropriate behavior of a classmate, identify the effects of the behavior, and engage in joint problem-solving (Arllen, Gable, & Hendrickson, 1996). Based on a model entitled "Positive Peer Culture" (Vorath & Brendtro, 1974), peer confrontation takes place both within a meeting format and during other times of the school day. The studies to date have taken place in small elementary schools and other self-contained set-

tings. In these respects the strategy is similar to *Group Goal Setting and Feedback* (see Chapter 6).

Table 8–5 describes the steps to carry out peer confrontation.

Conflict Resolution Strategies

To supplement social skills training, many schools have established conflict resolution training, calling on peers or adults to assist students with their conflicts. The research on these programs is mixed: Some studies have demonstrated a decrease in violent behaviors (Wilson-Brewer & Spivak, 1994; Goldstein & Huff, 1993), while others fail to show results (Webster, 1993).

Many schools are now adopting peer mediation programs, whereby students meet with classmates having a conflict and help the pair work things out. The peer mediator first learns skills, including active

TABLE 8–6 Peer Trainer Steps

Assess
1. Student will not speak aloud for at least 3 sec in order to assess the situation.
2. Student will ask the answer aloud, "What is going on?"
3. Student will ask and answer aloud, "Why did [he/she] do or say what [he/she] did?"
4. Student will ask and answer aloud, "Did [he/she] do this on purpose or is it something that just happened?"
5. Student will ask and answer aloud, "How does [he/she] feel about the situation?"
6. Student will ask and answer aloud, "Is [he/she] upset or just kidding?"

Amend
7. Student chooses an appropriate alternative response to anger. Example: Not responding verbally or nonverbally to the situation, initiating another topic for discussion, or walking away from the situation.
8. Student tells the other person how this situation makes him or her feel. Example: "I am upset that you would not just ask me for the paper or to see my homework. I considered you my friend and thought that you considered me your friend. Therefore, I am surprised that you took my notebook without asking me."
9. Student asks the other person to tell him or her how this makes him or her feel. Example: "How do you feel just taking my notebook without asking me?"

Act
10. Student responds to the situation, using ASSESS and AMEND steps. Example: Student waits, self-instructs, and then performs alternative response.
11. Student evaluates his/her initial response to the situation and makes changes, if necessary, in his or her response by using the ASSESS and AMEND steps. Example: Student speaks aloud that he or she has not followed the steps in the ASSESS and AMEND components. Student speaks aloud the steps to assess the situation and amends it.

Source: Presley, J.A., & Hughes, C. (2000). *Peers as teachers of anger management to high school students with behavioral disorders.* **Behavioral Disorders, 25(2), 118. Reprinted with permission.**

listening, identifying common ground, and maintaining impartiality and confidentiality. Although few peer mediation programs have undergone stringent evaluation, the results of some studies are promising (see Cartledge & Johnson, 1997).

Peers as Teachers of Anger Management

Presley and Hughes (2000) described how nondisabled teens successfully instructed their classmates with EBD to control their anger. Peer trainers received training on scripts (available from the senior author at jannpres@aol.com or at the Department of Teaching and Learning, Tennessee State University, Nashville). Using role-play situations, students practiced a three-step response adapted from the Walker Social Skills Curriculum (Walker, McConnell, Holmes, Todis, Walker, & Golden, 1983). Table 8–6 depicts the steps.

Group Goal Setting and Feedback

Group goal setting and feedback, a strategy explained in Chapter 6, has been applied to aggressive behaviors on the playground (Kerr, Strain, & Ragland, 1982). In this study, preadolescent students participated in daily group goal setting and feedback sessions to improve their recess activities, originally described by their teacher as follows:

> The kids go outside for a 30-min recess and start right off arguing about what game to play. Once that's settled, they bicker about who will pick teams. After teams are finally chosen, a fight breaks out over unfair membership on the two teams. About 10 min before the bell rings, they get down to playing baseball or something. By the time recess is over they've almost killed each other fighting about the rules. (E. Ragland, personal communication, 1980)

TABLE 8–7 Examples of Antecedents, Behaviors, and Consequences for Discrimination Training

("You" and "Your" refer to the student)
Antecedents (Triggers)
1. Your friend keeps throwing paper wads at you during seatwork.   2. You're supposed to be at work by 3:30, but your friends always want you to hang out after school.   3. Your teacher gives you a book report assignment that's due in 1 week.   4. Your dad tells you that you have to babysit Friday night.   5. The girl/boy that you want to go to the dance with asks you for help with homework after school.   6. You go out to the parking lot after school and find that you have a flat tire.   7. Your teacher gives you an assignment that you don't understand.   8. One of your teachers announces that there will be a chapter test on Friday.   9. Your mom asks you to come home right after school to help her out.   10. You're walking down the hall and someone you don't get along with comes up behind you and shoves you.
Behaviors
1. You punch your friend and yell swear words at him.   2. You get to work an hour late for 5 days in a row.   3. You schedule your study time so that you work on your report a little each night and have enough time to rewrite it neatly before it is due.   4. You really want to go out, but you stay home as you've been asked to do.   5. You really want to go shopping with your friend because you'd rather do that than school work.   6. You kick in your front fender and punch the side window, cracking it.   7. You go to a teacher during seatwork time and ask for clarification of the assignment.   8. You'd rather be out partying, but you decide to study each night between now and Friday.   9. Even though your friends are going out for sodas, you go right home and help out.   10. You're really angry, but you just walk away from him/her.
Consequences
1. Your teacher sends you to the principal's office.   2. Your boss fires you and you lose the income you were using to save for a car.   3. You get a B+ on your paper.   4. Your dad lets you borrow the car Saturday night and gives you $5.00.   5. When you ask your friend to go to the dance with you, he/she says, "Forget it!"   6. Instead of just having to change a flat tire, you have to come up with $100.00 for body work.   7. You are able to complete the assignment accurately and get a good grade.   8. Even though you missed a couple of nights out, you ace the test.   9. You are able to complete the assignment accurately and get a good grade.   10. The hall monitor sends the "other guy" to detention, but you're doing fine.

Source: *From Young, K. R., West, R. P., Smith, D. J., & Morgan, D. P. (1991). Teaching self-management strategies to adolescents (p. 35). Longmont, CO: Sopris West. Reprinted with permission.*

SELF-MEDIATED STRATEGIES

Because aggression is an interpersonal behavior, self-management strategies alone will not remediate the problem. However, self-monitoring in com-bination with contingency management and the learning of alternative behaviors may succeed.

Self-recording (described in Chapter 6) is a good way to teach students how to anticipate situations that trigger their aggressive behavior. Young, West, Smith, & Morgan (1991) have developed an excellent student handbook for teaching the ABCs of behavior. Through a antecedent-behavior-consequence analysis, students learn to discriminate between events that trigger appropriate and inappropriate responses; then students learn to self-talk about their behavioral choices (e.g., "If I do _____, then _____ will happen. But if I do _____, things will turn out better for me") Study the examples of antecedents, behaviors, and consequences for discrimination training in Table 8–7.

We believe that you will find self-control strategies especially helpful in supplementing the direct instruction, modeling, and role-play strategies included in your skills teaching programs.

SUMMARY

We hope you understand the importance of a thorough analysis of aggression attained through careful documentation early in a student's school career. As part of a larger team making your school safe, you can develop policies and school-wide strategies that discourage acts of aggression. Several environmental changes are available to solve specific problems. Most strategies, however, are teacher-mediated, requiring a high degree of control of your emotions and reactions. Solid management of contingencies and direct skills instruction are two of your best tools. Few studies have reported self-mediated strategies, but self-monitoring can contribute to a more comprehensive approach. Our chapter concludes with a case study depicting a multifaceted approach with sixth graders. Following the case study is a list of violence prevention resources. The list includes a brief description and ordering information for curricula, school safety projects, community programs, and other resources.

CHAPTER 8 CASE STUDY

Anger Management Skills Lessons

Dawn E. Cois

Background Information

A class of sixth-grade students exhibiting behavioral problems is in need of social skills training. In particular, these 10 students need to increase their social skills in interacting with adults. The faculty at this school is extremely cooperative and resourceful and will assist in the behavioral program for these students. Students are in my classroom for homeroom (15 min), third period (60 min), and at the end of the day (15 min), 5 days a week.

Behavioral Objective

When given a task request or directions from an adult, students will respond without talking back angrily or using inappropriate language (profanity).

Lesson Plan

Introduction

Students will be given an introduction on the target behavior (i.e., responding appropriately to adult requests or directions), its value to them and the consequences for noncompliance. Open discussion will follow with students' volunteering examples of good encounters and bad encounters with adults.

> *Teacher*: I need the class' help on a problem I have. Today Mrs. Lewis asked me to stay after school to help her finish the school newsletter. Well, I've stayed after school three times this week already to help with planning for the new weather station and

the Tropicana Speech Contest, and tonight I have company coming over. Besides, I was in a hurry to get to the office to run off some copies and only had a few minutes before I had to be back in the classroom, so I really didn't have time to talk. You know what that's like, don't you? When you're in a hurry and people are bugging you for time that you don't have? Well, I paused for a second and simply told her "No way! I'm not staying after school another day. I have a life too. Find someone else or do it yourself. Why is it that I have to do everything around here anyway?" Well, she looked kind of angry and replied, "Sorry I asked you! It won't happen again."

Well, I really like Mrs. Lewis and I felt sort of bad that I responded that way, but I didn't have time to apologize or explain myself so I just kept going. Anyway, remember how we talked about having an egg-drop contest next month? Well, Mrs. Lewis was going to help me with it since she's done this activity before. I really don't know much about it. Now she's mad at me and I don't know how to ask her for her assistance. What do you think she'll say if I ask her to stay after school next week to help me with this project?

What can I do to make things better so that our friendship isn't ruined?
How can I get her to still help me on this project?
Could I have avoided this problem if I had handled her request to stay after school differently?
What could I have said that would have sounded better and not made her angry?

We all do this sometimes, just blow up on people instead of talking politely and calmly when people ask us to do things, especially when they are things we don't really want to do. But in the end we just make people mad at us and then they don't want to help us when we need them. The funny thing about this is that if we would only take a moment to think the situation through, we could make our own lives a lot easier and know that the people around us will support us.

First, we need to think about what it is that the other person is asking of us. Is it a reasonable request? Is it something we can do? If not, what do we need that will better enable us to do it? Is it a fair request?

Second, we need to think about the consequences. What will happen if we do what is being asked of us? What will happen if we do not? Is there a good reason why we can't or shouldn't do this?

Third, we need to control our impulses to say things angrily. If we can do what is being asked of us, we should. If we can't, we need to calmly explain why we can't. Staying calm means that we don't say things that are offensive or use profanity. There's always a nice way to respond if we take the time to think about it.

Last, we need to reward ourselves for taking the time to think the situation through and responding appropriately.

This is especially important when dealing with adults. Adults make a lot of requests on kids, especially teachers. But their job is to help you get a good education and prepare you to undertake whatever careers you may choose when you leave school. When you are all adults, you'll find you'll have a lot of responsibilities and you'll need to rely on many of the skills you've acquired in school. Parents also ask a lot of you, but they usually have your best interests in mind.

Would anyone like to share a situation they may have encountered with a teacher in the past? What was asked of you and how did you handle it? Good and bad situations are encouraged to be shared. Bad situations are discussed with suggestions on ways that it could have been handled better.

Modeling

Teacher: Let's first review the four steps we just talked about to help us better deal with adults when they ask us to do something. (Students volunteer the four steps while the teacher writes them down.)

1. Is it a reasonable and fair request?
2. What will be the consequences of my actions?
3. I need to respond politely and calmly.
4. Reward myself for handling the situation well.

(Students are given index cards with these four steps written on them.)

Now Mrs. B. and I will demonstrate how to use these four steps in a situation that is a little worse than the one I had with Mrs. Lewis. In this situation, I'm going to play the role of a sixth grader who is being told by a teacher to take work detention for not completing an assignment that she knows she did. In this role-play I'm going to think aloud so that you can hear how I work through the four steps on your cards.

Mrs. B: Kathy, I'm really disappointed in you this week. You didn't hand in your book report even though I gave the class extra time on Monday to finish it. Here's your detention slip. You won't be allowed free time today with the rest of the class. Instead, you need to report to the detention room to finish your work. I want this detention slip signed by one of your parents and returned to me on Monday along with your completed book report.

Teacher (sixth grader): (1) Is this fair and reasonable? No! I did the assignment and I know I handed it in. (2) What will be the consequences if I do it? Well, I'll miss free time, my parents will be angry with me, and I'll have to do the assignment all over again. What will happen if I get angry and refuse to do it? Well, I'll be sent to the principal's office and my parents will be called. That will make them even angrier at me. I'll still have to go to work detention or possibly have to sit in the office during free time, the principal will be angry with me, and I'll still have to redo the assignment. Is there another alternative? Yes, I can explain to Mrs. B. that I did the assignment and already turned it in. If I'm nice, maybe she'll listen to me. (3) Be calm and polite. Mrs. B., I worked hard on that book report and finished it on Monday when you gave us that extra time in class to work on it. I'm sure I turned it in. I remember putting it in the homework box. Maybe you misplaced it?

Mrs. B.: No, if it was in the homework box with the rest of the book reports I would have gotten it. I don't lose papers. But . . . if you say you did it, maybe you thought you turned it in and didn't. Perhaps you should check your desk and see if you still have it.

Teacher (sixth grader): I don't think so, but I'll check anyway. Look, Mrs. B., you were right. It's here in my desk.

Mrs. B.: Well, it's late, but at least I know you did it and that it was an accident that it wasn't turned in, so I won't deduct any points. I'm glad we resolved this and that you don't have to take detention. Perhaps you should keep a record of your assignments and cross them off after you've turned them in rather than when you've completed them so that this won't happen again. I'll help you organize an assignment sheet if you'd like.

Teacher (sixth grader): OK. Thanks, Mrs. B. (4) Reward myself. Wow, I handled that great and got her to listen me. It got me out of detention and hot water with my parents.

Let's talk about that situation. (Students talk about how the four steps were used to help resolve the problem. Teacher also leads the class to discuss how that situation could have turned bad.)

Practice/Role-Play

Teacher: Now we're all going to have a chance to practice using these four steps with some practice situations that I've made up. First, we'll practice these skills as a class and then we'll pair up with partners to practice. I'll play the teacher role and let each of you respond to a situation using one of the four steps. Remember to think the steps aloud so that the rest of us know how you're working this out. When I walk next to you, it's your turn to respond, OK? If you get nervous and can't come up with something, then the person beside you can offer you some suggestions to help you out. Does anyone have any questions or comments before we begin?

Situation One Tommy is talking to Randy beside him about the football game last night while the teacher is giving instructions.

Teacher: Tommy, the rules of this classroom are that you shouldn't be talking when the teacher is talking. I want you to move your desk next to mine and stay in for 15 min of your recess.

(Students are each given a chance to respond to one of the four steps in responding appropriately in this situation.)

Situation Two Sam is being accused of writing on his desk when he knows he did not do it.

Teacher: Sam, why is there writing all over your desk? That's school property and you have no right to destroy or vandalize it! I want you to stay in at recess and wash not only your desk, but everyone's desk in this classroom!

Situation Three Rita is having problems understanding division problems. She put her best effort into her assignment but still did poorly.

Teacher: Rita, you missed 13 out of the 15 math problems on your homework assignment. I want you to redo this assignment for homework tonight and I want every problem done correctly. Do you understand?

Now I'd like you all to divide into pairs with the person sitting next to you. Mrs. B. and I will give you each a card with a situation. Each person will take a turn being the teacher for his or her own situation while the other person role plays a student. Remember to talk aloud through the four steps. The person playing the teacher will be the recorder. As the recorder, you will check off each step as the student does it. At the end of each role-play, the recorder will then compliment his or her partner on one thing he or she did well and then offer one suggestion on how else the situation could have been handled.

Practice Situations

1. You stayed after class to ask your teacher a question about the assignment. Now you're late getting to your next class and running down the hall.

Teacher: No running in the halls! Come here. I want you to go back to the end of the hall and walk this time.

2. You are Ralph. You and your grandparents flew in from California yesterday, and the

family all went to a relative's for a family get-together. Your family didn't get home till after 11:00 P.M. so you didn't have time to get your spelling assignment completed.

Teacher: Ralph, I don't have your spelling assignment. The test is tomorrow and it's important that you practice these words. I want you to stay in from recess and complete this assignment. I also want you to write each word five times tonight for homework and hand it in tomorrow.

3. Your name is Tommy, and you are anxious to get to gym class because they are playing basketball, a sport that you are real good at. Mrs. K. stops you in the hall and asks if you wouldn't mind helping her carry some boxes of books to the library. She promises you that she will write a note to your next teacher explaining why you are late.

4. You are Karen and your mother went into labor in the middle of the night. You were told this morning that she delivered a baby girl. You have not yet gone to the hospital to see your mother or your new baby sister. You're quite excited and haven't been able to pay attention in class.

Teacher: Karen, this is the third time that I've had to ask you to look up here and pay attention. Do I need to move you up to the front of the room to keep your attention?

5. You are running to catch a football on the playground when you accidentally collide with another student. The other student jumps up angrily and begins screaming accusations that you knocked him over on purpose. A teacher arrives promptly on the scene and hears the other student's accusations.

6. Your name is Dave and you're having a really bad day. You and your best friend are fighting, you got in trouble at home last night and are grounded for the weekend, and another student has just yelled at you for missing the ball in a volleyball game during gym class. You yell back at the student and push him.

Teacher: Dave, report to the office. No fighting is allowed in this school. I'll be up after class to give you a detention slip. (After class:) Dave, this kind of conduct is serious. Why did you push John?

7. Larry has found that he is missing his lunch money and accuses you (Tim) of stealing it. You brought your lunch but have extra money in your pocket that you brought to buy extra cookies with. You know that you did not take Larry's lunch money.

Teacher: Tim, Larry says that he saw you go into his desk when he went up to sharpen his pencil. He claims you have his lunch money in your pocket. Didn't you pack a lunch today? Stealing someone else's money is a crime and will have to be reported to your parents.

8. Yesterday's math assignment was really tough for you (Bob). You attempted the problems but just couldn't get it. Your mom's visiting the hospital a lot lately to see your grandma, so she wasn't around to help you, and your dad was too busy with your younger brothers. Now the teacher has asked you to put one of the problems on the board and explain it to the class.

Teacher: Bob, I asked you to come up and put problem 4 on the board and explain to the class how you got your answer. I want you to do it now!

9. While cleaning up at the end of art class, Andy accidentally bumped into you (Roy)

FIGURE 8–3
Practice session using the self-monitoring checklist.

Self-Monitoring Checklist

Name _____ Date _____

Class _____ Teacher _____

	Home room	1st period	2nd period	3rd period	lunch	4th period	5th period	6th period	Home room
1. Is it a reasonable and fair request?									
2. What will be the consequences of my actions?									
3. I need to respond politely and calmly.									
4. I need to reward myself for a good job.									
Total points (1 pt/situation)									

and made you spill your paint dish all over the floor and the walls.

Teacher: Roy, look at this mess! I want you to stay and wash the entire floor and walls until all this paint is cleaned up.

10. During reading class, Frank throws a spitball at Julie, which hits her directly in the head. The teacher has seen the direction that the spitball came from, but mistakenly thinks you (Danny) threw it.

Teacher: Danny, that was totally uncalled for. I want you to stay in the first 15 min of recess and sweep the entire floor. Also, I'd like you to apologize to Julie right now!

Generalization/Transfer Activities

To ensure generalization of the new skills taught (i.e., four self-management steps) and to better enable students to respond to requests or directions from adults in an appropriate way, it is important that these skills be practiced across settings, situations, and people. Thus, the other teachers in the building have agreed to "create" situations in which the student will be required to use these skills. Students will not be forewarned about these situations, but they will be told that they are expected to self-monitor their use of these skills in their other classrooms. Additionally, they will be told that their other teachers have been informed about this self-management program and have agreed to reward each student that successfully demonstrates the use of these skills in a situation with them, if one should occur. Students will be given a self-monitoring checklist that will be explained, modeled by the teacher, and then practiced by the students (see Figure 8–3).

Practice Session Using the Self-Monitoring Checklist

Teacher: I was told by a student from one of my other classes that someone in this classroom was given the answers to the math test yesterday. Since I don't know who it was, you will all have to retake a different math test that will be twice as hard. I'm very disappointed that someone from this class would cheat. Does anyone have any comments before we begin the test?

First Student: I don't think it's fair that we should all be punished for something that one person did. Besides, you don't know for sure whether the kid who told you that was telling the truth. How did he know?

(Students are prompted to check off the first step under third period if they have not already.)

Second Student: If we refuse to take the second test, we could get a failing grade. If we take the test, we could do poorly since it's twice as hard. If we get angry and yell, we might get in trouble plus a failing grade. But if we talk to the teacher nicely and convince her that it is wrong to punish us all, we might get out of it.

(Students are prompted to check off the second step under third period if they have not already.)

Third Student: Mrs. Cois, if someone from an earlier period gave someone in our class the answers to the test, wouldn't that be just as wrong as the person taking the answers? So why isn't that class being punished, too, since you don't know who gave the answers?

Teacher: I hadn't thought of that. You are quite right, Andy. Giving the answers is just as wrong as getting them.

Fourth Student: Couldn't you look at the tests with the same scores and see if there are any that have all the same right and wrong answers? Maybe you could talk to those kids and see if any of them did it.

Teacher: That's a good idea, too. Maybe I'd find some clues by looking at the tests.

Fifth Student: Instead of punishing all of us, why don't you just give different tests to each class from now on so that people can't cheat?

(Students are prompted to check off the third step under third period if they have not already.)

Teacher: That would certainly help to keep this from happening again. It may have happened before and I just didn't know about it. Well, you've all been pretty helpful with ways to identify the cheaters and keep this from happening again. And you're right that the other class shouldn't get off the hook if you're being punished. I guess it isn't fair to punish nine innocent people because of one student, so you won't have to take this other test. But be warned that future tests will be different for all classes.

Sixth Student: We did a great job. No one lost their cool or yelled swear words or anything nasty. We just stayed calm and came up with some good reasons why it wasn't fair and how she could find the cheaters.

(Students are prompted to check the fourth step under third period if they have not already.)

After students have been instructed on how to use the self-monitoring checklist, they will be instructed to record only situations where the teacher's request or direction makes them feel angry or upset. Students will be shown a video on "anger" so that they are more aware of the signs for anger. Discussion will follow with

Dear Parents,

   As previously discussed, you have agreed to assist _____ in practicing a new four-step strategy to assist him or her in dealing appropriately with adult requests or directions. This means that _____ will not talk back angrily, use offensive language, or refuse to do what is asked of him or her. The attached monitoring checklist is for you to complete. Please read the directions carefully. Additionally, you should have your child go over it with you since he or she has practiced completing it in school. Your child will also be completing his or her own monitor sheet.

   When finished with this homework assignment, you may compare your evaluation scores with his or her scores and talk about any discrepancies. If your child has the same score you have, you may give him or her an extra five points by writing your initials on the marked "5 bonus points."

   Thank you for participating with this program. Your support is essential to the success of any program. We hope this program will provide the participating students with better skills to deal with adults appropriately by encouraging them to think about their actions.

   Good luck and feel free to call me if you have any issues or concerns that you would like to discuss.

                                   Sincerely,

                                   Ms. D. Cois

FIGURE 8–4   Letter to parents.

students talking about their own warning signals of anger. Lastly, students will be instructed to use the self-monitoring checklist during all periods.

   Each of the five collaborating teachers will be instructed to set up situations with two different students a day to ensure that each student is receiving at least one practice session a day. Additionally, parents will be notified prior to implementing this behavior design and asked to sign an agreement to participate in assignments at home. The program, expectations, and monitoring system will have been explained to parents so that they can provide situations where their child(ren) can extend their practice to the home environments. Parents will be asked to monitor their child's performance utilizing these four steps and compare their evaluation with that of their child (see Figure 8–4). Parent signatures will be required on the parent's evaluation which will

Reprinted with permission of the author.

be returned to the school for bonus points (see Figure 8–5).

Group Contingency

Students will self-monitor their responses in all classes to adult requests and directions. Appropriate responses using the four-step strategy will earn one point for each situation. Inappropriate responses (talking back angrily or using inappropriate language) will earn a zero for each situation. For every point, students will earn a penny that will be put in the coin roller. If there are no inappropriate responses (zeros) from anyone during that week, an extra 5 pennies will be earned. When the class has earned 50 pennies, the class will be allowed to play a math game of their choice during third-period math class the following day and given a free homework ticket to be used at their discretion.

   Self-monitoring checklists will be randomly monitored. Any checklist found to be inaccurate will cost the individual a day without being able to earn any points.

FIGURE 8–5
Parent's Evaluation

Directions: Please complete the information at the top of the checklist. You have agreed to make **two requests** of your child and monitor his or her response. You may choose one or both of the requests already provided or fill in requests of your choice in the other boxes. These requests need to be *direct* and *specific* as to what you want and when you want it completed. An example might be, "Sam, I want you to set the table right now since dinner will be ready in five minutes. Please don't forget the napkins."

If your child responds as requested in a calm and polite manner, you may assume that she or he thought through the four steps before responding. You may then check each box under the appropriate request column. Four checks in a column for one situation earns two points. If your child fails to respond appropriately, remind him or her to follow the four steps. If he or she still does not comply with your request, place zeros in each of the boxes under that situation and fill out the comment section as to what your child's response was.

After two requests have been made and recorded on the checklist, you can compare your checklist with that of your child. If your child has the same scores you have, you may give him or her an extra five points by writing your initials on the line marked "5 bonus points."

Monitoring Checklist

Name_____ Date _____

Parent's Signature_____ 5 Bonus Points _____

Request/Direction

Four Steps	Assist with preparing dinner	Complete homework without TV on	Other	Other
1. Is it a reasonable and fair request?				
2. What will be the consequences of my actions?				
3. I need to respond politely and calmly.				
4. I need to reward myself for a good job				
Total Points (1 pt/situation)				

Comments _____

_____

_____

DISCUSSION QUESTIONS

1. What causes antisocial behavior?
2. When would you use an "After-the-fact" ABC analysis?
3. How do you select the right intervention(s) for your students with aggression?
4. List five actions to avoid when dealing with students who may have aggressive behaviors.
5. What can you do about bullying?
6. When should you use crisis intervention strategies?
7. Name four verbal de-escalation strategies.
8. Describe how self-management can help a student deal with his anger?
9. Why is role-playing important in social skills instruction?

REFERENCES

Alliance for the Mentally Ill. (1996). The Crisis. *Voice, 3,* 3, 6.

Arllen, N. L., Gable, R. A., & Hendrickson, J. M. (1996). Using peer confrontation to reduce inappropriate student behavior. *Beyond Behavior, 7*(1), 22–23.

Burnette, J. (1999). Critical behaviors and strategies for teaching culturally diverse students. ERIC/OSEP Digest E584. Reston, VA: ERIC Clearinghouse on Disabilities and Gifted Education.

Cartledge, G., & Milburn, J. F. (1996). Cultural diversity and social skills instruction. Champaign, IL: Research Press.

Cartledge, G., & Johnson, C. T. (1997). School violence and cultural sensitivity. In A. P. Goldstein & J. C. Conoley (Eds.), *School violence intervention: A practical handbook* (pp. 391–425). New York: Guilford Press.

Conroy, M. A., & Fox, J. J. (1994). Setting events and challenging behaviors in the classroom: Incorporating contextual factors into effective intervention plans for children with aggressive behaviors. *Preventing School Failure, 38,* 29–34.

Dodge, K. A., Bates, J. E., & Pettit, G. S. (1990). Mechanisms in the cycle of violence. *Science, 250,* 1678–1683.

Garrity, C., Jens, K., Porter, W., Sager, N., & Short-Camilli, C. (1994). *Bully-proofing your school.* Longmont, CO: Sopris West.

Goldstein, A. P. (1987). Teaching prosocial skills to aggressive adolescents. In C. M. Nelson, R. B. Rutherford, Jr., & B. I. Wolford (Eds.), Special education in the criminal justice system (pp. 215–250). Upper Saddle River, NJ: Merrill/Prentice Hall.

Goldstein, A. P. (1999). *The prepare curriculum: Teaching prosocial competencies.* Champaign, IL: Research Press.

Goldstein, A., & Huff, C. R. (1993). *The gang intervention handbook.* Champaign, IL: Research Press.

Gunter, P. L., Denny, R. K., Jack, S. L., Shores, R. E., & Nelson, M. (1993). Aversive stimuli in academic interactions between students with serious emotional disturbance and their teachers. *Behavioral Disorders, 24,* 180–182.

Hammond, R., & Gipson, B. (1994). *Dealing with Anger: Givin It, Takin It, Working It Out* (video). Champaign, IL: Research Press.

Hammond, R. W., & Yung, B. R. (1995). PACT-*Positive Adolescent Choices Training: A Model for Violence Prevention Groups with African American Youth (Video).* Champaign, IL: Research Press.

Hartman, R., & Sage, S. A. (2000). The relationship between social information processing and in-school suspension for student with behavioral disorders. *Behavioral Disorders,*25(3), 183–195.

Hohensee, J. B., & Derman-Sparks, L. (1992). Implementing an anti-bias curriculum in early childhood classrooms. ERIC *Digest.* Urbana, IL: ERIC Clearinghouse on Elementary and Early Childhood Education (ED 351 146).

Huesmann, L. R., Guerra, N. G., Miller, L. S., & Zelli, A. (1992). The role of social norms in the development of aggressive behavior. In A. Fraczek & H. Zumkley (Eds.), *Socialization and aggression* (pp. 139–152). New York: Springer.

Jensen, W. R. (1996). Reprimands and precision requests. In H. K. Reavis, M. T. Sweeten, W. R. Jensen, D. P. Morgan, D. J. Andrews, & S. Fister (Eds.), *Best Practices: Behavioral and educational strategies for teachers* (pp. 107–126). Longmont, CO: Sopris West.

Kellan, S. G., Rebok, G. W., Ialongo, N., & Mayer, L. S. (1994). The course and malleability of aggressive behavior from early first grade into middle school: Results of a developmental epidemiologically-based preventive trial. *Journal of child psychology and psychiatry,* 35(2), 259–282.

Keller, H. R., & Tapasak, R. C. (1997). Classroom management. In A. P. Goldstein & J. C. Conoley (Eds.), *School vi-*

olence intervention: A practical handbook (pp. 107–126). New York: Guilford Press.

Kerr, M. M., Strain, P. S., & Ragland, E. U. (1982). Component analysis of a teacher-mediated peer-feedback treatment package: Effects on positive and negative interactions of behaviorally handicapped students. *Behavior Modification, 2,* 278–280.

Loeber, R., & Farrington, D. P. (1998). *Serious and violent juvenile offenders: Risk factors and successful interventions.* Thousand Oaks, CA: Sage Publications.

Long, N. J., & Morse, W. C. (1996). *Conflict in the classroom.* Austin, TX: Pro-Ed.

Luckner, J. (1996). Juggling roles and making changes: Suggestions for meeting the challenges of being a special educator. *Teaching Exceptional Children, 28,* 24–28.

Meador, S. A. (1992). Changing youth's attitudes about guns. *School Safety* (Fall), 31.

Mulvey, E. (1993). Safe Schools Report. Unpublished manuscript. University of Pittsburgh, Pittsburgh, PA.

Mulvey, E., Arthur, M., & Reppucci, N. (1993). The prevention and treatment of juvenile delinquency: A review of the research. *Clinical Psychology Review, 13,* 133–167.

National School Safety Center. (1990). *School safety checkbook.* Westlake Village, CA: Author.

Penno, D. A., Frank, A. R., & Wacker, D. P. (2000). Instructional accommodations for adolescent students with severe emotional or behavioral disorders. *Behavioral Disorders, 25*(4), 325–343.

Presley, J. A., & Hughes, C. (2000). Peers as teachers of anger management to high school students with behavioral disorders. *Behavioral Disorders, 25*(2), 114–130.

Ramsey, E. (1995). Antisocial behavior in school: Strategies and best practices. Pacific Grove, CA: Brooks/Cole.

Reynolds, L. K., & Kelley, M. L. (1997). The efficacy of a response cost-based treatment package for managing aggressive behavior in preschoolers. *Behavior Modification, 21*(2), 216–230.

Rhode, G. (1996). In-school suspension program. In H. K. Reavis, M. T. Sweeten, W. R. Jensen, D. P. Morgan, D. J. Andrews, & S. Fister (Eds.). *Best Practices: Behavioral and educational strategies for teachers* (pp. 87–98). Longmont, CO: Sopris West.

Striepling, S. H. (1997). The low-aggression classroom. In A. P. Goldstein & J. C. Conoley (Eds.), *School violence intervention: A practical handbook* (pp. 23–45). New York: Guilford Press.

Vorath, H., & Brendtro, L. (1974). *Positive peer culture.* Chicago: Aldine Press.

Walker, H. M., Colvin, G., & Ramsey, E. (1995). Antisocial behavior in school: Strategies and best practices. Pacific Grove, CA: Brooks/Cole.

Walker, H. M., Hops, H., & Greenwood, C. (1993). RE-CESS: *A program for reducing negative-aggressive behavior.* Seattle, WA: Educational Achievement Systems.

Walker, H. M., McConnell, S., R., Holmes, D., Todis, B., Walker, J., & Golden, N. (1983). *The Walker social skills curriculum: The ACCEPTS program (a curriculum for children's effective peer and teacher skills).* Austin, TX: Pro-Ed.

Walker, H. M., & Severson, H. (1990). *Systematic screening for behavior disorders.* Longmont, CO: Sopris West.

Walker, H. M., Severson, H. H., Feil, E. G., Stiller, B., & Golly, A. (1998). First step to success: Intervening at the point of school entry to prevent antisocial behavior patterns. *Psychology in the Schools. 35*(3), 259–269.

Walker, H. M., Stiller, B., Golly, A., Kavanagh, K., Severson, H. H., & Feil, E. (1997). *First step to success: Helping young children overcome antisocial behavior.* Longmont, CO: Sopris West.

Wasserman, G. A., & Miller, L. S. (1998). The prevention of serious and violent juvenile offending. In R. Loeber & D. P. Farrington (Eds.), *Serious and violent juvenile offenders: Risk factors and successful interventions* (pp. 197–247). Thousand Oaks, CA: Sage Publications.

Webster, D. W. (1993). The unconvincing case for school-based conflict resolution programs for adolescents. *Health Affairs, 12,* 126–141.

Wilson-Brewer, R., & Spivak, H. (1994). Violence prevention in schools and other community settings: The pediatrician as initiator, educator, collaborator, and advocate. *Pediatrics, 94*(4), 623–630.

Yao, E. L. (1988, November). Working effectively with Asian immigrant parents. *Phi Delta Kappan,* 223–225.

Young, K. R., West, R. P., Smith, D. J., & Morgan, D. P. (1991). *Teaching self-management strategies to adolescents.* Longmont, CO: Sopris West.

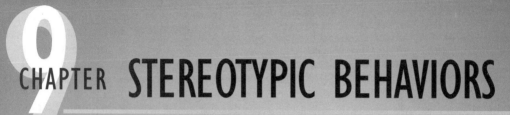

CHAPTER 9 STEREOTYPIC BEHAVIORS

OUTLINE

OBJECTIVES

After completing this chapter, you should be able to

- Define the various types of self-injurious and self-stimulatory behaviors.
- Conduct a functional analysis of a stereotypic behavior.
- Discuss the theoretical concepts underlying self-stimulatory behavior.
- Choose an effective intervention for self-injurious behavior.
- Discuss the ethical issues in carrying out aversive and restrictive interventions.
- Assist in conducting a sensory extinction intervention.

This chapter was written by Kristina Johnson and William J. Helsel

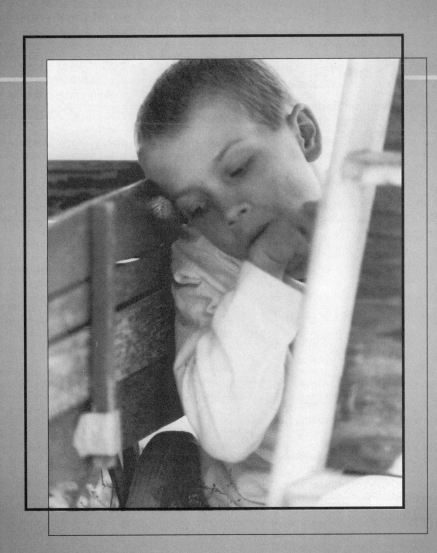

The behaviors described in this chapter may be the most complex that you will ever confront in teaching. Sadly, they are also serious—if not life-threatening—to the students who exhibit them. Let's look first at what is meant by self-injurious behavior (SIB) and self-stimulatory behavior (SSB) and the terms associated with them.

SELF-INJURIOUS BEHAVIORS

The terms self-injurious, **self-mutilating,** and self-destructive describe behaviors that hurt the person exhibiting them. These terms are commonly used for chronic, repetitive acts of individuals with severe disabilities (Favell, 1982). In this chapter we use self-injurious behavior, or SIB, because it is the term you are most likely to hear and use. Note that although this term conceivably consists of all acts of self-injury, including suicide and substance abuse (Schroeder, Schroeder, Rojahn, & Mulick, 1981), we do not refer to these behaviors in this chapter.

Favell (1982) summarized the various kinds of SIB reported in research literature into five categories :

1. Striking oneself (e.g., face slapping, head banging against objects)
2. Biting or sucking various body parts (e.g., "mouthing")
3. Pinching, scratching, poking, or pulling various body parts (e.g., eye-poking, hair pulling)
4. Repeatedly vomiting, or vomiting and reingesting food (i.e., "rumination")
5. Consuming nonedible substances (e.g., eating objects, cigarettes: **pica**; eating feces: **coprophagia**) (p. 1)

These generic categories are reflected in the research definitions of SIB in Table 9–1. These descriptions not only illustrate problem behaviors but give you and your multidisciplinary IEP team ideas for writing target behavior descriptions.

Also, note the measurement approaches used by the various authors. These may help you decide how to measure the SIB of your students.

The studies cited are attempts to resolve the serious problems of SIB individuals. This is a new area for researchers and classroom teachers, and you may find that your previous experience and training in the management of SIB are limited. Still, you must try to understand these often frightening behaviors because they can result in serious injury to a student, such as retinal detachment (Favell, 1982), loss of an appendage or of the use of a sensory modality, or a skull fracture. It is imperative that you recognize the significance of SIB and respect the highly systematic interventions designed to treat it.

Let's review some explanations for why these bizarre behaviors occur. Understanding the motivational conditions of SIB is a rapidly developing area for research, often called functional analysis (Carr & Durand, 1985; Durand & Carr, 1985).

Durand and Carr (1985) cited four motivational conditions for self-injury. The first, social attention, refers to the maintenance of the behaviors through the verbal or nonverbal feedback of others (Carr & McDowell, 1980). Second, self-injury may be maintained through tangible consequences (e.g., access to play activities). Third, the student may exhibit self-injury to avoid a situation he dislikes (e.g., a difficult self-help lesson). Finally, the sensory feedback a student receives from injuring himself may be reinforcing to him.

Durand and Crimmins (1987) developed a screening tool for determining the functional significance of self-injury, the Motivation Assessment Scale (MAS). You and your supervisor might use this instrument (available from V. Mark Durand, State University of New York at Albany) to gain a better understanding of a student's stereotypic behaviors.

A functional analysis of self-injury suggests the purpose for the behavior, and once we understand why a student injures herself, we can move to teaching her alternative behaviors for achieving

TABLE 9–1 Definitions of Self-Injurious Behaviors

Behavior	Definition	Measurement Procedure	Authors
Ear pulling and gouging	Closure of fingers, fingernails, or hand on ear. with a pulling or digging motion	Occurrence or nonoccurrence of self-injurious behavior during continuous, 10-sec intervals	Iwata, Dorsey, Slifer, Bauman, & Richman (1994)
Eye gouging	Any contact of any part of hand within the ocular area.		
Face slapping	Forceful contact of the open hand with the face.		
Hair pulling	Closure of the fingers and thumb on hair with a pulling motion away from the head.		
Hand mouthing	Insertion of one or more fingers into the mouth.		
Head banging	Forceful contact of the head with a stationary environmental object.		
Head hitting	Forceful contact of the hand with any part of the head.		
Neck choking	Forceful closure of both hands around the neck.		
Self-biting	Closure of the upper and lower teeth on the flesh of any portion of the body.		
Pica	Ingestion of, or attempt to ingest, nonnutritive items	10-second continuous interval record	Rojahn, McGonigle, Curcio, & Dixon (1987)
Self-injurious behavior (SIB)	Behavior directed against own body, which causes physical damage or presents a health hazard. These SIB types are likely to occur: head hitting (hit her head with her extremities), pinching, thigh slapping, hand pounding on hard surfaces, eye gouging with fingers		
Hand or arm biting	Insertion of the hand or arm into the mouth beyond the lips	Frequency, duration measures	Jenson, Rovner, Cameron, Peterson, & Kesler (1985)
Hand biting	Placing hands into mouth and biting down upon the skin with teeth	Frequency count	Luiselli (1984b)
Self-injurious behavior (SIB)	A tantrum that involves hitting head against the wall or floor, scratching at face, or hitting in the head or upper chest with clenched fists	Frequency count	Rolider & Van Houten (1985)
Mouthing objects	Placing any inappropriate objects such as rocks, napkins, cloth, part of toys, and dirt into the mouth		
Self-injurious behavior (SIB)	Striking face, head, neck, throat, torso, or extremities with closed hand (fist), open hand (palm), or extended fingers Striking face, head, neck, throat, torso, or extremities with any object held in the hand(s) Striking the head against any fixed surface such as a wall, floor, tabletop, or partition	Frequency count	Luiselli (1986)

(Continued)

TABLE 9–1 Definitions of Self-Injurious Behaviors—*Continued.*

Behavior	Definition	Measurement Procedure	Authors
Self-biting	Self-biting behavior was defined both in terms of frequency of daily occurrence and intensity of each occurrence and was scored when any part of the participant's body was pressed between her upper and lower teeth. The intensity of each occurrence was gauged according to the following five-point scale: 1. No teeth marks or lesions 2. Teeth marks not breaking skin 3. Scraping skin but no bleeding 4. Breaking skin and bleeding 5. Breaking skin, bleeding, and biting others attempting to restrain her	Frequency and intensity	Neufeld & Fantuzzo (1984)

the same goals. Carr and Durand (1985) illustrated this approach in a communication training program for children with developmental disabilities. Very carefully selected and trained phrases enabled the children to satisfy their needs without resorting to self-injury. Carr and Durand (1985) wrote of another illustration:

> As we have seen, it is essential to match the consequences involved in alternative behaviors to the assessed motivating conditions. Problems may arise if such a match is not made. For example, if a teacher chose to stand up and walk away from a boy who hit himself for attention, then his self-injurious behavior may very well decrease in frequency over time. However, if his self-injurious behavior were escape motivated, having the teacher walk away might produce an increase in self-injurious behavior since the teacher's leaving would be associated with removal of task demands. That is, the teacher would be providing the child with what he wanted, namely, a cessation of the task. This contingency would strengthen self-injurious behavior. The case just discussed illustrates the extreme importance of designing treatment intervention based on the specific motivation of the self-injurious behavior. (p. 175)

SELF-STIMULATORY BEHAVIORS

These actions, like SIB, are repetitive and frequent but do not cause physical injury. **Ritualistic** and **stereotypic** are global terms also used to describe self-stimulatory behaviors. For purposes of this chapter, however, we adopt self-stimulatory behavior (SSB), the term most commonly used, to describe "behaviors that are stereotyped and performed repetitiously, and that fail to produce any apparent positive environmental consequences or physical injury" (O'Brien, 1981, p. 117). Examples of self-stimulatory behaviors appear in Table 9–2.

Controversy surrounds (and may eventually alter the usage of) the term self-stimulation because it implies a questionable motivation for the behavior (Baumeister, 1978). Some Authors prefer the phrase "stereotyped movements" because it is "without inference and purely descriptive" (O'Brien, 1981, p. 118).

Like SIB, self-stimulatory behaviors are seen most often in those with severe behavioral disabilities. Research on the nature of SSB has revealed that this serious behavior problem may be maintained by the perceptual reinforcement that it

TABLE 9-2 Definitions of Self-Stimulatory Behaviors

Behavior	Definition	Measurement Procedure	Authors
Scream	Vocalization above normal conversational level that contains no words.	Response rate per minute, using a stopwatch during a 10-min session.	Bittle & Hake (1977)
Running and hopping	Normal running mixed with hops without any apparent attempt to move to a particular place.	Response rate per minute, using a stopwatch during a 10-min session.	
Arm waving	Extending arms at a 90° angle from one's side, moving them in a circular motion.	Response rate per minute, using a stopwatch during a 10-min session.	
Finger wiggling	Putting hands in front of face, spreading fingers apart, and then slowly flexing and extending them one at a time in sequence.	Response rate per minute, using a stopwatch during a 10-min session.	
Looking out the corner of eyes	Turning head in one direction while moving eyes in the opposite direction without any apparent attempt to focus on an object.	Response rate per minute, using a stopwatch during a 10-min session.	
Mouthing	Placing one or both hands, any fingers, or a toy in or on the mouth.	Scoring each 10-sec interval in a 10-min session as to whether self-stimulation or appropriate play occurred. (If both occurred, then only self-stimulation was scored.)	Coleman, Whitman, & Johnson (1979)
Head back	Tilting the head back at an angle of 45° to the normal upright position.		
Body motion	Any back and forth movement of the head and shoulders and the torso with the back moving away from and toward the chair back at least twice in a row.		
Bouncing	Bouncing up and down in the seat with up and down leg motion or kicking.		
Public masturbation	Putting either hand inside pants and directed toward penis. Hand was defined as in pants whenever one fingernail disappeared from view. Response ended when hand or fingers were removed from pants. Public masturbation meant that the behavior occurred anywhere outside the child's bedroom or bathroom.	Rate of masturbation responses per day, measured during six 5-minute time samples.	Cook, Altman, Shaw, & Blaylock (1978)
Rubbing saliva	Placing fingers into mouth for 1-2 sec, wetting them with saliva, and then rubbing the fingers together as student removed them from mouth.	Frequency count	Luiselli (1984a)

(Continued)

TABLE 9–2   Definitions of Self-Stimulatory Behaviors—*Continued.*

Behavior	Definition	Measurement Procedure	Authors
Tongue protrusion	Thrusting tongue of mouth and exposing it for several seconds.		
Stereotypy	Excessive manipulation of the environment (turning the water taps on and off, opening and closing doors, etc.), pacing back and forth or in circles, rocking back and forth or from side to side, finger pilling (a continuous motion of rubbing thumb and fingertips together or on her clothing), and continuous nonsense vocalizations (repeated out of context phrases at a rapid pace).	Occurrence or nonoccurrence of the behavior. If the behavior occurred at all during the minute, the interval was scored for the presence of stereotypy.	Rolider, Williams, Cummings, & Van Houten (1991)

provides to the self-stimulating individual (Lovaas, Newsom, & Hickman, 1987). Some of the important concepts put forth by these authors will help you understand why SSB is so difficult to eliminate in most individuals:

1. Many self-stimulatory behaviors are "so elaborate and idiosyncratic" (p. 46) that children must have learned them somehow. It is simply inconceivable that a child could be born with such complex behavioral preferences.
2. Children with SSB show a wide range of different kinds of SSB. These self-stimulatory behaviors are nearly identical, regardless of the culture in which the children were reared.
3. Withdrawal of social reinforcers and attention has not reduced these behaviors, which leads us to believe that these self-stimulatory behaviors are not the result of a "common social reinforcement history" (p. 46).
4. While engaged in SSB, children seem to be totally absorbed in their behaviors and become very difficult to interact with socially or instructionally.
5. When children do receive behavioral treatment, they often respond by developing new versions of SSB in place of the targeted behaviors.

6. "The most reliable and inevitable consequences of self-stimulatory behaviors are the perceptual or sensory stimuli that these behaviors produce" (p. 46).
7. SSB is a high-probability behavior, so SSB itself can be seen as a reinforcing event. (Review Chapter 5 on the concept of reinforcement.)

To better understand the particular role of perceptual reinforcement in SSB, consider these points made by Lovaas et al. (1987):

1. The child controls the perceptual reinforcers; these reinforcers are not controlled by others or the environment.
2. Perceptual reinforcers are primary reinforcers. Also, they are quite durable and not as vulnerable to satiation as other reinforcers.

When does a child begin to exhibit self-stimulatory behaviors? Research has shown that these behaviors begin in infancy in some individuals with developmental delays and, in most cases, before the age of two years (Berkson, McQuiston, Jacobson, Eyman, & Borthwick, 1985).

How does a child "learn" to engage in SSB? Consider this illustration (Lovaas et al., 1987):

An autistic child initially twirls a string in a variety of different ways. Sooner or later (through trial and error) a pattern of string movements is discovered that is particularly attractive to look at (i.e., that strongly reinforces twirling the string). With practice, he or she learns to perform exactly the right manipulation of the string to achieve the preferred pattern and tends to perform only that topography and closely related topographies most of the time. Consider another example: A child will retrieve and then skillfully manipulate a variety of objects (dishes, sinkstoppers, balls, etc.) to make them rotate or spin. Once the object comes to a resting position he or she will resume the behavioral sequence. In such an example, the child's spinning of various objects may be an acquired response, an operant, whose visual consequence (the spinning object) is the perceptual reinforcer that shapes and maintains the response. In the example of the child who repeatedly arranges (lines) objects such as toys, books, or shoes in neat rows across the living room floor, "objects in a line" may constitute a positively reinforcing perceptual consequence, shaping and maintaining the lining behavior. (p. 49)

How does SSB persist? SSB is highly reinforcing, and individuals engaged in SSB simply may not have other, alternative behaviors in which to engage.

As you study intervention possibilities later in this chapter, you will notice an emphasis on controlling the perceptual experiences of self-stimulating individuals. Also, you will learn how very carefully all assessments and interventions must be implemented if a program is to have any success with this difficult and durable set of behaviors. If you work with students with severe disabilities, the behaviors listed in Table 9–2 are probably familiar. Research has uncovered 50 types of SSB (LaGrow & Repp, 1984), only a few of which are included.

Self-stimulatory behaviors are not harmful in themselves but may, in time, change to self-injurious behaviors through a slight shift in topography (O'Brien, 1981). Furthermore, several researchers have reported that SSB dramatically limits an individual's attention to learning activities, thus reducing the potential skills repertoire of an already deficient learner (Foxx & Azrin, 1973). It would seem then that considerable effort should be expended toward the reduction of these troublesome behaviors. Indeed, this is now the generally accepted course of treatment.

A NOTE ABOUT SIB AND SSB ASSESSMENT AND INTERVENTIONS

The format of other chapters has been modified to accommodate the unusual issues surrounding the management of SIB and SSB problems. The major difference between this chapter and others is that fewer procedures are outlined in step-by-step fashion. We describe a few assessment and intervention procedures that you can implement with little supervision or outside help. Our exclusion of certain procedures will not be popular with many educators, who argue that "we already have these students in our classrooms, why not go ahead and tell us how to use all of the interventions available?" We can only reiterate our concern that you may inadvertently misuse a procedure because of problems with time, support personnel, supervision, effectiveness data, and approvals. As Judith Favell (1982) stated in her monograph on self-injurious behavior for the American Association of Behavior Therapy:

> The apparent simplicity of these techniques may be misleading. They are complex procedures which require a high degree of competence to design and conduct. The improper use of any procedure may place a self-injurious client at severe risk. (p. 20)

Despite their documented effectiveness, many interventions are prohibited in school settings because they create discomfort for the target student. Aversive procedures (always a last resort) have been replaced with more positive interventions in recent years (Van Houten, 1993; Iwata, Pace et al., 1994). Therefore, a second consideration is the use of alternative, nonaversive procedures that might be suggested through a good functional analysis. For example, you might discover that SIB occurs primarily when instructional demands are placed on the child—a finding described by Carr, Newsom, and Binkoff (1976). By changing the instructional schedule or the environmental demands, you may affect SIB. Iwata, Pace et al. (1994) studied individuals with visual impairments and reported that those who engaged in eye-poking may have increased their visual stimulation. Bright flashing lights or massages of the eye area contingent upon no self-injurious behaviors might work as interventions, if implemented properly.

Lovaas and Favell (1987) stated that

If a program cannot conduct alternative interventions in a high-quality fashion, then it should not employ aversive procedures. (p. 320)

. . . [T]he use of aversive and restrictive interventions should only be considered in the context of several issues surrounding their use. Such techniques are justified only when their effects are rigorously evaluated, caregivers are fully trained and adequately supervised in all dimensions of habilitative services, when a meaningful functional analysis of the child's problem has been conducted, alternative and benign treatments have been considered and are in place, parents and others are fully informed, and there is general agreement that the means justify the ends. (p. 324)

Furthermore, as Lovaas and Favell pointed out in their 1987 essay:

These complexities illustrate the need for a "functional analysis" of what is reinforcing a particular client's problem behavior in order to prescribe an adequate treatment, whether that treatment contains aversive consequences or not. This requirement raises again the question of whether a facility or agency has adequately trained staff to conduct such a functional analysis before any kind of treatment is employed. It is a serious concern that because some programs do not have the expertise and resources to functionally analyze problem behavior, they employ aversive procedures in an attempt to override the reinforcers maintaining them. Quite the opposite should be true. Only programs that are capable of conducting an adequate analysis of problem behavior should be allowed to employ aversive and restrictive treatments. (p. 318)

ESTABLISHING OPERATIONS

Assessment beyond function requires a look at motivative variables or establishing operations first identified by Keller and Schoenfeld (1995/1950) and further developed by Michael (1982). An establishing operation (EO) is an environmental event, operation, or stimulus condition that alters the reinforcing effectiveness of other events as well as the frequency of occurrence of the type of behavior that had been influenced by those other events (Michael, 1993). The behavior evoked by the EO is usually learned. There are many examples of day-to-day EOs that children with developmental disabilities or autism may experience. They may have difficulty in the afternoon as the day wears on. This could be called fatigue or referred to as the build-up of too many demands, pressures, or distress of unexpected events that are not part of their usual schedule. These same children are more likely to experience difficulty during the first six weeks of school, with changes in their daily schedules for the time period between Thanksgiving and Christmas, or an unexpected snow day.

There are two main types of EOs: unconditioned and conditioned. Both of these EOs are motivational because they increase the likelihood that a behavior will occur and at the same time increase the power of the reinforcer that follows the behavior. Unconditioned establishing operations (UEOs) are events, operations, and stimulus conditions whose reinforcer-establishing effects are unlearned (Michael, 1993). It is the unlearned aspect of the reinforcer-establishing effect that results in the EO being classified as "unconditioned." According to Michael (1993) many learned forms of reinforcement do not require learned EOs. The author states that there are variables that alter the reinforcing effectiveness of other events but only as a result of the individual organism's history. Michael (1993) refers to this definition as learned or conditioned establishing operations (CEOs). Here is an example to help you understand this concept. Teitelbaum (1977) defines thwarting (CEO) as "lack of reinforcement that are inevitable accompaniments of any reinforcement schedule" (p. 23). Thwarting is usually associated with anecdotal notes that state "he was aggressive out of the blue." For children with autism, we often recognize a statement like this is inaccurate after a functional analysis is completed. Oftentimes what happens is the child initiates a response, we may think "they want something," and we stop the child and tell him or her to wait. After you have thwarted an autistic child, depending on the time of day (i.e., UEO), one too many times, you will increase the likelihood that he is going to hit (behavior) you and escape negative reinforcement. Thus, that escape will be more powerful than usual in reinforcing the behavior and the occasion that it is contingent upon. Brown et al. (2000) investigated the effects of functional communication training in the presence and absence of EOs. They concluded that increases in relevant manding (i.e., making requests) were observed in the EO present condition; decreases in aberrant behavior were achieved when treatment was matched to the results of functional analysis. Kennedy and Itkonen (1993) investigated the effects of setting events (another way of looking at EOs) on problem behavior of students with disabilities. The authors concluded that the occurrence of preceding setting events was related to higher frequencies of problem behaviors and that the interventions designed to eliminate preceding setting events were associated with low rates of behaviors.

Now let's turn to the assessment procedures for SIB, followed by a discussion of interventions (environmental and teacher-mediated).

ASSESSMENT OF SIB

The data you collect in performing multilevel assessments of SIB will help you

- Recognize physiological and/or biological factors in SIB
- Analyze the interaction between SIB and environment variables
- Summarize information so that you can get assistance from a behavioral consultant
- Learn procedures that will prove useful in monitoring progress of subsequent interventions

The last is especially critical because, as Favell (1982) stated, "It is not possible to predict in advance if a given procedure or set of procedures will be effective in an individual case" (p. 21). Favell went on to recommend that thorough analysis of the behaviors precede any pinpointing of behaviors for intervention:

A prior analysis of biological and environmental conditions and consequences which may be maintaining the client's self-injury, and the explicit inclusion of that information in the design of [the intervention should be conducted]. . . . Such an analysis must be done situation by situation, since different situations control different rates and intensities of self-injury, and because even in situations in which self-injury does occur, the behavior may serve very different functions. For example, at times the behavior may serve to escape demands, at others it may function to obtain attention. (p. 18)

You may want assistance in conducting a comprehensive behavioral analysis; certain health-related information could be provided by the school nurse or physician with help from the student's parents. Complete this step before proceeding with any intervention, because this medical history is critical to determining whether the student has recently had or now needs a comprehensive physical and neuropsychiatric examination, as well as comprehensive testing for syndromes thought to cause SIB (Lesch-Nyan Syndrome, Cornelia de Lange's Syndrome). It is helpful to keep a daily log of bruises, cuts, and other injuries that may appear, as well as of SIB such as pica, vomiting, and rumination. Be sure to record any oral or topical medications (e.g., lotion for chapped or scratched skin) administered.

An environmental analysis calls for several items of information gathered in various settings and demand-situations. Figure 9–1 outlines components of an ecological approach. (See Iwata, Dorsey, Slifer, Bauman, & Richman, 1994, for a more detailed discussion of variables that contribute to SIB.) Because SIB varies within and across individuals, it is critical that you carry out a comprehensive individualized functional analysis (Iwata, Dorsey et al., 1994).

Naturally, the first item on the form requests a specific definition of the problem behavior or behaviors. Since SIB is rarely confined to one environment, say, school, we have included items that reflect different settings and different times of day. These variables are combined in question 4, which asks for information regarding possible alternative behaviors. Research on SIB individuals suggests that injurious behavior may be decreased by reinforcing alternative, noninjurious behaviors (Mulick, Hoyt, Rojahn, & Schroeder, 1978). Therefore, it is important for you to consider alternative behaviors to substitute for SIB.

Question 5 asks for demands on the individual. Again, studies have indicated that levels of SIB may be altered by the presence of demands (Iwata, Dorsey et al., 1994), or by activities the student finds particularly stressful. Questions regarding consequation for SIB (7 and 8) reflect the need for a thorough understanding of what has maintained, reduced, or increased SIB in the past. Before designing and initiating a new intervention, your consultant and multidisciplinary team should closely examine the data on prior attempts at intervention (see question 9).

A completed environmental analysis should provide your intervention team with specific settings, time, and adult actions for further examination. For a more complete review of SIB research on environmental variables, see Schroeder et al. (1981).

INTERVENTION STRATEGIES FOR SIB

Following are strategies to decrease self-injurious behaviors, some of which you will be able to implement by yourself, while other programs will require outside help.

Environmental Changes

As mentioned earlier, your multidisciplinary team, treatment team, or behavioral consultant may want to alter one or more of the following antecedent circumstances in order to determine their effects on SIB:

- The demands placed on an individual during a specific part of the daily routine (or the reinforcement the student receives for compliance with that demand)
- The available, reinforceable alternative activities that the student can engage in
- The physical restraints used with a client and the schedule for applying and removing them (see Favell, McGimsey, & Jones, 1978)
- The student's daily routine, with the possibility of rearranging stressful events

It is imperative to remember that any such alteration depends on a thorough analysis of each individual's behavior.

Environmental Safety Considerations

To prevent a self-injurious student from further harm, take safety precautions in your classroom. Remove any chemicals that may be toxic (e.g., typewriter correction fluid, cleaning supplies, medications, and paint). Take the position that a

Student _____ Age _____

Date _____ Teacher _____

1. What is (are) this student's self-injurious behavior(s)? Describe specifically.
   _____
   _____

2. List all the settings in which this behavior is exhibited.
   _____
   _____

3. At what times of day does the student engage in the SIB?
   _____
   _____

4. What activities could the student engage in, throughout the day, if he were not injuring himself?

Time	Alternative Activity
7–8 am	
8–9	
9–10	
10–11	
11–12	
12–1 pm	
1–2	
2–3	
3–4	
4–5	
5–6	
6–7	
7–8	
8–9	
9–10	
10–11 pm	

5. What demands are made of the student immediately prior to episodes of SIB? (Use an ABC analysis to determine this.)

Demand	Setting	SIB

6. Are there particular antecedent events that you associate with this student's SIB?
   _____
   _____
   _____

7. When the student engages in SIB, what happens?

Setting	Consequence

8. List all interventions you presently use to control the SIB (e.g., verbal statements, restraints, punishments, DRO).
   _____
   _____
   _____

9. Do you have data on these interventions? _____ Please provide, if yes.
   _____
   _____
   _____

FIGURE 9–1   Environmental analysis forms for SIB.

self-injurious child or adolescent does not possess the judgment necessary to determine what might be dangerous. Remove sharp objects such as scissors, pens, needles, paper clips, and thumbtacks. It may be necessary to cushion hard surfaces if the student pounds them with head or body.

Restraint Devices

SIB is sometimes treated through the application of various kinds of restraints (Dorsey, Iwata, Reid, & Davis, 1982; Irvin, Thompson, Turner, & Williams, 1998; Neufeld & Fantuzzo, 1984; Rincover & Devany, 1982; Van Houten, 1993). This intervention does not prevent self-injurious behaviors themselves, but it attempts to limit the harm of the stereotypic behavior. The disadvantages associated with restraints are (1) they do not teach new behaviors or eliminate the targeted ones, (2) they interfere with learning alternative behaviors (and may interfere with hearing and other senses), and (3) the appearance of a restraint may cause others to ostracize the child (Baumeister & Rollings, 1976). If your staff is considering a restraint procedure, consult Neufeld and Fantuzzo (1984) for the technical design of a "Bubble" restraint that does not interfere with other behaviors and that was successful in treating hand biting. This chapter's case study illustrates a safe alternative to restraints, which effectively reduced face slapping in one individual.

Irvin et al. (1998) demonstrated the use of a restraint procedure that allows for systematic fading. This case study illustrates utilizing increased response effort to reduce chronic hand mouthing with adjustable arm restraints. The arm restraints altered the amount of physical effort necessary to engage in hand mouthing, which successfully reduced levels of hand mouthing in children with profound disabilities.

Differential Reinforcement of Other Behaviors

Differential reinforcement of other behaviors (DRO) is a term frequently cited in descriptions of programs for SIB (or SSB) individuals. DRO procedures often accompany other interventions. Research has not proven DRO as successful as the "suppression interventions" in eliminating SIB (Dorsey, Iwata, Ong, & McSween, 1980; Iwata, Dorsey et al., 1994), but we often rely on DRO to teach the student vitally needed alternative behaviors (Jenson, Rovner, Cameron, Peterson, & Kesler, 1985). The basic notion of a DRO program is the reinforcement of intervals at a time during which the SIB (or other undesirable behavior) does not occur. For example, students might be reinforced initially each time they engage in 10 sec, then 15 sec, then 20 sec of non-SIB behavior.

In some programs based on the DRO procedure, reinforcement is administered for intervals of time during which certain behaviors incompatible with SIB are exhibited (e.g., putting together a puzzle without biting one's hand). These programs are then termed DRI, or differential reinforcement of incompatible behaviors. Table 9–3 provides a step-by-step procedure for conducting a DRO or DRI program.

Overcorrection

Overcorrection procedures have been used with conflicting results to modify self-injurious behaviors (Bierly & Billingsley, 1983; Carey & Bucher, 1986; Gibbs & Luyben, 1985; Iwata, Dorsey et al., 1994; Luiselli, 1984a, 1984b). During an overcorrection procedure, the student engages in practice of nonstereotyped behaviors while at the same time undergoing the removal of positive reinforcement for these behaviors. The goals of overcorrection programs, both restitutional and positive practice, have been described by their developers, Foxx and Azrin (1973).

In restitutional overcorrection, the self-injury is interrupted and the student is required to restore her immediate environment to an improved condition by practicing appropriate behaviors. To conduct a restitutional overcorrection procedure properly, you must first define the problem behaviors. Table 9–1 provides well-specified target be-

TABLE 9–3 Guidelines for Using a DRO or DRI Procedure

1. Set aside a block of time (e.g., 15 min daily or several such times per day) to conduct the training.
2. Arrange for a staff member to spend time with (or near, in later stages) the student during these sessions.
3. Record rate-per-minute baseline data on the problem behaviors, and chart them. Continue recording data throughout the program.
4. Select an appropriate behavior to reinforce (preferably one that is incompatible with the problem behavior). Be sure to choose a behavior that you can count easily by the frequency or interval method. If you cannot count it, you will have difficulty knowing when to reinforce it!
5. Select a powerful reinforcer for the student. Be sure you can remove the reinforcer from the student if response cost is to be incorporated into the procedure.
6. Gather the reinforcers, a container for them (e.g., clear plastic cup), and a data record sheet, and ask the student to sit across the table from you.
7. Say, "It's time to work (play)," and give the student the necessary items to engage in the appropriate (other) behavior (e.g., ballpoint pens to assemble and place in a tray, a toy car to roll toward you, a favorite stuffed animal to cuddle without self-stimulating).
8. Beginning with a "rich" schedule of reinforcement, provide the student with the reinforcer for each appropriate "other" behavior (each pen assembled) or for a brief interval of appropriate behavior (e.g., 5 to 10 sec of play with the teacher using a toy). If you use response cost, keep the reinforcers in the container until the end of the session.
9. If you desire, you can implement a response cost procedure at the same time. For this procedure, take away one (or two) of the reinforcers at each instance of the problem behavior after saying, "NO (*problem behavior*)!"
10. As the data indicate progress (e.g., a reduction in the response per minute of problem behaviors), you can "thin" the reinforcement schedule: you reinforce less frequently and require longer and longer intervals of time spent in the appropriate "other" behavior.
11. Be sure to praise the student at each time of reinforcement and to change the reinforcer if it no longer seems effective.
12. Do not use the verbal reprimand, "NO (*problem behavior*)!" at times when you cannot remove the reinforcer until you see definite, stable behavior improvement.

havior statements. **Restitutional overcorrection** is used for self-injurious and oppositional behaviors but not for self-stimulatory behaviors, which do not upset the environment. For example, restitutional overcorrection might be recommended for a child who smears feces, injures the inside of his mouth, or in some other way harms himself or damages his environment. Table 9–4 displays examples of overcorrection activities.

Correctly implementing overcorrection requires considerable staff time, so you will need help conducting this program. Review the guidelines, and once again, do not undertake this or any other SIB intervention without supervision from someone who has been trained to use overcorrection. Also, remember that overcorrection programs may require approval from the review committee and the student's parents. Check with your supervisor

about this. Table 9–5 provides guidelines for implementing restitutional overcorrection.

Positive practice overcorrection is similar to restitutional overcorrection (see Table 9–6). Unlike restitutional overcorrection, it does not require the learner to restore the environment. Positive practice overcorrection is used for behaviors that do not upset the environment or for behaviors for which no restitutional activity can be reasonably developed. Refer again to Table 9–4 for suggested positive practice activities. Positive practice overcorrection procedures are frequently described as successfully reducing the level of self-stimulatory or self-injurious behaviors. However, there is evidence to suggest that new forms of injurious behaviors may appear if they are not also included in the overcorrection procedure (Epstein, Doke, Sajwaj, Sorrell, & Rimmer, 1974). To avoid this negative side

TABLE 9–4   Suggested Restitutional and Positive Practice Activities for Self-Stimulatory and Self-Injurious Behaviors

Problem Behavior	Suggested Overcorrection Activity
Mouthing objects, injuring inside of mouth	Brush teeth with an oral antiseptic (mouthwash) and wipe lips with washcloth soaked in mouthwash. Periodically encourage student to spit out the rinse.[a]
Head weaving	Functional Movement Training for 5–7 min: Guide student to hold his head in each of three positions, up, down, and straight, for 15 sec. (Give instructions in a random order.)[a]
Clapping	Guide student through a series of hand positions, or Functional Movement Training. For example, have the student hold hands out, above her head, together, and behind back, holding each position for 15 sec.[a]
Hand flapping "airplaning"	Hold each of these positions for 15 sec, repeating the entire series 15 times: hands on head, hands straight up, hands on shoulders, hands on hips.

[a]Source: *These activities were taken from Foxx, R. M., & Azrin, N. H. (1973). The elimination of autistic self-stimulatory behavior by overcorrection.* Journal of Applied Behavior Analysis, 6, 1–14.

TABLE 9–5   Guidelines for Using Restitutional Overcorrection

1. Define the problem behavior or behaviors specifically.
2. Record baseline data on the rate or frequency of the problem behavior for at least three days. (Continue data collection during the program.)
3. Select a verbal cue to use when the student engages in the problem behavior. For example, "no throwing" or "no smearing."
4. Select a restitutional activity that is relevant to the problem behavior (see Table 9–4 for ideas). Be sure this activity sequence is long and extensive enough to have an impact on the student.
5. Decide when the program will be in effect each day, and then arrange an adequate amount of time and staff assistance to implement the program. An adult must be available for at least 45 min per problem behavior instance in the initial days of the program.
6. When the student engages in the problem behavior, give the verbal cue and proceed with the restitutional activity. Be prepared to prompt the student physically to complete the activities.
7. Avoid eye contact, unnecessary physical contact, and unnecessary conversation during restitutional overcorrection.
8. If the student reengages in one of the designated problem behaviors during the overcorrection procedures, start the activities again.
9. *Never* use the verbal cue without the restitutional overcorrection activities until the problem behaviors are reduced to a low and stable rate.
10. Be sure to provide ample opportunity during the rest of the day for the student to receive attention for appropriate behaviors.
11. *Remember:* This program may require parental-guardian permission and should be implemented under the supervision of a professional competent in this aspect of behavior modification. Medical approval of this program should be obtained prior to the student's participation in it.

Source: *The material in this table was taken from Foxx, R. M., & Azrin, N. H. (1973). The elimination of autistic self-stimulatory behavior by overcorrection.* Journal of Applied Behavior Analysis, 6, 1–14.

TABLE 9–6   Guidelines for Using Positive Practice Overcorrection

1. Define the problem behavior or behaviors specifically.
2. Record baseline data on the rate or percent of intervals of occurrence of each behavior. Continue collecting data throughout the overcorrection program.
3. Select a verbal cue to use when the student engages in the problem behavior.
4. Select a positive practice overcorrection activity, such as Functional Movement Training (see Table 9–4). Be sure the activity is sufficiently lengthy and intensive to modify the student's behavior.
5. Decide when the program will be in effect each day, and then arrange an adequate amount of time and staff assistance to implement the program. An adult must be available for at least 45 min per problem behavior instance in the initial days of the program.
6. When the student engages in the problem behavior, give the verbal cue and proceed with the positive practice activity. Be prepared to physically prompt the student to complete the activities.
7. Avoid eye contact, unnecessary physical contact, and unnecessary conversation during restitutional overcorrection.
8. If the student reengages in one of the designated problem behaviors during the overcorrection procedures, start the activities again.
9. *Never* use the verbal cue without the restitutional overcorrection activities until the problem behaviors are reduced to a low and stable rate.
10. Be sure to provide ample opportunity during the rest of the day for the student to receive attention for appropriate behaviors.
11. *Remember:* This program may require parental-guardian permission and should be implemented under the supervision of a professional competent in this aspect of behavior modification. Medical approval of this program should be obtained prior to the student's participation in it.

Source: *The material in this table was taken from Foxx, R. M., & Azrin, N. H. (1973). The elimination of autistic self-stimulatory behavior by overcorrection.* Journal of Applied Behavior Analysis, 6, *1–14.*

effect, be sure that your overcorrection procedure is closely monitored by a trained behavioral program specialist and that more acceptable replacement behaviors are reinforced.

Gibbs and Luyben (1985) showed that timeout from reinforcement (i.e., preventing the individual from engaging in the preferred stereotypic behavior) was a critical feature of successful overcorrection. Accordingly, we classify positive practice overcorrection as a restrictive procedure. This is in keeping with the advice of Foxx and Bechtel (1982) who suggested that the phrase *positive practice* be dropped from the term. (We have maintained the traditional title to assist readers who are acquainted with the two subtypes of overcorrection and who know of other, more purely educative uses of positive practice overcorrection.) However, one study suggested that you can maintain the effectiveness of the overcorrection by reinforcing the students for correctly practicing the designated behavior (Carey & Bucher, 1986). Correct responses,

performed without physical guidance from the adult, earned the child edibles and praise. The child received no feedback for approximate responses.

Remember that positive practice overcorrection is considered a punishment procedure that must be applied contingently after an episode of the target behavior, so you cannot schedule the practice sessions but must interrupt your classroom activities to conduct the practice contingently (Gibbs & Luyben, 1985). Moreover, the timeout from the preferred stereotypic behavior is a valuable component of the intervention and strengthens the view that overcorrection is a restrictive intervention requiring special consent and approval.

Positive practice overcorrection can be applied if the student is physically smaller than the adult in charge. Some students, however, are too strong and resistant to complete a functional movement training series. In the initial days of an overcorrection program, a student may struggle with you to continue self-injurious behaviors instead of following the positive practice activities (Luiselli, 1984a, 1984b). When working with a student whose physical stature prevents you from conducting the typical overcorrection functional movement exercises, your consultant may suggest exercises that only partially involve the student's body. For example, DeCatanzaro and Baldwin (1978) used a forced arm exercise, relying only on the arm involved in self-injurious acts. The teacher gently pumped the student's arm up and down once per second, repeating this action 25 times. Foxx (1978) offered the following guideline for using overcorrection with a counteraggressive individual:

> [I]f the overcorrection requires the involvement of two trainers instead of one, the danger of physical injury is greatly increased, and the procedure will not be implemented correctly. (Foxx, 1978, cited in Schroeder et al., 1981, p. 83)

Movement Suppression Procedure

The **movement suppression procedure** is a variation of timeout from reinforcement in which the student is punished for any movement or verbalization while in timeout (Rolider & Van Houten, 1985; Rolider et al. 1991). In the Rolider and Van Houten study, DRO alone (praise and candy every 15 min of no targeted behavior) was compared with movement suppression timeout plus DRO. The movement suppression intervention consisted of the parents or school staff placing the child in the corner, restraining his movements manually, and directing him not to move or talk. This lasted for 3 min. This procedure was replicated with slight modifications across cases of SIB in two other children; all reports were successful.

If you are on a team that is deciding which of several related interventions to try, review the Rolider et al. studies (1985; 1991); they provide comparative information on movement suppression plus DRO versus other treatments (e.g., contingent restraint, exclusionary timeout, corner timeout, and timeout in a wheelchair, respectively).

Some states have opted to prohibit selected treatment procedures based on their understanding of aversive and nonaversive procedures for purposes for protection (see Repp & Singh, 1990). To direct both the ethical and appropriate application of behavior treatment, Van Houten et al. (1988) propose that individuals who are recipients or potential recipients of treatment designed to change their behavior have the right to a therapeutic environment, services whose overriding goal is personal welfare, treatment by a competent behavior analyst, programs that teach functional skills, behavioral assessment and ongoing evaluation, and the most effective treatment procedure available.

ASSESSMENT OF SSB

Perhaps the first decision to be made with regard to referring a problem with SSB is whether it warrants treatment. In the event that a stereotypic behavior has become self-injurious, the decision is a quick "yes!" As pointed out by O'Brien (1981), there are types of SSB that, if repeated over time, are self-injurious: "tapping knuckles on hard surfaces . . . flipping fingers in front of eyes focused on the sun, keeping hands in a tight fist around the collar of a shirt" (p. 143).

An SSB individual may not gain access to less restrictive environments or to training programs within the present environment until the "annoying" SSB is reduced or eliminated (Baumeister, 1978; O'Brien, 1981). O'Brien illustrated this situation:

> Decreasing annoyance is a reason for treating self-stimulation. If parents, teachers, or peers reprimand, berate, or tease a client for self-stimulation, it should be treated. Similarly, treatment should be provided if clients are regularly required to accept less preferred sitting or sleeping arrangements because they self-stimulate. Requiring clients to sit in a position farthest from the television set, sit at the least preferred table in the dining room, sleep in a less-preferred bed, or sit in a less-preferred seat on the bus are examples of this. When these types of annoyance can be reduced, it seems reasonable to treat self-stimulation. (p. 143)

In classroom situations you may choose to pursue the assessment of the problem because SSB interferes with a student's ability to attend to appropriate instructional or adaptive behavior tasks (Foxx & Azrin, 1973; Lovaas et al., 1987). To define an SSB problem, use the questions in Figure 9–2 to assemble information gathered from the student's teachers and the student's family. The information listed on this form will help you complete your functional analysis of the student's SSB.

As you read about interventions for SSB, you will understand why certain items of information are important to a thorough definition and analysis of SSB. For example, questions regarding the type of sensory stimulation a student appears to gain from SSB (questions 3 and 4) provide initial information for a sensory extinction program, whereas questions 7, 8, and 9 target information for a DRO or punishment program. You should also complete a health history form or ask the student's parents to do this.

You need to record specific samples of SSB in preparation for (or to monitor the effects of) an intervention program. Review Table 9–2; the third column describes measurement procedures used for SSB. Notice that interval-based measurements are often used. We suggest you record SSB using an interval record such as the one in Figure 9–3. (If you have questions about designing or using an interval record, reread Chapter 3.)

These assessment activities should provide information to facilitate the design of an appropriate intervention, although the task is still not simple. O'Brien (1981) offers these guidelines:

> Should a decision be made to treat self-stimulation, a behavioral evaluation must be completed. The evaluation should determine the situations in which self-stimulation occurs, its topography, frequency, and duration, and its consequences. If during the evaluation it is found the self-stimulation occurred only under one condition (e.g., in front of a particular

---

Student _____   Date _____

1. What are the precise behaviors of concern?
2. Do these behaviors occur interchangeably, simultaneously, or separately?
3. Is any kind of sensory stimulation apparent (e.g., visual flickering, repetitive auditory signal)? In other words, what kind of *perceptual reinforcement* does the SSB provide the child?
4. Does the behavior appear only in selected settings (e.g., areas where there is a hard, smooth surface, well-lit areas)?
5. Do the behaviors prevent the student from engaging in an instructional activity? How?
6. Do the behaviors gain attention for the student from adults or peers? If so, what kind of attention? (Use an ABC analysis.)
7. Does the student cease self-stimulation when asked? For how long? When asked by whom? In what tone of voice?
8. Does the student stop these behaviors when alone? In the presence of whom?
9. Does the student stop the behaviors when engaged in certain activities? Specify these activities.
10. Could the self-stimulatory behaviors be considered developmentally age-appropriate for this student (e.g., masturbation)?
11. Is the student injuring himself?
12. Is the student presently involved in an intervention program? What is it? Where are the data on this program?

Name of person completing this form _____

FIGURE 9–2   Information-gathering form for SSB.

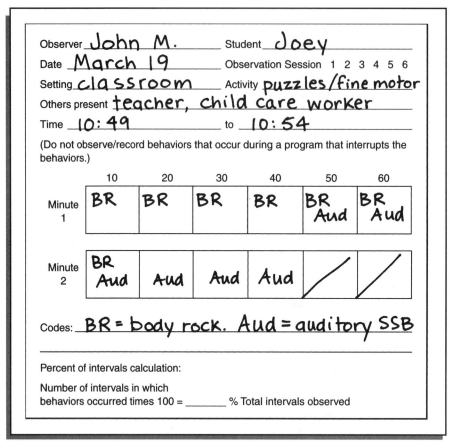

FIGURE 9–3 Interval record for self-stimulatory behaviors.

mirror, when wearing turtleneck sweaters), and it was reasonable to restrict the client from this condition, that might be the preferred treatment. Should it seem unreasonable to restrict the client from a particular situation in which self-stimulation occurred, it might be reasonable to apply sensory extinction. Should a behavioral evaluation determine that people regularly provide a consequence for the self-stimulation, that consequence should be reviewed as a possible reinforcer. Should the behavior evaluation determine that self-stimulation occurs in many different situations, that the sensory consequences would be difficult to modify, and that no other consequences are regularly provided, a program should be designed along the recommendations presented by Foxx and Azrin (1973), including

teaching and reinforcing adaptive behaviors, interrupting self-stimulation, and scheduling an annoying consequence to follow such. When designing a treatment based on these recommendations, planners must address themselves to two treatment concerns: providing the least restrictive (less intrusive) plan and providing treatment that is effective. (pp. 144–145)

INTERVENTION STRATEGIES FOR SSB

Research in the area of self-stimulatory behavior has important implications for your work as a classroom teacher. Some of the following interventions are effective with self-stimulatory behaviors, while others are not.

Social Reinforcement Approaches

Evidence has shown that self-stimulatory behavior does not extinguish with the withdrawal of social reinforcement (Lovaas et al., 1987; Newsom, 1974). In other words, ignoring a self-stimulating child will not affect her problem behavior. The attention of others is simply not powerful enough to compete successfully with the perceptual reinforcement the child receives from SSB. While SSB may not respond favorably to extinction, a child's other behaviors may improve with this withdrawal of social reinforcement. You do not want to eliminate this strategy for a self-injurious child.

Sensory Preferences

Children engaged in SSB appear to have strong preferences for particular sensory experiences (e.g., either auditory or visual) (Lovaas et al., 1987). This finding underscores the importance of a painstaking analysis of the student's behaviors and the circumstances that maintain them. See Hanley, Iwata, Thompson, and Lindberg (2000) for an examination of using an SSB individual's "stereotypy as reinforcement" for alternative behavior.

Reinforcing Alternative Behaviors

The DRO approach described earlier might prove helpful in teaching the child alternative behaviors, but it does not seem fruitful as an intervention to eliminate SSB. This is a bit confusing for you because you may notice that the stereotypic behaviors do lessen when the DRO is implemented. This problem arises when—as has been observed—the self-stimulatory behaviors return once the DRO is terminated (Lovaas et al., 1987).

Enriching the Environment

No matter how interesting you make your classroom, environmental manipulation alone will not reduce self-stimulatory behaviors (Favell, McGimsey, & Schell, 1982; Murphy, Carr, & Callias, 1986). However, there is evidence that self-stimulating individuals prefer objects (e.g., toys) that give them their preferred mode of perceptual feedback (Favell et al., 1982), so you might want to consider this variable as you plan your classroom activities.

Perceptual Reinforcement

As you will recall, the key to understanding SSB is to view it as a form of perceptual reinforcement to the individual. Therefore, we believe that forthcoming research will prove sensory manipulation strategies to be the most effective. Some interventions for reducing SSB require outside behavior change agents, but in many you may play a major role. (Several procedures are described in "Intervention Strategies for SIB," so we will only mention them here.)

Environmental Safety Considerations

In the discussion of SIB we mentioned safety precautions to take in the classroom, unless an individual is to be restrained (a last resort). For ethical reasons restraints usually are not recommended for SSB students. It is difficult to justify the deliberate restraint of an individual whose behavior is hurting no one. Nevertheless, students who engage in self-stimulatory behaviors may incorporate some aspect of the environment as a part of their behavioral syndrome, thus creating a safety risk. Do not permit self-stimulatory students to use sharp objects, breakable items, or damaged toys as a part of a self-stimulatory sequence, for example. Toys that are safe for normal youngsters may present a hazard for a student who will use them inappropriately.

Sensory Extinction Procedure

A development in the alteration of self-stimulatory behaviors, sensory extinction, is based on the notion that certain individuals have a strong preference for one aspect of sensory input (e.g., tactile, propriocep- tive, visual, or auditory) and engage in self-stimulatory behaviors to increase this sensory input (Aiken & Salzberg, 1984; Rincover & Devany, 1982; Rincover, Newsom, & Carr, 1979). For example, a child may spin objects for the auditory feedback (the sound of the plate spinning), may finger-flap (for the visual feed- back of watching his finger movements), or tap his fingers (for the proprioceptive stimulation).

The first step in a sensory extinction program is to determine the sensory input the student receives while engaged in the behavior. He may exhibit a be- havior that provides more than one type of sensory feedback; in that case, additional sensory analyses must be completed. One study described such an assessment procedure (Rincover, 1978):

> We observed each child throughout the day and consulted with the teachers in an attempt to identify possible sensory consequences of their self-stimulatory behavior. We found that Reggie would incessantly spin objects, particularly a plate, in a stereotyped, repetitive manner. How- ever, when he twirled the plate, he would also cock his head to the side and lean toward it, seeming to listen to the plate as it was spinning. This suggested that the auditory feedback may have been an important consequence of Reggie's self-stimulation. Robert engaged in excessive finger-flapping, in which he had one or both hands in front of his face and vigorously moved the fingers (but not the arms) back and forth. In this case, two sensory consequences were identi- fied for testing: the visual feedback from watching the finger movements, and the proprio- ceptive stimulation from the finger movement itself. Brenda's self-stimulatory behavior consist- ed of twirling objects such as a feather or string of beads in front of her eyes. For Brenda, as with Robert, both the visual and the proprioceptive components were targeted for testing.
>
> During sensory extinction sessions we at- tempted to eliminate a particular sensory conse- quence of a given self-stimulatory behavior. First, in order to eliminate the auditory feedback from Reggie's plate spinning, carpeting was installed atop the table in the classroom. The carpeting was .6 cm thick and completely covered the sur- face of the table. The surface of the carpet was hard and flat so as not to restrict the plate from spinning . . . no sound was audible from spinning the plate on the carpeted table. A second sensory extinction procedure was designed to mask the proprioceptive stimulation from finger-flapping (Robert) and object manipulation (Brenda). A small vibratory mechanism was taped to the back of each child's hand, generating a repetitive low- intensity, high-frequency pulsation. Significantly, the vibrator did not physically restrict self-stimu- latory behavior. The final sensory extinction pro- cedure involved removing the visual conse- quences for each of the three children. For this purpose a blindfold was introduced consisting of a handkerchief, once folded, snugly placed over each child's eyes and tied behind the head (pp. 302–303).

If you think an individual's self-stimulatory be- havior reflects a strong preference for one aspect of sensory feedback, talk with a behavioral consultant who is trained in this procedure. In the study just cited (Rincover, 1978), daily 20-min sessions were conducted in which the child sat in a separate room with an adult. The child's preferred self-stimulation object was placed on a table before him or her. These sessions provided the children with experiences in which the preferred sensory feedback was elimi- nated. An additional benefit in using the sensory ex- tinction procedure is that you may identify appro- priate activities involving the preferred sensory input as potential reinforcers. For example, if a stu- dent prefers auditory input, you might try music or noisemaking toys to reinforce appropriate re- sponses during teaching sessions.

Overcorrection

Overcorrection has been successful in some cases of SSB, as evidenced by a study by Luiselli (1984a), who targeted tongue thrusting and saliva rubbing (see Table 9–2). Positive practice was used, and the time period for each practice session was 30 to 40 sec. If you decide to try overcorrection, refer to Table 9–5 and remember to monitor for the possibility that other SSB may emerge. (This was not the case in the Luiselli study.)

Stimulus Variation

The purpose of stimulus variation is to increase the level of motivation and responsiveness exhibited by a student engaged in SSB. Although little research on this intervention has been conducted thus far, there is evidence to suggest that bored students may engage in SSB (Dunlap & Koegel, 1980). More recent early behavior analytic intervention for young children with autism supports these earlier findings (Maurice, Green, & Luce, 1996). Review carefully the sequence and length of activities you present to students. Try to intersperse two or three target tasks among other tasks rather than focusing on 15 min of one task followed by 15 min of another.

Response-Reinforcer Procedure

In a response-reinforcer procedure, the immediate environment is manipulated so that the student, as a result of completing a task, has immediate access to a reinforcer physically imbedded within the task. The following description of a manual task is an example of a response-reinforcer (Bittle & Hake, 1977):

> The manual task involved removing eight wing nuts that secured the transparent side of each of six boxes mounted on a wall at the child's eye level. Each box contained a small piece of bologna sausage and a cup with .25 ounces of Coke®, known reinforcers for this child. Because the child averaged eleven seconds to remove a single wing nut, approximately ninety seconds was required to open one box and about nine minutes was required to open all boxes. The child was shown how to open the boxes prior to the study. (p. 909)

Why might a response-reinforcer procedure result in rapid learning acquisition? Perhaps it is because the reinforcer becomes immediately available as soon as the student engages in the correct response (completes the task). In other words, ". . . a functional response-reinforcer relationship may serve to highlight the contingency between the reinforcer and the intended target behavior" (Williams, Koegel, & Egel, 1981, p. 59). See Thompson and Iwata (2000) for a more recent examination of direct and indirect contingencies.

Sensory Reinforcement

In contrast to the response-reinforcer intervention, a sensory reinforcement strategy provides the child with one or more sensory experiences that are deemed desirable to the child. Rincover and Newsom (1985) found that multiple sensory reinforcers were more effective than multiple edible reinforcers in increasing correct responses. When a single sensory reinforcer was compared with a single edible reinforcer, the results were about the same. The authors pointed out that "children may work longer and learn more when multiple-sensory events are used" (p. 245). Some of the sensory reinforcers they used include tickling, hand clapping, finger tapping, or drumming with sticks by the adult on a surface near the child, singing (by the adult), playing music very briefly, and caressing. To create the multiple-sensory reinforcement arrangement, the adult varied the reinforcers given for correct trials.

Automatic Reinforcement

In an **automatic reinforcement** procedure the reinforcement is produced independent of the social environment. Behaviors that are maintained by automatic reinforcement can present treatment challenges because of the difficulty in identifying, manipulating, and controlling the specific reinforcer produced by the response (Vollmer, 1994). Recent studies have focused on developing assessment procedures to facilitate the identification of the specific source of automatic reinforcement produced by behavior. Piazza et al. (1998) described the use of functional analysis and preference assessment to identify the specific source of reinforcement for automatically reinforced pica behavior. Functional analysis results indicated that pica behavior of three subjects was maintained in part by automatic reinforcement. The authors Piazza, Adelinis, Hanley, Goh, & Delia (2000) extended their investigation of comparing matched stimuli to aberrant behaviors. These aberrant behaviors consisted of dangerous climbing and jumping, saliva manipulation, and hand mouthing. Preference assessments were utilized to identify matched stimuli (items that provided the same or similar sensory consequence as the aberrant behavior) and unmatched stimuli (items that provided no actual sensory consequences). By integrating the results of the functional analysis which suggested that the behavior was maintained by automatic reinforcement and the structural observations, the authors were successfully able to develop treatment components for the aberrant behaviors of climbing, saliva play, and hand mouthing.

Differential Reinforcement of Other Behaviors

This procedure, described in an earlier section, is frequently applied to SSB as an accompaniment to behavior reduction procedures. Refer to Table 9–3 for steps in using DRO.

SUMMARY

Self-injurious and self-stimulatory behaviors are complex problems facing the teacher of students with developmental disabilities. Fortunately, new insights from research studies can provide new insights and relief to the classroom teacher seeking an end to stereotypic behavioral patterns. Consider the research-based interventions for self-injury and self-stimulation, fully respecting the complexity and intensity of some of these interventions and the assessments that must precede them. Our chapter closes with a case study about SIB.

CHAPTER 9 CASE STUDY

Behavioral and Naltrexone Treatment of Self-Injurious Behavior

Kristina Johnson, Cynthia R. Johnson, and Robert A. Sahl

The subject was a 7-year-old African-American boy with severe mental retardation and a long history of self-injurious behaviors. This was the first psychiatric hospitalization for this subject who had been diagnosed with autism at age 2. The subject's self-injurious, aggressive, and noncompliant behaviors began to worsen approximately 1 year prior to hospitalization, to the point where the subject sustained injury to his face (i.e., a large, swollen hematoma under his left eye due to repetitively striking this area

with a closed fist). The parents, most recently, had been simply holding him on their laps to prevent self-injurious behaviors. The parents reported that he had become combative when they attempted to interrupt the self-injurious behaviors. The subject had lost interest or the ability to engage in the few self-help care skills that he had mastered, including eating skills.

The subject was initially evaluated at the ages of 2 and 3. These evaluation results included observations that the subject exhibited a wide scattering of abilities, many autistic-like behaviors, and a strength in gross motor areas. Another evaluation conducted at the age of 5 years confirmed the diagnosis of autistic disorder, and noted poor progress in the subject's development over the previous year. At that time, a trial of Haldol 0.5 mg was initiated to assist in improving the subject's activity level, tantrums, and to hopefully improve his social-relatedness. Apparently this was somewhat effective, and he was followed at the medical center on a regular basis for approximately 1 year. At this point, his aggression and head-slapping began to increase and his attention span decreased. Haldol was increased 1 mg b.i.d. and this was effective for approximately another year. When the aggression and head-slapping began, Haldol was once again increased to 1.5 mg/l mg b.i.d., following another increase to 1.5 mg b.i.d. However, due to the sedating effect, it was decreased back to 1.5 mg/l mg on a b.i.d. schedule. At this point, after the discontinuation of the Haldol, Tofranil was initiated at a dosage of 25 mg hs. This medication was then increased to 50 mg hs. and again increased to 75 mg hs., but it was apparently felt to be ineffective and was discontinued. At that time, the referral to Western Psychiatric Institute and Clinic had been made, and further treatment was deferred pending an inpatient evaluation. Upon admission, consent for treatment was obtained from the parents.

During inpatient hospitalization, psychoeducational evaluation utilizing the Bayley Infant Development Scale showed an age-equivalent of 5 1/6 months, indicative of severe to profound mental retardation. On the Vineland Adaptive Behavior Scale, the subject earned a behavior composite standard score of 23, with subtest scores as follows: Communication = 24; Daily Living Skills = less than 20; and Socialization = 24. A speech and language evaluation was also completed utilizing the Receptive Expressive Emergent Language Scale (REEL). His expressive score was 3 months and his receptive score was 4 months. The patient was able to vocalize approximately 3 sounds, was unable to imitate, had object permanence for food, and overall low sensory skills.

Self-injurious behavior was defined as the forceful contact by the subject to the left side of his face, under his eye, with his fist. Ethical considerations precluded allowing unrestrained self-injurious behaviors to continue without intervention; therefore, physical and verbal interruption and redirection were implemented throughout all phases of the study. Due to the severity and frequency of the self-injurious behaviors, pediatric "no-no" arm splints were applied within 48 hours of the subject's admission to the hospital. Data were collected during structured periods by milieu-trained staff, with ongoing frequency counts of the subject's self-injurious behaviors across all settings, from wakeup to bedtime.

Procedures

Baseline

Due to the intensity and frequency of the subject's self-injurious behaviors, baseline was necessarily brief. The frequency of the subject's self-injurious behaviors and attempts to self-injury were collected across a day.

Phase I Phase I involved a behavior treatment package of systematic splint fading, a faded differential schedule, and a 15-sec hand restraint contingent on self-injury. Systematic splint fading began with the pediatric "no-no" splints being removed for 15 min twice per day, once in the morning during structured classroom time, and once in the afternoon during structured play activity. During this and all subsequent treatment phases, the subject was reinforced at the beginning of the session on a fixed interval schedule of 10 sec, with verbal praise and edible reinforcers for the absence of self-injurious behaviors. Edible reinforcement (i.e., soda, cookies, candy, chips, crackers, and pretzels) was delivered and paired with the verbal statement, "Nice hands down." When the subject had achieved 10 consecutive intervals of 10 sec with no self-injurious behaviors, the fixed interval was faded to 30 sec. After 10 consecutive intervals of 30 sec with no self-injury, the fixed interval was faded to 60 sec. This continued again for 90 sec and 120 sec. Along with the faded differential reinforcement schedule, a brief hand restraint program was implemented. Whenever the subject engaged in self-injurious behaviors when his splints were off, a brief hand restraint was implemented for 10 sec. This consisted of milieu staff citing, "No hitting," and holding the subject's hands on a flat surface without conversation for 15 sec when the behavior occurred.

Phase II During this phase, naltrexone 50 mg b.i.d. (3.8 mg/kg) was administered. The behavioral treatment package was continued as described above in Phase I.

Phase III During this phase, placebo was administered as well as a continuation of splint fading, faded differential reinforcement schedule, and the brief hand restraint. This allowed for the removal of splints due to the reduction of the self-injurious behaviors. The subject had his splints off from 9 A.M. until 11 A.M., with a constant one-to-one supervision period. At 11:30 A.M., his right splint was replaced during lunchtime, leaving his left one off so that he could eat. Both splints were replaced at the end of lunch, from 12:15 P.M. to 1:00 P.M., and then from 1:00 P.M. until 3:30 P.M. both splints were removed. From 3:30 P.M.

until bedtime both splints remained on, with the exception of being removed every hour for a total of 10 min for range of their motion exercises.

Phase IV In the final phase the naltrexone-placebo trial was discontinued, as well as the removal of splints, continuation of the brief hand restraint for 15 sec was implemented whenever the self-injurious behavior occurred, the reinforcement being changed to a variable interval schedule of every 2 to 5 min.

Follow-Up Follow-up data were recorded for 2 months after the subject's discharge to the school setting. The classroom aide collected frequency counts across each school day of self-injurious behaviors of the subjects. The contingent hand restraint for 15 sec was implemented whenever the self-injurious behavior occurred, with reinforcement being delivered every 3 to 5 min.

Results

Mean total frequencies per day of self-injury across phases were recorded. At baseline, the subject engaged in self-injurious behaviors almost continuously during the initial two observation sessions, requiring splints to be applied within 48 hours of hospitalization. During unstructured settings, mean total frequency of self-injurious behaviors during baseline assessment was 544. In Phase I, mean total frequency of self-injurious behavior was 197 (range = 1–1426). Hence a significant decrease in self-injurious behavior was observed to occur following implementation of splint fading, the brief restraint program, and a faded differential reinforcement schedule. The mean total frequency of self-injurious behavior in Phase II was 424 (range = 0–2051). In Phase III, mean total frequency was 226 (range = 0–1488). In

Phase IV, the behavioral treatment alone, mean total frequency was 34 (range = 0–377). During the last 12 days of hospitalization, the patient maintained zero rates of self-injurious behaviors across all settings. In follow-up, the subject's school personnel continued collecting total frequency counts of self-injurious behaviors on a daily basis. These data indicated that the mean total frequency for month one was 9.6, and the mean total frequency for month two was 5.1.

Discussion

The combined use of splint fading, differential reinforcement, and a brief hand restraint successfully eliminated self-injurious behaviors in one child with severe profound mental retardation and autistic disorder. These results are similar to earlier reports of success with the combined use of DRO and restraint fading in the reduction of self-injurious behaviors (Cowdery, Iwata, & Pace, 1990; Parrish, Iwata, Dorsey, Bunick, & Slifer, 1985). This was in contrast to the lack of behavioral change noted during the naltrexone trial and is consistent with other reports (Szymanski, Kedesdy, Sulkes, Culter, & Stevens-Our, 1987; Davidson, Keene, Carroll, & Rockowitz, 1983), but differed with the results supporting the efficacy of naltrexone (Barrett, Feinstein, & Hole, 1989; Campbell, Adams, Smolt, Tesch, & Curran, 1988; Herman et al., 1987).

One of the major challenges associated with the successful treatment of self-injurious behavior is to systematically program for maintenance and generalization of treatment in the home and school environment. In this study, attempts were made to promote generalization through (a) systematic fading of the use of restrictive physical restraints and simultaneous fading of reinforcement schedules to one that could be implemented in the child's natural environment, (b) intense training with the parents and school personnel in the implementation of treatment procedures prior to the subject's discharge from the hospital, and (c) follow-up phone calls to the home and school setting in order to promote continuance of treatment and provide performance-based feedback and consultation.

Throughout the subject's hospitalization, the intensive training of parents and school personnel included the education of possible motivational factors for the subject's self-injurious behavior, a use of differential reinforcement, brief hand restraint, and strategies to promote maintenance of the program in their environments. The parents, as well as the school personnel, were quite active, motivated, and involved in this subject's hospitalization, although they lived some distance away. Phone contact with parents 1 day after discharge was made, reporting that they were consistently able to implement the behavior treatment package. School personnel collected total frequency counts across a day, and at the 1- and 2-month intervals, the generalization of treatment gains substantially continued in the school environment. Along with observed decreases in the frequency of SIB, anecdotal reports from school indicated decreased irritability, and increased ability of this boy to sit in his seat for long periods of time. Significant gains in playing independently with toys for longer periods of time were also noted.

In the home environment, anecdotal reports from the subject's mother emphasized continued treatment gains at the 6-month period. Phone contact 1 year after discharge was made, with parental report that the subject's rate of SIB was minimal and the behavior treatment package that was recommended from his inpatient hospitalization was consistently being utilized. School personnel reported the subject was also doing well in their environment with minimal SIB rates. The schedule of reinforcement had been extended to every 8–10 min while the brief hand restraint was continued contingent on any SIB.

A number of limitations of this study should be noted. Optimally, reliability data should have been collected throughout all four treatment phases. In addition, as in many cases with self-injurious behavior, high variability makes any interpretation of treatment efficacy difficult. Admittedly, variations in the data collection may be accounted for by problems such as measurement error of observers. Another limi-

tation of the study consisted of the medication only being administered at one dose over a short period of time. The dose was also higher than that used in some previous investigations (Barrett et al., 1989). Hence, the dose may have not been optimal and the medication trial might have continued longer with titrating dosages of medication.

Reprinted with permission from Johnson, K., Johnson, C. R., & Sahl, R. A. (1994). Behavioral and naltrexone treatment of self-injurious behavior. *Journal of Developmental and Physical Disabilities*, 6, 2, 193–202.

DISCUSSION QUESTIONS

1. What are the major concepts of a perceptual reinforcement theory of self-stimulatory behavior? Discuss them.
2. What are the steps in conducting a functional analysis for self-injurious behavior and for self-stimulatory behavior? Describe each.
3. How would you use sensory extinction to reduce the auditory SSB of a child with developmental delays?
4. What is the importance of contingent practice and timeout in an overcorrection procedure for self-injurious behavior? Discuss it.
5. How is DRO best used for individuals with stereotypic behaviors? Will it suppress the stereotypic behaviors?
6. What criteria should you meet before trying an aversive or restrictive intervention?
7. What interventions have not proven effective in suppressing SSB? Why?
8. What seems to be the most effective reinforcer for a child who engages in SSB?

REFERENCES

Aiken, J. M., & Salzberg, C. L. (1984). The effects of a sensory extinction procedure on stereotypic sounds of two autistic children. *Journal of Autism and Developmental Disorders*, 14 (3), 291–299.

Barrett, R. P., Feinstein, C., & Hole, W. T. (1989). Effects of naloxone and naltrexone on self-injury: A double-blind, Placebo-controlled analysis. *American Journal of Mental Retardation*, 93, 644–651.

Baumeister, A. A. (1978). Origins and control of stereotyped movements. In C. E. Meyers (Ed.), *Quality of life in severely and profoundly mentally retarded people: Research foundations for improvement.* (AAMD Monograph, No. 3). Washington, DC: American Association on Mental Deficiency.

Baumeister, A. A., & Rollings, P. (1976). Self-injurious behavior. In N. R. Ellis (Ed.), *International review of research in mental retardation* (Vol. 9). New York: Academic Press.

Berkson, G., McQuiston, S., Jacobson, J. W., Eyman, R, & Borthwick, S. (1985). The relationship between age and stereotyped behaviors. *Mental Retardation*, 23, 31–33.

Bierly, C., & Billingsley, F. F. (1983). An investigation of the educative effects of overcorrection on the behavior of an autistic child. *Behavioral Disorders*, 9 (1), 11–21.

Bittle, R., & Hake, D. F. (1977). A multi-element design model for component analysis and cross-setting assessment of a treatment package. *Behavior Therapy*, 8, 906–914.

Brown, K. A., Wacker, D. P., Derby, M., Peck, S. M., Richman, D. M., Sasso, G. M., Knutson, C. L., & Harding, J. W. (2000). Evaluating the effects of functional communication training in the presence and absence of establishing operations. *Journal of Applied Behavior Analysis*, 33, (1) 53–57.

Campbell, M., Adams, P., Smolt, A., Tesch, L., & Curran, L. (1988). Naltrexone in infantile autism. *Psychopharmacology Bulletin*, 24, 35–139.

Carey, R. G., & Bucher, B. D. (1986). Positive practice overcorrection: Effects of reinforcing correct performance. *Behavior Modification*, 10 (1), 73–92.

Carr, E. G., & Durand, V. M. (1985). Reducing behavior problems through functional communication training. *Journal of Applied Behavior Analysis*, 18 (2), 111–126.

Carr, E. G., & McDowell, J. J. (1980). Social control of self-injurious behavior of organic etiology. *Behavior Therapy*, 11, 402–409.

Carr, E. G., Newsom, C. D., & Binkoff, J. A. (1976). Stimulus control of self-destructive behavior in a psychotic child. *Journal of Abnormal Child Psychology*, 4, 139–152.

Coleman, R. S., Whitman, T. L., & Johnson, M. R. (1979). Suppression of self-stimulatory behavior of a profoundly retarded boy across staff and settings: An assessment of situational generalization. *Behavior Therapy*, 10(2), 266–280.

Cook, J. W., Altman, K., Shaw, J., & Blaylock, M. (1978). Use of contingent lemon juice to eliminate public masturbation by a severely retarded boy. *Behaviour Research & Therapy*, 16(2), 131–133.

Cowdery, G. E., Iwata, B. A., & Pace, G. M. (1990). Effects and side-effects of DRO as treatment for SIB. *Journal of Applied Behavior Analysis*, 23, 497–506.

Davidson, P. W., Keene, B. M., Carroll, M., & Rockowitz, R. J. (1983). Effects of naloxone on self-injurious behavior: A case study. *Applied Research in Mental Retardation*, 4, 1–4.

DeCatanzaro, D. A., & Baldwin, G. (1978). Effective treatment of self-injurious behavior through a forced arm exercise. *American Journal of Mental Deficiency*, 82, 433–439.

Dorsey, M. F., Iwata, B. A., Ong, P., & McSween, T. E. (1980). Treatment of self-injurious behavior using a water mist: Initial response suppression and generalization. *Journal of Applied Behavior Analysis*, 13, 324–333.

Dorsey, M. F., Iwata, B. A., Reid, D. H., & Davis, P. A. (1982). Protective equipment: Continuous and contingent application in the treatment of self-injurious behavior. *Journal of Applied Behavior Analysis*, 15, 217–230.

Dunlap, G., & Koegel, R. L. (1980). Motivation of autistic children through stimulus variation. *Journal of Applied Behavior Analysis*, 13, 619–627.

Durand, V. M., & Carr, E. G. (1985). Self-injurious behavior: Motivating conditions and guidelines for treatment. *School Psychology Review*, 14 (2), 171–176.

Durand, V. M., & Crimmins, D. B. (1987). Assessment and treatment of psychotic speech in an autistic child. *Journal of Autism and Developmental Disorders*, 17 (1), 17–28.

Epstein, L. H., Doke, L. A., Sajwaj, T. E., Sorrell, S., & Rimmer, B. (1974). Generality and side effects of overcorrection. *Journal of Applied Behavior Analysis*, 6, 1–14.

Favell, J. (1982). *The treatment of self-injurious behavior.* New York: American Association for Behavior Therapy.

Favell, J. E., McGimsey, J. F., & Jones, M. L. (1978). The use of physical restraint in the treatment of self-injury and as positive reinforcement. *Journal of Applied Behavior Analysis*, 11, 225–241.

Favell, J. E., McGimsey, J. F., & Schell, R. M. (1982). Treatment of self-injury by providing alternate sensory activities. *Analysis and Intervention in Developmental Disabilities*, 2, 83–104.

Foxx, R. (1978). An overview of overcorrection. *Journal of Pediatric Psychology*, 3, 97–101.

Foxx, R. M., & Azrin, N. H. (1973). The elimination of autistic self-stimulatory behavior by overcorrection. *Journal of Applied Behavior Analysis*, 6, 1–14.

Foxx, R. M., & Bechtel, D. R. (1982). Overcorrection. In M. Hersen, R. M. Eisler, & P. M. Miller (Eds.), *Progress in behavior modification* (Vol. 13). New York: Academic Press.

Gibbs, J. W., & Luyben, P. D. (1985). Treatment of self-injurious behavior: Contingent versus noncontingent positive practice overcorrection. *Behavior Modification*, 9 (1), 3–21.

Hanley, G. P., Iwata, B. A., Thompson, R. H., & Lindberg, J. S. (2000). A component analysis of "stereotypy as reinforcement" for alternative behavior. *Journal of Applied Behavior Analysis*, 33, 285–297.

Herman, B. H., Hammock, M. K., Aither-Smith, A., Egan, J., Chatoor, I., Werner, A., & Zelnik, N. (1987). Naltrexone decreases self-injurious behavior. *Annals of Neurology*, 22, 550–552.

Irvin, D. S., Thompson, T. J., Turner, W. D., & Williams, D. E. (1998). Utilizing increased response effort to reduce chronic hand mouthing. *Journal of Applied Behavior Analysis*, 31, 375–385.

Iwata, B. A., Dorsey, M. F., Slifer, K. J., Bauman, K. E., & Richman, G. S. (1994). Toward a functional analysis of self-injury. *Journal of Applied Behavior Analysis, 27,* 197–209.

Iwata, B. A., Pace, G. M., Dorsey, M. F., Zarcone, J. R., Vollmer, T. R., Smith, R. G., Rodgers, T. A., Lerman, D. C., Shore, B. A., Mazaleski, J. L., Goh, H. L., Cowdery, G. E., Kalsher, M. J., McCosh, K. C., & Willis, K. D. (1994). The functions of self-injurious behavior: An experimental-epidemiological analysis. *Journal of Applied Behavioral Analysis, 27,* 215–240.

Jenson, W. R., Rovner, L., Cameron, S., Peterson, B. P., & Kesler, J. (1985). Reduction of self-injurious behavior in an autistic girl using a multifaceted treatment program. *Journal of Behavior Therapy and Experimental Psychiatry, 16,* 77–80.

Johnson, K., Johnson, C. R., & Sahl, R. A. (1994). Behavioral and naltrexone treatment of self-injurious behavior. *Journal of Developmental and Physical Disabilities, 6* (2), 193–202.

Keller, F. S., & Schoenfeld, W. N. (1995/1950). *Principles of Psychology.* Acton, MA: Copley Publishing Group for The B. F. Skinner Foundation.

Kennedy, C. H., & Itkonen, T. (1993). Effects of setting events on the problem behavior of students with severe disabilities. *Journal of Applied Behavior Analysis, 26* (3), 321–327.

LaGrow, S. J., & Repp, A. C. (1984). Stereotypic responding: A review of intervention research. *American Journal of Mental Deficiency, 88,* 595–609.

Lovaas, O. I., & Favell, J. E. (1987). Protection for clients undergoing aversive/restrictive interventions. *Education and Treatment of Children, 10* (4), 311–325.

Lovaas, O. I., Newsom, C., & Hickman, C. (1987). Self-stimulatory behavior and perceptual reinforcement. *Journal of Applied Behavior Analysis, 20* (1), 45–68.

Luiselli, J. K. (1984a). Therapeutic effects of brief contingent effort on severe behavior disorders in children with developmental disabilities. *Journal of Clinical Child Psychology, 13* (3), 257–262.

Luiselli, J. K. (1984b). Effects of brief overcorrection on stereotypic behavior of mentally retarded students. *Education and Treatment of Children, 7* (2), 125–138.

Luiselli, J. K. (1986). Behavior analysis of pharmacological and contingency management interventions for self-injury. *Journal of Behavior Therapy and Experimental Psychiatry, 17* (4), 275–284.

Maurice, C., Green G., & Luce, S. C. (Eds.). (1996). *Behavioral intervention for young children with autism: A manual for parents and professionals.* Austin, TX: Pro-Ed.

Michael, J. L. (1982). Distinguishing between discriminative and motivational functions of stimuli. *Journal of the Experimental Analysis of Behavior, 37,* 149–155.

Michael, J. L. (1993). Concepts and principles of behavior analysis. *Society for the Advancement of Behavior Analysis* (pp. 57–72). Michigan: Leadership Research Publication Education.

Mulick, J., Hoyt, R., Rojahn, J., & Schroeder, S. (1978). Reduction of a "nervous habit" in a profoundly retarded youth by increasing toy play: A case study. *Journal of Behavior Therapy and Experimental Psychiatry, 9,* 381–385.

Murphy, G., Carr, J., & Callias, M. (1986). Increasing simple toy play in profoundly mentally handicapped children: II. Designing special toys. *Journal of Autism and Developmental Disorders, 16,* 45–58.

Neufeld, A., & Fantuzzo, J. W. (1984). Contingent application of a protective device to treat the severe self-biting behavior of a disturbed autistic child. *Journal of Behavior Therapy and Experimental Psychiatry, 15* (1), 79–83.

Newsom, C. D. (1974). The role of sensory reinforcement in self-stimulatory behavior. Unpublished doctoral dissertation, University of California, Los Angeles.

O'Brien, F. (1981). Treating self-stimulatory behavior. In J. L. Matson & J. R. McCartney (Eds.), *Handbook of behavior modification with the mentally retarded* (1st ed., pp. 117–150). New York: Plenum.

Parrish, J. M., Iwata, B. A., Dorsey, M. F., Bunick, T. J., & Slifer, K. J. (1985). Behavior analysis, program development, and transfer of control in the treatment of self-injury. *Journal of Behavior Therapy and Experimental Psychiatry, 16,* 159–168.

Piazza, C., Adelinis, J. D., Hanley, G. P., Goh, H. L., & Delia, M. D. (2000). An evaluation of the effects of matched stimulation on behaviors maintained by automatic reinforcement. *Journal of Applied Behavior Analysis, 33,* 13–27.

Piazza, C. C., Fisher, W. W., Hanley, G. P., LeBlanc, L. A., Worsdell, A. S., Lindauer, S. E., & Keeney, K. M. (1998). Treatment of pica through multiple analyses of its reinforcing functions. *Journal of Applied Behavior Analysis, 31,* 165–189.

Repp, A. C., & Singh, N. N. (1990). *Perspectives on the use of nonaversive and aversive interventions for person with developmental disabilities.* Sycamore, IL: Sycamore Publishing Company.

Rincover, A. (1978). Sensory extinction: A procedure for eliminating self-stimulatory behavior in developmentally disabled children. *Journal of Abnormal Child Psychology, 6,* 299–310.

Rincover, A., & Devany, J. (1982). The application of sensory extinction procedures to self-injury. *Analysis and Intervention in Developmental Disabilities*, 2, 67–81.

Rincover, A., & Newsom, C. D. (1985). The relative motivational properties of sensory and edible reinforcers in teaching autistic children. *Journal of Applied Behavior Analysis*, 18 (3), 237–248.

Rincover, A., Newsom, C. D., & Carr, E. G. (1979). Using sensory extinction procedures in the treatment of compulsive-like behavior of developmentally disabled children. *Journal of Consulting and Clinical Psychology*, 47, 695–701.

Rojahn, J., McGonigle, J. J., Curcio, C., & Dixon, M. J. (1987). Suppression of pica by water mist and aromatic ammonia: A comparative analysis. *Behavior Modification*, 11, (1), 65–74.

Rolider, A., & Van Houten, R. (1985). Movement suppression time-out for undesirable behavior in psychotic and severely developmentally delayed children. *Journal of Applied Behavior Analysis*, 18 (4), 275–288.

Rolider, A., Williams, L., Cummings, A., & Van Houten, R. (1991). The use of a brief movement restriction procedure to eliminate severe inappropriate behavior. *Journal of Behavior Therapy and Experimental Psychiatry*, 22, 23–30.

Schroeder, S. R., Schroeder, C. S., Rojahn, J., & Mulick, J. A. (1981). Self-injurious behavior: An analysis of behavior management techniques. In J. L. Matson & J. R. McCartney (Eds.), *Handbook of behavior modification with the mentally retarded* (pp. 141–180). New York: Plenum.

Szymanski, L., Kedesdy, J., Sulkes, S., Culter, A., & Stevens-Our, P. (1987). Naltrexone in treatment of self-injurious behavior: A clinical study. *Research of Developmental Disorders*, 8, 179–190.

Teitelbaum, P. (1977). Levels of integration of the operant. In J. E. R. Staddon and W. K. Honig (Eds.), *Handbook of operant behavior* (pp. 7–27). Englewood Cliffs, NJ: Prentice Hall.

Thompson, R. H., & Iwata, B. A. (2000). Response acquisition under direct and indirect contingencies of reinforcement. *Journal of Applied Behavior Analysis*, 33, 1–11.

Van Houten, R. (1993). The use of wrist weights to reduce self-injury maintained by sensory reinforcement. *Journal of Applied Behavior Analysis*, 26, 197–203.

Van Houten, R., Axelrod, S., Bailey, J., Favell, J. E., Foxx, R. M., Iwata, B. A., & Lovass, O. I. (1988). The right to effective behavioral treatment. *Journal of Applied Behavior Analysis*, 21, 381–384.

Vollmer, T. R. (1994). The concept of automatic reinforcement: Implications for behavioral research in developmental disabilities. *Research in Developmental Disabilities*, 15, 187–207.

Williams, J. A., Koegel, R. L., & Egel, A. L. (1981). Response-reinforcer relationships and improved learning in autistic children. *Journal of Applied Behavior Analysis*, 14, 53–59.

PART III BEYOND THE CLASSROOM

CHAPTER 10 PSYCHIATRIC PROBLEMS

OUTLINE

OBJECTIVES

After completing this chapter, you should be able to

- Describe the steps for interviewing a student who may have an emotional problem.
- Define each of the following terms: anorexia nervosa, bulimia nervosa, suicide, depression, drug and alcohol abuse, school and other phobias, anxiety disorder.
- Identify a student who is showing signs of a psychiatric problem.
- Make an informed referral for a student showing signs of a psychiatric problem.

This chapter was written by Deborah Lange Lambert, with Kristina Johnson, Ph.D., and David E. O'Connor, M.D.

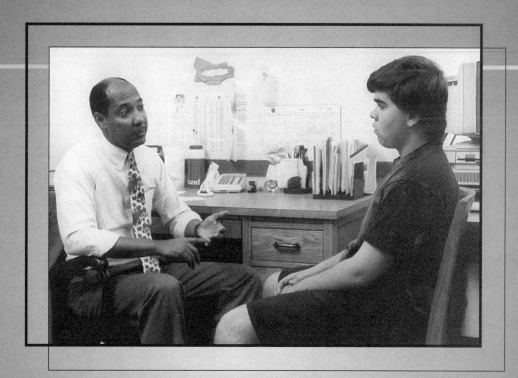

This chapter deals with psychiatric or emotional problems that require treatment outside of school. Your role is one of collaborator, usually with in-school professionals and those from a mental health agency. Although we do not cover all of the possible psychiatric problems of children and adolescents, we hope to make you aware of those you are likely to identify in school-age children. The problems covered in this chapter include depression, suicide, drug and alcohol abuse, eating disorders, anxiety disorders, and specific phobias and extreme fears.

This chapter highlights some of the signs of psychiatric problems and offers you guidelines for recognizing and referring these disorders. Classroom teachers are good observers of children's normal and abnormal behaviors (Kerr & Schaeffer, 1987; Hoier & Kerr, 1987). After all, educators are the one professional group constantly in touch with normal child and adolescent behavior. You can decipher when a student's actions fall outside these norms.

Therefore, your primary role in helping children with serious emotional or psychiatric problems is to identify and refer them for more intensive services. Moreover, you may be called on to collaborate in the student's subsequent treatment, especially if you are a special educator, school counselor, psychologist, or social worker.

RECENT TRENDS IN SCHOOL PROGRAMMING

Student Assistance

A recent addition to many schools is the Student Assistance Program (SAP). SAPs are a response to the many and varied personal problems that students bring with them to school. The motivation behind the implementation of these programs is fundamentally educational. The sheer magnitude of many students' emotional predicaments makes working to their academic potential impossible. Initially, Student Assistance programs sprang up

in response to the increasing concern of problems related to alcohol and other drug use. Now SAP is designed to identify the needs of individual students and refer them, for the *assessment* of treatment. The SAP is not meant to diagnose mental health illness or addiction but rather to refer students for possible counseling or treatment. At the heart of the SAP is the core team: a group of trained school professionals who meet daily to identify youngsters who could benefit from school support and outside help. The team identifies issues that pose a barrier to a student's learning and success. When working in a new school, ascertain whether or not a SAP or its equivalent exists.

IDENTIFYING PSYCHOLOGICAL PROBLEMS

Consider these general warning signs of a psychological problem:

1. A sudden change in behavior or mood
2. A prolonged sad, unhappy mood
3. Fatigue and lethargy, or excessive energy and euphoria
4. A disinterest in activities that once were enjoyable
5. A change in sleep (being sleepier or having difficulty sleeping)
6. A change in appetite or a remarkable weight loss
7. Making statements about hurting oneself
8. A sense of worthlessness or hopelessness
9. A decline in grades

We review these signs in our discussion of specific disorders, but first we offer some assessment strategies.

Interview Strategy

Before a student is interviewed, the SAP can gather information. A two part behavioral checklist can be sent to each teacher with a list of questions pertaining to the student's academics, behavior, and attitude. The SAP can also review the student's current grades, transcript, attendance, and discipline record. Then, if you interview a student who says that everything is going great, you have data to support or challenge the information being offered during the interview.

Interviewing is a good way to learn about a student's psychological problems. Have a conversation with the student. See the student privately and allow enough time (no less than 30 min). Let the student know that you are concerned and want to help.

1. If the student hesitates, gently offer an example of the worrisome behavior.
- "You seemed to have lost your interest in the track meet."
- "I've noticed that you seem more excited than usual. . . ."
- "You look as if you have dropped a lot of weight recently."
- "I notice you've been sleepy a lot lately."
2. Resist the urge to explain the symptom and/or offer advice. Refrain from comments like
- "I guess your track team is not doing as well this year. No wonder you're less interested."
- "Maybe you should eat more."
- "Kids sometimes sleep too much when they're bored. Maybe you need to. . . ."
After all, you may guess incorrectly and throw the conversation off track.
3. Be a good listener so the student feels comfortable talking. Pay attention to how much you are actually listening versus counseling.
4. Do not badger! Here are some ways we badger:
- "I took time to talk with you, and this is all you have to say?"
- "Why don't you face facts; something is wrong with you!"

- "If you don't want help now, then don't come to me later."
- "Stop making excuses, and get your work done."
5. If the student does not want to talk, try another option.
- "Maybe this isn't a good time. We could meet after school."
- "I know you and Dr. Robb are rather close. Do you feel you might want to talk with him? I could check to see when he is available."
- "If you ever want to talk, just let me know."
- "Sometimes students are more comfortable expressing their problems in writing. Would that make things any easier for you?"
6. Be patient! Students with problems are not always articulate. It may take a little while for them to explain how they feel. Do not interrupt. Show the student that you are interested by looking at him and nodding your head.
7. Avoid judgments. This is no time to evaluate the student's perceptions.
- "Well, that is nothing to worry about."
- "How did you ever get into such a mess anyway?"
- "I hope you've learned your lesson."
8. Name some action that you can take with the student. If you cannot immediately think of a plan, at least show your acceptance and willingness to help.
- "I am not sure how to tackle this problem, but we can think it through."
- "Gee, this is a real problem. Let me give this some thought. We'll talk Wednesday, okay?"
- "Now I see. How about if I share some of this with the counselor? I think she could help."
- "I'd like to help you through this. How would you like to proceed?"
9. Close the conversation with reassurance (even if you cannot genuinely show acceptance of the student's views). Some students need information to help them view their situations more hopefully. If this is the case, offer it.

- "I see why you were so worried about the quiz. You did not realize that everyone did poorly. I have decided to adjust everyone's grades."
- "Suspension is serious, but no, it does not mean you fail the course."
- "I know the seniors said they could vote you off the team, but that decision is made only by the coach."

10. Follow-up on your commitment. Even if you have promised only to talk again, be sure you do. If you offered specific help, get it quickly.
11. Know how to help. Your work obligates you to know child and adolescent referral procedures, to understand the mental health services in your community, to know warning signs, and so forth.
12. Know how to handle confidentiality. Do not promise total confidentiality to a student; you may not be able to keep your word. Do not promise confidentiality, for example, in the case of suicidal or homicidal threats.

For very young children, you will need to interview the parents. Your school social worker or guidance counselor can assist you, or you can informally ask questions based on your concerns. One helpful strategy is to share your concerns with the parent and ask if the same or other problems have been apparent at home. Sometimes this approach cues the parents to recall events that may not have seemed problematic to them at the time. Remember, follow the same guidelines in talking with a parent that you follow in talking with a student. Do not badger, explain the symptom, or pass judgment! Instead, listen with empathy. You will be in a better position to effect positive change if you focus on building a partnership with a parent without passing judgment.

Teacher Interview for Psychiatric Symptoms

One instrument for identifying psychiatric problems in children is the Teacher Interview for Psychiatric Symptoms (TIPS) developed by Kerr and Schaeffer (1987). Figure 10–1 displays some questions from this interview, designed for counselors to ask teachers about worrisome students. The interview lasts approximately 45 min and can be conducted by telephone. Before using this or any mental health assessment, or instrument, check the regulations for your state and secure any needed consents (students and parent/guardian).

Teacher's Report Form of the Child Behavior Checklist

Developed by Achenbach and Edelbrock (1979), this checklist is commonly used around the world to screen children for psychiatric problems. The teacher completes the checklist in about 30 min, rating each problem statement as not true, somewhat or sometimes true, or very true or often true for the target student within the past two months. Here are some sample items:

- Clings to adults or too dependent
- Is not liked by other pupils
- Gets hurt a lot, accident-prone
- Feels or complains that no one loves him/her
- Is unhappy, sad, or depressed
- Is afraid of making mistakes
- Worries

Frequently schools have their own assessment tools that require a minimal amount of time to complete while providing meaningful information. Figure 10–2 displays a student assistance form that goes to the student's teachers, administrator, counselor, and school nurse. Comparing a summary of this data to a student's perception of his performance can provide additional insight. With older students it is especially important to access the guidance counselor's transcript, where you can observe trends in grades, attendance, and tardiness. If you have referred students to a mental health clinic, you probably have completed one of these instruments.

The TIPS and the Child Behavior Checklist are only two of many available psychiatric screening instruments. Refer to Chapter 1 for a screening procedure (Walker, Severson, Haring, & Williams, 1986) for problem behaviors.

1. One of the feelings I'd like to know about is sadness. (This item refers to a mood of depression, sadness, "feeling bad.") Has (student's name) been feeling sad, unhappy, or miserable in school?
2. Does (student's name) appear to worry about things? Do you know of any current stressors that the student may be experiencing (at home or at school) that may be the reason for his or her worrying (e.g., parental divorce, boy/girlfriend problems, pending disciplinary action)?
3. Do you have a sense that (student's name) feels hopeless or pessimistic? Does she or he ever indicate that she or he has things to look forward to (e.g., movies, outings with family, basketball games, weekends)?
4. Does (student's name) have several friends with whom she or he plays or associates? If *no*, ask, does the student have a special friend with whom she or he plays or associates? When was the last time you noticed this student with a friend(s)?
5. When students are upset, sad, or angry, sometimes they think about hurting or killing themselves. Has (student's name) ever made a statement about wanting to hurt or kill herself or himself? Has she or he ever made a statement about not wanting to live?

FIGURE 10–1   Excerpts from the Teacher Interview for Psychiatric Symptoms.

Direct Observations

For some psychiatric problems, you will be able to use a direct observation approach—or at least rely on your informal observations and impressions of a student.

DEPRESSION

Childhood depression is extremely difficult to diagnose, but it may be a warning of a serious psychiatric disorder. The diagnosis of depression begins with the criteria listed in the **Diagnostic and Statistical Manual of Mental Disorders** (DSM-IV), published by the American Psychiatric Association.

Depression in children and adolescents is marked by these warning signs: sadness (sometimes called dysphoria), low self-esteem, irritability, changes in appetite or sleep, impaired concentration, anhedonia (loss of pleasure in activities the child previously enjoyed), somatic complaints, and antisocial behaviors. If you observe any of the warning signs for two weeks or more, you should be concerned about the possibility of depression (American Psychiatric Association, 1994; Shaffer, 1985).

Consider this excerpt from a 7-year-old boy's hospital file:

Eli returned to school after the death of his grandparents. His mother complained that in addition to becoming more withdrawn, he had been engaging in self-destructive and aggressive behavior. He had been running in front of automobiles and jumping down long flights of stairs in their apartment building. He had been increasingly aggressive toward his mother to the point that she had become quite fearful of him. She noted that for no reason he would come up to her and slap her. He would often call her a pig or a liar and have frequent tantrums. Other times, he would ignore his mother and refuse to eat.

Eli's affect is depressed, and he has admitted to feeling sad. He spent his entire physical examination and first two therapy sessions sitting in a constricted manner, sobbing throughout. Eli related that sometimes in the (psychiatric) hospital he wakes up crying because he misses his mom so much (Mendelsohn, personal communication, 1981).

Eli's agitated depression—temper tantrums and acting-out behavior—rarely leads a lay person to think of depression. He may have a bipolar disorder. According to Dr. Robert DeLong (1990), a

Teacher _____ Subject _____ Period _____

Student _____ Grade _____ Date _____

Check appropriate responses

A. Academic Performance

_____ Present grade (this nine weeks)

_____ Declining grades, declining achievement

_____ Course grade to date

_____ Decrease in class participation

_____ Failure to complete assignments

_____ Disinterest in academic performance

_____ Short attention span, easily distracted

_____ Poor short-term memory (i.e., can't remember from one day to the next)

Specific Comments

_____

_____

_____

_____

B. School Attendance

_____ Absenteeism (total absences)

_____ Number of absences in the last month

_____ Tardiness (please list dates)

_____ Absent from school; present at work

_____ Skipping class

_____ Frequent schedule changes

_____ Frequent visits to health office

_____ Frequent visits to counselor's office

Specific Comments

_____

_____

_____

_____

C. Extracurricular Activities

(Specify activity: _____)

_____ Attendance

_____ Withdrawal

_____ Performance level

Specific Comments

_____

_____

_____

_____

D. Physical Symptoms

_____ Weight loss

_____ Reported insomnia

_____ Paleness, tiredness

_____ Alcohol or marijuana smell*

_____ Frequent complaints of nausea*

_____ Glassy, bloodshot eyes*

_____ Slurred speech*

_____ Inability to concentrate*

_____ Deteriorating personal appearance*

_____ Sleeping in class

_____ Physical injuries, bruises, cuts*

Specific Comments

_____

_____

_____

_____

E. Illicit Activities*

_____ Possesses drug paraphernalia (roach clips, etc.)

_____ Carries a weapon

Specific Comments

_____

_____

_____

_____

F. Disruptive Behavior*

_____ Defiance of rules

_____ Alcohol- and/or drug-related clothing or jewelry

_____ Irresponsibility, blaming, denying

_____ Fighting

_____ Cheating

_____ Sudden outbursts of anger; verbal abuse to others

_____ Obscene language gestures

_____ Attention-getting behavior

_____ Extreme negativism

_____ Hyperactivity, nervousness

*****Please provide comments when checking these behaviors.**

FIGURE 10–2 Behavior Assessment Form.

Specific Comments

_____

_____

_____

_____

G. Atypical Behavior*
_____ Model child, perfectionist
_____ Free talk about alcohol and other drug use
_____ Avoidance of contact with others
_____ Change in friends
_____ Erratic behavior/mood changes as viewed on day-to-day basis
_____ Abnormal interest in food/dieting
_____ Sudden popularity
_____ Constant adult contact
_____ Older or significantly younger social group
_____ Obsessive/compulsive behavior
_____ Extremely disoriented
_____ Unrealistic goals
_____ Inappropriate responses
_____ Depression
_____ Seeking adult advice without a specific problem
_____ Defensive attitude
_____ Social withdrawal, difficulty in relating to others

_____ Change in dress

Specific Comments

_____

_____

_____

_____

H. Home Problems*
_____ Family
_____ Runaway
_____ Job

Specific Comments

_____

_____

_____

_____

Additional Comments

_____

_____

_____

_____

_____

_____

_____

_____

_____

_____

FIGURE 10–2   Behavior Assessment Form—*Continued.*

renowned authority, the most prominent feature of a childhood bipolar illness is that emotions are extremely intense, especially irritability, anger, and rage. Fortunately, many of these children can be treated successfully with medication.

While childhood and adolescent depression has become an accepted clinical entity, one still finds professionals and others who argue its existence. Depression can be mistaken for other illnesses. When you learn about a child's lethargy, you often assume the child is merely bored in school or you look for medical reasons. You can overlook depression because some of the symptoms are considered "normal." For example, a parent may overlook his child's periodic school re-

fusal or poor grades and chalk it up to a "bad phase." Generally, parents have extreme difficulty identifying a mood disorder such as depression. There continues to be a stigma associated with psychiatric illnesses. Hopefully, once medical reasons are ruled out, psychiatric possibilities are considered.

Age plays an important role in identifying childhood depression. As children get older, their chances of becoming depressed increases. Besides looking at characteristics that mark adult depression such as fatigue, suicidal ideation, and low self-esteem, you also need to look at failure to thrive, temper tantrums, school avoidance, withdrawal, daydreaming, and irritability. With younger students, you see less of the guilt, hopelessness, and despair that may accompany depression in adults. Appreciate the fact that depressive symptoms change with a child's developmental level.

How does a depressed student appear at school? What should you look for? Here are some examples of teacher-reported behaviors from a study by Kerr and Schaeffer (1987):

1. Dejected/Dysphoric Mood
"Susan has been very depressed since she learned that her mother has cancer. She cries often and has difficulty completing schoolwork."
"Bill has stated repeatedly that he is never happy but does not give a reason for his unhappiness. He lays his head down in class and does not complete his work."

2. Irritability/Temper
"Cindy's defiant and irritable moods have become more severe as the year has progressed. She becomes angry at her classmates over the littlest thing. Although she does not harm other students, her behavior has warranted her removal from the classroom. This disciplinary action usually provokes more anger; she frequently slams her books down on a desk."
"Michelle is easily irritated by many things and displays her temper by slamming a locker door or throwing books down on her desk."

3. Low Self-Esteem
"After receiving a compliment about her appearance, Mary responded, 'I am not pretty at all.' She does not express pride in her academic accomplishments. Mary sees herself as unimportant and not worthy of attention."

4. Hopelessness
"During a discussion of future plans, Ellen said, 'What is the future? Who knows if we have one?' She frequently comments, 'What does it matter?' or 'What's the use?'"

5. Anhedonia
"Mark no longer seems to be interested in his favorite activities. He used to enjoy listening to music and being on the swim team but now avoids participating in those activities."

Schools are taking an active stand in identifying depression in youth. Depression in kids is not a passing phase; the average episode lasts 7 months. Compare that to a student's calendar year of 9 months. According to Maria Kovacs (1985), a chief researcher in this field, when childhood depression is not identified and treated early, the prognosis for recovery is less promising. Likewise, there is a high rate of recidivism among children with episodes of major depression. When mood disorders go untreated, they get worse. Depression interferes with everything in and out of school.

Because mood disorders affect intellectual functioning, depressed students often perform below their cognitive abilities. With depression, concentration is difficult and student motivation suffers. One may see a "Swiss cheese" learning pattern. Doing poorly scholastically can affect one's self-esteem dramatically. Parents often have a difficult time identifying depression in their child. More often, a school person notices academic or social problems that differ from the norm and makes a referral. When depression is treated, academic improvement occurs and self-esteem increases.

Another negative side effect of depression involves peer relations. Children and adolescents who are depressed tend to have fewer friends. Joaquim Puig-Antich (Puig-Antich et al., 1985), the first psychiatric researcher to devote his career to childhood depression, remarked that while all psychiatric disorders affect children's social relationships, depression is by far the most impairing. Depression is damaging to school performance, friendships, and family relations. Even with therapy, social relationships do not improve as quickly as school performance. Typically treatment consists of therapy accompanied by medication.

Let us turn our attention from major depression to dysthymic depression. **Dysthymia** is a classification of depression. Dysthymia generally lasts an average of 1 year in children and may be accompanied by other psychiatric conditions. According to Dr. Kovacs (1985), dysthymia in children is "the most chronic and the most complicated" type of depression to diagnose and treat (p. 389). Symptoms are not always severe enough to warrant medical or psychiatric attention, so youth suffer in silence while adapting to their chronic pain. While the symptoms of a dysthymic disorder are less severe than with those of major depression, they are longer lasting. If you suspect a student suffers from dysthymia, identify the behaviors and seek outside help.

SUICIDE

The incidence of suicide attempts reaches a peak during the midadolescent years; suicide completion, which increases steadily through the teens, is the third leading cause of death at that age (Centers for Disease Control [CDC], 1999). From 1980 to 1997, the rate of suicide among young persons aged 15–19 years increased by 11% and among persons aged 10–14 years by 109% (CDC, 1997). In 1996, 4,656 young people between the ages of 10 and 24 committed suicide (CDC, 1997). Among persons aged 15–19 years, firearm-related suicides accounted for 62% of the increase in the overall rate of suicide from 1980 to 1997 (CDC, 1997). As you can see from these statistics, suicide is a problem you must be prepared to deal with if you work with adolescents.

What are the risk factors for suicide? A previous suicide attempt is a serious risk factor (Brent, 1997), as is threatening to take one's life. Seek professional help immediately for any student who talks about suicide or makes an attempt, regardless of how "serious" you think the student is. Drug and alcohol abuse are often implicated in a suicide (Brent, Perper, & Allman, 1987). Under their influence, a vulnerable student may engage in risk-taking behaviors that she would otherwise avoid; these risks can include the fatal use of firearms (Brent et al., 1987; Brent, 1997). Access to firearms greatly increases the likelihood of suicide in adolescents who are already vulnerable (Lester & Murrell, 1982). Exposure to a suicide or suicide attempt is another risk factor,

sometimes referred to as contagion (Davidson & Gould, 1986). This contagion effect has prompted schools to adopt carefully planned postvention efforts when a suicide takes place among the student body. **Postvention** (as compared to prevention) refers to a set of actions that we take to prevent contagion after a suicide. Your school may have a postvention policy designed to lessen the risk of cluster suicides. Family variables in suicide include family conflict and a history of family psychiatric problems (including alcoholism). Indeed, a high percentage of suicide completers themselves had psychiatric problems, usually depression.

This finding underscores the importance of your early recognition of the signs of depression. First, increase your understanding of each risk factor. Try to learn about the families of your students. Second, know how to use your community mental health resources and drug rehabilitation agencies. Remember the warning signs for suicide:

- Hopelessness
- Chemical abuse
- Changes in eating or sleeping
- Isolation from friends and family
- A drop in academic achievement
- Giving away valued possessions
- Talking or writing about suicide or not wanting to live
- A recent loss, such as divorce or death in the family, or a close friend moving away

Reinforce the teenager's support network—family members, friends, and adults whom the student views as supportive. "Help in strengthening the [individual's] support system will be beneficial, as it is with all other psychiatric problems: with suicidal [individuals] it may be lifesaving" (Strayhorn, 1982, p. 480).

Following are specific steps to take with a teenager who discusses or threatens suicide:

1. Listen!
2. Help the student reach a mental health service, even if you must accompany the student there.

3. Contact the student's family.
4. Do not leave the student alone.
5. Do not underestimate the student's situation or expressed intent to end her life or hurt herself.

DRUG AND ALCOHOL ABUSE

Educators and parents consistently identify drug use as a paramount problem confronting our schools. When 13- to 18-year-olds were asked to name the biggest problem facing them today, drug use was number one on their list. Educators and parents do not always agree on how schools should go about educating our students about alcohol and drugs, but both groups agree that open discussion in the classroom and at home is needed. Recognizing this widespread problem, most school districts have undertaken in-service training on drug and alcohol abuse prevention for their faculty and staff. School and community task forces have also joined hands to assess what works and what does not. Following are some important aspects of identifying and referring students at risk for drug and alcohol abuse. We begin with a review of the behaviors you might see in students who are engaged in substance abuse.

ALCOHOL AND OTHER DEPRESSANTS.
Remove from the class any student who is intoxicated or in any identifiable stage of withdrawal. Do not confront the student with an accusation of drug use in front of peers. This may lead to opposition, resistance, or combativeness. When the student has been removed from the class, explain why and ask if you can be of help. School authorities and parents should be notified (and medical agencies if intoxication or withdrawal is severe). Refer the student to a counseling or rehabilitation program as soon as possible.

MARIJUANA.
It is the responsibility of frontline school personnel to provide adequate supervision to prevent marijuana use during school hours. Teachers, counselors, school

psychologists—all of the individuals who have regular direct personal contact with the student—share this responsibility.

The most effective means of prevention of marijuana-related problems is the creation of a system of peer control based on educating students and families, the ability to convey an attitude of openness to communicate about drug and personal problems, and the appropriate structure in planning daily activities. It is important to demonstrate to the young person that you are concerned with his academic and social success and are not trying to control him unreasonably or remove his freedom in any other way. Pay attention to your students who are extremely interested in obtaining specific information about marijuana and other drugs. Information presented in textbooks or by the media may be inconsistent, fueling student debate and justification of usage. Also, students may seek knowledge to provide them with a means to "get high." In a nonjudgmental way, ask students about their curiosity.

To identify an acute marijuana episode, closely observe student behavior. A sudden uncharacteristic change in appearance, academic performance, or social functioning may be indicative. Apathy, drowsiness, and taking on drug culture mannerisms also alert you that marijuana use is being initiated or has become a significant problem.

STIMULANTS.
Intense agitation, unreasonable suspiciousness, and bizarre behavior may be indicators of stimulant use. Hostility and aggression may result. Extreme talkativeness and flushed skin that are uncharacteristic of a student may also indicate stimulant use. Avoid physical confrontation if possible.

HALLUCINOGENS AND INHALANTS.
These chemicals usually severely disorganize behaviors so that medical or law enforcement intervention is necessary.

NARCOTICS.
Overt intoxication or narcotic withdrawal can be identified through close observation. Drowsiness and slurred speech may appear to be simple fatigue, except that the

person cannot become fully alert when confronted and his pupils are constricted. Aggressiveness is unlikely to be a reaction of an individual under the influence of narcotics; however, agitation and impulsiveness are likely to accompany narcotic withdrawal. Significant withdrawal episodes require proper medical management. Do not rule out such intervention.

Do not attempt a power struggle with a student who appears to be under the influence of a drug. Certain drugs elicit combative behavior that can often be avoided if you do not respond impulsively to a physical threat.

Do not hesitate to seek emergency medical treatment for a student who appears to be experiencing a physical or emotional crisis. Sources of emergency care services, such as poison control, crisis intervention, and the police department, are often listed in the human services section of the telephone directory.

The classroom is not a place in which to attempt treatment of drug abuse. Prevention and identification are important activities for educators. It is appropriate to make individual referrals to proper agencies once drug use has been established, especially if it is the basis for disruptive behavior or poor academic performance. Table 10–1 summarizes the major drugs of abuse and their effects.

EATING DISORDERS

Professionals who work with adolescents need to know of the three major **eating disorders: anorexia nervosa, bulimia nervosa,** and **eating disorder, not otherwise specified**. With any eating disorder there is preoccupation with weight, size, and body image. Generally feelings of guilt and shame are associated with the behavior. The following vignette describes a teenager with anorexia nervosa:

Katherine states that in February she went on a diet. At that time she was 127 pounds and 5 feet 8 inches tall. She decided to cut down because she felt she didn't look good at that weight. She was surprised that she had so much willpower, and she was able to get down to 100 pounds. Katherine reports that around April her mother became uncomfortable with her dieting. By the end of April, her mother was really getting angry about her diet. She said that she exercised about half an hour each night and she would not eat sweets. She found herself being too occupied with counting calories. Katherine does not currently see herself as being too thin, so she does have a distorted body image. Katherine has always felt herself to be different from the other kids. She has always been tall and was especially bothered by this in the seventh and eighth grades. When she was in ninth grade, her periods began. Her mother told her about periods and talked to her about sex. She also viewed some informational movies at school. Katherine was somewhat uncomfortable talking about this area. She reports that her periods stopped several months ago. Katherine reports a change in her personality since going on the diet. Before February she would become depressed only if her mother yelled at her, and her mother often became angry and upset. Now she becomes depressed over nothing, or so she feels, and just wants to be by herself, but she does no excessive crying. She does not feel that her current problems have had any effects on her friendships, though she has only one close friend, Natalie.

The *Diagnostic and Statistical Manual of Mental Disorders* (DSM-IV) (American Psychiatric Association 1994) defines the criteria for Anorexia Nervosa to include the following:

A. Refusal to maintain body weight at or above a minimally normal weight for age and height (e.g., weight loss leading to maintenance of body weight less than 85% of that expected; or failure to make expected weight gain during period of growth, leading to body weight less than 85% of that expected).

B. Intense fear of gaining weight or becoming fat, even though underweight.

C. Disturbance in the way in which one's body weight or shape is experienced, undue

TABLE 10–1   Common Drugs Abused by Youth

Tobacco: Nicotine, a stimulant, is the main ingredient in tobacco; it is more addictive than alcohol or marijuana. All tobacco products, even smokeless chewing tobacco and snuff, are addictive. Students are smoking in record numbers. Seventy percent of cigarette smokers who begin as teenagers will continue to smoke for forty years. Provocative advertisements appeal to young people and can influence their decision to start smoking.

Alcohol: Alcohol remains the number one drug of choice of teenagers. Teens receive very mixed messages about alcohol that creates a false sense of safety for some. The alcohol industry is targeting children and youth with media blitzes using talking frogs, party animals, and horses kicking footballs during major sporting events, and this recreational drug is filtering down to younger children. Newer products such as wine coolers and pre-mixed drinks make alcohol more palatable to the inexperienced user. The dangers of alcohol include dependency, automobile accidents involving people driving while under the influence, depression, accidental death, and suicide.

Marijuana: Marijuana is the first illicit drug that children and teens use. A generation ago, it was viewed as a "harmless" weed. With improved cultivation techniques, the most active chemical, delta-9-tetrahydrocannabinol (THC), has increased significantly. It would have taken twenty-five joints in the 1970s to equal the strength of one joint today. Hashish, a purified resin from the marijuana plant, has an even higher concentration of THC. Physical symptoms of users include reddening of the eyes, increased heart rate, relaxation, and increase in appetite. Dangers include loss of motivation, feelings of indifference, and developmental latency. Marijuana can be laced with PCP, cocaine, arsenic, or other chemicals.

Cocaine: Cocaine is a powerful central nervous system stimulant readily available to teenagers. The drug can be smoked or used intravenously. An added risk cocaine presents is its unpredictability in the effect on the user. Crack, which is smoked, is a less expensive, easy to procure, but more powerful form of the drug. The dangers of these drugs include dependency, weight loss, inability to concentrate, paranoia, cardiac arrest, and suicide.

LSD: Lysergic acid diethylamide (LSD), a popular hallucinogen, is practically considered a mainstream drug because of the high rates of experimentation. Typically, the drug is sold on small squares of paper saturated with the liquid. LSD is easy to hide and easy to use, while difficult to detect. The dangers related to its use include bizarre behavior, distorted thoughts, hallucinations, paranoia, "bad trips," feelings of invincibility, and dependency.

Inhalants: Inhalant abuse is the deliberate misuse of chemicals to attain an intoxicated state, or "high"; it is becoming popular with young children. The "high" associated with certain chemicals, coupled with the lack of awareness of their harmful effects, is dangerous. Inhalants include a broad array of cheap and easily obtainable household products including aerosols, glue, paint thinner, gasoline, and nitrites (poppers). Problems may include irritability, headaches, drowsiness, confusion, memory loss, and unconsciousness. Using inhalants, even once, can be fatal.

Over-the-Counter/Look-Alike Substances: These druglike substances are sold as diet aids, asthma/breathing medication, or "energy" supplements. Trade names include Minithins, Megatrim, Buzz, TurboTabs, and Heads Up. Each product stimulates the central nervous system. Dangers include overstimulation of the heart, stroke, mood swings, insomnia, dizziness, loss of appetite, and irritability.

Designer Drugs: There has been an upsurge in designer drugs, which can be produced in illegal labs. Typically, these drugs offer euphoric effects. Methamphetamine, known as crack, ice, or poor man's coke, is half the price of cocaine and easy to manufacture. Ecstasy or MDMA is a combination of a stimulant and a hallucinogen. The "party pill," or the Moroccan Quaalude, is especially popular in the West. These street drugs are a special threat to our society. Users cannot be certain about what they are popping, snorting, or smoking. Because these chemical compounds are so varied, hospitals and treatment centers have difficulty detecting their presence with today's standard screening measures.

Other Drugs: Phencyclidine (PCP) or angel dust, mushrooms, anelobolic steroids, and heroin are dangerous. Anelobolic steroids are synthetic derivatives of testosterone that students use to enhance their physical performance in sports. Problems related to their use include aggressiveness, "roid rages," acne, high blood pressure, and damage to most body organs. Do not minimize the effects of these drugs.

influence of body weight or shape on self-evaluation, or denial of the seriousness of the current low body weight.

D. In postmenarcheal females, amenorreha, (i.e., the absence of at least three consecutive menstrual cycles) (p. 251).

Bulimia nervosa, which often follows anorexia nervosa, is evidenced by these criteria from the *Diagnostic and Statistical Manual of Mental Disorders* (DSM-IV) (American Psychiatric Association, 1994):

A. Recurrent episodes of binge eating. An episode of binge eating is characterized by both of the following:
(1) Eating, in a discrete period of time (e.g., within any 2-hour period), an amount of food that is definitely larger than most people would eat during a similar period of time and under similar circumstances.
(2) A sense of lack of control over eating during the episode (e.g., a feeling that one cannot stop eating or control what or how much one is eating).

B. Recurrent inappropriate compensatory behavior in order to prevent weight gain, such as self-induced vomiting, misuse of laxatives, diuretics, enemas, or other medications; fasting; or excessive exercise.

C. The binge eating and inappropriate compensatory behaviors both occur, on average, at least twice a week for 3 months.

D. Self-evaluation is unduly influenced by body shape and weight.

E. The disturbance does not occur exclusively during an episode of Anorexia Nervosa (p. 252).

Erin recalls her painful journey with bulimia:

Back in the seventies no one was talking about bulimia. In high school I was 5 feet 2 inches and weighed 96 lbs. As a teen I received a lot of positive attention because of my petite size. I attended a private all-girls school where eating was a popular social activity. I quickly learned how much I enjoyed binging. Soon my weight escalated, and one night after devouring 15 hot fudge sundaes I laid on the bathroom floor retching in pain. For relief, I made myself throw up. I discovered something magical. I could overindulge with my friends and then go off by myself to purge and prevent the weight gain.

Unfortunately I was not always able to purge after binging. For the next years I tried every crazy diet and my weight fluctuated between 94 and 130 lbs. One week I gained 17 lbs. after eating nothing but junk food—hot buttered donuts with bacon, chocolate milk, Oreos®, ice cream, Vanilla Wafers® with icing, and more. Little did I know that this activity would become chronic and progressive. Besides my weight fluctuating, my moods were all over the board. While I viewed myself as basically a happy person, I knew something was seriously wrong. This vicious preoccupation with food ended up dominating my life for the next 22 years until I sought help after feeling depressed, suicidal, and "out of control."

The Eating Disorder, Not Otherwise Specified category is for disorders of eating that do not meet the criteria for any specific eating disorder (American Psychiatric Association, 1994). Examples include:

1. For females, all of the criteria for anorexia nervosa are met except that the individual has regular menses.
2. All of the criteria for anorexia nervosa are met except for current weight loss; the individual's current weight is in the normal range.
3. All of the criteria for bulimia nervosa are met except that the binge eating and inappropriate compensatory mechanisms occur at a frequency of less than twice a week or for a duration of less than 3 months.
4. The regular use of inappropriate compensatory behavior by an individual of normal body weight after eating small amounts of food (e.g., self-induced vomiting after eating the consumption of two cookies).

5. Repeatedly chewing and spitting out, but not swallowing, large amounts of food.
6. Binge eating disorder: recurrent episodes of binge eating in the absence of the regular use of inappropriate compensatory behaviors characteristic of bulimia nervosa (p. 253).

The following vignette describes an adolescent's problems with binge eating and alcohol abuse.

A 16-year-old found solace in comfort food (i.e., foods high in fat and sugar) and alcohol. He has clear memories of reaching for Coca Cola®, cookies, and his honey bear as a small child. As a teen he began to self-medicate with junk food and alcohol. Both of his parents were obese. When he was 10, he knew he was fat, but he did not want to diet even though the school nurse made the recommendation.

As an adolescent he recalls the euphoria he felt after drinking his first beer. He described the calmness as a feeling reminiscent of the feeling he had after binging on high-calorie food. He loved numbing himself and then drifting off to sleep.

At school, things seemed normal enough. He tried eating like everybody else but had trouble resisting pizza and cheeseburgers. Everyday he arrived home to an empty house. After walking through the door he went straight to the refrigerator and then to the pantry. He rarely brought his bookbag inside because he was too tired to bother. He began with milk and cereal and then moved on to cookies, cake, ice cream, leftovers, or anything available. Three hours later he would have a large meal with his family.

On Thursday and Friday his ritual changed as his parents worked later and there was no family dinner. On those nights he went to his parents' liquor cabinet and had a few drinks, climbed upstairs to his bedroom, and passed out. As the amounts of food and alcohol increased, his social life decreased. He began isolating himself from his friends. He felt more relaxed with food and alcohol than with people, even his friends. Once a counselor suggested he might be depressed. He did not understand what that meant. He did not care about much and wished people would leave him alone. He was not ready for help.

As Russell (1985) stated, "The very nature of the illness [is] that the [individual] tries to avoid measures that are aimed at reducing a gain in weight" (p. 632). Therefore, you will probably not succeed by encouraging or admonishing the student to eat better. Rather, your role is to inform parents and mental health professionals of your concerns. Above all, do not ignore the problem; the mortality rate for eating disorders can be as high as 10% (American Psychiatric Association, 1994). Oftentimes students who are compulsive overeaters are seen by the school nurse. Generally the nurse will work with the family and the students. She will attempt to involve outside agencies who treat this disorder as an illness rather than as a lack of willpower.

ANXIETY DISORDERS

There are several types of anxiety disorders that children and adolescents may experience: separation anxiety disorder, generalized anxiety disorder, social anxiety disorder, obsessive compulsive disorder, and post traumatic stress disorder (American Psychiatric Association, 1994). The primary feature of **separation anxiety disorder** is developmentally inappropriate anxiety sufficient to cause the child or adolescent to experience distress or impairment when faced with separation from home or major attachment figures in their lives (American Psychiatric Association, 1994). Children and adolescents with anxiety disorders may refuse to go to school because of difficulty making friends and then complain that they are mistreated by their peers at school. They may engage in repeated complaints of physical symptoms such as headaches or stomachaches when they anticipate separation from major attachment figures. Children and adolescents may exhibit persistent refusal or reluctance to transition into a classroom because of fear of separation from a major attachment figure, their favorite homeroom teacher.

Generalized anxiety disorder is experienced by children and adolescents as multiple excessive, persistent worries and fears about life occurrences, as well as their competence or the quality of their performance (American Psychiatric Association, 1994). They may worry about a poor grade they made weeks ago or worry in advance about who will be their math teacher the next school year. Children and adolescents with anxiety disorders may be conforming and perfectionist. They are unsure of themselves and tend to re-do tasks because they are dissatisfied with their less-than-perfect performance, which leads them to require excessive reassurance about their performance from their teachers, friends, and families.

Social anxiety disorder in children and adolescents is represented by avoidance of unfamiliar places and people, secondary to the concern of unwarranted scrutiny towards themselves (American Psychiatric Association, 1994). Your students may experience a common social phobia of public speaking. Sometimes they may fear using public bathrooms, eating in the cafeteria, or going to a party. They may feel lonely and develop a low self-esteem and begin to see themselves as different from the other children in the classroom.

Obsessive compulsive disorder in children and adolescents is represented by the presence of an obsession (persistent, disturbing, intrusive thoughts or impulses that are illogical or irresistible) or a compulsion (obsessive rituals or actions that the child or adolescent feels urgently compelled to engage in) (American Psychiatric Association, 1994). In the school environment teachers might observe their students engaging in repeated hand washing because of their obsession with dirt and germs. They may be preoccupied with counting the lines of the story instead of focusing on the content, or they may feel the need to check things or arrange things in a certain symmetrical order. Such perfectionism from children or adolescents may interfere with the progression and completion of homework, classroom time, and extracurricular activities.

Post-traumatic stress disorder (PTSD) is an anxiety disorder that may be present in children and adolescents who have had a traumatic experience in their life (kidnapping; serious car, plane, or bus accident; violent attacks such as rapes, torture, or physical or sexual abuse) (American Psychiatric Association, 1994). Children and adolescents who experience PTSD may lose interest in their favorite things, or they may avoid going to places or seeing things that remind them of the traumatic event. Anniversaries of traumatic events are often very difficult. In addition, some children and adolescents with PTSD repeatedly may re-experience their trauma in the form of reenacting the behaviors about the trauma as well as reliving the trauma through nightmares, flashbacks, or intrusive images of the traumatic event.

When a child's anxiety interferes with normal school and social functioning, consider a referral to a mental health professional.

Treatment for anxiety disorders can be multifaceted, including various psychotherapeutic techniques, cognitive behavioral therapy, individual psychotherapy, behavioral relaxation, desensitization techniques, psychopharmacological interventions as well as psychoeducation for supporting teachers, families, and friends of the child or adolescent.

In terms of classroom interventions, you may find the school survival skills described in Chapter 7 helpful in alleviating children's anxieties about school demands and deadlines. Time management can be especially helpful for an overanxious child. Other classroom suggestions will come from the child's therapist. Be sure to keep the person informed about the student's progress and problems.

SPECIFIC PHOBIAS AND EXTREME FEARS

A "specific phobia" is an intense and persistent fear of a particular object or situation that may include irrational fears of certain things or situations such as heights, animals, escalators, receiving an injection, storms, enclosed places, tunnels, flying, insects, death, water, and seeing blood (American Psychiatric Association, 1994).

Consider this illustration of a phobic child:

> The presenting complaints at the time of the initial visit centered on Brenda's multiple fears. She is afraid of rain and lightning and is fearful of leaving the house without . . . one of her parents. While Brenda does attend school, she expresses discomfort at being there. Furthermore, her school performance is poor: Brenda has considerable difficulty with all school subjects.
>
> Brenda acknowledged the first two fears—her being afraid of lightning and of leaving the house alone—but she would not expand on either. However . . . Brenda's fear of being alone became evident. So that she would not have to be without her parents in the waiting room, Brenda instructed her mother to request that the social worker finish talking with the mother prior to Brenda's completing her session with me.
>
> With regard to school, Brenda did say that she disliked going to school. Brenda does not like her teacher, saying that her teacher is mean and always yells. (Mendelsohn, personal communication, 1981)

Psychotherapeutic treatment of phobias may be categorized into four components described by Miller, Barrett, and Hampe (1974): development of a helping relationship with the therapist, clarifying what the feared object or situation is, helping the child become desensitized to the feared object or situation, and helping the child face the feared object or situation. Your role as an educator would be defined by the child's therapist.

In the case of school refusal, sometimes called school phobia, your role could be extensive. Children and adolescents may avoid attending school due to their anxiety or fear. Anxiety-based school refusal is a clinical problem in which children and adolescents avoid going to school due to their specific fears. Over the years several terms have been utilized to describe school attendance. First, let's differentiate between school refusal and truancy. Truant students are not fearful of the school situation, whereas a school refuser may show fearfulness and anxiety such as somatic complaints,

withdrawal from social interactions with other children, and a general inability to cope with demands to be independent of the family (Hersov, 1985). Consider this description by Hersov (1985):

> Once back to school, on the first day contact must be maintained with child and parents by means of telephone calls to or from parents to gauge their own and the child's reactions to this first school attendance. Suggestions are made on how to deal with any new anxieties or attempts to manipulate parents to avoid school. If parents can manage unaided on successive mornings, they are praised and encouraged to take total responsibility for this, but support from the clinic or school must be available if there are signs of faltering or loss of resolve in either child or parents. The child should be interviewed again after one week at school to sort out any existing or potential sources of stress and anxiety in the school or home situation which can then be discussed with teachers and parents. All concerned should be warned that the times of potential danger of breakdown of school attendance are after a weekend, after an illness requiring more than a day or two at home, the beginning of a new term, family illness or bereavement, and change to a new class or school. (p. 395)

INTERNET RESOURCES

For more information on psychiatric problems, check one of these websites:

American Academy of Child and Adolescent Psychiatry (Facts for Families): www.aacap.org/web/aacap/factsFAM

American Anorexia Bulimia Association, Inc.: www.aabainc.org

American Psychiatric Association: www.psych.org

American Psychological Association: www.apa.org

Centers for Disease Control and Prevention, National Center for Injury, Prevention and Control: www.cdc.gov/ncipc

Eating Disorders Awareness and Prevention, Inc.: www.edap.org

Health Resources and Services Administration:
www.hrsa.dhhs.gov

Mental Health Net: www.cmhc.com

National Alliance for the Mentally Ill:
www.nami.org

National Clearinghouse for Alcohol and Drug
Abuse Information: www.health.org

National Institute of Mental Health:
www.nimh.gov

Office of the Assistant Secretary for
Health/Surgeon General: www.surgeon
general.gov

Substance Abuse and Mental Health Services
Administration: www.samhsa.gov.

SUMMARY

We hope that you have gathered information from
the clinical vignettes and guidelines to help you
identify and refer students at risk for psychiatric
disorders. Do not hesitate to discuss a worrisome
child with a colleague; you do not need to be absolutely sure about your concerns to make this in-
quiry. Be sure to document your concerns so that
future professionals working with the child will
have a better understanding of her history. Evaluation of results is discussed in Chapter 4; you
might want to review this material before making
notes in a child's record.

DISCUSSION QUESTIONS

1. How would you talk with a student who
   appears to be depressed?
2. Why is the identification of depression so
   important?
3. What are the warning signs for suicide?
4. What are the psychotherapeutic treatments
   for phobias?
5. How do truancy and school refusal differ?
6. What is an anxiety disorder?
7. What behavioral indicators might alert you
   to a student's use of alcohol, marijuana,

cocaine, stimulants, narcotics,
hallucinogens, or inhalants?
8. What are the warning signs for anorexia
   nervosa and bulimia nervosa?
9. What are the steps to take when an
   intoxicated student comes to your class?

REFERENCES

Achenbach, T. M., & Edelbrock, C. S. (1979). The child behavior profile: II. Boys aged 12–16 and girls aged 6–11
and 12–16. *Journal of Consulting and Clinical Psychology*,
47(1), 223–233.

American Psychiatric Association. (1994). *Diagnostic and
statistical manual of mental disorders* (4th ed.). Washington, DC: Author.

Brent, D. A. (1997). Practioner review: The aftercare of
adolescents with deliberate self-harm. *Journal of Child
Psychology and Psychiatry*, 38, 277–286.

Brent, D. A. Perper, J. A., & Allman, C. J. (1987). Alcohol,
firearms, and suicide among youth—Temporal
trends in Allegheny County, Pennsylvania, 1960 to
1983. *Journal of the American Medical Association*, 257,
3369–3372.

Centers for Disease Control. (1997). Unpublished mortality data from the National Center for Health Statistics (NCHS) Mortality Data Tapes.

Centers for Disease Control and Prevention. (1999). Suicide deaths and rates per 100,000 [On-line]. Available:
http://www.cdc.gov/ncipc/data/us9794/suic.htm.

Davidson, L., & Gould, M. S. (1986). Contagion as a risk
factor for youth suicide. Unpublished manuscript.

DeLong, R. (1990). Lithium treatment and bipolar disorders in childhood. *North Carolina Medical Journal*, 5,
152–154.

Hersov, L. (1985). School refusal. In M. Rutter & L.
Hersov (Eds.), *Child and adolescent psychiatry: Modern ap-
proaches* (2nd ed., pp. 382–399). Oxford, England:
Blackwell Scientific Publications.

Hoier, T., & Kerr, M. M. (1987). Extrafamilial information
sources in the study of childhood depression. *Journal
of the American Academy of Child Psychiatry*, 27, 21–33.

Kerr, M. M., & Schaeffer, A. L. (1987). Teacher interview
for psychiatric symptoms (TIPS). (Available from
Mary Margaret Kerr, Ed.D. at Western Psychiatric Institute and Clinic, University of Pittsburgh, 3811
O'Hara Street, Pittsburgh, PA 15213.)

Kovacs, M. (1985). *The natural history and cause of depressive disorders*. Washington, DC: American Psychiatric Association.

Lester, D., & Murrell, M. E. (1982). The preventive effect of strict gun control laws on suicide and homicide. *Suicide and Life-threatening Behavior*, 12, 131–139.

Marks, I. M. (1969). *Fears and phobias*. London: Heinemann.

Miller, L. C., Barrett, C. L., & Hampe, E. (1974). Phobias of childhood in a prescientific era. In A. Davids (Ed.), *Child personality and psychopathology: Current topics*. New York: Wiley.

The Pennsylvania Statistical Abstract. (1986) (28th ed.). Harrisburg, PA: Department of Commerce, Bureau of Statistics, Research and Planning.

Puig-Antich, J., Lukens, E., Davies, M., Goetz, D., Brennan-Quattrock, J., & Todak, G. (1985). Psycho-social functioning in prepubertal major depressive disorders. *Archives of General Psychiatry*, 42, 500–507.

Russell, G. F. M. (1985). Anorexia and bulimia. In M. Rutter & L. Hersov (Eds.), *Child and adolescent psychiatry: Modern approaches* (2nd ed., pp. 625–637). Oxford, England: Blackwell Scientific Publications.

Rutter, M., Tizard, J., & Whitmore, K. (Eds.). (1970). *Education, health and behavior*. London: Longman. (Reprinted, 1981, Huntingdon, NY: Krieger.)

Shaffer, D. (1985). Depression, mania, and suicidal acts. In M. Rutter & L. Hersov (Eds.), *Child and adolescent psychiatry* (2nd ed., pp. 698–719). Oxford, England: Blackwell Scientific Publications.

Shaffer, D. (1986). Developmental factors in child and adolescent suicide. In M. Rutter, C. E. Izard, & P. B. Read (Eds.), *Depression in young people: Clinical and developmental perspectives* (pp. 383–396). New York: Guilford Press.

Smith, K., & Crawford, S. (1986). Suicidal behavior among "normal" high school students. *Suicide and Life-threatening Behavior*, 16(3), 313–325.

Strayhorn, J. M., Jr. (1982). *Foundations of clinical psychiatry*. Chicago: Year Book Medical Publishers.

Thomas, A., Chess, S., & Birch, H. G. (1968). *Temperament and behavior disorders in children*. New York: Universities Press.

U.S. Department of Health and Human Services. (1991). *The international classification of diseases* (4th ed.). Washington, DC: Author.

Walker, H. M., Severson, H., Haring, N., & Williams, G. (1986). Standardized screening and identification of behavior disordered pupils in the elementary age range: A multiple gating approach. *Direct Instruction News*, 5(3), 15–18.

EXTENDING INTERVENTION EFFECTS

CHAPTER 11

OBJECTIVES

After completing this chapter, you should be able to

- Describe the relationship between the restrictiveness of treatment settings and the extent to which intervention effects generalize to other environments.
- Identify and describe obstacles to the maintenance and generalization of treatment effects.
- Describe strategies for achieving the maintenance and generalization of specific target behaviors.
- Describe procedures for assessing the expectations and tolerances of less restrictive settings for desired and maladaptive behaviors.
- Indicate factors to consider when planning for the transition of students to less restrictive school or post-school environments.
- Suggest strategies for accomplishing the successful transition of students to less restrictive educational or post-school environments.
- Explain the role of the special education teacher in working with families and other professionals.

Up to now, the major focus of this text has been on accomplishing changes in students' problem behaviors in settings where the primary intervention agent directly implements or supervises intervention procedures. In many cases, these **primary treatment settings** are individual classrooms that afford a high degree of stimulus control over pupils' behavior. Remember that there is a varied and powerful technology for accomplishing desired behavioral changes in settings in which intensive treatment may be applied. However, as we emphasized in Chapter 1, problem behaviors may occur in many different settings throughout the school. Furthermore, the effects of carefully designed and implemented interventions often do not generalize to other settings, nor do they tend to persist in primary treatment settings once intervention procedures are withdrawn. The failure of intervention effects to maintain and generalize is a serious problem, especially for students whose behavior poses significant challenges to school personnel. This failure has been observed across many populations and age levels. For instance, Lane and Burchard (1983) conducted an extensive review of behavioral interventions with delinquent youth and observed an apparent relationship between recidivism and the restrictiveness of the treatment setting. Their conclusion is relevant to all professionals who attempt to serve children and youth in restrictive environments: "To the extent that delinquents and criminals are locked up in institutions, the rationale for doing so should be to punish, and/or to temporarily protect the community, not to rehabilitate. *Very restrictive environments make rehabilitation less likely to happen*" (p. 273, emphasis added). The task of educators is habilitative (i.e., improving capability by developing new skills) rather than rehabilitative (i.e., restoring previous capacity). Nevertheless, research concerning the maintenance and generalization of behavioral changes accomplished in single settings (e.g., special classrooms, residential treatment programs) indicates that the "albatross of generalization" (O'Leary & O'Leary, 1976) also plagues those who attempt to modify the behaviors of school-age children and youth in restrictive environments.

Thus, extending intervention effects beyond individual classrooms is a critical task. For students with academic and behavioral challenges, including EBD, this task is rendered more complex by the difficulties of including them in general education programs (Kauffman & Hallahan, 1995). Nevertheless, there are several practical reasons for attempting to generalize behavioral changes across settings and over time. First, as we have just suggested, many pupils with EBD have problems in other settings as well. They clearly need help in these environments too, and persons in these settings need assistance in dealing with them constructively. Second, the school environment actually is composed of many different settings. This is obvious in secondary schools where pupils move from classroom to classroom and may participate in a variety of extracurricular activities. But even in elementary schools composed of self-contained classrooms, pupils function in a variety of settings. It is important both to assess these environments to determine what problems, if any, the student is having in them and to generalize behavior changes accomplished in the primary treatment setting to these environments as well. Third, a behavioral problem is a complex interaction of the characteristics of the setting and the child; thus it is not "owned" exclusively by the student and therefore, it is inappropriate to expect all the change to occur in the student alone. In order for the pupil's behavior to change in the presence of persons in settings where problem behavior occurs, their behavior must change as well. This is particularly important for generalizing behavioral changes to other settings. A fourth reason for extending treatment effects is to socially validate that real behavior changes have occurred. For example, if you eliminate a pupil's stealing in your classroom but her parents still find her stealing at home, the problem has not been solved.

Finally, if you teach in a restrictive setting (such as a self-contained classroom or day treatment program in a regular school building, a special day school, residential program, or juvenile correctional facility), we hope that you plan to move your pupils into more natural environments. If you are working with secondary-level pupils, you must think about their successful transition to adult living and working environments. To accomplish these goals, you must involve a variety of other persons (e.g., other teachers, school administrators, bus drivers, family members, human service agency representatives, employers) in planning and implementing transition procedures.

This chapter describes strategies for extending the effects of interventions to other settings in which behavior changes also are needed. These interventions are discussed in three sections. The first describes maintenance and generalization procedures that have been developed through research. The second section presents educational strategies for the successful transition of pupils to less restrictive school and adult environments. The last section describes strategies for working with parents and professionals outside of primary treatment settings, and therefore is a logical extension of the preceding chapter. Obviously, the sets of procedures described in the following sections overlap considerably. Our discussion emphasizes issues that affect attempts to work across educational and other settings.

MAINTENANCE AND GENERALIZATION PROCEDURES

The question of whether desired behavior changes extend across settings is one of generality. As Baer, Wolf, and Risley (1968) explain, "A behavior change may be said to have generality if it proves durable over time, if it appears in a wide variety of possible environments, or if it spreads to a wide variety of related behaviors" (p. 96). Generality therefore may be defined in terms of three effects. **Response maintenance** is the continuation or durability of behavior in treatment settings after the intervention has been withdrawn. Thus, if the social skills

a student has acquired through instruction in the classroom continue to improve after social skills training procedures are discontinued, response maintenance has occurred. **Stimulus generalization** refers to the transfer of behaviors that have been trained in one setting, or in the presence of specific discriminative stimuli to settings or stimuli in the presence of which they have not been taught. An analogous term, **transfer of training,** more aptly describes the process of transferring behavior changes accomplished in training to new settings or in the presence of new discriminative stimuli (e.g., cues, persons, physical objects). For example, a student may use a social skill taught in the classroom with his peers in the cafeteria. **Response generalization** involves changes in untreated behaviors that are related to those behaviors targeted for intervention. For example, if a pupil is taught to suppress her physical attacks on other students, and her rate of verbal aggression also decreases (even though this behavior was not treated directly), response generalization has occurred. Such generalization across behaviors is more likely in responses that serve the same function (i.e., produce the same outcomes) as the target behavior.

For educators, the critical questions regarding the maintenance and generalization of intervention effects include the following (Rutherford & Nelson, 1988):

1. Will desired behavior changes persist when students leave structured, highly controlled training settings?
2. Will students exhibit newly learned behaviors in nontraining settings, in the presence of other teachers or peers, and over time?
3. Will learning new skills facilitate the acquisition of similar behaviors that were not targeted for training in the original setting?

Strategies to promote maintenance and generalization may be approached on two fronts: one focusing on procedures that influence the student's behavior during intervention so that it will maintain in other settings, and the other focusing on preparing other settings to support the pupil's new behaviors. If you are unable to influence what goes on in other classrooms, for example, you still can select strategies that can be used in your own classroom. However, it is clear that maintenance and generalization programming is most effective when employed on both fronts, especially with students with more severe disabilities (Nelson & Rutherford, 1988). One such strategy is **transenvironmental programming** (Anderson-Inman, Walker, & Purcell, 1984), which includes four component strategies: assessing the behavioral expectations of specific generalization settings, teaching skills related to these expectations to students in the special education environment, selecting and using techniques for promoting the transfer of skills across settings, and monitoring and evaluating student performance in generalization settings. Only the second component can be accomplished entirely in the primary treatment setting, and even so, it requires assessment data from the generalization setting. Anderson-Inman et al. (1984) observed that monitoring and evaluating pupil behavior in generalization settings is the most difficult aspect of transenvironmental programming because of the lack of training and support available to general education personnel. Consider these issues when reviewing the maintenance and generalization strategies presented later in this chapter.

Stokes and Baer (1977) identified nine strategies in the research literature that address generalization and maintenance. A decade later, Stokes and Osnes (1986) refined these into 11 tactics grouped into three categories that emphasize the general principles underlying the classification:

1. Take advantage of natural communities of reinforcement.
   a. Teach relevant behaviors.
   b. Modify environments supporting maladaptive behaviors.
   c. Recruit natural communities of reinforcement.
2. Train diversely.
   a. Use sufficient stimulus exemplars.
   b. Use sufficient response exemplars.
   c. Train loosely.
   d. Use indiscriminable contingencies.
   e. Reinforce unprompted generalization.
3. Incorporate functional mediators.
   a. Use common physical stimuli.
   b. Use common social stimuli.
   c. Use self-mediated stimuli. (pp. 417–418)

TAKE ADVANTAGE OF NATURAL COMMUNITIES OF REINFORCEMENT. The strategies incorporated in this principle emphasize using reinforcement normally available in natural settings. For instance, appropriate social behaviors usually are followed by pleasant social responses from other persons, which is reinforcing to most individuals. Thus, the first strategy, *teach relevant behaviors*, involves adding skills to the pupil's social repertoire that are likely to set up reciprocal social interactions that strengthen further social initiations on the student's part. Examples include greetings and other positive social initiations, and effective language, communication, and interpersonal skills (Stokes & Osnes, 1986). Behaviors that are useful in generalization settings for gaining attention, inviting interactions, or generating praise effectively "trap" reinforcement; thus, the term **trapping effect** is used to describe the tactic of increasing behaviors that effectively capture naturally contingent reinforcement. When using this strategy, however, follow these suggestions.

First, assess generalization settings to determine what skills and behaviors are required or are likely to result in reinforcement. A skill that is taught in one setting (e.g., greeting every pupil in the class with a handshake) may not be necessary or even desirable in another setting. Although this strategy is implemented in the primary treatment setting, the trainer obviously must assess the generalization setting to identify relevant behaviors.

(A procedure that may be used for this purpose is described in the next section.)

Our second recommendation is to make sure that the student acquires sufficient proficiency in the skill. If the pupil does not use the skill fluently (i.e., as well as other students in the generalization setting), he is less likely to be reinforced when he does use it. One way to increase the probability of reinforcement in generalization settings is to prompt it. In one study teachers had to prompt preschool children to interact with a withdrawn child in order to increase her social initiations enough to occasion their responses naturally (Baer & Wolf, 1970). Some pupils' social behaviors may not come under the control of peer responses without considerable training (e.g., see Gunter, Fox, Brady, Shores, & Cavanaugh, 1988), pointing out the need to carefully monitor settings in which generalization is desired. It also is important to go beyond providing training in only the primary treatment setting and simply hoping that the target behavior occurs in other environments. In fact, it is much more efficient and logical to train social skills in the settings where they are needed from the start (Scott & Nelson, 1998). Third, do not assume that the apparent existence of a natural community of reinforcement for one student's behavior assures that the same naturally occurring consequences will be reinforcing to another pupil (Stokes & Osnes, 1986).

As most teachers and parents know, peers sometimes provide consistent reinforcement of undesired student behaviors, and adults and peers in generalization settings may not adequately reinforce desired target behaviors. In such cases, it may be necessary to *modify environments supporting maladaptive behavior.* This tactic entails controlling the consequences that peers provide for undesired behavior. Managing peer reactions can be extremely difficult, given the number of students and settings that may be involved. Use peer-mediated procedures, such as dependent group contingencies and peer feedback, to shift reinforcement contingencies so that desired replacement behaviors are supported instead. Under such contingency conditions, desired behavior becomes the discriminative stimulus for peer group reinforcement. However, you also may need to prevent reinforcement of undesired behavior by training peers, other staff, or parents to ignore maladaptive behavior and to attend systematically to replacement behaviors (Stokes & Osnes, 1986). Obviously, this strategy requires intervention in generalization settings, and conducting a functional behavioral assessment (FBA) will improve correspondence between the function of target and replacement behaviors.

Another strategy that can be used is to teach the target pupil to *recruit natural communities of reinforcement.* This consists of training the student not only to emit behaviors desired in the generalization setting but also to draw positive adult or peer attention to these behaviors. This strategy has been effective in recruiting adult attention (e.g., Graubard, Rosenberg, & Miller, 1971; Hrydowy, Stokes, & Martin, 1984), but its success with peers has not been as well documented. However, Gaylord-Ross, Haring, Breen, and Pitts-Conway (1984) taught autistic adolescent boys to operate socially desirable objects (e.g., a video game and a tape player) and then to use them in social interactions with typical peers. The researchers observed generalized maintenance of those students' social interactions with typical pupils. Dependent group contingencies, in which the target pupil's desired behavior earns reinforcers desired by peers, also have been observed to increase peers' positive attention to the targeted student (Shores, Apolloni, & Norman, 1976). Initial training may be provided only in the primary treatment setting, but the trainer must be able to assess the pupil's skill in recruiting reinforcement in the generalization setting in order to adjust training procedures as needed.

TRAIN DIVERSELY. The objective of this group of strategies is to arrange training conditions and response and reinforcement criteria to cover a range of possible circumstances that occur in generalization settings. As with other strategies, those in this category (except reinforce unprompted generalization) may be applied in the primary treatment setting, but they are much more effective when training occurs in generalization settings as well. The first strategy, *use sufficient stimulus exemplars*, tells you to arrange for more than one or a small set of discriminative stimuli to control the target behavior. Thus, conduct training in more than one setting or under more than one set of training circumstances (Stokes & Osnes, 1986). An application of this strategy that has been used successfully with pupils exhibiting autism involves typical peers as discriminative stimuli for targeted social behaviors (Simpson, 1987); however, this tactic is much more effective with trained, as opposed to untrained, peer confederates (Hollinger, 1987; McEvoy & Odom, 1987). You also should augment peer-mediated strategies with direct instruction in generalization settings (Shores, 1987). Stokes and Osnes (1986) stress the importance of having a generalization plan to guide training across stimulus examples. Decide where and with whom generalization is desired and tailor your strategy according to the characteristics of these persons, stimuli, and settings.

The response analogue of the above strategy is to *use sufficient response exemplars*, which involves including more than one example of the target behavior(s) in the training. Using multiple-response examples is particularly important when attempting to generalize a complex behavior such as holding a conversation (Stokes & Osnes, 1986). In applying this strategy, the pupil is taught a range of correct responses that are appropriate for the situation and is reinforced for using them. Teaching several acceptable response variations also is useful for situations in which students may be required to exhibit different response topographies in different stimulus settings. For example, some greeting behaviors may be appropriate for a male coming up on a group of adolescent boys (e.g., "How's it going?" or "Hey, what's happening?") while other expressions are preferred for use in greeting members of the opposite sex (e.g., "Hi!" or "Hello, Sandy."). Getting a drink of water requires different response topographies when at a drinking fountain, a restaurant, or a garden hose.

Train loosely is closely related to the previous two strategies. Control over the training conditions and acceptable responses is loosened intentionally to permit greater flexibility in both the stimuli occasioning target behaviors and the reinforced behaviors. More tightly controlled initial training conditions will require proportionately greater attention to loosening stimulus control. Consequently, Stokes and Osnes (1986) recommend that the least tightly controlled yet effective initial training environment be used. Therefore, teachers who have students work in study carrels, who provide daily work in folders, who time seatwork assignments, and who have very specific response requirements for reinforcement may not be facilitating their pupils' success in less structured environments.

The objective of the strategy *use indiscriminable contingencies* is to loosen control over the consequences of behavior. The most common application is to use intermittent schedules of reinforcement to lessen the predictability of reinforcement while increasing the durability of target behaviors. Koegel and Rincover (1977) demonstrated that even noncontingent reinforcement maintained the imitation and direction-following behaviors of children with autism after systematic treatment contingencies were withdrawn. However, we do not recommend this approach unless pupils can be supervised continuously in generalization settings. Another application is to use vicarious reinforcement. For example, if one student is praised for appropriate behavior, other pupils who observe this model are more likely to imitate the desired behavior (Kazdin, 1977; Strain, Shores, & Kerr, 1976). This has been referred to as a *ripple* or *spillover effect*. To make reinforcement less predictable, delay its delivery for some time after the target behavior has occurred or reinforce the behavior when it occurs simultaneously with other nontarget responses (Stokes & Osnes, 1986). One note of caution, however: you should be certain that desired responses are well established under systematic and plentiful schedules of reinforcement before making the discriminative stimuli for reinforcement less easy to identify. The last strategy in this category, *reinforce unprompted generalization*, involves monitoring in generalization settings and reinforcing spontaneous generalization of desired target behaviors when they occur or reinforcing the absence of maladaptive behaviors (Stokes & Osnes, 1986). Obviously, this strategy requires that persons in generalization settings be aware of target behaviors, monitor their occurrence, and apply the appropriate reinforcers contingently.

INCORPORATE FUNCTIONAL MEDIATORS. The strategies included in this group attempt to take advantage of potential discriminative stimuli that are common to training and generalization settings. Again, assessment and training in generalization settings are critical to the success of these strategies. U*se common physical stimuli* means to ensure that physical discriminative stimuli are present in all settings in which target behavior is desired. Common work or play materials may be used to facilitate generalization. Marholin and Steinman (1977) found that by reinforcing the academic response rate and accuracy of special education students when the teacher was present, the academic materials became discriminative stimuli that occasioned working even when the teacher was not present. On the other hand, when the teacher merely reinforced on-task behavior, work productivity dropped when the teacher was out of the room, apparently because the adult was the discriminative stimulus for academic responses in this condition. Peers are logical common stimuli in the next strategy, *use common social stimuli*. Significant peers and adults present in generalization settings may participate in training sessions in the primary treatment setting, either early in training or later, when transfer of training is contemplated (Stokes & Osnes, 1986). For example, Gunter et al. (1988) used typical peers who were present in generalization settings as discriminative stimuli in the training environ-

ment for the appropriate social initiations of students with disabilities. This tactic is an option when trainers cannot work in generalization settings, but assessment is necessary to ensure that interactions in these settings are consistent with the generalization plan.

A readily available source of common stimuli is the student herself. Thus the final strategy, *use self-mediated stimuli*, involves having the student carry or deliver stimuli that are discriminative of appropriate responses. Instructions, reminders written on a card, or a string on a finger are tangible discriminative stimuli, whereas teaching the student to self-administer a verbal instruction or cue is intangible but more natural to generalization settings. Self-recording, self-evaluation, and self-reinforcement are procedures that also employ self-mediated stimuli. This set of strategies is potentially one of the most useful and least intrusive for promoting transfer of training, but it also is hard to evaluate the extent to which students use self-mediated procedures. Consequently, it is difficult to say that these procedures are responsible for some of the gains attributed to them. It also is important to realize that prior training in using self-mediated strategies is critical to ensuring their effectiveness in generalization environments (Polsgrove, 1979). Nevertheless, a number of studies have involved teaching students to self-monitor their performance. For example, Clees (1995) taught students with learning and behavioral disorders to self-record their daily schedules and observed significant and durable increases in the number of teacher-expected behaviors exhibited, even after withdrawing the self-recording intervention. Levendoski and Cartledge (2000) improved the on-task behavior and academic productivity of four elementary students with EBD by teaching them to use a simple self-monitoring strategy. Reid and Harris (1993) found that self-monitoring of performance and self-monitoring of attention had varied effects on students with learning disabilities. They concluded that a "best" strategy for teaching self-monitoring does not exist for all students and all tasks.

Cognitive behavior modification involves teaching students cognitive strategies to help them solve problems. These strategies incorporate an analysis of the tasks to be performed (or the social problems to be solved) and teaching the strategy through modeling, self-instruction, and self-evaluation (Meichenbaum, 1977). For example, if a student needs to learn how to control his temper, the teacher might teach him—through modeling, role-playing, and individual or group discussions—a set of steps to rehearse when he finds himself losing control (e.g., count to ten, leave the situation, repeat to himself that the other person is not trying to "get" him).

Such tactics frequently include an evaluation component. For example, Maag (1994) taught a girl to self-monitor situations that led to feelings of frustration. Her self-monitoring sheet included a description of the situation resulting in frustration, her expectations of that situation, her reactions, and whether the outcome was satisfactory to her.

The strategies that you design to extend treatment effects to other settings, persons, or specific discriminative stimuli, or over time, will depend on your objectives for the student and situation. It is likely that a combination of strategies will be more appropriate to specific circumstances than a single procedure. Develop a generalization plan to guide your efforts and facilitate your evaluation of its effects. Figure 11–1 provides a format for this purpose. Use checklists like that illustrated in Figure 11–2 to identify resource persons to assist in generalization programming. Once you have gained fluency in writing intervention and generalization plans, you may find it more convenient to incorporate the latter into your intervention plan from the beginning.

In discussing maintenance and generalization training strategies, we have emphasized the importance of assessment and intervention in the environments where skills are expected or needed. Interventions that fail to address the demands and idiosyncrasies of generalization settings are not likely to produce effects that persist in these environments. Thus, severe limitations are imposed on intervention agents who are unable to gain access to these settings because their direct teaching responsibilities prohibit it, because other teachers will not tolerate other adults in their classrooms, or because staff members will not cooperate with training procedures. The organization of most public school environments can be a significant obstacle to effective maintenance and generalization of treatment effects. Although you may have no authority to change factors such as teaching loads, you may be able to identify resources in the school in order to accomplish generalization objectives. Your own enthusiasm and dedication to helping your students will assist in recruiting reinforcement and support for your efforts. We have known educators who, by modeling hard work and determination, evoked similar efforts from their colleagues. As more school districts adopt teaming strategies that support both students and teachers, better mobilization of the many resources available in schools (and communities) will follow.

PROGRAMMING FOR TRANSITION OF STUDENTS TO LESS RESTRICTIVE EDUCATION AND ADULT ENVIRONMENTS

This section describes strategies directed toward moving students to less restrictive educational settings,[1] to other programs or facilities where services are delivered, or to post-secondary school environments. Of course the maintenance and generalization procedures just presented may be applied to this goal. Our rationale for presenting transition strategies in a separate section is that movement of pupils to less restrictive environments is a common educational goal, and it involves transferring students and their entire repertoires of behavior to new settings. Thus it is a

---

[1]Recall that the concept of least restrictive environment is not synonymous with placement in a general education classroom.

Student _____   Target Behavior _____

Primary Treatment Setting _____

Intervention Plan (Include objective, procedures, data decision rules, review dates, etc.)

Outcome   (Narrative description, dates plan reviewed/revised, data summaries or
          graphs, etc.)

Generalization Plan

  Objective

    Terminal Behavior

    Conditions (Settings, persons, reinforcers, schedule, etc.)

    Criteria

  Strategy (Procedures used, resources needed, etc.)

  Evaluation Plan   (Data to be collected, when it will be collected, who will
                    collect it, who will summarize/evaluate data, data decision
                    rule, etc.)

  Outcome   (Narrative description, dates plan reviewed/revised, data summaries
            or graphs, etc.)

FIGURE 11–1   Sample generalization plan format.

broader task than that of programming for the maintenance and generalization of specific target behaviors. In addition, the movement of students among instructional settings is an activity peculiar to schools. Although it is desirable to generalize changes in those behaviors targeted in the primary treatment setting to these environments, each classroom teacher also has individual expectations for the behaviors required in his setting. Transition planning must take these expectations into account, and strategies for accomplishing the movement of pupils into less restrictive settings must involve a broad range of activities. Procedures have been developed for the specific

Personnel Agencies	Willing to work with pupils?	Supportive of your program?	Cooperated with you previously?	Willing to collect data?	Supervision required?	Training required?	Willing to devote time above normal duties?	Reliably carried out procedures with pupils before?	Comments (Phone numbers, etc.)
Teachers									
Aides and volunteers									
Speech clinician									
Guidance counselor									
School psychologist									
Vice principal									
Principal									
Secretaries									
School nurse									
Custodian									
Bus driver									
Cafeteria workers									
Others									

FIGURE 11–2 In-school resource checklist.

purpose of facilitating this movement, especially in the case of students with disabilities. We describe strategies to facilitate transitions to less restrictive educational settings, other educational or treatment settings, and to adult environments separately, although many procedures, including those discussed in the previous section, are appropriate for any of these goals. We also consider follow-up assessment procedures because these are important for evaluating both pupils' status after leaving treatment settings and the effectiveness of the programs they received.

The key element in all transition activities is a **transition plan.** In effect, the eligibility assessment and multidisciplinary team (MDT) process conducted prior to students' entry into special education programs constitutes transition planning from general to special education. All systematic transitions must include strategies for moving both the student and appropriate data from one location to another. Transition plans most often are associated with movement of students with disabilities from secondary school programs to post-secondary settings, but the components of all transition plans are the same: a statement of the goals and objectives to be achieved by the transition, and the procedures for their implementation, including the responsibilities of the sending and receiving program, the information to be transferred, and follow-up procedures (Edgar, Webb, & Maddox, 1987).

Transitions to Less Restrictive Educational Settings

While the movement toward including students with disabilities in general education settings has had dramatic effects on the classroom placement of many pupils with special education needs, recall that students who exhibit emotional and behavioral challenges are the least likely to be successfully included of any group. Furthermore, claims that inclusion settings are beneficial for all students with disabilities, while more restrictive settings are never beneficial, are not supported by

research (MacMillan, Gresham, & Forness, 1996). Nevertheless, returning students with EBD to general education classroom settings is a laudable, but complex, goal. If you are the practitioner who is contemplating such a transition for a student, you must not only evaluate and develop appropriate pupil behaviors; you also must coordinate a number of environmental variables: schedules, curricula, materials, school staff, and other students, just to name a few. A technology for achieving this change on behalf of students with disabilities is developing; however, as Kauffman and Hallahan (1995) caution, the attitudes, strategies, and resources needed for achieving the successful full inclusion of students with significant behavioral challenges are not in place in the vast majority of school districts in the United States. Kauffman and Hallahan indicate that until such systems change, "full inclusion can provide only an illusion of support for all students, an illusion that may trick many into jumping on the bandwagon but is sure to produce disappointment, if not outrage, in its riders when the juggernaut crushes the students it was supposed to defend." (p. x).

A recommended strategy for accomplishing the reintegration of students into regular classrooms is *transenvironmental programming* (Anderson-Inman et al., 1984). As explained earlier, transenvironmental programming consists of four steps. Following is a detailed description of each step.

ASSESSING MAINSTREAM CLASSROOMS. The task of locating an appropriate general education class into which to reintegrate a student is greatly facilitated in schools with a climate that supports full inclusion. It is true that the mechanics and dynamics of such a climate are not in place on a large scale. Until they are, students who are hard to teach and to manage will not be welcome or successful in general education classes, regardless of lip service given to having "full inclusion school programs."

Fortunately, research is beginning to identify the factors that characterize such a climate. For example, Rock, Rosenberg, and Carran (1994) conducted a large-scale study in Maryland that identified variables that influence the reintegration[2] rate of students with EBD. They found three sets of variables that predicted higher rates of reintegration. Set 1 consisted of a "positive reintegration orientation," which included the following combination of program components:

1. Multiple options for reintegration, such as part-day, trial, and transitional reintegration.
2. Opportunity for special education teachers to learn reintegration class expectations.
3. Authority for the special teacher to participate in selecting the reintegration placement for a particular student.
4. Program-wide reintegration goals, including goal setting for students, when they are admitted to the program, and reintegration planning at the annual IEP review of each student.
5. Reintegration procedures that are written, documented, and easy-to-implement.
6. Training in reintegration that is provided to special teachers, including annual training in procedures and methods; regular, formal meetings to update reintegration information; and informal reintegration training sessions given by administrators to individuals or groups.

The best single predictor from this set was the ability of special education teachers to select the particular class into which the student would be reintegrated. In this regard, Wong, Kauffman, and Lloyd (1991) have developed procedures for selecting mainstream teachers to work with students certified as having EBD. On the basis of the effective teaching literature, they identified the following sets of characteristics of teachers who are likely to be successful with students with EBD:

- High expectations for students' academic performance and conduct.
- Selection of activities to maintain high rates of correct responding and low rates of off-task behavior.
- Frequent praise of desired student behavior.
- Infrequent use of criticism or punishment.
- Self-confidence in helping students learn and behave appropriately. (Wong et al., 1991, p. 111)

However, recall that interactions between teachers and students with serious problem behavior tend to be aversive, and that teachers tend to avoid them, resulting in significantly fewer instructional interactions than experienced by students with less demanding behavior (Carr, Taylor, & Robinson, 1991; Gunter, Jack, DePaepe, Reed, & Harrison, 1994). This suggests that as much work must go into preparing a classroom teacher to receive the student with EBD as in preparing the student for the transition.

The second set of variables identified by Rock et al. (1994) consisted of the following combination of specific demographic characteristics:

1. The special education program was located in a wing of a comprehensive school building, as opposed to a separate building.
2. Program was within 1 mile of the most likely reintegration site.
3. Multiple reintegration sites were available, including less restrictive classes in the same building, in nearby public schools, in students' home school or previous school, or in another setting (such as a vocational center).
4. Program was public rather than private, and in a county that had a significantly higher rate of reintegration than others.
5. Program served students who were older rather than younger.

[2]Students with EBD are the last of any group of students with disabilities to be identified—in terms of age and grade level—and placed in special education programs (U.S. Department of Education, 2000). Therefore, their entry into the educational mainstream is more accurately characterized as reintegration.

6. Program had smaller mainstream class sizes.
7. Classes were departmentalized or rotating, rather than self-contained.

Of this set, the best demographic predictors of reintegration rates were (1), (2), and (3) (Rock et al., 1994). Thus, the political climate regarding the reintegration of students with EBD as well as the social and physical demographics of the school are important factors in reintegration rate.

Set 3 consisted of a combination of teachers' characteristics and experiences:

1. Greater number of places a teacher had received reintegration training, including undergraduate school, graduate school, in-school training, in-service courses, access to professional literature, and other sites.
2. Higher number of students who have been reintegrated from a given teacher's class, and a higher number of students for whom the teacher had primary (case manager) or secondary (team member) reintegration planning responsibilities.
3. More years worked with children certified as EBD.
4. An "Advanced Professional" certificate from the Maryland State Department of Education (as compared to Standard, Temporary/Provisional, or none).
5. State certification in special education.
6. A higher level of overall teacher education (e.g., Master's as compared to Bachelor's degrees).
7. Teacher's educational specialization in special education.

The best single predictor in this set was the teacher's experience with reintegration. As the authors of this study pointed out, many other variables contribute to how much of this expertise a teacher has, including previous training, administrative and community support, and programmatic resources.

Another set of variables, consisting of special education teachers' opinions and attitudes, did not add significantly to the prediction of reintegration rate. However, as we have just mentioned, these variables were related to other factors that already were predictive of reintegration rate (Rock et al., 1994).

Rock et al. (1994) also observed that a number of these variables are influenced by school administrators, who should ensure that (a) reintegration procedures are clearly defined and in writing, (b) school-wide reintegration goals and expectations exist for all students, and (c) in-service teacher training is implemented as described in set 1. However, as a classroom teacher, you may sit on a school council or site-based management team that makes decisions regarding such policies and staff training. As a special education teacher, you should be involved in the selection of classes into which your students are reintegrated and you should familiarize yourself with reintegration expectations and procedures in your school (Rock et al., 1994).

A lively and sometimes contentious debate has developed regarding the participation of students with EBD in full inclusion programs (Kauffman & Hallahan, 1995; MacMillan et al., 1996). We believe that full inclusion is a desirable goal for these students but is not an appropriate strategy for all. Rather, as Edgar and Siegel (1995) observed, the needs of many pupils with EBD (and their families) require a wide range of services that exceed those typically provided by the schools. Furthermore, without extended services, school programs are not likely to be successful. Edgar and Siegel (1995) also advised that teachers should argue "for programs that achieve desired outcomes regardless of the degree of inclusion, concede that no one program will ever meet the needs of all students, and advocate for the proactive testing of many program types rather than continued debates on what should be" (p. 252).

PREPARING THE STUDENT. In describing strategies for developing students' competence with regard to the expectations and freedoms of the general education classroom, we begin with the assumption that you have improved the student's academic and social functioning to the point where he is able to profit from a less restrictive environment. If this assumption is met, the issue is one of generalization and maintenance of behavior change, which of necessity involves arrangements with other persons.

To help the student prepare for inclusion in a mainstream class, develop a hierarchy of student competencies and classroom structure that increasingly approximates the pupil behaviors and teacher expectations found in general education classrooms (Maag & Katsiyannis, 1998). One strategy to organize these variables is to establish a *levels* or *phase system*. Ideally, a levels system is coordinated with a continuum of placements in the school building. The probability that critical behaviors will be maintained and generalized outside restrictive settings is enhanced by having a complete continuum of services available in the building (MacMillan et al., 1996; Rock et al., 1994). That is, rather than going directly from a self-contained, highly individualized program into a group-oriented general education classroom, students enter a class that more closely approximates the setting, demands, and expectation of the regular classroom (e.g., a resource room) and are phased into mainstream classrooms from there.

Entry and exit competencies for each level of program in this continuum can be specified. For example, Taylor and Soloway (1973) devised a service delivery system consisting of four levels of student competence. *Pre-academic competencies* include such skills as paying attention, starting an assignment immediately, working continuously without interruption, following task directions, doing what one is told, taking part verbally in discussions, getting along with others, and demonstrating adequacy in perceptual-motor and language skills. *Academic competencies* include proficiency in all core subjects, as well as being accurate, being neat, efficient, and well organized. *Setting competencies* involve learning to profit from instruction provided in settings found in mainstream classrooms (independent work, large and small group work,

etc.), and *reward competencies* range from responding to tangible reinforcers at the most basic level to being reinforced by social recognition and the acquisition of new knowledge and skills. Pupils are grouped according to their level of competence in these skill categories. They move up through the levels as they demonstrate more advanced competencies. The environments corresponding to each level consist of a self-contained setting, a resource room (with increasingly greater time spent in general education classrooms), and the mainstream classroom. Table 11–1 illustrates Taylor and Soloway's (1973) level system of student competencies leading to functioning in a regular classroom.

Similar levels systems have been developed for secondary programs (e.g., Braaten, 1979; Vetter-Zemitsch et al., 1984) and for children and adolescents with severe behavior disorders in residential programs (e.g., Bauer & Shea, 1988; Hewett & Taylor, 1980; LaNunziata, Hunt, & Cooper, 1984). Within a given level, progress upward is maximized by a curricular emphasis on those competencies needed for the next higher level.

More than likely, you will not have the prerogative of developing a complete delivery system. However, most levels systems are designed to operate in the context of an individual classroom. Therefore, you can arrange your own expectations for student behavior in terms of a hierarchy of competencies. If progress through the levels is associated with increasing independence and powerful (and naturalistic) reinforcers, student motivation to advance will pose few problems.[3] However, your system will work only if it is based on skills your pupils actually need for success in the less restrictive environments within your school or institution. Therefore, as suggested by

[3] One cautionary note: levels systems are patently ineffective if progress is less reinforcing to students than the peer and adult attention they receive for exhibiting problematic behaviors, if they do not receive meaningful reinforcement for advancement through the levels, including those levels that involve participation in mainstream classes, or if they lack the skills needed for success at higher levels. Recall too that levels systems may impose restrictions on students' legal rights (e.g., access to the general education curriculum).

TABLE 11–1   A Level System of Student Competencies Leading to Regular Classroom Functioning

	Continuum of Settings and Competencies Required			
Levels	**Pre-academic I Self-Contained Setting** ——➤	**Pre-academic II Resource Setting** ——➤	**Academic I Resource Setting** ——➤	**Academic II General Education Setting**
Pre-academic	*Major emphasis* Paying attention Beginning work immediately Working continuously Following directions Doing what one is told	*Minor emphasis* Behavior stressed in pre-academic *Major emphasis* Taking part in discussion Getting along with others	*Minor emphasis* Pre-academic behaviors stated in pre-academic I & II	Mainstream classroom
Academic	*Minor emphasis* Academic assignments Being accurate Being neat	*Major emphasis* Presenting basic school subjects Supplementing remediation with special materials and resources	*Major emphasis* School subjects Some remedial Some grade-level curriculum	Mainstream classroom
Setting	Student works independently at desk or booth 1:1 relationship with teacher	Student works in teacher/small group setting Student works independently in shared desk space Group interaction and cooperation emphasized	Regular classroom simulated Large group receives instruction from teacher Opportunities presented to function independently	Mainstream classroom
Reward	Checkmark system linked to tangible rewards for appropriate social and academic behaviors Any incentive considered that will motivate child	Checkmark system linked to free time Increased emphasis on social approval	Numerical grading system for effort, quality of work, and citizenship	Mainstream classroom

Source: This information is taken from Taylor, F. D., & Soloway, M. M. (1973). The Madison School Plan: A functional model for merging the regular and special classrooms. In E. N. Deno (Ed.). Instructional alternatives for exceptional children. Reston, VA: Council for Exceptional Children, pp. 147–149.

the findings of Rock et al. (1994), you should begin by determining the minimum requirements of each environment. For example, what skills do pupils need to be manageable in mainstream classes in your building? Which behaviors are more likely to successfully trap reinforcement in the less restrictive environment? In general, we believe these consist of appropriate social behavior, compliance with teacher requests and directions, and basic language proficiency.

These general skills, as well as the school survival skills described in Chapter 7, suggest some target behaviors for students you are considering moving to less restrictive settings. However, each classroom teacher's specific skill requirements vary, just as competence in and motivation to perform these skills vary from student to student; therefore, assess each environment separately. Thus, steps one and two of transenvironmental programming are ongoing and interactive.

In selecting target behaviors for intervention with the goal of the full inclusion of pupils with EBD in mind, assign appropriate social skills a high priority. The social skill deficits of students with disabilities, particularly EBD, are well documented. For example, Gresham, Elliott, and Black (1987) found that teacher ratings of social skills alone could be used to classify accurately 75% of a sample of mainstreamed pupils with mild disabilities. In other words, lack of social skills appears to be a factor that discriminates between children with disabilities and their peers who are not disabled. Use social skills rating scales such as those discussed in Chapter 2 to evaluate pupils' social skills relative to normative standards and to select target behaviors for training prior to mainstreaming placement.

Of course, students also should be prepared to meet the academic expectations of less restrictive environments if they are to have successful experiences in these settings. The delineation of academic instructional strategies is beyond the scope of this book (see Kameinui & Darch, 1995; Mercer & Mercer, 2001). However, the general approach should be the same as for preparing students to meet the social demands of less restrictive settings: identify the academic expectations, assess the student with regard to these expectations, teach the pupil in the more restrictive setting up to the criterion levels expected in the less restrictive environment, provide generalization training in the new setting, and follow up to determine whether the student is meeting expectations and to provide ongoing support and technical assistance to the general education teacher.

IMPLEMENTING TRANSITION STRATEGIES.   In the process of assessing the less restrictive classroom environment and establishing a match between the student's characteristics and the reintegration setting, you will develop relationships with the other building staff. Your relationship with the potential receiving teacher will be strengthened if you plan the student's academic program with her. In view of the likely possibility that the pupil may need special support and assistance not available to other students in the setting, you may need to help the teacher adapt instruction by providing special materials, tutoring the pupil, or training the teacher in errorless or mastery learning procedures. If your school has formed behavior support teams, staff may be available to assist teachers in adapting instruction and management practices.

Use these teacher support services to facilitate the transition of your pupils to less restrictive settings. The more that dealing with students with behavior problems is seen as a responsibility shared by all professional educators and not just by those who are certified as "special," the more quickly professionals will learn the necessary skills and accept responsibility for guaranteeing these students their educational rights.

The settings in which social skills instruction takes place are important to consider. Whereas it is desirable to provide initial social skills training in settings that ensure a high level of stimulus control over instructional and response variables, the most effective maintenance and generalization strategies involve training in generalization settings. For instance, the use of multiple peer exemplars is a critical social skill generalization strategy, and research clearly supports using typical peers as confederates, who are specifically trained to prompt and support appropriate social interactions (Gresham, 1998; Hollinger, 1987; McEvoy & Odom, 1987; Simpson, 1987). In turn, more durable patterns of confederate interactions occur when students with disabilities are taught to make social initiations toward these peers (Gaylord-Ross & Haring, 1987; Gresham, 1998). These strategies require that reciprocal social interactions between students be trained in generalization settings. This requirement is difficult for many school districts to implement because their other responsibilities restrict the staff members with expertise in social skills training (e.g., special education teachers) from working in settings with students who are not disabled. The most economical solution to this dilemma is to make social skills training the responsibility of general education staff, but given the current pressures on general educators, this is not likely to happen. The development of collaborative teaching models, in which general and special education teachers work together in full inclusion classrooms, is a promising compromise (Hallahan & Kauffman, 1995; Idol, Paolucci-Whitcomb, & Nevin, 1986). Whether you seek employment as a general or special education teacher, we strongly recommend that you investigate the amount of time and opportunity you will have to work with mainstream educators, as well as the school's strategies for promoting collaborative relationships.

Wong et al. (1991) developed procedures, based on the effective teaching literature, for establishing a match between the characteristics of teachers in general education classrooms and students who are being considered for inclusion. A Mainstream Classroom Observation form is completed by the special education teacher either during or immediately after directly observing a potential mainstream classroom (see Figure 11–3). Teachers who demonstrate recommended teaching behaviors then are interviewed to determine who would be a better match for a particular student. Following this interview, the special education teacher completes a Student-Teacher Match form (see Figure 11–4), which is based on the SBS *Inventory of Teacher Social Behavior Standards and Expectations* (Walker & Rankin, 1980b) for selecting regular classroom teachers for mainstreamed students with EBD. This form also asks for information regarding the amount and kind of technical assistance the teacher would need for the student to be placed, as well as supportive plans for the student and teacher.

MONITORING AND FOLLOW-UP ASSESSMENT. The purposes of follow-up assessments are to monitor and evaluate the student's current status with regard to IEP or intervention objectives, to evaluate how well the program prepared the student for integration, or to evaluate the accuracy with which staff members implement transition procedures. Follow-up data thus serve three func-

tions: to certify that objectives have been reached; to provide feedback for use in revising programs for future students; and to determine whether strategies are being properly implemented.

If the student has been certified previously as having a disability, follow-up data regarding IEP goals and objectives may be used as a basis for deciding that special education classification is no longer needed. In Chapter 1 we recommended that IEP teams specify criteria for decertification of pupils once conditions that caused them to be certified are remediated. The IEP should contain goals and objectives related to successful integration or reintegration into the educational mainstream; therefore, follow-up assessment in mainstream settings is needed for making decertification decisions. Follow-up evaluation of the maintenance and generalization of intervention effects is more specific and precise because the focus of assessment is on targeted behaviors. These assessments may or may not occur in settings outside the educational program.

The specific follow-up assessment procedures used depend upon the student's current educational placement. If the pupil is in your classroom, follow-up may involve conducting measurement probes of targeted behaviors after an educational program or intervention strategy has been terminated. If the student has been moved to a less restrictive setting, the same behaviors should be monitored, but the measurement strategy used will be influenced by the setting and the person using it. For example, if you must rely on a mainstream classroom teacher to do the assessment, you probably will select a less technically demanding procedure than you would if you were monitoring the behavior yourself. In such circumstances you may elect to have the teacher complete a behavior rating scale or evaluate the student against criteria for behaviors in her classroom (e.g., is the target pupil's frequency of disruptive behavior higher than, about the same as, or lower than that of the average student?). Frequency counts of discrete behaviors are preferable, and these data are even better when rates of similar

General Classroom Teacher K. C. Kray   Date of Observation 3/18/98

A. Use of Classroom Time
1. Percentage of time spent on academic learning   90   %
2. Percentage of time spent on group work   75   %
3. Percentage of time spent on independent work   25   %
4. Average amount of time spent in transition from one activity to the next   2   min or sec
5. Average amount of time unassigned   5   min or sec
6. Systematic way teacher deals with student wait-time   __X__ Yes   _____ No

B. Instruction
1. Teacher gives clear and complete directions and instructions   __X__ Yes   _____ No
2. Teacher's lessons are highly structured and clearly presented   __X__ Yes   _____ No
3. Teacher's instruction is responsive to individual needs and the readiness
   levels of students   __X__ Yes   _____ No

C. Questioning/Feedback/Student Involvement
1. Teacher encourages students to take an active role in learning   __X__ Yes   _____ No
2. Teacher asks primarily low-order, content-related questions   _____ Yes   __X__ No
3. Students are able to respond correctly to most of the teacher's questions __X__ Yes   _____ No
4. Teacher gives frequent positive feedback to correct student responses   __X__ Yes   _____ No
5. Teacher gives sustaining feedback to incorrect student responses   _____ Yes   __X__ No
6. Teacher seldom uses criticism in responding to student answers   __X__ Yes   _____ No

D. Classroom Management
1. Teacher articulates positive expectations for students' academic success _____ Yes   __X__ No
2. Teacher monitors students' work during independent seatwork   __X__ Yes   _____ No
3. Teacher communicates clear standards and expectations for behavior   __X__ Yes   _____ No
4. Teacher consistently applies consequences for meeting standards and
   expectations   _____ Yes   __X__ No
5. Teacher keeps students engaged in lessons   __X__ Yes   _____ No
6. Teacher seldom has to intervene in behavioral problems   __X__ Yes   _____ No
7. Teacher seldom uses punitive intervention   __X__ Yes   _____ No
8. Teacher uses supportive interventions   __X__ Yes   _____ No
9. Teacher's interventions appear to be effective   __X__ Yes   _____ No

E. Classroom Climate
Teacher demonstrates the following characteristics (check if yes):

_____ Flexibility   __X__ Consistency   _____ Warmth   __X__ Active Involvement with Students
__X__ Fairness   __X__ Responsiveness _____ Humor
__X__ Firmness   __X__ Patience

FIGURE 11–3   Mainstream classroom observation (MCO) form.

Source: Wong, K. L. H., Kauffman, J. M., & Lloyd, J. W. (1991). *Choices for integration: Selecting teachers for mainstreaming students with emotional or behavioral disorders.* Intervention in School and Clinic, 27, 108–115. Copyright PRO-ED. Used with permission.

behaviors collected on nontarget peers are available for comparison (see Chapter 2). However, such procedures require trained observers.

Although data obtained from these procedures cannot be compared to the graphs and charts used

to analyze the student and his program while in your classroom, they can serve to socially validate that behavioral changes have taken place. Because others' perceptions of the student in his natural environment is the ultimate test of success in

General Classroom Teacher _____Mrs. K. C._____   Date _____3/19/01_____

Student To Be Mainstreamed _____Michael_____

	Teacher Willingness		Student Performances		
A. Types of Behavior Teacher Deems Critical for Success	Is Willing to Work on Behavior	Is Not Willing To Work on Behavior	Exhibits Behavior Consistently	Exhibits Improving Behavior	Lacks Appropriate Behavior
1. Following directions	X	___	___	X	___
2. Completing assignments	X	___	___	___	X
3. Cooperating with peers	X	___	___	X	___
4.	___	___	___	___	___
5.	___	___	___	___	___

	Teacher Willingness		Student Performances		
B. Types of Behavior Teacher Deems Intolerable	Is Willing to Work on Behavior	Is Not Willing To Work on Behavior	Does Not Exhibit Behavior	Exhibits Behavior but Improving	Frequently Exhibits Behavior
1. Hitting and fighting	___	X	X	___	___
2. Disrupting others in class	X	___	___	X	___
3. Refusing to follow directions	X	___	___	X	___
4. Whining	X	___	X	___	___
5.	___	___	___	___	___

C. **Kind and Amount of Technical Assistance Teacher Desires** Help in designing a behavior management program for student: ongoing support in helping student reduce intolerable behaviors; daily monitoring of student's performance in mainstream classroom.

   Desired Technical Assistance Can Be Provided __X__ Yes _____ No

   Comments Student's current behavior contract program can be modified for use in mainstream classroom.

D. **Supportive Plans for Moving Student into Mainstream Classroom** Special education teacher will meet general classroom teacher before placement date to discuss specific needs of student; student's behavior contract program will be reviewed. Special education teacher will introduce student to general classroom teacher and student will visit mainstream classroom before actual placement date. Special education teacher will monitor student's adjustment and progress on a daily basis (during resource period).

E. **Contingency Plans in Case Student is Not Successful in Mainstream Classroom** General classroom teacher and special education teacher will discuss presenting problems and try to address these without having to remove student from mainstream classroom. If difficulties persist, student will be taken out of the mainstream classroom and returned to special class.

FIGURE 11–4   Student/teacher match (STM) form.

Source: Wong, K. L. H., Kauffman, J. M., & Lloyd, J. W. (1991). Choices for integration: Selecting teachers for mainstreaming students with emotional or behavioral disorders. Intervention in School and Clinic. 27, 108–115. Copyright PRO-ED. Used with permission.

readjusting, these data should not be treated lightly. However, if you can obtain measures that are more comparable to the data you collected during intervention phases, a more specific analysis of the student's current status is possible. This can be important if target behaviors once again are problematic and you need to assess their occurrence in the new environment. If you are unable to collect these data, or if your presence in the environment influences the pupil's behavior, follow the guidelines presented in Chapter 3 for training other observers.

Finally, the length and schedule of follow-up assessments should be geared to the student, the behaviors, and the settings in which assessments are conducted. If you follow the suggestions in Chapter 3 (collect data that are sensitive to the changes you want to occur; measure only behaviors to which you will respond), follow-up data collection should not be unduly time consuming. You may want to monitor some behaviors closely (e.g., verbal threats having a history of leading to physical aggression); others may require less regular scrutiny because they are less important to the pupil's success in the new setting. Some data are easy to collect (e.g., number of assignments completed), whereas other data require more time and effort (e.g., time on-task). In general, use data that are readily available and that the classroom teacher, employer, or caregiver keeps and uses anyway.

Data pertaining to the student's adjustment to the expectations of the mainstream classroom environment thus can be as specific or general as necessary. The important point is to establish, and use, a feedback loop, in which you and your colleagues collect and respond to information about the student's performance. Figure 11–5 illustrates a simple daily evaluation form. The format may be adapted to suit the student's age, grade, or subject, or the student may evaluate himself and have the mainstream teacher sign it. Depending on circumstances, the student can bring the cards to you or the classroom teacher may keep them for periodic review with you. You also may ask the classroom teacher to rate the frequency of behaviors he previously identified as critical or unacceptable. For example, you can construct a three-point checklist of the behaviors that a teacher indicated as critical to success in her classroom: (1) indicates that the student is acceptably skilled, (2) indicates less than acceptable skill, and (3) indicates much less than acceptable skill. If you are monitoring specific target behaviors, however, you or

the classroom teacher should be able and willing to collect direct observation data. It is critical that you and the teacher meet regularly to review these data and design collaborative strategies to intervene when needed. As students demonstrate increasingly consistent adjustment, decrease the frequency of monitoring. Another strategy is to have the student rate or count her own behavior (see Chapter 3).

If the student has been transferred out of your building or even further away, follow-up will be sporadic, at best. Few agencies are interested in the status of clients once their direct service responsibilities have ended. Still, you may make telephone, e-mail, or conventional mail contacts to assess your former pupils' present status. No matter where former students are located, schedule follow-up contacts on your calendar so you will not forget. Initially, follow-up intervals should be brief (1 to 3 weeks). Thin the schedule as time passes (e.g., 1-, 6-, and 18-month intervals). At some point, you will be able to decide to discontinue evaluation. As with other phases of assessment, your data will suggest when you reach this point.

Another reason for conducting follow-up assessments is to evaluate the implementation of maintenance and generalization training procedures. These evaluations address the question of **procedural reliability** (Tawney & Gast, 1984), or the extent to which intervention procedures are being followed. The recommended format for such assessments is a behavioral checklist containing a list of intervention procedures that are checked (by an observer familiar with the intervention) according to whether they are implemented properly. Figure 11–6 illustrates a procedural reliability checklist for a DRO intervention. Intervention steps that are not being properly implemented indicate a need for feedback or retraining of the responsible persons. Assessment of procedural reliability is important, especially for identifying implementation failures when staff members report that a procedure "is not working." Having a plan for sustaining accurate implementation of the intervention

Student's Name ______________ Date ______ Class ________

Yes	No		Comments
____	____	Followed classroom rules	
____	____	Demonstrated appropriate social behavior	
____	____	Completed work on time	
____	____	Tried his/her best	

Teacher's Signature ____________________

FIGURE 11–5 Sample daily teacher report card.

Observer ____________________ Observation Dates ________

	Observations		
	1	*2*	*3*
1. Length of DRO interval is set (interval length _____ secs/mins)	____	____	____
2. Teacher accurately observes occurrence/nonoccurrence of target behavior during interval.	____	____	____
3. Behavior *does not* occur during interval.	____	____	____
3.1 Teacher delivers reinforcer immediately upon end of interval.	____	____	____
3.2 Teacher resets interval timer.	____	____	____
4. Behavior *does* occur during interval.	____	____	____
4.1 Teacher does not respond to behavior.	____	____	____
4.2 Teacher resets interval timer.	____	____	____

FIGURE 11–6 DRO procedural reliability checklist.

procedures also is important, especially when procedural reliability data indicate that procedures are not being implemented as planned. Noell et al. (2000) demonstrated that general education teachers improved their implementation of a peer tutoring reading comprehension program when they received brief daily performance feedback from consultants.

Obviously, effective transition to less restrictive educational environments is much more than simply placing students who appear ready to make the necessary adjustments. To improve the educational performance of students with EBD, it is necessary to work closely with general education staff, acknowledging and responding to their expectations and needs for support. Few individual special education teachers have the time or authority to serve in this capacity. This is another reason for having behavior support teams in schools.

Transitions to Other Settings

As a group, children and youth with significant behavior challenges are involved in numerous transitions. Although they are the last group of students with disabilities to be identified and placed in special education programs (U.S. Department of Education, 2000), they often have histories of multiple placements in the regular educational system prior to their referral to special education (Walker, Shinn, O'Neill, & Ramsey, 1987). The transitions they make include changes in school districts, classrooms, and programs (e.g., Chapter 1, remedial classes). Presumably, these alternate placements are attempts to meet students' needs, but it is likely that the motivation is to reduce disruptions to the settings from which the students were removed.

Students who have been identified as having EBD also are extremely mobile. Although in the previous section we discussed transitions to less restrictive educational settings, their transitions typically involve movement to more restrictive educational settings (Rock et al., 1994; Stephens & Lakin, 1995). Moreover, in their study of students in separate facilities for children and youth with disabilities, Stephens and Lakin (1995) found that facilities primarily serving students with EBD reported considerably greater turnover and shorter average lengths of stay than did facilities serving children with varying disabilities. Also, compared with day programs for students with varying disabilities, nearly twice as many students leaving day programs for students with EBD either had no next placement or the placement was unknown to the staff. Approximately 20% of those leaving day or residential programs for students with EBD were transferred to another separate facility.

As these findings suggest, the teacher of children and youth with EBD, whether in public school or separate day or residential programs, should expect the management of transitions to be a significant component of her job. Next, we describe transitions to more restrictive settings and to adult life.

TRANSITIONS TO MORE RESTRICTIVE SETTINGS. As we have just indicated, a typical movement of public school students with EBD is toward more restrictive environments. These settings include segregated special classes, special day programs in the public schools, day treatment programs, residential school programs, residential psychiatric facilities, and juvenile correctional programs. Unfortunately, such transitions often appear to be made for the convenience of the school and community rather than to meet the needs of the student.

Frequently, movement to more restrictive settings entails transitions between separate agencies (e.g., public schools and juvenile correctional or residential treatment programs). Edgar et al. (1987) identified three components to the transition process: (a) a sending agency, which has the student who is being transferred elsewhere, (b) a receiving agency, which gets the student, and (c) the hand-off, which is a process and a set of procedures for moving the student and his records from one agency to another. According to Edgar et al. (1987), six issues are involved between agencies when making transitions:

1. *Awareness.* Sending and receiving agencies need to learn about each other's programs and services. Unfortunately, most agencies operate without such information.
2. *Eligibility criteria.* The sending agency should have a working knowledge of the eligibility criteria of the agencies whose services may help their students or clients. Obviously, a lack of information about other agencies suggests that knowledge of eligibility criteria also is lacking.
3. *Exchange of information.* The receiving agency needs information before the client arrives. The transfer of student records is a

universal problem. Often, records do not arrive in time to be used in placement or planning, and in many cases, the student has left the agency before her school records are obtained.

4. *Program planning before transition.* This should involve both sending and receiving agencies so that students are prepared for the programs they are about to enter and so their new programs will capitalize on the gains made in the old ones.

5. *Feedback after transition.* Feedback to the sending agency is essential for program evaluation and modification. Without it agencies are left to repeat the mistakes of the past, which often is the case.

6. *Written procedures.* Formal written procedures ensure that important hand-off activities take place. If only one staff person knows the procedures, there will be nothing in place should that person leave, unless procedures are formalized in writing.

If these issues are not addressed, students experience a lack of continuity in their educational programming, which may express itself in terms of repeating a curriculum they have completed already or being exposed to a curriculum that is inappropriate for their skills and needs. As a classroom teacher, you should be involved in transition activities at either the sending or receiving level to help ensure continuity of instructional and behavioral interventions. Your participation in site-based management teams will help you ensure that your agency's policies include important collaborative interagency linkages.

TRANSITIONS TO POST-SECONDARY SCHOOL ENVIRONMENTS. PL 94-142 mandated that schools serve children and youth with disabilities through age 21, and subsequent amendments have added specific emphasis to the provision of transition services to help these people adjust to adult living. The law now requires that, when students reach the age of 14, their IEPs must include a statement of transition needs, and that IEPs of students 16 or younger must contain a statement of needed transition services, including, where appropriate, interagency responsibilities or needed linkages (Maag & Katsiyannis, 1998). Unfortunately, follow-up studies of the post-school status of youth with disabilities indicate that the special education enterprise has not been overwhelmingly successful in terms of preparing these young persons for successful post-school adjustment, particularly students with EBD (Frank & Sitlingtonm 1997; Malmgren, Edgar, & Neel, 1998; McLaughlin, Leone, Warren, & Schofield, 1994).

For over two decades, the **criterion of ultimate functioning** (Brown, Nietupski, & Hamre-Nietupski, 1976) has influenced curriculum planning for pupils with moderate to severe disabilities. This top-down approach to curriculum design begins with the assessment of the skill demands of the least restrictive adult environments in which the student is likely to function, and the curriculum is developed around pupils' skill deficiencies based on these expectations. However, determining which adult environments are least restrictive for students exhibiting widely varying levels of cognitive, academic, and social functioning is complex in itself and must be accomplished before the expectations of these settings can be assessed. Therefore, specific post-school objectives for students with less severe disabilities, based on assumptions about the limits of their future capabilities, are more difficult to develop while they are still in school. We are not suggesting that objectives relevant to post-school living cannot be established for these youth; appropriate social behaviors are useful in all adult settings and are needed by persons at all levels of cognitive functioning. Students who interview for jobs or admission to post-secondary schools, who go out on dates, or who visit their local hair salon need to employ these skills every day.

Unfortunately, it is apparent that the lack of such skills is a common denominator among individuals who display chronic emotional and behavioral problems. For example, Walker and his colleagues (Shinn, Ramsey, Walker, Stieber, & O'Neill, 1987; Walker et al., 1987) identified behavioral differences between fifth-grade boys who were designated antisocial (on the basis of familial variables) and a control group of boys who were designated at risk for engaging in antisocial behavior. The behavior patterns that differentiated the antisocial group included less time engaged in academics, higher rates of negative interactions with peers, more school discipline contacts, and lower teacher ratings of social skills. The behavioral characteristics of older youth and adults who are at risk for criminal behavior or who are incarcerated reveal similar patterns (Nelson & Pearson, 1994; Nelson, Rutherford, & Wolford, 1987). Walker & Stieber (1998) found that teacher rating of social skills in grade 5 were significant predictors of police contacts and arrest status through grade 11. Thus, early maladaptive social behavior patterns appear to be predictive of lifelong patterns of social failure (Robbins, 1966; Van Hasselt, Hersen, Whitehill, & Bellack, 1979). Early identification and remediation of social skills deficits in children who are at risk should be a major educational priority.

Planning for transitions to adulthood may not prevent the failure of all, or even many, students with behavior problems, but neither should it be assumed that the existence of problem behaviors condemns pupils to lives of crime or institutionalization. Transition programs for adolescents are useful for bridging the gap between school and productive adult experiences. If a transition plan is to be meaningfully linked to the student's post-school life, it should be initiated well before graduation. Maag and Katsiyannis (1998) identified several promising transition practices, which included: (a) interagency collaboration; (b) the presence of a strong transition coordinator; (c) comprehensive educational programming that includes vocational preparation, social skills, and self-awareness training as well as effective academic instruction; (d) identification of school and community services to meet individual needs; (e) parental involvement; and (f) supported employment.

Transition plans must be developed with persons who have a stake in the pupil's post-school adjustment (e.g., parents, the student himself), and they should involve agencies and service providers who can address the student's likely post-school needs. Transition plans also should take into account the wide range of options the student may consider as an adult. Therefore, a team of persons who know and care about the student should develop transition plans, and community-based service providers should be involved well before the student leaves school. Maag and Katsiyannis (1998) argue that school personnel are best suited to assume the role of transition coordinator because of their greater familiarity with the student, and because IDEA requires that transition strategies be initiated well before students leave school. Unfortunately, as Maag and Katsiyannis also point out, the high drop-out rate of students with EBD poses a significant barrier to the implementation of school-based transition activities. Therefore, a critical element of effective transition is keeping the student in school.

As we have emphasized throughout this text, an effective strategy for keeping students engaged in school is meaningful and effective academic and social skills instruction. In addition, instruction in daily living skills, vocational planning, and individual counseling should be part of the services offered in school. Rylance (1997) found that students with EBD who received counseling and vocational education had significantly higher graduation rates than those who did not receive these services.

It would be naive to assume that school-based interventions alone are sufficient to enable adolescents with emotional and behavior problems to successfully enter adult living and working environments. Ideally, they also should have the benefit of **community-based training** during their public school years. Community-based instruction has played an important role in the curriculum of pupils with moderate and severe disabilities, and many good models are available (e.g., see Goetz, Guess, & Stremel-Campbell, 1987; Taylor, Bilken, &

Knoll, 1987). Much less attention has been paid to teaching social skills to students with so-called "mild" disabilities in the community settings where these skills are critical to their successful adjustment. Given that many adolescents with EBD fail to make adequate adjustments to adult life (Frank & Sitlington, 1997; Malmgren et al., 1998; McLaughlin et al., 1994), appropriate changes in the secondary school curriculum for these students clearly are needed.

It is important to recognize that EBD is extremely durable and has deleterious long-term effects (Bullis & Paris, 1996). Therefore, one aspect of post-school transition is maintaining service coordination with agencies and the family to ensure that students continue to receive adequate support. Sample (1998) observed that, relative to students with other disabilities, fewer adult services are available to students with EBD after they leave school, and these individuals are more likely to refuse to attend eligibility meetings with potential adult services providers. As Walker and Bullis (1996) indicate, the goal for working with older adolescents and young adults with EBD probably should be accommodation; that is, to reduce the negative impact of their disability on successful adjustment. Alarm regarding the costs of a community-based support system to achieve the necessary level of accommodation should be balanced by the realization that these are no greater than the staggering costs of long-term institutionalization. At this level, the transition plan might better be conceptualized as a *wraparound plan*, because it emphasizes providing ongoing support to the individual across multiple life domains. Moreover, the client in a community-based *system of care* is far less likely to be a financial burden to his family or society.

Including the student's parents or primary caregivers throughout the process provides greater assurance that the transition plan will address life domains that are relevant, and this strategy also increases the likelihood of their ongoing involvement and cooperation. The provision of opportunities for paid work experience while in school also is more likely to keep the youth productively engaged after leaving school. Sample (1998) found that parent involvement and student work experience were factors that differentiated former students with EBD who had better post-school outcomes.

Clark, Unger, & Stewart (1993) describe four domains that should be considered in transition planning for students with EBD (see Table 11–2): Alternatives such as college, military service, and independent living should be considered in addition to employment. Support services likely to be needed (e.g., mental health counseling, daily living support, vocational training) should be indicated, and representatives from agencies that provide services (e.g., community mental health, developmental disabilities council, vocational rehabilitation) should participate in drafting the transition plan. Implementation of the plan should begin during the pupil's secondary school experience and should continue until the structure and support provided by the plan are no longer needed. Bearing in mind that individuals with EBD appear to be extremely resistant to intervention (Sample, 1998), including transition-related activities, ensure that the plan is relevant, supportive, and responsive to the youth's evolving needs. If you are in a position to be involved in post-secondary school transition planning, consult Brolin (1995). A transition plan for a student with EBD is illustrated in the case study at the end of this chapter.

EFFECTIVE COLLABORATION

As we have emphasized throughout this chapter, the successful maintenance and generalization of behavioral improvements requires the involvement of other persons in other settings. Even if you serve students with behavior problems in a single classroom setting, your work will lead you into other environments, both within and outside the school. In this section we present a number of suggestions and strategies to increase your effectiveness with other professionals and lay persons in these settings.

TABLE 11–2 Transition Domains

A. Employment
   1. Competitive employment
   2. Supported employment (individual and enclave)
   3. Transitional employment opportunities
   4. Work experience opportunities
B. Education opportunities
   1. Workplace educational programs
   2. High school completion of GED certificate
   3. Vocational or technical certification
   4. Associate's degree
   5. Bachelor's degree or beyond
C. Independent living
   1. Independent residence
   2. Residence with natural, adoptive, or foster family
   3. Semi-independent living (e.g., nonlive-in case manager assists)
   4. Supported living (e.g., supervised apartment)
   5. Group home or boarding home
D. Community life: Skill development and activities related to domains A, B, and C
   1. Leisure time activities and fun
   2. Social interaction and problem-solving skills (e.g., self-advocacy)
   3. Relationship development (e.g., friendships, intimate relationships)
   4. Peer support groups
   5. Emotional/behavioral management (e.g., anger control, relapse prevention, self-medication management)
   6. Safety skills (e.g., prevent victimization, avoid dangerous situations)
   7. Daily living skills (e.g., eating nutritious food, leasing an apartment)
   8. Health care and fitness (e.g., stress management, physical activity)
   9. Substance abuse prevention and maintenance
   10. Sex education and birth control (e.g., prevention of sexually transmitted diseases and unwanted pregnancies)
   11. Community resources (knowledge and utilization)
   12. Transportation skills
   13. Cultural/spiritual/religious resources

Source: Clark, H. B., Unger, K. V., and Stewart, E. S. (1993). Transition of youth and young adults with emotional/behavioral disorders into employment, education and independent living. Community Alternatives: International Journal of Family Care, 5(2), 19–46. Copyright Human Services Associates, Inc. Reproduced with permission.

Working with School Personnel

In a typical school building, residential facility, or institution, there are a number of people who can be resources for students with emotional and behavioral problems. The extent of their involvement may range from praising a student's achievement to taking pupils on after-school trips, from simply rating performance as acceptable or unacceptable to taking frequency data, and from following a plan worked out by you to collaborating in the development of a complete intervention strategy. Different persons may prove useful for different func-

tions, and we hope the checklist in Figure 11–2 helps you develop a profile of your various personnel resources.

Before you approach anyone to assist you with a pupil or program, get your objective clearly in mind. Do you want to assess the generalization of change in a target behavior? Do you want to evaluate a trial mainstream placement? Do you want to establish other persons as social reinforcers? Do you want to increase the availability of reinforcement outside your classroom? Do you need assistance with a potential emergency situations?

Each objective dictates a different tactic. When you enlist the cooperation of other people, explain clearly what you would like them to do, as well as when and how they are to communicate to you regarding their work with the pupil or pupils.

Once again, a written plan is the best approach if the program is complex. Conflicts may arise between involved parties, such as teachers and school administrators; each party may want to impose its agenda on your program (the teacher wants the student to suit up for gym; the principal wants him to arrive at school on time). Remember, though, that the *student* is your client (the person who is to benefit from the program). This focus is somewhat different from the one you use when you are serving as a consultant, where your client is the person who comes to you with the problem. Many a good teacher has been rendered ineffective by trying to serve too many clients with conflicting demands. A written plan should specify objectives and roles at the outset, thereby preventing such episodes.

One such planning tool is a school-based wraparound plan.[4] This format is useful for planning the structure and support for students who need the most intensive level of positive behavior support, as described in Chapter 1. Like a transition plan, this individualized plan is developed and implemented by a team of professionals and family members who know the student best. The wraparound plan must address the student's typical day and provide behavioral support where it is needed, as well as systematic reinforcement in settings in which the student typically behaves appropriately. It is driven by the needs of the student rather than the services traditionally available in the school. It also typically addresses services and supports that extend to life domains beyond the school. Thus, the resources, structure, and supports for each targeted student must be flexible and creative. For example, if managing un-

structured times and settings (e.g., hallways, cafeteria, bus waiting areas) is a difficult task for the student, a wraparound plan might consist of enlisting the aid of a member of the school staff to escort him to his locker and then the classroom. Several peer "buddies" or mentors may be recruited to accompany him on the bus, in the halls and cafeteria, and to the restroom. Or teachers may stand outside their classroom doors during class breaks to monitor his behavior during transitions. As he makes progress, this structure may be loosened so that the pupil maintains a self-monitoring checklist, which is reviewed several times daily with his wraparound coordinator. Figure 11–7 (Eber, 1995) describes more of the features of a wraparound plan.

In working with school staff, remember that adults need support and reinforcement too; therefore, find out what teachers need, set up communication channels, and be sure to show your appreciation for their assistance. You can increase the likelihood of a wraparound plan being followed by meeting the teacher's need (e.g., arrange to help supervise difficult transition times) or providing needed materials (e.g., a checklist for classroom teachers to complete, a roll of smiley-face stickers for the cafeteria cashier or bus driver to put on the shirts of well-behaved students, a wrist counter for the librarian to use in counting disruptions).

The school principal traditionally is regarded by pupils (and teachers) as the major disciplinarian for a building. In view of this, having the principal deliver reinforcement can be a potent tactic, as several studies demonstrated. Copeland, Brown, and Hall (1974) found in three separate studies that contingent principal recognition and praise increased attendance and academic performance. Brown, Copeland, and Hall (1972) involved a principal in administering tokens, playing basketball with pupils, and providing the opportunity to work on bicycles in the school basement, contingent upon appropriate school behaviors. The school counselor also can provide reinforcement or other services. Clore (1974) had a school-phobic child

[4]As explained in Chapter 2, wraparound is an approach to planning and implementing services to students with needs in multiple life domains. It is not a set of services or an intervention strategy.

The wraparound process is based on individualized, needs-driven planning and services. **It is not a program or a type of service.** It is a value base and an unconditional commitment to create services on a "one student at a time" basis to support normalized and inclusive options for students with complex needs.

A child and family team, consisting of the people who know the student best, develop an **individualized plan.**

This plan is **needs driven** rather than service driven. Services are not based on a categorical model but on specific needs of the student, family, and teacher.

The plan is based on **needs identified by the family.**

The plan is based on **teacher expectations.**

The plan is **strengths based.** Human services traditionally have relied on the deficit model, focusing on pathology. Positive reframing to assets and skills is a key element in all individualized planning.

The plan focuses on **normalization.** Normalized needs are those basic human needs that all persons (of like age, sex, and culture) have.

The team makes a commitment to **unconditional care.** Services and interventions are changed to meet the needs of the student rather than referring her to another setting.

Academic and support services are created to meet the unique needs of the student. Though many plans rely on blending and reshaping categorical services, teams have the capacity to **create individualized supports and activities.**

Services are **based in natural school environments.** Restrictive settings are accessed only for brief periods of stabilization.

Services are **culturally competent.** The composition of the team ensures a fit to the person's culture and community.

Planning and services are **comprehensive,** addressing needs in three or more domain areas. These life domains are family, living situation, vocational/educational, social/recreational, psychological/emotional, medical, legal, and safety/crisis.

The plan is financially supported by **flexible** use of existing categorical resources or through a **flexible funding mechanism.**

Outcome measures are identified and measured often and are generated by parent and teacher expectations.

FIGURE 11–7 What is wraparound?

report to the counselor's office each morning, and the counselor assisted in successfully phasing the student back into his classroom.

The school administrative staff may be helpful in other ways as well. For example, many reinforcing activities occur around the school office: pupils can deliver attendance slips or notes, answer the telephone, run the ditto machine, file, or perform other office tasks as reinforcement for desired behaviors. The main reason such opportunities are not taken is that teachers seldom think of them. Few persons will refuse to provide such experiences if you ask them (and remember to follow up with reinforcement).

Involving yourself has the further advantage of increasing your visibility to, and interaction with, school staff, which lessens the stigma attached both to teachers and students who spend much of the day in segregated special classrooms. Volunteering to sponsor all-school activities such as clubs and social events will improve your standing with pupils outside your classroom. Also, do not shirk cafeteria or bus duty, and don't do all your work in the classroom where you are isolated from your colleagues. Instead, spend some of your time working in the teachers' lounge. In our experience, the more successful special education teachers are actively involved in the total school environment. When you are working with pupils with EBD, visibility and involvement are especially important because of the fear and misconceptions regarding persons with mental disabilities.

In developing intervention plans that wraparound a student and her school day, it is important to recognize that schools are rich in intervention resources. In addition to the school staff mentioned previously, other students may be used as models, tutors, reinforcing agents, and monitors for wraparound plans. For students who need this level of structure, it is essential that environmental assessments be performed to identify those settings and times of the day when wraparound support is needed. It also is important to schedule regular meetings with the wraparound team to ensure that the plan is being implemented properly and the student is making progress.

Working with Families

Those who provide daily care of children with EBD, as well as those who live with them, need as much, if not more, support than do professional service providers. They also have unique perspectives on the strengths and issues these children present. At the same time, the blame that has been assigned to parents of students with EBD, as well as the disruptions created by living with children who exhibit such great challenges, has caused them to refrain from vigorously advocating for their children. The development of community system of care approaches for children and families with the most intensive level of needs, and the emergence of strong family organizations (e.g., the PACER Center, the Alliance of Families for Children's Mental Health) are changing this picture for the better. Family members now are acknowledged as essential to effective wraparound teams. Two specific ways in which professionals can improve outcomes for students and assist families include (a) helping them address a child's behavior in their home or neighborhood, and (b) helping families support academic and behavioral improvements made at school. Each goal calls for a slightly different approach.

FAMILY IMPLEMENTATION OF POSITIVE BEHAVIOR SUPPORT. If you and the parents agree on the need to use behavioral support at home, you are putting yourself in a consultative relationship. Because caregivers have learned to expect teachers to deal directly with their children and, consequently, may be less prone to let you help them, this relationship can be a difficult one. Also, parents of children with behavior problems (especially children who have been certified as having EBD) may be defensive about admitting their problems because, in the past, it was fairly common to attribute children's behavior disorders to faulty parenting. Fortunately, as mentioned above, families are becoming empowered to work actively on behalf of their children and are being included as equal partners with professionals in planning and implementing services (DeChillo, Koren, & Schultz, 1994; Friesen & Wahlers, 1993). Comprehensive systems of care have a distinctly family-centered focus, in which families are regarded as a source of support and strength, not of dysfunction and pathology (Duchnowski, Berg, & Kutash, 1995). Such national organizations as the Federation of Families for Children's Mental Health and the National Alliance for the Mentally Ill—Children and Adolescent Network have provided strong political advocacy where none has existed before.

Nevertheless, some professionals still hold the view that parents are the cause of their children's emotional and behavioral disorders and, because parents' interactions with school personnel tend to be negative, they may avoid working with school staff. One way around this problem is to treat the task of helping parents more effectively address the needs of their child as an educational issue, rather than as a problem requiring psychotherapy or analysis. Parents are essential partners for students who need the structure of wraparound service plans. As Eber (1995) emphasizes, such plans should be based on needs identified by the family, as well as on teacher expectations. By including parents on the wraparound service team for their child, professionals not only gain important information about the child and her needs, but they also enlist an important ally in their efforts to help the student. When families are full participants in developing a team-based wraparound plan, their resistance tends to disappear. The wraparound emphasis on strength-based planning, and the focus on strengthening desired replacement behaviors that is inherent in positive behavior support, also help to break down barriers. Another suggestion is to maintain a focus on the child. Presenting ideas and techniques to help the parents address their child's behavior problems at home is likely to meet with less resistance than giving them the impression that their parenting skills need a major overhaul.

When parents do recognize a problem or agree to help, the team has several options. One is to set up a specific home-based positive behavior support program, following the steps delineated in Chapter 2. There is evidence that parents can successfully implement such procedures with professional guidance. For example, Christophersen, Arnold, Hill, and Quilitch (1972) taught two sets of parents who had five children between them to administer a token economy in their homes. The parents successfully altered 21 problem behaviors, including refusing to perform chores, bickering, teasing, whining, and refusing to go to bed. However, as the authors observed, these were not severe behavior disorders. Strain and Danko (1995) taught caregivers to implement a social skills training program and to encourage positive interactions between three 3- to 4-year-old children with autism and their siblings. The caregivers were quite successful in applying the interventions and reported that they were simple to learn, easy to apply, and enjoyable.

If you have several interested parents, a parent education group may be a useful strategy (Rinn, Vernon, & Wise, 1975). Several formats have been used. The format we prefer combines instruction in behavioral principles and procedures with specific problem-solving consultation. Parents show more interest in learning principles when they can immediately apply them to their children's behav-

iors. However, as Ferber, Keeley, and Shemberg (1974) found, a short-term parent course may be insufficient without long-term follow-up consultation for other problem behaviors. Also, aggressive children who display problems in the community may not be helped at all through parent education (Ferber et al., 1974). For these individuals, more extensive community-based intervention may be required. If you need to go this far, consider developing a comprehensive wraparound plan or referring the problem to another agency (see Chapter 12).

PARENTAL SUPPORT OF CLASSROOM GOALS.
If caregivers are to support classroom goals, they should have input in identifying target behaviors and interventions. It also requires a school-home communication system, for parents can hardly be expected to support the objectives of a behavior change program if they do not understand them or have little access to information regarding their child's progress.[5] Traditional reporting systems (e.g., grade cards) are unsuitable for this type of communication because they are infrequent and they tend to communicate little useful information. Parental response to an unsatisfactory report card may be inappropriate, or caregivers may fail to respond at all to good reports. Therefore, we suggest a frequent (daily or weekly) reporting system that conveys meaningful information to parents and to which they may respond in a systematic manner. This implies that you have worked out a plan with the family beforehand. Tell them what to expect (e.g., a daily or weekly report containing points their child has earned for academic work and for social behavior each day), when to expect it (e.g., every day after school), and how to respond to each report (e.g., praise when the point total is above 35, and for each subject or area for which four or more points are awarded).

---

[5]IDEA requires that individual program objectives be developed in collaboration with parents and guarantees parents access to their child's school records.

Where more solid home support is needed, work with parents to set up explicit home contingencies based on their child's school performance. For example, they may provide extra privileges for good reports (specify the criteria for a "good" report) or lose privileges for a poor report. If required, you may even work out a menu of back-up home consequences similar to the classroom menu presented in Chapter 6. This provides for differential reinforcement and long-term savings for special privileges or treats (e.g., a movie, a fishing trip). It is preferable to work out the details of more elaborate systems with a simple contract among the pupil, parents, and you. All parties should sign and receive copies of the contract.

Figure 11–8 shows a variety of daily report cards (these also could be weekly). Panels A and B present forms useful for preschool and primary-age students. Panel C is a simple checklist for middle-grade students, and Panel D shows a form for reporting daily points. Panel E is a checklist for upper-level or secondary pupils and may be used with students in general education classrooms. One problem with daily report cards is that students may lose them. If you advise parents to respond to a missing report as though it were poor or below criterion, this problem seldom persists. If you are concerned that parents fail to read the report, include in the contract an agreement that they are to sign reports and return them the next day. Graphs and charts such as those presented in Chapter 3 also may be sent home on a daily or weekly basis.

Home-school communication systems that use back-up home contingencies offer several advantages. First, they provide contingent consequences at home for performance in school. This can be a great help for students who do not respond well to school consequences (e.g., pupils who "do not care" if they miss recess or back-up reinforcers available at school). Second, they keep caregivers informed of their child's progress and get them involved in what is going on at school. Third, by emphasizing reinforcing consequences for good performance, they break down the common expectation among parents of children with behavioral problems that all school reports are bad reports. Furthermore, by teaching parents to reinforce their children, you may help break the criticism-punishment cycle that is prevalent in families with children who exhibit behavioral problems.

If properly used, school-home communication systems can be very effective. For instance, Ayllon, Garber, and Pisor (1975), sent a good behavior letter home with students in a third-grade class for meeting criteria for good conduct. Receipt or non-receipt of these letters resulted in differential consequences by the parents. Disruptive behavior, which averaged 90% during the baseline period and did not appreciably decrease in response to a school-based contingency system, dropped to 10% when the letter was instituted.

Strategies for working with parents can be as varied as the students and caregivers themselves. Each situation calls for different measures, but behavior in the home obeys the same principles as in school. Several excellent texts on working with parents of exceptional children are available (e.g., Kroth, 1975; Kroth & Edge, 1997; Kroth & Simpson, 1977; Maag, 1996; Rutherford & Edgar, 1979; Wagonseller & McDowell, 1979), and we suggest you consult these sources for additional ideas and information.

Working with Community Professionals and Agencies

Your work with children and youth exhibiting behavior problems will lead you into the domain of other professionals and agencies. Recent federal, state, and local efforts have been launched to reform the system of children's services toward greater coordination and integration (Nelson & Pearson, 1991). A system of care for children and youth with EBD and their families emphasizes more community services, less reliance on restrictive child placements, prevention of hospitalization and out-of-home placements, interagency collaboration, flexible and individualized services,

Date _____

Classroom Work

☐ Good ☺

☐ Bad ☹

_____
Teacher's Signature

A

Date _____

Classroom Behavior

☐ Good ☺

☐ Bad ☹

_____
Teacher's Signature

B

Date _____

Social Behavior
☐ Acceptable
☐ Unacceptable

Academic Work
☐ Completed on time
☐ Not completed
☐ Accuracy acceptable
☐ Accuracy unacceptable

_____
Teacher's Signature

C

Date _____

Reading _____
Math _____
Spelling _____
Science _____
P.E. _____
Lunchroom _____
Playground _____
Social Behavior _____
Bonus Points _____
Fines _____   Total _____
Total Points _____   Possible _____

_____
Teacher's Signature

D

Subject _____   Date _____

_____ Is doing acceptable work and is keeping up with assignments
_____ Is not doing acceptable work
_____ Is behind on assignments
_____ Exhibits acceptable social behavior
_____ Exhibits unacceptable social behavior

Comments:

_____
Teacher's Signature

E

FIGURE 11–8 Daily report cards.

and cost containment and efficiency (Stroul, Goldman, Lourie, Katz-Leavy, & Zeigler-Dendy, 1992).

The lack of interagency collaboration has been a major obstacle to achieving continuity of programming between public schools and other human service agencies. Remember that discontinuity in services contributes to the failure of treatment effects achieved in one setting to be generalized and maintained in other settings where these effects are expected and needed. As a professional attempting to extend the effects of interventions applied in educational settings or attempting to plan interventions across settings, you may work with a number of agencies such as the juvenile court, child welfare agencies, mental health centers, organizations serving children and youth with developmental disabilities, vocational rehabilitation agencies, medical clinics, and service organizations such as Big Brothers or Big Sisters, in addition to working with parents and family groups. The professionals in these agencies (or in private practice) include social workers, psychologists, psychiatrists, physicians, dentists, and lawyers. These individuals should be included on wraparound planning and implementation teams when students' needs extend beyond the school day. It is well beyond the scope of this book to acquaint you with the workings of these professions and agencies. However, we can provide a few guidelines for effective interaction and collaboration.

First, you should be aware of political realities. One of the foremost of these is that outside the school, special education is not viewed as the salvation of children with emotional and behavior problems. Do not expect other professionals to greet your suggestions and views with automatic respect and admiration. Your credibility with these people will come from your record with their clients. If you succeed in accomplishing goals with students and parents that are in accord with the agency's goals, or if you have solved problems addressed by the agency or professional, you are more likely to be viewed as effective. However, it is foolhardy to set up programs that oppose those established by another agency if you want to enjoy credibility with that agency. For example, if you develop a behavioral program with parents to deal with their child's enuresis while a psychiatrist is using psychoanalysis to treat the same problem, you are not likely to establish a good working relationship with that psychiatrist. A better tactic would involve demonstrating the effectiveness of your programs with other behaviors or students, and to offer suggestions as requested. Alternately, a strategy developed collaboratively by a wraparound planning team that includes the psychiatrist could provide greater consistency throughout the child's day.

Second, learn to channel credit away from yourself and toward the other professional whenever appropriate. However, do not suggest that the other professionals possess qualities or powers they do not have, and do not give credit where credit is not due. A good strategy is to follow the principle of contingent reinforcement of practices with which you concur. For instance, if you approve of a psychologist's plan for dealing with school phobia, say, "I like this plan," not "You're a terrific psychologist" or "You have so much insight into this client." At times you need to overlook that it was you who suggested a particular plan in the first place.

Third, you should recognize that other professionals may not speak your language. You must be tolerant of the jargon of other professions while minimizing the use of your own. This is particularly important in the case of behavior analysis terminology. By selecting nontechnical but meaningful words (e.g., reward instead of positive reinforcement), you can avoid both semantic confusion and value clashes (Reppucci & Saunders, 1974).

Fourth, you should realize that most human service agencies often do not communicate well with one another. That is, juvenile court personnel may seldom contact the school, and there may not be an automatic communication link between the school and the local mental health clinic. Communication among agencies requires someone who will initiate it and maintain it. Although interagency linkages are improving rapidly, frequently effective communication results from a dynamic individual rather than from agency policy. So, if you desire communication with other agencies, be prepared to take the initiative and follow through. Also, remember that communication will continue only as long as it is reinforced and functional. Therefore, you need to acknowledge your appreciation of others' attempts to communicate and to make use of the communicated information. Further, be sure to communicate information that is useful to the treatment program being followed by the other agency. Irrelevant comments about a child's social history or the criminal record of his brother only serve to cloud issues and professional judgment.

Finally, whether you approach another agency or professional or they approach you, clarify the purposes of the involvement and your mutual responsibilities. Interagency memoranda of agreement formally commit agencies to working together, but these do not ensure effective collaboration among frontline staff and parents. A major advantage of a written integrated (or wraparound) service plan for a particular child and family is its clear delineation of roles and responsibilities. If an agreement is plainly spelled out and understood by all (you are to count the frequency of Ronnie's appropriate bids for social attention during school hours, his parents are to record it at home, and both parties are to call in their data to the mental health service coordinator every Friday), there is a greater likelihood that interactions will be efficient, productive, and mutually reinforcing.

As you work with other professionals and human service agencies, you will learn which are most useful for specific purposes. You may find it helpful to maintain a checklist, using the format presented in Figure 11–9, to keep track of your contacts and the outcomes of your involvement. When working outside the school, keep in mind the limitations of your role. If you overextend yourself or intrude too far into another's territory, you may ex-

perience unpleasant consequences. At the least you are apt to find that your efforts do not produce the effects you desire. (Some limitations of the educator's role are discussed in Chapter 12.) The range of persons and professional or volunteer agencies in the local community that can assist your students is virtually endless. Each community has its own array of resources. These may be enlisted in the same manner as parents or in-school resources, and the guidelines we presented for working in those settings apply here as well. Particularly when working with professional agencies, make your requests consistent with the functions and philosophy of those within the agency (do not ask a psychoanalytically inclined social case worker to follow a sophisticated overcorrection procedure) unless you are able to provide sufficient training and supervision to ensure reliable performance.

An early study by MacDonald, Gallimore, and MacDonald (1970) illustrated how a variety of persons may be used. They taught a parent and two school staff members (a counselor and a registrar) to contact persons in the communities of chronic school nonattenders. These community contacts (mediators) established contingencies for the target pupils. The mediators arranged contracts between pupils and the mediators, making reinforcement contingent upon school attendance. The mediators included relatives, a girlfriend, the guidance counselors themselves, and a pool hall proprietor. The reinforcers included privileges, money, and access to persons or places (time with a girlfriend, permission to enter a pool hall). This arrangement improved the school attendance of 26 nonattenders, whereas the attendance of a control group of 15 pupils who received personal counseling by a trained school counselor did not improve.

Again, we must emphasize that the complex issues faced by many students with EBD, their families, and the educators who serve them are such that schools are not, nor should they be, able to deal with them alone. As public schools become

Personnel Agencies	Willing to work with pupils?	Supportive of your program?	Cooperated with you previously?	Willing to collect data?	Supervision required?	Training required?	Willing to devote time above normal duties?	Reliably carried out procedures with pupils before?	Comments (Phone numbers, etc.)
Mental Health									
Child Welfare									
Juvenile Court									
Other Social Service Agencies									
Physicians									
Dentists									
Scout Club Leaders									
Local Merchants									
Parents									
Volunteers									

FIGURE 11–9 Outside school resource checklist.

more active participants in developing integrated, comprehensive services for children and youth with EBD, new models of service delivery are emerging in the schools. These include intensive wraparound planning, collaborative day treat- ment programs, and family-linked services (see Illback & Nelson, 1996). These models compel educators to learn new skills and to assume increasingly more collaborative roles with parents and other professionals.

SUMMARY

Extending the effects of interventions that have been successfully applied in primary treatment settings is a complex task requiring intensive programming within these settings as well as assessment and intervention in those settings where these behavior changes also are needed and desired. We have described a variety of strategies addressing the goals of achieving the maintenance and generalization of treatment effects and the transition of students to less restrictive environments. Although the technology for achieving these goals has advanced, helping students make desired behavior changes that endure over time and across settings continues to be difficult. A major factor seems to be the tendency to provide educational treatments, especially with pupils who are certified as having disabilities, in restrictive settings. Extending effects beyond the school environment is further complicated by problems of communication and the lack of collaborative relationships among educators, parents, and other professionals. However, research has demonstrated that generalization of desired intervention outcomes can occur when it is systematically planned and implemented. The challenge of the future is to alter the ways in which human service programs work to achieve better coordination and greater consistency on behalf of students and clients.

CHAPTER 11 CASE STUDY

Transition Case Study

Kristine Jolivette
University of Kentucky

Eileen, now 16 years old, has received special education services since the third grade as a student with EBD. In her school records, Eileen was described as "having experienced significant difficulties during her transition from middle school to high school. As a result, she was suspended for a day due to hitting, pushing, and kicking a peer in the hallway and was in in-school suspension for a total of 6 days her first month in high school for making verbal threats toward her math and English teachers and overt noncompliance in other academic subjects." During this transition period, Eileen's grades were lower than expected but steadily improved over the course of the year. Given her difficulty during this transition, Eileen's parents have begun to voice concern over her impending transition from school to a work environment.

From the age of 14, Eileen has had a transition plan embedded in her IEP. The purpose and goals of that transition plan centered on Eileen and her family beginning discussions regarding what Eileen will do after she completes high school, where she will live, and whether she wants to further her education. The goals on this transition plan were purposely written in vague yet measurable terms so as to provide Eileen and her family a starting point in their discussions on Eileen's future. Now that Eileen is 16 and 2 years from her expected graduation date, teachers, support staff, Eileen, and her family are meeting once again for her yearly IEP review and to more precisely outline responsibilities for the transition component.

Eileen has been present at her IEP meetings since the seventh grade as her parents and teachers felt that allowing her to have an active voice in her schooling may positively affect her rates of noncompliance and aggression. In the past several years, Eileen has been charged with detailing her strengths, preparing academic and social goals, and providing input on her future goals. This year, Eileen and the guidance counselor she meets with twice weekly have been working on Eileen's presentation of her transition goals and areas in which Eileen has concerns. In addition, Eileen's teachers and vocational counselor have assessed her strengths and weaknesses in the areas of academic, social, and vocational skills and begun to assess community options in the domains of employment, housing, recreation, medical services, higher education, and post-school support systems (i.e., social services, rehabilitation services). At home, Eileen and her family have begun talking about what each sees the other doing after her graduation. Following are brief summaries of the actions/decisions and information from Eileen, her teachers, and family.

EILEEN. Eileen has told both her family and guidance counselors that she is apprehensive about her life after graduation. She is unclear as to her specific career goals, whether she wants to attend the local community college, and where she would like to live. Eileen accurately portrays her job skills, as she is currently working at various employment sites in her hometown in the afternoons with support from a job coach. She has done well at the sites where she is permitted to work independently on repetitive tasks. In these situations, she has received positive evaluations, most notably for her accuracy and attention to detail. In addition, at these sites she has displayed positive and proactive social skills during "down" times. However, she has had difficulties, mostly social in nature, when the job requires her to work as part of a team or when she needs to rely on another individual to complete a task. When Eileen has experi-

enced situations like these, she has verbally threatened her coworkers, thrown supplies or products on the floor, and left the site without permission. She states that when she has questions and cannot find someone to help her she gets mad and will then find a coworker to "be mean to." She also acknowledges that she does not seem to get along with coworkers if she has to work directly with them on a common goal. Eileen is unsure about her work preferences with regard to responsibilities, supervision, etc.

Eileen has stated that she wants to remain in her community; however, she would like to live as independently as possible in her own apartment, mobile home, or house with or without roommates. In addition, she has expressed concern regarding what she will do for "fun" after graduation and wants to explore recreational opportunities. Eileen also has identified her inability to maintain long-term friendships and is willing to continue to work on her social skills in the community to improve employment and social options.

EILEEN'S TEACHERS. Based on assessments recently conducted with Eileen, her teachers conclude that Eileen will be able to make a successful transition into the community post-school as well as reach goals she sets for herself. Since her involvement in her IEP team meetings has steadily increased the past couple of years, her teachers report that Eileen is learning to be an effective self-advocate. Moreover, in doing so, she has been more compliant with her IEP goals and more strident in her desire to improve her social skills. Eileen's most recent data suggest the following: (a) that she has the motivation and commitment to support herself in post-school employment; (b) that she has significantly improved on the skills of turn-taking, problem-solving, asking for help, and clearly stating needs; and (c) that she has many prerequisite skills needed for independent to semi-independent living, securing full-time employment, and pursuing further educational opportunities. These data also suggest that Eileen needs improvement in the following: (a) anger management and problem-solving in work settings, (b) interview skills and how to accurately complete job applications, and (c) support in exploring community options matched with her long term goals.

EILEEN'S FAMILY. Eileen's family states that they are having difficulty viewing Eileen as an independent adult able to successfully and independently live in the community and who also is happy. As a result, the family admits that they have spent little time formally preparing Eileen for life after high school. When asked to describe Eileen's responsibilities at home, her family stated that (a) she independently cleans her room, (b) she can be left alone, (c) she helps her mother grocery shop once a week and can stay within the budget, (d) she pays for her own phone line with babysitting money, (e) she takes turns with her sibling with the dinner dishes and vacuuming, and (f) she has to tell her parents where she is and who she is with. The family also stated their concerns regarding Eileen's lack of friends, future living options, and inability to independently seek out and follow through with recreational activities. In addition, her family expressed concern over their lack of knowledge of what their community has to offer Eileen.

Based on this information, the school, family, and Eileen wrote a year-long transition plan. It was decided that the specific goals to be achieved would be broken into three areas (school, family, Eileen) so as to empower Eileen and clarify family responsibilities with the understanding that they all share responsibility for goal achievement. Eileen's transition plan is shown in Figure 11–10.

Transition Plan

Student: <u>Eileen Jacobs</u>   **D.O.B.:** <u>12/20/80</u>   **Grade:** <u>10th</u>

Goal Statement: The purpose of this transition plan is to better prepare Eileen for her transition from school to work in terms of the following domains: academics, employment, housing, and recreation. The specific goals are categorized by domain and the person(s) primarily responsible for action. These goals will be assessed at each grading period (3 per year) and each participant has agreed to meet at such times for follow-up.

Persons Invited	In Attendance	Agree with Plan
Special education teacher	yes	yes
Vocational counselor	yes	yes
Guidance counselor	yes	yes
Business manager	yes	yes
Eileen	yes	yes
Eileen's mother	yes	yes
Eileen's father	yes	yes
Job coach	no	N/A
Rehabilitation counselor representative	yes	yes

ACADEMICS

Eileen
1. Eileen will self-enroll in the courses outlined in her program of studies (see IEP course list).
2. Given a three-ring binder and dividers and after visiting various community agencies as part of community-based instruction, Eileen will organize agency materials by domain employment, housing, recreation.
3. Eileen will continue to work with the guidance counselor on social skills and anger management 2 hours 2x/week.
4. Eileen will continue to participate in the assistive employment program at school.

School
1. Given a weekly budget and a shopping list, Eileen (via classroom simulation) will purchase the groceries within the budget.
2. Given the family weekly budget, money, and a shopping list, Eileen (with the special education teacher) will purchase the groceries within the budget.

Family
1. Eileen's family will continue to provide Eileen with a math and reading tutor 3x/week.

EMPLOYMENT

Eileen
1. Given Eileen's interests and past employment experiences, she will write a goal statement for post-school employment.
2. Given a list of Eileen's past and current employment history, she will identify preferred employment characteristics for each placement.
3. Given the list of preferred employment characteristics created by Eileen, she will write a job description for her post-school employment.
4. Given the list of employee attributes, Eileen and the vocational counselor will circle the attributes in which she has demonstrated competency.
5. Given the list of employee attributes, Eileen and the guidance counselor will work on areas to improve.

(Continued)

FIGURE 11–10 Transition Plan.

Transition Plan (*cont.*)

School

1. In partnership with local businesses and community outreach, the special education teacher and vocational counselor will list supported employment options for Eileen and her family.
2. The guidance counselor will make three joint appointments throughout the school year with Eileen and a rehabilitation counselor to discuss short- and long-term goals and support systems available to Eileen in the community.
3. In partnership with local businesses, the special education teacher, vocational counselor, and business managers will create a list of employee attributes prospective employers seek.
4. Given local community agencies, the special education teacher and vocational counselor will list community contacts (agency, contact name, address, phone) for various supported and nonsupported employment options for Eileen and her family.

Family

1. Eileen's family will continue to encourage and reinforce Eileen's independent securement of babysitting jobs.

HOUSING

Eileen

1. Given Eileen's housing options, she will write a goal statement for post-school living arrangements.

School

1. Given local community agencies, the special education teacher and vocational counselor will list community contacts (agency, contact name, address, phone) for various housing options for Eileen and her family.

Family

1. Given the local newspaper rental section, Eileen's family will cut out housing options (mobile homes, apartments, assistive living, rental homes) for Eileen's three-ring binder.
2. Given the housing options notebook section, Eileen's family, with Eileen, will visit two options per month.

RECREATION

Eileen

1. Given the local recreational newsletter and paper, Eileen will sign up for one recreational class provided by the community per semester.

School

1. Given local community agencies, the special education teacher and vocational counselor will list community contacts (agency, contact name, address, phone) for various recreation options for Eileen and her family.

Family

1. Eileen's family will provide Eileen with transportation to and from evening and weekend recreational classes.

FIGURE 11–10 Transition Plan—*Continued.*

DISCUSSION QUESTIONS

1. Given that the generalization of treatment effects is much more difficult when interventions occur in restrictive settings, how could treatment procedures be designed to facilitate generalization within school environments? How might educational services be reorganized to make generalization of intervention outcomes more likely to occur?

2. Assume that you have reduced a student's aggressive behavior to an acceptable level in a special classroom environment, but he still exhibits verbal and physical aggression in other school settings. How would you

assess these behaviors in other settings, and what strategies would you use to accomplish a generalized reduction in her aggression?

3. How would you prepare a student with EBD for inclusion in a general education classroom? Describe the procedures you would use in the special education setting and the strategies you would apply in the mainstream environment.

4. A parent of one of your students complains that his child is "unmanageable" at home (refuses to do chores, disobeys rules and direct requests, and fights with siblings). List some strategies that the student's wraparound team can suggest.

REFERENCES

Anderson-Inman, L., Walker, H. M., & Purcell, J. (1984). Promoting the transfer of skills across settings: Transenvironmental programming for handicapped students in the mainstream. In W. R. Heward, T. E. Heron, D. S. Hill, & J. Trap-Porter (Eds.), *Focus on behavior analysis in education* (pp. 17–39). Upper Saddle River, NJ: Merrill/Prentice Hall.

Ayllon, T., Garber, S., & Pisor, K. (1975). The elimination of discipline problems through a combined school-home motivation system. *Behavior Therapy, 6,* 616–626.

Baer, D. M., & Wolf, M. M. (1970). The entry into natural communities of reinforcement. In R. Ulrich, T. Stachnik, & J. Mabry (Eds.), *Control of human behavior: Vol. II. From cure to prevention* (pp. 319–324). Glenview, IL: Scott, Foresman.

Baer, D. M., Wolf, M. M., & Risley, T. R. (1968). Some current dimensions of applied behavior analysis. *Journal of Applied Behavior Analysis, 1,* 91–97.

Bauer, A. M., & Shea, T. M. (1988). Structuring classrooms through level systems. *Focus on Exceptional Children, 21*(3), 1–12.

Braaten, S. (1979). The Madison School program: Programming for secondary level emotionally disturbed youth. *Behavioral Disorders, 4,* 153–162.

Brolin, D. (1995). *Career education: A functional life skills approach* (3rd ed.). Upper Saddle River, NJ: Merrill/Prentice Hall.

Brown, L., Nietupski, J., & Hamre-Nietupski, S. (1976). The criterion of ultimate functioning and public school services for severely handicapped students. In A. Thomas (Ed.), *Hey, don't forget about me: New directions for serving the severely handicapped* (pp. 2–15). Reston, VA: Council for Exceptional Children.

Brown, R. E., Copeland, R. E., & Hall, R. V. (1972). The school principal as a behavior modifier. *Journal of Educational Research, 66,* 175–180.

Bullis, M., & Paris, K. (1996). Competitive employment and service management for adolescents and young adults with emotional and behavioral disorders. In R. J. Illback & C. M. Nelson (Eds.), *Emerging school-based approaches for children and youth with emotional and behavioral disorders: Research on practice and service integration* (pp. 77–96). New York: Haworth Press.

Carr, E. G., Taylor, J. C., & Robinson, S. (1991). The effects of severe problem behavior in children on the teaching behavior of adults. *Journal of Applied Behavior Analysis, 24,* 523–535.

Christophersen, E. R., Arnold, C. M., Hill, D. W., & Quilitch, H. R. (1972). The home point system: Token reinforcement procedures for application by parents of children with behavior problems. *Journal of Applied Behavior Analysis, 5,* 485–497.

Clark, H. B., Unger, K. V., & Stewart, E. S. (1993). Transition of youth and young adults with emotional/behavioral disorders into employment, education, and independent living. *Community Alternatives: International Journal of Family Care, 5*(2), 19–46.

Clees, T. J. (1995). Self-recording of students' daily schedules of teachers' expectancies: Perspectives on reactivity, stimulus control, and generalization. *Exceptionality, 5,* 113–129.

Clore, P. (1974). Chris: "School phobia." In J. Worell & C. M. Nelson, *Managing instructional problems: A case study workbook* (pp. 212–217). New York: McGraw-Hill.

Copeland, R. E., Brown, R. E., & Hall, R. V. (1974). The effects of principal-implemented techniques on the behavior of pupils. *Journal of Applied Behavior Analysis, 7,* 77–86.

DeChillo, N., Koren, P. E., & Schultz, K. H. (1994). From paternalism to partnership: Family/professional collaboration in children's mental health. *American Journal of Orthopsychiatry, 64,* 564–576.

Duchnowski, A., Berg, K., & Kutash, K. (1995). Parent participation in and perception of placement decisions. In J. M. Kauffman, J. W. Lloyd, D. P. Hallahan, & T. A. Astuto (Eds.), *Issues in educational placement:*

Students with emotional and behavioral disorders (pp. 183–195). Hillsdale, NJ: Lawrence Erlbaum Associates.

Eber, L. (1995, April). LASDE EBD *network training developing school-based wraparound plan.* LaGrange, IL: La-Grange Area Department of Special Education.

Edgar, E. (1987). Secondary programs in special education: Are many of them jusifiable? *Exceptional Children, 53,* 555–561.

Edgar, E., & Siegel, S. (1995). Postsecondary scenarios for troubled and troubling youth. In J. M. Kauffman & D. P. Hallahan (Eds.), *The illusion of full inclusion: A comprehensive critique of a current special education bandwagon* (pp. 251–283). Austin, TX: PRO-ED.

Edgar, E. B., Webb, S. L., & Maddox, M. (1987). Issues in transition: Transfer of youth from correctional facilities to public schools. In C. M. Nelson, R. B. Rutherford, Jr., & B. I. Wolford (Eds.), *Special education in the criminal justice system.* Upper Saddle River, NJ: Merrill/ Prentice Hall.

Ferber, H., Keeley, S. M., & Shemberg, K. M. (1974). Training parents in behavior modification: Outcomes of and problems encountered in a program after Patterson's work. *Behavior Therapy, 5,* 415–419.

Frank, A. R., & Sitlington, P. L. (1997). Young adults with behavior disorders—Before and after IDEA. *Behavioral Disorders, 23,* 40–56.

Friesen, B. J., & Wahlers, D. (1993). Respect and real help: Family support and children's mental health. *Journal of Emotional and Behavioral Problems, 2*(4), 12–15.

Gaylord-Ross, R., & Haring, T. (1987). Social interaction research for adolescents with severe handicaps. *Behavioral Disorders, 12,* 264–275.

Gaylord-Ross, R. J., Haring, T. G., Breen, C., & Pitts-Conway, V. (1984). The training and generalization of social interaction skills with autistic youth. *Journal of Applied Behavior Analysis, 17,* 229–247.

Glogowger, F., & Sloop, E. W. (1976). Two strategies of group training of parents as effective behavior modifiers. *Behavior Therapy, 7,* 177–184.

Goetz, L., Guess, D., & Stremel-Campbell, K. (Eds.). (1987). *Innovative program design for individuals with dual sensory impairments.* Boston: Paul H. Brookes.

Graubard, P. S., Rosenberg, H., & Miller, M. B. (1971). Student applications of behavior modification to teachers and environments or ecological approaches to social deviancy. In E. A. Ramp & B. L. Hopkins (Eds.), *A new direction for education: Behavior analysis:* 1971 (pp. 80–101). Lawrence, KS: University of Kansas Support and Development Center for Follow Through.

Gresham, F. M. (1998). Social skills training: Should we raze, remodel, or rebuild? *Behavioral Disorders, 24,* 19–25.

Gresham, F. M., Elliott, S. N., & Black, F. L. (1987). Teacher-rated social skills of mainstreamed mildly handicapped and nonhandicapped children. *School Psychology Review, 16,* 78–88.

Gunter, P. L., Fox, J. J., Brady, M. P., Shores, R. E., & Cavanaugh, K. (1988). Nonhandicapped peers as multiple exemplars: A generalization tactic for promoting autistic students' social skills. *Behavioral Disorders, 13,* 116–126.

Gunter, P. L., Jack, S. L., DePaepe, P., Reed, T. M., & Harrison, J. (1994). Effects of challenging behavior of students with E/BD on teacher instructional behavior. *Preventing School Failure, 38,* 35–46.

Hallahan, D. P., & Kauffman, J. M. (1995). From mainstreaming to collaborative consultation. In J. M. Kauffman & D. P. Hallahan (Eds.), *The illusion of full inclusion: A comprehensive critique of a current special education bandwagon* (pp. 5–17). Austin, TX: PRO-ED.

Hewett, F. M., & Taylor, F. D. (1980). *The emotionally disturbed child in the classroom: The orchestration of success* (2nd ed.). Boston: Allyn & Bacon.

Hollinger, J. D. (1987). Social skills for behaviorally disordered children as preparation for mainstreaming: Theory, practice, and new directions. *Remedial and Special Education, 8*(4), 17–27.

Hrydowy, E. R., Stokes, T. F., & Martin, G. L. (1984). Training elementary students to prompt teacher praise. *Education and Treatment of Children, 7,* 99–108.

Idol, L., Paolucci-Whitcomb, P., & Nevin, A. (1986). *Collaborative consultation.* Rockville, MD: Aspen.

Illback, R. J., & Nelson, C. M. (Eds.). (1996). *Emerging school-based approaches for children and youth with emotional and behavioral disorders. Research or practice and service integration.* New York: Haworth Press.

Kameinui, E. J., & Darch, C. B. (1995). *Instructional classroom management: A proactive approach to behavior management.* Reston, VA: Council for Exceptional Children.

Kauffman, J. M., & Hallahan, D. P. (Eds.). (1995). *The illusion of full inclusion: A comprehensive critique of a current special education bandwagon.* Austin, TX: PRO-ED.

Kazdin, A. E. (1977). Vicarious reinforcement and direction of behavior change in the classroom. *Behavior Therapy, 8,* 57–63.

Koegel, R. L., & Rincover, A. (1977). Research on the difference between generalization and maintenance in extra-therapy responding. *Journal of Applied Behavior Analysis, 10,* 1–12.

Kroth, R. L. (1975). *Communicating with parents of exceptional children: Improving parent-teacher relationships.* Denver, CO: Love.

Kroth, R. L., & Edge, D. (1997). *Strategies for communicating with parents and families of exceptional children* (3rd ed.). Denver, CO: Love.

Kroth, R. L., & Simpson, R. L. (1977). *Parent conferences as a teaching strategy.* Denver, CO: Love.

Lane, T. W., & Burchard, J. D. (1983). Failure to modify delinquent behavior: A constructive analysis. In E. B. Foa & P. M. G. Emmelkamp (Eds.), *Failures in behavior therapy* (pp. 355–377). New York: Wiley.

LaNunziata, L. J., Hunt, K. P., & Cooper, J. O. (1984). Suggestions for phasing out token economy systems in primary and intermediate grades. *Techniques: A Journal for Remedial Education and Counseling, 1,* 151–156.

Levendoski, L. S., & Cartledge, G. (2000). Self-monitoring for elementary school students with serious emotional disturbances: Classroom applications for increased academic responding. *Behavioral Disorders, 25,* 211–224.

Maag, J. W. (1994, November). Teaching students self-control: From theory to practice. Workshop presented at the Seventeenth Annual Conference on Severe Behavior Disorders of Children and Youth. Tempe, AZ.

Maag, J. W. & Katsiyannis, A. (1998). Challenges facing successful transition for youths with E/BD. *Behavioral Disorders, 23,* 209–221.

MacDonald, W. S., Gallimore, R., & MacDonald, G. (1970). Contingency counseling by school personnel: An economical model of intervention. *Journal of Applied Behavior Analysis, 3,* 175–182.

MacMillan, D. L., Gresham, F. M., & Forness, S. R. (1996). Full inclusion: An empirical perspective. *Behavioral Disorders, 21,* 145–159.

Malmgren, K., Edgar, E., & Neel, R. S. (1998). Postschool status of youths with behavioral disorders. *Behavioral Disorders, 23,* 257–263.

Marholin, D., & Steinman, W. (1977). Stimulus control in the classroom as a function of the behavior reinforced. *Journal of Applied Behavior Analysis, 10,* 465–478.

McEvoy, M. A., & Odom, S. L. (1987). Social interaction training for preschool children with behavioral disorders. *Behavioral Disorders, 12,* 242–251.

McLaughlin, M. J., Leone, P. E., Warren, S. H., & Schofield, P. F. (1994). *Doing things differently: Issues and options for creating comprehensive school-linked services for children and youth with emotional or behavioral disorders.* College Park, MD: University of Maryland and Westat, Inc.

Meichenbaum, D. (1977). *Cognitive-behavior modification: An integrative approach.* New York: Plenum.

Mercer, C. D., & Mercer, A. R. (2001). *Teaching students with learning problems* (6th ed.). Upper Saddle River, NJ: Merrill/Prentice Hall.

Nelson, C. M., & Pearson, C. A. (1991). *Integrating services for children and youth with emotional and behavioral disorders.* Reston, VA: Council for Exceptional Children.

Nelson, C. M., & Pearson, C. A. (1994). Juvenile delinquency in the context of culture and community. In R. L. Peterson & S. Ishii-Jordan (Eds.), *Cultural and community contexts for emotional or behavioral disorders* (pp. 78–90). Boston: Brookline Press.

Nelson, C. M., & Rutherford, R. B., Jr. (1988). Behavioral interventions with behaviorally disordered students. In M. C. Wang, H. J. Walberg, & M. C. Reynolds (Eds.), *The handbook of special education: Research and practice* (Vol. 2, pp. 125–153). Oxford, England: Pergamon.

Nelson, C. M., Rutherford, R. B., Jr., & Wolford, B. I. (Eds.). (1987). *Special education and the criminal justice system.* Upper Saddle River, NJ: Merrill/Prentice Hall.

Noell, G. H., Witt, J. C., LaFleur, L. H., Mortenson, B. P., Ranier, D. D., & LeVelle, J. (2000). Increasing intervention implementation in general education following consultation: A comparison of two follow-up strategies. *Journal of Applied Behavior Analysis, 33,* 271–284.

O'Leary, S. G., & O'Leary, K. D. (1976). Behavior modification in the school. In H. Leitenberg (Ed.), *Handbook of behavior modification and behavior therapy* (pp. 475–515). Englewood Cliffs, NJ: Prentice-Hall.

Polsgrove, L. (1979). Self-control: Methods for child training. *Behavioral Disorders, 4,* 116–130.

Reid, R., & Harris, K. R. (1993). Self-monitoring of attention versus self-monitoring of performance: Effects on attention and academic performance. *Exceptional Children, 60,* 29–40.

Reppucci, N. D., & Saunders, J. T. (1974). Social psychology of behavior modification: Problems of implementation in natural settings. *American Psychologist, 29,* 649–660.

Rinn, R. C., Vernon, J. C., & Wise, M. J. (1975). Training parents of behaviorally disordered children in groups: A three-year program evaluation. *Behavior Therapy, 6,* 378–387.

Robbins, L. N. (1966). *Deviant children grown up: A sociological and psychiatric study of sociopathic personality.* Baltimore: Williams & Wilkins.

Rock, E. E., Rosenberg, M. S., & Carran, D. T. (1994). Variables affecting the reintegration rate of students with serious emotional disturbance. *Exceptional Children, 61,* 254–268.

Rutherford, R. B., Jr., & Edgar, E. (1979). *Teachers and parents: A guide to interaction and cooperation.* Boston: Allyn & Bacon.

Rutherford, R. B., Jr., & Nelson, C. M. (1988). Generalization and maintenance of treatment effects. In J. C. Witt, S. N. Elliott, & F. M. Gresham (Eds.), *Handbook of behavior therapy in education* (pp. 277–324). New York: Plenum.

Rylance, B. J. (1997). Predictors of high school graduation or dropping out for youths with severe emotional disturbance. *Behavioral Disorders, 23,* 5–17.

Sample, P. L. (1998). Post-school outcomes for students with significant emotional disturbance following best-practice transition services. *Behavioral Disorders, 23,* 231–242.

Scott, T. M., & Nelson, C. M. (1998). Confusion and failure in facilitating generalized social responding in the school setting: Sometimes 2 + 2 = 5. *Behavioral Disorders, 23,* 264–275.

Shinn, M. R., Ramsey, E., Walker, H. M., Stieber, S., & O'Neill, R. E. (1987). Antisocial behavior in school settings: Initial differences in an at risk and normal population. *Journal of Special Education, 21,* 69–84.

Shores, R. E. (1987). Overview of research on social interaction: A historical and personal perspective. *Behavioral Disorders, 12,* 233–241.

Shores, R. E., Apolloni, T., & Norman, C. W. (1976). Changes in peer verbalizations accompanying individual and group contingencies. *Perceptual and Motor Skills, 43,* 1155–1162.

Simpson, R. L. (1987). Social interaction of behaviorally disordered children and youth: Where are we and where do we need to go? *Behavioral Disorders, 12,* 292–298.

Stephens, S. A., & Lakin, K. C. (1995). Where students with emotional or behavioral disorders go to school. In J. M. Kauffman, J. W. Lloyd, D. P. Hallahan, & T. A. Astuto (Eds.), *Issues in educational placement: Students with emotional and behavioral disorders* (pp. 47–74). Hillsdale, NJ: Lawrence Erlbaum Associates.

Stokes, T. F., & Baer, D. M. (1977). An implicit technology of generalization. *Journal of Applied Behavior Analysis, 10,* 349–367.

Stokes, T. F., & Osnes, P. G. (1986). Programming the generalization of children's social behavior. In P. S. Strain, M. J. Guralnick, & H. M. Walker (Eds.), *Children's social behavior: Development, assessment, and modification* (pp. 407–443). Orlando, FL: Academic Press.

Strain, P. S., & Danko, C. D. (1995). Caregivers' encouragement of positive interaction between preschoolers with autism and their siblings. *Journal of Emotional and Behavioral Disorders, 3,* 2–12.

Strain, P. S., Shores, R. E., & Kerr, M. M. (1976). An experimental analysis of "spillover" effects on the social interaction of behaviorally handicapped preschool children. *Journal of Applied Behavior Analysis, 9,* 31–40.

Stroul, B., Goldman, S., Lourie, I., Katz-Leavy, J., & Zeigler-Dendy, C. (1992). *Profiles of local systems of care for children and adolescents with severe emotional disturbances.* Washington, DC: Georgetown University Child Development Center, CASSP Technical Assistance Center.

Tawney, J. W., & Gast, D. L. (1984). *Single subject research in special education.* Upper Saddle River, NJ: Merrill/Prentice Hall.

Taylor, F. D., & Soloway, M. M. (1973). The Madison School plan: A functional model for merging the regular and special classrooms. In E. Deno (Ed.), *Instructional alternatives for exceptional children* (pp. 145–155). Reston, VA: Council for Exceptional Children.

Taylor, S. J., Bilken, D., & Knoll, J. (Eds.). (1987). *Community integration for people with severe disabilities.* New York: Teachers College Press, Columbia University.

U.S. Department of Education. (2000). *21st annual report to Congress on the implementation of the Individuals with Disability Education Act.* Washington, DC: U.S. Department of Education, Office of Special Education and Rehabilitative Services.

Van Hasselt, B. B., Hersen, M., Whitehill, M. B., & Bellack, A. S. (1979). Social skills assessment and training for children: An evaluative review. *Behavior Research and Therapy, 17,* 413–437.

Vetter-Zemitsch, A., Bernstein, R., Johnson, J., Larson, C., Simon, D., Smith, D., & Smith, A. (1984). The on campus program: A systematic/behavioral approach to behavior disorders in high school. *Focus on Exceptional Children, 16*(6), 1–8.

Wagonseller, B. R., & McDowell, R. L. (1979). *You and your child: A common sense approach to successful parenting.* Champaign, IL: Research Press.

Walker, H. M. (1986). The assessment for integration into mainstream settings (AIMS) assessment system: Rationale, instruments, procedures, and outcomes. *Journal of Clinical Child Psychology, 15,* 55–63.

Walker, H. M., & Bullis, M. (1996). A comprehensive services model for troubled youth. In C. M. Nelson, B. Wolford, & R. B. Rutherford (Eds.), *Developing comprehensive systems that work for troubled youth* (pp. 122–148). Richmond, KY: National Coalition for Juvenile Justice Services.

Walker, H. M., & Rankin, R. (1980a). *The SBS Checklist of Correlates of child handicapping conditions*. (Available from Hill Walker, Center on Human Development, Clinical Services Building, University of Oregon, Eugene, OR 97403).

Walker, H. M., & Rankin, R. (1980b). *The SBS Inventory of teacher social behavior standards and expectations*. (Available from Hill Walker, Center on Human Development, Clinical Services Building, University of Oregon, Eugene, OR 97403).

Walker, H. M., Shinn, M. R., O'Neill, R. E., & Ramsey, E. (1987). A longitudinal assessment of the development of antisocial behavior in boys: Rationale, methodology, and first year results. *Remedial and Special Education*, 8(4), 7–16; 27.

Walker, H. M., & Stieber, S. (1998). Teacher ratings of social skills as longitudinal predictors of long-term arrest status in a sample of at-risk males. *Behavioral Disorders*, 23, 222–230.

Wong, K. L. H., Kauffman, J. M., & Lloyd, J. W. (1991). Choices for integration: Selecting teachers for mainstreaming students with emotional or behavioral disorders. *Intervention in School and Clinic*, 27, 108–115.

THE CHALLENGES OF WORKING WITH STUDENTS WITH EBD

CHAPTER 12

OUTLINE

OBJECTIVES

After completing this chapter, you should be able to

- Identify circumstances in which universal, targeted, and intensive intervention strategies are needed.
- Identify the major limitations that apply to educators working in school settings and describe the consequences of exceeding these limitations.
- Identify potential sources of conflict for educators working on behalf of students exhibiting behavioral disorders.
- Discuss strategies for working effectively within professional role boundaries.
- Identify signs of stress and burnout and suggest appropriate strategies for their reduction.
- Describe the advantages of participation on an interactive team.

Previous chapters have described a broad range of intervention strategies for dealing with an equally wide range of students' behavioral needs and issues. In these chapters we have discussed the need to plan and implement interventions in noneducational settings and described procedures for assessment and intervention in these settings. The present chapter considers the need to work collaboratively with other professionals and families to implement intensive interventions for students who often are affected by multiple service delivery systems. We begin with a brief discussion of universal, targeted, and intensive approaches, which are used as a basis for making decisions regarding when to expand the scope of intervention planning through interactive teaming and wraparound planning. Next is a description of some of the limits to the classroom teacher's role that indicate a need for collaboration. The role of team member is an important extension of the functions traditionally served by educators; in view of the professional support and technical assistance needed by those who serve children and youth with EBD, a section has been added on this role. The relatively high attrition rate of teachers of students with EBD must be considered by any professional in this field. Therefore, the final section presents information on teacher stress and burnout.

POSITIVE BEHAVIOR SUPPORT REVISITED

In Chapter 1 we described three levels of intervention that are needed to address the full range of student behavior in educational settings. This model is based on the concept of positive behavior support (Sugai et al., 2000). Universal interventions are applied to all members or a group or population (e.g., a school-wide discipline plan, changes in scheduling, and student monitoring procedures) and focus on preventing initial occur-

rences of behavior problems. Targeted interventions are directed at specific pupils and behaviors that are not responsive to universal interventions, and targeted intervention methodology is based on the technology of applied behavior analysis. This includes the development of behavior intervention plans based on functional behavioral assessment. We cited research demonstrating that the need for multiple targeted interventions is reduced dramatically when effective universal interventions are in place. Universal interventions are presented in numerous methods texts, chapters, and articles on effective schools, and this literature has been cited throughout this text. Examples of targeted interventions also are plentiful in the professional literature. Interventions at this level can be delivered, supervised directly, or orchestrated by school personnel with appropriate training in behavioral interventions.

In previous chapters we have described characteristics and features of a third level of intervention, which represent the most intensive strategies that can be designed to support students with the most severe emotional and behavioral needs. It may appear convenient to assume that *all* students who are identified as EBD require this level of intervention. However, a more efficient method for identifying candidates for intensive interventions is to document which students are receiving targeted interventions and the results. Just as students who need targeted interventions may be identified as those for whom universal interventions have not been effective, candidates for intensive interventions may be identified on the basis of the failure of targeted interventions to meet their needs. A recommended strategy is to organize a network of support for these students through wraparound planning. As we have mentioned previously, this approach to intervention planning involves teams of professionals and family members who jointly create strategies that wrap around a given child and her needs in school, home, and community settings. Using the wraparound approach, a comprehensive interagency plan is developed that crosses multiple life domains.

Wraparound planning involves identifying the student's strengths and other resources in the settings that make up the student's typical day. Both traditional and nontraditional intervention strategies are created and evaluated in terms of their impact on the progress and comfort of both the pupil and those who provide services for her (Eber, 1996). The wraparound process developed from the system of care approach for children and youth who were involved with multiple human services agencies (Stroul & Friedman, 1986). The goal of this approach has been to increase the intensity and effectiveness of services to children with EBD and their families in their home schools and communities, thereby reducing the need for out-of-community placement (Skiba & Polsgrove, 1996). The core values and guiding principles of a system of care are presented in Table 12–1. These values and principles are reflected in school-based wraparound planning (see Table 12–2).

Recently, the wraparound process has been applied to planning and delivering more proactive services to children not at immediate risk for out-of-community placement. Many strategies presented in this text are appropriate for delivery through a wraparound approach; however, the policies, procedures, and technical assistance needed to ensure the effectiveness of this approach are beyond the scope of this text.[1] If school practices include effective universal and targeted interventions, the need for intensive interventions, implemented through wraparound planning, will be reduced significantly, *but they will not be eliminated.* Therefore, it is necessary to have school-based staff who are capable of determining when this level of intervention is needed, and who can initiate interactions with families, other school staff, and other agencies to develop comprehensive wraparound plans.

As explained in Chapter 1, this three-tiered model of positive behavior support derives from a public health conceptualization of primary, secondary, and tertiary prevention strategies. Primary prevention involves efforts to prevent initial occurrences of emotional and behavioral problems. The focus of secondary prevention is on preventing reoccurrences of problem behavior, while tertiary prevention attempts to reduce the impact of chronic emotional and behavioral problems on the student's life functioning. Figure 12–1 shows a different way of looking at this model, one that focuses on the proportion of the student population that is likely to need services at each level. Each level of intervention is entered by students for whom interventions have not been successful at previous levels. Therefore, progress toward more intensive intervention planning involves the compilation and analysis of data regarding what has worked and what has not worked in previous systematic attempts to address problem behaviors. In effect, each level of positive behavior support functions as a screening gate for successive levels of intervention. That is, students who do not succeed when universal interventions are in place may be considered at-risk for failure and, therefore, should receive academic and behavioral support through targeted interventions. Students who are not able to succeed even with targeted behavioral support are identified as needing intensive interventions. Intensive interventions may be school-based (e.g., placement in a special classroom or alternative program), or they may entail programs and services that address other life domains. In the latter case, the school may serve as a liaison in calling other agencies, service providers, and the family together to initiate a wraparound plan. Information regarding school-based interventions and their outcomes will be invaluable to interactive teams who have the responsibility for wraparound planning and service coordination.

[1]For information regarding wraparound planning and outcomes, consult Burns & Goldman (1998), Eber (1996), Eber (1997), Eber, Osuch, & Redditt (1996), Katz-Leavy, Lourie, Stroul, & Zeigler-Dendy (1992); or visit the Illinois State Board of Education Emotional and Behavioral Disabilities Network web page (www.ebdnetwork-il.org).

TABLE 12–1   Values and Principles for the System of Care

Core Values
1. The system of care should be child-centered and family-focused, with the needs of the child and family dictating the types and mix of services provided.
2. The system of care should be community based, with the focus of services as well as management and decision-making responsibility resting at the community level.
3. The system of care should be culturally competent, with agencies, programs, and services that are responsive to the cultural, racial, and ethnic differences of the populations they serve.

Guiding Principles
1. Children with emotional disturbances should have access to a comprehensive array of services that address each child's physical, emotional, social, and educational needs.
2. Children with emotional disturbances should receive individualized services in accordance with the unique needs and potentials of each child and guided by an individualized service plan.
3. Children with emotional disturbances should receive services within the least restrictive, most normative environment that is clinically appropriate.
4. The families and surrogate families of children with emotional disturbances should be full participants in all aspects of the planning and delivery of services.
5. Children with emotional disturbances should receive services that are integrated, with linkages between child-serving agencies and programs and mechanisms for planning, developing, and coordinating services.
6. Children with emotional disturbances should be provided with case management or similar mechanisms to ensure that multiple services are delivered in a coordinated and therapeutic manner and that they can move through the system of services in accordance with their changing needs.
7. Early identification and intervention for children with emotional disturbances should be promoted by the system of care in order to enhance the likelihood of positive outcomes.
8. Children with emotional disturbances should be ensured smooth transitions to the adult service system as they reach maturity.
9. The rights of children with emotional disturbances should be protected, and effective advocacy efforts for children and youth with emotional disturbances should be promoted.
10. Children with emotional disturbances should receive services without regard to race, religion, national origin, sex, physical disability, or other characteristics, and services should be sensitive and responsive to cultural differences and special needs.

Source: *Stroul, B. A., & Friedman, R. M. (1986). A system of care for children and youth with severe emotional disturbance. Copyright CAASP Technical Assistance Center. Used with permission.*

TABLE 12–2   Some Major Elements of School-Based Wraparound Care

- Is responsive to the needs of the individual student and her family
- Provides strength/support, not deficits/fix orientation
- Delivers flexibly in terms of time, quantity, and approach
- Is typical of age/culture/environment
- Is comprehensive for all domains and entire school day
- Integrates formal school services with informal school-based supports
- Is unconditional
- Ensures that resources are delivered on the basis of need rather than program or setting definitions
- Analyzes school or special education operations on the basis of the single student

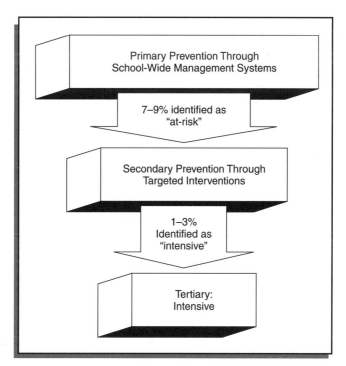

FIGURE 12–1   School-wide management as a screening system to identify students in need of individualized management.

Copyright 2000 by T. M. Scott. Used with permission.

LIMITATIONS ON THE EDUCATIONAL ROLE

Working effectively with students who have challenging emotional and behavioral needs requires a great deal of communication and coordination with other service providers, human services agencies, family members, and other persons who are, or could be, significant influences. In particular, when working with other professionals and their agencies, these interactions may present some risk of conflict. While not all conflict can (or should be) avoided, it is wise not to be the cause of such issues. The consequences of overextending oneself or of overstepping one's professional boundaries can be unpleasant. Therefore, we provide guidelines derived from research, litigation, au-

thoritative discourse, and experience. Recognizing the limits of the educational role not only helps you avoid aversive personal and professional consequences but also benefits you in two ways. First, you avoid overextending yourself in areas beyond your scope, which helps reduce your stress. Second, you function more effectively and more flexibly as a student advocate and as a member of an interactive team.

Our discussion of limitations is organized into three categories: ecological constraints, role constraints, and legal constraints. This division is arbitrary; in practical situations, the categories overlap considerably. Moreover, we believe the philosophy of services for persons with diverse needs in this country is shifting toward a more comprehensive and integrated focus, which demands that education become part of a system of care. The implication is that educators, especially those who work with children and youth who have become alienated and disempowered because of their economic, cultural, and behavioral characteristics, no longer can function in isolation. The final section discusses teacher stress and burnout and the potential of wraparound planning to support the important work of the classroom teacher.

Ecological Constraints

OVEREXTENSION AND INTRUSION. Remember that problem behaviors do not occur only in educational settings. In particular, students with EBD display maladaptive behaviors or deficits in appropriate social skills across many settings. Caregivers and other persons who must deal with these individuals may lack the skills needed to design and implement sophisticated and effective intervention procedures. As a professional educator, you are constrained by the practical limits of your role. This means that you are sure to encounter circumstances in which you cannot manage all the student's environmental contingencies and reinforcers, nor can you train and supervise all those who do. It is important that you recognize these facts, even though you may have the expertise to deal with the student's problems. For example, there may be serious difficulties in the pupil's family interactions, or the student may be involved in a gang. If you know or think you know how to attack such problems, it may be tempting to try to manage them yourself. However, this tactic presents several dangers. First, you may be overextending yourself; your official responsibility is to the student's educational program, unless you are acting in another professional capacity. If you are in a consulting role or have released time for parent education or community work, there is less conflict; nevertheless, one can easily become overextended when working with multiple-problem situations.

A related risk is that of intruding upon another professional's domain. If a family receives counseling from a mental health agency or if a proba-

tion officer is working on the pupil's delinquent behavior, do not initiate interventions without the prior consent of the other professional or agency. Then too you may risk providing ineffective treatment: You may find yourself working in areas or on problems for which you are not trained adequately. Paradoxically, the dangers of overextension are increased by your own effectiveness. That is, the better you are at your job, the more you may be called upon to help in other areas. It is very tempting to respond to the social reinforcement offered by your students, their families, and other professionals by increasing your participation in areas beyond your jurisdiction. However, this pattern may lead to undesired consequences for you and your pupils; thus, you should recognize this as a limitation on your role.

Extending yourself beyond your role and professional skills is more likely if you are the only resource in the geographic area for a pupil or a family, as in rural locales. In more urban areas where other professionals are available, you may be the only one the student or family trusts. Providing assistance in these instances may represent a difficult decision.

Interagency and family collaborative service planning and delivery offer a viable solution to the problems of overextension and intrusion. School-based wraparound plans should include the use of family and community resources to support educational goals for individual students, as well as other life domains. At the same time, school services and resources should facilitate the achievement of family and community goals. Integrated service planning is, of course, a team effort. One way to identify the needs to be addressed in multiple life domain planning is to assess the pupil's ecology. An ecological assessment can be accomplished by interviewing the student or his caregivers. Wahler and Cormier (1970) developed three behavior checklists, reproduced here in Figures 12–2, 12–3, and 12–4, that can be used to map student ecological settings. Neither the problem behaviors nor the situations listed here are exhaustive, and you may note that they fail to identify strengths in either the setting or the child.

The following checklist allows you to describe your child's problems in various home situations. The situations are listed in the column at the left and common problem behaviors are listed in the row at the top. Examine *each* situation in the column and decide whether one or more of the problem behaviors in the row fits your child. Check those that fit the best—if any.

	Always has to be told	Doesn't pay attention	Forgets	Dawdles	Refuses	Argues	Complains	Demands	Fights	Is selfish	Destroys toys or property	Steals	Lies	Cries	Whines	Hangs on or stays close to adult	Acts silly	Mopes around	Stays alone	Has to keep things in order	Engages in sexual play
Morning																					
Awakening																					
Dressing																					
Breakfast																					
Bathroom																					
Leaving for school																					
Play in house																					
Chores																					
Television																					
Afternoon																					
Lunch																					
Bathroom																					
Play in house																					
Chores and homework																					
Television																					
Company arrival																					
Evening																					
Father comes home																					
Dinner																					
Bathroom																					
Play in house																					
Chores and homework																					
Television																					
Company arrival																					
Bedtime																					

FIGURE 12–2 Child home behavior checklist.

Source: Wahler, R. G. & Cormier, W. H. The ecological interview: A first step in outpatient therapy. Journal of Behavior Therapy and Experimental Psychiatry, 1, 279–289. Copyright 1970. Pergamon Press, Ltd. Reprinted with permission of the Journal of Behavior Therapy and Experimental Psychiatry.

The following checklist allows you to describe your child's problems in various situations outside the house. The situations are listed in the column at the left and common problem behaviors are listed in the row at the top. Examine *each* situation in the column and decide if one or more of the problem behaviors in the row fits your child. Check those that fit the best—if any.

	Always has to be told	Doesn't pay attention	Forgets	Dawdles	Refuses	Argues	Complains	Demands	Fights	Is selfish	Destroys toys or property	Steals	Lies	Cries	Whines	Hangs on or stays close to adult	Acts silly	Mopes around	Stays alone	Has to keep things in order	Sexual play
In own yard																					
In neighbor's yard or home																					
In stores																					
Public park																					
Downtown in general																					
Church or Sunday school																					
Community swimming pool																					
In family care																					

FIGURE 12–3 Child community behavior checklist.

Source: *Wahler, R. G. & Cormier, W. H. The ecological interview: A first step in outpatient therapy. Journal of Behavior Therapy and Experimental Psychiatry*, 1, 279–289. Copyright 1970. Pergamon Press, Ltd. Reprinted with permission of *Journal of Behavior Therapy and Experimental Psychiatry*.

However, the service coordination team can use these checklists as models to develop their own. Focus on specific behaviors and ask the interviewee in which of the settings they occur, or ask which behaviors present problems in each of the student's ecological settings. By entering checks in the appropriate rows and columns, you can develop a map of the student's problem behaviors and strengths in various settings and thereby gain a general understanding of their extent, as well as which behaviors the student displays in specific settings. Further questioning may reveal specific persons in whose presence problems occur, typical reactions or approaches to handling problem behaviors, and who observes or supports desired behaviors.

Again, note that the illustrated checklists depart from the philosophy of wraparound planning in that they do not probe for strengths and resources in the student or her ecology. Therefore, remember to identify these and to incorporate them into service plans. A focus on building positive behavioral supports, as opposed to one that concentrates exclusively on reducing undesired behaviors, has been a major breakthrough in approaches to intervention and is much more likely to improve cooperation and collaboration with both families and community agencies.

If your school building or district has not implemented an integrated, team-based planning process for students with EBD, you may need to

The following checklist allows you to describe your student's problems in various situations. The situations are listed in the column at the left and common problem behaviors are listed in the row at the top. Examine *each* situation in the column and decide if one or more of the problem behaviors in the row fits your student. Check those that fit the best—if any.

	Out of seat	Talks to others	Always has to be told	Doesn't pay attention	Forgets	Dawdles	Refuses	Argues	Complains	Demands	Fights	Is Selfish	Destroys toys or property	Steals	Lies	Cries	Whines	Hangs on or stays close to adult	Acts silly	Mopes around	Stays alone	Has to keep things in order	Sexual play
Morning																							
Teacher explains lesson																							
Teacher discusses with group																							
Silent work time																							
Cooperative work with other students																							
Oral reading or class presentation																							
Line up for lunch or recess																							
Hall																							
Playground																							
Lunch																							
Afternoon																							
Teacher explains lesson																							
Teacher discusses with group																							
Silent work time																							
Cooperative with other students																							
Oral reading or class presentation																							
Line up for recess or dismissal																							
Hall																							
Playground																							

FIGURE 12–4   Child school behavior checklist.

Source: *Wahler, R. G. & Cormier, W. H. The ecological interview: A first step in outpatient therapy.* Journal of Behavior Therapy and Experimental Psychiatry, 1, 279–289. Copyright 1970. Pergamon Press, Ltd. Reprinted with permission of the Journal of Behavior Therapy and Experimental Psychiatry.

conduct the ecological assessment independently. If this is the case, after your interviews with caregivers and service providers you can make a decision whether to approach the problem situation yourself, to collaborate with other providers and family members, or to refer the student or caregiver elsewhere. The practice of referring students and families to other providers has been a common approach to dealing with children exhibiting significant emotional and behavioral problems. In many cases, this process has been a one-way ticket to "deep end" services (e.g., residential treatment) that remove the child from his community. The enormous costs and relative ineffectiveness of this strategy (Epstein et al., 1993) have driven the search for approaches to treatment that are not based on removal and containment. The system of care strategy for delivering intense treatment in natural settings has enabled many children to remain in their schools and communities (Rivera & Kutash, 1994; Stroul, 1993). The wraparound approach to service planning and delivery is a critical component of a system of care. Wraparound requires a team approach involving partnerships among parents and service providers. Therefore, participation in a service coordination team is an important addition to the role of special educators working with students with EBD.

Thus, collaboration with other professionals is an important part of your role, and you should learn to function as a team member. Obviously, both you and your students will experience greater support if the professionals and agencies with whom you collaborate render high-quality service. Maintain a list of agencies and persons who have proven their worth to you and to your students. This list should include a variety of human service agencies to allow maximum flexibility in wraparound planning. For example, your local Agricultural Extension Office may employ a home economist or family nutritionist who can consult with families and help with such diverse problems as budgeting income or providing a diet that meets basic nutritional requirements. In several instances we have collaborated with field nursing services on such problems as hygiene, diet, and general health care. Recreational therapists can help children gain access to camping programs and afterschool and recreational activities.

Even sparsely populated areas may be served by a variety of such professionals, and you may begin to develop a community resource guide by contacting your county courthouse or your state's department of human services to find out what services are locally available.[2] As suggested in the previous chapter, whenever you work with other professionals and parents, you should communicate your goals and objectives clearly.

Formal training and technical assistance regarding integrated service delivery and the wraparound process are beginning to emerge (for information, contact the CASSP Technical Assistance Center, Georgetown University Child Development Center, 2233 Wisconsin Avenue, N. W., Suite 1204, Washington, DC 20007 or access the Illinois State Board of Education EBD Network web page, www.ebdnetwork-il.org). Seek out such training and encourage others in the school community to do so as well. As the integration of services becomes more prevalent for children and youth with emotional and behavioral problems, educators will need to expand their information and skills in such areas as managed care (Malloy, 1995), child and family resources, and the effective use of human services in communities.

If you do not have the support of a building- or community-based interagency team and lack the opportunity to team informally with other providers, you may find yourself facing one of the most difficult solutions to the problem of being overwhelmed or overextended: saying no. If you or your school board have carefully defined and explained the limits of your services to your clientele initially, this should not alarm you. Nevertheless, there are tactful ways of declining, and there are

---

[2]Trained volunteers are used extensively in the system of care developed in Alaska (the Alaska Youth Initiative). See Burchard, Burchard, Sewall, and VanDenBerg (1993).

ways that reinforce people coming to you without building up false hopes that you will solve all their problems. Ideally, when you must say no, you will be able to refer the person or family to an appropriate service.

ADVOCACY. In your role as an advocate for students exhibiting problem behavior, you undoubtedly will find many shortcomings in the systems that serve them. These may include gaps in special educational provisions, or the lack of needed related services. When confronted by these problems, you have two choices: to campaign for the services your pupils require or to make do with what you have. The first option poses several questions: What educational or related services are most critical? Is the school or another agency responsible for providing these? What are the consequences to you of advocating for these services? IDEA obligates the agency responsible for each pupil's educational program to provide a free and appropriate educational program in the least restrictive environment. In addition, the agency must obtain the necessary related services, which include transportation and such developmental, corrective, and other supportive services as may be required to assist a student with a disability to benefit from special education.

Guthrie (1993) offered guidelines for determining whether related services are needed to accomplish the goals and objectives specified on a student's IEP. These are reproduced in Figure 12–5. In determining the need for related services, be aware that additional educational and related services cost money, and traditionally IDEA's mandate has been interpreted as requiring the education agency (e.g., local school district) to be accountable for these services.[3] In the absence of specific interagency agreements, your school district may be responsible for providing or funding

[3]The process of implementing a system of care typically involves planning how costs and resources are to be shared among agencies. Interagency memoranda of agreement are the vehicles used to establish fiscal and programmatic responsibility (see Skiba & Polsgrove, 1996).

related services included on the IEP. If this is the case, we suggest that you advocate for an interagency planning group in your community to deal with the complex issues of multiagency services. (Alternately, you may contact the Federation of Families for Children's Mental Health, 1021 Prince St., Alexandria, VA 22314–2971, which may have an active chapter in your state, for suggestions regarding how parents can facilitate the development of appropriate related services.)

Role Constraints

Role constraints apply to those interventions not suited for a person in your professional role, so the limitations in this category overlap considerably with ecological constraints. Related services such as psychotherapy or family counseling fit this category. Although you may feel qualified to provide informal counseling and the service you provide may be effective, you may not possess the professional authority (credentials or training) to render the service.

Another constraint exists if you are working in a day treatment or residential setting where the treatment program is prescribed and supervised by another professional. For example, a pupil may be institutionalized for treatment of a severe emotional or behavioral disorder or delinquency. In such a case, the treatment program probably will be developed and supervised by a mental health or correctional worker, and the education program will be only part of the total treatment package. In these situations, you may not be free to make unilateral treatment decisions or to implement programs that affect the student outside the school program.

Failure to recognize role constraints can result in wasteful duplication of effort. This often happens with children and youth with EBD because they come to the attention of several agencies. Another undesirable consequence results in the provision of conflicting treatment programs. For example, a psychiatrist may give a pupil cathartic play therapy for aggressive behavior while you use

Related services are supplemental, corrective, developmental, or therapeutic resources other than basic educational services needed by the child or youth with an educational disability in order for the child to benefit from, participate in, or be provided specially designed instruction.

After IEP goals, objectives and implementers and services are identified, MDT members discuss the objectives and services designed for the child or youth and decide whether:

a. Specially designed instruction alone will facilitate mastery of the IEP goals and objectives
b. Related services are needed.

MDT members determine the need for any related service based on answers to the following questions:

1. Will the child or youth be required to receive an education in a more restrictive environment if the related service is not provided?
2. Will personnel assigned to any objective be unable to implement strategies and activities leading to mastery of the objective without the related service?
3. Does the related service need to be provided within school facilities and during school hours in order for the child or youth to benefit from specially designed instruction?
4. Does the related service directly affect the acquisition of skills or information identified as a goal or outcome of public education for all children?
5. Is the related service required to allow the child or youth access to a public school program?

If the CST answers **yes** to **any** of these five questions, the need is a related service, and that service is included on the IEP.

If the CST answers **no** to **all** of these five questions or finds that the service requires provision by a licensed physician, the service being considered is determined to be solely for medical, health, or asthetic reasons. This service cannot be a related service and is not included on the IEP.

If a related service is identified, the CST members check the appropriate box on the IEP. Then the service is identified by type and nature (e.g., health services, catheterization; special transportation, bus with lift; physical therapy, strengthening exercise) and such a statement is written in the comments section on the Conference Summary Report.

FIGURE 12–5   IEP team determination of a related service.

Source: *Adapted from P. Guthrie (1993).* ARC determination of a related service. *Bowling Green, KY: Warren County Public Schools. Reprinted with permission of the author.*

contingency management for the same problem. If you assume too much of another professional's treatment responsibility, you may face professional sanction or at least suffer bad public relations in certain quarters. However, the most harmful consequence of overstepping role boundaries is that it erodes the effectiveness of all treatment or educational programs through professional conflict and disharmony. Students exhibiting severe behavior problems need consistency in their environment, and this is impossible when differ-

ent agencies or professionals pull in different directions or haggle with each other over territorial issues.

The suggestions for working with other professionals that were provided in the last chapter, as well as several of the responses to the ecological limitations discussed in the previous section, also will help you deal with role constraints. For example, you can clarify the goals and purposes of your program and concentrate on doing a credible job within your specific role. This point is well illustrated in the history of education programs for children and youth with EBD. Many early educational programs were established in residential treatment or psychiatric settings. Initially, these educational programs were regarded as little more than day care or as an adjunct to medically oriented treatment. However, such professional leaders as Bettelheim, Berkowitz, Rothman, Fenichel, Hobbs, Redl, Long, Morse, Haring, Phillips, Whelan, Wood, and Hewett have been instrumental in the development of an uniquely educational perspective and have helped establish credibility for the educator's role in treatment programs (see Kauffman, 2001; Kauffman & Lewis, 1974).

Hewett and Taylor's (1980) description of the opening of an educational program at the University of California at Los Angeles' Neuropsychiatric Institute (NPI) illustrates how educators have had to reconceptualize their role as distinct from that of other professionals. The school program originally was viewed as a babysitting service by the psychodynamically oriented staff. The teachers were not considered part of the powerful triumvirate composed of the psychiatrist, clinical psychologist, and psychiatric social worker. In time the educational staff began to see that their low status was caused by their failure to conceptualize the unique contribution of their role to the overall treatment program. The school staff then formulated their concept of an educational program in this setting in terms of teaching the skills pupils needed in order to function in less restrictive environments, making them better able to communicate with other professionals and contribute to the overall NPI program. As this example suggests, you should not try to imitate other human service providers; instead, you should provide educational services that are not available through any other professional group (instruction in social and academic skills).

If you are not working within an interdisciplinary facility, such as a hospital or residential treatment center, you will need to facilitate the student and family's access to services available from other agencies or persons (the question of whether these services are considered "related" under IDEA is not at issue here; assume, for the present, that your employing agency or the child's parents will pay for the service). Figure 12–6 is a checklist you may find useful in deciding whether to go outside your program for help with specific problems or to refer the student/family to a different treatment program (remember that all decisions to move a student toward a more restrictive environment or to alter a student's IEP must follow due process). Use Figure 12–6 in conjunction with Figures 12–2, 12–3, and 12–4 to gain a comprehensive picture of the problem, the student, and the student's ecological settings when contemplating a referral decision. (This figure also may be used to guide the MDT's decisions about the need for related services.) The questions in Figure 12–6 are intended to be illustrative rather than exhaustive. Those behaviors encompassed in the first question may suggest a request for related services, or interagency collaboration, whereas subsequent questions imply difficulty in reaching educational objectives with the pupil.

If your decision involves seeking assistance from other service providers, the questions of whose assistance you seek and for what services depend on the needs of the student (e.g., participation in an afterschool therapeutic program) and the parents (e.g., respite care for their child).[4] As indicated earlier, it is wise to maintain a log of your requests for collaborative assistance with appropriate evaluative comments. Keep this log confidential unless there are compelling professional reasons for making portions of it public (e.g., being subpoenaed in litigation against a professional who has worked with some of your pupils).

Fortunately, as stressed throughout this text, the notion of education as a treatment agency operating in isolation is giving way to the concept of a system of care, in which education works collaboratively with other agencies and families to help

[4]Refer back to Chapter 10 for additional guidelines about making referrals.

	Yes	Comments

1. Does the following apply to the pupil in any, in most, or, all of his ecological settings?

Language disorder (echolalia, pronomial reversal, mutism, etc.)? _____

Self-stimulation, self-mutilation, hallucinations, catastrophic reactions? _____

Rumination? _____

Encopresis, enuresis, obsessive-compulsive behaviors (e.g., rituals, preoccupying thoughts?) _____

Chronic depression? _____

Phobias? _____

Generalized anxiety? _____

Suicidal behavior? _____

Sleep disorders? _____

Gang delinquency? _____

Interpersonal aggression? _____

Excessive masturbation? _____

Chemical intoxication? _____

Seizures? _____

2. Are you unable to control the consequences, or are unable to gain the cooperation of those who do control consequences affecting the pupil's target behaviors? _____

3. Is (are) the pupil's problem behavior(s) not under the control of antecedent stimuli arranged by you? _____

4. Does the pupil fail to respond (appropriately or inappropriately) to consequences administered by you? _____

5. Are you unable to work with the parent? _____

6. Are you unable to identify or control any of the pupil's reinforcers? _____

7. Have you been ineffective in achieving meaningful gains with the pupil? _____

Specify goals not met: _____

_____

_____

_____

_____

8. Are there other reasons why you cannot or will not work with the pupil and/or his caregivers? _____

Note: If these problems are targeted on the student's IEP, you may be responsible as the primary treatment agent. However, you may also need to work with other agencies or professionals on these problems.

FIGURE 12–6 Checklist to identify the need for collaborative assistance.

students access a full range of services that meet their needs. Edgar and Siegel (1995) propose

> . . . an adequately funded comprehensive social services system for all those with special needs (i.e., persons with disabilities, teen parents, drug-involved youth, sexual minority youth, adjudicated youth, youth in group and foster homes, dropouts, low-income youth, homeless youth, and newcomers) that asks a simple and direct question: Does the individual need services? If the answer is yes, the services (based on an empowerment dynamic, meaning that the recipient's needs will diminish over time) are provided, and no further questions need be asked. (p. 279)

Edgar and Siegel also argue that the role of education should be to prepare youth for a place in society, which includes helping them to cope with the inequities of our culture; collaborate with other agencies; provide a range of services and options; and advocate for change outside the education arena. They observe that educators should recognize that 25% to 30% of U.S. citizens are disenfranchised by poverty and lack of opportunity and that we cannot pretend to serve children if we remain silent on the issue of change.

Legal Constraints

CONSTRAINTS ON THE ROLE OF TEACHERS. Today's newspapers contain numerous stories involving allegations of improper and illegal conduct by educators. The long-standing common law doctrine of in-loco parentis, giving teachers authority equivalent to that of parents, has been increasingly tested in the courts. As a teacher, you may be liable for injury sustained by a pupil as a result of negligence on your part or for defamatory material regarding students or fellow employees (contributory negligence must be ruled out in the case of older or more mature students). You or your agency also may be liable for negligence in depriving a student of appropriate treatment or due process (Yell, 1998).

The Council for Exceptional Children (CEC) has developed a code of ethics and professional stan-

dards to guide practitioners and define their professional responsibilities (Council for Exceptional Children, 1995). These consist of eight principles that form the basis for professional conduct.

1. Special education professionals are committed to developing the highest educational and quality of life potential of individuals with exceptionalities.
2. Special education professionals promote and maintain a high level of competence and integrity in practicing their profession.
3. Special education professionals engage in professional activities that benefit individuals with exceptionalities, their families, other colleagues, students, or research subjects.
4. Special education professionals exercise objective professional judgment in the practice of their profession.
5. Special education professionals strive to advance their knowledge and skills regarding the education of individuals with exceptionalities.
6. Special education professionals work within the standards and policies of their profession.
7. Special education professionals seek to uphold and improve where necessary the laws, regulations, and policies governing the delivery of special education and related services and the practice of their profession.
8. Special education professionals do not condone or participate in unethical or illegal acts, nor violate professional standards adopted by the Delegate Assembly of CEC.

The professional standards derived from these principles are grouped into seven categories: Instructional Responsibilities, Management of Behavior, Support Procedures, Parent Relationships, Advocacy, Professional Employment Certification and Qualification, and Professionals in Relation to the Profession and to other Professionals. It is important to become familiar with these standards because they will affect your professional obligations and influence critical decisions. You may download these standards from CEC's web page (www.cec.sped.org).

As you study these standards, you will see the potential for conflict with your employing agency. Thus, in following them you may be on sensitive ground. In general, teachers' rights as private citizens (freedom of speech, right to action, right to due process) have been upheld by the courts. The chief reasons for the dismissal of a teacher have included insubordination, incompetence, neglect of duty, inappropriate conduct, subversive activity, or decreased need for the person's services (Yell, 1998). If your behavior with respect to the above principles causes your employer to level charges against you, be prepared to seek legal counsel. You also may be named in a suit brought by a child's caregivers for failing to act in accordance with these principles. It is difficult to advocate for children while simultaneously maintaining allegiance to your employing agency.

Public Law 94–142 and its subsequent amendments address constraints on agencies providing educational services in that they declare and protect the civil rights of students with disabilities. The law guarantees these students the right to treatment, which encompasses procedural and substantive due process and equal protection, the right to equal educational opportunity, the right of access to their records, and the right to an individualized education. In addition, Thomas (1979) identified provisions that must be guaranteed by each state in their annual program plans. This list remains valid today:

1. Extensive child-find or child identification procedures. (The first priority is to identify children who are not receiving any type of education. The second priority is to identify those who are receiving an inadequate education).
2. A full-service goal and detailed timetable designed for the education of each child.

3. A guarantee of complete due process procedures.
4. The assurance of regular parent or guardian consultation.
5. Maintenance of programs and procedures for comprehensive personnel development, including in-service training.
6. Assurance of special education being provided to all children with disabilities in the least restrictive environment.
7. Assurance of nondiscriminatory testing and evaluation.
8. A guarantee of policies and procedures to protect the confidentiality of data and information.
9. Assurance of the maintenance of an individual program for all children with disabilities.
10. Assurance of an effective policy guaranteeing the right of all students with disabilities to a public education, at no cost to parents or guardians.
11. Assurance of a surrogate to act for any child when parents or guardians are either unknown or unavailable, or when the child is a ward of the state. (p. 10)

Your state department of education and employing agency are accountable for the implementation of policies, procedures, and safeguards. You are accountable for providing specific educational services in accordance with these guidelines. In the event that caregivers bring suit for failure to meet these provisions, you may be named as codefendant. If your professional behavior can be construed as negligent or unethical, you may be sued by the caregivers and not supported by your agency.

As a special educator, it also is necessary to have an understanding of IDEA and Section 504 of the Rehabilitation Act of 1973 (Yell, 1995). Most special education teacher preparation programs now include information concerning IDEA as part of their curriculum.[5] Information regarding the le-

---

[5]Several excellent books are available on special education law. See, for example, Weber (1992), and Yell (1998).

gal requirements of Section 504 is offered less frequently; nevertheless, it is incumbent upon both general and special educators to know about the provisions and requirements of the latter legislation. Under Section 504, a student is considered to have a disability if he has a physical or mental impairment that substantially limits one or more major life activities, *or is regarded as having such an impairment.* Students eligible for services under Section 504 may be eligible for related services even if they do not need special education. This law provides due process and procedural requirements similar to IDEA; however, it is broader and it is administered by the U.S. Department of Education's Office of Civil Rights instead of the Office of Special Education and Rehabilitation Services (Fossey, Hosie, Soniat, & Zirkel, 1995). Consult Fossey et al. for a succinct discussion of Section 504 and its implications for educators.

CONSTRAINTS ON THE USE OF BEHAVIORAL INTERVENTIONS. Legal constraints have been applied specifically to the use of aversive procedures in educational programs. (These issues were discussed at length in Chapter 4.) Although aversive procedures involve the presentation of a noxious stimulus or infringement of students' bodily or human rights, litigation generally has been restricted to corporal punishment in the form of spankings or beatings (Wood & Lakin, 1983). The school's right to use moderate corporal punishment has been upheld and is approved by most states. However, it has not been advocated in the special education literature (Wood, 1983), and the American Federation of Teachers, the National Education Association, the Council for Exceptional Children, and the American Psychological Association have issued statements opposing it.

The use of seclusion timeout also has been argued in the courts, although until recently, litigation has involved mental health facilities rather than public schools (Wood & Lakin, 1983; Yell, 1998). As indicated previously, a growing number of states and school districts are issuing policies regulating the use of behavioral interventions, particularly those involving restrictive or intrusive procedures.

Solutions to the problems posed by legal constraints are easier to suggest than to implement. With respect to your professional conduct, we suggest that you clarify your role and specific responsibilities and stay within them. By all means, follow the Code of Ethics and Professional Standards adopted by the CEC (1995), but in so doing, make it clear that your goal is to improve pupil services, not to subvert the system or its administrators. Also carefully study IDEA, Section 504, and, particularly if you are working in settings that involve the employment of persons with disabilities, the Americans with Disabilities Act.

Guidelines for the use of aversive procedures are provided in Chapter 4, but here we emphasize that punishment is justified when the behavior it suppresses is more injurious to the individual or to others than the punishment itself and when no alternative exists (Wood, 1983). Do not use corporal punishment; it is too subjective and is likely to have a long history of misapplication with your students. Instead, apply planned, objective, and systematic procedures such as extinction, verbal reprimands, response cost, or timeout in conjunction with positive reinforcement of incompatible behavior. If you must use a more extreme technique (overcorrection, aversive consequences), see Wood's (1983) suggestions:

1. All reasonable alternatives should be considered, if not tried, first. This consideration should be documented.
2. Do not apply punishment of any type without first becoming thoroughly familiar with your state and local regulations.
3. The lines of authority for the punishment procedure should be clear.
4. Punishment should be adequately supervised, monitored, and externally reviewed.
5. All persons using punishment should understand its dynamics and complexities.

In addition, remember that prior parental consent to use punishment in an educational program is required by IDEA, and parents have the right to withdraw consent at any time.

INTERACTIVE TEAMING

Chapter 11 indicated that approaches based on school staff collaborations show great promise for delivering effective interventions for students who exhibit significant problem behavior. In this and previous chapters, we argued for a wraparound approach to service planning and delivery for students who present significant behavioral and emotional challenges to educators and other service providers. Interactive teaming (Thomas, Correa, & Morsink, 1995) is a process that structures the coordination of decision making among professionals who engage in collaborative planning on behalf of children and their families. An interactive teaming model is a new concept based on equal partnerships and shared decision making. Figure 12–7 illustrates the differences between the present system of serving students with special needs and this new model.

In a relatively short period of time, much has been learned about effective teamwork in educational decision making. Teaming greatly increases the ability to implement sound interventions on behalf of students and their families while at the same time providing support and technical assistance to teachers.

Team membership should be based on who can help meet the student's needs rather than on who occupies roles traditionally associated with decision making for students (e.g., building principal, guidance counselor, school psychologist). It is important to realize that merely requiring that persons function as members of teams will not ensure their effectiveness. In order for teams to be successful, ongoing, accountable training and technical assistance are required. Table 12–3 contrasts the characteristics of effective and ineffective teams. Phillips and McCullough (1992) have de-

veloped an in-service curriculum for preparing both staff and parents to work as effective student/staff support teams. Thomas et al. (1995) provided thoughtful guidance for team development. Use these resources to increase the ability of school staff to form and maintain effective teams with parents and other providers on behalf of children and youth with emotional and behavioral needs. Recognize that teaming not only supports children and families, but also the professionals who work with them daily. Therefore, the presence of interactive teams in schools is an important benefit to you and your colleagues, and we strongly encourage you to seek training in this area and to take a leadership role in the formation of such teams.

STRESS AND BURNOUT

Factors such as low pay discourage many young people from entering the field of education. Teachers' salaries have not kept pace with those of comparable professions. In his seventh annual address on the state of American education, Secretary of Education Richard W. Riley noted that teachers with master's degrees earn an average of $32,000 less per year than their counterparts in other fields (*Lexington Herald-Leader*, February 23, 2000). Special education has been particularly affected by teacher shortages. Throughout the country, many school districts are unable to find qualified professional special educators. For example, in Kentucky, 916, or 15% of, teachers certified to teach students with Learning and Behavioral Disorders (the category in which students with EBD are served) currently have emergency or probationary certificates (Scott Smith, personal communication, March 16, 2000). Moreover, low pay and the conditions under which education professionals must work discourage many teachers from remaining in the field. Six percent of all teachers leave the field each year, and 9.3% of teachers in urban schools leave at the end of their first year of teaching (Boyer & Gillespie, 2000). Attrition among spe-

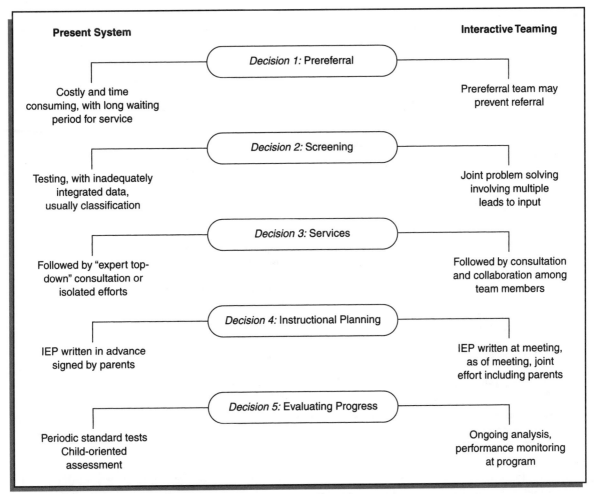

Present System   **Interactive Teaming**

Decision 1: Prereferral

Costly and time consuming, with long waiting period for service

Prereferral team may prevent referral

Decision 2: Screening

Testing, with inadequately integrated data, usually classification

Joint problem solving involving multiple leads to input

Decision 3: Services

Followed by "expert top-down" consultation or isolated efforts

Followed by consultation and collaboration among team members

Decision 4: Instructional Planning

IEP written in advance signed by parents

IEP written at meeting, as of meeting, joint effort including parents

Decision 5: Evaluating Progress

Periodic standard tests Child-oriented assessment

Ongoing analysis, performance monitoring at program

FIGURE 12–7 Contrasts between the current system and the proposed model for interactive teaming.

Source: Thomas, C. C., Correa, V. I., & Morsink, C. V. (1995). Interactive teaming: Consultation and collaboration in special programs. (2nd ed.). Copyright Prentice Hall. Used with permission.

cial educators, including teachers of students with EBD, is particularly acute. For example, Wrobel (1993) reports that 1,355 licensed EBD teachers in Minnesota chose not to work in programs for this student population, despite 303 position vacancies. Boyer and Gillespie (2000, p. 10) report that special education teachers leave the field for the following reasons:

- Insufficient certification
- Excessive paperwork

- The stress of working with students with disabilites
- The lack of balance between extrinsic rewards and demands
- Unfulfilled intrinsic rewards
- Personal change factors
- Perceptions of high stress
- Frustrations with school climate

Burnout has been defined as "emotional exhaustion resulting from the stress of interpersonal

TABLE 12–3 Characteristics of Effective and Ineffective Teams

An Effective Team	An Ineffective Team
A team is a unified group of people who join in a cooperative problem-solving process to reach a shared goal.	• Goals are unclear. • Members are unprepared. • Leadership is poor. • Commitment to task is lacking.
Effective	**Ineffective**
Participation and leadership are distributed among all members.	Participation is unequal, leadership is delegated and based on authority.
Goals are cooperatively formed to meet individual and group needs.	Members accept imposed goals.
Ability and information determine influence and power.	Position determines influence; obedience to authority is stressed.
Two-way communication.	Communication about ideas is one-way; feelings are ignored.
Decision-making steps are matched with situation: consensus is sought for important decisions.	Decisions are made by highest authority with minimal member involvement.
Conflict is brought out and resolved.	Conflict is ignored, avoided, or denied.

Source: *Reprinted with permission from the publisher. Anderlini, L. S. (1983). An in-service program for improving team participation in educational decision-making.* School Psychology Review, 12, 163.

contact" (Maslach, 1978, p. 56). How well you are able to maintain a healthy perspective of your job and your students in the face of stress depends on a number of factors. Researchers are just beginning to study and delineate these variables for educators working with children and youth with EBD. However, because a person's emotional reactions to job stresses are subjective and highly individualized, it is difficult to obtain reliable, objective data on the subject.

Causes and Effects of Stress

Since stress is an integral part of working with pupils who exhibit challenging behavior, be aware of other variables that can be emotionally and physically draining, for these may influence your decision to accept a job, change your place of employment, or leave the field entirely. Pullis (1992) administered a questionnaire to 244 teachers of students with EBD, using the Pullis Inventory of Teacher Stress (PITS). The teachers in his sample rated school or setting factors, such as inadequate school discipline policy, attitudes and behavior of administrators, evaluation by administrators/supervisors, attitudes and behavior of other teachers/professionals, and too much work to do, as more stressful than pupil characteristics. Pullis observed that these results supported those of Schmid, et al. (1990), in that teachers report feeling greater emotional exhaustion and emotional distancing when they saw their program as not having adequate resources or support.

Pullis (1992) also found that his sample of teachers most frequently experienced exhaustion, frustration, feeling overwhelmed, carryover to outside life, guilt, and irritability. These effects were similar to those reported by learning disability resource teachers in an earlier study (Pullis, 1983), except that teachers of students with EBD reported carryover to life outside of school.

The causes of stress among teachers of students with behavioral challenges reflect conditions that occur frequently in their workplaces. Trying to deal with the educational system; spending hours working outside the classroom; encountering nonsupportive school administrators and staff; and negative attitudes by professional colleagues have had a negative impact on the recruitment and retention of special education professionals. Fortunately, a number of initiatives are being launched to address these problems.

Coping with Stress

One part of the PITS consists of 15 strategies for coping with stress. Respondents to Pullis' (1992) study rated activities in the workplace (e.g., time management and discussions with colleagues), in addition to strategies used away from work (e.g., hobbies, nutrition, and exercise) as most effective. Interactions with other special education professionals was mentioned specifically as a factor contributing to job satisfaction. Respondents also indicated a desire for more courses and workshops to improve or update their skills. Unfortunately, substantial numbers of teachers reported using strategies that are not healthy coping mechanisms, including smoking; taking alcohol, drugs, or prescription medication; and excessive eating.

Many of the variables that should be changed to reduce stress are controlled by your employing agency, not by you. For example, Zabel and Zabel (1980) indicated that the probability of burnout may be reduced by lowering the student-teacher ratio, reducing working hours, providing opportunities for time away from the job, sharing student loads through team teaching, and training in dealing with stress. All of these tactics require organizational change, which involves policy decisions at higher administrative levels. Wrobel (1993) indicated that an important addition to the curriculum for teachers of children with EBD consists of skills in working effectively with the school administration.

Developing teacher mentor networks is a strategy for supporting and retaining special education teachers. Beginning teachers indicate that having access to an experienced mentor as one of the most important contributors to their early job satisfaction (Conderman & Stephens, 2000; McCaffrey, 2000; Whitaker, 2000). A mentor is a special educator who knows and understands the needs of the students being taught by the new special educator (Boyer & Gillespie, 2000). Other important supports include the following (Boyer & Gillespie, 2000):

- Providing the new teacher with released time for guided observations of experienced special educators who serve students with the same needs.
- Ensuring that the new teacher has access to communication technology that allows for communication with experienced special educators.
- Scheduling regular group sessions that provide an opportunity for new teachers to share experiences and ask advice of experienced teachers, teacher educators, or specialists.
- Ensuring that new teachers have access to content training on such topics as developing IEPs, working with paraprofessionals, managing behavior, adapting curriculum, determining appropriate accommodations, differentiating instruction, and coordinating diagnostic results with the selection of instructional methods.
- Helping new teachers to reflect on teaching practices and their impact on student progress.

Beginning special education teachers report that their mentors were instrumental in helping them to feel, and be, more effective at their jobs (Conderman & Stephens, 2000). In addition, mentors benefit from such relationships through learning about new methods and research information from their mentees, as well as from being acknowledged as a skilled and experienced practitioner.

Conderman and Stephens (2000) offer several potential strategies for responding to some of the issues that are faced by beginning teachers. These are presented in Table 12–4. Bear in mind that these issues and their alternate solutions apply equally as well to experienced special educators who, for example, are re-assigned to a new school or school district.

Perhaps the best deterrent to stress and burnout is feeling competent in one's role. Maroney (2000) identified a number of resources for beginning (or experienced) special educators. These include books, manuals, and web pages addressing topics related to effective instruction, behavior management, and developing interests and activities outside one's professional role. A number of these resources have been cited in earlier chapters of this text. Additional information may be obtained from

TABLE 12–4 Possible Issues and Responses Faced by Beginning Special Education Teachers

Possible Issues	Possible Responses
Unsure how to approach general educators who appear unsupportive of having students with disabilities in their classrooms.	• Do not make assumptions about general educators' knowledge of students with disabilities • Be realistic and stay focused • Be patient with colleagues • Initiate and maintain effective communications systems
Unfamiliar with successful inclusion practices or models.	• Use flexible learning objectives • Use multiple adaptations • Consider consultation, team teaching, involving paraprofessionals, and limited pullout services • Evaluate the inclusion program
Lack of experience in working collaboratively with families and other service providers.	• Provide information to parents • Talk with parents, not at them • Avoid stereotyping students and their families • Establish and maintain effective communication systems • Use a variety of group process strategies
Unsure how to work with a paraprofessional.	• Understand your roles and those of your administrator regarding your paraprofessional • Develop clear roles and responsibilities • Consider the training and skills of the paraprofessional • Employ the steps of delegating • Engage in continuous planning, training, coaching, and feedback
Experiencing feelings of inadequacy or loneliness.	• Assess personal psychological needs • Create a personal development plan • Acquire new coping skills • Enhance personal growth through the use of communication skills and preventative measures

Source: Adapted from Conderman, G., and Stephens, J. T. (2000). Reflections from Beginning Special Educators. Teaching Exceptional Children, 33(1), pp. 16–21. Copyright 2000 by the Council for Exceptional Children. Used with permission.

the following web sites (Conderman & Stephens, 2000; Maroney, 2000; Whitaker, 2000):

- Best Practices in Mentoring (http://www.teacherementors.com)
- The Council for Exceptional Children (www.cec.sped.org)
- Education World (http://www.education-world.com)
- ERIC Clearinghouse on Disabilities and Gifted Education (www.ericec.org)
- ERIC Clearinghouse on Teaching and Teacher Education (http://www.ericsp.org)
- IDEA Practices (http://www.ideapractices.org)
- The International Mentoring Association (http://www.umich.edu/conferconces/mentoring)
- Mentoring Leadership and Resource Network of ASCD (http://www.mentors.net)
- National Foundation for the Improvement of Education (http://www.nfie.org)
- National Information Center for Children and Youth with Disabilities (http://www.nichy.org)
- Special Education Services on the Internet (http://www.hood.edu/seri)
- TeacherNet.com (http://www.teachernet.com)
- Teachers Helping Teachers (http://www.pacificnet.net/~mandel)

It is true that while the skills needed to be effective with pupils who exhibit emotional and behavioral challenges can be learned, not everyone is cut out for this work. Effective teachers who remain in the field share a commitment to their students, and this is one of their major sources of satisfaction. Wood (1995) interviewed teachers about their profession. A few of their representative comments help to put our work in perspective:

> "Most of my satisfaction comes from the kids—seeing them feel as if they belong, seeing them feel good doing something. I also love the freedom to try new, different things, figuring out how to do whatever it takes [to help someone learn]. Also I'm not stuck teaching boring subjects. My role affords me the opportunity to have fun and be a little bizarre myself from time to time."

> "If you don't like these kinds of kids, then don't even consider teaching students with EBD. You'll know pretty quick if you like it. If you have a negative attitude about these kids, then forget it."

> "They can drive you nuts, but they're never dull." (pp. 13–14).

As we have tried to demonstrate throughout this text, and especially in this chapter, working with problem students, their families, and their communities is difficult. Remaining psychologically fit and professionally effective requires that you know your role and its limitations. This is not sufficient, however. To be a successful educator who works with pupils with challenging behavior, regardless of whether they have been formally identified as having EBD, you also must be highly skilled. We hope this text has helped you acquire the skills you need to feel, and be, effective.

CHAPTER 12 CASE STUDY

Developing a Wraparound Plan

Pamela Johnson and Donna T. Meers
The Bridges Project, Kentucky Division of Mental Health

In an effort to redesign and enhance the comprehensive system of care for children with emotional disturbance (ED) and their families, the Kentucky Department of Mental Health and Mental Retardation Services, Division of Mental Health, obtained a 5-year grant from the Center for Mental Health Services. This project, "Building Bridges of Support: One Community at a Time," (or Bridges), serves three rural Appalachian regions of southeastern Kentucky. The Bridges project builds on a strong interagency infrastructure known as Kentucky IMPACT, in partnership with public schools, to address children's needs via a family-focused, culturally competent, flexibly-funded, community-based, and accountable system of care.

In coordination with the local education agencies' Family Resource and Youth Service Centers, Student Service Teams (SSTs) develop, implement, and organize school-based wraparound planning in each identified elementary, middle, and high school in all target regions. The SSTs are comprised of three core team members: (1) a student service coordinator, who oversees effective case management, service coordination, and access to appropriate service components; (2) a family liaison, who ensures that the caregivers of children receiving services are engaged as true partners with professionals, empowered to effectively care for and to support their child; and (3) an intervention specialist, who helps design and model appropriate interventions, including but not limited to behavior intervention plans. These wraparound plans build upon the strengths that exist in the student, his or her family, and the service providers to increase the likelihood that the child will succeed in school, home, and community environments. In addition to these core team members, the SST identifies extended team members who are key members of the school staff (i.e., teacher(s), counselor, and principal), parents, and other members of the community who may be influential in the student's life.

The following case example illustrates a school-based wraparound plan developed by a SST for Joe. Joe is a 16-year-old Caucasian male referred to the Bridges Project due to his frequent angry outbursts and verbal aggression when asked to follow adult directions both at school and in his home. Joe was referred to an alternative educational setting by his home school for refusing to attend classes, but continued to have poor attendance even after he was placed in this setting.

The wraparound process began with the identification of core team members, consisting of Joe, his mother, a student service coordinator, family liaison, and an intervention specialist. Other persons joined the team as extended team members, individuals likely to be most invested in working collaboratively to meet Joe's needs and toward mutually agreed upon goals. These persons were identified through informal initial conversations with Joe, his mother, and core team members.

The first step of the wraparound process was to facilitate discovery of strengths. Each team meeting began with the identification and review of strengths from the perspective of each team member. This process provided a framework for using the strengths of Joe, his family, and other stakeholders to design intervention strategies that addressed the issues that prompted Joe's referral to the Bridges Project. The team then prioritized three needs by consensus and developed action steps to be taken to address each need. Again, the action steps were developed using the strengths identified earlier in the process. After the action plan was developed, roles and responsibilities were assigned and documented for each team member by consensus of the wraparound team.

The team developed a plan to be implemented by Joe's mother. This plan addressed school attendance, anger, and verbal aggression (see Figure 12–8). Joe's mother used a behavior checksheet to document when Joe got up for school by the third request, used appropriate language, and demonstrated respect for property. Joe's mother tracked these behaviors for 5 days. If Joe met the goals of the plan, he received a reward. Also, the mental health specialist on the team taught Joe self-calming strategies. These strategies were to be used when Joe became anxious about new situations or tasks, which typically led to an angry outburst. Joe was taught to use a self-monitoring form to track when he used his self-calming strategies. Joe rated his behavior daily and received a gift certificate from the intervention specialist after he completed 10 days of accurate self-monitoring. The self-monitoring process reinforced Joe's use of self-calming strategies. This plan was successful in improving Joe's attendance from an average percent of daily attendance of 40% prior to intervention to 95% after intervention.

Joe's team met five times during the school year. The composition of his team changed during the academic year as extended team members were added in response to new strengths, issues, and concerns identified over time. Needs and outcomes also changed as Joe made progress and reached desired outcomes. For instance, the concerns and issues at the first team meeting were "refusing to go to school" and "not attending class when he did attend school." At the fourth team meeting, the need for appropriate clothing to promote peer acceptance, and transportation to school field trips were identified. By the fifth meeting, the team noted that the needs identified in the first wraparound planning meeting were now identified as strengths: Joe had good attendance and liked school.

Name <u>Joe S.</u>   Social Security # _____

I. Planning Step 1: "Getting the Family Story/Initial Conversations"

A. *Identify the Core Team Members*

Members	**Role**
Susan S.	Mother—Advocate—Provider
Kathy H.	Coordinate resources for student and family
Pam J.	Behavior Planning—Facilitate wraparound process/plan/support
Alice M.	Family Liaison

Extended Team Members	**Role**
Mrs. Thompson	Language Arts Instructor—Support—General Education
Ms. Stephens	Special Education Instructor—Support
Mr. Hamic	Instructor of science—Support
Dr. A.	Evaluate for medication
Mary Ellen M.	Provide therapy for anger management and social skills
Sally G.	Special Education Coordination
Howard S.	Protection, coordinate resources for family, assist mother via system support with safety issues, limit setting, liaison to court

B. **Signs to Look For**

Signs to Look For	**Planned Response**	**Contacts/Support**
Verbal Aggression	Out-of-class cool down	Intervention Specialist, Guidance Counselor, Mrs. Thompson
Angry Outburst	Contact Mother—She will come to school to request appropriate assessment and intervention	Susan J., Mental Health Clinician/Intervention Specialist, School Principal, social services

C. *Strengths Discovery* (Try for multiple perspectives in multiple domains)

Date	Perspective Y=Youth F=Family S=School C=Community	Domain Key on page 435	Strengths/Interests
9/28	S	ev	Good verbal skills
9/28	S	pe	Can manage anger at times
9/28	S	sr	Participation in intramural sports
9/28	S	ev	Likes to read aloud in class
9/28	Y/F	fs	Good relationship with brother
11/15	Y/F	fs,ls,pe	Has begun to help mother with chores at home

FIGURE 12–8   Bridges project wraparound planning form.

Date	Perspective Y=Youth F=Family S=School C=Community	Domain Key at bottom of page	Strengths/Interests
11/15	Y/S	ev,pe	Joe is able to express concerns and ask for help from teacher in an appropriate manner
12/16	F/S	fs,pe	Joe has been able to complete behavior plan at home and school. He met objective and received reward.
12/16	S	ev,sr,pe	Teacher relates positive communication and interaction when Joe taught him how to play an electronic game. Rapport and trust building facilitated. Teacher represents positive male role model.
2/2	S	ev	Eager to participate
2/2	F	ev,pe	Has been up early and ready to go to school
2/2	F/Y	hm	Glasses have been ordered and will be paid by Medicaid. Improved in using anger management strategies.
3/4	F/Y/S	ev	Attendance has improved to 95%. Joe is able to use self-monitoring to track angry episode and volume of voice indoors.
5/12	Y/F/S	ev,pe	Attendance at school is GOOD!
5/12	Y/F/S	ev,pe	Student likes school!

Domain Key: fs= family support; l=legal; ls=living situation; hm=health/medical; s=safety; ev=educational/vocational; sr=social/recreational; csp=cultural/spiritual;

D. *Issues and Concerns*

Date	Perspective Y=Youth F=Family S=School C=Community	Issues/Concerns
9/28	F/S/C	Absent from school (school attendance 40%)
9/28	F/S	Refuses to go to school
9/28	F/S	Refuses to go to class when at school
9/28	F	Defiant with his mother
9/28	S	Fidgety in class
9/28	F/S	Poor peer relations, lacks social skills, problems making friends

FIGURE 12–8   Bridges project wraparound planning form—*Continued*.

Date	Perspective Y=Youth F=Family S=School C=Community	Issues/Concerns
11/15	Y/F/S	Court date for truancy and beyond parental control
11/15	Y/F	Anxiety in new situations
2/2	F/S	Tone of voice; high volume of voice indoors
2/2	Y/F/S	Anger
2/2	F/S	Impatient
3/4	F	Agitation due to ban on smokeless tobacco at school
5/12	F	Clothing to assist with self-esteem and socialization with peers
5/12	F	Money for field trip
5/12	F	Transportation for 7:30 A.M. to leave for field trip

II. Planning Step 3: First Meeting and Follow-up Meetings

Develop Team-based Mission Statement

> Mission Statement:
> To provide support and planning to assist Joe in meeting the goals to graduate from high school.

III. and IV. Planning Steps 4 and 5: First Meeting and Follow-up Meetings

A. Identify Needs/Outcomes in all Applicable Life Domains (Comprehensive)

B. Prioritize Specific Needs/Outcomes by Indicating Date for Strategizing

> Domain Key: fs=family support; l=legal; ls=living situation; hm=health/medical;
> s=safety; ev=educational/vocational; sr=social/recreational.

> Team Choices: 2–3 Needs/Outcomes as Most Immediate or Critical. Signify by Date Prioritized. Priorities will likely change over time. Code Follow-up Status as: C=Continuing; M=Met; NA=No Longer Priority or Discontinued.

Date of Meeting: 9/28

Domain	Need	Outcome	Prioritized Date	F/U Status
ev	Improved Attendance	Joe will get up and get ready for school by 3rd request from his mother	9/28	

FIGURE 12–8 Bridges project wraparound planning form—*Continued*.

Domain	Need	Outcome	Prioritized Date	F/U Status
pe,s	Decrease angry outburst	Joe will replace explosive behaviors with self-calming strategies	9/28	
fs	Decrease defiant behavior at home	Joe will begin to make friends at school	9/28	

V, VI and VII. Planning Steps 6, 7, and 8: First Meeting and Follow-up Meeting(s)

V.   Develop Action Plans Addressing Prioritized Needs (Connect to Strengths)

VI.   Solicit Commitments/Assign Tasks

VII.   Review Prioritized Needs/Outcomes, Assess Status, Modify Action Steps to Address Identified Barriers-Ongoing

Date	Prioritized Needs	Outcome(s)	Strength(s)	Time Specific Action Steps	Responsible Team Member	Review Date & Status
9/28	Increase attendance at school	Joe will get up and get ready for school by 3rd request from mother.	Verbal @ school; likes to read; responds to positive reinforcement.	Attendance plan: Joe will receive reward at 10th day. Received: 10/10.	Joe, Intervention Specialist	10/28 C
9/28	Decrease angry outbursts	Joe will replace explosive behaviors with self-calming strategies.	Joe has demonstrated ability to manage anger.	Prompts for "out of class" "cool down." Psychiatric Evaluation scheduled, 9/28.	Teacher, Joe, Intervention Specialist, Therapist, and Psychiatrist	10/28 C Psy. Eval- M
9/28	Decrease defiant behavior at home	Joe will respond in appropriate manner to mother's request to get up for school.	Joe's mother is interested in doing behavior plan at home.	Behavior plan developed for home. Joe receive positive reinforcement.	Joe, Joe's mother, Intervention Specialist	10/28 C
9/28	Decrease problems with peers Increase making friends skill.	Joe will begin to make friends at school.	Verbal skills.	Peer tutoring to provide opportunity to interact with peers.	Teacher (general ed.), Mrs. Thompson and Mr. Hamic	10/28 C

FIGURE 12–8   Bridges project wraparound planning form—*Continued.*

SUMMARY

The complexity and intensity of working with students exhibiting behavioral problems require high levels of dedication and expertise by professional educators. To function effectively, these persons need adequate support systems in their working and personal environments; they must recognize and work within the limitations of their roles. The foundation of effective instruction and behavioral interventions for students with or at-risk for EBD is a system of school-wide positive behavior support, which addresses the full range of student behavior, from primary prevention through universal interventions to the most intensive level of support. Optimal programming for children and youth with EBD should address their needs and the needs of other persons who care for and work with them across many different ecological settings. Our culture's practice of institutionalizing human services according to specific settings and agencies constrains those who must work within formal professional roles. This chapter has described some of these constraints and has suggested guidelines and strategies for working more effectively within them. Ultimately, the success of interventions on behalf of students with emotional and behavioral disabilities will depend upon our ability to bridge professional and political boundaries. Our responsibility is to design strategies for students that provide meaningful habilitative or rehabilitative experiences to ensure the skills acquired in educational settings are retained and used to facilitate lifelong patterns of success.

DISCUSSION QUESTIONS

1. What are the constraints that affect educators working in each of the following roles: special education resource teacher, special education self-contained classroom teacher, school psychologist, school social worker?

2. As a special education teacher, how would you deal with the problem of a regular classroom teacher who uses corporal punishment with one of your students?

3. How would you respond to parents who request your help in managing their child's behavior outside of school? (The student is being seen by a psychologist in private practice.)

4. The principal of your school wants to refer one of your pupils to a residential treatment program. You disagree with this action, but the principal insists. What should you do?

5. A psychiatrist has prescribed an antipsychotic drug for a student with EBD in your school. You have observed that the student is lethargic, withdrawn, and experiencing trouble concentrating. The parent, however, is pleased with the child's improved behavior at home and will not consider asking the psychiatrist to adjust the dosage. What course of action will you take?

6. You have been asked to participate in designing a study of burnout in your school district. How would you assess staff to identify signs of stress and burnout? What recommendations could you offer to reduce or prevent it?

REFERENCES

Boyer, L., & Gillespie, P. (2000). Keeping the committed: The importance of induction and support programs for new special educators. *Teaching Exceptional Children, 33*(1), 10–15.

Burchard, J. D., Burchard, S. N., Sewall, R., & VanDenBerg, J. (1993). *One kid at a time: Evaluative case studies and description of the Alaska Youth Initiative demonstration project.* Department of Mental Health/Mental Retardation, State of Alaska, Center for Mental Health Services Substance Abuse and Mental Health Services Administration, U.S. Department of Health and Human Services.

Burns, B. J., & Goldman, S. K. (Eds.). (1998). *Promising practices in wraparound for children with serious emotional dis-*

turbance and their families: Systems of care: Promising practices in children's mental health 1998 series, Volume IV. (Report No. EC307 170). Washington, DC: National Technical Assistance Center for Children's Mental Health Services Administration. (ERIC Document Reproduction Service No. ED 429 422).

Conderman, G., & Stephens, J. T. (2000). Voices from the field: Reflections from beginning special educators. Teaching Exceptional Children, 33(1), 16–21.

Council for Exceptional Children. (1995). What every special educator must know: The international standards for the preparation and certification of special education teachers. Reston, VA: Author.

Eber, L. (1996). Restructuring schools through the wraparound approach: The LADSE experience. In R. J. Illback & C. M. Nelson (Eds.), Emerging school-based approaches for children with emotional and behavioral problems: Research and practice in service integration (pp. 135–149). New York: Haworth Press.

Eber, L. (1997, Winter). Improving school-based interventions through use of the wraparound process. Reaching Today's Youth (pp. 32–36), National Education Service.

Eber, L., Osuch, R., & Redditt, C. A. (1996). School-based applications of the wraparound process: Early results on service provision and student outcomes. Journal of Child and Family Studies, 5, 83–89.

Edgar, E., & Siegel, S. (1995). Postsecondary scenarios for troubled and troubling youth. In J. M. Kauffman, J. W. Lloyd, D. P. Hallahan, & T. A. Astuto (Eds.), Issues in educational placement: Students with emotional and behavioral disorders (pp. 251–283). Hillsdale, NJ: Lawrence Erlbaum Associates.

Epstein, M. H., Nelson, C. M., Polsgrove, L., Coutinho, M., Cumblad, M., & Quinn, K. (1993). A comprehensive community-based approach to serving students with emotional and behavioral disorders. Journal of Emotional and Behavioral Disorders, 1 (2), 127–135.

Fossey, R., Hosie, T., Soniat, K., & Zirkel, P. (1995). Section 504 and "front line" educators: An expanded obligation to serve children with disabilities. Preventing School Failure, 39(2), 10–14.

Guthrie, P. (1993, November). ARC determination of a related service. Bowling Green, KY: Warren County Public Schools.

Hewett, F. M., & Taylor, F. D. (1980). The emotionally disturbed child in the classroom: The orchestration of success (2nd ed.). Boston: Allyn & Bacon.

Katz-Leavy, J. W., Lourie, I. S., Stroul, B. A., & Zeigler-Dendy. C. (1992). Individualized services in a system of care. Washington, DC: CASSP Technical Assistance Center, Georgetown University Child Development Center.

Kauffman, J. M. (2001). Characteristics of children's behavior disorders (7th ed.). Upper Saddle River, NJ: Merrill/Prentice Hall.

Kauffman, J. M., & Lewis, C. D. (Eds.). (1974). Teaching children with behavior disorders: Personal perspectives. Upper Saddle River, NJ: Merrill/Prentice Hall.

Malloy, M. (1995, April). Mental illness and managed care: A primer for families and consumers. Arlington, VA: National Alliance for the Mentally Ill.

Maroney, S. A. (2000). What's good? Suggested resources for beginning special education teachers. Teaching Exceptional Children, 33(1), 22–27.

Maslach, C. (1978). Job burnout: How people cope. Public Welfare, 36, 56–58.

McCaffrey, M. E. (2000). My first year of learning: Advice from a new educator. Teaching Exceptional Children, 33(1), 4–8.

Phillips, V., & McCullough, L. L. (1992). Student/staff support teams. Longmont, CO: Sopris West.

Pullis, M. (1983). Stress as a way of life: Special challenges for the LD resource teacher. Topics in Learning and Learning Disabilities, 3, 24–36.

Pullis, M. (1992). An analysis of the occupational stress of teachers of the behaviorally disordered: Sources, effects, and strategies for coping. Behavioral Disorders, 17, 190–201.

Rivera, V. R., & Kutash, K. (1994). Components of a system of care: What does the research say? Tampa, FL: University of South Florida, Florida Mental Health Institute, Research and Training Center on Children's Mental Health.

Schmid, K. D., Schatz, C. J., Walter, M. B., Shidla, M. C., Leone, P. E., & Trickett, E. J. (1990). Providing help: Characteristics and correlates of stress, burnout, and accomplishment across three groups of teachers. In R. B. Rutherford, Jr., & S. A. DiGangi (Eds.), Severe behavior disorders of children and youth (Vol. 13) (pp. 115–127). Reston, VA: Council for Children with Behavioral Disorders.

Skiba, R., & Polsgrove, L. (1996). Developing a system of care: Interagency collaboration for students with emotional and behavioral disorders. Reston, VA: Council for Exceptional Children.

Stroul, B. A. (1993). Systems of care for children and adolescents with severe emotional disturbances: What are the results? Washington, DC: CASSP Technical Assistance Center, Georgetown University Child Development Center.

Stroul, B. A., & Friedman, R. M. (1986). A system of care for children and youth with severe emotional disturbances.

Washington, DC: Georgetown University Child Development Center, CASSP Technical Assistance Center.

Sugai, G., Horner, R. H., Dunlap, G., Hieneman, M., Lewis, T. J., Nelson, C. M., Scott, T., Liaupsin, C., Sailor, W., Turnbull, A. P., Turnbull, H. R. III, Wickham, D., Wilcox, B., & Ruef, M. (2000). Applying positive behavior support and functional behavioral assessment in schools. *Journal of Positive Behavior Interventions*, 2, 131–143.

Thomas, C. C. (1979). *PL 94–142: An instructional module for inservice training*. Frankfort, KY: Office of Education for Exceptional Children, Kentucky Department of Education.

Thomas, C. C., Correa, V. I., & Morsink, C. V. (1995). *Interactive teaming: Consultation and collaboration in special programs* (2nd ed.). Upper Saddle River, NJ: Merrill/Prentice Hall.

Wahler, R. G., & Cormier, W. H. (1970). The ecological interview: A first step in outpatient behavior therapy. *Journal of Behavior Therapy and Experimental Psychiatry*, 1, 279–289.

Weber, M. C. (1992). *Special education law and litigation treatise*. Horsham, PA: LPR Publications.

Whitaker, S. D. (2000). What do first year special education teachers need? Implications for induction programs. *Teaching Exceptional Children*, 33(1), 28–36.

Wood, F. H. (1983). Punishment and special education: Some concluding comments. In F. H. Wood & K. C. Lakin (Eds.), *Punishment and aversive stimulation in special education: Legal, theoretical, and practical issues in their use with emotionally disturbed children and youth* (pp. 119–122). Reston, VA: Council for Exceptional Children.

Wood, F. H. (1995). Emotional/Behavioral disorders and the Zeigarnik Effect. *Education and Treatment of Children*, 18, 216–225.

Wood, F. H., & Lakin, K. C. (1983). The legal status of the use of corporal punishment and other aversive procedures in the schools. In F. H. Wood & K. C. Lakin (Eds.), *Punishment and aversive stimulation in special education: Legal, theoretical, and pracical issues in their use with emotionally disturbed children and youth* (pp. 3–27). Reston, VA: Council for Exceptional Children.

Wrobel, G. (1993). Preventing school failure for teachers: Training for a lifelong career in EBD. *Preventing School Failure*, 37 (2), 16–20.

Yell, M. L. (1995). Editorial: The law and education of students with disabilities and those at risk for school failure. *Preventing School Failure*, 39(2), 4–5.

Yell, M. L. (1998). *The law and special education*. Upper Saddle River, NJ: Prentice Hall.

Zabel, R. H., & Zabel, M. K. (1980). Burnout: A critical issue for educators. *Education Unlimited*, 2, 23–25.

APPENDIX

INTERVENTION RESOURCES

Systematic Screening to Identify At-Risk Children and Youth

Walker, H. M., & Severson, H. (1990). *Systematic screening for behavior disorders.* Longmont, CO:Sopris West.

Walker, H. M., Severson, H., & Feil, E. G. (1995). *Early screening project.* Longmont, CO:Sopris West.[1]

Universal Interventions

Alberg, J., Petry, C., & Eller, S. (1994). *A resource guide for social skills instruction.* Longmont, CO:Sopris West.

Beck, R., & Williamson, R. (1993). *Project RIDE for preschoolers.* Longmont, CO:Sopris West.

Black, D. D., & Downs, J. C. (1990).*Administrative intervention: A discipline handbook for effective school administration.* Longmont, CO:Sopris West.

Colvin, G., Sugai, G., & Kameenui, E. (1994). *Curriculum for establishing a school-wide discipline plan.* Eugene, OR: Project PREPARE, Behavioral Research and Teaching, College of Education, University of Oregon.[2]

Kameenui, E. J.,. & Darch, C. B., (1995). *Instructional classroom management: A proactive approach to behavior management.* Reston, VA: Council for Exceptional Children.[3]

Mayer, G. R., Butterworth, T. W., & Spaulding, H. L. (1989). *Constructive discipline: Building a climate for learning—A resource manual of programs and strategies.* Los Angeles: Los Angeles County Office of Education.[4]

Targeted Interventions

Algozzine, B. (1992). *Problem behavior management: Educator's resource service* (2nd ed.). Gaithersburg, MD: Aspen Publishers.[5]

Brown, W., Conroy, M. A., Fox, J. J., Wehby, J., Davis, C., & McEvoy, M. (1996). *Early intervention for young children at risk for emotional/behavioral disorders: Implications for policy and practice.* Reston, VA: Council for Exceptional Children.

Cipani, E. (1993a). *Disruptive behavior: Three techniques to use in your classroom.* Reston, VA: Council for Exceptional Children.

Cipani, E. (1993b). *Non-compliance: Four strategies that work.* Reston, VA: Council for Exceptional Children.

Hops, H. H., & Walker, H. M. (1988). CLASS: *Contingencies for learning academic and social skills.* Seattle, WA: Educational Achievement Systems.[6]

Hops, H. H., Walker, H. M., & Greenwood, C. R. (1988). PEERS: *Procedures for establishing relationship skills.* Seattle, WA: Educational Achievement Systems.

[1]Sopris West, 1140 Boston Avenue, Longmont, CO 80501. Phone: (303) 651-2829.

[2]For information concerning this curriculum, contact George Sugai, Project PREPARE, Behavioral Research and Teaching, Division of Learning and Instructional Leadership, Room 235 College of Education, University of Oregon, Eugene, OR 97403.

[3]Council for Exceptional Children, 1920 Association Drive, Reston, VA 20191-1589. Phone: (800) 232-7323.

[4]Division of Evaluation, Attendance, and Pupil Services, 9300 East Imperial Highway, Downey, CA 90242-2890. Phone: (310) 922-6381.

[5]Aspen Publishers, Inc., 200 Orchard Ridge Drive, Suite 200, Gaithersburg, MD 20878.

[6]Educational Achievement Systems, Inc., 319 Nickerson, Ste. 112, Seattle, WA 98109.

Mathur, S. R., Quinn, M. M., & Rutherford, R. B., Jr. (1996). *Teacher-mediated behavior management strategies for children with emotional/behavioral disorders.*

McIntyre, T. (1989). A *resource book for remediating common behavior and learning problems.* Boston: Allyn & Bacon.[7]

Phillips, V., & McCullough, L. (1992). *Student/staff support teams.* Longmont, CO: Sopris West.

Polsgrove, L. (Ed.)(1991). *Reducing undesirable behavior.* Reston, VA: Council for Exceptional Children.

Rhode, G., Jenson, W. R., & Reavis, H. K. (1992). *The tough kid book.* Longmont, CO: Sopris West.

Rutherford, R. B., Jr., Quinn, M. M., & Mathur, S. R. (1996). *Effective strategies for teaching appropriate behaviors to children with emotional/behavioral disorders.* Reston, VA: Council for Exceptional Children.

Simpson, R. L., Myles, B. S., Walker, B. L., Ormsbee, C. K., & Downing, J. A. (1991). *Programming for aggressive and violent students.* Reston, VA: Council for Exceptional Children.

Sugai, G. M., & Tindal, G. A. (1993). *Effective school consultation: An interactive approach.* Pacific Grove, CA: Brooks/Cole.[8]

Walker, H. M. (1994). *The acting-out child: Coping with classroom disruption* (2nd ed.). Longmont, CO: Sopris West.

Walker, H. M., Colvin, G., & Ramsey, E. (1995). *Antisocial behavior in school: Strategies and best practices.* Pacific Grove, CA: Brooks/Cole.

Watson, R. S., Poda, J. H., Miller, C. T., Rice, E. S., & West, G. (1990). *Containing crisis: A guide to managing school emergencies.* Bloomington, IN: National Educational Service.[9]

School-Based Integrated Services

Illback, R. J., & Nelson, C. M. (Eds.). (1996). *Emerging school-based approaches for children with emotional and behavioral problems: Research and practice in service integration.* New York: Haworth Press.[10]

Skiba, R., Polsgrove, L., & Nasstrom, K. (1996). *Developing a system of care: Interagency collaboration for students with emotional/behavioral disorders.* Reston, VA: Council for Exceptional Children.

---

[7]Allyn & Bacon, A Division of Simon and Schuster, 160 Gould Street, Needham Heights, MA 02194.

[8]Brooks/Cole Publishing Company, a Division of Wadsworth, Inc., Pacific Grove, CA 93950.

[9]National Educational Service, 1610 West Third Street, P.O. Box 8, Bloomington, IN 47402. Phone: (812) 336-6768. FAX: (812) 336-7790.

[10]The Haworth Press, Inc., 10 Alice Street, Binghamton, NY 13904-1580.

GLOSSARY

Academic assessment. Classroom-based component of comprehensive assessment; may include standardized academic achievement tests as well as curriculum-based measures.

Activity reinforcement. Providing opportunities to engage in preferred or high-probability behaviors contingent upon completion of less preferred or low-probability behaviors.

Addiction. Compulsive use of a drug, characterized by a behavior pattern that centers on drug use, procurement, and continued use. According to this definition, evidence of physical tolerance and dependence is not necessary for establishing that a person is addicted.

Admissions and release committee. *See* child study team.

Advocacy. To campaign for services your students need; to protect their legal rights.

Aggression. A category of behavior that involves harm, injury, or damage to persons or property (e.g., kicking, pushing, throwing school books).

Alcohol abuse. The voluntary intake of alcohol in spite of adverse physical and social consequences.

Analogue measure. A role-play or behavioral rehearsal in which an individual demonstrates how he or she would respond in a given social situation.

Anger control training. An approach to help juveniles reduce aggressive behavior using modeling, role-playing, visual cues, and homework.

Anorexia nervosa. Extreme self-starvation with no known physical cause brought about by an abnormal aversion to eating in which the weight of an individual with anorexia nervosa (usually an adolescent girl) falls at least 25 percent below normal.

Antecedent-behavior-consequence analysis (A-B-C analysis). A technique used to systematically identify functional relationships among behaviors and environmental variables.

Antecedent stimulus. A stimulus that precedes a behavior; stimulus may or may not serve as a discriminative for a specific behavior.

Antisocial behavior. Behavior that violates socially prescribed norms or patterns of behavior.

Applied behavior analysis. A systematic, performance-based, self-evaluative technology for assessing and changing behavior.

Assessment. The process of gathering data for the purpose of making educational decisions.

Assessment-based intervention (curriculum-based intervention). Systematic behavior change plan based on data provided by ongoing probes of a student's progress towards a specific goal or objective.

Attempted suicide. Includes some of the elements of completed suicide (i.e., having the conscious intent to die but not dying); attempters wish both to live and to die.

Autism. Condition characterized by extreme social withdrawal and communication skill deficits.

Automatic reinforcement. The reinforcement is produced independent of the social environment.

Aversive procedure. Any procedure involving the use of an aversive stimulus to modify behavior (e.g., lemon juice applied to a pupil's mouth following an episode of rumination).

Aversive stimulus. A noxious stimulus having the effect of decreasing the rate or probability of a behavior when presented as a consequence (punishment); alternately, it may have the effect of increasing the rate or probability of a behavior (negative reinforcement) when that behavior allows the student to escape or avoid contact with the stimulus.

Avoidant disorder. Experienced by children who go to great lengths to avoid contact with any strangers.

Back-up reinforcer. An object or event received in exchange for a specific number of tokens or points in a token economy.

Bar graph. A method of visually displaying data; may be used to show progress toward a specific goal or objective.

Baseline data. Data points that reflect an operant level (the level of natural occurrence of the target behavior before intervention); serves a purpose similar to a pretest; provides a level of behavior to which the results of an intervention procedure can be compared.

Behavior intervention plan. A formal, written plan for addressing problem behavior that is based on a functional behavioral assessment and includes strategies for teaching and supporting appropriate or desired behavior to replace the problem behavior, as well as strategies to decrease the problem behavior.

Behavioral context. External environmental events that precede and follow a specific behavior, including setting events, immediate antecedents, and consequences or outcomes for the behavior. These events may be physical (e.g., time of day, class activity) or the behavior of other persons.

Behavioral contract (behavior change contract, contingency contract). Written, signed agreement between the teacher, parent, therapist, or other behavior change agent and the child, specifically and positively stating in an if-then format what consequence will result from the child's performance of the desired target behavior.

Behavioral-ecological assessment. The evaluation of observable student behaviors across the range of settings in which they occur.

Behavioral interview. An important part of the assessment process, interviewing students, their parents, and teachers to gather information about a student's strengths and needs.

Behavioral momentum. Proactive strategy to promote compliance; involves a low-probability request preceded by a series of high-probability requests in the same or a similar response class.

Behavioral objective. A statement of the behavior to be achieved following intervention, the conditions under which the behavior will occur, and the criterion for acceptable performance.

Behavioral standard. An acceptable level of behavior based on the expectations of other persons.

Behaviorally disordered. Behavior characteristics that deviate from educators' standards of normality and impair the functioning of that student or others; manifested as environmental conflict or personal disturbances.

Bulimia nervosa. An eating disorder in which eating binges are accompanied by vomiting, often self-induced.

Burnout. Emotional exhaustion (sometimes experienced by teachers).

Caffeine. A stimulant drug found in some coffees, teas, and soft drinks; belongs in a chemical class named xanthines (pronounced "zanthenes") and is a methyl-xanthine compound.

Certification. A decision to classify a pupil for special education placement.

Changes in the environment. Environmental changes that can affect behavior, such as schedule changes, seating changes, changes in teaching staff or the class roll, changes in placement, and changes in the home environment.

Changing criterion design. A single-subject experimental design that involves successively or gradually changing the criterion for reinforcement, systematically increasing or decreasing in a step-wise manner.

Chart. A method of visually displaying data using several to many data-representation symbols.

Checklist. A quick, informal, yet systematic tool used to inventory behavior patterns and risk factors that may be associated with behavior disorders; a checklist may be completed by a parent, teacher, sibling, peer, or the target student.

Chemical abuse. The self-administration of a psychoactive chemical that has not been prescribed by a physician; or the compulsive use of a chemical, persisting at a high level in spite of extreme disruption of physical well-being, psychological integrity; and/or social functioning.

Child Behavior Checklist. A checklist developed by Achenbach and Edelbrock (1980), used to screen children for psychiatric problems.

Child study team. A group of persons designated to oversee the assessment of a student with a disability, as well as the implementation and evaluation of the student's IEP.

Childhood psychosis. Term that denotes a wide range of severe and profound disorders in children, including autism, schizophrenia, and symbiotic psychosis.

Classroom adjustment code (CAC). A five-second interval recording system that measures three categories of pupil and teacher behavior; used to evaluate the adequacy of students' classroom and peer social adjustments in less restrictive settings.

Classroom density. The number of students per amount of classroom space.

Clinical syndrome. DSM-IV classifies psychological disorders along five axes, or dimensions; Axis I consists of the major pattern of symptoms or clinical syndrome that the student exhibits.

Clock light. An environmental intervention that signals on- and off-task behavior.

Cocaine. A mood-altering drug, originally prescribed as a topical anesthetic, now widely abused; the physiological effects of cocaine use are very similar to that of amphetamines.

Cognitive behavior modification. An approach that involves teaching students to apply cognitive strategies in interpersonal problem solving.

Collaborative approach. A transdiciplinary team approach to assisting a student in self-management of problem behaviors.

Collaborative consultation. An interactive process involving a team of persons who jointly address mutually defined problems.

Collateral effect. One intervention affecting several target behaviors.

Communicative function. Maladaptive behaviors can occur because students lack or do not use more effective means of communicating their needs or obtaining reinforcement; replacement behaviors which serve the same communicative function must be taught.

Community-based training. Behavioral interventions implemented in natural settings rather than in the classroom in order to promote skill transfer.

Competing explanations. In single-subject design, the uncontrolled factors that influence the behavior simultaneously with the intervention; confounding variables.

Compliance training. Reducing oppositional behavior and training students to respond quickly to adult directions.

Conditioned reinforcer (secondary or learned reinforcer). A stimulus that has acquired a reinforcing function through pairing with a previously established reinforcer; most social, activity, and generalized reinforcers are conditioned.

Conditions. Within a behavioral objective, the part that specifies where, when, and with whom a target behavior will occur; description of the antecedents, including prompts and setting events, that will signal the behavior to occur.

Consensual observer drift. Two observers gradually changing their response definitions while recording data.

Consequence. Any stimulus that is presented contingently following a particular response.

Consultation. Providing indirect services to pupils by helping their teachers or parents directly.

Contiguity. The timing of reinforcement or punishment immediately contingent upon the target behavior, so that a connection between the behavior and its consequence is readily apparent.

Contingency. The relationship between behavior and its consequences; contingencies are often stated in the form "if-then."

Contingency contract. Placing contingencies for reinforcement (if-then statements) into a written document; creates a permanent product that can be referred to by both teacher and student.

Contingent observation. A form of timeout in which a child is removed from reinforcement while observing others receiving reinforcement.

Contingent teacher attention. A type of social reinforcer in which the teacher responds with smiles, praise, attention, and physical proximity when a student performs a desired behavior.

Continuous. A term used to describe behaviors that do not have clearly identifiable beginning and ending points (e.g., on task).

Continuous measurement. Continuous data collection for the purpose of monitoring and evaluating student progress.

Continuum of services. A range of special education service options with consideration given to more restrictive educational placements only after interventions have proven unsuccessful in less restrictive settings.

Contract. *See* contingency contract.

Controlled procedures. Disciplinary interventions permitted by the courts only in accordance with specific legal guidelines.

Cooperative learning. An instructional activity, in which students work in small, structured learning groups with a common goal or purpose.

Coprophagia. The eating of feces.

Council for Children with Behavioral Disorders (CCBD). Major professional organization for special educators serving students with emotional and behavioral disorders.

Criteria. The part of an instructional objective that specifies the requirements for acceptable performance of the target behavior.

Criterion-based assessment (CBA). Assessment of a pupil's status with regard to specific curriculum content and objectives.

Criterion of functioning in the next environment. Identifying the skill requirements and expectations of less restrictive environments and teaching these in order to increase students' chances of successful participation.

Criterion of the least dangerous assumption. When conclusive data are not available regarding the effectiveness of an intervention, educational decisions should be based on assumptions that, if incorrect, will have the least dangerous effect on the student.

Criterion of ultimate functioning. The functional skills needed by adults to participate freely in community environments.

Cubicle. *See* study carrels.

Cumulative graph. A graphic presentation of successive summed numbers (rate, frequency, percentage, duration) that represent behavioral occurrences.

Curriculum-based assessment (CBA). Informal, teacher-made tests used to measure progress towards IEP and other classroom goals and objectives.

Curriculum modification. Revision or change in curriculum to provide appropriate instruction based on individual needs.

Data-based decision making. Using direct and frequent measures of a behavior as a basis for comparing student performance to a desired level and making adjustments in the student's educational program based on these comparisons.

Data decision rules. Rules that suggest how to respond to patterns in student performance; developed by the teacher to facilitate the efficient and effective evaluation of instructional and behavior management programs.

Data level change. The amount of relative change in the data within or between conditions.

Data stability. The degree of variability of individual data points above and below the trend line.

Data trend. The general path of graphed data. A trend line often must be interpolated by the teacher, since data paths seldom follow straight lines, nor do they increase or decrease in even increments.

Decertification criteria. The goals and objectives for a student's special education program; when goals are met, the student should be returned to regular education.

Dependence. Compulsive drug use to ward off physical or emotional discomfort; the person depends on the drug to prevent withdrawal or abstinence-related distress; physical and psychological dependence are determined on the basis of overt and predictable withdrawal symptoms.

Dependency. The need for maximum adult support, accompanied by minimal independent skills.

Dependent group-oriented contingency. The performance of certain group members that determines the consequence received by the entire group.

Dependent measure. A variable that is measured while another variable (the independent variable) is changed in a systematic way, with the goal of establishing a relationship between the two variables.

Dependent variable. The behavior that is changed by intervention, through manipulation of an independent variable.

Depressants. Drugs belonging to the classes of barbiturates (phenobarbital, hexobarbital), benzodiazepine and propanediol minor tranquilizers (Librium, Valium, meprobamate), and antihistaminic sedatives. Barbiturates are commonly prescribed for sleep facilitation and for control of seizures. Benzodiazepines and propanediols are anti-anxiety agents. Benzodiazepines are also used to control seizures and promote muscle relaxation. Antihistamines are used to control allergies and respiratory ailments.

Depression. A behavioral disorder characterized by prolonged feelings of sadness, hopelessness, emptiness, or discouragement that are out of proportion to reality; physical symptoms may include eating, sleeping, or sexual excesses or deficits; affect can range widely from listless apathy to suicidal recklessness.

Detention. A behavioral correction intervention in which a student must stay for 30 to 90 min before or after school to complete assignments.

Developmental regression. A temporary lapse in an individual's social skills.

Diagnostic and Statistical Manual of Mental Disorders, 4th edition (DSM-IV). A manual that defines and classifies mental disorders according to American Psychiatric Association guidelines (APA, 1994).

Differential reinforcement. Four strategies that involve reinforcement applied differentially to reduce undesired behaviors while increasing desired behaviors; see DRL, DRO, DRI, and DRA.

Differential reinforcement of alternative behaviors (DRA). A procedure in which reinforcement is delivered for behaviors that are alternatives to the target behavior.

Differential reinforcement of incompatible behaviors (DRI). Systematically reinforcing a response that is topographically incompatible with a behavior targeted for reduction.

Differential reinforcement of low rates of behavior (DRL). A procedure in which reinforcement is delivered when the number of responses in a specified period of time is less than or equal to a prescribed limit; encourages maintenance of a behavior at a predetermined rate lower than the baseline or naturally occurring rate.

Differential reinforcement of other behavior (DRO). A procedure in which reinforcement is delivered when the target behavior is not emitted for a specified period of time; also referred to as differential reinforcement of the omission of behavior.

Direct observation. Observation of a student in those settings in which the target behavior occurs.

Direction/adult involvement. Leadership, structure, and quality of interactions provided by a teacher, parent, or other significant adult in a child's life.

Discrete. A term used to describe behaviors having a distinctly identifiable beginning and ending point (e.g., hand raising, talking out).

Discrete learning trial. A learning trial that has a discriminable beginning and end; involves the presentation of a prompt or discriminative stimulus, a pupil response, and subsequent teacher feedback.

Discrimination. Demonstration of the ability to differentiate among stimuli or environmental events.

Discriminative stimulus (S^D). An antecedent stimulus that is likely to occasion a particular response because it signals the probability that reinforcement will follow the response.

Distributed trials. Individual instructional trials are spread out over a number of sessions in a given period of time (e.g., a school day).

Drug. Any chemical that is consumed and is present in abnormal concentration in the body; includes substances such as insulin or other hormones found naturally within the body, which can dramatically influence emotion and behavior if their concentrations are not kept within normal limits.

Drug abuse. The voluntary intake of a chemical in spite of adverse physical and social consequences.

Drug tolerance. Physical adaptation to the effects of a drug so that more of the drug is necessary to produce the same effect with repeated use.

Due process. Procedural safeguards established to ensure the rights of exceptional students and their parents.

Duration recording. Recording the amount of time between the initiation of a response and its conclusion; total duration recording is recording cumulative time between the initiation of a response and its final conclusion (e.g., one may record cumulative time out-of-seat across several instances); duration per occurrence is recording each behavioral event and its duration.

Dysphoria. Sadness, a symptom of depression.

Dysthymia. A persistent mood of depression or irritability, more days than not, for most of the day, for at least a year.

Eating disorders. Maladaptive, health-threatening behaviors that involve food; *see* anorexia nervosa, bulimia.

Echolalia. Parroting repetition of words or phrases; observed in children with autism, schizophrenia, or psychosis.

Ecological approach. An approach to assessment that focuses on the student's interactions with the environment rather than on the deficits of the student.

Ecological ceiling. Acknowledgment that it is unrealistic to expect target behaviors to increase or decrease to rates above or below those of peers in the same settings.

Ecological model. Assumption that behavior disorders primarily result from flaws in a complex social system in which various elements of the system (e.g., child, school, family, church, community) are highly interdependent, and that the most effective preventative actions and therapeutic interventions will involve changes in the entire social system.

Ecological settings. Various subsettings in which a student's behavior occurs.

Edible reinforcement. Providing edible items that are reinforcing for the student, contingent upon the performance of desired behavior.

Education of the Handicapped Act (PL 94–142). The public law that guarantees appropriate educational experiences for children and youth with disabilities.

Effective behavior support. Behavior change strategies which involve the teaching of appropriate alternative behavior that serves the same communicative function as the undesirable target behavior.

Elective mutism. Refusal to talk by an individual who is able to talk; may occur in one setting and not in others.

Emphysema. A disease in which the alveoli or air sacs of the lung are destroyed, thus preventing the normal exchange of oxygen and carbon dioxide; resulting in breathlessness, expansion of the rib cage, and possible heart impairment.

Environmental analysis. A technique used to provide the intervention team with information on specific settings, times, and adult actions for further examination.

Environmentally mediated strategy. Changing of some aspect of the environment to prevent or manage behavioral problems.

Equal interval graph paper. A form for presenting behavioral data: vertical lines represent training sessions or calendar days, and horizontal lines may represent number, percentage, or rate (frequency); emphasizes absolute differences among data points.

Equal ratio graph paper. A form for presenting behavioral data in terms of rate per minute or percent; semilogarithmic rather than additive, therefore changes in rate of performance that are proportionately equal are visually presented as equal.

Establishing operations (EO). An environmental event, operation, or stimulus that alters the reinforcing effectiveness of other events as well as the frequency of occurrence of the type of behavior that had been consequated by those other events.

Event recording. Recording a tally or frequency count of behavior as it occurs within an observation period; an observational recording procedure.

Expulsion. A disciplinary consequence that involves exclusion from school.

Externalizing. A pattern of behavior characterized by acting out against persons or objects in the environment.

Extinction. Systematic withholding of reinforcement for a previously reinforced behavior in order to reduce or eliminate the occurrence of the behavior.

Facial screening. A procedure for reducing stereotypic behaviors by covering the student's face with a hand or a cloth bib when the student engages in the target behavior.

Fading. Gradually taking away the prompt that had preceded a target behavior.

Fair pair rule. Teach and/or positively reinforce desired social behavior to replace the behavior to be reduced.

Feedback. Providing the student with descriptive information regarding his or her behavior; includes specific praise as well as specific error correction.

Follow-up assessment. Evaluating the student's current status with regard to IEP or intervention objectives, and evaluating the effectiveness of the educational program.

Formative evaluation. Evaluation that occurs as skills are being developed.

Frequency (rate). The number of times a behavior occurs during an observation period.

Frequency polygon. A noncumulative frequency graph; may be used to report frequency, rate, or percent data.

Functional analysis. A technique used to systematically identify functional relationships between behaviors and environmental variables.

Functional behavioral assessment. A process of assessing identified problem behavior in its environmental contexts to identify the antecedent and consequent events that may explain its repeated occurrence.

Functional mediation. A strategy that takes advantage of potential discriminative stimuli common to acquisition, fluency, and generalization training.

Functional relationship. In applied behavior analysis, demonstrated when a behavior varies systematically with the application of an intervention procedure; sometimes called a *cause-and-effect relationship*; change in a dependent variable due to a change in an independent variable.

Functional response class. Behaviors grouped because they have the same effect on the environment (e.g., attention-seeking behaviors).

Generalization. Expansion of a student's capability of performance beyond those conditions set for initial acquisition; *stimulus generalization* refers to performance under conditions—that is, cues, materials, trainers, and environments—other than those present during acquisition; *maintenance generalization* refers to continued performance of learned behavior after contingencies have been withdrawn; *response generalization* refers to changes in behaviors similar to those directly treated.

Generalization training. Intervention specifically directed at achieving generalization across settings, time, or responses.

Good behavior game. An independent, group-oriented contingency that applies consequences to a group, contingent upon each member reaching a specified level of performance.

Grandma's Law. *See* Premack Principle.

Graph. A method of visually displaying data; typically uses only one or two symbols to represent data.

Group contingency. A peer-mediated strategy in which several peers and the target student work with the teacher to modify behaviors; behavioral consequences are applied to all group members according to teacher-made rules.

Group goal setting and feedback. An intervention that consists of two major components: (1) the teacher assists each student in establishing a social behavior goal; and (2) each student receives teacher and peer feedback on progress toward that goal during highly structured group discussions.

Group-oriented contingency. Contingencies related to the behavior of groups of persons.

Hallucinogens. A chemically heterogeneous group of drugs with the common property of altering sensory experiences and mood; marijuana, LSD, PCP, and psilocybin are hallucinogens.

Hashish. A purified resin of the marijuana plant.

Heroin. Ciadetylmorphine; an addictive narcotic opiate.

High-probability behavior. Behavior that has a high likelihood of occurrence; preferred activity.

Home-based contract. Written contingencies for reinforcement in which parents have agreed to participate.

Host environment. A broad setting or context (e.g., a school building) that supports a system of policies or interventions, such as positive behavioral support.

Ignoring. Withdrawing social attention in response to an undesired behavior.

In loco parentis. Legal doctrine giving the school parental authority over and responsibility for students during school hours.

Independent group-oriented contingency. Group behavior management strategy in which the same response contingency is in effect for all group members, but is applied to each student's performance on an individual basis.

Independent variable. The treatment or intervention under experimenter control that is being manipulated in order to change a behavior.

Indiscriminable contingencies. Consequences that are made less predictable, more natural, and less teacher-controlled through the use of intermittent, gradually thinned schedules of reinforcement.

Individualized education plan (IEP). A written educational plan developed for each student eligible for special education.

Inhalants and volatile solvents. Chemicals that mix easily with air and can be inhaled, includes hydrocarbons (benzene, carbon tetrachloride), freons (trichlorofloromethane), ketones (acetone), esters (ethylacetate), alcohols (methyl alcohol), glycols (etylene glycol), and gasoline; common sources of these chemicals are aerosols, fingernail polish, household cements, lacquer thinner, lighter fluid, cleaning fluid, and model cement.

In-school suspension. A school intervention that includes a reinforcing setting from which the student is removed, a nonreinforcing environment to which the student goes, and contingencies that govern the student's passage from one environment to the other.

Instructional dimensions of the environment. Variables such as the type and sequence of instructional methods, materials, and activities.

Instructional time. The amount of time that students are engaged in active learning and instruction.

Instructional trial. A systematic sequence of instruction, consisting of a prompt, the student's response, and a consequent event (e.g., error correction, reinforcement).

Integrated service plan. *See* wraparound plan.

Intellectual assessment. The process of gathering data through IQ testing and adaptive behavior measurement to see if a behavior problem may be due to a cognitive impairment.

Intensity. A measure of behavior that involves recording both its frequency and its duration.

Interactive teaming models. Collaborative intervention methods such as the use of teacher assistance teams to promote the effective education of students with behavior problems in the least restrictive environment.

Interdependent group-oriented contingency. Group behavioral intervention in which each student must reach a prescribed level of behavior before the entire group may receive positive reinforcement for that behavior.

Intermittent schedules of reinforcement. Schedules in which reinforcement follows some, but not all, correct or appropriate responses, or follows when a period of appropriate behavior has elapsed; these include ratio, interval, and response-duration schedules of reinforcement.

Internalizing. A pattern of behavior characterized by social withdrawal, extreme shyness, sad affect, fears, or depression.

Interobserver agreement. Comparison of observation data between two or more observers to check reliability.

Interval recording. An observational recording system in which an observation period is divided into a number of short intervals, and the observer counts the number of intervals during which the behavior occurs rather than instances of the behavior.

Interval schedule of reinforcement. A schedule for the delivery of reinforcers contingent upon the occurrence of a behavior following a specified period of time; in a fixed interval (FI) schedule, the interval of time is standard (e.g., FI5/min indicates the delivery of reinforcement for the first occurrence of behavior following each five-minute interval of the observation period); in a variable interval (VI) schedule, the interval of time varies (e.g., VI5/min indicates the delivery of reinforcement for the first response that occurs after intervals averaging five minutes in length).

Intervention. Systematic involvement with a student in order to improve his or her performance socially, emotionally, or academically.

Intervention plan. The components include a behavioral objective, what will be done, who will do it, how it will be done, when it will be done, when it will be reviewed, who will review it, and what will happen if the plan is ineffective or if undesired side effects occur.

Interview. Informal method for obtaining assessment data from both children and adults.

Intrusiveness. The extent to which interventions impinge or encroach on students' bodies or personal rights.

Juvenile delinquency. Pattern of illegal activities exhibited by a youth.

Latency recording. Recording the amount of time between the presentation of the S^D (discriminative stimulus) and the initiation of a response.

Learned helplessness. Passivity, a lack of drive or initiative to problem-solve which may result from fears of failure or success, or from a lack of trust, habitual put-downs (verbal abuse), or patterns of overprotectiveness by adult caregivers which can lower a child's self-confidence.

Least intrusive alternative. *See* least restrictive alternative.

Least restrictive alternative. Using the simplest yet most effective intervention based on available data regarding the effectiveness of a procedure.

Least restrictive environment (LRE). The placement imposing the fewest restrictions on a student's normal academic or social functioning.

Level. Quantity of behavior as represented on a graph.

Levels system. A method of differentiating hierarchically any aspect of an individual's performance (e.g., in a token economy or for assessment purposes); also referred to as *phase system*.

Limiting behaviors. Behaviors that limit the student's access to regular education programs or other less restrictive settings.

Line of desired progress (aim line). A line drawn on a behavior graph to depict the desired rate of pupil progress toward a terminal goal.

Long-term objective. A statement describing the ultimate desired outcome of intervention or instruction (*see* behavioral objective).

Low-probability behavior. Less preferred behavior; unlikely to occur without contingent reinforcement.

Lysergic acid diethylamide (LSD). The prototypical hallucinogen.

Magnitude of behavior change. The quantity by which a behavior increases or decreases with respect to some prior amount of behavior.

Mainstreaming. The integration of exceptional children with typical peers.

Manifestation determination. An assessment process, required under IDEA, in which a student's IEP team must demonstrate that a problem behavior or school disciplinary infraction is not a manifestation of the student's disability before a change in educational placement can be made.

Manipulating antecedent stimuli. Strategic control of setting events such as classroom physical arrangement, teacher proximity, and scheduling in order to facilitate desirable behavior.

Marijuana. The dried leaves and flowers of the hemp plant (genus cannabis, cannabis sativa).

Massed trials. All instructional trials are presented in a single session.

Measurement probes. Periodic data samples used in making intervention decisions.

Mediator. Parent, teacher, or other person who provides direct services to a child with the support of a consultant.

Medical model. An assessment and intervention model used by mental health professionals; based on the identification of physiological, emotional, or cognitive pathology that is presumed to underlie the student's behavior problems.

Memoranda of agreement. Documents produced at interdisciplinary team meetings that specify what services are to be provided, when, where, and by whom; signed by all team members.

Mental health assessment. The identification of emotional or cognitive pathology that is presumed to underlie a student's behavior problems.

Modeling. An instructional procedure by which demonstrations of a desired behavior are presented in order to prompt an imitative response.

Momentary time sampling procedure. Recording the occurrence or nonoccurrence of a behavior immediately following a specified interval of time.

Monitoring teacher verbal behavior. A teacher's self-monitoring to gain awareness and increased control of verbal messages.

Movement suppression procedure. A variation of timeout from reinforcement in which the student is punished for any movement or verbalization while in a timeout area.

Multidisciplinary team. A team that includes, at minimum, a student's parents or guardians (if they are not available, a parent surrogate may be appointed), the referring general education teacher, a school administrator, the special education teacher, and a person able to interpret the results of the diagnostic procedures which determines whether a student should be identified as having a disability and served in special education, the types and extent of special education and related services to be provided, and implements the student's individual education plan.

Multiple baseline design. A single-subject experimental design in which a treatment is replicated across (1) two or more students, (2) two or more behaviors, or (3) two or more settings; functional relationships may be demonstrated as changes in the dependent variables occuring with the systematic and sequenced introduction of the independent variable.

Multiple probe design. A variation of the multiple baseline design in which data are collected periodically rather than continuously across settings, behaviors, or students.

Narcotics. Drugs that dull the senses, block painful sensations, and induce sleep.

Natural community of reinforcement. A child's family and peers who provide reinforcement that maintains his or her behavior.

Negative reinforcement. The increase in rate or future probability of a behavior that occurs when the behavior successfully avoids or terminates contact with an aversive stimulus.

Nicotine. A habit-forming drug found in tobacco; nicotine is chemically classified as an alkaloid and is physically toxic, causing nausea, salivation, abdominal pain, vomiting, diarrhea, cold sweat, headache, dizziness, confusion, convulsions, and respiratory failure at high doses; a common active ingredient in several insecticides.

Noncompliance. Refusal to obey teacher directions; behavior that is not under the verbal stimulus control of an adult.

Norm-referenced standardized test. A test that compares a student's performance to that of the students in a norm group; standard scores are identified on the basis of this group's performance.

Observer drift. A change in the observer's response definition while observing behavior and recording data.

Off-task behavior. Behavior exhibited by a student who is not attending to or participating in a classroom activity; not working on an assignment.

On-task behavior. Behavior exhibited by a student who is working on an assignment or paying attention during a classroom activity.

Operational definition. Describing a behavior in terms of its observable and measurable component parts.

Oppositional behavior. A pattern of refusal to follow directions, even when the refusal is destructive to the interests and well-being of the oppositional individual.

Organized games. Structured play directed by the teacher; an intervention intended to reduce aggression during recess.

Overanxious disorder. Experienced by children who are chronically fearful or worried about future events, demands made of them, their health, or their social and academic skills.

Overcorrection. A procedure used to reduce the occurrence of an inappropriate behavior; the student is taught the appropriate behavior in which to engage through an exaggeration of experience; in *restitutional overcorrection* students must restore or correct an environment they have disturbed to its condition before the disturbance and must then improve it beyond its original condition, thereby overcorrecting the environment; in *positive practice overcorrection*, students, having engaged in an inappropriate behavior, are required to engage in exaggerated practice of appropriate behaviors.

Parent surrogate. An adult appointed to take the role of the parent and to make decisions regarding the most appropriate educational program and placement.

Peer coaching. A procedure involving peers and adults who provide instruction to train social isolate pupils in social skills.

Peer imitation training. An intervention that requires an isolate child's classmate to model social behaviors and encourages imitation.

Peer manager strategy. Young socially withdrawn students being trained to play "class manager" to increase their social interactions and sociometric ratings.

Peer-mediated intervention. An intervention that requires a member of the individual's peer group, rather than an adult, to take the primary role as the agent of behavior change.

Peer modeling. Having the student model or imitate the behavior exhibited by peers.

Peer monitoring. Having students observe and record the behavior of a classmate.

Peer-rating method. Sociometric screening method in which students rank one another in terms of popularity or other perceived social attributes.

Peer reporting. An intervention designed to help students improve their social interactions and reduce aggression.

Peer social initiation. An intervention strategy to improve the social skills of withdrawn children.

Peer tutoring. Formal instruction of one child by another.

Percent of interobserver agreement. Measure of the reliability or consistency of data collection across two observers, calculated as

$$\frac{agreements}{(agreements + disagreements)} \times 100$$

Perceptual reinforcement. Reinforcement by engaging in particular perceptual experiences; a key to understanding self-stimulatory behaviors is to view them as a form of perceptual self-reinforcement.

Performance deficit. A skill that a student can perform but does not because of a lack of motivation.

Performance feedback. Providing the student with descriptive information regarding role-playing activities or academic performance.

Performance graph. A graph that plots a change in a single task or behavior.

Permanent product recording. A measurement strategy based on tangible evidence of behavior (e.g., written work, numerical count, videotape, physical injury, or property damage).

Permitted procedures. Disciplinary measures included in a school district's discipline plan for use with all students.

Phase line. Vertical lines drawn on a behavior graph to designate where program changes have been made.

Phencyclidine (PCP). Frequently abused hallucinogen likely to promote aggressive behavior with concurrent increased physical vigor and lack of response to pain.

Phenobarbital. A barbiturate sedative hypnotic; also used as anti-seizure medication in children; it and other types of anti-epileptic medication such as phenytoin (diphenylhydantoin), Cylert (pemoline), and Tegretol (carbamazepine) also

have potentially negative side effects (e.g., depression, insomnia, weight loss, confusion, hallucinations).

Phobia. An abnormally intense dread of certain objects or specific situations which may severely limit activities related to the fear reaction.

Physical aversives. Unpleasant or painful physical stimuli, such as foul tastes and odors, electric shock, slaps, and pinches, used to punish dangerous maladaptive behaviors (such as SIB) when less intrusive methods have failed.

Physical dimensions of the environment. Variables such as lighting, temperature, seating arrangement, noise level, and time of day that can affect behavior.

Pica. The persistent eating of nonfood substances (i.e. paper, paint, dirt, etc.).

Pinpoint. Specifying in measurable, observable terms a behavior targeted for change.

Placheck. Recording which students are engaged in a particular activity at the end of specified intervals.

Planned ignoring. A variation of timeout in which social proximity and attention are consistently withheld for a specific length of time immediately contingent on a pupil's undesirable behavior.

Point-by-point reliability. A method used to assess the agreement between two observers when discrete units of observation are compared. Formula:

$$\frac{Number \text{ of } agreements}{Number \text{ of } agreements \text{ } plus \text{ } disagreements} \times 100$$

Portfolio. Collection of representative samples of a student's work used to measure proficiency, rate of skill development, and effectiveness of teaching methods.

Positive behavioral support. An approach to intervention that is based on functional behavioral assessment and results in an intervention plan that includes strategies for increasing desired behavior as well as to reduce the occurrence of undesired behavior.

Positive practice overcorrection. A procedure in which the student is required to engage in a period of exaggerated alternative behaviors (e.g., exercises) after an episode of an unwanted behavior.

Positive reinforcement. The presentation of a stimulus contingent on the occurrence of a behavior that results in an increase in the rate or future probability of that behavior over time.

Postvention. Actions taken by school psychologists, counselors, administrators, and educators to prevent contagion after a suicide and to help students and staff deal with bereavement.

Praise. Giving positive verbal attention contingent upon appropriate behavior.

Pre-correction. Adjustment in academic instruction based on the teacher's anticipation of student error and intended to prevent errors by providing supportive prompts.

Predictability. Familiar daily classroom routines and a teacher's consistency in applying consequences can help students gain stability by letting them know what to expect.

Premack Principle. An empirical observation that, when access to a high-probability activity (behavior that occurs at a higher rate in the natural environment) is made contingent upon the exhibition of a low probability behavior (one that occurs at a lower rate in the natural environment), the latter will increase in rate (also called *activity reinforcement* and *Grandma's Law*).

Prereferral interventions. Straightforward and relatively easy program modifications implemented by the regular classroom teacher to see if behavior problems can be solved without referring the student for formal evaluation for special education placement.

Primary prevention. Efforts directed at preventing initial occurrences of a condition or pattern of behavior.

Primary treatment setting. The setting in which the intervention is applied directly.

Principle of hierarchical application. Educational tenet stating that more intrusive and restrictive discipline procedures may be used only after less intrusive and restrictive procedures have been applied and have been unsuccessful in promoting student compliance.

Problem behavior pathway. Events that occur before and after an identified problem behavior that, when identified, contribute to the predicting the antecedent and consequent events that contribute to its occurrence.

Procedural reliability. The extent to which intervention procedures are being consistently followed.

Progress graph. A graph that shows progress toward mastery of a set of objectives.

Prohibited procedures. Unlawful disciplinary actions, such as a unilateral change in the placement of a special education student.

Projective technique. A psychological assessment procedure in which the client "projects" thoughts and feelings through responses to ambiguous stimuli such as pictures or ink blots.

Prompt. An added stimulus that increases the probability that the S^D (discriminative stimulus) will occasion the desired response.

Psychological problems. Problems characterized by sudden changes in behavior or mood; feelings of sadness, fatigue, anhedonia; changes in appetite and sleeping habits, feelings of worthlessness.

Psychopathology. Mental illness; in psychiatry, the study of significant causes and development of mental illness; more generally, behavior disorder.

Psychosis. Behavior disorder characterized by a major departure from normal patterns of acting, thinking, and feeling.

Public posting. Publicly listing the names of persons who have (or have not) engaged in a target behavior.

Punisher. A consequent stimulus that decreases the future rate or probability of a behavior.

Punishment. Presentation of an aversive stimulus, or the removal of a positive reinforcer (response cost) as a consequence for behavior which reduces the future rate of the behavior.

Rate. The frequency of a behavior during a defined time period. Formula:

$$\frac{\text{frequency}}{\text{time}} = rate$$

Rating scale. A scale using information supplied by a teacher, parent, sibling, peer, or the target student to describe the child's behavior.

Ratio schedule of reinforcement. A schedule for the delivery of reinforcers contingent upon the number of correct responses; in a fixed ratio (FR) schedule, the number of appropriate responses required for reinforcement is held constant (e.g., FR5 indicates the delivery of reinforcement following every fifth appropriate response); in a variable ratio (VR) schedule, the number of appropriate responses required for reinforcement varies (e.g., VR5 indicates that reinforcement is delivered on the average of every fifth appropriate response).

Reinforcement. Provision of a reinforcing consequence or removal of an aversive stimulus contingent upon the occurrence of a behavior, resulting in an increased or maintained rate of the behavior in the future.

Reinforcer sampling. Prior to the start of a behavioral intervention, the student is provided with samples of reinforcers which may be earned during the intervention.

Reinforcing event menu (RE menu). A pictorial or verbal list of a variety of reinforcing events.

Relevant behaviors. Student's social repertoire behaviors that are likely to evoke reciprocal social interactions that strengthen further social initiations on the student's part.

Reliability. Consistency of measurement; the extent to which an observation holds true across time and observations; types of reliability include test-retest, alternate form, split-half, and interrater.

Replacement behaviors. Desirable skills that are strengthened as undesirable maladaptive behaviors are reduced; often replacement behaviors serve the same communicative function as the maladaptive behavior.

Reprimand. A verbal aversive used by adults to influence children's behavior by telling them their behavior is inappropriate.

Response class. Behavior definitions including several related responses which serve the same or similar functions.

Response cost. A procedure for the reduction of inappropriate behavior through the withdrawal of specific amounts of reinforcers contingent upon the behavior's occurrence; fine or penalty.

Response definition. The definition or description of a behavior in observable, measurable terms.

Response generalization. Changes in untreated behaviors related to those behaviors targeted for intervention.

Response latency. Time that elapses between the presentation of a discriminative stimulus and the initiation of the desired response.

Response latency recording. A measurement strategy in which a timer is started when a task request is given and stopped when the pupil begins to comply with the request.

Response maintenance. The continuation or durability of behavior on a naturally occurring reinforcement schedule after an intervention has been withdrawn.

Response-reinforcer procedure. An intervention in which the immediate environment is manipulated so that the student, as a result of completing a task, has immediate access to a reinforcer physically imbedded within the task.

Restitutional overcorrection. The student must restore an environment which he or she has disturbed to its condition before the disturbance and must then improve it beyond its original condition, thereby overcorrecting the environment.

Restraint. Limiting physical movement to prevent injury to self or others.

Restrictiveness. The extent to which an intervention inhibits a student's freedom to live like other students.

Reversal design (ABAB design, similar to withdrawal design). A single-subject research design in which an intervention condition is reversed in order to verify the existence of a functional relationship; its four phases include baseline (A),intervention (B),contratherapeutic reversal of intervention, which may be similar but is not identical to baseline (C), and reinstatement of intervention (B).

Reverse tolerance. Increased sensitivity to a drug; may be the result of metabolic factors that produce a build-up in the body over time with regular use.

Ripple/spillover effect. A spreading effect in which an intervention with one student, one behavior, or in one setting influences change in another student, behavior, or setting; *see* generalization.

Ritualistic behaviors. Repetitive, stereotypic acts that appear to have no function in the environment.

Role-playing. A therapeutic procedure that helps introduce new behaviors to enhance social relationships (the adult attempts to recreate certain situations for the student in an effort to help that student practice skills that have been difficult).

Rule. A basic component of a school's discipline code, communicating student and teacher expectations; rules should be few, clear, and stated positively.

Rumination. Self-induced regurgitation and rechewing of food with loss of weight or failure to thrive.

SBS Checklist of Correlates of Child Handicapping Conditions. A checklist by Walker and Rankin (1980) describing conditions and characteristics commonly associated with disabilities in children.

SBS Inventory of Teacher Social Behavior Standards and Expectations. A rating scale by Walker and Rankin (1980) describing adaptive and maladaptive student classroom behavior.

Scatter plot. A type of graphing used to determine if there is a significant relationship between two variables.

Schedule of reinforcement. A schedule for the delivery of reinforcers for the purpose of increasing or maintaining behavior.

Scheduling. Posting daily activities in a clear schedule that reflects how students should spend their time.

Schizophrenia. A psychotic disorder characterized by distortion of thinking, abnormal perception, and bizarre behavior and emotions.

School phobia. Fear of going to school, usually accompanied by indications of anxiety about attendance (abdominal pain, nausea, or other physical complaints) just before leaving for school in the morning.

School records. Archival information helpful in assessing social skills and problem areas.

School survival skills. Skills necessary to do well in school, such as classroom deportment and time-management strategies.

School-wide intervention. Universal intervention in which a behavior management system is applied consistently across the student population.

Scopolamine. One of a class of drugs known as anticholinergics, because they inhibit the activity of the brain chemical acetylcholine, which is considered important for mood and sensory regulation; scopolamine is derived from plants in the nightshade family; has been used as a sedative and a truth serum.

Screening. Identification of students at risk for behavioral problems.

Secondary prevention. Efforts to prevent or reduce reoccurrences of a pattern of behavior.

Selected intervention. Behavioral change procedure chosen to suit the needs of a particular student.

Self-evaluation. A procedure in which the student assesses his or her own behavior by rating.

Self-injurious behavior (SIB). Behaviors that hurt the person exhibiting them; also referred to as "self-mutilating" or "self-destructive" behaviors.

Self-instruction. A procedure in which students use self-talk in the form of "coping statements" as an aid to problem-solving.

Self-management. An intervention in which the target individual plays the primary role in changing her or his own behavior.

Self-mediated stimuli. A strategy that involves having the student carry or deliver stimuli discriminative of appropriate responding.

Self-mediated strategies. Strategies for behavior management in which the student controls his or her own planned intervention.

Self-monitoring. Recording one's own behavior to increase one's time on-task, academic productivity, or appropriate social interactions.

Self-mutilation. Self-injurious behavior that results in tissue damage.

Self-recording. Students recording data on their own performance.

Self-regulation. A range of procedures (e.g., self-monitoring, self-evaluation, and self-reinforcement) in which the student acts as his or her own behavior change agent; self-regulation is relatively nonintrusive, nonrestrictive, and allows classroom activities to proceed with a minimum of interruptions.

Self-reinforcement. A procedure whereby students reinforce their own behavior.

Self-report. A procedure whereby students report their own performance.

Self-stimulatory behavior (SSB). Any repetitive, stereotypic activity that appears to serve no purpose other than to provide sensory feedback.

Self-verbalization. A strategy used with socially immature and impulsive students to improve their academic performance by self-instruction or verbalization.

Sensory extinction. A procedure designed to eliminate a particular sensory consequence of a given behavior; based on the hypothesis that certain individuals have a strong preference for one aspect of sensory input (e.g., tactile, proprioceptive, visual, or auditory) and engage in self-stimulatory behaviors to increase this sensory input.

Sensory preferences. Sensory experiences that are desirable to the child.

Sensory reinforcement. Providing the child with preferred sensory experiences contingent on behavior.

Separation anxiety disorder. Intense fear and worry when separated from significant others or familiar surroundings; separation anxiety is typical of a developmental stage in toddlers, but is of concern when it persists or occurs in older students.

Sequential modification. Replicating intervention procedures in other settings in which the desired behavior change is relevant without systematically programming for the durability of treatment effects once intervention is withdrawn.

Serious emotional disturbance. Exhibiting one or more characteristics over a long period of time and to a marked degree which adversely affects educational performance: (1) an inability to learn that cannot be explained by intellectual, sensory, or health factors, (2) an inability to build or maintain satisfactory interpersonal relationships with peers and teachers, (3) inappropriate behavior or feelings under normal circumstances, (4) a general pervasive mood of unhappiness or depression, or (5) a tendency to develop physical symptoms or fears associated with personal or school problems.

Setting events. Antecedent stimuli such as the time of day, transition periods, or the behaviors of peers and teachers that set the occasion for certain behaviors.

Shaping. Behavior change process in which a new or unfamiliar behavior is taught through rewarding successive approximations of the behavior, progressing step-by-step toward a terminal objective.

Short-term objective. A statement describing intermediate steps or approximations toward a long-term objective (*see* behavioral objective).

Single-subject research design. Experiment intended to establish a functional relationship between dependent and independent variables; in a single-subject design the target individual serves as his or her own control.

Skill deficit. A target behavior that cannot be performed due to a lack of appropriate skills.

Social competence. An ability to establish satisfactory social relationships.

Social dimensions of the environment. Variables such as the number of peers and adults in the classroom, proximity to others, and frequency and types of social interactions.

Social interaction code (SIC). Assessment of three major classes of events associated with a student's peer interactions.

Social isolation. Behavior of individuals who seldom interact with their peers or with adults.

Social learning theory. Assumption that antecedent or setting events (e.g., models, prompts, instructions), consequences (rewards and punishments), and cognitive processes (perceptions, thoughts, feelings) combine to influence behavior; includes features of applied behavior analysis with additional emphasis on cognitive factors.

Social maladjustment. Predelinquent or delinquent behavior patterns which may indicate the existence of an emotional or behavioral disorder.

Social performance deficit. Refers to a student's knowing how to perform a specific social skill while being unmotivated to do so.

Social reinforcement. Teacher or peer attention (feedback, attention, and approval) given contingent on behavior which maintains or increases the behavior.

Social skills. Specific social behaviors (e.g., a greeting, a nod during a conversation, a handshake) that facilitate interpersonal interactions.

Social skills deficit. Inability to perform a particular social skill.

Social validation. Degree to which significant others agree that a behavior should be changed, approve of a particular behavioral intervention, or concur that intervention has been effective.

Social withdrawal. A cluster of behaviors that result in an individual's escaping or avoiding social contact.

Sociometric procedure. A technique used to evaluate the social status or position of individuals in a particular social reference group.

Special education admissions and release committee (ARC). A team that decides when assessment information indicates a need for special education placement; the team also decides if goals have been met and a student should be decertified.

Standardized test. A formal assessment instrument in which a student's score may be compared to scores of a norm group.

Static measures. Assessments that provide a report of progress at discrete points in time (e.g., annual or semiannual reassessments).

Stereotypic behaviors. Repetitive, apparently nonfunctional movements (e.g., rocking, hand-flapping) characteristic of autism and other severe behavior disorders.

Stimulants. Drugs which accelerate pulse and respiration, such as amphetamines (speed), cocaine, caffeine, nicotine, phenylpropanolamine, methylphenidate, and pemoline.

Stimulus change. Altering the discriminative stimuli for a particular response.

Stimulus control. The relationship between behavior and its antecedent in which the antecedent occasions the behavior; repeated occurrences of the behavior are dependent upon its being reinforced; an antecedent that occasions a response and therefore results in reinforcement is known as a discriminative stimulus (S^D); an antecedent that does not occasion a response and therefore does not result in reinforcement is known as an S-delta (S^D).

Stimulus fading. The gradual removal of discriminative stimuli.

Stimulus generalization. The transfer of behaviors that have been trained in one setting or in the presence of specific discriminative stimuli to new settings or the presence of stimuli for which they have not been taught.

Stimulus variation. A procedure to increase social responsiveness in a student who habitually engages in self-stimulatory behavior.

Stress. Real or imagined physiological, mental, or emotional strain or pressure that is a typical aspect of everyday life; each individual must develop his or her own personal repertoire of coping skills to deal with stress. Development of optimistic yet realistic expectations, good health habits, organization and time-management skills, humor, religious faith, and a network of social support are a few of the ways people cope well with stress. Overwork, overeating, and abuse of alcohol, tobacco, and other drugs are a few of the maladaptive ways people react to stress. Depression, anxiety attacks, displaced hostility, physical ailments, and burnout are some of the negative outcomes which can occur when stress exceeds an individual's ability to cope.

Structured learning. Approach to teaching prosocial behaviors to students using modeling, role-playing, performance feedback, and transfer of learning.

Structuring. Clarifying the relationship between a behavior and its consequences.

Student prompting of teacher praise. Students solicit praise contingent upon their own behavior.

Study carrels or cubicles. A study area for isolating easily distracted pupils so they can concentrate better.

Successive approximations. Systematic increases in behavioral expectations leading to a desired terminal level of performance.

Sufficient stimulus exemplars. A strategy that involves arranging for more than one, or for a small set of, discriminative stimuli to control the target behavior.

Suicidal ideation. Having thoughts about killing oneself.

Suicide. When someone takes his or her life with conscious intent.

Summative evaluation. Evaluation done at the end of a program.

Suspension. A temporary exclusion from school to manage behavior.

Syndrome. Recurring actions or symptoms that combine to form a disordered pattern.

System of care. Multidisciplinary approach to meeting the needs of a child with a behavior disorder in which several agencies collaborate to provide individualized services that wrap around the child and family.

Systematic desensitization. A systematic procedure to help a person relax when engaging in activities that previously were anxiety-provoking; involves gradual, controlled exposure to the anxiety-producing stimulus accompanied by positive reinforcement.

Tactile (sensory) reinforcement. The application of tactile or sensory consequences to reinforce behavior; used primarily with students with severe and profound disabilities.

Tangible reinforcement. Contingent provision of nonedible items to reinforce behavior.

Target behavior. A behavior identified for change that is observable, measurable, defined so that two persons can agree as to its occurrence, and stated so that a criterion can be set for a desired level of performance.

Task analysis. The process of breaking down a complex behavior into its component parts so that it can be taught in small, easy steps.

Teacher assistance team. Staff who assist the regular educator with prereferral interventions; the team may also assist teachers with behavior management problems involving special education students.

Teacher expectations. The rating of important adaptive behaviors and teachers' tolerance for maladaptive behaviors in terms of how they affect their willingness to work with students in their classroom; a vital consideration for the mainstreaming and inclusion of special education students.

Teacher interview. An informal method for screening and identification of students with behavior problems.

Teacher Interview for Psychiatric Symptoms (TIPS). Instrument for identifying psychiatric problems in children (Kerr & Schaeffer, 1987).

Teacher-mediated strategy. Behavior management strategy that involves a teacher's direct interaction with students.

Teacher ranking. Sociometric screening procedure in which the classroom teacher generates an ordered list representing his or her perceptions of students from lowest to highest risk of either internalizing or externalizing behavior problems.

Terminal behavior. The desired end product or goal for change in a student's behavior.

Tertiary prevention. Efforts to reduce the negative impact of a condition or pattern of behavior on the ability of an individual to function normally in his or her least restrictive environments.

Therapy. A procedure for bringing about positive social adjustment.

Time delay. An errorless teaching procedure in which the time interval between a task request and an instructional prompt is systematically increased until the pupil emits the correct response before the prompt is given.

Time management. The organization of time for school tasks; a key to stress management and academic success for both students and teachers.

Time sampling. Observational recording system in which behavior is observed for a limited time period (e.g., 5 min of a 60-min period).

Timeout. A procedure for the reduction of inappropriate behavior whereby the student is denied access, for a fixed period of time, to the opportunity to receive reinforcement.

Timer game. Using a kitchen timer to shape pupil behavior and train teachers to use tokens and praise.

Token economy. A system of behavior modification in which tangible or token reinforcers such as points, plastic chips, metal washers, poker chips, or play money are given as rewards and later exchanged for back-up reinforcers that have value in themselves (e.g., food, trinkets, play time, books); a miniature economic system used to foster desirable behavior.

Topographic response class. A class of behaviors that are related in terms of their form, or the movements comprising the response (e.g., handraising).

Topography. The physical form or description of a motor behavior.

Total reliability. A method used to assess the agreement between the total numerical counts of behaviors obtained by two independent observers. Formula:

$$\frac{\text{smaller frequency}}{\text{larger frequency}} \times 100$$

Train loosely. Teaching principle for generalization in which trainers, settings, situations, prompts, and so on are varied across all phases of the learning process.

Transenvironmental programming. A strategy consisting of four components: (1) assessing the behavioral expectations of specific generalization settings, (2) competency training in the special education environments, (3) selection and use of techniques for promoting the transfer of skills across settings, and (4) monitoring and evaluating student performance in generalization settings.

Transfer of training. *See* stimulus generalization.

Transition plan. A program designed to help students cope with the move from one setting to the next, usually including annual goals and short- and long-term plans.

Transition services. Services and agencies designed to aid students in the move from one setting to another, including helping the individual make work and social contacts, helping him or her become established, and following up with the individual and his or her progress in the new environment.

Transition strategies. Strategies that involve transferring students and their entire repertoires of behavior to new settings.

Trapping effect. Behavior is "trapped" in the natural environment when it is relevant to the student's lifestyle and needs and is reinforced by naturally occurring schedules of reinforcement, usually in the form of social attention.

Trend. Data points on a graph which show whether a behavior is increasing, decreasing, or remaining stable (an ascending or descending trend is defined as three consecutive data points in a single direction).

Trend lines. Lines of "best fit" that are drawn to represent the path shown by graphed data—increasing, decreasing, or level.

Triadic model. A description of the relationship between a behavioral consultant, a mediator (primary intervention agent), and the target pupil.

Trial-by-trial recording. Recording student responses to individual prompts given by the teacher over a set of discrete trials.

Trials to criterion recording. A measurement strategy for monitoring progress through a task-analyzed sequence or for measuring skill generalization.

Universal intervention. Behavior change procedure applied to an entire class or school.

Unprompted generalization. A strategy that involves monitoring in generalization settings and reinforcing spontaneous generalization.

Validity. The degree to which a test measures what it purports to measure; types of validity include content, criterion-referenced (predictive and concurrent), and construct validity.

Variable reinforcement. Observing and reinforcing students after varying time intervals, which average a designated time interval.

Verbal aversive. Unpleasant verbal behavior (i.e., yelling, scolding, whining) that may serve as an aversive stimulus.

Vicarious reinforcement. Reinforcement of a student for appropriate behavior so that observing students will imitate the behavior.

Visual analysis. Evaluating the significance of behavior change through visual inspection of a behavior graph.

Visual screening. A procedure for reducing stereotypic behaviors in which the teacher covers the student's eyes with his or her hand when the student engages in the target behavior.

Volatility. Drug inhalants mixing readily with air in high concentrations.

Walker-Rankin Child Behavior Rating Scale. A criterion-referenced scale on which the teacher in the sending setting assesses the target student's behavioral status on the items designated as critical or unacceptable (Walker, 1986).

Window of variance. The amount of desired stability around the trend; found by drawing parallel dotted lines representing a 15-percent range above and below the trend line.

Withdrawal design (ABAB or ABA design, similar to reversal design). A single-subject research design that involves collecting baseline data (A), followed by an intervention condition (B), a withdrawal of intervention procedures, or return to baseline conditions (A) and a reinstatement of the intervention (B).

Wraparound plan (integrated service plan). A multi-agency plan of care designed to meet the individual needs of a youth with an emotional or behavioral disorder in his or her family.

REFERENCES

Achenbach, T. M., & Edelbrock, C. S. (1991). *Child behavior checklist—teacher's report.* Burlington, VT: University Associates in Psychiatry.

Kerr, M. M., & Schaeffer, A. L. (1987). *Teacher interview for psychiatric symptoms* (TIPS). (Available from Mary Margaret Kerr, at Western Psychiatric Institute and Clinic, 121 University Place, University of Pittsburgh, 3811 O'Hara St., Pittsburgh, PA 15213).

Walker, H. M., & Rankin, R. (1980). *The SBS inventory of teacher social behavior standards and expectations.* Eugene, OR: SBS Project, University of Oregon.

INDEX

465